History of the Clan Gregor, From Public Records and Private Collections; Compiled at the Request of the Clan Gregor Society Volume 1

E IN ƆO BAIT   SPAIR NOCHT

LOZD MAKGZEGOVZ OFould,

HISTORY OF
THE CLAN GREGOR

FROM PUBLIC RECORDS AND
PRIVATE COLLECTIONS

COMPILED

AT THE REQUEST OF THE CLAN GREGOR SOCIETY

BY ONE OF ITS VICE-PRESIDENTS

AMELIA GEORGIANA MURRAY MACGREGOR

OF MACGREGOR

VOLUME FIRST—A.D. 878-1625

WILLIAM BROWN
26 PRINCES STREET, EDINBURGH

1898

To the Clan Gregor

To the Memory of the Courage and Fortitude of

OUR ANCESTORS

To the Clan yet Flourishing and Faithful to

THE NAME

To the Future Generations who will still uphold its

HONOUR

This Record is dedicated

By an Attached

DAUGHTER OF GREGOR

Don Chloin Ghriogair;

Do Chuimhne Gaisge agus Treuntais

AR SINNSEAR;

Do'n Chloinn nis a soirbheachadh agus dileas

D'AN AINM;

Do na Ginealaich ri teachd a chumas suas fathast

A CHLIÙ

Tha an Leabhar so air a choisrigeadh

LE

NIGHEAN GHRADHACH GHRIOGAIR.

CONTENTS

Contents

Contents xi

Chapter XI

Chapter XII

Chapter XIII

Chapter XIV

b o

Contents

Contents

Chapter XXIII

Chapter XXIV

Chapter XXV

Chapter XXVI.

Chapter XXVII.

Contents

Chapter XXVIII

Chapter XXIX

Chapter XXX

Contents

Chapter XXXI

Chapter XXXII

Chapter XXXIII

Chapter XXXIV

Contents

ERRATA.

Page 17—5th line, *instead of* " 37," *read* " 38."
,, 44—3rd line, *instead of* " from page 12," *read* " from page 22."
,, 50—1st line of footnote *for* " Glensbrae," *read* " Glenstrae."
,, 119—Line 4 from last line, *instead of* " bann," *read* " Lann."
,, 128—2nd line within brackets, *instead of* " Lan," *read* " Ian," and line 17 *for* " Lagfarme," *read* " Lagfarne."
,, 129—1st line, *instead of* " priviledge," *read* " privilege."
,, 174—Line 10, from foot of page *delete* the quotation mark preceding " Notwithstanding his tyranny."
,, 226—Line 14 from top of page, the reference wanting at the mention of Duncan na Glen as to page is 171.
,, 255—Footnote, *instead of* " Chapter IV., page 161," *read* " Chapter XX., pages 236, 237."
,, 311—Lines 7 and 5 from foot of page, *for* " Earll," *read* " Earl."
,, 373—Line 3, *delete* 2nd footnote.
,, 398—In the list of names it should be observed that the signs × and * in each case precede the names so distinguished.

Introduction

THE following pages contain the eventful chronicles of a Highland Clan, not one of the most numerous or most powerful, but remarkable as occupying a distinct place in the history of Scotland. The narrative may doubtless be considered a record of crime, sometimes tragical, sometimes trivial, yet a careful study of the Race, of the circumstances and of the times, must forcibly bring out many claims for a lenient judgment. Early and native inhabitants of the country, with pride of ancestry and an indomitable spirit, the MacGregors in the fourteenth century found themselves dispossessed of the lands whereon they dwelt, by reason of Charters, instruments inexplicable to them, bestowed upon others. From that time a sense of wrong and of injustice pervaded their minds. Yet they might possibly have been content to maintain themselves on lands held by heritable tacks from the landlords in possession, but for two causes. First, the natural increase in the numbers of the Clan, hemmed up in glens and straths where the means of subsistence were necessarily limited. Secondly, the enmity of certain neighbours determined to dispossess them. In other countries the turmoils of the sixteenth and seventeenth centuries were equally violent, but the art of war on a larger scale afforded an outlet to the belligerent qualities of their inhabitants, and tended also to decrease the population. The MacGregors without any other channel for their energy, cramped in the means of livelihood, totally ignorant, and goaded by those anxious to profit by their fall, lived by forays and raids. Many other Highland Clans and many Lowlanders did the same, but most of them had more power to make their struggles against each other effective in forcing support from the Government, whereas the ClanGregor, through the wiles of their adversaries, became the object of the strongest persecution and the most severe penal enactments. Had the opportunity occurred, the MacGregors, as was proved later, would have fought for their Sovereign with devoted loyalty, but they could not easily understand that their

A

personal enemies, through misrepresentations, had become armed with the King's authority. The conflict of Glenfruin, in which the ClanGregor gained a victory, eventually fatal to themselves, against vastly superior numbers, was punished by numerous executions. the Name was proscribed, the men were hunted down with bloodhounds, the women branded on the cheek with a red-hot iron, and yet the Clan clung to the only virtues they knew, courage, endurance and fidelity. Their unquenchable spirit was never broken, and when the time of persecution was over, they revived and brought their noble qualities to a better use. The British Army has numbered many heroes from this lion-hearted race.

The article on MacGregor in Sir Robert Douglas's "Baronage," published in 1798, was probably the first accessible history of the Clan, with the exception of the short notice in Buchanan of Auchmar's "History of Scottish Surnames," first published in 1723 Douglas's "Memoir of the MacGregors and the MacAlpins" was written by the late Sir John MacGregor Murray, Bart., before he went to India in January 1770.[1] He is styled by the editor "An ingenious gentleman who hath been at great pains in collecting the materials, and with much care and accuracy hath ranged the vouchers and put them into their proper order" This tribute was well merited, and Sir John's accuracy both in public and private life was afterwards well known, but modern researches, and facilities of access to public records, have thrown a different light on some parts of the narrative, whilst on the other hand many circumstances familiar to the writer of the account one hundred and twenty-five years ago have now slipped beyond recall.

In the year 1822 the Rev William MacGregor Stirling, at that time minister of the Port of Monteith, undertook the compilation of a history of the ClanGregor, for the late Sir Evan Murray MacGregor, who himself revised the MSS. till he went to the West Indies as Governor of the Leeward Islands in 1832 The work, which had the able assistance

---

[1] Douglas's "Baronage" was not published till 1798, after the death of the author, Sir Robert Douglas of Glenbervie A MS note on the margin of a copy in the possession of the late Sir John MacGregor Murray's family fixes the period when the MacGregor notice was written, viz, in the lifetime of his father, Major Evan MacGregor Murray, and uncle, Duncan MacGregor Murray, the Chief at that time (see subsequent history), who both supplied him with materials For the correspondence between Sir John (then Mr) Murray and Sir Robert Douglas, see appendix.

and co-operation of the late Mr Donald Gregory, was not finished or in a form ready for publication at the time of Mr MacGregor Stirling's death in 1833, but a great portion of it has been of infinite service to the present compilation. Mr MacGregor Stirling had collected an elaborate series of Excerpts from the Register of the Privy Council of Scotland, and other Records which were afterwards enlarged, carried forward and critically analysed by Mr Gregory, and which embodied every known authentic passage regarding the Clan. These were comprised in three large folio volumes entitled "The Chartulary[1] of the ClanGregor." It was understood that this valuable collection was made with the view of assisting the history of the Clan, which Sir Evan wished to have published at his expense, and several letters from Mr Gregory to Sir Evan allude to the intended publication, but the death of Mr Gregory in 1836, and of Sir Evan in 1841, put a stop to the work.

On the death of Mr Gregory the Iona Club, which had been founded by him in conjunction with Mr W. F. Skene in 1833, "to investigate and illustrate the History, Antiquities and early literature of the Highlands," made an arrangement with his executors by which the Club acquired his collections, and amongst them the three volumes of the so-called Chartulary, together with three companion volumes of pedigrees. When the Iona Club was dissolved Mr Skene deposited these collections in the Library of the Antiquarian Society, with the stipulation that any papers claimed by the families to whom they related were to be restored.[2] Circumstances delayed the following up of a claim which seems to have been made nearly fifty years ago, but through the courtesy of the President and Council of the Society of Antiquaries of Scotland, with the consent and advice of the late Mr Skene, the six MS. books relating to the ClanGregor were in March 1890 handed over to Sir Malcolm MacGregor of MacGregor, as representative of his great grandfather Sir Evan, on whose daughter the privilege of giving to the Clan the results of former zealous Clansmen's labours now devolves.

In addition to these most important collections, and the materials

---

[1] This title is adopted for reference throughout the present work, but MacGregor Stirling's Collection cannot correctly be styled a chartulary.

[2] Letter from late Dr W. F. Skene to Editor.

which are to be found in the Dean of Lismore's MS., the "Black Book of
Taymouth," and the published "Records of the Privy Council," (the first
two volumes edited by Dr Hill Burton, and the subsequent volumes by
Dr Masson), etc., etc., the papers of many of the Clan have been placed in
the hands of the compiler. The admirably preserved traditions of the
Rannoch MacGregors, and their different branches, have been supplied by
Mr Alexander MacGregor, Crosshill, Glasgow, now in America, to whom
thanks for most valuable assistance are due; also to Mr Gregor MacGregor,
S.S.C, Edinburgh, for much kind aid, including the revision of the Gaelic
portions of the work; to Dr W. D. Cameron and others, whose information
will be acknowledged in the course of the work.

One of the objects of the ClanGregor Society, instituted in 1822, is—
"To publish ancient or interesting documents or articles on interesting
events connected with, and to compile an authentic history of, the Clan
and of the different families belonging to it." In furtherance of this
object, the present work has been undertaken at the request of the
Society, and with the hope that the facts and traditions here collected will
prove of interest to the whole ClanGregor.

DUNKELD, *January* 1897.

Chapter I

Early Origin

THE renowned ancestor to whom we look as the Founder of our Race was King Gregory, who reigned from 878 to 890. No documentary evidence can be adduced to prove descent from a source so remote; and allusion to it is not made here as to an established historical fact, but because the tradition has been constantly handed down that Gregory, of the race of Scotland's early kings, was the ancestor of the Clan which bears his name.[1]

Modern authorities on early Scottish History state that Ciricius, or Girig, or Girg, afterwards known as Gregory, whatever may have been his connection with Alpin's Royal line, was not King Alpin's son. According to the most trustworthy chronicles, his father was Dungaile, or Dungallus, grandfather of Run, King of the Britons of Strathclyde, who married the daughter of Kenneth McAlpin. After the death of Aedh, or Heth, the last of Kenneth's sons, Eocha, son of Run, was placed on the throne of the Picts, and another king, Girig, was associated with him as his Governor. It is recorded that he liberated the Scottish Church from various secular exactions, in gratitude for which good offices the later chronicles, connected with the Religious Houses, afterwards revered him as Gregory the Great, a Ruler of remarkable wisdom, as well as a successful Commander.[2]

---

[1] Our Scottish Historiographer, the late Dr Skene, to whose valuable works frequent reference must at the outset be made, while deducing the race from another source, to be hereafter quoted, remarks that the ClanGregor, having recognised Gregory "as their eponymous ancestor, their descent from him is now implicitly believed in by all the MacGregors" ("Celtic Scotland," vol. iii. p. 364). After this record we may surely preserve our belief, which is thus itself established as a matter of history (see Appendix).

[2] Taken from "Celtic Scotland," *first edition*, vol. i. p. 329, 330. Mention is there made also of a "Church in the Mearns" with the name of "Eglisgirg," which still preserves a memorial of Girig.

It may be frankly confessed that, where even the most prominent historical characters are involved in considerable uncertainty, it must be impossible to trace the lineage of the Clan through the tenth, eleventh, and twelfth centuries with any certainty. Such an attempt was indeed made in a "Latin History of the Alpinian Family, formerly in the Scots College at Paris, and recovered from it by David Mallet" the Poet, who died in 1765 It is exceedingly unlikely that the date of this history, now undiscoverable, can have been earlier than the seventeenth century, before which time, the History by Hector Boece (1570) had given rise to much spurious tradition, but it is probable that there may have been threads of truth woven into the more elaborate narrative. It may be interesting to give a list of the generations, as enumerated in the article on MacGregor, in Sir Robert Douglas's "Baronage," based, in the early part, on this Latin document, of which Sir John MacGregor Murray possessed an authentic copy, although no trace of either the original or the copy can now be found [1]

Two very old MacGregor pedigrees have been brought to light since Douglas's "Baronage" was written, one occurs in an ancient Gaelic parchment MS, dated 1467,[2] which contains genealogies of most of the Highland Clans. In this document, the ClanGregor is deduced from Fearchar Fada, King of Dalriada, of the Lorne line, who reigned in the early part of the eighth century, through a certain Anrias connected with the Earldom of Ross. This pedigree has been printed in full in the "Collectanea de Rebus Albanicis," and again in "Celtic Scotland," vol. iii From these works it is here transcribed in Gaelic and in English.

"Genelach Clann Grigair   Maelcolaim ic Padruic MᶜEoin ic Grigair ic Donch MᶜMaolcolaim ic Gillacrist MᶜFearchar ic Muiredaig ic Ainreas MᶜCormac ic Oirbertaig ic Fearchair MᶜFearchair fada ic Fearadaig fin —

---

[1] Mr Donald Gregory in 1825 states that the copy was unfortunately missing. (Chartulary.) One reason for here reproducing the greater part of the article in Douglas's "Baronage" is, that as it has served as a basis for small sketches of the Clan history, readers may have an opportunity of comparing it with other studies on the subject, and observe how far its views have now to be modified.

[2] Discovered by Dr Skene among the MSS in the Collection of the Faculty of Advocates, and considered to have been written by a MᶜLachlan, 1450 (See Skene's "Highlanders," vol ii p. 8.) Reference is made to the MS having been printed in the "Collectanea de Rebus Albanicis," edited by the Iona Club, first number. The genealogies from this MS. are also to be found in "Celtic Scotland," vol iii, Appendix, p. 487.

Malcolm, son of
Patrick, son of
John, son of
Gregor, son of
Duncan, son of
Malcolm, son of
Gillchrist, son of
Ferchard, son of
Murdoch, son of
Annreas, son of
Cormac, son of
Airbertach, son of
Ferchar og, son of
Ferchar fada, son of

Feradach finn."

[A King of Dalriada of the line of Lorn, early part of eighth century.]

Dr Skene holds that, previous to the eleventh century, this document is of no authority. His own theory is that, "previous to the thirteenth century, the Highlanders of Scotland were divided into a few great tribes, which exactly corresponded with the ancient earldoms, and that, from one or other of these tribes, all the Highlanders are descended" ("Highlanders of Scotland," vol. ii.).

The other ancient pedigree is to be found in a MS. Latin Chronicle, chiefly an obituary,[1] composed by Sir James MacGregor, Dean of Lismore,[2] in the sixteenth century, and containing a genealogy of John MacGregor of Glenstray, dated 1512. With regard to this list of ancestors (to be given later in detail), Dr Skene remarks :—

"Besides the genealogy of this Clan contained in the Irish MS., Dean MacGregor furnishes us with one which may probably be viewed as the native tradition. In it Gregor, the eponymus of the Clan, has a different ancestry, and his pedigree is taken up to a certain Aoidh Urchaidh, or Hugh of Glenurchay, which, as Glenurchay was an old possession of the MacGregors, may be viewed as the native tradition and more probable descent. The usual calculation would place him in the end of the twelfth century, but the Dean connects him at once

---

[1] Sir John MacGregor Murray was acquainted with this obituary.—*Ed.*

[2] Communicated to the Society of Antiquaries of Scotland by Donald Gregory, Honorary Secretary of the Society, January 1831, and printed in vol iii. of the "Archæologia Scotica."

with Kenneth McAlpin in the ninth century,[1] and thus the supposed royal descent of the MacGregors must be relegated to the same category with the descent of the other Clans from the Kings of Dalriada."[2]

"To the great tribe of the Moravians, or 'Men of Moray,' belong, in the main, the clans brought in the old Irish genealogies from the Kings of Dalriada of the tribe of Lorn, among whom the old Mormaers of Moray appear. . . . The group containing the McNabs, ClanGregor, and McKinnons, appear to have emerged from Glendochart, at least to be connected with the old Columban monasteries. The Clans, properly so called, were thus of native origin, the surnames partly of native and partly of foreign descent."[3]

It would seem unavailing to discuss at further length the question of the origin of the clan, always reckoned in the past as the "Siol Alpin"— the old motto, "'S RIOGHAIL MO DHREAM," "My tribe is royal," will suffice as a memorial of our traditions. We may now pass on to a period when the family history begins to be more distinct.[4]

At the outset it may be desirable to recall circumstances which, although well known, require to be borne in mind, rightly to comprehend the subsequent position of the ClanGregor, their difficulties and struggles.

Amongst the continental nations there arose, in the early Christian centuries, the institution of feudalism. To protect themselves against hostile armies of foreigners, or against assaults by enemies of their own nation, the principal men turned their houses into fortified castles, and agreed with the peasants to protect them and their families on condition of their surrendering themselves entirely to their liege lord or suzerain. The sovereign gave land to his nobles on condition of military service to himself, with a certain number of their men, the nobles adopted some of their less powerful neighbours, and gave off portions of land to them on similar conditions, thus establishing a system of mutual advantage

---

[1] "It is obvious that a number of generations are omitted, not even excepting the ancestor who gave his name to the Clan "—Note to the Dean of Lismore's MS., by Mr Gregory.

[2] Celtic Scotland, *first edition*, vol iii. p 362, 363

[3] *Ibid*, p. 365 In the "Highlanders of Scotland," vol ii pp. 4, 5, Dr Skene seeks to demonstrate that the modern Highlanders are the same people with those who inhabited the Highlands of Scotland in the ninth or tenth centuries, the descendants of the great northern division of the Pictish nation, unaffected by the Scottish conquest of the Lowlands in 843

[4] The hereditary belief in royal ancestry, and in an inheritance of the highest courage and truth, is shown in the poems from the Dean of Lismore's book, quoted chapter vii.

between the lord who granted protection, the vassals who gave their military service in return, and lastly the peasants who received protection and entirely gave up their freedom to obtain it

Amidst the pressing necessities of the age which gave rise to it, the institution undoubtedly had its value, till the nations outgrew it. The feudal laws were brought to England by the Saxons about A.D. 600, and were made more stringent under the Norman William the Conqueror, in 1068. The system was introduced into Scotland by Malcolm II. in 1008, but it took a long time before it could absorb the tribal organisation then prevalent Certain burdens on land proper to the old Celtic tenures gradually became assimilated to feudal forms in the eastern districts, whilst in the northern and western the great tribes broke up into clans about the thirteenth century.[1]

The Clan, a Gaelic word meaning children, consisted originally of the children of a common ancestor, bound together by the ties of blood, loyal to the Chief of their race, and sharing his good or bad fortune. Personal attachment united each to the other in this family system, which in different degrees has subsisted in most primitive nations, such as the Israelites, and even in the present day amongst the Arabs. In the High-lands the chiefship was generally hereditary and belonged to the repre-sentative of the main stem, but to this there were frequent exceptions The next cadet often became the captain, and transmitted that honour to his descendants. Occasionally in cases where the actual chief was prevented from taking an active part in warfare, the clan chose a leader on elective principles. The chieftains or heads of the different houses which had branched off from the main stem were also powerful, and exerted great influence over the chiefs ; moreover, every clansman had his birthright of kindred blood, which gave him dignity and enthusiasm, so that it is incorrect in any way to liken members of a clan to the serfs of the feudal system. Doubtless there must have been cases of abuse and hardship, and the two systems running parallel, where they did not clash, sometimes overlapped. The feudal superiors, in some circumstances, won

[1] For details as to the breaking up of the old earldoms and tribes, see " Celtic Scotland," vol III p. 287.

the affections of the occupants of their lands, and were accepted in the same position as chiefs of race, but this was the exception.

The struggle between the Gaelic population of the Highlands clinging to the old clan system on the one side, and the feudal overlords, who, having obtained crown charters of the lands, occupied by the native races, sought to dispossess them, was a long source of trouble and dispeace, and the MacGregors, especially, were for centuries irreconcilable to the change

It may be observed that neither at the period under present considera-tion, nor for some time later, does the name of MacGregor, so passionately loved and so powerful a talisman in the future, appear to have existed as a surname, although individuals[1] of the race can be traced   There must early have been numerous descendants of the same ancestor, allied in blood and interests, for by the fifteenth century they had become a very large clan.   The custom of distinguishing different families of the same clan by their patronymics—i e, as the son of so-and-so—also of giving a "byname," or "to-name," to individuals, prevailed amongst Highlanders in very early days, and continued long after surnames became general in other places.

The following is taken from a sympathetic article on the ClanGregor, published by Dr Joseph Anderson in 1890 .—[2]

" There are some minor episodes in Scottish history that illustrate with singular force the native intensity of character and fervour of attachment to traditional systems, which so often made the nation's progress towards the universal reign of law a bloodstained path.   The case of the ClanGregor is perhaps the most typical of these episodes, which marked the transition from the old Celtic system of the military organisation of the clans under the chiefs of their name to the territorial system, by which the men of the tribes became the men of their feudal landlords But though its tragic and romantic elements have often been dealt with, the true story of the doings and sufferings of the devoted clan has yet to be dug from the dry-as-dust sources of historic narrative in contemporary records, and the purpose of this paper is merely to show that the records contain material for such a narrative

" There is no indication of the reason why the numbers of the clan when they

[1] In 1260 Gilcolm Makgrigir, probably a churchman, is mentioned in the proceedings of a court held by the Prior of St Andrews at Dull, in Atholl   Quoted from " Transcript of Chartulary of St Andrews," Advocates' Library, by Mr MacGregor Stirling
[2] Published in the *Scottish Review*, October 1890

first appear in record are found scattered over such a wide area of the Perthshire and Argyleshire Highlands, unless it be simply that they had spread over the adjacent lands and baronies as best they could, in consequence of their chiefs holding no land of the Crown. We find them located in Glenurchy and Glenlochy, Strathfillan and Glendochart, Breadalbane and Balquidder, Glenlyon and Rannoch. Although by the immemorial custom of the Highlands, to which they most tenaciously clung, they owed military service to the chief of their own name only, he was not at any time within the ken of record in a position either to provide them with homesteads or protect them in their possessions. While the lands on which they had settled remained in the Crown they might be safe from eviction, but when the lands came to be granted out to local barons, the grantees naturally desired to settle their new estates with their own men, on whom they could depend for thankful service and punctual payment of rents. The MacGregors, on the other hand, in all such cases immediately found themselves in the position of occupants of the lands of owners to whom they were unacceptable as tenants, and who desired nothing better than to be rid of them at any price. The inevitable consequences followed—eviction, resistance, and retaliation. The evicted tenants sought shelter among their kinsmen who still possessed lands, as sub-tenants or squatters; or they became "broken men," and betook themselves to the hills to live on the plunder of the lands from which they had been ejected."

Referring to the Act passed in 1488

"For the stanching of theft and other enormities in the Highlands," Dr Anderson adds, "this was the first of a long series of similar enactments by which the MacGregors were placed entirely at the mercy of their natural enemies."

Chapter II

Early Ancestry

EXCERPTS from the "Baronage of Scotland," by Sir Robert Douglas of Glenbervie, Baronet, Edinburgh, 1798:—

"I Gregor[1] (third son of King Alpin) was brother to Kenneth, Donald, and Achaius MacAlpin, the two former of whom reigned successively, *inter annos* 834 *et* 859

"II Dongallus or Doun-gheal,[2] so called from his light brown complexion. Martin (who, by mistake, says he was son to Gregory the Great,[3] though all historians are agreed that that monarch never had any issue), relates of this Doun-gheal, 'that he behaved most gallantly in the wars which King Gregory had in Ireland'[4] 'He married' (says the same learned antiquarian) 'Spontana, sister to Duncan, a king in Ireland, and their posterity got the name of MacGregor, all of them in this kingdom being descended from him.'[5] He died about 900, leaving two sons—

    1 Constantine.

    2. Findanus, of whom the MacFindons, MacFingons, or MacKinnons are descended

"III Constantine married his cousin Malvina, daughter to King Donald VI.[6]

"IV 'Gregor na Bratich' (Bratach), 'Gregor of the Standard,' so called from his office of standard-bearer to his uncle, King Malcolm I., son of Donald VI

---

[1] See introduction, page 1, as to article on MacGregor. Many observations therein not required for the genealogy are omitted in present work —*Ed*

[2] This name, believed to be that of Gregory's father rather than of his son, shows due search had been made in the ancient chronicles —*Ed*

[3] Mr MacGregor Stirling derives the family from King Gregory, whose historical existence is acknowledged (see page 1), whilst no Prince Gregor, brother of Kenneth, can be traced. He disputes the assertion that King Gregory did not marry, as the wives of the kings were frequently not mentioned, unless with reference to dynastic connections —*Ed*

[4] Martin's collection —Douglas' Baronage

[5] "Genealogical Collections in a Tree of the Family of Glenurchay or Breadalbane Title, MacGregor, vol. 11, page 22."—Macgregor Stirling.

[6] History of the Alpinian family in Latin, recovered from the Scottish College at Paris by David Mallet, Esq Authentic extract, *penes* Evan Murray, Esq.—Douglas' Baronage

He married 'Dorviegeldum[1] filiam hostiarii,'[2] and was killed in battle with the Danes, 961, with King Malcolm, leaving two sons—

1 Eoin or John.
2 Callum nam feidh, or 'Malcolm of the Deers,' keeper of the royal forests of Corrygeig.[3]

"V. Joannes, vocatus Eoin Mor MacGregor na Bratich (of the Standard), who married Alpina, daughter of Angus, or Eneas, great-grandson of Achaius, brother of Kenneth the Great. Eoin Mor is said to have been 'a comely man of great stature,[4] and an excellent bowman.' He fought under King Malcolm II. against Grimus, or Gruamach, so called from his surly looks, and was killed in battle, *circiter annum* 1004, leaving a son.

"VI Gregor Garbh, or the Stout, designated of Glenurchay, a man of martial spirit and great renown in Malcolm's time. He also fought under King Duncan I. against the Normans and Danes, *inter* 1035 and 1040, and promoted the restoration of his son, Malcolm III. He married a daughter[5] of the ancient house of Lochow,[6] by whom he had two sons—

1 Sir John
2. Gregorious, or Gregor, bred to the church, 'obiit electus episcopus St Andria '

"VII. Sir John MacGregor, Lord of Glenurchy, a person of very good account in the reign of King Malcolm III.,[7] *inter* 1057-1093, and because of his warlike achievements, was called 'Shir Ian borb an Cath,' 'Sir John forward in battle.' He married an English Lady of great beauty, who came to Scotland in the retinue of Princess, afterwards Queen Margaret. He died *circa* 1113, leaving two sons—

1 Malcolm who succeeded him.
2 Gregor or Gregory, who having been bred to the Church travelled to foreign parts for improvement, from whence having returned, he became

---

[1] History of the Alpinian family in Latin, recovered from the Scottish College at Paris by David Mallet, Esq   Authentic Extract, *penes* Evan Murray, Esq.—Doug. Bar.
[2] Professor Gregory writes this " The King's Hostarius " or " Doorward "
[3] Mamlorn called (in Gaelic) " The Glen of the Mist," " Corri-cheathich "—Doug. Bar
[4] The Latin History and Songs of the Bards —Doug Bar
[5] Buchanan's " History of the Clans."—Doug Bar
[6] " I find in the genealogical account of the surname of Campbell that Sir Colin Campbell of Lochow, who had divers great offices from King Malcolm II, had a daughter married to McGregor, Laird of Glenurchay; of this marriage was Sir John, a person of very good account in the reign of King Malcolm III." (Buchanan)   The Chartulary has the following entry —"He (Gregor Garbh) married a daughter of ' Paul na Sporan' or ' Paul of the Purse,' treasurer to King Malcolm II , and whose female descendant carried the estate of Lochow, by marriage, into the family of Campbell, now Argyle." (Comparison of Buchanan with genealogical table prefixed to Campbell of Kirnane's life of John, Duke of Argyle and Greenwich)—Macgregor Stirling.
[7] Buchanan and said heroic Poems.—Doug Bar

Abbot of the Monastery of Dunkeld.[1] Being a person of great piety and learning, and because of his father and grandfather's services to King Malcolm, St David the King changed that monastery into a Cathedral Church, *anno* 1127, and promoted the Abbe or Abbot Gregory to the new see, of which the Bishop obtained an ample ratification from Pope Alexander III. as well as an apostolical protection[2] to himself. He is witness to several Charters in the reign of King David and of Malcolm IV. From him the McNabs or the 'Sons of the Abbot' are undoubtedly descended. He lived to be the oldest Bishop of his time, and died *circiter* 1169 "

The notice of Bishop Gregory, to which reference is made, is thus given by Myln, who was a Canon of Dunkeld in the sixteenth century. The work is a Latin MS of which there are several translations :—

"Gregory, who was at that time Prior of the Convent, and afterwards a Privy Counsellor, was the first Bishop. It was by his interest that the lands of Auchtertoul and thirty prebends were granted to the Bishop and Chapter of Dunkeld, as is contained in King David's Charter, Gregory procured in the strictest form, from Pope Alexander III., a protection for himself and his Church, in which writing all the possessions are reckoned which they held at that time He sat in this see forty-two years, and died in the year 1169, which was the third year of the reign of King William "

From the "Chartulary" —

"Gregory, Abbot of Glendochart (where from early in the eighth century there had been a house of Culdees), next Abbot of Dunkeld, and on the erection of Dunkeld into an Episcopal see, the Bishop is said to have been a younger son of Sir John MacGregor of Glenurchay, and to have been the progenitor of the MacNabs, whose surname signifies 'Son of the Abbot,'[3] 'the pale Abbot, MacGregor's son from Stronuidhme' (a place in Glenfalloch where he resided at

---

[1] Dicta historia, Keith's Bishops   Cart. Scone, Dalrymple's Collection.—Doug Bar.
[2] Mill's MS (Lives of the Bishops of Dunkeld) —Doug Bar.
[3] A note by MacGregor Stirling explains that Abbots in the time of the Culdees were allowed to marry, which, however, according to Myln, must have been altered directly afterwards, as he states that the "good King David changed Dunkeld into a Convent of Seculars, at the same time he got appointed a Bishop and Canons, about 1127 " Dr Skene's investigations alter the date, places, and persons   "Mylne is however wrong, both in the date and in the name of the Founder" ("Celtic Scotland," vol ii page 370)   Alexander III created, 1107, two additional Bishoprics for the more remote and Celtic portion of his Kingdom, the first was that of Moray, to which he appointed a Bishop named Gregorius; and the second was that of Dunkeld, which he revived in the person of Cormac." Note, "They are first mentioned by name when they confirm the charter of erection of Scone, 1115," *ibid.*, page 368

no great distance from St Phillans Church), is still proverbial in the Highlands" ("Baronage," Keith's Catalogue of the Scottish Bishops, etc.).

The following passages from Celtic Scotland by Mr Skene are here quoted to shew the conclusions to which he has arrived on the subject of the MacNabs.—

"The name of MacNab certainly means the son of the Abbot. In the seventh century St Fillan founded a monastery in Glendochart the upper part of which took its name of Strathfillan from him, and in the reign of King William we find the Abbot of Glendochart ranking along with the Earls of Atholl and Menteith. As the property possessed by the MacNabs lay in Glendochart, and we find the name of Gillefaelan, or servant of St Fillan, occuring in their oldest genealogy, we may certainly recognise in them the descendants of the lay Abbots of Glendochart"

Mr Skene goes on to say that as the son of Aoidh Urchayidh or Hugh of Glenurchay bore the name of Gillafaelan or servant of St Fillan, and as the MacGregors also possessed property in Glendochart, they were probably connected with the MacNabs

"VIII. Sir Malcolm MacGregor of Glenurchy, eldest son of Sir John, was a man of reputation and authority in St David's time He married Marjoriam, juniorem filiam Wilhelmi hostiarii, domini rigis nepotis 'Marjory, youngest daughter of William,[1] Chief of the Army and nephew of our Lord the King'

" Sir Malcolm was a man of incredible strength of body Being of the King's retinue at a certain hunting party, in a forest, his Majesty having attacked a wild boar, or some other animal of prey, was like to be worsted, and in great danger of his life, when Sir Malcolm coming up, demanded his Majesty's permission to encounter it, the King having hastily answered, 'In,' or 'e'en do, bait spair nocht,' Sir Malcolm is said to have torn up a young oak by the root, and throwing himself between his Majesty and the fierce assailant, with the oak in one hand, kept the animal at bay till with the other he got an opportunity of running it through the heart. In honour whereof his Majesty was pleased to raise him to the peerage by the title of Lord MacGregor, to him ' et hæredibus masculis ', and in order to perpetuate the remembrance of the brave action, gave him an oak tree eradicate, in place of the fir-tree which the family had formerly carried We have his arms blazoned by an ancient herald[2] in these words · 'Lord MacGregor of old,

---

[1] The lady's father, as appears, was William, Earl of Murrayse, son of King Duncan II Chronicon Cumbrae —Chartulary.

[2] Workman's MS , blazoned, p. 37, illuminated, p. 249, *penes* Mr Cumming, Herald printer in Edinburgh —Doug Bar.

Argent, a sword in bend *azure* and an oak tree eradicate, in bend sinister *proper*, in chief a crown *gules*. *Crest*, a lyon's head crowned with an antique crown, with points.—Motto In do, bait spair nocht. Supporters, on the dexter an unicorn *argent* crowned, horned *or*, and on the sinister a deer *proper* tyn'd *azure*.'[1]

"Sir Malcolm[2] was called 'Morefhir Callum nan Caistel,' 'Lord of the Castles,' because of the several castles which he built, as those of Caol-Charn (now Kilchurn), beautifully situated at the north-east end of Lochow, and that of Finlarig, and the chapel which last was consecrated to the Blessed Virgin, and the old Castle of Taymouth, at least to have had their residence there and to have built Castle Coal Churn "

The " Chartulary " has the following remarks regarding this Sir Malcolm, styled in Gaelic " Morair " (Lord) —

" He is asserted to have saved the life of the Sovereign, who must have been either Alexander I., or David I. or Malcolm IV , in the act of hunting, and when attacked by the wild boar, and to have then obtained in reward for his service that armorial bearing which, being emblematical of the exploit, forms, amid the wreck of written documents, one of the muniments of the Family

With regard to the Arms the late Mr Donald Gregory sent to Sir Evan MacGregor a certified paper, signed by himself and his brother, John Gregory, Advocate, after a search made in the British Museum (9th June 1825), of which the following is a slightly abridged transcript —

"The MS. No. 1371 of the Harleian Collection,[3] in the British Museum, said to have been written and painted by Scotch, but bearing internal evidence of having been done by English hands, is titled 'Scotica Nobilitas, 1589 ' The MS contains .

   1 The Atchievements of King James VI , fo 1
   2 The Atchievements of the Earls of Scotland, twenty-four in number, fo 2 to 25.
   3 The Atchievements of the Barons, forty in number, fo. 26 to 67.
   4 The Shires of Scotland.
   5 The Stewartries of Scotland, &c , &c.
  10 Elenchus Baronum, of which the following is a copy "

---

[1] This blazon was copied by Sir John MacGregor Murray, before 1710 The book was, about that time, exposed for sale, " with the late Mr Goodall's effects," and others believed to have belonged to the family of the former librarian of the Advocate's Library

[2] In the poem by Duncan MacDougall Maoil, in the Book of Lesmore, reference is made to " Malcolm who his wealth ne'er hid," and in another poem to " Malcolm of unbending truth,"— see chapter ix , but his ancestry differs from that given in the " Baronage."

[3] This MS , and the coloured sketch of arms, has been verified by Sir Malcolm MacGregor of MacGregor, at the British Museum, Feb. 1897.

In this list of forty, unnecessary to be given here, MacGregoyre is placed thirty-eighth, not preceded, like all the others with one exception, by the letter L for Lord, thus—

Harleian MS. *continued*—

> " 37. MacGregoyre.
> 39. MacCloyd Heris.
> 40. L. of Lorne."

"The Atchievement of Macgregoyre as painted fo 64 is *Argent* a Pine Tree eradicate in bend sinister *proper*, surmounted of a sword in bend *azure*, hilted *gules*: in Chief an antique crown with points of the last; Crest a lyon's head erased *proper*, langued *gules* and crowned *or*. Supporters on the dexter an unicorn *argent* crowned and horned *or*, and on the sinister a deer *proper* crowned of the last."

In Mr Gregory's letter of the same date he writes:—

"I am inclined to think that Workman may have taken his blazoning of Arms from this very MS, and from the company in which MacGregor is there placed have called him Lord MacGregor of Old."

This conjecture is not altogether correct. The arms of MacGregor, as "Lord MakGzegour of Ould," occur also in an illuminated MS in the Lyon's office, Edinburgh, compiled about 1565-66 by an unknown hand. It became the property of James Workman, a Herald painter, whose name, with the date, 1623, it bears. This MS. has been reproduced in facsimile in the valuable book entitled "Scottish Arms, being a collection of Armorial Bearings, A.D. 1370-1678," by W. R. Stoddart, published in 1880. The frontispiece of the present volume is taken from a plate in this work, a reproduction of the Arms in Workman's MS. It is remarkable that the shield in the Harleian Collection bears a pine tree eradicate, whilst in Workman's MS. (which is the oldest) a young oak tree is represented, also eradicate. The family of the present Chief carry the oak tree. There is a tradition that the pine tree was the original armorial "charge," but that after the above related prowess of Sir Malcolm it was changed for the oak tree, which consequently pertained specially to his descendants and representatives. The Chiefs of Highland clans have the right to bear supporters, which right in other countries pertains generally to Peers only. On the title-page is given the shield, crest and motto to which all gentlemen of the ClanGregor are entitled.[1]

Although there may be no historical evidence as to this Sir Malcolm, the grant of armorial bearings, commemorating some hunting exploit, and the well established tradition of the MacGregor " Morar" (Lord) who built the Castles enumerated, affords reasonable probability to the main narrative. The actual date when the Arms were first given or first used is undiscoverable   But it was not till the reign of King William the Lion, 1165-1214, that arms were first borne in Scotland, and that King William chose as his cognisance the red "Lion rampant," which constitutes the Arms of Scotland.

"Baronage" *continued*—

"Sir Malcolm died, *circiter* 1164,[2] leaving three sons—
  1 William, his heir
  2. Gregor, called "Gregor more graund," more because of his large stature, and "graund" on account of his being ill-favoured or ugly. Of him all the Grants are said to be descended.
  3. Achaius (Hugh), of whom, by the traditions of the family, the Clan Achaius—now corruptly called Maccays or Mackays—are descended.

This theory of the descent of the Mackays is undoubtedly an error. They are now understood to be derived from the old Earldom of Sutherland. (See Skene's "Highlanders") In the old MacGregor genealogy, given in the Dean of Lismore's MS, to be quoted farther on, one of the ancestors of the main stem of the Macgregors bears the name of Hugh, and appears to have flourished in the twelfth century   It is probable that this Achaius, or Hugh, was a more prominent representative than a third son, as stated in the "Baronage"

With reference to the derivation of the Grants, a family copy of the "Baronage" has a note, apparently in Mr MacGregor Stirling's handwriting.

----

[1] Crests are not considered to come under the same fixed rules as other armorial bearings, but the Lion's head is generally adopted by all MacGregors.—*Ed*

[2] Probably the time when he flourished was thirty or forty years later, and it is possible that the two generations of Duncan a Straileadh, and his son, Duncan Beg, came in between Ian Borb nan Cath and Malcolm of the Castles.—*Ed*

"In a history of the Family of Grant—in the possession of a respectable Cadet (Grant of Bonhard), composed before 1719, and denying the traditional account of the descent of the Grants from a younger son of the Laird of MacGregor—there is the following passage regarding the parents of Patrick Grant of Freuchie and Bellachastell, born about 982 —'Anlaw, or Allan, the eldest son and representative of Heming Grandt, a man of desirable accomplishments, is married to Mora, daughter to Neil MacGregor, a man lineally descended of Gregorious Magnus, King of Scotland. This Anlaw (others call him Avelass) got with Mora MacGregorie, in portion or tocher, the Barony of Bellachastell and Freuchie in Straspey.' The grandson of Patrick (son of Mora MacGregor) was 'Gregory Grant of Freuchie'[1] The same passage occurs also in the 'Chartulary' with the remark : 'This account, which differs materially from the title Grant of Grant, in Douglas's Baronage—but is obviously preferable, and is confirmed by the other MSS. quoted—may serve to account for, and, at the same time, to correct the extant tradition of the common origin of the MacGregors and the Grants, whose armorial bearings have a strong affinity."

In consequence of this passage (found, however, only in a modern genealogy), the date of A.D 980 is assigned as the time when Neil MacGregor flourished, and he is conjectured to have been a son of Gregor of the Standard [2]

"Baronage" *continued*—

"IX William, Lord Macgregor, who flourished in the reign of William the Lyon, and Alexander II   He married filiam domini de Lindsay, and died *ad annum* 1238, leaving two sons and a daughter—

1 Gregor, his heir
2. Alpin ; who, being bred to the Church, was promoted to the Bishoprick of Dunblane, *inter annos* 1232 and 1290 "[3]

The "Chartulary" notices—

"From a collation of circumstances, a strong presumption arises that William's wife was daughter of Lindsay of Bonhill, or Buchnull as it was anciently called. These Lindsays in the thirteenth century were hereditary Toschsadorachs, and Forresters of the Earls of Lennox."

---

[1] "The foundation of the Grant story seems merely to be that the earliest Grant known was Gregory le Grant, whose sons Laurence and Robert, called Grant (dicti Grant), witness an agreement between the Bishop of Moray and John Bisset in 1258."—"Celtic Scotland," vol. III. p 350.
[2] Chartulary   (See page 13.)   [3] Historia familiæ et Keith's Bishops.—Doug. Bar

"Baronage" *continued*—

"X Gregor,[1] Lord[2] of MacGregor (or, according to the 'Chartulary,' Gregor of Glenurquhay) succeeded, and joined King Alexander II *anno* 1248 with his followers when that Monarch went upon his expedition for recovery of the western Isles from Haco, King of Norway He also flourished in the reign of Alexander III (*inter* 1249 *et* 1296). By his Lady Marion, filiam de Gilchrist, he was father of Malcolm XI"

The "Baronage" adds a note that the writer has been unable to discover who the Gilchrist was, but the "Chartulary" has a remark—

"*Circiter* 1286   Died Gregor of Glenurchy, who married a daughter of Gilchrist (4th son as is believed of Aulin, 2nd Earl of Levenax), founding this belief on a Charter by Malduin, 3rd Earl of Lennox, 1238-9, of certain lands which is witnessed, it is to be remarked, by John Glendochir, Amalech my Brother, &c."

In the "Baronage" the successor to Gregor No. 10 is given as—

"XI. Malcolm (styled Dominus de MacGregor), a person of great loyalty, strongly attached to Bruce, whom he is said to have relieved from the chief of Lorn at Dalreogh, and to have been mounted on a milk-white steed[3]   Thereafter the King harboured in a large cave in MacGregor's lands, near Craig-Chrostan, which is to this day called "Uamh an Riogh" (the King's cave), from which he crossed over Loch Lomond, and met the Earl of Lennox

"Malcolm fought at the battle of Bannockburn, and is said to have been the person who brought the relics of St Fillansarum from the country of that name, then part of his lands, to King Robert's chaplain, who passed it for a miracle, in consequence of which the Bruce founded a priory in Strathfillan[4] (*anno* 1314) This Malcolm[5] is much celebrated by several bards   He fought under Edward Bruce in Ireland, and having received a wound at the battle of Dundalk, of which he was ever afterwards lame, he retired home, and was known by the name of "Morfhear bachdach," or the lame lord.

[1] There is ground to suppose that Gregor's father's name was John, believed to be William's second brother, omitted in "Baronage"   (See chapter vii)—*Ed*

[2] The writers of the "Chartulary" do not consider that the title "Morer" (equivalent to Lord), by which Sir Malcolm was designated, was hereditary, even if it was ever formally bestowed ; but after No VII , styled Lord of Glenurchy in the "Baronage," the "Chartulary" continues to quote the territorial designation —*Ed*

[3] Collection of ancient heroic poems, *penes* Mr John Murray —Doug Bar

[4] The ruins of this priory can still be traced near Crianlarig —*Ed*.

[5] Said heroic poems —Doug Bar

"He died at an advanced age, *anno* 1374, leaving by his wife Mary, daughter to Malise McAlpin of Finnich, two sons—

    1 Gregor, his heir.

    2. Gilbert, of whom it is said the Griersons of Lag descended"

The Griersons of Lag claim this descent, which is quite probable although it may not be susceptible of actual proof

The existence of this second Malcolm seems to be well established by tradition and Highland poems. It is said that "Malcolm, chief of the family of MacGregor, had a command at the army of King Robert Bruce at Bannockburn," but the authority for this statement is not conclusive [1] There is also mention of a Malcolm of Glendochart doing fealty to Edward of England, 28th August 1296 As Gregor (X.) is said to have flourished in the thirteenth century, it seems improbable that his son should have lived till 1374. Possibly one or two generations have been missed out before or after Malcolm The MSS of the Dean of Lismore contains a very interesting genealogy by an old Highland seannachie, giving the Glenstray pedigree. It is difficult to identify the list recorded in the "Baronage" with the names found therein, but in a subsequent chapter this genealogy will be transcribed

From the unquestionable authority of the Obituary, known as the Chronicle of Fortingal,[2] the following entries are here given in chronological order —

"1390, April 19. Died John, son of Gregor of Glenurquhay, and was buried in Dysart, north of the High Altar.

Dysart, q d Tigh sart—in English, "House of the Highest"—is the old name of the Church of Glenurquhay, which was annexed to Dalmally John, son of Gregor, was surnamed Cham, or "blind of an eye," as appears from the two entries under 1415

It is believed that he was the latest MacGregor in recognised possession of Glenurquhay, for his son is styled "in," not "of," that land, but "there does not seem ground to suppose that they ever had what alone, according to Saxon ideas of landed property, could secure continued possession, a charter of confirmation on their resignation into the King's hands. ("Chartulary.")

1415 Died Gregor, son of John Cham, in Glenurquhay, and was buried as first mentioned

1415. Died John the Black (dhu), son of John Cham, son of Gregor at Stronmelochan, and was buried at Dysart

Stronmelochan was a fortalice at the north-east extremity of Lochaw, near the entrance of Glenstray.

---

[1] "Catalogue of Chiefs," *penes* Major-General David Stewart of Garth.

[2] Translation of Dean MacGregor's Chronicle, printed with the *Historical Review*, 1831.

The above entries, the Bard's genealogy, and others from "The Black Book of Taymouth," enable us to define positively that the house of Glenstray descended in direct line from this John Dhu, and as he had a brother, Gregor, who coincides with Gregor, surnamed Aulin, in the "Baronage," we are led to believe that these two Gregors were identical.

From the "Baronage".—

"XII Gregor, called Aulin (Aluinn)—*i e*, "perfectly handsome"—succeeded. He married Iric, daughter of his uncle Malcolm McAlpin, son of the said Malise, and died *circiter annum*, 1413 leaving by his said lady five sons and several daughters—

1. Malcolm, his heir
2. John, first designed of Breachd-shabh, who eventually became Laird of MacGregor.
3. Gillespie, or Archibald, who married and had issue.
4. Gregor, of whom the family of Ruath shruth, or Roro (as will be shown later, the name of this son was probably Duncan).[1]
5. Dugal Ciar "

In the course of this, the fourteenth century, the sovereigns had given many lands to those who supported them, and amongst these were territories occupied by the ClanGregor as Crown tenants—*i.e*, settled on the Crown lands by royal favour, either as a reward for military services, or connected with the royal house, which tradition asserts, or the tribe may have enjoyed allodial occupation of these localities from time immemorial.

From the "Chartulary" —

"Before 1340, Alexander Menzies, son and heir of the deceased Alexander Menzies,[2] gave a grant to 'Avunculo meo,' Yvaro Campbel, of all his lands in the Barony of Glendochart.

"In A.D. 1340, July 30th.   Charter by Alexander Menzies, son and heir of Alexander de Menzies, Lord of Glendochart, to Ewar Campbell and his heirs, of 20 merks of land in Glendochart, dated at Kilmarnock, 30th July 1340.

"1368-9, 12th March.   Charter by King David II. at Perth to John of Lorn, of the district of Glenlyon, in Atholl   (Robertson's "Index of Missing Charters," 80-141)

[1] See chapter xi.
[2] In 1374-6 Campbell is mentioned as having received it from the Crown, it is supposed on the forfeiture of Malcolm of Glendochart

"1374, April 20th. Charter by King Robert II. to Arthur Campbell, son of Ewar Campbell, of the lands of Strathquhir, resigned by the said Ewar.

"1376, Feb. 9th. Charter by King Robert II., confirming one by his son Robert, Earl of Fife and Menteith, to Arthur Campbell of Strathquhir, of certain lands in the Barony of Glendochart, viz., amongst others, Kyleters, mor, and beg, Inner-hardgowrane, with the Lake of Glendochart, and the Island of Garwhelane, and Wester Hardkell (Ardchalzie). "Mag. Sig.," v. 50.

A pause may here fittingly be made, to clear the ground before proceeding to more historic times.

Chapter III

Sketch of Scottish History, 1285-1390

THE period succeeding the death of King Alexander III, in 1285, and of his young granddaughter, the Maiden of Norway, who died in September 1290, was the darkest of Scotland's history, only illumined by the patriotism of William Wallace, and subsequently of Robert Bruce. After a miserable reign of four years, John Baliol attempted to contend against Edward I. of England, but sustained a severe defeat at the battle of Dunbar, 28th April 1296. Wallace, after a few years of heroic struggles to deliver his country, was eventually captured, and beheaded on the 22nd August 1305 Bruce, King Robert I., was crowned at Scone, 29th March 1306, and gained the victory of Bannockburn 23rd June 1314 After his early death (June 1329) Scotland's troubles were again renewed, his son, David II., being only four years old at the time Edward Baliol, son of John Baliol, invaded the country, gaining a victory at Dupplin, 1332, and Edward III. of England coming to his support, won the battle of Halidon Hill, near Berwick, 19th July 1333 But brave and skilful warriors were not wanting in Scotland, and having succeeded in winning back the castles and towns taken from them, they welcomed home in 1341 the young King David, who had taken refuge in France. Having subsequently invaded England, he was made prisoner at the battle of Neville's Cross, near Durham, 17th October 1346, and remained in captivity till Scotland was able to ransom him in 1359. Peace was at length restored, till the death of David II., February 1370-71.

The dynasty of the Stewarts now came to the throne. Walter, the Lord High Steward of Scotland, having married Lady Marjory Bruce, eldest daughter of King Robert I., their son Robert Stewart succeeded his uncle as King Robert II., and reigned till his death, April 1390.

All that is known of the ClanGregor during this stormy period is ably discussed in a paper by Mr Donald Gregory, entitled "Historical Notices of the ClanGregor," which Essay was read to the Society of Antiquaries of Scotland, 22nd March 1830, and printed in the "Archæologia Scotica," vol. iv. As this paper is now out of print, and not in general circulation, quotations may here be freely given.[1]

"An early, if not the original, seat of the ClanGregor (one of the few families in the Highlands which, so far as male descent is concerned, can be regarded as purely Celtic), a family which is generally allowed to be one of the most ancient and re-nowned of the Highland tribes, was the valley of Glenurchy, in the district of Lorn. From Glenurchy, accordingly, they took their style for many generations

"It appears that John of Glenurchy—the chief, probably, of the family—was made prisoner by King Edward of England at the battle of Dunbar, *anno* 1296, and that he had afterwards his lands and possessions restored by order of that monarch, on condition of going to France to serve him in his wars in that kingdom. In the public instruments connected with the fate of those of the Scottish leaders captured at Dunbar, John de Glenurchy is ranked as one of the "Magnates Scotiæ," a proof that his possessions holding of the Crown were far from incon-siderable This individual had—as would seem—died in France; for his name does not again appear in any of the transactions of the period He left a daughter and heiress, Margaret, who carried the Barony of Glenurchy to her husband, John, son of Sir Neil Campbell of Lochawe, by Lady Mary Bruce, sister of King Robert. This John Campbell, on whose mother her Royal brother had conferred the Earl-dom of Athole, became in her right Earl of Athole. He fell in the battle of Halidon Hill, *anno* 1333, leaving issue by his wife,[2] a child, who survived a few years only On the death of this child, the Barony of Glenurchy appears to have returned to the family of MacGregor, for there is undoubted evidence of the death, so late as 1390, of John MacGregor of Glenurchy I have been thus minute in tracing the history of this barony, as I conceive it to have been the last freehold possession of any consequence held by the name of MacGregor."

In the "Chartulary," the documents connected with Edward I's prisoners are given at full length

"Johannes de Glenurchart, one of several 'Scottish Magnates' is taken prisoner in the battle of Dunbar   ⸴

"Mandate by Edward I of England, 31st of July 1297, bearing the title, 'King

---

[1] Taken from a MS. copy of this Essay presented to Sir Evan Murray MacGregor in 1830
[2] Margaret de Glenurchy must have been his first wife —See p 28.

Edward commands that the Scottish Magnates captured in the battle of Dunbar, and about to fight for him in France and elsewhere, be liberated from prison.— (Rotuli Scotiæ)—1297, July 31st.' 'The King (Edward I) to the Constable of the Castle of Berkhamsted, greeting   Whereas John de Glenurchart, lately captured in the conflict that took place betwixt us and the Scots at Dunbar, and by our command detained in the prison of the said castle, hath found before our beloved and faithful Walter de Bello Campo (Beauchamp), Steward of our household, sufficient bail that he shall immediately pass with us in our service to the countries beyond seas, and that he shall well and faithfully serve us against the King of France, and other Rebels and Enemies to us in time to come, as in the foresaid Bail Bond, recorded in presence of the said Steward, is fully contained.   We command you that ye cause ye body of the foresaid John to be liberated from our prison of the said castle without any delay whatsoever in the foresaid manner.'" —Rotuli Scotiæ.

The following remarks from the "Chartulary" relate to the same personage.—

"Charter by King David II. of Scotland 'To Margaret de Glenurchy and to John Campbell, her spouse' (Earl of Atholl), 'of the lands of Glenurchy.'"[1]

Between 1329, June 28th, death of King Robert Bruce, and 1333, July 19th, battle of Halidon Hill

"John Campbell, younger son of Sir Neil Campbell of Lochaw by Lady Mary Bruce, sister of King Robert I, was created Earl of Atholl on the forfeiture of David de Strathbogie, *arciter* 1314.   He married Margaret, heiress of Glenurchy, daughter, most probably, of John de Glenurchart, captured at the Battle of Dunbar, 1296, who had, in virtue of a warrant by Edward I of England, 31st July (same year), been ordered to deliver up his eldest son (if he had one) as a hostage   It is unknown whether he had a son.   John Campbell, Earl of Atholl, was killed at the Battle of Halidon Hill."

The "Historical Notices" proceed —

"Glendochart is another district with which the Clan appears to have been connected at an early period   John Glendochir witnesses a charter by Malduin,

---

[1] Index of missing charters by William Robertson, Esq, one of the Deputies of the Lord Clerk-Register for keeping the Records of Scotland, 1798   The terms of this missing charter are not known   All the charters extant in the general Register House, Edinburgh, in the reigns of Robert I, David II, Robert II and III, and in the regency of Robert, Duke of Albany, have since been printed.   The charter quoted in the text is not among them   Those reigns, and that regency, comprehend the period over which Mr Robertson's index extends.   A MS. index in 1629 is the source of the information regarding this missing charter.—Note in "Chartulary"

third Earl of Lennox, 3d March 1238, and Malcolm and Patrick de Glendochart, probably sons of John, do homage to Edward I at Berwick-upon-Tweed, 28th August 1296, being a short while after the disastrous conflict of Dunbar. In the lists of the Scots on this occasion, printed by Prynne, Malcolm de Glendochart is mentioned twice, and in separate places, once as Malcolm de Glendochart simply, and again, in company with amongst others Alexander de Argyle (Lord of Lorn), as King's Tenant in Perthshire From these facts the obvious inference is, that Malcolm de Glendochart held lands both as a free baron and as a kindly tenant. That the individuals designed of Glendochart were Mac-Gregors appears highly probable, when, in addition to the well-known fact of the long settlement of the Clan in this quarter, we find that the names Malcolm and Patrick were common in the tribe

"But these were not the only territories in which the ClanGregor succeeded in gaining a footing The numbers of the name that have for centuries been found in the adjacent districts of Rannoch, Glenlyon, Glenlochy, Strathfillan, and Balquhidder, and in Breadalbane generally, to all of which there is easy access from Glenurchy, testify the ancient power of the family, and warrant the supposition that parts at least of these ample territories were held as free baronies by the chieftains of the Clan

"If this supposition be thought not unreasonable, it will not be difficult to account for the loss of many of these possessions under the reign of Robert Bruce

"The Lord of Lorn, who married a sister of John Cumin the Black, brother-in-law of King John Baliol, took, as is well known, a very active part in favour of Baliol, and after the dethronement of that unfortunate prince, attached himself to the Cumin party, displaying a constant and energetic opposition to the claims of Bruce. The family of MacGregor, from the situation of their principal property, Glenurchy, in Lorn, and probably through their possessions in Perthshire also, were necessarily in strict alliance and otherwise closely connected with the house of Lorn, and would naturally follow the fortunes of that very powerful family, in a question more especially admitting of so much dispute as that of the succession to the Scottish Crown. We find, accordingly, that Bruce had no sooner established himself on the throne, than the house of Lorn, with all its followers and allies, suffered severely by forfeiture Nor were the MacGregors exempted from their share of the loss. Glenurchy could not be forfeited, being the property of an heiress and a minor, but the wardship and the marriage were probably given by the King to Sir Neil Campbell of Lochawe, his brother-in-law Glendochart was granted to Alexander Menzies, who had married Egidia, sister to the High Steward, husband to the Princess Marjory Bruce. The barony of Fortingal became, by the royal bounty, the property of Thomas Menzies, son, probably, of Alexander, and part of Rannoch fell by the same process to the ancestor of the family of Strowan Robertson, who had been a staunch adherent to Bruce To the power of the Clan

Gregor these various grants must have given a fatal blow; and it is from this reign that we must date the downfall of this ancient tribe

"Some of the Clan however appear to have taken the other side, for in 1293 John Baliol, then King of Scotland, issued a mandate to Alexander de Ergadia (Lord of Lorn), and to the Bailie of Lochawe, charging them to summon 'Sir Angus MacDonald, Knight, Lawmund MacGregor, and Angus, son of Duncan MacGregor,' to appear in the royal presence on a specified day, to do homage, and various other things obligatory upon them   The first of these three individuals is evidently the son and heir of the Lord of the Isles, and the same as he who proved afterwards so steady a friend to Robert Bruce   It would thus seem that Sir Angus, and the two MacGregors mentioned along with him, and who, from the terms of the writ, are evidently free barons holding their lands of the Crown, had not acquiesced in the award which placed Baliol on the Scottish throne, an inference which, as it seems perfectly legitimate, will serve to account for Glenurchy's being, as we have seen, in 1390, the property of John MacGregor   This, however, did not prevent the chiefs of the Campbells who, by their close alliance with the new dynasty, had now commenced that rise which has not been less permanent than it was rapid, from acquiring a superiority over the MacGregors, which was improved by every succeeding generation "

Dr Joseph Anderson has the following remarks or "resumé" on this subject ·—[1]

"The earliest notice of the ClanGregor shows them settled in Glenurchay, Glendochart, Breadalbane, Glenlochy, Glenlyon, Rannoch, and Balquhidder, but not holding their lands of the Crown. Before the date of Robert Bruce there are incidental notices of the MacGregors of Glenurchay, but the forfeiture of the House of Lorn, with all its followers and allies, with whom undoubtedly the MacGregors were closely allied, deprived them of their possessions   Glenurchay was at that time the property of an heiress and a minor, and the ward and marriage of Margaret de Glenurchay[2] seems to have been given to John Campbell,[3] son of Sir Nigel (or Neil), who was created Earl of Atholl, and fell at Hallidon Hill, 1333   There was one child of the marriage, who survived a few years only, and the Barony of Glenurchay seems to have returned to the MacGregors, for there is a John MacGregor of Glenurchay in 1390

[1] Copied by permission from a note-book of Dr Joseph Anderson in connection with the "Chartulary."

[2] After the death of this Margaret de Glenurchay, the Earl of Atholl must have married again, for Mr Skene quotes a "dispensation in 1339 for the marriage of Johanna, Countess of Stratherne, widow of John, Earl of Atholl, to Maurice de Moraira."—Celtic Scotland, vol iii, appendix, page 452

[3] 5th April 1357-8.—Charter of whole lands of Glenurchy by King David II in favour of Mariota of Glenurchy, daughter of John of Glenurchy, and spouse of John Campbell —Dr Anderson

"Immediately after this we find the Campbells of Lochaw in possession of Glenurchay, and a family of MacGregors as vassals of the Earl of Argyle in Glenstrae. There is no evidence to show how the barony of Glenurchay passed from the MacGregors to the Campbells, but in the Black Book of Taymouth . it is stated that Colin Campbell, second son of Sir Duncan Campbell of Lochaw, was the first Laird of Glenurchay of the line of Lochaw. In point of fact he had a charter from his father in 1432 of the barony of Glenurchy, and afterwards, by marriage with the heiress, acquired a third of the great Lordship of Lorn This Sir Duncan Campbell was King's Lieutenant in Argyleshire "

Continuing the Historical Notice of the Clan, the account of their possessions may now be followed ·—

"At what time the barony of Glenurchy was finally lost to the MacGregors by becoming, as it did, the property of the Campbells, is a point on which, so far as I can learn, there is no extant evidence Nor is it certainly known how the change took place. It has been stated from good authority that John MacGregor of Glenurchy died in 1390, this individual was contemporary with Sir Colin Campbell of Lochawe, of whom I find it said, in a manuscript history of the Campbells, that he added greatly to the property of his family The words of the manuscript are :—' But never any of that family showed himself a more worthy man than he, according to the times he lived to see ; and although, by every one of his predecessors, some lands were added to the estate and honours of that family, yet none of them purchased more of both than he In effect, he it was (as the proverb is) who broke the ice and opened a door to all the after grandeur of the family, by suppressing the Islanders and curbing all oppressors.' Duncan, first Lord Campbell, son of Sir Colin above mentioned, married a daughter of Robert, Duke of Albany, brother of King Robert III., and many years Governor of Scotland This Duncan, Lord Campbell, long known as Sir Duncan Campbell of Lochawe, was one of the wealthiest and most powerful of the Scottish barons. He held, under the Jameses I and II., the office of King's Lieutenant in Argyleshire, which invested him with very extensive powers against rebels to the King's authority Whether he exercised those powers to strip the MacGregors of the territory of Glenurchy, or inherited this possession from his father, are points on which it is impossible to come to a decision. This much however is certain, that he possessed Glenurchy, and gave it in patrimony to a younger son, Sir Colin, founder of the House of Breadalbane, who is mentioned in a Charter by the style of Glenurchy, *anno* 1442

"I have now brought down the history of the ClanGregor to the time when I find them in a situation totally different from that of any other Clan in the Highlands, namely, without an acre of land held free of the Crown. Although, however, this was a very singular situation for a Clan so numerous, and so long and extensively established, I have not discovered, from any authentic source whatever, that they had at this time become distinguished any more than the neighbouring tribes for a predatory disposition. In Perthshire the Crown still possessed extensive lands on which the Chieftains of the tribe were seated, nominally as Crown tenants, but in reality, from the unsettled state of the country, as absolute proprietors, their numbers, and their warlike habits, making it very difficult, or next to impossible, for the Crown to enforce payment of their rents. Such a state of things could not last.   During the government of Albany accordingly, and in the minorities of the four immediate successors of James I, owing to the above, and other causes not less important, these lands gradually passed into the possession of the various powerful barons in that part of the country whom it was the interest of a weak government to conciliate.

"Although it be well known that the Duke of Albany, in order to strengthen his party during the captivity of James I, dilapidated the royal revenues to a very great extent by bribing the most powerful families with grants of the Crown-lands on very favourable terms in every part of the kingdom, yet I have not been able to trace any such transactions relating to that part of Perthshire of which we speak, while he held the government. It appears, however, that the Governor himself, besides the lands which he held in the Highlands as Earl of Menteith, and as heir to the earldom of Fife,[1] acquired extensive possessions in Breadalbane. He had, in 1375, a royal charter of the lands and barony of Glendochart, proceeding on the resignation of Alexander de Menzies   A large portion of this territory, comprehending Glenfalloch, Strathfillan, and the upper half of Glendochart, was held under Albany, by Arthur Campbell of Strachur,[2] the representative of a family which had long been seated in this part of the country   The lands conveyed to Campbell (afterwards erected into the barony of Glenfalloch) were in later reigns, and we may therefore presume, at this time also, almost exclusively occupied by the ClanGregor

"The mischievous system, introduced by Albany, of granting the Crown-lands to those whose support he wished to gain, without reference, as may be easily supposed, to the antiquated claims of the Celtic occupants, was checked for a time under the active and vigorous sway of James I, but during a century after the untimely death of that monarch, and particularly under the long minorities with which Scotland was afflicted during this melancholy period of her history, we can trace the rise of several distinguished families, through their acquisition, principally, of the hereditary property of the Crown   A contemporary writer of undoubted

---

[1] Isabell, Countess of Fife, resigned into the hands of King Robert II. (amongst other lands) the barony of Strathurd, Strathbrand, Discher, Toyer, with the Isle of Loch Tay, in Perthshire, 22nd June 1389 —Note in " Historical Notices."

[2] See Charters on page 23

authority says, under the year 1452, 'Ther wes sindrie landis gevin to sindrie men oe the Kingis Secreit Counsall, the quhilk men that is to say, the Lord Campbell, to Schir Colyne Campbell, to Schir Alexander Hwme, to Schir Dauid Hwme, to Schir James Keyr, and to uther sindrie, quha wer rewardit be the said Secreit Counsall, the quhilk men demyt wald nocht stand.'[1] Many such grants having been made during the minorities of the respective sovereigns were, on their attaining their majority, revoked; whilst others, according to the influence of the grantees, were confirmed. The uncertainty attending these new titles to the Crown-lands must doubtless have encouraged the actual occupants to despise the authority of the charters by which overlords were imposed upon them, and in many cases, from families with whom they had long been at mortal feud. The MacGregors, as may be supposed, soon rendered themselves obnoxious to such of the families as had been fortunate enough to obtain charters to any of these lands; and consequently it became, in almost every instance, an object of the new proprietors to expel them Resistance, though natural enough, became in the end ruin to the weaker party, and it may, I think, be safely affirmed that, in proportion as the MacGregors, from being kindly tenants of the Crown, became subject to their neighbours, who had a greater interest and better opportunities, and were consequently more successful than the King and his Bailies had been formerly, in depriving them of lands to which they could produce no better title than occupancy, the Clan grew remarkable for opposition to law and order.

" This position will appear to have a better foundation if we enter a little more into detail as regards the history of the Campbells of Glenurchy, the family of Menzies, and of others of the Perthshire families closely connected, in one way or another, with the ClanGregor.

" In the reign of James III , but in what year is uncertain, Sir Colin Campbell, first of Glenurchy, acquired the large barony of Lawers, on Loch Tay, in the hands of the Crown since the forfeiture of Thomas Chalmer, who had been executed for aiding in the murder of James I. He acquired also the lands of Achriach or Achinrevach[2] in Glendochart, which, along with Lawers, he gave to his youngest son John, ancestor of the Campbells of Lawers.

" In 1473 John Stewart of Fortingal, and Neil Stewart[3] his son and heir, had from the King a nineteen years' lease of the lands and lordship of Apnadull, Glen

---

[1] Short chronicle, chiefly of the reign of James II , by a contemporary author, in the archives of Boswell of Auchinleck, printed by Thomas Thomson, Esqre, Deputy Register of Scotland. —Note in " Historical Notices."

[2] Malcolme Johnsoun of Auchinrevach (supposed to be a MacGregor) disponed his lands of Auchinrevach, lying in the barony of Glendochir and shire of Perth, to Colin Campbell of Glenurchay, K^t, by charter dated 6th July 1463 —Chartulary

[3] The father died at Garth, 10th December 1475, and the son at the same place, 31st Jan 1499-1500 —" Chronicle of Fortingal." The Stewarts of Fortingal were descended from a natural son of the celebrated Wolf of Badenoch, by Johaneta de Menzies, heiress of Fortingal

coich, Glenlyon, Strathbrawin, and Rannoch, all in Perthshire.[1] They had, besides, a royal grant, for the same term, of the office of bailiary of those lands, and it was at the same time provided that they should have the lands of Rannoch free of all duties and services during the whole of the period above mentioned—a plain proof that, so far as Rannoch was concerned, it was not expected to prove, in any other way at least, beneficial to the lessees   This lease expired in 1492, and, to Stewart's mortification, was not renewed   A great part of the power which it had conferred on this family passed, as we shall have occasion to see, into the hands of Glenurchy

"In the minority of James IV, *anno* 1488, being the first of his reign, a Parliamentary Act was passed for the 'stanching of thift, reiff, and uther inormiteis throw all the realme,' and amongst others of the barons, the following became bound to seek out and punish such as should be guilty of those crimes in the districts over which their authority *in cumulo* extended, and they were for this purpose furnished with extensive powers—viz, Duncan Campbell of Glenurchy, Neil Stewart of Fortingal, and Ewyne Campbell of Strachur (proprietor of Glenfalloch).   The districts were Disher and Toyer,[2] Glenurchy, Rannoch, Apnadull, Glenlyon, and Glenfalloch.   It is evident that if this Act was enforced at all, it must have fallen with accumulated severity upon the landless and consequently desperate ClanGregor. It is much to be doubted, however, if the morals of this now obnoxious race would be greatly improved by such discipline, and whether it was not rather to be expected that their feelings, in the situation in which they found themselves placed relatively to these powerful barons, must, in even a people far less high-spirited, have been indignation and the thirst of vengeance

"Sir Duncan Campbell of Glenurchy, in this reign, made vast additions to the property of his family in Perthshire   He acquired the King's lands of Balloch (now Taymouth), and others on Loch Tay, in 1492   About the same time he obtained the important office of Bailiary of the Crown-lands of Disher and Toyer, Glenlyon and Glendochart, in most of which he was moreover the principal tenant The acquisition of the office of bailiary was in this, as in most other cases, merely a prelude to the lands becoming hereditary in his family.   Accordingly, in 1502, he had a charter of the lands of Glenlyon, which he gave to his son Archibald, founder of the family of Campbell of Glenlyon   Some years later he acquired, from private

---

[1] *Mag. Sig* —The lands of Rannoch mentioned here must not be confounded with that part of the ancient Lordship of Rannoch granted by Robert Bruce to the ancestor of Robertson of Strowan, the former being in fact what remained to the Crown of the Lordship after that grant, and comprising (probably) the greater part of it

[2] The Lordship of Disher and Toyer comprehended the lands on both sides of Loch Tay (with some exceptions), and likewise the rich valley of Glenlochay, lying between Glenlyon and Glendochart.   Disher and Toyer are Gaelic, the former signifying a tract of country having a southern exposure, the latter a northern.   The three last notes occur in the "Historical Notices"

individuals, the barony of Fynlang, at the west end of Loch Tay; the lands of Scheane (Shian) and others, and the lands of Crannych—all in the same district; so that before his death (in the battle of Flodden) in 1513, he had undoubtedly become one of the most influential barons of Perthshire, and if we take into account his possessions in Argyle, there were few barons of greater power in Scotland.

"Whilst the Laird of Glenurchy was thus extending the influence of his house in one part of the territory occupied by the ClanGregor, the head of the ancient family of Menzies followed his example in another Robert Menzies of that Ilk had (1502) a royal charter of what remained to the Crown of the lands of Rannoch, a district claimed by the Clan as more peculiarly their own

"It may naturally be supposed that these proceedings were viewed with a favourable eye, neither by the MacGregors (the actual occupants) nor by the Stewarts of Fortingal, so lately all but proprietors of Glenlyon and Rannoch. Deadly feuds immediately arose; and the ink on his charter of Rannoch had scarcely dried when Menzies's Castle of Weyme was burnt to the ground by Neil Stewart and his associates, and all his lands laid waste [1]

"These dissensions attracted the attention of the Government, and in 1504 the Earl of Athole, a near kinsman of Stewart, Stewart himself, and the Lairds of Glenurchy and Strowan Robertson, with MacGregor, were summoned to attend Parliament on a charge of treason What the final result was does not appear Rannoch was still the theatre of intestine broils, nor could the chartered holder make good his title by actual possession To strengthen himself, he, in 1505, entered into a contract with the Earl of Huntly, which contained, among others, the following stipulations.—(1) Menzies's eldest son, Sir Robert, became bound to marry Lady Jean Gordon, the Earl of Huntly's daughter (2) The lands of Rannoch were by Menzies let to Huntly for five years, the latter binding himself to stock it with the best and most obedient tenants that could be found; and also to assist and maintain the Laird of Weyme and his son in the peaceable enjoyment of their lands in Perthshire, to aid them in all cases of need, and to help them in getting tenants for their lands."

The "Chartulary" gives, under date 1504-5, March 15th, the following —

"In the actioun and causs persewit be Robert Menzies of that Ilk Kny[t] aganis Nele Stewart of Fothergilt, for the wranguss destruction and down casting of his Mansion place and Fortalice of the Weme, and for the burning and destruction of divers vittualles in sicht gudes &c."—with details of the same. The "Chartulary"

---

[1] Chronicle of Fortingal (1502, September—Weym was burned by Neil Stuart of Gart) The Lord High Treasurer's books contain the following entry under 12th October 1502 —"Item to Robert Wallace, Messenger to pass in Stratherne to warne the Lordis of the countrie to pas to freithe the Lord of Weyme quhen Neill Stewart segit him, vij s "—Note in "Historical Notices."

remarks of another Decreet ("No MacGregors unless Duncan Patrikson be one.")[1]

"About this time Neil Stewart resigned his lands of Fortingal to Huntly [2] All the power, however, of this nobleman, which the acquisition of Fortingal tended to increase in relation to the projected settlement of Rannoch, failed to put his ally Menzies in quiet possession of this turbulent territory In 1523, Menzies having by Janet, Countess of Athole,[3] been charged to expel thence the Laird of MacGregor and his Clan, on account of some depredations alleged to have been committed by them upon the Countess's tenants, stated to the Lords of Council that it was impossible for him to comply, '*seeing that the said MacGregor on force enterit the said Robertis landis of Rannoche, and withhaldis the samyn from him maisterfullie, and is of fer gretar powar than the said Robert, and will nocht be put out be him of the saidis landis*'[4] Upon this statement he was absolved from all liability till the matter should be further investigated Several years appear to have passed over before any very vigorous measures were taken against the ClanGregor in this quarter In 1530 the Laird of Enoch, Menzies of that Ilk, 'askit instrumentis that without sum gud rewle be fundin for the ClanGregour, he may nocht ansuer for his landis, nor be bundin for gud rewle in the samin as he allegit.' It was probably in consequence of this representation that, in 1531, John, Earl of Athole, was sent by the King against the offenders, and succeeded in taking the Castle in the Isle of Loch Rannoch, and in expelling thence the 'brokin men of the ClanGregour' The negligence of the government, however (which can only be accounted for from the King being engaged at this time in reducing the Islemen to obedience), neutralised any good effects that might have been expected to result from Athole's success, for in December 1531 we find the Earl complaining that his expenses in this expedition, which he states to have been very high, had not been reimbursed

---

[1] Mr Duncan Campbell, in the "Lairds of Glenlyon," gives further explanations, of which the following is an abridgment —"In 1473, John Stewart of Fortingall and Neil, his son, had a nineteen years' lease from James III of the Royal lands and lordships of Apnadull, Glenquaich, Glenlyon, Strathbrawin, and Rannoch The MacGregors of Roro, and others of the Clan, aided Neil Stewart in his struggles in aid of the King, after whose death he attacked some of the Barons who had sided with the Prince against his father. On the accession of James IV, Neil Stewart's lease was not renewed, the Barony of Glenlyon was given to the Laird of Glenurchy, and the north side of Loch Rannoch to Sir Robert Menzies of Weem. Neil Stewart died at Garth, early in 1499, and his son, 'Niall Gointe of Garth,' burnt Weem Castle and took Sir Robert Menzies prisoner in September or October 1502 "

[2] "The person who burned the Castle of Weyme, and who resigned Fortingal to the Earl of Huntly, was grandson to John and son to Neil Stewart of Fortingal."—"Historical Notices "

[3] "This lady is omitted in both editions of Douglas's 'Peerage'" She was apparently Janet, youngest daughter of sixth Lord Forbes, second wife of John Stewart, third Earl of Atholl, who died 1542; but as the Earl's first wife, Grizel Rattray, did not die before March 1537, there seems to be an error in dates —*Ed*

[4] "Full Transcript," chapter viii

to him, and that the whole charge of garrisoning and keeping the Castle, from the time of the siege in October preceding, had been defrayed by him in addition, notwithstanding repeated applications to the Council on the subject; and finally, making a solemn protest that any inconvenience that might arise from the Council refusing or delaying to receive the Castle from him should not be laid to his charge. It may be presumed that his complaints still passed unheeded, and that the Earl in disgust left the Island Fortress to be occupied by the former inhabitants; for no great time elapsed before the Laird of Weyme found himself under the necessity of obtaining an exemption from answering for the police of his lands of Rannoch, on the score of the alleged untameable insubordination of the ClanGregor dwelling therein. This state of things was in full force so late as the year 1684, when Sir Alexander Menzies of Weyme obtained an exemption of this kind, which refers to two former exemptions granted by Mary of Guise, Queen-Regent, and by her daughter, Queen Mary, respectively. It was long after even this late period ere the family of Menzies succeeded in enforcing all the rights of free property in this large barony." [1]

[1] The "Historical Notices" are continued in chapter xiv.

Chapter IV

Sketch of the Reign of King James I

KING JAMES I., born in 1390, was captured by the English on his way to be educated in France, shortly before his father, King Robert III's death, which took place 4th April 1406. The first part of his reign the sovereign power was exercised by the King's uncle, the Duke of Albany, who was succeeded as Regent by his son Murdoch. King James I. returned from his captivity in England in 1424 He was an energetic ruler who sought to curb the power of his nobles, and also to crush the Highlands by severe measures. Tytler in his "History of Scotland," regarding this reign, gives the following description of the country at that time ·—

"Besides such Scoto-Norman barons, however, there were to be found in the Highlands and Isles, those fierce aboriginal chiefs who hated the Saxon and the Norman race, and offered a mortal opposition to the settlement of all intruders within a country which they considered their own They exercised the same authority over the various clans and septs, of which they were the heads or leaders, which the baron possessed over his vassals and their military followers, and the dreadful disputes and collisions which perpetually occurred between these distinct ranks of potentates, were accompanied by spoliations, ravages, imprisonments and murders which at length became so frequent and so far extended that the whole country beyond the Grampian range was likely to be cut off, by these abuses, from all regular communication with the mere pacific parts of the Kingdom."[1]

Amongst sundry enactments in the Parliament held in March 1424, the following was issued —

"46 Anent remissions to be given, and assithment or partie, Item it is ordained be the Parliament, that quhair the King gives remissiones til onie man, with condition to assyth the partie skaithed and compleinand, That consideratioon be had

[1] Tytler's "History of Scotland," *first edition*, vol III. page 215.

of the Hieland men, the quhilkis before the Kingis hame cumming commonlie reft and slew ilk ane utheris, bot in the Lawlands quhair the skaithes done may be kend of all, or of part that there be chosen gud men and leil sworne thereto, to modifie amendis after the qualitie and quantitie of the person, and of the skaithes, gif the parties cannot concorde be themselves; or the quhilks modificationes, baith the parties sall hald them content."[1]

Mr Tytler thus comments on this part of the Act :—

"It was declared to be the intention of the sovereign to grant a remission or pardon of any injury committed upon person or property in the lowland districts of his dominions, where the defaulter made reparation, or, according to the Scottish phrase, 'assythement,' to the injured party, and where the extent of the loss had been previously ascertained by a jury of honest and faithful men, but from this rule the Highlands were excepted, where on account of the practice of indiscriminate robbery and murder which had prevailed, previous to the return of the King, it was impossible to ascertain correctly the extent of the depredation, or the amount of the assythement. The condition of his northern dominions, and the character and manners of his Highland subjects, whose allegiance was of so peculiar and capricious a nature, had given birth to many anxious thoughts in the King, and led not long after this to a personal visit to these remote regions, which formed an interesting episode in his reign "[2]

The murder of King James I. by the traitor Graham, in February 1436, again plunged Scotland into the troubles of a long minority amidst rival factions seeking their own interests.

The following entries relating to the fifteenth century are taken from the " Chartulary " :—

"1436-7, Feb. 18   King James I. murdered at Perth. Henry MacGregor appears to have been an actor in the murder, and to have suffered death for his share in that barbarous deed. The proof of this is contained in a charter[3] of King James III. in favour of Robert de Ros, dated 14th August 1479. 'James (III) by the Grace of God, &c.. Whereas it hath lately come to our knowledge that the late Henry McGregour, father of the late Murdac Henrisoune, was present at the traiterous and most cruel death of our late most serene grandfather, the most illustrious James I., King of Scots, and for this was executed, and the said Murdac, son of this traitor,

---

[1] Acts of Scottish Parliament, King James I , March 1424.
[2] Tytler's "History," vol iii., page 197.
[3] From the same Charter it appears that Murdac had no lawful issue

had one tenement with pertinents lying in our Burgh of Perth, acquired by the said Murdac, &c.' The name Murdac affords a slight presumption that Henry McGregour had been a partisan of the late unfortunate Regent Murdac, part of whose offences is understood to have been the alienation (in imitation of his father, the previous Regent) of the Crown lands.

" 1440-1, 21st June. Charter by King James II. to John Menzies, son and heir of David Menzies Kt: and monk of the Monastery of Melrose and to his heirs, of the barony of Rawir, Lands of Weyme, Aberfallibeg, of Cumrey, and the lands of the Thanage of Crennich &c.

" 1440, Jan. 8. Charter by John Lockart of Bar to his son Robert of the lands of Bar in Ayrshire witnessed among others by ' Gilb· Greresoun ' Register of Great Seal, 111-148

" 1463, July 5th   Malcolme Johnsoun of Auchrevach disponed his lands of Auchinrevach,[1] lying in the barony of Glendochir and shire of Perth, to Colin Campbell of Glenurchay Kt by charter. The charter by Johnsoune is signed at Perth, and one of the witnesses to it is ' Murdacus Henrisoun '

" King James II., who had succeeded his father at the age of six, in 1436 was killed by a splinter from the explosion of a gun at the siege of Roxburgh, 3d August 1460, having shown himself a sovereign of vigour and capacity.

" 1483, Feb. 19th. Donald Balloch MacGregor with several others ordered by the Lords Auditors 'to content and pay to the Prior and Convent[2] of the vale of Virtue beside Perth the soume of fourty pund, aucht be him for the mailes of their landis in Athol.'

" 1484, Oct 21st   In the action and cause pursued by Schir Duncan McGregore, Vicar of Drumman, against James Arthursoune, for the wrongous occupation and detention of the mansion of Drumman, and taking up the fermeze and profits of the said mansion, and for the withholding of 'ane vmast cloth ' pertaining to the said Vicar by the decease of Jonet Badly and for the withholding of 10s of borrowed silver. The Schir Duncan being present, and the said James being lawfully called and not compeired, the Lords decree and deliver the said James does wrong in the occupation of the said mansion

1484, Oct 11   In an action by Margaret Lady Torre against Lioune of Logyalmond and others for wrongous occupation of the Manys of Logy, &^a occur the names of Alane Grigsoune and Johne Gregorsoune."

---

[1] The Lands of Auchintevach are believed to have been the earliest MacGregor possession in Perthshire.—*Ed*

[2] "Charterhouse of the Vale of Vertu." This and the next three entries occur in the " Acta Dominorum Auditorum," formerly at Perth.

King James III. was killed at the battle of Sauchie Burn, 18th June, 1488. The notices of the Clan during the previous stormy period are meagre. The Obituary has the following entries :—[1]

> "1440, April 20th. Death of Malcolm, son of John dhu MacGregor, at Glenurquhay, on the 20th of April; he was buried in the manner formerly mentioned.
>
> "1461. Death of Patrick MacGregor, Laird of Glenstray,[2] at Stronemelochane; he was buried in Dysart, in the way before mentioned.
>
> "1477, February 17th. Death of Duncan Beg MacGregor, at Roro."[3]

In the first Parliament after the accession of James IV., held in Edinburgh, 17th October 1488,

> "A determined effort was made for the putting down of theft, robbery, and murder—crimes which were at this moment grievously prevalent—by dividing the kingdom into certain districts, over which were placed various Earls and Barons, to whom full authority was entrusted, and who promised on oath that they would, to their uttermost power, exert themselves in the detection and punishment of all offenders.[4]
>
> "On this occasion, the districts of 'Renfrew, with Dumbarton, the Lennox, Bute and Arran,' were entrusted to the Earl of Lennox, Lord Lisle, and Matthew Stewart; Stirlingshire to the Sheriff of Stirlingshire and James Shaw of Sauchie; Menteith and Strathgartney to Archibald Edmonston; Glenurquhart, Glenlyon, and Glenfalloch to Neill Stewart, with Duncan and Ewin Campbell; Athole, Strathern, and Dunblane to the Earl of Athole, Lord Drummond, and Robertson of Strowan."[5]

The following is the text of part of the enactment :—

> "Item anent the stanching of Theft, Reft, and other enormities through all the realm; the Lords underwritten have made faith and given their bodily oaths to our Sovereign Lord in this his parliament, that they, and each of them, shall diligently with all care and besinace, search and seek where any such trespassers are found or known within their bounds, and to take them and justify them, or make them to be sent to our Sovereign Lord to be justified. And they shall have power of our Sovereign Lord, under his white wax, to take and punish the said trespassers without favour according to Justice. And also to give them power to cause others, small Lairds within their bounds, to mak faith likewise; And to

---

[1] See chapter vi.
[2] Son of the preceding, and the first mentioned under the designation of Glenstray.
[3] The first mention of the family of Roro in the Obituary. See chapter vi.
[4] Tytler's "History," vol. iv. p. 293.
[5] Abridged from *ibid.*

rise and assist them in the taking of the said tresspassers; and this Act to endure to our Sovereign Lord's age of xxi years, &ᵃ"

"Among these Lords we find Duncan Campbell, Neille Stewart, and Ewyne Campbell for Discher, Toyer, Glenurquhar, Rannoch, Apnadule, Glenhoun, Glenfalloch." ("Parliamentary Record," first Parliament of King James VI)[1]

"In 1491, Duncan Campbell of Glenurchy had a Charter of the Port and Isle of Loch Tay, and certain of the King's lands adjacent to Loch Tay In 1498 he had the 'Balliary' of all the King's lands of Discher, Toyer, Glenlyon, and the Barony of Glen Dochart "—(Dr Joseph Anderson)

"1499-1500. Precept of Remissioun to Patrick McGregor, Remittand to him the slauchter of umquhill Gillaspy McNeluss, &ᵃ" (all after crime).

Continuation of the notices in the public Records, after the Act of James IV.'s first Parliament, as taken from the "Chartulary" :—

"1499-1500. Decree at the instance of Alexander, Earle of Menteith, against his tenants of certain lands, Ledard, Franach, Dowlochcon, &ᶜ, and amongst those tenants are Malcolm MakGregour and John Dow Malcolmson, whose names immediately follow that of the others Acta Dominorum Concilis and Secessionis.

"1499-1500, February 20th A precept of Remissioune for Patrick McGregor Remittand him the slauchter of vmquhile Gillaspy McNeluss, and for all crime that may be imputed to him zairfoir alanerlie, &ᶜ, the usual exceptions for capital crimes, treason, &ᶜ, following de data xx Februarij anno Regis xij Registrum Secreti II 4

"1500, December 16th. Charter by King James IV. at Stirling to Robert Porterfield, son and heir to John Porterfield of that Ilk, and to Janet Maxwell, spouse to the said Robert, and lawful heirs of their body of the forty shilling lands of Porterfield, with the liberty of the Burgh of Renfrew, reserving to the said John a free tenement, and to Katherine 'Macgregor' ('Nighean Vic Gregor' that is daughter of MacGregor) a reasonable tierce, Register of Great Seal.

"1501, June 14th (13th year of the reign of James IV.). Duncan Campbell of Glenurchy having compounded with the King, and bound himself for the good order of the inhabitants of Discher, Toyer, Glenlyoun, Glendochart, Glenlochy, and Glencoich, obtains a general Remission to them all, of all crimes committed by them before the above date, with the usual exceptions of Treason, Murder, Fireraising, and Rape

"1502, September 1st. The following lands let on feu to Robert Menzies of that Ilk by Charter of our Lord the King, 'Rannauch,' viz, Downane, Kin-

---

[1] Given in "Chartulary"

claucher, le twa Cammysyrochtis, Ardlaroch, Kilquhonane, Laragne (Learan ?), Ardlar, Laragan, Insula de Lochranach, the louchies of Rannach Yrouchy (Ericht)[1] cum aliis lacubus et Insulis eiusdem cum pertinentibus Rentale Supremi Domini nostri Regis [2]

"1503, April 22. Charter by James IV. confirming one of same date by John Lord Drummond of the lands of Fynlarg (Finlarig) in the Lordship of Glendochart, to Duncan Campbell of Glenurquhay.

"1503, April 22 Charter by James IV of certain lands in Lordship of Strathire and Stewartry of Buchquhidder sold to the Earl of Argyle in a cause 'Argyle *versus* Walter Buchanan of that Ilk.'

"1503, September 21st. Item ye xxi day of September to Makgregoris man which brect venisoun to the quene x. s Compot Thesaur

"On the 8th June 1504 'Alexander Robertson of Strowan' and 'MacGregor Inenvich'[3] were noticed by the Parliament as charged with Treason Parliamentary Records of this date 'Probation of the summondis of Alexander Robertson of Strowan and Makgregor Inenvich The said day Thomas Chisholm, Sheriff deput, swor in jugement that he execut the summons of tresson upon Makgregor Inenvich befor the said witnesses sworne in jugement' Continuatio summonitionis Makgregor Inenuyck et Alexandri Robertsone de Strowane. Quo ecciam die Makgregore Inenuyck et Alexro Robertson de Strowane sehe vocat per tras dui Regis sub testimonio Magni Sigilli et tenore eiusd ad respondere dicto supremo domino nostro Regis super certis proditoriis actionibus in eisdem literis contentis, et non comparentibus continuantur ad decimam diem Octobris, &c "—Parliamentary Records

"1504, August 1st. Item the first day of August to ane man to pas with the Kingis writing to Makgregor 9 shillings, Lord Treasurer's books, commonly called 'Compot Thesaur,' doubtless the same as he who had sent venison to the Queen the previous year

"1505, Novr. Sir Robert Menzies sublet Rannoch for five years to Earl of Huntly, whose daughter he married.

"1506, August 28th. Item the 28th day of August to the Vicar of Balquheder quhair the king lugeit, 28 shillings

"Item for a cloke to the King in Balquheder, 27 shillings and 8 pence.

"Item the 1st day of September in Inchcalloun to ane Clarscha ('Clarsair,' harper), 13s.

---

[1] Errochd, "around which were many broken men of the ClanGregor."—Red and White Book of Menzies.

[2] These lands were at some time erected into the free Barony of Rannach.—Red and White Book of Menzies.

[3] Inenvuyche or Innervucht in Glenlyon.

"Item the 2d day of September to Makgregouris men hed corn etin tua nychtis, £6, 13s 4d.

"Item to Makgregouris servandis brocht tua surches to the King, 4 shillings

"Item to ane man to turs (pack up) tua surches of deir to the Quene at Linlithgow, 4s "

Lord Treasurer's Books :—

"1506, September 8th   Item to Makgregouris man of bridil silver of ane horss giffen to the King, 13s.   Compot Theasaur

"King James IV had been on a hunting expedition at Balquhidder and Strathfillan in September 1502. 'Item the samyn nycht (Sep 13th). To the King at ye park of Buquheder to play at ye cartes xviijs ' He had that day received a present from Duncan Campbell whose servant, the bearer, got nine shillings from the King's Treasurer. The Countess of Argyll had sent a present to the King on the same day, and her messenger received the same sum 'Item ye xvj. day of September for four hors in Strafilane to ye King to rede to ye sete of ye hunting ixs ' 'Item to the men of the place quhair ye king lay, and for hay that was taen fra him xiijs ' On September 18th is the following entry—'Item to ye man that gydit the king fra ye fote in (of) Bynemore to Buquhedder iijs,' and the following, 'Item the samyn day to ye vicar of Buquheder quhaire the King baited xiijs ' The King's horses had on their way to the hunting been turned, as would seem, into the vicar's cornfield, as under 14th September the following entry occurs—'Item to ye priest hes his corne etin with ye court hors, be the Kingis command xiijs ' Bards and minstrels had flocked to the Sovereign, who gave them various sums of money [1]

"1507, 4th July   Preceptum Remissionis Nigelli McAne Moil, ane McFinlason et Johannis McLeache pro receptatione Patricii [2] Duncanbegsone et Johannis Dow sui fratis &   Apud, Perth, 4th July 1507 (Privy Seal, iv 113).

"1510, September 6th   Preceptum Remissionis Donaldis Robertsoun pro communicatione cum Johanne Moill McGillaspy, Gilberto Moil, et eorum complicibus et pro omnibus aliis actionibus (with the usual exceptions)

[1] A well-known tradition relates that on the occasion of a Royal visit to MacGregor, the Sovereign, surprised at his large following, asked how he could afford to keep so large a retinue, to which the now landless Chief replied "My wash hand bason is sixteen miles long, and my towel twelve yards," alluding to Loch Tay and to his belted plaid "Thou art greater than a King," is said to have been the reply—Rev Wm. MacGregor Sterling

[2] This Patrick, son of Duncanbeg (probably he who died at Rorow, 1477), may have been the Patrick MacGregor who is said to have got possession of Dunan in 1480. He died in Morinch, 1522.

le data apud Tympane (Tempar) prope Lochrannoch, vj Septembris anno
pro-edicte (1510) gratis Jacobo Redeheugh ex mandato Domini per A.
Galloway (Privy Seal, iv. 113).

" 1511, September 18th.   Charter[1] by Robert Menzies of that Ilk to Sir
   Duncan Campbell of Glenurquhay, among other witnesses has Domino
   Jac. McGregoure, Notario Publico,[2] and Dugallo Johneson, of same family.

" 1512, October 31st.   Charter by Sir Robert Menzies to his eldest son of other
   lands at the west end of Loch Tay.   Kynnaldy, now called Kinnell, which
   embraced Killin at this time and also the lands of Moreyinche."—Red and
   White Book of Menzies, by D. R. Menzies, F.S.A., Scot., 1894.   The
   quotations are given by express permission of the Author.

In the reign of James IV. great progress was made towards the general
pacification of the country.

" The policy which he adopted was, to separate and weaken the clans by
arraying them in opposition to each other, to attach to his service by rewards and
preferment some of their ablest leaders, to maintain a correspondence with the
remotest districts, and gradually to accustom their fiercest inhabitants to habits of
pacific industry, and a respect for the restraints of the laws."   For the purpose of
quieting the lowland districts the king adopted a system of engaging the most
powerful of the resident nobles and gentry in a covenant or band which under
severe penalties obliged them to maintain order throughout the country."[3]   Proud
of the success attending his efforts James IV. set out " on horseback unaccompanied
even by a groom, with nothing but his riding cloak cast about him, his hunting
knife at his belt, and six and twenty pounds for his travelling expenses in his purse.
He rode, in a single day, from Stirling to Perth across the Mounth, and through
Aberdeen to Elgin."

But in the disastrous year 1513 King James IV. and the " flower of his
nobility" unfortunately fell at Flodden, while his only son was still an infant.

The minority of James V. was a time of great trouble to the nation,
and little heed was taken of the Highlands.   In 1528 many contentions
occurred in the Isles, and the King showed much skill in conciliating the
island chiefs.   But other troubles occupied the King's short life, and
wearied and worn he expired in the thirty-first year of his age, on the 13th
December 1542.

---

[1] The lands conveyed by this Charter were those of Crandyncht or Crannoch, north-west side
of Loch Tay.
[2] See later, Sir James McGregor, Dean of Lismoir.
[3] Tytler's " History," 1st edition, vol. v.

Chapter V

15th Century—Various Conflicts

" Baronage," *continued from page* 12

" MALCOLM (son of Gregor Aulin) succeeded his father, but dying soon after unmarried, in 1420, was succeeded by his second brother

" XIII.[1] John MacGregor of that Ilk (formerly of Brackly), a man of very martial spirit In his days the Knight of Lochow found means to stir up the McNabs to insult the MacGregors, in consequence of which, a party of the latter fought the Clan an Abba at Chrianlarich, and cut them off almost to a man. Lochow, having on that pretence obtained letters of fire and sword against both Clans, got military force to assist him in reducing them, and, after many bloody skirmishes, fought in conjunction by both, in which many of their enemies were destroyed, they in the end lost part of their lands, which the Knight of Lochow and his friends assumed possession of (" *Scots Magazine*, May 1768, p 226, observation on Act 4, Parliament 1st —James I)

" John married a daughter of the Laird of McLachlan, and died in 1461, leaving three sons—

    (1) Malcolm, his heir

    (2) Gregor of Breachd-shabh

    (3) John

" Margaret, his daughter, married Lauchlan mor Macquarie, Chief of that Clan John died *anno* 1461, and was succeeded by his eldest son,

" XIV Malcolm, who lived in the reigns of King James III and IV In this Laird's days, the MacGregors lost many more of their lands They had been provoked to chastise the MacNabs, in a manner not at all unusual in every corner of the Highlands in those days, but, as they had never been disloyal to the Royal Family, they considered the letters of fire and sword, obtained as above, as marking them rebels, "not by their own acts, but by the act of their sovereign or of his ministers," and because they did not tamely yield possession of their lands to the King's forces, whom they looked upon as the executive tools of ambitious in-

---

[1] The numbers in the "Baronage" refer to the different generations, not to individual successors

dividuals, his Majesty, by insiduous information (and because the MacGregors had been formidable adherents to his father, James III., against the faction which he, while Prince, had headed, and which proved the death of his late Majesty), was much incensed against them.

"In consequence of which they lost great part of their lands. Seumas Beg, descended from a natural son of the Duke of Albany, possessed himself of the country of Balquhidder, and several other lands, and Sir Colin Campbell, as second son of the Knight of Lochow, became Laird of Glenurquhay   They lost the lordship of Glendochart, the extensive lands and Baileries of the countries of Desser (Deasser) and Tuar (Tuath)—the south and north sides of Loch Tay—Glenlyon, the Port of Loch Tay, the country of Rannoch, the Barony of Finlarig, "with the Castle, town, and fortalice," the lands of Shian, Balloch—now called Taymouth— and Achnoch, &a , &a.," *inter annos* 1465 and 1504 [1]

The "Baronage" states that Malcolm was first married to a daughter of MacIntosh, by whom he had a son, James, his heir (and several daughters), but this is an error explained on next page.   His immediate successor was his brother, Gregor Mor.

The Latin history of the Alpinian family appears to have ended about the time of Gregor X , 1248.[2]   After Malcolm XIV the article in the " Baronage " falls unintentionally into misleading errors for several generations   The genealogy is very complicated, but the patient investigations of Mr MacGregor Stirling throw considerable light upon it.   The care with which he worked out his researches, and the conclusions to which they led, can be exemplified from his correspondence with the late Sir Evan. In December 1824 Mr MacGregor Stirling had drawn up a genealogical tree, in which Malcolm, No. XIV. of the "Baronage," is shewn succeeded by a son James as above mentioned, and that James, followed by two legitimated sons   But in a letter of the 16th March 1825 he wrote that "Dominus Jacobus MacGregor, 31st January 1557-8," who he and Mr Gregory had imagined to have been "James MacGregor of that Ilk," turned out to be the Dean of Lismore.   Again, on the 14th April 1825, Mr MacGregor Stirling wrote—

" The accident of an inaccurate copy of a voucher, dated 1571 instead of 1671, has, in the printed history of the Gregorian race, perplexed the genealogy for more

---

[1] Many of these lands had been granted to others much earlier than this period.

[2] *Vide* page 20

than a century. It is now ascertained that James MacGregor of that Ilk, who entered into a bond of friendship with Lachlan McFingon of Strathardle, was that Laird of MacGregor who had Malcolm Douglas for tutor, and for whose name we were at a loss."[1]

Returning to the "Baronage," and passing over the two next erroneous personages, we have this account of Gregor Mor :—

"XIV Gregor Mor or the Great, second son of John MacGregor of that Ilk, to whom his father gave the lands of Breachd-sliabh, commonly called Brackly, in Glenurchy, with a numerous following of men [2] He lived in the reigns of King James III. and IV., and, grieved at the oppression of his family and friends, he raised his men, and, making several successful expeditions against their enemies, recovered possession of a large tract of country called Glen Lochy, the forest of Corrychaick, the lands of Ardeonaig, and several others on the side of Loch Tay, which his descendants enjoyed till the reign of James IV

"Gregor took to wife Finvola or Flora, daughter to McArthur of Strachur, by a daughter of the family of Argyll, ancestor of the present Colonel Campbell of Strachur

" By this lady he had four sons and several daughters
    1. Duncan, his heir
    2. Gregor, a captain of great reputation, who, having come to the south country, performed several valiant actions against the English Borderers in conjunction with his cousins the Griersons of Lag
    3 Malcolm, a man of great prudence and valour, famous for his dexterity in all manly exercises, and in great esteem with Alexander, Earl of Mar, at whose request he raised his patrimony from his brother, and acquired the lands of Inverey, with several others in Brea-Mar, where he settled. He married a daughter of Dougal Lamont of Stiolaig (by a daughter of the family of Bute), by whom he had several children, the eldest of whom, Alexander, acquired the lands of Cherry, Killach, Dalcherz, Balachby, &c

        There are several good families, and some hundreds of commoners, of this branch of the MacGregors in Brae-Mar and the adjoining countries to this day, but during the general persecution they lost their lands, and betook themselves to several different names, as Ogilvies, Gordons, &a [3]

---

[1] I e , James MacGregor, last of the line of John Dhu Nan Lurag ; died, probably about 1678
[2] The "Baronage" does not quote its authority for these statements If Gregor Mor survived his brother and became chief, it would account for his numerous following.
[3] Curious history of this family, by John Gregory penes Mr John Murray. (Extant)
—Ed.

4. John, who afterwards got the lands of Brackly from his eldest brother.[1]

"XV Duncan, called Ladasach, or "the complete hero,"[2] succeeded—a man of resolution, much celebrated by the bards He lived for some time with his uncle Strachur, in the Island of Orann in Glenfalloch, and did him the good service of reducing the Macilvanes, a tribe who possessed some lands of Strachur's, without any acknowledgment Thereafter he acquired the lands of Ardchoill[3] (which belonged to Strachur), and several others in Breadalbane, besides his former possessions, upon which he gave those of Brackly to his younger brother, John,[1] as before observed. He took to wife Mary,[4] daughter to the Laird of Ardkinlas, ancestor of Sir James Campbell of Ardkinlas, by a daughter of the family of Argyll, by whom he had two sons ·—

    1 Gregor, his heir."

Another son, John, is mentioned on the authority of a charter witnessed by "domino Joanne MacGregor, militi," but this is a mistake, as the John in question was John MacEwin Vic Allaster of Glenstray, see page 32. Details of the history and tragical end of Duncan and his eldest son will be given farther on There were other sons :—

    " 2 Malcolm, who perished with his father and brother.[5]
    3 Duncan Oig Laddosoun.[5]
    4 Patrick Dow McGregor Vic Duncan Laddosach, murdered in Balquhidder, 4th Oct 1574, by the Clan Dowilchayr "

Sir John MacGregor Murray, with the scanty sources of information then in his possession, had not only been led by the wrongly dated voucher into the error of giving a son James as the successor to Malcolm XIV., but supposed this James to have been the father of the Alexander MacGregor who was the leader in the celebrated battle of Glenfruin ; whereas that leader was Glenstray, of a different line. Re-

---

[1] His descendants continued on the lands of Brackley for many generations, and his line is often mistaken for that of Duncan Ladasach.

[2] The Gaelic word signifies rather "rich," " Lordly "—*laoch* is the Gaelic for " hero."

[3] From the name of this property came the " slogan" or war cry of the ClanGregor, although some of the families, according to a MS by Pont, preserved in the Lyon Office, used the motto, " Bad Guibhas " or "Clump of Firs "—" Chartulary "

[4] It is probable that there may have been a confusion of names here, as a Glenstray is known to have married into this family.

[5] *Vide* Notice in the Obituary, as given later, and Duncan Oig (Young) Ladossoune (son of Laddeus) is also mentioned in the Records, 1562 63, &c. See Chapter XVI

turning to Chapter IV., where the entries are given from the Obituary under date 1415, mentioning the deaths of two sons of John Cham (see page 16), there appears some reason to believe that Gregor Aulin, whose line has been traced on as far as Duncan Ladosach and his son, was the *elder* brother, and the argument sustained by Mr MacGregor Stirling is that Gregor's descendants, eventually Glencarnoch, and through him the present Chief, Sir Malcolm, carry down the representation from the early Chiefs by right of blood as the eldest line[1]

We have now to trace the House of Glenstray, or Clan Dowlagneir, a distinctive name occurring in the Black Book of Taymouth, and supposed to be derived from "Dubh Lag an Iar"—Black Hollow of the West. The authority for the Founder of the House, and for the first succeeding generations, is the repeatedly quoted Obituary, or Chronicle of Fortingal (See Chapter VIII.)

> "I John dhu McEan Cham Vic Gregor, brother of Gregor (Aulin), and mentioned (page 21) as having died at Stromelochane, 1415
>
> "II Death of Malcolm, son of John dhu MacGregor, at Glenurquhy, on the 20th April in yhe year 1440; he was buried in the manner formerly mentioned."

There is evidence that he had a brother Allaster (to be noticed farther on).

> "III Death of Patrick MacGregor of Glenstray, at Stronemelochane, on the 24th of May in the year 1440 He was buried at Dysart in the way formerly mentioned.
>
> "IV Death of John dhu MacGregor of Glenstray, son of Patrick, at Stronemelochane, on the 24th May in the year 1519.

His son predeceased him, and is thus mentioned in the Obituary—

> "Death of Malcolm MacGregor, son and heir of John MacGregor of Glenstray, at Glenlyon. He was buried in Dysart, South of the Altar, in a stone coffin, on the 22nd of June 1498.[2]

On the death of John Dow, in 1519, the representation of this line

---

[1] Sir John MacGregor Murray recognised Glenstray as the Chief, but supposed him to be a grandson of Malcolm XIV

[2] It is remarkable that all of this line continued to be buried at Dysart in Glenurchy.

passed to his heir and successor, John McEwin McAllaster, his second cousin.[1] Contemporary with Gregor Mor, XIV.

In the Dean of Lismore's Book,[2] the genealogy of this John dhu McGregor of Glenstray is given in old Gaelic,[3] with the following translation :—

"John, son of Patrick, son of Malcom, son of John, the black son of John, son of Gregor, son of John, son of Malcom, son of Duncan the little, son of Duncan from Srulee, son of Gilelan,[4] son of Hugh of Urchy, son of Kenneth, son of Alpin; and this Kenneth was head King of Scotland, in truth, at that time; and this John is the eleventh man from Kenneth, of whom I spoke. And Duncan the servitor, son of Dougal, son of John the grizzled, wrote this from the books of the genealogists of the kings, and it was done in the year of our Lord one thousand five hundred and twelve."

The genealogy is here reversed for greater distinctness :—

"Alpin.
Kenneth.
Hugh of Urchy.
William (see "Baronage," No. IX.), or Gillefealan.
Duncan a Strwlee (see p. 14); he was probably the second son.
Duncan beg (see same page).
Malcolm (see No. XI. of "Baronage," and page 11, or, more probably, Malcolm VIII.).
John (not mentioned in "Baronage").
Gregor   do.   do.
John (Cham). (Died 1390, page 15.)
John Doef (or dhu). (Died in 1415. Had a brother Gregor, who also died in 1415.)
Malcolm. (Died in 1440 as above. Had a brother Allaster.)
Patrick. (Died May 1440 as above.)
John (dhu). (Died in 1519 as above.)

[1] See Genealogical Table at end of chapter.

[2] From the MS. collection made by Sir James MacGregor, Dean of Lismore, in the beginning of the sixteenth century; edited with translation by Revd. Thomas McLauchlan, 1862. The Obituary had been previously printed in the "Archæologia Scotica," vol. iii. (see page 25).

[3] "Eone Macphadrick vec Voylchallum vec Eonedoef vec Gregor vec Eone vec Woilchallum vec Conquhy veg vec Conquhy a Strwlee vec Illehane[4] vec Ey Urquhaych vec Kennane vec Alpen."

[4] Mr Skene reads this name as Gillefealan (it seems probable): William in modern Gaelic is Uilleam.

The Bard may be assumed to have had accurate information about the late generations, although he skipped over several ancestors prior to Hugh of Urchy The Latin MS. followed in the "Baronage," was probably the labour of a monk or ecclesiastic of the name of MacGregor. It has been found, by the scrutiny of sundry ancient chronicles, that the monks sometimes drew on their fertile imaginations ; but, although some generations may have been omitted by them also, and the names mixed up, the accounts of the various Chiefs, as related in this MS., were probably founded on old traditions ; and thus the two pedigrees embody all that can now be known about the early days of the Clan's heroes. We reach solid and perfectly reliable ground in the Obituary of the Chronicle of Fortingall On the next page a Genealogical Table of Ian Cham's immediate descendants is given.

`As remarked by Mr Skene in a note to the genealogy—

" It is obvious that a number of generations are omitted, not even excepting the ancestor who gave his name to the clan. The omission of generations is by no means an uncommon feature in traditional genealogies "

The circumstance that Malcolm MacGregor of Glenstray, who died in 1440, had a brother, and that his name was Allaster, has been made out from the patronymics of his grandson, given in a genealogy occurring in the Black Book of Taymouth.

We therefore return to the said

II Allaster, younger brother of Malcolm,[1] and thus younger son of John Dhu McEan Cham VicGregor   (See previous page)

III Ewine, cousin-german of Patrick of Glenstray, his existence being traced in the same way

IV. John MacGregor of Glenstray, second cousin and heir to the last of the same name, who died in 1519.

Against this individual, as John Macgregor of Glenstray, a claim was brought by the widow of his predecessor.

---

[1] The evidence of the connection of John MacGregor of Glensbrae with his predecessor is sufficiently clear to all who have studied Highland genealogies and their patronymics. Finding that John, son of Ewan, son of Alastair, is heir to John, son of Patrick, son of Malcolm, son of John Dhu, the conclusion to be drawn is, that Alastair must also have been a son of John Dhu, and that through him came the claim to the property See page 52

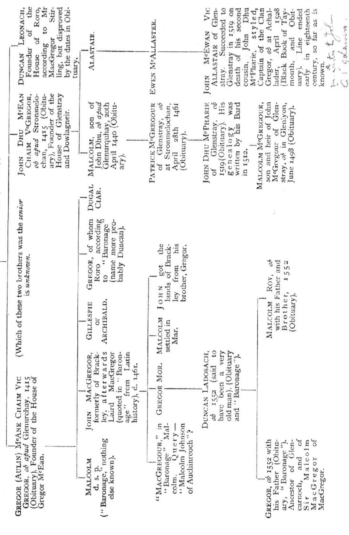

JOHN CHAM M^cGREGOR of Glenurchay, *ob* 1390 (Obituary).

GREGOR (AULIN) M^cFANE CHAIM VIC GREGOR, *ob apud* Glenurchay, 1415 (Obituary), Founder of the House of Gregor McEan.

(Which of these two brothers was the *senior* is *unknown*.)

JOHN DHU M^cEAN CHAIM V^cGREGOR, *ob apud* Stronmelochan, 1415 (Obituary), Founder of the House of Glenstray and Dowaigneir.

DUNCAN LEONACH, Founder of the House of Roro, according to Mr MacGregor Stirling, but disproved by the dates in Obituary.

MALCOLM d. s. p. ("Baronage," nothing else known).

JOHN MACGREGOR, formerly of Brackley, afterwards Laird MacGregor (quoted in "Baronage" from Latin history), d. 1461.

GILLESPIE or ARCHIBALD.

GREGOR, of whom Roro according to "Baronage" (name more probably Duncan).

DUGAL CIAR.

MALCOLM, son of John Dhu, *ob apud* Glenurquhay, 20th April 1440 (Obituary).

ALASTAIR.

"MACGREGOUR," in "Baronage" "Malcolm. Query—"Malcolm Johnson of Auchinreoch"?

GREGOR MOR.

MALCOLM settled in Mar.

JOHN got the lands of Brackley from his brother, Gregor.

PATRICK M^cGREGOR of Glenstray, *ob* at Stronmelochan, April 28th 1461 (Obituary).

EWEN M^cALLASTER.

DUNCAN LADOSACH, *ob* 1552 (said to have been a very old man). (Obituary and "Baronage").

JOHN DHU M^cPHARIE of Glenstray, *ob* 1519 (Obituary). His genealogy was written by his Bard in 1512.

JOHN M^cEWAN VIC ALLASTAIR of Glenstray. Succeeded to Glenstray in 1519 on death of his second cousin, John Dhu McPharie, styled, Captain of the Clan Gregor, *ob* at Achallader, April 1518 (Black Book of Taymouth, and Obituary). Line ended early in eighteenth century, so far as is known.

GREGOR, *ob* 1552 with his Father (Obituary, and "Baronage"). Ancestor of Glencarnoch, and of Sir Malcolm MacGregor of MacGregor.

MALCOLM ROY, *ob* with his Father and Brother, 1552 (Obituary).

MALCOLM M^cGREGOUR, son and heir of John McGregor of Glenstray, *ob* in Glenlyon, June 1498 (Obituary).

"1522-23, February 9th   Anent the actioune and causs persewit be Marioune
Stewart ye Relict of umq^le Johnne M'Gregour of Glenstra his air and successor" the reduction relates to the "fermes and profittis of the lands of
Edindarnycht," being, as appears, part of the estate of Glenstrae ("Chartulary")

"1522, Feb. 9   Action pursued by Marioune Stewart, relict of Jon M'Gregour of
Glenstra, against John M'Gregor, his heir and successor, to content and
pay to the said Marioune the fermes and profits of the lands of Glendarnycht,
in the Earldom of Argyle, and shire of the same, pertaining to her in
conjunct fee, of the terms of Whitsunday and Martinmas 1519, extending
to seven bolls of oatmeal, price of the boll 16s , four bolls of beir, price of
the boll 20s , twelve stone of cheese, price of the stone 40d , one mart,
price 40s , and four wedders, price of the piece 6s. and 8d.   The said
Marioun, compeared by Robert Leslie, her procurator, and the said John
M'Gregor did not compear.   The Lords of Council continued the action
to the 24th May next to come "—From the "Acta Dominorum Concila "

He married a daughter of Sir Colin Campbell of Glenurchy, Knight, by
a daughter of Luke Stirling of Keir, Sir Colin's fourth wife.[1]   From the
Obituary :—

"1528, April 12th.   Death of John MacGregor M'Ewine, Captain of the Clan-
Gregor of Glenstray, who died of good memory, at Achallader in Glenurquhay, on Easter Day, the 12th of April, in the year 1528 ; he was buried
in Dysart, as others of his name used to be.   May God have care of his
soul."

This family of the ClanGregor having become connected with the
Glenurchay family, the Black Book of Taymouth gives a genealogy of
it   According to this the marriage of

"'Johnne Makewin Vic Allaster M'Gregour with Helene Cambell, dochter to
Sir Coline Campbell of Glenurchay, Knight, and widow of Lochbuy,' was not perfectly regular, but it must have been condoned, for the Campbells of Glenurchay
afterwards favoured the Glenstray family , and it may have been in consequence of
the Campbell support that Glenstray became Captain   With regard to Sir Colin's
son-in-law the Black Book has the following notice : ' The foresaid Johne wes not
righteous air to the M'Gregour, bot wes principal of the Clandowlagniar.'"[2]

---

[1] "Black Book of Taymouth" and "Stirlings of Keir," by William Fraser, 1858

[2] In another part of the "Black Book of Taymouth," enumerating the wives of Sir Colin
Campbell, first of Glenurquhay, it is stated that Sir Colin married fourth "Margaret Stirling,
dochter to the Laird of Keir, by whom he had ane dochter callit Helene Campbell, quha wes first
mareit on Makeane of Arnamurroch, and thairefter on Makgregoure "

This remark on John M'Ewin's position is not understood as casting a doubt on his legitimacy, but as implying that he was head of his branch only of the Clan.[1]

"Details of the Glenstray Family, from the Black Book of Taymouth, Johne Makewin V'Allaster M'Gregour, in anno . . . ravischet Helene Campbell, dochter to Sir Coline Campbell of Glenurquhay, Knight. This Helene Campbell wes widow and lady of Lochbuy, and scho wes ravischet. The foresaid Johne wes not righteous air to the M'Gregour, bot wes principall of the Clan-Doulagnear.

"This Johne M'Ewin begat upon the foirsaid Helene, Allaster M'Gregour of Glenstray, quha mariet ane dochter of the laird of Ardkinglass, being widdow to M'Nachtan of Dundaraw.

"This Allaster M'Gregour of Glenstray begat upon the said dochter of the Laird of Ardkinglass, Johne M'Gregour of Glenstray and Gregour Roy, his brother. The said Johne diet of the hurt of an arrow going betuix Glenlyoun and Rannoch.

"Gregour Roy, his brother, succeidit to him. The said Gregour Roy mariet the Laird of Glenlyoun's dochter, and begat upon her Allaster Roy M'Gregour and Johne Dow M'Gregour, his brother. This foresaid Gregour Roy wes execute be Coline Campbell of Glenurchay.

"Allaster Roy M'Gregour succeidit to the foirsaid Gregour, his Father, and had no children bot ane dochter. This Allaster Roy M'Gregour wes execute and hangit at the mercat Croce of Edinburgh, and forfaultit in anno 1604.

"Johne Dow M'Gregour, brother to the said Allaster M'Gregour, mariet ane dochter of the Laird of Strowane Murrayis, and begat upon her Gregour, Patrik and Ewin M'Gregouris. This Johne Dow M'Gregour wes slaine in Glenfrune be the Laird of Luss, anno 1602."

By the said Helen Campbell, relict of Lochbuy (M'Lean), John MacGregor of Glenstray left three sons :—

1. John, who with his father witnessed a grant by the Earl of Argyle to —— Campbell, of the lands of the Phanans, but nothing is known of him beyond this solitary notice.

2. Allaster, who succeeded his father, as is believed.

3. Gregor, who predeceased his father, and whose death is thus recorded in the Obituary :—

[1] See Chapter X.

" 1526, July 31. Death of Gregor, son of John MacGregor,
     alias M°Ewine M°Allaster of Glenstray, at the Isle of
     Loch Rannoch ; he was buried in Dysart, in a stone
     coffin, on the north side of the High Altar of Glenstray,
     on the last day of July in the year 1526.   May his soul
     rest in peace."

This Gregor left a son, Allaster, who became ancestor of the MacGregors
of Ardlarich,[1] a very important branch of the Clan in Rannoch.[2]

V. Allaster[3] M°Gregor of Glenstray, son of John M°Ewine MacGregor,
was formally infeoffed in Glenstray in 1528, which, including Stronmelochan, amounted, as appears from the enfeoffment, to twenty merks
old extent.   He "mariet ane dochter of (Campbell) the Laird of Ardinglass, being widdow to M°Nachtan of Dundaraw "—B. B. of Taymouth—
and left four sons, or more—

   1. John, his heir.
   2. Gregor Roy, who succeeded his brother.
   3. Ewin, Tutor of Glenstray.
   4. Allaster Galt (or the Travelled), mentioned in Record as the
     " Brother to the Laird of MacGregor."   He lived in Culquhirrilan.
     He had five sons—

      1. Allaster.
      2. John Dhu M°Allaster, in Cannoquhan.
      3. Duncan M°Allaster Galt.
      4. Patrick M°Allaster Galt.
      5. Gregor M°Allaster Galt, executed at Edinburgh, 28th
          July 1612

   5. Duncan na Glen of Phanean, so styled in Bail Bond, 22nd April
     1601, by his nephew, Alexander M°Gregor of Glenstray, and
     mentioned elsewhere as " Duncan M°Gregor in Glen, Brother to
     the Laird of M°Gregor."   He had sons—

[1] Mr MacGregor Stirling's MS. History of the House of Glenstrae, from which this list is
adapted.
[2] To be hereafter enumerated.
[3] Born, according to the Chronicle of Fortingall, in 1525.

1. Gregor, a famous soldier.
2. Patrick.

6. Patrick our (or Dun) (and Mor), in Cadderlie or Caddernoch in Glencorf.

1. Allaster McPatrick in Cadderine.
2. John Dhu.
3. Duncan.

It is recorded in the Continuation of the Chronicle of Fortingall that—"1543, 31st August. The House of Trochray in Strathbran was burnt by Alexander McGregor of Glenstray."

VI. John MacGregor of Glenstray, in which property he never was infeoffed. He died of the hurt of an arrow, without issue, and was succeeded by his brother.

VI. Gregor Roy of Glenstray, who was never enfeoffed in the property either. Of him hereafter.[1]

[1] See Chapter XVIII.

Chapter VI

THE so-called Chronicle of Fortingall, compiled by James MacGregor, Vicar of Fortingall and Dean of Lismoir, contains a most valuable abstract of the contemporaneous history of the ClanGregor, and therefore it is here given, omitting many entries not connected with the Clan. The Chronicle was continued from 1531 by the Curate of Fortingall The first portion was published in the original Latin, with a translation by Mr Gregory, in 1831, and advantage of this translation has been taken on the next page, whilst the latter part has been copied from the Black Book of Taymouth, merely translating the few words of Latin.

Translation of Dean MacGregor's Chronicle,[1] by Donald Gregory, Esq .—

" 1092 Death of Malcolm Kenmoir, the elder[2] King of Scotland, at Alnwick And Qwiene Margret heir and the deid of hir husband died within thre dais thairefter in the said year. The translation of Queen Margaret was in the year 1092.

" 1107. Death of Edgar, King of Scotland, at Dundee. He reigned nine years and three months.

" 1124 Death of Alexander I., King of Scotland, in Striweleich He reigned eighteen years and three months.

" 1153 Death of David I., King of Scotland, at Carlisle. He reigned twenty-nine years and twenty days. He died on the 9th of the Kalends of June, and was buried at Dunfermlyne before the great altar

" 1165 Death of Malcolm the younger (IV), King of Scotland, in Gedwart[3] He reigned twelve years six months and twenty days.

" 1213 Death of William, King of Scotland, at Streulyne. He reigned fifty-one years.

---

[1] From a document in the Archives of the Highland Society, and published in their Transactions The notes marked with *letters* are Mr Gregory's own. A duplicate (of the Gaelic and Scotch part) is to be found in the Black Book of Taymouth, and it is known as the Chronicle (or Obituary) of Fortingall

[2] In contradistinction to Malcolm IV.

[3] Jedburgh.

"1247. Death of Alexander II king of Scotland at Kerueroy,[1] he reigned thirtyfive years.

"1250. The re-enterment of the said Margaret Queen of Scotland (Queen of Malcolm Kenmore) took place.

"1285. Death of Alexander III at Kyngorne; he reigned thirtysix years and eight months.

"1314. Battle of Bannochburn.

"1328.[2] Death of Robert I King of Scotland at Cardross he reigned twentythree years.

"1333. Battle of Hallidonhill.

"1345. Battle of Durayme.

"1370. Death of David King of Scotland at Edinburgh. he reigned forty-three years.

"1388. Battle of Ottyrburn.

"1390, April 19 (first notice). Death of John MacGregor of Glenurquhay. he was buried at Dysart on the north side of the High Altar.[3]

"1390. Death of Robert II King of Scotland at Dundownald; he reigned nineteen years and two months.

"1396. Combat of the sixty men at Perth.

"1402. Battle of Homilton.

"1405. Death of Robert III King of Scotland. he reigned thirtyone years.[4]

"1411. Battle of Hayrlaw.

"1415. Death of Gregor McAnecham in Glenurquhay, he was buried as above noted in Dysart.

"1415. Death of John dhu McAnecham VcGregor at Stronmelochane; he was buried in Dysart.

"1424. Death of Darwayll daughter of Ewyn V. Lachlan—John dhu McGregor (his wife ?).

"1425. May 27. Death of Lord Murdac Duke of Scotland and his sons Walter and Alexander.

"1431. Battle of Inverlocha.

"1435. July 26. Death of Alexander Earl of Mar and Gareoch Lieutenant of our Lord the King. he was buried in Inverness.

"1436. Jan. 17. Death of Mr Robert Cardny Bishop of Dunkeld.

"1436. Feb. 21. Death of James I King of Scotland at Perth. he reigned thirtyone years.

"1440. April 20. Death of Malcolm son of John dhu MacGregor, at Glenurquhay; he was buried in the manner formerly mentioned.

[1] Kerrera, off Oban.   [2] True date said to have been 7th June 1329.
[3] Clachan Dysart—now the Church of Glenurquhay, close to Dalmally.
[4] True date 1406.

" 1443   Death of John Gorm Stewart who was killed on the north Inch of Perth on the birthday of John the Baptist.

" 1452   Oct 8.   Death of William Cardny Laird of Foss.

" 1460   Death of James II King of Scotland at Roxburgh, he reigned twenty-three years   He was interred in Dunedin

" 1461   Death of Patrick MacGregor of Glenstray at Stronmelochane.   He was buried at Dysart, in the way before mentioned (first notice of Glenstray)

" 1463   Dec 20   Death of John Stewart Lord of Lorn at Dunstaffnage

" 1475   Sept 26   Death of Sir Colin Campbell of Glenurquhay Knight   he was buried in Kilmartin

" 1475.   Dec. 10.   Death of John Stewart of Fortingal, at Garth, he was buried at Dunkeld ;

" 1477   Feb 17   Death of Duncan Beg MacGregor at Roro (first notice of Roro).

" 1482   Cochrane was hanged at Lauder

" 1482   August 30.   Death of John Grant son and heir of Sir Duncan Grant of Freuchy, Knight, at Kindrochit in Mar, he was buried in the Cathedral Church of Murray, having died three years before his father

" 1483   Feb 4   Death of Donald Robertson of Keirquhin [1]

" 1488   Death of Patrick Macnab of Bowayne at Auchline [2]

" 1488   June 11   Death of James III King of Scotland at Bannockburn on the feast of St Barnabas the Apostle, he reigned twenty-seven years and upwards

" 1488   Battle of Stirling where James III King of Scotland was killed.

" 1491   March 10   Death of John Duncanson MacGregor at Bellicht[3] he was buried in Inchadin [4] on the north side of the Great Altar

" 1493   August 14   Death of Katrine Cardney daughter of the Laird of Foss and widow of the late John Duncanson MacGregor.   she was buried in the Church of Dull before the step of the Great Altar

" 1494   16 May.   Duncan son of Charles at Loch Dochard ("Black Book of Taymouth ")

" 1494   July 24   Death of Terloch Keir son of Duncan MacGregor   he was buried in Dysart

" 1494   Oct. 17   Death of Donald McCauss, in the Crag   ·

" 1496   Nov.   Death of Margaret Douglas, Lady of Glenurquhay

[1] Keirquhin, Carwhin, a property belonging to the Robertsons, to the west of Crannoch , but there was another Carwhin in the parish of Balquhidder belonging to a family of Campbells —*Ed*

[2] This property in Glendochart belonged to the MacNabs till acquired by Sir Colin Campbell of Glenurchy (as also Bovaine) in 1552 —*Ed*

[3] Probably Balloch near Taymouth

[4] Now Kenmore   (An old church lower down the river than Kenmore, destroyed by the third Earl of Breadalbane , there was also a village and ford over the Tay —*Ed*)

"1498. Death of Donald Macqueen at Fortingal.

"1498. June 22. Death of Malcolm MacGregor son and heir of John Mac-
Gregor of Glenstray, at Glenlyon ; he was buried in Dysart in a stone
coffin.[1]

"1499. Jan. 31. Death of Neill Stewart at Garth, he was buried in Dunkeld.

"1502. Weyme was burnt by Neill Stewart [2] in the month of Sep.

"1503. july 25. Entrance (into Scotland) of Margaret Queen of Scotland
spouse of King James IV.

"1503. Sep. 10. Death of Gregor Duncanbegson at Morinch.[3]

"1505. March 18. Death of Alexander Robertson of Strowan at Dunmakcarf;
he was buried in Dunkeld.

" „ Oct. 20. Death of Eugenius (Ewine) MacGregor, son of Gregor Duncanson in Roro.—(" Black Book of Taymouth.")

"1507. Death of Andrew Cardney Laird of Foss, at Inchewin he was buried
in the Aisle of (St Ninian).

"1509. March 31. The (Religious House) on the Island of Loch Tay [4] was
burned owing to the negligence of servants on Palm Sunday.

[1] In taking down many years ago the old church of Dysart, several stone coffins were found at
the north part of the east end of the church, where the M°Gregors appear chiefly to have buried.
Several of their old tombstones, much defaced, were likewise discovered, which are still appropriated
by such of the clan as bury in the churchyard (1831). Note by Compiler.—Pennant, in his book
"A Tour," in 1769 writes :—"The church is seated on a knowl. . . . In the churchyard are
several gravestones of great antiquity, with figures of a warrior, each furnished with a spear or two-
handed sword ; on some are representations of the chase, on others elegant fretwork, and on one—
said to be part of the coffin of a M°Gregor, is a fine running pattern of foliage and flowers, and,
excepting the figure, all in good taste." At a meeting of the Society of Antiquaries of Scotland in
Jan. 1897, Mr Brydale read a paper describing a group of seven carved grave slabs in the churchyard at Dalmally, which is stated to have been the burying-place of the Chiefs of MacGregor from
1390 to 1528. "The Chronicle records the burial of no fewer than twelve of these Chiefs successively in stone coffins at the north side of the east end of the church. When the old church was
demolished about 1811, a number of stone coffins and carved grave slabs were found in this position."
. . . Of the seven stones now described three are of the same type, showing in a panel the figure
of an armed man with sword and spear, and wearing a pointed bascinet and short tunic, the rest of
the surface being filled in with foligeous ornamentation. A fourth is curious as showing this type
superimposed on a larger figure obliterated, and having a cross at the top of the stone. Of the
other two of this type one is curious from its small size, and the other is much mutilated. The
seventh is apparently the front slab of an altar tomb, and bears a finely carved scroll of foliage, but
no armed figure. Drawings of all the slabs were exhibited."—Abridged from an account of the
meeting in the *Oban Times* of 23rd Jan. 1897.

[2] Son of the preceding entry.

[3] Marinch or Morenish, on the north side of Loch Tay, near the Killin Pier. It was at one
time in possession of the Menzieses, but was acquired by Sir Duncan Campbell, seventh Laird of
Glenurchy, 1602.—*Ed.*

[4] There was a Nunnery, the ruins of which are still to be seen (1831) on the island at the east
end of Loch Tay.

"1510   Oct. 27.   Death of Janet Stewart Countess of Huntly at Strathbogie she was buried in the Church of Strathbogy

"   „   Nov 28   Death of Gregor Patrickson at Innerchattane

"1511.   June 3   Death of Gilbert Duncanson vicar of Kilmartin.

"   „   July 22.   Death of Katrine Neyndonil [1] wife of Dougal Johnson at Tullichmullin,[2] she was buried in the choir of Inchadin [3] on the south side of the Altar   Dominical Letter E.

"   „   Oct 9   Death of William Johnson MacGregor, at Garth; he was buried in Inchadin on the south side of the Altar   Dominical E

"1512.   May 2   Death of Gregor Neilson at Crannych.[4]

"   „   Death of Patrick McCarb.

"   „   July 13.   Death of Duncan Macdougall who was killed who was son and heir of Alexander Macdougall of Dunnolych   This Duncan was buried in Ardchattan

"   „   Sep 15   Death of John Stewart, Earl of Atholl.

"1513   Sep 9.   Death of James IV King of Scotland in Northumberland near Branstone in England   Dominical A   He reigned twenty-six years three months and eight days.   On which day there were slain in the said field many noblemen on both sides   On the side of Scotland divers Bishops, Abbots, Lords, Knights, Nobles, and other gentlemen

   "On which day were slain the most prudent Lord Archibald Earl of Argyle, Lord Campbell and Lorne, Duncan Campbell of Glenurquhay, and John Campbell of Lawers   May God have care of their souls.

"1515   April   Death of Gregor Duncanson at Roro   he was buried in Killin

"1516   Death of William Strowan Robertson, who was beheaded at Tulymat   Dominical Letter B

"   „   Dec 12   Death of Elisabeth neyn Donald V^cCauss [5] at Garth

"1517   Dec 15   Death of John Lord Gordon and Badenoch at Killoss he was buried in the monastery of Kinloss

"1518.   July 9   Death of Patrick MacGregor at Auchinchallane,[6] he was buried in Dysart [7]

---

[1] McClaw, alias Grant.   [2] Glenlyon House

[3] The ancient name of Kenmore

[4] Crannych or Crannich, on Loch Tay; anciently a thanage, and now a district in the parish of Kenmore, but formerly a detached part of Weem   The old "tuelf merk land" was purchased in 1602 by Sir Duncan Campbell, from Menzies of Weem —From "Lairds and Lands of Loch Tayside," by John Christie, 1892

[5] Wife of Gregor Dhu.   She was buried at Inchadin.   [6] Aychincschecall.

[7] It is stated that a very old Charter in reference to Auchinchallane, and other papers connected with the subsequent sale of this property to the Campbells, exist in private hands, but the compiler has not access to them.

"1518. July 19. Death of Duncan MacGregor Captain of the Castle of Glenurquhay; he was buried at Dysart.

"1519. May 24. Death of John dhu MacGregor of Glenstray son of Patrick of Stronemelochane, he was buried in Dysart on the 26. of May 1519 on which day a great meteor was seen in Glenurquhay.

"1520. Death of Malcolm Cam MacGregor son of Neil at Thegyrmith [1] .... Dow and buried in Killin 14th Jany.

"1521. June 9. Death of Donald McNacht; Vicar of Fortingall

"1522. Death of the Lord Earl of Errol in the month of July.

" ,, Sep. 16. death of Mr John Laycock Canon of Dunkeld.

" ,, March.[2] Death of John McNicoll he was buried in Inchaddin.

" ,, August 12. Death of a venerable man Sir Robert Menzies Knight at Weyme; he was buried in the Church of Weyme.

" ,, Oct. Death of Patrick Duncanbegson in Morinche.

" ,, Nov. 6. Death of Duncan McOlchallam VcKerlich (son of Malcolm son of Charles) at Drumcharre.—(" Black Book of Taymouth.")

"1523. Aug. 12. Death of Sir Colin Campbell Knight Laird of Glenurquhay at the Castle of Glenurquhay. He was buried in the chapel of Finlarg.

" ,, Sep. 1. Death of Gilbert Borricht Vicar of Dysart at Eddergoill [3] he was buried on the south side of the Church near the door of the Choir.

" ,, Sep. 20. Death of Sir John Stewart of Stuekis Knight. He was buried in Dunkeld.

" ,, Oct. 31. Death of Mr Walter Leslie in Dunkeld.

" ,, Nov. 6. Death of the Vicar of Inchaddin Sir Duncan McNachtane who died at Perth and was buried in Inchadin.

" ,, feb. 9. Death of John Malloch McHustone at Tullichcamin. he was buried in Killin.

" ,, March 4. Agreement of John MacGregor and of Sir John St John [4] his son and Mariot his daughter at Killasse.[5]

"1524. July 26. Death of Margaret Stewart Lady of Glenurquhay at the Island of Loch Tay; she was buried in the Chapel of Finlarg, near her husband.

" ,, Nov. 9. Death of Neill son of Duncan MacGregor in Glenurquhay, at the Castle of Glenurquhay.

" ,, Feb. 15. Death of Christian neyn Varrone McKerross wife of John Dougalson, at Ardtrasgart.

[1] Tegarmuchd Island on the Tay, between Kenmore and Aberfeldie.—From " Lairds and Lands of Loch Tayside," by John Christie, 1892.

[2] Till 1600 the year began in March.

[3] Eddergoll, ancient name of a district extending from Auchroich Burn, at Callelochan, to the east end of Loch Tay.—From " Lairds and Lands of Loch Tay."

[4] More probably Sir John Stewart.   [5] Killiechassie.

"1524 March 15 Death of a provident and famous man Gregor Macanemoill at Easter Innervar in Glenlyon early in the morning; he was buried on the 17. day of the same month in Killin on the south side of the High Altar

"1525. April 13 Death of Finlay Macnab of Bowayne at Ilanran[1] he was buried at Killin.

"   „   April 19 Death of Hugh McEwin VcNeill at Fernay he was buried on the 21st of the same month in Inchadin before the step of the great Altar, on the south side of the church

"   „   August 17 Death of John mor McEan Vec Condochy alias Maknecht at Ewchirvlairris[2] he was buried in Inchadin before the step of the Choir on the south side of the Church, on the 18 of August.

"   „   Oct 16. Death of John Neilson at Fernay, he was buried at Inchadin

"1526. Jan. Death of Malcolm McWilliam,[3] he was buried in Branvo.

"   „   April 12 Death of Robert Cokburne at Dunkeld, in the Palace there, he was buried in the Choir of Dunkeld.

"   „   April 20. Death of Duncan Reoch McGillechonnyll

"   „   July 31 Death of Gregor,[4] son of John MacGregor, alias McEwine McAllaster of Glenstray at the Isle of Loch Rannoch; he was buried in Dysart in a stone coffin on the north side of the High Altar of Glenstray. May his soul rest in peace

"   „   Sep 3. Battle near Glenvchow alias Lithkow striken betwixt the Lords William Douglas and John Earls of Angus and Arran on the one side- and   Earl of Lennox where the said Earl of Lennox was slain and there was slain many on his side

"1527 Oct. 31 Death of Mariot Forester, Lady Lawers, wife of James Campbell of Lawers She died of good memory at Fordew in Strathearn, and was buried in the parish Church of Stirling, in the Aile of St Andrew at 7 p.m. May her soul rest in peace. Dominical letter F

"1528. April 12. Death of John MacGregor M'Ewine[5] Captain of the Clan-Gregor of Glenstray, who died of good memory at Achallader[6] in Glenurquhay on Easterday. he was buried in Dysart as others of his name used to be   May God have care of his soul

"1529 Death or slaughter of Alexander McPatrick roy and Duncan his son by Duncan Brek, at West Culdar, they were buried in the cemetry of Fortingall near the window of the High Altar Alexander was buried on the 28 May and Duncan on the 4 June Dominical letter C. May God have a care of their souls Amen

---

[1] An island at the west end of Loch Tay, near Killin.   [2] Uachddarblairis   [3] At Glenlyon
[4] Son of John McEwine McAllaster of Glenstray, who died 1528, 12th April (see next page).
[5] John McEwin McAllaster of Glenstray, who had succeeded his second cousin in 1519
[6] "Ayethachallodor" in the Black Book of Taymouth

"1529. Death of William Robertson of Keirquhin at that place. on the day of St Michael the Archangel he was buried in Inchadin in the nave of the Church on the north side near the door of the Choir.

"1529. Oct. 9. Death of an honourable man Colin Campbell Earl of Argyll, Lord Campbell and Lorn, who died at Inverary. and was buried at Kilmun. May God have care of his soul.

"1530. April 18. Death of Finlay McVorricht.

"1531. Feb. 28. Death of Alexander McAyr Rawyr   at Aulich in Rannoch, and buried at Killechonan.

"1531. August 11. Death of Duncan McConnilgorme at Rayn in Eddirgowill. he was buried in the Church of Inchadin on the north side of the door of the Choir.

"1536. Sep. 5. James V. King of Scotland passit and salit in France, accumpaneit with Archabald Earl of Argyle the Earl of Rothess Sir John Campbell of Calder, schipit with diu Lordis and Knychtis, bot nocht returned to his Kingdome till the 5. day of Sep. 1526.

"1538. June 1. Death of Christian Stewart Lady of Garth. She was buried at the altar of St Ninian (of Dull?).

"1542. Oct. 30. In the year 1542. there was a great army of Scots at Jedburgh to fight the Saxons invaders of the Kingdom of Scotland thay remained there for fifteen days, and returned without fighting on the 30. of Oct.[1]

"1531. Death of Duncan McConilgorme in Eddergowyll.

"The quhilk yer I sayd my first mes on Wytsunday afoyr. *Memorandum.*—Rannoch was hareyd the morne eftir St Tennenis day in harist be John Erlle of Awthoell and be Clan Donoquhy, and at the next Beltane eftir that the quhilk was XXXII yer, the Bra of Rannoch was hareyd be them abowin wryttin, and Alexander Dow Albrych war heddyth at Kinlochtrannoch the quhilk Belten and yer I com tyll the cwyr (cure) of Fortyrgill fyrst, and Alexander McGregor of Glenstra our Scheiff was bot ane barne of 7 yer that tyme.

"1542. Dec. Death of Katherine Neyn Ayn Neill, wife of John McAyn Rawych V^cGewycar (McVicar) in Achlie (Auchline).

" ,,   Feb. 20. Death of Katherine McChastyllan, wife of Alexander McOlchallum V^cGregor, at Slattich in Glenlyon.

"1545. August 25. The House of Gordalis Throchchdare apud Strythbrawyn (Trochrie in Strathbran) was burnt by Alexander MacGregor of

---

[1] It is assumed by Mr Gregory that Dean MacGregor's death must have taken place soon after this period. But the Curate of Fortingall continued the Obituary from 1531, and the entry on August 11 is therefore repeated with a memorandum added, and the Chronicle is henceforward quoted from "Black Book of Taymouth."

Glenstray[1] on which day Robert Robertson of Strowan was captured and four of the servants of Robert were slain.   God the just render unto each according to their works.

" 1547.   March 6   Death of Gregor Patrickson MacGregor in Glenurquhay at Aychinchechallan, and buried in Dysart.

" 1548   Death of Mariote Neyn Olchallum V^cGregor Wife of Duncan McAyn V^cCowyll and afterwards wife of James——McJames V^cRobert at Slattich.

"   „   May 4   Death of Mary daughter of Duncan V^cAyn V^cCowyll who was 'affedator' with Joanne Cam McDuncan V^cGregor at Roro, and buried in Rannoch.

" 1549.   Sep. 3.   Death of Christian Murra, wife of Gregor Dougalsoun at Balloch   She was buried in Inchadin

" 1552   Expulsion of Gregor Dougallson from Balloch by Colin Campbell at Whitsunday.

"   „   June 16.   Murder and decapitation of Duncan MacGregor and his sons Gregor and Malcolm Roy by Colin Campbell of Glenurquhay and Duncan Roy Campbell of Glenlyon and Alexander Menzies of Rannoch with their accomplices on which day John Gour McDuncan V^cAlexander Kayr were murdered by Alexander Menzies at ——.   Murder of Gregor, Clerk by Ewine McDuncan V^cGour de Roro and buried in Straythfelen

"   „   Nov 27   Death of Katrine Nyn Velyem (William) V^cOlchallum wife of John Leyche, at Kynnalde, she was buried at Inchadin

„ 1554.   April 30   Death of Katherin Neyn Dowyll V^cAyn wife of the Baron of Kyrquhurn (Colchurn ?) and afterwards wife of Alexander Maxtone of Cultoquhay who died at Cultoquhey.

"   „   Jan 26.   Death of Ewine McCondoquhy V^cGregor of Roro at Crythgarff in Parish of Fortingal, and buried in the Choir of Branvo with great lamentations of men and women.

"   „   There was a most severe snowstorm this winter

" 1555.   May 1.   Death of Gregor Dougalson at Carsdall "propre Dow" he was buried in Inchadin with a large congregation.

"   „   Jan 12.   Death of Dougal Dougalson at Farna in the house of his brother John Dougalson.   He was buried in Inchadin

'   „   Jan 26.   Death of Margaret Robertson wife of William MacGregor, at Port of Bofrak and buried at Weyme

" 1556   Sep 27.   Death of John Challarmore at Eddergovyllit and buried at Inchadin the night of St Michael the Archangel.

"   „   Jan 11.   Death of Mariota Barre, wife of quondam Gregor Duncanson

[1] According to the age of the young Chief mentioned in 1532, Glenstray can at this time have been only twenty —Ed

of Roro and afterwards wife of ——— McAllexander V^cJames. She died
at Kallwyng (Calvine) in Atholl and was buried at Strowane.

"1557. Juje 16. Death of William MacGregor at Port of Bofrak he was
buried at Inchadin in the Choir.

"1558. Feb. 8. Death of Malcolm McNeill McEwine at Lagfarne in Farna in
his own house and was buried in the Church of Inchadin.[1]

    "Quhilk sammyr Schir Dougal McGregor byggit . . . ew hous besyd
the kirk of Fortyrgill and . . . iugn yer Schyr Dougall gat the seneellarie.
. . . Lessmoyr fra Collin Campbell of Glenurquhay.

"1562. May 21. Murder of Allaster McEwin Dow V^cGregor by Patrick McAyn
VycOlchallum alias McGregor Kyllejiese (Killiehassie?) he was buried
at Foss.

"   Feb. 2. Death of John Dow McCondoquhy V^cGregor at the Castle of
Glenurquhay.

"1563. Item death of Neyn Glas in month of Feb.

    "Yer of God 1563. ane gud symmer and gud harist pece and rest
excep the Lard of Glenwrquhay wyryth aganis ClanGregor.

"1564. Sep. 10. Death of John Dougallson at Ferna. in his own house and
was buried on the 7. in Inchadin.

"   May 28. Death of Rinalda McArtna wife of Angus Dow McAyn Voyr
at Rannoch and was buried at Fortyrgill.

"   Nov. 5. Death of John Dow McEwin V^cCondoquhy at Bunrannoch
he was buried in the Choir of Fortingall.

"   Murder of Patrick McAyn V^cCouill V^cAyn by James McGestalcar at
Ardewynnek Dec. 7. and buried on the 8. of the same in the grave of
his kindred at Inchadin.

"1565. Murdered were Gregor son of the Dean of Lismore, alias MacGregor,
and Robert McConil V^cGregor on the 11. of June viz on Penticost
day in the afternoon and night, and the house was burnt and those
murdered by James McGestalkar with his accomplices. They were
buried in the same grave in the Choir of Inchadin. God will judge the
hidden just and punish whom He wills to the second and third
generation.

"   July 27. James McGestalcar V^cPhatrik was slain with his accomplices
by Gregor McGregor of Stronmelecan with his companions at
Ardowenec.

"1565. Jan. 31. Death of Christian Cunygem wife of John Dougallson at
Stronferna, and buried at Inchadin.

"1565. yeris. Item ane gud symmer and harist gret hayr schippis in mony

---

[1] "Pray for the soul of him who did good to God and man," added in the Latin version.

partis of Scotland, in Stratherne, in Lennox, in Glenalmond, in
Breadalbane, bayth slattyr and oppressyon beand mayd in syndry vdr
partis be the Erl of Ergyll and McGregor and ther complessis Siklyk
in Strathardill mony men slayn be the men of Atholl and the Stewartis
of Lorn.

" 1568. April 13   Death of Duncan McAllestyr V^cOlchallum V^cGregor at
Slattich in Glenlyon. He vas bot 26 yer alld

" 1568   Death of Janet Neyn Gregor at Fortyrgill and buried in the Choir
there Oct 12

" 1570   April 7 Gregor of Glenstra heddtt at Belloch

"   „   Aug. 12 John McConil Dow V^cGeglas V^cKessok slayn besyd Glenfalloch and thirteen men of the lardis of Glenurquhais men slayn that
da be ClanGregor, and ther complisis   Gud in hawin stance them of
ther vykgytnes   So be it.

" 1571. Nov 16. Death of Gregor son of the Vicar of Fortingall in the house
of his father in Fortingall ; he was buried there

' 1572   Sep 24   Allaster McAllestyr slain and his son ane yonge barne of
sewin yer ald callyt Gregor, and Duncan brodyr tyl Allestyr al slain
in Stronfarna be Patrik Dow McGregor V^cCondoquhy Lawdossyt with
his complesis, and be the drath of Allestyr Gald V^cGregor. The saidis
Allestyr and his son and brodyr zyrdith in Fortyrgill the 28 day of Sep

" 1572   Nov 30 Death of Donald Elder McQuhewin at Theneff in the house
of his son Donald and buried in the Choir of Fortingall.

" 1572. Jan 9   Death of Katherine neyn Allestyr V^cOlchallum V^cGregor wife
of Patrick McQuhewin at Ardtrasqyr ' in Gallocante ' (mad?)   She
was buried in the Choir of Fortingall

" 1573. Death of Donald McGregor V^cCouil in the nordland March 13   He
was buried in the Church of Taldow in Strathdayn

" 1574   April 7 Item Donald Dow McConil V^cQuhin heddyt at the Kenmore
be Collyn Campbell of Glenurquhay and zirdyt in Fortyrgill that
samyn day.

"   „   Item gud Mald N^cAyn Vay in Glenlyon spouse till the clerk
McNevin zirdit in Branwo the April 28

"   „   Death of Ellyssat Neyn Huston V^cEwyn wife of Donald McCondoquhy
Voyr at Fortingall

"   „   Oct 4 Patrick Dow McGregor V^cDuncan Lawdossyt was slain in
Bofudyr (Balquhidder) by Clandowilchayr (Clandougalciar).

" 1576   July 1   Death of Janet Neyn Duncan V^cGregor wife of Donald
McQuhewin at Thyneff June 31. and buried July 1 in the Choir of
Fortyrgill.

Chapter VII

Book of the Dean of Lismore

IN connection with the preceding Obituary, some poems from the Collection known as the Dean of Lismore's Book[1] now follow. They are written in praise of some of the MacGregors, whose deaths are recorded in the Obituary, and they show the traditional Genealogies current in the fourteenth and fifteenth centuries. Some remarks by Dr Joseph Anderson on this subject are interesting :—

"There are three separate Genealogies of MacGregor given by the MacGregor Bards in the collection of Sir James MacGregor Dean of Lismore. The oldest of them is introduced in the matter of fact manner of these old Sennachies. The author of this is McGillinduk the man of songs, as if all the world ought to have heard of his fame. He commences the genealogy with Duncan Beg and carries it down to Malcolm whom he styles son of Derval and names his wife as Mary. Malcolm son of Derval may be recognised from the obit in the 'Chronicle of Fortingall' as the Malcolm son of John Dhu McAin Cham who died in 1440. This Genealogy as he is the last mentioned and is spoken of as in life, was probably composed before that time. Derval his mother is mentioned in the 'Chronicle of Fortingall' as Dervogill Nyn Ean VcLachlan wife of John Dhu MacGregor as dying at Glenurchy in 1424. The second Genealogy written by Duncan MacDugal Moill in the lifetime of John Dhu Macpatrick, Grandson of the Malcom who died in 1519, carries the Genealogy up to Kenneth McAlpin. Both are the same up to Duncan Beg, Great-Grandfather of that Gregor who was father to the John MacGregor whose obit is 1390. John Dow McPatrick's mother may have been a Grant as the blood of Grant in thy apple-red cheeks and the death of John Grant in 1480 is noticed in the 'Chronicle.'"

---

[1] "A Selection of Ancient Gaelic Poetry from a MS. Collection." Edited, with a Translation and Notes, by the Rev. Thomas McLauchlan, and an Introduction and additional Notes by William F. Skene, Esq., 1862. Particulars about the Dean and his family are given in Chapter XIII.

FIONNLADH RUADH AM BARD.

"Fad a taim gun bhuaidh, 'fhaigheal domh is mithich,
Thainig time thàmhach, as an aoradh dhligheach,
Is e conair a theighinn, d' iarraidh slait mhir,
Gu flath treun nan Gaidheal, far nar fhaighear luchd suaill.
Gu Mac Grigoir dion, is ceann air na sgoilibh,
Ni bhi neomhin falamh, dlighear dhomh a mholadh.
Gu fear is treun coir, an toiseach gach samhradh,
Ni an samhach dha bhi, bithidh an amhaich gach h-amhuil.
'N uair theireas iad uime, Grigoir nan ceuda,
Bithidh a chail am fogradh, gu trath os na treudaibh,
Eoin is ceann do 'n treud sin, rìgh fhuair creach a ghabhail,
Theireas féin ceol, beul ri beul 's a chamhar.
'N uair a chi teaghlach armgheur, Mhic Grigoir am Bealach,
Slighe mhin 'n a choire, ni b' eire riu an eallach
'N uair chinneadar a chomhrag 'g a ghairm an cridhe namhaid,
Is ris féin do theigheadh, an riochd goile 'us bhràghaid
De mhaisibh Mhic Grigoir, tothair chath r' a chulthaobh
Gun diol ri daoinibh, 'us gach meodhar 'n a dhuna,
'N uair dh' fhagam mo bhuaidh, am eis air lar trod,
Mi ag innseadh mo mhùc 's e is millse le 'm oide.
Ge h-olc an loch mhir mo dheileanas innseadh,
Gon chath làn loingsich 's e air la cath is millse.
Cuimhnich gun bitheam romhad, Mhic Grigoir gun agadh,
Ri aghaidh gach trod an dail siad fada fada.
Ealasaid uasail iompaich mo mheuda,
A bhean nan ciabh boga, dh' am buin an clàr fada.
                           Fada."

IS E ÙGHDAIR SO DUGHALL MACGHILLE GHLAIS.

"Righ ghaisge ei reachd Eoin,
    is asdaireach do dhuan a dhroing,
Ni nach bheil a amhra do chàch,
    fhuair an fhioradh an sàidhe rìgh
MacGrigoir nan greas geur,
    toiseach is treine air gach tir,
Eadar or 'us creach a Ghall,
    is dòigh a bhi gu mall min;

FINLAY THE RED-HAIRED BARD.

" I am a stranger long to success, 'tis time that I should have it,
 'Tis time now to desist, from satire justly due.
 The way that I shall take, to seek a noble branch,
 Is to the Prince of the Gael, where are no worthless guests.
 To MacGregor the brave, head of all the schools ;
 He's neither cruel nor sparing, to praise him is our duty.
 To whom courage is a right ; when summer time comes round,
 Peace he never knows, he's in the throat of all his fellows
 When men of him do speak, as Gregor of the blows,
 'Tis his delight to drive, flocks and herds before him.
 Of that flock John's [1] the head, the king at lifting cattle.
 I myself will sing, mouth with mouth at daybreak,
 When his sharp-armed men see, MacGregor at the Bealach,
 His way so gently soft, no weight to them their burdens.
 Then when war arises, proclaimed in enemies hearts,
 It is to him they'd gather, clothed in martial dress.
 'Tis of MacGregor's fame, when fighting's left behind,
 To men not to be cruel, his castle full of mirth ;
 When victory I had left upon the field of war,
 When of the fight I spoke nought loved my patron more
 Though sad, on the stormy lake, to tell of my grief,
 To have a crew of mariners, is best in battle's day.
 Remember I'll be with thee, MacGregor without stain,
 In face of any foe, long, long's the time.
 Gentle Elizabeth, change thou my state ;
 Woman of softest locks, and of the loftiest brow."

THE AUTHOR OF THIS IS DOUGALL MAC GILLE GLAS.

" Bold as a Prince is John in each gathering
 'Twere long to sing his race's glory ;
 Of this there is no doubt 'mong men,
 That he is the first of the race of kings,
 Mac Gregor of the bravest deeds,
 Is the boldest chief in any land ;
 Between his gold and the Saxon spoil,
 Well may he live in ease and peace.

---

[1] Supposed to be John dubh MacGregor of Glenstrae, died May 24, 1519.—Obituary.

Aon roghainn ghaisge Ghaidheil Ghreige,
    leis nior meathaich meud achliù
Fear is fearr agh 'us iochd,
    an laimh an tir sliochd nan righe.
Seabhag deud gheal nan tri ghleann,
    leis an leughar goil gach gniomh,
Lamh is crodha an cathaibh cinnidh
    flath a 's còir dhe 'n t-slioch rìgh
Air-Mac Phadruig nan gruaidh dearg,
    'n uair athfhasas fearg an uaireachd
Na h-alaich a bheir 'n a dheigh
    nocha slàn an luadh cath ;
Ogha Mhaoil Chaluim nan dearc corr,
    ni sgaradh ri òr gun dìth,
Gille daimheach, sothrach, seang,
    an lamh a 's fearr um gach ni ;
Aicme Ghriogoir timchioll Eoin,
    ni mar chaillte a bhuille s'a mhèin
Droing bhreagh air nach leughar lochd,
    is gnath gort mar a thì ;
Clann Ghriogoir an dream nach treig,
    an àm nach bitheas réidh ri rìgh,
Gaidheil ge fulachdach na fir,
    ni chuireadh siad sin am br 'gh ;
Ni mo leo Gaidheil no Goill,
    na saoir fhir o chuain an rìgh ;
Aicme Ghrigoir nan colg cruaidh,
    o bhorb shluagh ni 'n gabh sniomh
Brainean foirne nam fear fiala,
    oighre Ghrigoir nan srian òr,
Olc do dhuine air an dean creach,
    miosad do neach theid 'nan toir ;
Flath Ghlinne Liobhainn nan lann,
    sgiath bhrignmhor nach gann ri cléir
Lamh mar Osgar anns gach cath,
    is da is cosmhuil am flath fein ;
Urram eanaich d' a ghruaidh dheirg,
    a fhuair gun cheilg mar is coir
Air ghabhail 'einich do gach neach,
    air thiolacadh each 'us òir ;

Choice for courage of the Grecian Gael
Whose meed of praise shall ne'er decay,
Abounding in charity and love,
Known in the lands of the race of kings.
White-toothed falcon of the three glens,
With whom we read the bravest deeds,
The boldest arm 'midst fight of clans,
Best of the chiefs from the race of kings.
When on Mac Phadrick of ruddy cheeks
Wrath in battle's hour awaked,
The men who with him share the fight
Are never safe amidst its blows.
Grandson to Malcolm of bright eyes,
Whom none could leave but felt their loss,
The generous, gentle, shapely youth,
The readiest hand when ought's to do.
The race of Gregor stand round John,
Not as a weak one is their blow ;
The famous race without a fault,
Round him like a fence they stand.
Clan Gregor who show no fear,
Even when with the king they strive,
Though brave Gael may be the foe,
That they count of little weight.
Gael or Saxon are the same,
To these brave men of kingly race,
Sons of Gregor bold in fight,
Bend not before the fiercest foe,
Prince of the host of generous men,
To Gregor of golden bridles, heir,
Pity the men whom you may spoil,
Worse for them who you pursue.
Chief of GlenLyon of the blades,
Shield and benefactor of the Church,
His arm like Oscar's in the fight,
To whom in all things he is like.
Kindness mantles on his red cheek,
Thy praise he justly wins ungrudged,
Benevolence when to men he shows,
Horses and gold he freely gives.

Mac Grigoir an teaghlaich ghrinn,
    ni h-ioghnadh leinn 'n a chuirt cliar,
Ni bheil coimeas d' a uchd geal,
    ach am fear dhe 'n robh an fhiann ;
Aigesan tri freiceadan fionn,
    braigh a ghille ni facadh riamh,
Lamh bu mhaith iorghuil an greas,
    do b' ionmhuinn leis fuileach fiadh
Cosmhuil a mhein's mhodh,
    ris an righ 'g a robh an Fhiann,
Ri h-agh Mhic Grigoir nan creach,
    bheir roghadh gach neach am mian ;
Maith is cumha a rosg gorm,
    ri Mac Cumhail nan corn fial,
Ionann an or fa dhuinn,
    agus an run diolaidh cliar ;
Ionann an suiridh 's an sealg,
    riu 'us Cu ceaird nam Fiann,
A ta an rath air sliochd nan righe,
    is maith an cliu 'us an ciall ,
Eineach 'us eangnath 'us iochd,
    do cheangladh air an shochd righ,
Fion 'us ceir, agus mel,
    am miann sin le sealga fhiadh ;
Fine Eoin is gasda gniomh,
    iad mar mhacaibh righ na Feinn,
Agus Eoin mar am Fionn fein,
    'n a cheann air gach daimh a. . . . .
Ge dhurachd leo flaitheas Feinn,
    do chathaich ri linn na Feijn,
Is air Mhac Phadruig a ta an rath
    sharuich se gu maith. . . . . .
Mac Grigoir nan dochair a t' ann,
    ceann sochair ceall 'us cliar,
Taobh seang air am breithbbean,
    o Gleannsrath nam fear fial ;
Comhrad dhuinn breth le Eoin,
    is ni g' a dheoin do ni,
A tiodhlacadh each 'us or,
    fa 'n seach mar is coir do righ ;

Mac Gregor of the noble race,
No wonder though bards should fill thy court ;
To his white breast there is no match,
But he so famous 'mong the Feinn.
Three fair watches him surround,
Never as captives were his men ;
His arm in battle's struggle strong,
Well did he love to hunt the deer.
In mien and manners he was like
The king who ruled amongst the Feinn.
MacGregor of the spoils, his fortune such
That choicest men do covet it.
Good and gentle is his blue eye,
He's like Mac Cumhail of liberal horn,
Like when giving us his gold,
Like when bestowing gifts on bards,
Like in wooing or in hunt,
To the Cu Caird [1] among the Feinn.
Fortune attends the race of kings,
Their fame and wisdom both are great,
Their bounty, prudence, charity,
Are knit to them, the race of kings ;
Wine, and wax and honey,
These, with the stag hunt their delight.
Famous the actions of John's clan,
Like to the sons of the Fenian king ;
John himself was like to Finn,
First and Chief 'mongst all his men,
Though many sought to have Finn's power.
'Mongst those who fought against the Feinn,
On Patrick's son fortune attends,
His enemies he has overcome.
Mac Gregor who destroys is he
Bountiful friend of Church and bards ;
Of handsome form, of women loved,
He of Glenstay of generous men.
Easy 'tis to speak of John
His praise to raise loud in the song,
Giving his horses and his gold,
Just as a king should freely give.

K

Righ neimh, Mhuire oigh,
    dlighe mar is doigh mo dhion,
Mo bhreith 's a chaithir gun chealt,
    's a bheil Athair Mhic an Aig
                Righ."

IS E ÙGHDAIR SO DUNCHADH MAC DHUGHAILL MHAOIL.

" Aithris fhreumh rùna Eoin Mhic Phadruig,
    no 'r creud cheileam,
Na bhitheann 'g a fhine mor fhanna,
    mu 'm a chinnidh do char sinn
Teirc ri aithris fhine fhanna
    dh' uailsibh Gaidheal nan glan dhàil
Fochd na freumh gu bheil,
    do luchd leughaidh nan leabhar.
Barail dileas doibh 'us domh,
    feadh ard an fheasgair orra,
An fhuil rìgh an caomh,
    chur an fhior dhream Ghrigoir ;
Mi réidh ri d' àros glas,
    eisd Eoin ri 'd sheanchas,
Riamh de fhreumh tamaid,
    righ seimh saor-theist.
Padruig athair, aithne dhuit,
    Maolcholuim athair Phadruig,
Mac Eoin duibh na 'r dhubh bràigh,
        dligheach a chuire 's a chreadradh
Eoin eile athair Eoin duibh,
    Mhic Grigoir, Mhic Eoin aghmhoir,
Ta triar feara fa feile,
    triar teamhaireach mu thromchleir,
Athair an Eoin sin oileanaich,
    Maolcholuim na 'r cheil a nì,
Mac Dhunchaidh mhuiginir bhig reim,
    onchoin air nach tig toibheum.
Dunchadh eile athair-san
    Mac Gillfhaolain oirchill,
Do shaor leat 'n uair dh' fhoir ri daimh,
    Mac Aoidh ùr o Urchaidh.

King of heaven, Mary Virgin,
Keep me as I should be kept.
To the great city fearless me bring
Where dwells the Father of the King.
                              Bold.

THE AUTHOR OF THIS IS DUNCAN MAC DOUGALL MAOIL.

The history of the secret origin of John Mac Patrick
Why should I conceal it?
What belongs to his race is not feeble,
The bearing of that race we love,
Seldom of a feeble race it is,
Among the Gael of purest fame,
That inquiry of their origin is made,
By the men who read in books
Firm the belief to them and me,
During the evening time so dark
That in the blood of noble kings
Were the rights of true ClanGregor
Now that I'm by thy green dwelling,
Listen John to thy family story.
A root of the very root are we
Of famous kings of noble story.
Know that Patrick was thy Father,
Malcolm father was to Patrick.
Son of Black John, not black his breast,
Him who feasts and chariots owned.
Another John was Black John's father,
Son of Gregor, son of John the lucky.
Three they were of liberal heart,
Three beneficent to the Church.
The father to that learned John,
Was Malcom who his wealth ne'er hid,
Son of Duncan surly and small,
Whose standard never took reproach.
His father was another Duncan,
Son of Gillelan of the ambush,
Noble he was, giving to friends,
Son of the famous Hugh from Urquhay.

Ceanan nan corr gatha,
 athair Aoidh Urchaidh,
O Alpain a gharg mhein ghlan,
 ardrigh nam balg bheum brioghmhor.
So an ceathramh tuaraisg a 's tug,
 umad a oighre Phadruig,
Cuimhnich ceart bheil fa 'd chaomh
 dream o Alpain oighre Dhughaill,
Fear an fhichead is tu fhein,
 Eoin dubh nach dubh cre,
Do cheart sheanchas is e sin,
 gu Fearghus Mac Eirc aghmhoir.
A 'd chinneadh nach crion ri fodhair,
 sé linn do ghabh coron,
Da fhichead agus triur righ,
 dlighear an fhuil 's an ardfhreumh,
Tri tuathruidh, tri deasruidh,
 an deigh Mhaolcholuim Chinnmhoir,
Da choigear choron a chinnidh,
 o Mhaolcholum gu Alpain,
O Alpain suas is e bhitheas,
 ceithir deug fir gu Ferghus,
Do cheart sheanchas is e sin,
 riamh gu Ferghus Mac Eirc aghmhoir.
Cia lion de sheanchas
 imar sin riamh gu Ferghus faighidir,
Iomadh fine oll fa d' fhuil tathas,
 nach àireamar n' uair àirmheas,
Do bu sgith sgoil d' an sgeulaibh,
 gach righ a bheil fa d' ur fhreumh
Fuil Artuir fa d' urla fann,
 maith do chuid 'do chuislean ;
Fuil Chuain, fuil Chuinn fa 'd chneas,
 da shuthain sothrain n' fhine
Fuil Ghrantach ma 'd ghruaidh mar ubhal,
 fuil Neil nimheil neart-mhoir
Garg mhin a ceum 's a gach greas,
 de reim ard righ an aithris.
     Aithris."

Kennan of the pointed spear,
Of Hugh from Urquhay was the father.
From Alpin of stately mien and fierce,
Mighty king of weighty blows.
This is the fourth account that's given
Of thee who art the heir of Patrick.
Remember well thy backbone line,
Down from Alpin, heir of Dougal
Twenty and one besides thyself,
John the black not black in heart.
Thy genealogy leads us truly
To the prosperous Fergus McErc.
Of thy race which wastes not like froth,
Six generations wore the crown.
Forty Kings there were and three,
Their blood and origin are known.
Three there were north and three to the south,
After the time of Malcom Kenmore.
Ten of the race did wear the crown,
From the time of Malcom up to Alpin.
From Alpin upwards we do find
Fourteen kings till we reach Fergus.
Such is thy genealogy
To Fergus, son of Erc the prosperous.
How many are there of thy race
Must there have been from thee to Fergus.
Noble the races mix with thy blood,
Such as we now we cannot number.
The Schools would weary with our tale
Numbering the kings from whom thou 'rt sprung.
The blood of Arthur is in thy bosom
Precious is that which fills thy veins;
The blood of Cuan, the blood of Conn,
Two wise men, glory of the race.
The blood of Grant in thy apple-red cheek,
The blood of Neil the fierce and mighty.
Fierce and gentle, at all times,
Is the story of the royal race.

IS E ÙGHDAIR SO MAC GILLIONDAIG AM FEAR DÀN.

"Buaidh thighearn air thoisichibh,
        a ta o thùs an cinne,
Airidheach de na h-oig fhearaibh,
        gach aon fhear a breith fios,
Ceud tighearn na tir-sa,
        Dunchadh beag fa mòr aigne,
Do dh' fhag mar a chuid dilib,
        aig clann Ghriogoir an gaisge.
Dunchadh mòr de mhileadhaibh,
        athair beannaichte Mhaolcholuim,
Seanair Eoin aonfhlaith nior gheill,
        cunradh'n uair a chunbhail.
Grigoir deagh-mhac Dhunchaidh,
        mac o Eoin do b' e oighre,
Fear aibheasach o'n chontath,
        o Loch thaobh sholuis Tulaich.
Eoin dubh angoilgeillte,
        mac aireadhach Eoin mhic Grigoir,
Sealgair dhamh dhreachach,
        tùs gach cogadh do fhritheal.
Maolcholum go dheagh chunbhal,
        aithnichte Eoin d' éis a athar,
Deisceart glinne geal Urchaidh,
        maiseach do chaidh m'a cachta,
A ta toiseach an uibhireachd,
        do chloinne Ghrigoir o Ghallaibh,
'Ga bheil tri thighearn beò,
        gràdh sealga, 'us beò ghaisge.
An aimsir Chuinn cheud chatha,
        do chuala mi a mhac samhail,
Fionn ni ghabh o gheur lannaibh,
        Mac Cumhail nan grath calm.
Sealg Eirinn's thighearnas
        aig Mac Cumhail 'n a coillich
Aoibh dha no tighearnas,
        air criochaibh clanna Ghuill
D' fhiodh r' a linn da 'n leigeadh,
        o Charaidh gu Carn Bhalair.

THE AUTHOR OF THIS IS MAC GILLINDAK, THE MAN OF SONGS.

The Lords have precedence of chiefs,
It has been so from the beginning;
It is commendable in young men,
That each should have knowledge of this,
The first who was Lord of this land,
Was Duncan beg (little) of the great soul,
He who as a legacy has left,
Their bravery to the ClanGregor.
Duncan, great by many spoils,
Was the blessed father of Malcom;
Grandfather he was to Princely John,
Him who never broke his pledge.
Gregor, excellent son of Duncan,
Was son to John and was his heir;
Famous man he was of the country,
From the bright shore of Loch Tullich,
Swarthy John,[1] so pure in speech,
Princely son of John M\^cGregor,[2]
Hunter of the well formed deer,
He like a king aye led the fight,
Malcom of unbending truth,
Know thou John, succeeds his father,
Southwards in fair Glenurchay,
Handsome he was amongst its valleys.
The first place 'mong their ancestors
Is given by the Saxon to ClanGregor,
Of whom were three chiefs loved the hunt,
And were most active in the fight.
In the days of Conn of hundred battles,
I heard something like this,
Of Finn of spears and sharp sword,
Cumha's son of famous deeds,
That of Erin the hunting and lordship
Belonged to Mac Cumhal of long locks,
Patrimony and lordship he had not
Over the lands of the race of the Gaul.
Forest right they had all his life,
From Kerry north to Carn Valair.

[1] John Dhu, *ob.* 1415.   [2] John Cham M\^cGregor, page 21.

Roimhe ghabh na seisir,
    bha aig 'n a fhiodha.
O shamhainn gu bealltainn, bhuineadh,
    air ni gach tì d' a Fhianaibh,
An t-sealga fa soimheamh samhradh,
    aig an inbhe in fhiodha
Iomadh cis nach airmhear,
    aig Fionn no aig fear a àirmhidh.
Fiacha Eirinn da roinn,
    air Mhac Cumhail 'n a fhiodh.
Fiodh mhoir ridir dh' Fhiantaibh,
    air bruachaibh gach buinne,
Aig sin ni bheil diongairean,
    Mhaoilcholuim aig Mac Muirne.
Ni dheaadh Fionn fein sealg,
    gun sireadh a cheada,
Sealg Albainn gun fharraid
    aig Maolcholum 's a chreacha.
Cunbhalach 'n an coshealg
    Mac Grigoir is garg daoine,
Nior mhince coin cro-dhearg,
    gu longphort cloinne Bhaoisgne.
Linn trodach de thoisichibh,
    eiridh leis an la catha,
Fir iad air oirleachaibh
    'g luchd ti 'san tàchair.
Ceannas fion 'us fiùdhantais,
    coitchinn is cliù dh' a chinneadh,
Air barn ghaisge ghlé dhearbhas,
    Mac Grigoir gràdh ni bheil.
Iomadh 'n a chuirt coluath,
    saolaim cuideachd a 's colg teann,
Or dearg air an dornairibh,
    airm leoghain Loch Abh.
Co sheirm eadar clàrsaichibh,
    na doine an léich 'n an lamhaibh,
A luchd ti o thaibhlisibh
    a dol far gheibhear gadhar.

But he possessed the old rights,
Which previously were his.
From Hallowmas on to Beltin,
His Feinn had all the rights.
The hunting without molestation.
Was theirs in all these forests.
Many the tributes I cannot tell,
Belonged to Finn and his men,
Tribute in Erin possessed,
By Mac Cumhail from the forests.
A noble forest's right to the Feinn,
On the banks of every stream.
But Malcom's[1] large tributes
Did not belong to Mac Muirn ;
Finn himself would never hunt
Without first asking leave.
The hunting of Scotland, without leave
Belongs, with its spoil, to Malcom.
Constant in the hunt together
Are MacGregor and his fierce men ,
No oftener did the blood-red hounds
Enter the fort of Clan Boisgne.
A fighting band of chieftains
Arose with him in battle's day,
Men whose dress sparkled with gold,
Men who conquered in the fight.
The heads of clans and of huntsmen
In the common fame of his race.
No trial of bravery of skill
Will show weakness in McGregor.
Many in his halls are found together,
Men who carried well-sharped swords,
Red gold glittered on their hilts,
The arms of the lion of Loch Awe.
Harmonious musick among harps,
Men with dice-boxes in their hands
Men who leave the game of tables,
Go and lead forth the hounds.

[1] Assumed to be Malcolm, son of John Dhu McGregor.   He died on the 20th April 1440, and the poem appears to have been written in his lifetime.   From the references in the poem, Malcolm's mother was Dervogil (*ob.* 1424), and his wife Mary.

L

Mac Grigoir bos barr chorcuir,
   Mac Diarbhuill buaidh a Ghallaibh,
Aon chara na calmachd a lamh,
   le 'r ràinig gach rath buaidh.
Buaidh feile ri filidhibh,
   a ni Mac Laomuinn a chosnadh,
Do mhadaibh a chliù ceann-aigh,
   air thiolacadh a lamh luath.
Mairidh muime ollamhan,
   mingheal is maith com,
Na char 'g a comoladh,
   corcra a gruaidh no sugh."

Mac Gregor of red-pointed palms,
Son of Dervail, the Saxon's terror,
No hand like his amidst the fight,
He 'tis that ever victory won,
Liberal he ever was to bards,
Gifts which Mac Lamond knows to earn,
Famous for managing his hounds,
A hand so ready with its gifts.
Mary who stands by his side,
Of noble mind and handsome form,
Poets unite to give her praise,
Her with cheeks as berries red.

Chapter VIII

1513 to 1548

KING JAMES IV having lost his life at the fatal Field of Flodden, 9th September 1513, the long minority of a child-king again began Sir Duncan Campbell of Glenurquhay fell with most of the Scottish nobility, and was succeeded in his lands by his son Sir Colin There does not appear to be any authentic record of the ClanGregor at Flodden During the reign of James V, when both Highlands and Lowlands were convulsed with incessant troubles, the Clan was not more conspicuous for feuds than its neighbours.

The following Band of Manrent from the "Black Book of Taymouth," is curious as showing the customs as to receiving foster children .—

"1510 April 29 Obligation by Johne McNeill Vreik (breac, freckled) in Stronferna and Gregoure his brother to receive Coleyne Campbell lawful 3d son to Coleyne Campbell the eldest son and heir of Sir Duncane Campbell of Glenurquhay Knight in fostering and to give him a bairns part of gear, and giving to the said Sir Duncane and his heirs their bands of manrent and calps that is the best aucht in thair housis the tymes of thair deceiss ; the said Sir Duncane and Coleyne his son being bound to defend the saids John and Gregour in the lands of Stronferna and the rest of the rowmis they possess as law will. Johne Campbell of Lawers brother to Sir Duncane, Sir Robert McNair Vicer of Killin Alexander Maknachtan Tuldonycht Talzeour Macfale and Gillechreist Clerk witnesses. Signed at the Isle of Loch Tay. Schir Maureis McNauchtane Vicar of Inchedin notar."

From the "Chartulary" .—

"1514 31st May In lykewiss the Lord Dromond hes takin upoun him the inbringing of ye Kingis and Quenis propirte w'in the boundis of Buchquhidder and Stratherne sua that he have authorite of in and furth putting of the Chalmerlane —Acta Dominorum Concilii xxvi

"1522-23 February 16. Anent our Soverane Lordis Letters purchest at the instance of Robert Menzies Knicht against Jonet Countess of Athole[1] makend mentioun That quhair Sche and hir tenentis of Athole hes laitlie be sinister and wrang information purcheist uther letters direct be deliuerance of the lordis of Counsale chargeing the said Robert to put and hald McGregor his Clan and Complices, out of the said Robertis landis of Rannach haldin be him of our Soverane Lord in feuferm, and feubying thairof, the said Robert to answer for the haill skaith done be the said McGregor and his Clan to our Soueran Lordis Lieges of Athole and utheris nixt adjacent yairto quhilk is unpossible to the said Robert to doo, considering the said McGregor on force enterit on the said Robertis landis and withhaldis the samyn fra him maisterfully, and is of fer greater power than the said Robert and will not be put out be him of the saidis landis.' . . . 'The Lords of Counsale suspendis the letters purchest be the said Jonet Countess of Athole charging the said Robert to put and hauld McGregor his Clan and Complices out of the said Robertis landis of Rannoch and ordainis the effect of theme to ceiss, ay and quhill thai be producit befoir the Lordis of Counsell and the party warnit to the production yairof and letters to be direct yairupoun as effeirs.—Acta Dominorum Concili xxxiii.

"1524-5. Early in the morning of 25th March Annunciation of the Blessed Virgin and by the then reckoning New Year's day 1524, (1525 by the modern computation) Makintosh of that Ilk went to a fatal hunting seat, for John McCallum Milmor, and his brother William, with three others, their associates in wickedness surround him and so soon as they descried Makintosh alone in the hunting seat, they attack him from their lurking places and treacherously run him through the body, in his 34th year. In revenge for this murder, Donald Makintosh (otherwise 'glas,' or wan complexioned) son of Makintosh's brother William and Donald Makintosh (otherwise son of William, son of Allan) his kinsman, by the help of Dominus[2] MakGregor who had married the deceased's sister apprehend John McCallum near Anakelt &^a. A M.S. History of the Makintoshes in the archives of Moy Hall states of the lady that she married first 'Lord MacGregor' and afterwards 'the Baron Kincarne.' De origine et incremento Macintoshiorum M.S. in MacFarlane's Papers.

"1527. Item Johnne McGregour of Glenstray, ten pundis to be pait at Lammas in anno &^a xxvij for x ky, a mere, a foil, vi lib aittis[3] sawin of the guidis of Duncan Gromache, not provin, and the rest of the said Duncan Gromache's guids gif there be ony to be reseruit to my lord's will,

---

[1] See Chapter III., page 34.

[2] How called Lord is not known, it may have been a mistake for Laird, and so translated into Latin.

[3] Pounds of oats sown.

bot gif my Lord be pleisit yrfor.—Erle of Argyll's 'Book of Casualties,' preserved in Register House, Edinburgh.

"1527. August 14th at Edinburgh.   Quo die Johannes, Comes Atholie plegins devenit ad intrandum Donaldem Campbell nominatum ad Abbacium de Cowper & &   Archibald Campbell son of Duncan Campbell Knight, James Campbell of Lawers, John Campbell his brother, Neill Stewart, John Stewart, son of John Stewart Kt. Gregour Dougalsoune,[1] John and William Dougalsoune,[1] John Makewin Makalester Captain of the Clangregour, Duncan Bayne his cousin, Duncan Brek his Cousin, Donald Patricksone Duncan Donaldsone, Gregor Patricksone, Patrik Duncansoun in Dundwrne,[2] James his brother, Duncan Campbell, son and heir of Duncan Campbell Kt ad subcundum leges pro arte et parte convocationes ligeorum Domini Regis ad magnum numerum vemendi super, Patricium Charteris Prepositum de Perth die festi Corporis Christi ultimo elapso, ipsum invadendo et pergarte et parte mutilationis   Duncan Cameron et Patricii Rutherford Servitorum dicte Patricus —Record of Justiciary

"1527 Sept 2   Decreet of Removal, obtained at the instance of Andro Lord Avondale, who has the gift of the Ward, Relief and Non entry of the lands and Earldom of Lennox against the tenants of the said ward lands charging them to cease occupying the same, among whom are mentioned Patrick McGregour Malcolm McGregour, and others —Acta Dominum Concilii

"1528. 12 April   John McEwen McAllaster Captain of the Tribe of Glenstray died at Achallader in Glenurquhay and was succeeded by his son Allaster.

  "Glenurquhay.   Item Gregor McPatrick McGregour sall pay to my Lord for the ward of Johnne McGregouris landis of Glenstray lx merkis at yir termes efter written viz xx merkis at the Natuiite of our Lady (8th September) in anno &c xxviij, xx merkis at Andromas (30th November) eodem anno, and xx merkis at the Natuiite of our Lady in anno &a xxix. Plages for the said soume Johnne Campbell, McAne vic Ewin, and John McDonachie McGregour conjunctim et divisim.

  "Kinlochgoyle.   Duncan Campbell Robertsoun Captain of Carrik sall pay to my lord for the marriage of McGregour soun and ayr sewyn scoir of merkis at yir termis efter wrytin the thrid part of the said soume at the fair of Lukemas in anno &a xxviij the thrid part of the said soume at the fair of Lukemas in anno &a xxix and the tother thrid part at the nixt Patrikmass yairefter eodem anno Regij for the said soume.—Earl of Argyll's 'Book of Casualties.'

---

[1] Probably sons of Dougall Maol, father of Dean of Lismore, as they do not appear to have been of the Dougal Ciar family.   [2] Family of Dundurn.

"1530. May. Slaughter of Alexr. McPhatrick Roy and Duncan his son by Duncan Brek at West Culdar."

In the course of 1528 Allaster MacGregor, son and heir of John McEwin McAllaster, was formally infeoffed in Glenstray (General Register House of Sasines, as quoted by MacGregor Stirling), but at that time he can only have been three years old, because in 1532 the Curate of Fortingall states that "Alexander McGregor of Glenstra our Scheiff was bot ane barne of 7 yer that tyme." Thus the provision appointed for the "marriage of McGreger son and heir" was evidently a sum to be set aside for the future event.

"1530. December 2d. James Campbell of the Lawers askit instrumentis that he denyit yat he is Bailie of Ardowny or has any doo yairw^h and y^{t}foir renunceit all bailzeri gif he ony has in pins of the Kingis Grace, and Lordis foirsaidis of Ardownie. The Laird of Enoch askit instrumentis yat w^{t}out sum gud reyle be finden for ye ClanGregor yat he may not ansuer for his landis nor be bund for gud reule in the samyn as he allegeit.—Acta Dom. Con.

"1531. March. Respite by James V. for Rebellioun, slaughter to McGregor, McClane, Cayme, Buquhannane, fynne Colquhoun Layn.—Privy Seal, ix. 44.

"1531. October 10th. Before certain authorities and 'Domini Campbell et Lorne Justiciarij Generalis.' 'Quo die Gillespy Makmakky Finlaiius McClintokech Johannes Dow Makgregor, Duncansoune, Duncanus McGregor[1] ejus frater in Moreynche, Duncanus Dow McFarlane, Gillespie Dow McKinlay, pro arte et parte fuote, trium bovium et duarum vaccarum a David Drummond et suis pauperibus tenentibus extra terras sue assedationis terrarum de Myllenab.' Outlawed for non-appearance.—Record of Justiciary.

"1532. June 25th. Johannes Campbell, frater Duncani Campbell de Glenurquhy et Gillechristus Makchernay Tarloch[2] w^t ye ax. Duncanus Dow McTarloch, Johannes Dow McNab, Finlaius McWay, Donaldus McWane Duncanus the Maris sone in Auchrio^r, Finlaius ejus filius, Parlane Aquanite (of the cudgell i.e. player at the quarter staff) in Killearne, summoned before the Justice for convocating the lieges. cum Gregorio owr, Duncano McPhatrik vore, Donaldo McCallich voy (roy), Tarloch Beg in Ardewnan, Donaldo McKessak, Donald[3] vardno (mischancy) McGillip, rebellibus. All

---

[1] MacGregors in Morinch—at the North-West end of Loch Tay. Their ancestor was Gregor, son of Duncanbeg of Roro. There was another brother, Patrick.

[2] "Tearlach" Charles.

[3] May not this word rather be "fortanach" *fortunate*, on the contrary.

including John Campbell (afterwards Sir John Campbell 5th Laird of Glenurquhay of his family, and father of Sir Colin 6th Laird) fugitated. —Record of Justiciary

"1532 18th July. Johannes MacGregor alias Williamson in Auchindothy et Finlaius Rede in Monze, for stealing xxx milch cows from William Drummond of Ballakin in Strathern, fugitated —Record of Justiciary

"1533 Nov 15th. Quo die Malcolmus McCoule Kere McGregour, Duncanus McGregour et Petricius McGregour fratres[1] for theft 'Cum diver sis rebellibus Domini Regis de la Clangregour in October last from Alexander Earl of Menteith and fugitated —(1st distinct notice of this tribe)

"1534-5 Item sauld to Gregor McDonche VcGregour of my Lordis former meal of Lochaw ewer of the crop of anno 1534 for xxvj sl viij pence to be pait to my lord at Sanctandrosmess day anno 1535. ij bols of meal. plege Johnne McArthour officer of Lochaw ewer.—Earl of Argyll's 'Book of Casualties'

To Duncan McGregour of my lordis fermes meal of Lochaw ewer of the said crop for xxvj shillings viij pence to be pait to my lord the said day ij bols —*Ibid.*

"1535 July 20 List of persons fined in £10 for not compearing on the assize of Sir John Colquhoun of Luss for intercommuning with Humphrey Galbraith and his Complices, Campbells, Buchanans and Patricius McGregour. —Record of High Court of Justiciary.

"1537-8 March 8th John Menzies of Comrie plege for entering Andrew McWiccar, pro arte et parte incendis and combustionis certarum domorum infa terres de Weme in compatina de ClanGregor &ᵃ —Justiciary Record

"1541 April 11th Dischere et Toyer. half of Dalgardy to John McGillireoch Corricarmyk assedatur Patricio McGregour for five years paying yearly 3 pund 6 and 8 pence grassum 3 pund 6 and 8 pence absque pastura et Intromissione cum foresta de Balmakane parts of the lordship to Duncan McCarbery part of Clochrane to Gregour, Dougalstoun, Skeag to him —Rentale Supremi Domini nostri Regis in Register House

"1541. August 26 A Charter Granted by Archibald Campbell de Glenlyoun dated at Elgin May 1538 is witnessed by, among others, Duncane Makgregour.

"1541. September 13 Gevin to William Straitherne for his expensis passing with twa closs writings to Walter M'Farlane, and M'Gregour with diligence, xliijs.

"1541. Nov Item gevin to Alexander hutoun for passing to McGregour and Allane Stewart of Baquhidder[2] with twa closs writingis . iij li "—Lord High Treasurer's Books

[1] Dougall Kier Family.
[2] M'Gregour thus appears to have lived in or near Balquhidder

After the disastrous defeat of the Scottish Army at Solway Moss, Nov. 25, 1542, King James V. expired on the 13th Dec. same year, leaving a daughter only six days old, to begin her life of trial as our Queen Mary.

"1543. Dec. 11. Anent the summondis raisit at the instance of Duncane MacGregour present tenant to Johnne Campbell of Calder Kt for spoliation of his corns, Delayed till 24. Jan.—Register Decreet of Court Session.

"1546. August 14. Letter to Archibald Erle of Ergyle Escheit of McFarlanes, Buchanans, John Bane McCallane, in Corroclaid, Dougal McGregour sone thair, Duncan McCoulekerry McGregour George (Gregor) McRobb alias McGregour there &^{c}. &^{c}. killing 50 persons servants of the Governor at the Townend of Dumbartone in July last.—Record of the Privy Seal.

"1549-50. Jan. 29. Joannes McGregour Clavigeris (q. d. Chamberlain or Secretary.) along with Alexander Menzies of Rannoch witnesses a discharge by Elizabeth Colquhoun relict of Duncan Campbell of Glenurchay.—General Register of Decreets of Council and Session in Register House.

"1546. August 14. Gift of Escheat to Archibald Earl of Argyle, of all goods &^{a} which pertained to Walter MacFarlane of Ardlesc Andro McFarlane his son and heir &a John Bain McAllane in Carronclaid, Dougall McGregour son there, Duncan McCowlekerr (Dougalkeir) McGregor Robert Roy McGregour his man George McJok alias McGregour in Cragcrostan and many others at the horn for being 'art and part in the tressonable cuming to the townend of Dumbertane in the month of July bypast and crewall slauchter of fifty personis, servantis to mylord Governour and Lordis, being with him in cumpany and for the reiffing steling and thiftuous awaytaking of four scoir 80 of hors at the samyn tyme apertening to my Lord Governour and Lordis foresaidis. and for sorning, reiff and oppressioun done be thame upoun the inhabitants of the Levenax and utheris pairtis thairabout and for thair tressonable being in company with the auld inymies of Ingland (?) in burning of divers pairties of Hir Graces realme and specialie of the town of Dunune, or be quhatsumevir manner of way sall happin or may pertene to hiv Hienes, with power &a.

"1547. March 6. Gregor Patrikson MacGregor—died in Glenurquhay at Aychinchechallen.

"1548. Gift of Escheat to Margaret Nykferlane relict of Donald MacGregor in Glenlochye, John Dowsoun, her heirs &a of all goods which pertained to the said deceased Donald MacGregour her spouse and now through his decease in her Majesteis hands be reason that the said Donald was born bastard. Edin. Sep. 28.

"1548. Nov. 15. Gift to Hugh Morye commendator of the priory of Strathfillan his heirs &a which pertained to the deceased .   Johnstoun MacGregour son natural to John Dow Duncanson M⁽c⁾Gregour in Mureloganemore in Glenlochy in the shire of Perth, escheat through the said John being born bastard

John Dow Duncansoun was himself a natural son of Duncan MacGregor in Moreloganemore, but in 1528 a royal letter was given to enable him to inherit property the same as if he were legitimate.[1]

The country of Rannoch had been inhabited by MacGregors from early days, and confident in what they conceived to be their right of possession and their position as king's tenants, they became undoubtedly thorns in the side of those who had been given charters over their heads. The Clan Menzies [2] do not appear to have been very exacting, but the Campbells lost no opportunity of endeavouring to sow strife between the ClanGregor and their neighbours   The following passages are taken, by permission, from the "Red and White Book of Menzies," by D P. Menzies, F.S Scot [3]

After stating that the left wing of the English was cut to pieces at Flodden by the Clans, including Menzies, MacGregors, &a, it continues :—

"On Campbell of Glenurchy receiving all he could from Sir Robert in connection with his liferent of the lands of Crannoch, which gave him a footing on Loch Tayside, he then, for the purpose of forcing the Menzies to sell these lands, secretly, by misrepresentations and other influences, stirred up the MacGregors and other unsophisticated kindly tenants of the Menzieses to violate the laws of the land, and thereby embroiling Sir Robert into difficulties with the Crown for the acts of his tenants   These lawless men were not all MacGregors, but they were saddled with these crimes by their would be friend Campbell

"   .   Sir Robert 'therefore on giving his son a grant of Rannoch bound him not to let these lands in life rents or long leases   It had been made clear to Sir Robert that the Campbells had in secret made use of the MacGregors to ravish his lands so that he would get disgusted with such a state of affairs, and would therefore let or sell the lands on easy terms to the Campbells   This is quite obvious, as there never was any difference between the Menzies and the MacGregors who

[1] A copy of the letter which was written in Latin is given in the "Chartulary," but is omitted here as unimportant

[2] Charter of the lands of Rannoch, to Robert Menzies of Menzies, 1st Sept 1502, on lease See Chapter IV , page 40

[3] Published October 1894

were their kindly tenants and kinsmen (?). until the crafty Campbells came as evil spirits among those peaceful Celts.' Sir Robert therefore procured a second obligation from his son William Menzies not to let his lands of Roro [1] in Glenlyon, to the Campbells or the Chief MacGregor.

"Obligation not to set Rorow to Campbells nor the Chief of MacGregor :— [2] Perth, 22. Feb. 1518. We William Menzies and Jonat Campbell my spouse binds and oblissis vs, and the langer levand of vs tua to ane honourable man Schir Robert Menzeis of that ilk, knyght, that we sal gif na takkis nor set in assedatioun the tuelf merkislands of Rorowis, with the pertinentis liand in the barony of Menzeis and Schirefdom of Perth, quhilkis we haif of the said Sir Robert to nane berand the surname of Campbell, nor to the Chief of the ClanGregor, vnder pain of ane hundreth pundis to be payt to the said Robert for costis, scathis, and expenses. Indorsed The oblygatioun that Rorow sall nocht be set to the Campbells na Scheyff of the ClanGregour.—Charter Room of Castle Menzies."

It is stated in the "Lairds of Glenlyon," by Mr Duncan Campbell, that the second daughter of this Sir Robert Menzies (who died in 1523) married MacGregor of Roro.

"For every theft or violation of the law done by the MacGregors (or by caterans or outlaws) the government held Sir Robert responsible as Lord of Rannoch. He petitioned the government to be relieved of this burden. This he urged in 1530. by 'asking instruments that without some good rule be found for the ClanGregor he may not be to answer for them on his lands, nor be burden for good rule in the same.'—Book of Menzies.

"The MacGregors of Glenstray seem to have been on the best of terms with Sir Alexander Menzies (son and successor to Sir Robert) and for years they held the lands of Archty east and others in Rannoch where they had power from Sir Alexander to sublet these lands to any of the ClanGregor with the exception of Duncan Ladosach.

"Lease by Alexander Menzies of Rannoch to John MacGregor of Glenstray of the twenty merkland of Rannoch 'fra the watter of Aracty est' which had been held by the father of the said John for seven years for the payment of £20 yearly and for the other customary service. The right is given to sublet the lands to any person except 'Duncan McGregor McPhadrick,[3] and his barnis.' Perth, 4. Oct. 1548.—Menzies."

[1] Mention is made of the "Roros and Glenlyoun" in a charter to Sir Robert Menzies, 1510.

[2] Duncan Ladosach.

[3] This was not Duncan Ladosach, as his patronymics were Duncan MacGregor mor VcGregor VcIan.

Chapter IX

Duncan Ladasach

DUNCAN LADASACH, who the "Baronage"[1] mentions as having acquired the lands of Ardchoill,[2] seems to have been an object of peculiar terror and aversion to Sir Colin Campbell of Glenurquhay, the 6th Campbell Laird   In the "Black Book of Taymouth" there is a satirical ballad entitled "Duncen Laideus alis Makgregouris Testament," the writer of which is not known, but throughout which the gall of the penman in abuse of the warrior, with whom his Clan was at deadly feud, is virulently displayed.

A passage from an interesting work entitled "The Lairds of Glenlyon"[3] may explain the Laird of Glenurquhay's position at this time.   Quoting first from the "B B of Taymouth" where it is said of

"Colene sext Laird of Glenurquhay" that he "was Laird induring the space of threttie-thre zeiris, in the quhilk tyme he conquesit the few of the kingis landis and Charter-hous landis in Braydalbane, the tackis quhairoff his predecessouris obtenit,"

the writer continues—

"In addition to this he had acquired the 'superioritie of McNab his haill landis'   He was actually possessor of the greater part, and with the exception of Struan's small Barony of Fernay, or Fernan, and a few other small bits of land, was Lord Superior and Bailie of the different Baronies and Lordships of Breadalbane.   With the most ample feudal privileges, and though his predecessors had land and manrent in the district for nearly a century, he was still but a stranger in a strange land, in which his footing was but precarious, and the authority granted by the King far from being satisfactorily acknowledged and obeyed   At that time the feudal charter, until the title of the holder was recognised and confirmed by the so-called vassals, according to the old Celtic custom, that is, by acknowledging

---

[1] See page 30
[2] In Glen Dochart
[3] "The Lairds of Glenlyon," historical sketches contributed to the *Perthshire Advertiser*, 1855 58 by Mr Duncan Campbell, parish schoolmaster of Fortingall, and now editor of the *Northern Chronical*, Inverness.   The sketches have been collected by Sir Donald Currie, M.P., in a volume printed for private circulation, together with another volume of the same nature entitled "The Book of Garth and Fortingall," and are quoted here by the kind permission of Mr Campbell

him as chief, and granting him the calp[1] of chieftainship, was little else than a piece
of useless parchment.   A landlord in order to have the use and mastery of his possessions, must either conciliate or extirpate the inhabitants.   The Laird of Glen-
orquhay was not in a position to adopt the latter alternative, and he therefore
eagerly and skilfully seized upon the former.   Breadalbane was at that time
inhabited mostly by several old colonies or sections of distant clans, who had come
under the auspices of different lord-superiors, to occupy the places of those ancient
inhabitants upon whom confiscation and death had fallen on account of their
accession to the long sustained, and to Bruce almost fatal, opposition of McDougal
of Lorn.   The inhabitants of Breadalbane were thus made up from five or more
separate sources, and except the McNabs, a supposed branch of the ClanGregor,
none of the sections had a chieftain.   This gave the Laird of Glenurquhay the
precious opportunity of establishing his judicial authority, and the band of manrent
and calp of Ceann-Cinne naturally followed, from men alive to feelings of gratitude,
for having been by the aid of the Bailie rescued from oppressors, and confirmed in
their rights.   Every act of judicial authority added what was both absolutely
necessary for the safe exercise of that authority and the gradual vindication of
feudal possession, a willing recruit to the standard of the 'justiciar.'   It may
sound strange to present landlords that, three hundred years ago, a proprietor
could exercise no privilege of property till mutual kindness produced a bond of
brotherhood between him and his vassals, till a democratic election confirmed the
royal charter and the calp of clanship superseded the feudal enfeoffment.   No
suspicion appears to have crossed the Celtic mind that despicable parchment right
to the soil was sufficient to confer the personal pre-eminence which, in the absence
of hereditary chiefs, they, even they, with their wild notions of unrestrained freedom, had for the sake of internal union, and for giving edge to defensive or
offensive policy, found it at all times requisite to support, but which as uniformly
they had insisted upon creating for themselves, through means of a rude
election."

The preceding able description of the then state of matters will best
explain the following bonds of "Manrent," which are to be found in the
"Black Book of Taymouth," corresponding with this period :—

"The second day of Junii anno domini 1547 zeris at the castell of Glenurquhay
Donald McGillekeyr, Fynla McGillekeyr his son, Duncan McGillekeyr and Neill
McCoull V^cIllekeyr, Mylcallum McCoull V^cIllekeyr, Finlay McAne V^cKyndlo,

---

[1] "An exaction made by a superior, especially by the Head of a Clan, on his tenants and other
dependants, for maintenance and protection. This was generally the best horse, ox, or cow the
retainer had in his possession" (Jamieson's "Dictionary"). It seems only to have become due at the
decease of the clansman. Calpach or Colpach in Gaelic means a Heifer.—*Editor.*

Donald MᶜHewin VᶜIllekeyr, John oyr MᶜCoull VᶜIllekeyr for thame and thair successioun.[1]

"Thai and ilk ane of thaym hes . . . chosyn of thayr awyn fre motywe . . . . ane honorable man Jhon Cambell of Glenurquhay and his ayris to their cheyf to be thair protector   in all just actionis . . . as ayne cheyf dois in the contreis of the helandis and sall haif landis of me in assedatioun for the payment afor wderis   . . and quhen ony of thaym decessis sall leyf to me or my ayris ane cawylpe of kenkynie[2] as is usit in the contreis aboutis, befor thir witnesses &ᵃ &ᵃ . . And atour thay hayf promest to bryng all the layf of thair kyn that thay may to the sammyn effek . . . and for the mair securite the pairt remanent witht Jhon Cambell the saydis persones aboun hes subscriuit witht thair awyn handis led at the pen . . be the viccar of Inchadyn

    Donald MᶜGillekeyr with my hand led at the pen
    Fynla MᶜGillekeyr and Duncan his broder our hands
        ~   led at the pen.
    Neill MᶜCoull VᶜIllekeyr and Malcum his broder do. do.
    Fynla MᶜAne VᶜIndlo do do
    Donald MᶜHewin VᶜIllekeyr do. do
    Jhon Oyr MᶜCoull VᶜIllekeyr siclyk.

And in 1550 another interesting bond[3]—

Alexander MᶜPatrick VᶜCondoqhuy is becumyn of his awin fre will ane faythtfull seruand to Collyne Cambell of Glenwrquay and his ayris for all the dais of his lyftyme   incontrar all . . persomis the authorite beand excepit alanerly baith till ryd and gang on horss and futt in Heland and Lawland upon the said Collynys expenses   And gif it happinnys ony difference betuixt the said Collyne his ayries and MᶜGregour his Cheyff . . . the said Alexander sall nocht stand with ane of theme bot he sall be ane ewinly man for baith the pairties. Attour the said Alexander hes made . the said Collyne and his ayris his . assingnaris to his takys . . . . of ony landis and specially of the ten merkland of Wester Morinche[4] now occupyit be the said Alexander and his subtennendis and allse hes nominat the said Collyne and . . . . his ayris . . . his execuitours and intromittours witht all . . . his gudis mowible and immowible that he happinnis to hef the tyme of his decess, and that in cace he hef nay barnis lewand at that tyme

[1] These all belong to the Dougall Ciar Family, to be considered later

[2] "Ceann Cinnidh"—"Head of the Tribe"

[3] Descendants of Duncan Beg (see Obituary 1477) settled at Moreninch at the south-west end of Loch Tay   Moreninch was the property of Menzies of Menzies of Weem at that time and till about 1600 when it was bought by Sir Duncan Campbell of Glenurchy

[4] Allusion is made to this Alexander twenty years later as son of Patrick, son of Duncan , he was probably nephew of the two brothers, Duncan MacGregor in Moreynche and John Dow, son of Duncan, mentioned in entry October 1531

lauchtfully gottyn. . . . For the quhilk the said Collyne and his ayris sall defend the forsaid Alexander in all his just actionis . . . . the authorite my Lord of Argyle and thair actionis alanerly excepyt. . . . Acta meridiem presentibus ibidem Alexandro Menzies de Rannocht, Joanne McEmeweyr et magistro Willelmo Ramsay notario publico testibus. 10th Julii 1550."

Notwithstanding this band with Glenurquhay, Alexander McPatrick VcCondoqhuy seems to have acted on his own account in some encounter as shown by the following, found in the "Chartulary":—

"1550, October 31st. 'Gregour Dougalsoune' Pledge for 'Alexander Oure (dun or sallow) McPatrick McGregor,' and Nicol McKintaylzeor for art and part of the slaughter of the late John McDonald Bayne. Not appearing fugitated.—Record of Justiciary."

In the preface to the "Black Book of Taymouth," Mr Cosmo Innes gives an indictment which shows that Duncan Ladosach resented either this slaughter, or Allaster Our's defection to an adopted Chief.

"On the 26th of November 1551, 'The Queen's advocate set forth that Duncan Laudes and Gregour his sone recently, namely opoun Sounday the 22nd day of November instant at sex houris at even under silence of nycht, be way of hamesukin, cam to the hous of Alaster owir, alias McGregoure, servand to Coline Campbell of Glenurquhay of the lands of Moreis and be force tuke him furth of his said hous, and be way of murthure straik him with whingearis and crewellie slew him and spulzeit and tuke fra him his purs, and in it the soume of fourty poundis incontinent thireftir past to the landis of Killing to the hous of ane pure man callit Johnne McBayne Pipare, and thair assegit the said hous and brak the durris thairof and be force tuke the said Johne furth of the samyn, and straik his heid fra his body and crewellie slew him and gaif him divers uther straikis with whingearis in his body.'"

Duncan Ladosach and his son were afterwards outlawed and put to the horn.[1] Sir Colin Campbell engaged certain persons to pursue the said Duncan; in this case, as in many others, the Laird of Glenurchy having recourse to strangers and not to his own Clan.

"Band to pursue to the deid Duncane Laudosach.

"Be it kend till all men, We James Stewart sone to Walter Stewart of Ballindoran, Alexander Dormond and Malcolme Dormond, yonger to hawe gewin our

---

[1] *To put the horn,* in Scotch Law is to denounce as a rebel; to outlaw a person for not appearing in the Court to which he is summoned. This is done by a messenger-at-arms, who proceeds to the cross of Edinburgh, and amongst other formalities gives three blasts with a *horn*, by which the person is understood to be proclaimed rebel to the King for contempt of his authority.—Dr Ogilvie's "Imperial Dictionary."

band of manrent to . . . Colline Campbell of Glenurquhay and his ayns, Duncan Campbell sone and apperand air to Archibald Campbell of Glenlioun and his airis . . for all the days of our lyvetyme in all actiones . . . and in speciale that we sall dispone owrselffis at our haill power wytht our kyn, freyndis and part takeris to invade and persew to the deid Duncane Laudosach McGregour, Gregour his sone, thair seruandis, part takeris and complices in all bundis and cuntreis quhair euer thai sall happyn to mak resydens be reasoun that thai are our deidlie enemies and our Souerane Ladeis rebellis. And lykwiss salbe redye   to serve the .   saidis Colline and Duncane and thair airis upon thair .   expenssis baytht in the Heland and Lawland aganes all maner of . . persones, the Quenis Grace hir authorite, the Earl of Menteytht and the Lord Drummond, allanerlie exceptit.   In witness of the quhilk thing because we culd nocht subscrywe our selffis we have for us causit the notare onder wrytin subscrywe the samyn witht our handis tuechand the pen, at the Ile of Loch-Tay the xi day of Marche the zeir of God M V fifty ane zeir (1551) befoir thir witnesses Allexander Menzies of Rannocht, Thomas Graham of Calzemuk, Andro Toscheocht of Monze, Patrick Campbell, Johnn Mawire and Andro Quhit notar publicus.

> James Stewart wytht my hand at the pen.
> Alexander Dormond wytht my hand led at the pen
> I ta est Andreas Quhit notarius publicus."

It is impossible to fathom the reasons which led Sir Colin, the following year, to reconcile himself to McGregor.

"Be it kend to all men—Me Colyne Campbell of Glenurquhay grants me to have ressavit Duncane McGregour and Gregour his sone into my menteinance in all thir just actionis in so far as I may of law, and gude conscience and atour to have forgevine the saidis Duncane and Gregour thair sarvandis complices and part takers the zeil of luf and gude conscience moving me to the samyn, all manner of actionis and faltis thay ony of them hes committit to me providing alwais that the saidis Duncane and Gregour fulfill thair band and manrent maid to me and my airis in all pointis   Forquhilkes grantis me to have given to the saidis Duncane and Gregour thair eschitis of all thair gudis movabill and unmovabill, quhilkis I purchist at my Lord Governouris handis, tha beand for the tyme our sourane Ladeis rebellis and now ressavit to hir heiness peace and my favouris.   In witness wherof I hes subscriuit this my letter of meintenance at the Ile of Lochtay the secund day of Maii the year of God Mvc fifty tua yeris befor thir witnesses Alexander Menzies of Rannocht, Patrick Campbell, David Tosheocht, and Alexander Maknab, Gregour Clerk [1] and Andro Quhit notar publico

> COLYN CAMPBELL of Glenurquhay.

[1] Slain by Ewin McDuncan V^cGregor de Roro, Sept. 22, 1552.—Chron Fort.

This letter of maintenance is the more remarkable because, within a
month afterwards, Sir Colin succeeded (by treachery, it is said) in getting
both his recently-accepted friends into his power, and slaughtering them.

The following tradition is told in the "Lairds of Glenlyon"[1] as a
legend, which may possibly explain Glenurchay's temporary reconciliation
with Duncan Ladosach :—

"MacGregor of Dunan, in Rannoch, had committed great herships on the lands
of the Campbells in every direction, and particularly on those of Campbell of
Glenurchay. The latter did all in his power to take him dead or alive; but
M⁣ᶜGregor, notwithstanding, not only eluded his enemy, but continued to commit
greater depredations. At last Glenurchay offered terms of amity and peace, and
proposed a conference at the newly-built Castle of Balloch (Taymouth), with a
certain number of friends on both sides, to settle disputes, and ratify the relations
of friendship into which the parties were about to enter. Glenurchay did all this
deceitfully, thinking thus to capture MᶜGregor and his principal followers when off
their guard. MᶜGregor, not suspecting the snare, set off for Balloch at the time
proposed, accompanied by the number of men agreed upon. On the top of
Drummond, the hill overlooking the castle and meadows of Taymouth, they
encountered an old man, who, on bended knees, before a huge, grey stone,
appeared to be repeating his orisons in a state of great perturbation. Struck
with a thing so unusual, MᶜGregor, drawing near, discovered the old man was
repeating the prayers for the dead, with which ever and anon the following sentence
mixed : 'To thee, grey stone, I tell it, but when the black bull's head appears,
MᶜGregor's sword can hardly save the owner's fated head. Deep the dungeon,
sharp the axe—and short the shrift.' MᶜGregor saw at once the toils were set for
him, and that the old man had taken this round-about way of apprising him of the
vile conspiracy, for fear of the laird, and in consequence of being sworn to secrecy.
He proceeded on his way, however. Glenurchay received him with the most
cordial appearance of kindness. Dinner was laid for them in the great hall of the
Castle, each Campbell having a MᶜGregor on his right hand—a circumstance giving
the latter a very decided advantage in the melée which followed. The introduction
of the black bull's head, and a simultaneous clatter of armed men in an adjoining
chamber, put the MᶜGregors into an attitude of defence. Snatching the dagger
stuck in the table before him, which a few moments previous he had used in cutting
his meat, MᶜGregor held its point within an inch of the heart of Glenurchay, while

---

[1] The author of this work, Mr Duncan Campbell, supposes throughout that Duncan Ladosach
was acting as tutor for the young Glenstray Chief, but we do not find any evidence or mention
of Duncan as tutor. It was Gregor MᶜPatrick who, in 1528, got the ward of the lands of
Glenstray.

with the other hand he compressed his throat. His men following promptly the example of the leader . the M⁣ᶜGregors carried off captive the Baron and some of his principal retainers, the armed vassals, at the earnest request of the Baron himself, whose life the least attempt on their part to rescue him would endanger, offering no resistance. M⁣ᶜGregor crossed by the boat at Kenmore, dragged his captive to the top of Drummond, and there and then forced Glenurchay to subscribe an ample pardon and remission for all past injuries, and a promise of friendship for the future "

The legend is characteristic of the times, but although the writer suggests that the hero may have been Duncan Ladosach, it would hardly have been possible at his supposed advanced age.

The " Baronage " gives the following narrative :—

" Some disputes having occurred between Gregor, eldest son of Duncan, and Doncha Dubh a Churic (this is a mistake, it was his father, Colin), ancestor of a great family in the neighbourhood, about some marches, a friendly meeting was appointed to be held at Killin for adjusting those differences ; but Doncha Dubh (Colin) in the meantime having hired no less than eight assassins, they were concealed in a closet off the room, where the meeting was held ; from which upon a certain signal they rushed out upon the too credulous and unguarded Gregor, however he made shift to get out of the house, and jumping into a deep pool of the water of Lochy which ran close by, he dragged several of the assassins after him, but from the number of stabs he had received from their dirks, and the loss of blood in swimming, he was so weak when he got to the opposite bank, that the ruffians easily finished his life But not yet satisfied with this cruelty, Gregor's horse was sent as a token to his father, and though it is said he dreaded some evil, he went, and was also murdered in the venerable 100th year of his age Several mournful songs made on this occasion are still preserved. At this time Doncha Dubh seized upon the whole estates of this family which with some interruptions, his posterity enjoyed ever since "

Mr MacGregor Stirling in the " Chartulary," supposes this event to have taken place in 1559-60 or 61 ; but by the following entry in the Obituary of the " Chronical of Fortingal," continued by the curate,[1] the date of their deaths is shown clearly to have been in the month of June 1552

" 1552. Interfectio et decapitio Duncani M⁣ᶜGregor et filiorum eius vidilicet Gregorii et Malcolmi Roy per Colinum Campbell de Glenwrquhay et per Duncanium Roy Campbell de Glenlyon et Allexandrum Menzheis de Rannoch cum suis com-

---

[1] The continuation of the Obituary, from October 1542 to 1576, is not printed with the first part of the " Chronicle of Fortingal," but is to be found in the " Black Book of Taymouth."

plicibus, quo die Joannes Gour McDuncan V^cAllexandrum Kayr fuit interfectus per Alexandrum Menzies de apud   in mense Junii vidilicet xvi anno Domini ave M.V. Lij.

The Black Book has a memorandum in regard to this Sir Colin :—

"He was ane greit justiciar all his time, throcht the quhilk he susteinit thee deidlie feid of the Clangregour ane lang space. and besydis that he causit execute to the death, many notable lymnaris, he beheidit the Laird of McGregour himself at Kenmoir in presence of the Erle of Atholl the justice clerk and sundrie other nobillmen."

It is probable that it was to Duncan Ladosach that the compliment of personal decapitation was paid by Sir Colin out of his "zeil of luf." As will be noticed later, Duncan Ladosach was undoubtedly much feared and detested by his enemies, and was turbulent and reckless of shedding blood in his quarrels. In that respect he was no worse than his neighbours. Not till the publication of the "Black Book of Taymouth" was his career looked upon as blamable, and those who enjoyed the venom of the scurrilous doggerel about him adopted its views. If Duncan Ladosach openly slew, perhaps, several men, Sir Colin, his executioner, compassed the death of many more.

In farther illustration of this dire event, so full of interest to the descendants of Duncan Ladosach, the following may be related, given by Mr MacGregor Stirling as a traditional account gathered from "an aged native of Glendochart"[1] :—

"Glenurchay, having some disputes with Gregor, son and heir of the aged MacGregor, about some marches (it is supposed in reference to the properties of Ardchoille Easter and Wester), proposed a friendly conference for adjusting these. The parties therefore met at the village of Kincauser, on the river Lochy, and in the near neighbourhood of Glenurquhay's seat, Finlarig ; when Sir Colin caused some armed men, whom he had concealed, to rush suddenly upon Gregor. These, having overpowered their single opponent (for he had no attendant), proceeded towards his and his father's residence, Ardchoille Wester, and getting the old Chief in their power, killed him on the spot. The son was reserved for a more publick and mortifying triumph at Kenmore, whither he was dragged all wounded and bleeding, and there, in the presence of several noblemen, beheaded."

This version makes the son survive the father. It seems probable

[1] MS. by Mr MacGregor Stirling.

however, that the earlier tradition may have been the more correct, the father being reserved for the solemn execution [1]

It has been supposed by Mr MacGregor Stirling and others that Gregor younger of Ardchoille was identical with Gregor Roy, named "Bassen Gheal" ("Red Gregor of the White Palm or Hand"), celebrated in a mournful Gaelic song, but this song, which is supposed to have been composed by a lady of the Campbell race lamenting the death of her beloved Gregor, must apply to Gregor Roy of the Glenstray line, beheaded in 1570, whose wife was a Campbell, instead of young Ardchoille. This will be shown farther on

Gregor XVI, eldest son of Duncan Ladosach, according to the "Baronage," married Isabel, daughter of Cameron of Stronhead, and left two sons —

1. Duncan, who succeeded him, and who, after his father's death, was sent to Lochaber, whence he was called Duncan Lochaber or Abarach, as afterwards appears

2 Patrick, brought up in Athole, and thence known as Parig Adholach or Aulich, "of whom the Drummonds, *alias* MacGregors, of the Bows, and many other tribes."

Daughter, More (probably Mairie, Mary), married to a MacGregor.

Patrick Adholadh was executed in Edinburgh with Glenstray, February 1604 He left five sons, frequently mentioned in the Register of Privy Council, *i.e.*—

Duncan,	. .	took name of Livingstoun.	
Allester,	.	Do.	Do.
Patrick,[2]	.	Do.	Do
Donald,		took name of Balfour.	
John,		Do	Do

[1] In the "Lairds and Lands of Loch Tay Side," by John Christie, published in 1892, it is stated that Duncan Ladasoch and his sons, Gregor and Malcolm Roy, were executed at *Finlarig*. This is quite possible, as the place of their deaths is not mentioned in the "Black Book of Taymouth"

[2] Patrick "Beg" and "Callum Baine," another son, slain in skirmish at Leny, 1626; as also Donald, son of the above Duncan

Chapter X

Genealogical

TAKING a retrospective view of the notices of the Clan during the reigns of James IV. and V., and up to the tragic deaths of Duncan Ladosach and his son Gregor in 1552, it may be observed that mention is repeatedly made in 1503-1506 of "MacGregor," a style which it is well known pertained always to the Chief of a Clan. At this period he appears to have lived in the neighbourhood of Balquhidder, and had rights of forestry and facilities for the pursuit of deer, which James IV. countenanced. It is not possible to affirm with certainty who was at that time the Chief. Following the "Baronage" in point of chronology, it may have been Malcolm Nr XIV., or possibly his brother, Gregor, his next heir.

Mr MacGregor Stirling, in one of his MS. papers, gives the following note :—

"Inchcalloun (see entry, 1st Sept. 1506, regarding the king having been there) was the residence of Gregor Mor, formerly (during his elder brother's lifetime) styled of Brackly, and now styled 'Makgregour.'

"Patrick MacGregor died at Auchinchallane, '9th July 1518, and was buried in Dysart in Glenurchy (Obituary). This was Gregor Mor's youngest brother,[1] the place of whose death shows that Inchcalloun was still in MacGregor's possession. Gregor Mor, indeed, had most probably been succeeded by his eldest son at this date, 1518."

The additional note rests, perhaps, on firmer grounds :—

"Inchcalloun, or Auchinchialloun,[2] as it was also called, was soon after, along with Brackly (in Glenurchy), held by a descendant of a younger son of Gregor Mor, as a feu under the Campbells of Glenurquhay, and continued to be held by this line till some time after the beginning of the last century."[3]

[1] No evidence is adduced in the "Chartulary" in support of this statement.

[2] From the entry in the Obituary, Auchinchall is shown to have been in Glenurchay, therefore cannot well have been identical with Inchcalloun, mentioned in King James IV.'s visit to Balquhidder.

[3] A very early parchment regarding the lands of Auchinchallane, and papers connected with

There is, however, reason to believe that Malcolm XIV. of the "Baronage" survived till about the year 1525-6　The history of the murder of Macintosh in 1524-5, and the help given in the capture of the murderers by the deceased's brother-in-law, "Dominus MacGregor,"[1] as quoted from the "Chartulary," from a private MS at Moy Hall, may connect this date with the said Malcolm, who the "Baronage" states to have married the sister of Macintosh

Up to this period we find Johnne McGregour of Glenstray still called by that territorial designation (see an entry as to "Duncan Gromach's Guids," in 1527)　After his death, 12th April 1528, and already previous to that date—i e, in 1527—his cousin, and eventual successor, John Makewin Makalester, is styled Captain of the Clan Gregour. The circumstances which led to the elevation of John Makewin to this important office are unknown　The office became hereditary in the family of Glenstray for at least six generations　If the representative by right of blood of the eldest line, why was he styled Captain ?[2]　It has been already remarked that possibly the line of Gregor Aulin was the eldest, and of that line Gregor Mor, his son Duncan Ladasach, and grandson Gregor, were men such as the Clan would have been proud to follow.　It has already been observed, chapter v p 48, that Sir John MacGregor Murray believed Glenstray, the leader at Glenfruin, to have been the Chief.

The Campbells of Glenurquhay at this time strongly supported the Glenstray family, but that circumstance would not have recommended them to the rest of the Clan

In the Obituary occur these notices :—

"1518　July 19　Death of Duncan MacGregor, Captain of the Castle of Glenurquhay ; he was buried in Dysart.
"1523　August 12th.　Death of a venerable man, Sir Robert Menzies, Kt He was buried in the church of Weyme.

the sale of it subsequently to the Campbells has found its way into the hands of a private collector, who is understood to be averse to communicating it to this work.

[1] So styled by the Macintosh Historian, probably as a mere recognition of his place of influence in the Clan

[2] The Captain in this instance may occasionally have been styled MacGregor, but in the history of Highland Clans the actual Chief rarely was styled Captain

" 1523. August 12. Death of Sir Colin Campbell Kt., Laird of Glenurquhay, at the Castle of Glenurquhay. he was buried in the Chapel of Finlarig.

" 1524. November 9. Death of Neill son of Duncan Macgregor, in Glen-urquhay, at the Castle of Glenuraquhay.

" 1529. October 9. Death of an honourable man, Colin Campbell, Earl of Argyle, Lord Campbell and Lorn who died at Inverary, and was buried at Kilmun."

The following "Tak" in connection with the keeping of the Castle of Glenurquhay is interesting. It occurs in the "Black Book of Taymouth":—

" 1550. Tak of Kincrakin and utheris set to Johne McConoquhy V^cGregour. Be it kennd be thir present letteris, me Johne Campbell of Glenurquhay to have set and for malis and seruice lattin the keping of my Castell of Glenurquhay to my weil belouit seruand Johne McConoquhy McGregour [1] the four merkland of Kincrakin for all the termis of fyfe yeris to the said Johne alanerlie, with the Croft of Polgreyich and the Croft of Portbeg, and the Croft that Ewin McEwir wes wont to have, with all the Croftis within Kincrakin, the malt Croft exceptit quhilk Patrik McKeirmoil hes, and the Yarde Croft, and the Turnour exceptit, and the said Johne sall gif gress fre to the yard Croftis for samany sowme as the said Croft wes wont to have, and the auld warde callit the Quosche exceptit in this assedatioun; the said Johne his interes beand at Whitsounday (1550) he pay and thairfor yeirlie fourtie aucht bollis gude victuall, the thrid part quhite meale fre fra all thingis and dewities, the victuale mett with ane inst. firlott brount with the stand of Perth, in the Castell of Glenurquhay in tyme of yeir as us is, and to the Lairdis misteris [2] quhen it is requirit be him or his seruandis, with his awin trew seruice and keiping of my Castell of Glenurquhay, and he sall haif the merkland of Arrècastellan and the merkland of Arrenabeyne, for the keiping of the Castell foresaid, fre fra all hosting as us was wont to be, except the defence of me and the cuntretht quhen misteris beis; and siclyke for the landis of Kyncrakkyn half stenting and hosting to the Quenis grace and Mylord of Argylis quhen mister beis and als requirit; and that he and his seruandis sall ansuer me quhen I have ado; and the said Johne sall hald ane sufficient wetchmen on his awin expensis yeirlye indurand his takis and I sall pay yeirlie for his fie sex schillingis aucht penneis and meat quhen I am in the place, he keipand the tour heid cleyn, and failyiend the

---

[1] Probably John McConoquhay or Duncanson, mentioned in the Records, 1531, with his brother, Duncanus, in Moreynch. He appears, however, to have held lands on Loch Fyne. (See next page.)

[2] Musters.

tour heid be not cleyn, he sall tyne his fie; and I sall gif the said Johne
and his wife and tua honest seruandis of thair awin, or his tua sonis meat
quhen I am in the place of Glenurquhay, and the wetchman to be their
boy, and the said Johne or his wyfe sall find me als oft as I cum to the
Castel elding[1] to the hale chalmer and kitcheine and bakhous for the first
nicht and fodder to my chalmer to mak beddis and uther dewities as us is,
and I sall giff leif to the said Johne to hald on the Quosche sex new calffit
kye, on his awin expensis and keip it fra all guidis except my guidis, and
the guidis specifiet abonewrittin, and gif thair beis ony uther guidis funden
upoun the samyn, thai salbe escheatit to me fre but ony process of law,
attoure the said Johne sall na guidis pasture in the warde fra Sanct Patrikis
day furtht quhill the Lairdis awin gude will cum to it under the pane foirsaid and stop not my weddens fra Kyncrakkyn and gras thairof, nor yit fra
the grass of Portbeg, nor yit the Portarig Kye quhen thay may not be on
the Quosche, and the said Johne sall have leiff to sett foure nettis within
the Dowloch and not farder, that is to say thrie small nettis and ane greit
nett, and attoure the Mylne of Kencrakyn sett to the said Johne for the
space of the yeiris above writtin, he payand yeirlie for it, fouretene bollis
gude meale, of that the tane halfe quhite meile weill schittit and tua dassoun
of pultrie, and gif the Laird bringis ony malt of his awin furth of utheris
cunthreis it sall be grundin multer fre be the said Johne, and the said Johne
sall laif sawin in the best gudet land of Kyncrakkan fourtie aucht bollis
sufficient eattis mett with the firlott abone writtin and failyeand thairof with
ane uther firlott of the samyn stand foirsaid, and attoure the said Johne
McConochie VcGregour for the getting of the tak abone expremit, hes givin
me my airis or assignanaris ane bairnis part of geir of all his kye and hors
efter his deceis that may pertene to him be ony maner of way and siclyke
the said Johne McConochie VcGregour hes givin ouir in my handis[2] the
markland of Drimleyart, the half markland of Glenkinglas, and the half
markland of Corrcoran with the Ile of the samyn, and with the consent of
Gregour his sone hes renuncit all rychtis that the said Johne and Gregour
his sone micht haiff into the saidis landis but ony reuocatioun, and mair-
ower the yaird set to Johne McConochie with the Croft of the samyn for
fyve yeiris, he haldand ane sufficient gardner upon his awin expensis to
amend and graith baith the yairdis and plant treis in the new yaird of
Portbeg, and big ane sufficient dyk about ilkane of the saidis yairdis, and
the said Johne sall saw quhite kaill seid, reid kaill and unzeoun seid, I send-

---

[1] Fuel, especially peats

[2] It is to be observed that John Duncanson MacGregor held previously the half merklands of
Drimleyart, Glenkinglas, and Corrcoran, with the Isle of the same, which lands, with consent of
his son Gregor, he renounced.

ing him seid in dew tyme of yeir, and he sall find himself to the yairdis sege and heyntoungis, and he sall give yeirlie to me or my deputis the iast tua partis of the proffittis of the yairdis under ane aith, and the thrid part to himself for his trauell and labouris of the saidis yairdis: and attoure my stabill, peithous, kyill and barne exceptit out of his takis and assedatioun fra the said Johne McConnochie, bot I to us the samyn to my behiuff as I think expedient, quhilkis housis lyis to Portbeg and I have subscriuit this present assedationn with my hand at the Castell of Glenurquhay the xvii day of May (1550) befor thir witness. Alexander Menzies of Rannoch. Johne McNab of Bowane, Johne Reddoch, Johne McDonichie Roy McAllan, Johne Tailyour Moir alias McNachtane, Johne McIllespy McPhatrik officer and Johne Clerk Messinger with uther diueress.

" 1544. 17th April. Item the xvij day of Aprile gevin to McFarlane efter the siege of Glasgow in xxx crowns of the sone. Item the samyn day to McGregor in xx crowns of the sone. (Lord High Treasurers Books Minority of Queen Mary and Regency of the Earl of Arran.)

"Note The Earl of Glencairn having joined the Earl of Lennox in a rebellion against the Government under the Earl of Arran was besieged in Glasgow from whence he made a sally on the besiegers and was defeated by them and forced to fly: the Action being known as the Battle of Glasgow Moor, 16th March 1543-4, when the town was recovered by Arran. the Siege according to Pitscottie had lasted from the 8th."

Shortly after the death of the English Sovereign Henry VIII. in 1546, an attempt was made on the part of the English to compel a marriage between the young King Edward VI. and our Queen Mary, an alliance which was resisted by the patriotic party in Scotland, because of the policy pursued by the English Kings, of trying to subjugate Scotland. The Duke of Somerset led an army over the Border in August 1547, to attain the object desired by force of arms. The Earl of Arran in this moment of peril

"Sent the Fiery Cross throughout the country—a warlike symbol of Celtic origin, constructed of two slender rods of hazel formed into the shape of a cross, the extremities seared in the fire and extinguished when red and blazing, in the blood of a goat slain for the occasion. From this slight description it is evident that the custom may be traced back to Pagan times and it is certain, that throughout the highland districts of the country, it's summons wherever it was carried was regarded with awe, and obeyed without hesitation. Previous to this we do not hear of it's being adopted in the lowlands; but on the present emergency, being fastened to the point of a spear, it was transmitted by the heralds and poursuivants through-

out every part of the realm , from town to town, from village to village, from hamlet
to hamlet, the ensanguined symbol flew with astonishing rapidity, and such was it's
effect, that in a wonderfully short space of time an army of thirty-six thousand men
assembled near Musselborough "[1]

But through the fortunes of war this gallant army sustained a severe
defeat in the battle of Pinkie, 10th September 1547, followed by the return
of the English Protector to England soon afterwards, to attend to matters
nearer home, and eventually in August 1548 the young Queen Mary, then
in her sixth year, was conveyed to the Court of France, and affianced to
the Dauphin, afterwards Francis II. of France.   Reinforcements having
been sent from France and the invaders repulsed, peace with England was
at last concluded in April 1550.[2]

The " Chartulary" has the following extract —

"1547 September 10th   Order of the Scottish Army at the Battle of Pinkie
    'To witt the Erll of Angus in the vanguard withe ten thousand mene in guid
    ordour   The Erll of Hunthe in the rereward witht tuell thousand men of
    the north pairts of Scotland   The governour himself in the greyt staill oist
    and withe him all the haill gentilmene of Louthien, Fyf, Angus, Strathern,
    Stirlingschyr, and the haill borrowis of Scotland to the number of tuentie
    thowsand mene and upon the richt hand and wing the Erll of Argyll and all
    the wast hilandmene of Scotland and on the left hand Maklain and Mak-
    riggour with all the Illsmene of Scotland'   M S of Pitscottie's Chronicles in
    the Library of Innerpaffray of date 23 April -30 July 1600. folio 123, a b[3]

Mr MacGregor Stirling has the following remarks in the "Chartulary" —

"'In connection with the military history of McGregour' in 1544 and 1547. it
is impossible to overlook the circumstance that whatever 'Slogan' was used by the
Glenstrays during the long period of their Captaincy, originally elective, and
ultimately by prescription hereditary (for it lasted from 1552 down to the death
of Kilmannan about 1706) the more accepted Slogan of ClanGregor is derived
from the estate or 'roume' of McGregoure 'Ardchoill'   That the Glenstrays used
a different Slogan is presumable from the very nature of the case   Nor does it
seem irrelevant to mention that James Pont a Herald contemporary with the

---

[1] Tytler's History of Scotland—Reign of Queen Mary
[2] Taken from *ibid*
[3] In the printed copy, date 1728, the account is much the same, only mentioning—" On the
left Macleod, MacGregor and the Islesmen."

Captaincy of the Glenstrays, and whose Manuscript preserved in the Lyon Office of Scotland is dated 1600, gives the armorial Bearing of MacGregor without supporters and states the motto as being 'Bad Giubhas' which is being interpreted 'Clump of Firs.'[1] In the atchievement of 'MacGregoure' from the Lislebourg M.S. in the British Museum date 1589[2] there is no motto; a circumstance leading to the inference, that the Slogan of Ardchoill had been first used in 1544 for the obvious reason already stated that there had been previously no established Slogan; and that the Slogan alluding to the Clump of Firs had been substituted by those who did not chuse to adopt the other. It is further remarkable that the Arms of McGregor of Stucknary, the penult representative of the Elective Captains of the Glenstray line, as exhibited on his tombstone in the Island of Inch Caileoch in Loch Lomond, want supporters; a presumption amongst many others that the Glenstrays did not affect to possess the right of Blood as Representative of McGregoure of Old."

An unfinished MS., by the same writer, may also here be quoted :—

" Duncan Ladosach was during the lifetime of his father or elder brother, styled of Ardchoille a small estate in Glendochart which he had obtained from a near kinsman of another Clan[3] for military service, and which, from being McGregor's seat during two armed expeditions and the earliest which the Clan made in defence of the Crown, under Duncan's son and heir, became it's war cry, and is still a scroll in MacGregor's Armorial Bearing. As the Gregorian Race had now by the severity of the Stewart Dynasty on the one hand, and by it's bounty to the other families on the other, become in comparison of their former state, landless; so although the Lineal Chief of a Family that existed towards seven centuries, and was originally royal, must have been tacitly acknowledged, yet from the absence of the grand link of Superior and vassal on Land property, subordination to the Chief had been much relaxed. We shall in the sequel find that the conscious tie of blood had overcome generally the policy of quiet settlement among strangers; that the ClanGregor had in a turbulent state of society preferred a predatory warfare under an elective Captain, to the obscure industry prescribed by a government, unjust in the first instance and tyranical in the second. We shall find that Clan-Gregor's subsequent efforts to defend the Crown at the expense of it's best blood, were but inadequately rewarded and that when the person possessed of the largest portion of it's Chief's ancient territory, had by the slaughter of Ardchoille Elder and by the publick decapitation of Ardchoille younger, and by the dispersion of the sons of the latter (which deprived the Clan of a lineal Chief), it rallied under a

---

[1] See Note, page 47.

[2] See pages 16 and 17. In the Harleyan Collection, under the title, the word Lyslebourg is written, for which reason Mr MacGregor Stirling thus quotes it.

[3] Campbell of Straquhir. See page 30.

Captain who by his armed excursions for the recovery of the ancient territory (which by a plausible fiction was held to be the right of the Chief whether by blood or election) drew down upon his followers the utmost vengeance of a government trembling for it's own existence He was himself put death in the cause and became the first of a line of hereditary Captains under whom the Clan (now most unruly it must be owned) experienced from the Government the greatest severities, in an attempt to root out the names Gregour and McGregour, and to abolish them in all time coming under pain of death   We shall have occasion to witness a general though fruitless revolt of the now nameless Clan for the purpose of bursting the bands of their political death, and those bands which the 'Secreit Council' had imposed, rivetted by the Act of Parliament   The next important scene will display the nameless Clan stepping forth in defence of that Throne, whence had emanated the decree for annihilating it, and which was now menaced with annihilation, the Clan earning a reward, (which on the re-establishment of the Throne, it actually received), in the repeal of the obnoxious decrees " [1]

From the " Red and White Book of Menzies " :—

" Letter by Mary of Guise Queen Regent of Scotland exempting Alexander Menzeis of that Ilk from finding caution for MacGregors his tenants in Rannoch for seven years—

" 1559. Feb. 7. Regina. We understanding that it is not within the power of Alexander Menzies of that Ilk to ansuer for the gud reule of the Clan-Gregoure inhabitantis of the Rannoch and that our chozing the Erle of Ergyle and Coline Campbell of Glenurquhay hes the seruice of that clann and that thai will do thare deligens to caus gud reule kepit be the said clann and for dieuers other resonable causis and considerationis moving vs, grantis an gevis licence to the said Alexander to set in tak and assedatioun all and haill his tuentie pund land of Rannock liand within the sherefdome of Perth, to the auld tenentis and inhabitantis thairof of the ClanGregour for the space of seven yeris ; and will and grantis that he nor his airis sall nocht be haldyn to our derrest dochter, nor us, to ansuer for thair gud reule during the said sevin yeris, nor to enter them to our lawes, our justice airis nor justice courtis for thair demeritis, notwithstanding the general band maid be the lordis and landit men of the said S- our said derrest dochter and us thereupon &a. Marie R. (Menzies Charter Room)."

This was a kind and gracious concession, and might have conduced to peace under more favourable circumstances.

[1] MS. Sketch of History of the Clan, by Mr MacGregor Stirling

Chapter XI

NOTICES of some of the other branches of the Clan have now to be given, as they henceforward become more prominent in the general history.

The family of Grierson of Lag, following the account given in the "Baronage," trace their descent from Malcolm (XI.) the Lame Lord (see page 20). It is supposed that they branched off the end of the 14th century, and probably before the death of Ian Cam, who died in 1390. Their immediate ancestor Gilbert, Laird of Ard and Lag, took the name of Grierson in accordance with charters from George Dunbar, Earl of March, of the Netherholme of Dalgarnoch, to him and his heirs male, to be called by the surname of Grierson, before 1400 ; and another charter, dated at Dunbar 1400, of the lands of Airdes &a lying in the barony of Tyberis and shire of Dumfries, to the said Gilbert for his many good deeds done to the said Earl. The lands of Lag were conveyed by his cousin Henry Sinclair, 2nd Earl of Orkney, by charter dated 6th December 1408. Confirmation of lands of Garryhorn and Sandokhill dated 17th May 1410. Charter from Archibald Earl of Douglas to Gilbert Grierson his armour-bearer of the lands of Drumjoan, confirmed by his Relict the Princess Margaret, Duchess of Touraine, dated 9th April 1425. Lag Castle was built circa 1460.[1] It is averred that there is no legal proof connecting the Gilbert Grierson of the Charters with MacGregor ancestry.[2] Granting that the required link is missing, yet most Highlanders will accept the tradition.

MacGregor of Ardinconnell was one of the oldest offshoots of the Clan, and this branch must be noticed as most involved in subsequent disputes with Colquhoun of Luss. Its earliest recorded existence was in 1429, as in a deed of Resignation by John MacRoger of "Gleane Mackerne (Mackurn)

---

[1] Genealogical Table of Grierson of Lag—printed for private circulation.

[2] On this ground the Griersons are not admitted as Members of the ClanGregor Society.

in favour of John Colquhoun of Luss, dated 7th February 1429 One of the
witnesses is Johanne MacGregor Dominus de Ardinconwell."—"Chiefs of
Colquhoun," by William Fraser, 1869, vol II. page 28

Returning to the "Chartulary":—

> "1479 Oct 27 Before the lords compeired Umphra Colquhoun of that ilk,
> Patrik Noble, Patrik McGregour and Johnne of Douglas, and protested
> that because Christian Lady Grahame 'gert sumond theme that therefore
> they should be assoilzied &a &a'—Acta Dominorum Concilii vol 1. folio 58
> in Register House

> "1483 June 20 Before the Lords Auditors compeired Robert Flemyng for
> himself and as procurator for Vmphra Culquhon, Alex, Ardincapil brief of
> inquest purchased by Robert Flemyng foresaid upon two merks worth of
> land of bannory and protested that Umfra Colquhon of Luss, gert summonde
> them at his instance for certain actions, contained in the summonds and
> would not follow them &a"—Acto Dominorum Auditorum, p. 179.

About 1502, Sir John Colquhoun of Luss, who had lately acquired
Porterfield's Lands, vide page 40, purchased from Patrick MacGregor of
Ardinconnell the "Middle third of Ardinconnell" Original Charter, dated
February 20th, 1501, and original Instrument of Sasine, dated April 1501,
at Rossdhu Chiefs of the Colquhouns, Patrick MacGregor of Ardinconnell, was afterwards tenant of Sir John Colquhoun, and the following
bond in which Patrick calls him his "darast Master" is curious.

> "Discharge and Obligation by Patrick MacGregor of Ardyncuwall to Sir John
> Colquhoun of Luss Knicht for forty merks of the duties of the said lands
> "1513 May 3 Be it kende tyll all men be thir present lettres me, Patriek
> MacGregar of Ardynconwall, to be bwndyn andoblest and be the faytht and
> the trewtht in my body, letely and trewly bindis and oblesis me tyll ane
> nobyll man and my darast master, and Schir Johne of Luss, Knycht, in the
> sovme of forty markis of gud and vsual mony of the Kynrik of Scotland
> 'for the runnyne maillis, fermes, and wderis dewuytis of the lands of Ardin-
> convall, with part of lent mony of the foirsaid forty markis to me be the said
> Schir Jhone Culquhone, in my mester and neide, off the quhilkis forty
> markis I halde me weyll content and payt, ande attowr, I the said Patrik
> byndis and oblesis me my executouris and assingnays, for tyll pay the said
> sovme of forty markis, at twa termys, next and immadiat efter the dayt of
> this vrit, viz at Lammes next to cum xx markis, and at Mertymes next there-
> efter vder xx markis be equayll porcionyss lelely and trewly but fraude or
> gyill onder the payne of dowbelling of the forsaid sovm, all remeid of law,

civyll or canone, in the contrare to be maid or ellegit. In vitnes of the theng, I haf set to my seill to thir present lettris, and subscibit the samyne witht my hand, at Rosdw, the third day of Maij, in the zeir of God M.V. and thratenys zeris, befoir thir vetnes, Master James Culquhone Vicar of Dunlope, Robart Culquhone, son and aperand ayr to Robart Culquhone of Camstrodane, James Akynros, Wmfra Lang and Schir George Fallusdayll, chapyllane, witht overis byueryss (divers) vitht Patrik MacGregar his sone.

"'Patik McGregar of Ardynconvall. manu propria.'"[1]

From the "Chartulary":—

"1527. Notice of a raid by Patrik McGregors Elder and Younger of Lagris upon the lands of Strone, in the barony of Luss.

"1527. September 2. Mention is made in the Record of an Action at the instance of Andrew Lord Auvandale, who had obtained a gift of the ward of the Earldom of Lennox against the Colquhouns &a and among them Patrick Malcom, and Patrick MacGregor. (Acta Dominorum Concilii xxxvii, M.S. 2369.) These were probably of the Ardinconnell family.

"1527. Nov. Patrick MacGregor younger of Ardinconnal had letters of reversion of 8 merkland of Ardinconnal from Sir John Colquhoun of Luss Kt. and at the same time, the ward of these lands was given by Andrew (3) lord Evandale to Walter Colquhoun brother of the said John. —Records of the Burgh of Dumbarton.

"1541. Patrik MacGregor of Lagris was pursewed by John Colquhoun of Luss oye and successor to Sir John Colquhoun of Luss in the 28th year of King James V (1541) for 8 oxen, price of each 3 lib, and of 12 'grete mylk ky' price of each . . . 'thiftuilie stowin and cancelit fra the lands of Strone in Glenfruiune 1527 and for the yeirlie profits thereof since that time at 6 firlotts of oatmeal, at 12s per boll, for each ox and 13s 4p. for each cow yeirlie.' His father Patrik McGregor also had shared in the raid, and in 1531 found Walter McFerland his son suretie for the damages, at the Justice Assize of Dumbarton.

"1544. Dec. 21. 'The 4 merkland of Laggarie, belonging in property to Patrick McGregour, and holding of the Earl of Lennox, and the 8 merkland of Ardinconnal,' are thus specified in a charter by Queen Mary 27. July 1545, being one of appreciation of the Earl's estate for the damage done in his late rebellion to James Stewart of Cardonald 4, Jan. 1543-4. Mag: Sig: xxxx 22. By the Laird of Ardinconnal is meant obviously the person to whom it was mortgaged by McGregour of Laggary, formerly of Ardinconnal.

[1] "Chiefs of Colquhoun," vol. ii., page 324.

"1544. Dec. 21. John Colquhoun of Luss complains that 'Duncane McFarlane of Arrochar Andrew McFerlane, Robert M^cferlane and Duncane M^cferlane his fader bray^r viz., Campbell of (Strachur) James Stewart sone to Walter Stewart in Buchquhidder and certain uthir grete thevis, lymaris, robaris, qmoun (common) sornaris upoun the liecis, throtcuttaris, murtharis slaaris of men's wiffis and barnis and y^r complices to ye novmer of vj (7 score?) men w^t ye maire come to ye said John's lands and place of Rossdew and lands and barony of Luss and yare crellie slew and murdrest nyne of his pure tennents in y^r beddes ans hereit his hale cuntrie baith his self and his pure men alswele of all insy gude w^t in houss as of nolt and schap and vyir (other) bestiale laitlie in ye monet of December instand dailie (ar) persewaries in plain reif and sorning vpoun ye pure liege of ye realme, and ar gaderand to yaim (them) ma thevis and lymmares, tending to hery ye haill cuntre to Glasgow and Striveling and yai be not resisted in yis temptioun (contemptioun) of ye: authrite and lawis giff salbe.' Whereupon the Sheriffs of Argyle Dunbarton Renfrew and Stirling are charged to summon all the lieges within their bounds 'to ryss and cum togidder for resisting of the saidis thievis and revaris to sik ptis (parties) as yai sal happin to cum uponn and yai tak plane pairt w^t ye said Johnne or ony uyer gentilmen yat rysis for resisting of ye saidis theves and lymaris and tak and apprehend yame and bring yame to ye Justice to be punist for yr demeritis qform (conform) to ye lawis. And giff ony of yame beis slane or hurt in ye taking or resisting of yame to cum upoun o (our) privelege yat na cryme salbe impuitt to yame y^rthrow.' "—Luss Papers quoted in the "Chartulary."

The following passage is from "The Chiefs of Colquhoun"[1]:—

"The first trace of that enmity between the MacGregors and the Colquhouns, which at length became so inveterate, to be found in the Luss family writs, occurs in a document dated in the year 1541. So far back as the year 1527, one of the Macgregor clan, Patrick Macgregor of Laggarie, had despoiled the father of the then Laird of Luss of a considerable number of oxen and cows. To obtain redress for this theft committed on his father's property, John Colquhoun of Luss summoned him on 27 Dec. 1540, to appear before the Lords of the Privy Council, to hear their decreet, ordaining him, in terms of the summons, to restore to the pursuer eight oxen and twelve milk cows, or the price of them with the profits of the same since the year 1527, when he had stolen them from the lands of Strone, in Glenfruin. And on 30th May 1541, Patrick Macgregor of Laggarie was at the instance of John Colquhoun of Luss inhibited from selling any of his lands or heritages until he had satisfied John for the spoil which he had reft from him.

[1] Vol. I., page 110-111.

These proceedings we may not be entitled to consider as evidence of the existence of a formed feud between the MacGregors and the Colquhouns; but they are symptomatic of growing bad feelings between them, and they explain some of the causes which contributed to produce and to intensify the hatred which afterwards proved so disastrous to both."

MacGregor of Roro, a very ancient house, from whence sprang also Leragan, Dunan, Balhaldies, &a., falls to be taken next.

The first authentic notices are to be found in the "Obituary of Fortingal,"[1] 1477. Death of Duncan Beg MacGregor at Roro. There must have been another previous Duncan, probably his father, because there is a notice in 1491 of the death of John *Duncanson*. Later, in 1503, Gregor *Duncanbegson* dies at Morinch and Gregor *Duncanson*, in 1515, at Roro.

The "Baronage" and the Roro traditions state that the founder of the family was Gregor, fourth son of Gregor Aulin, who is believed to be identical with Gregor MᶜAne Cham, whose death is recorded in the Obituary in 1415. Another generation is required between Gregor Aulin and Gregor who died at Roro in 1515, and it is clear that the name of the father of the latter was Duncan. It seems, therefore, most probable that the first of the Roro House was grandson of Gregor Aulin instead of his son.

The following is from a MS. Memoir formerly in the possession of the late Colonel Hugh MacGregor of the 63rd Regiment, himself a descendant of the Leragan Family, and thus from Roro. Several copies of this Memoir are extant, and it is probable that it embodied all the oral tradition that Colonel Hugh could collect :—

"I. Gregor MacGregor 4th son (more probably Grandson) of Gregor Aulin, and (more probably Great) Grandson of MacGregor of Glenurchy, got possession of Roro (Ruaraidh) in Glenlyon, from his father, about the year 1390. which property remained in the possession of his family by right of occupancy, feu, or wadset, until the 1st of April 1760. Gregor was married to his cousin, by whom he had eleven sons and several daughters, he was succeeded by his eldest son.

"II. John MacGregor who fought the MᶜKays in Glenlyon with such personal courage and success as acquired him the proud distinction of 'Ian dubh-nan-Lann' 'Black John of the spears.'[2] He and the Laird of Garth afterwards fought the

---

[1] Chapter VI. pages 56, 57.

[2] Allusion is made to this "John of the Spears," "Chief of Glenlyon of the Blades," in an early poem by Dougal MacGille glas in the Lismore collection.—See Chapter VII. page 71.

powerful Chief of the McIvers at Laggan-a-Chatha, and having obtained a complete victory, they shared their lands between them, by which John was enabled to take possession of Carnban Castle,[1] where he resided for many years   He married Margaret, daughter to Luke Stirling of Keir and widow of Campbell of Glenurchy, by whom he had six sons, and a daughter, but all of these having died before himself he left the greater part of his lands to a son of his wife by her former Husband   The remaining part he left to his brother Duncan with the superiority of the whole, by which he was enabled to raise the men of Glenlyon, in time of war, by a tune of the bagpipe, a privilege, which in those days was considered a greater honour, than the possession of lands   He died aged ninety nine years "

Mention is made in the book of the "Stirlings of Keir" that Lukas of Strevelyn, the first acquirer of Keir, who died in 1452, had one daughter, Margaret, married to Sir Colin Campbell, but nothing is said of a second marriage

Here follows from Colonel Hugh MacGregor's narrative the traditional account of how Ian-dubh-nan-Lann disposed of his lands to his step-son :—

"Ian Dubh was proprietor of the whole north side of Glenlyon, as well as of Roro, and resided much in the vicinity of the Kirkton of Fortingall, where the ruins of Baile-mor mhic-Gregair, is still pointed out on the east side of the Burn called Aldour below the publick road

"He is said to have had six sons and a stepson, whose name was Campbell It seems that while he meditated on getting his right to the lands which he possessed confirmed by a Charter, he had employed his stepson who was considerably older than any of his own sons to get it executed for him. It was no easy matter in those days.   Before setting out upon his important embassy Campbell obtained his stepfather's permission to insert his own name in the Deed, as next heir, failing that of MacGregor   John calculating on the improbability of all his six sons dying without heirs, unhesitatingly gave Campbell his full consent to insert his own name as required.   Owing to what fatality is not known the said John and his sons died without heirs. The last of the sons while hunting in the Braes of Glenlyon was overnight at a hunting seat called Lub-Sheas-Garnich, where he lay upon a bed of rushes covered with his plaid, and it is said that whilst turning over upon his bed, a stump of rushes penetrated into his stomach, and killed him on the spot   In

---

[1] The castle of that name was not, however, built and so called till long afterwards —*Ed.*

consequence of which his maternal Brother Campbell succeeded to the whole north side of Glenlyon which his family have enjoyed ever since." [1]

A very picturesque account of the same tradition is given in "The Lairds of Glenlyon." The writer gives the date as the end of the reign of David Bruce, and in regard to Ian dubh's marriage says :—

"From some domestic feud in the family of the Knight of Loch Awe his widowed daughter-in-law and her infant son, were forced to abandon their native Halls. and flee for refuge to Glenlyon. Black John [2] married the widow, and by her had a family of seven sons. The young Campbell his 'dalta' was carefully nurtured."

A tale is next told of a victory over the Chisholm who had made a raid into Glenlyon, and a relation of the circumstances under which the "dalta" succeeded to the lands, which agrees with the foregoing, continuing afterwards—

"The name of the first laird of the family of Campbell was Archibald. We have reason to believe he was not John Dubh's dalta, but the dalta's heir He lived during the first part of the 16th century. He was a wise man and fully conciliated the people to whose rule he had succeeded. The MᶜGregors of Roro, who appear in some way to have been closely connected with the family of Ian Dubh did not dispute his rights, they received him as the heir of the Chieftain, a kindness afterwards well repaid by the Campbells of Glenlyon."

Colonel Hugh's Memoir continued :—

"I I I. Duncan MacGregor of Roro, likewise styled Baron of Glenduibhe now Glenlyon, Brother of Ian-dubh-nan-Lann' He married Elisabeth daughter to the Laird of MᶜNaughton of Dun-da-ramh, by whom he had seven sons all of whom were married and had children. and several daughters."

Another traditional account appears among Sir John MacGregor Murray's papers, which at all events gives an interesting view of the adventures of the time.

"Traditional notes taken down 15. October 1814. from the recital of John MacGregor from Ruadhsruthmore :—

[1] Till 1806, when by the death of the last laird the property devolved on his great-nephew Francis Gordon of Troup.

[2] In another part of the work Mr Campbell assumes this Ian dubh to have been identical with a John of Lorn, a M'Dougall, and disputes his having been a MacGregor. His identity seems scarcely susceptible of proof.

" The first [1] person of the name of MacGregor who settled in Ruora was John the Tanister, or second son of MacGregor of Breachdslrabh who was a very handsome man   A daughter of MacNaughtan of Strath Tay fell in love with him

"Macnaughtan is said to have possessed at a remote period the tract of country between the Cross of MacDuff near Perth and Tigh an Druim, excepting some properties which held of him, of which that of MacNab of MacNab is said to have been one.

"MacNaughtan had seven Farms in Glenlyon which he used as grazings in summer   When the young lady declared her partiality for John MacGregor he told her that he had not the means of supporting a Family as he was not his father's eldest son   In consequence of this remark the Lady proposed that they should take possession of the said lands in Glenlyon which her father used for rearing cattle.   They were privately married and proceeded to Glenlyon and settled at Ruarumore one of the said farms   MacNaughtan was highly offended and vowed that he would put his son-in-law to death

"In the mean time Robert the Bruce came to that country and in consequence of the Battle of Dalrigh MacNaughtan and MacNab lost their Lands. MacNaughtan took refuge at Dundrave near Inverary where he built a place of strength   After the lapse of some years he determined to fulfil his vow against his son-in-law.

"In the interim the son-in-law conciliated the Inhabitants of Glenlyon and its vicinity by his bravery and heading them occasionally in resisting the depredations of various tribes who wished to plunder the country

"MacNaughtan having asembled threescore chosen men set out on his enterprise to put his son-in-law to death   Some of his party who secretly disapproved of this intention, sent notice of it to MacGregor of Breacdslrabh in Glenurchay, who apprised his son of the circumstance stating the route the MacNaughtans were to take   On receipt of this intelligence Ruara told some of his friends and neighbours what was in agitation, and proposed to abscond till the danger was over The inhabitants answered that they owed him many a day for the manly protection that he had afforded them by his prowess and guidance   that he must not abscond but allow them to select threescore men to meet MacNaughtan man to man.   This advice was adopted and MacGregor with his party set off to Innermherran at the west end of Glenlyon, where he put his men in ambush at the east side of a rising ground, and went forward himself very much against the inclination of his followers but he assured them that neither MacNaughtan nor any of his followers could know him as none of them had ever seen him   He had not proceeded far when he met the advance of MacNaughtan's party, with whom he entered into conversation in the course of which they told him that none of them had ever been in that country

---

[1] This does not agree with Colonel Hugh's tradition, as he makes the third of the Ruora lairds the husband of a MacNaughton lady

before. He observed that they appeared like a party bent upon some hostile expedition, and added that if it were not an improper question he would be glad to know to what place they were proceeding. The answer was that as none of them had ever been in these parts before, they did not know how far they were going, but that they knew the object of the expedition and asked if he was of that country, as in that case he might be of great use to them as a guide if he would undertake to be so. He replied that he was perfectly acquainted with the country but that his undertaking to be their guide would depend upon the nature of the service they had in view. They answered that they were accompanying MacNaughtan to put to death a person of the name of MacGregor who had run away with his daughter and that they were sure that MacNaughtan would give him a handsome reward if he would be their guide. John MacGregor acknowledged that he knew the man they were in search of; that he was a fierce and formidable man who would not be easily overcome, and certainly not without bloodshed but they asserted that if they could find him they would accomplish MacNaughtan's object. He then asked where MacNaughtan was and was informed that he was coming up on horseback. When he came up he was informed that this man (Ruara) was well acquainted with the country and knew his son-in-law and he would guide them to him. Upon hearing this MacNaughtan promised that if he would guide the party to the place where his son-in-law resided he would give him the seven farms possessed by his son-in-law. This induced MacGregor to say that he would certainly show them the man they were in quest of, but that he would not undertake to seize him. MacNaughtan was satisfied and the party proceeded towards the place where Ruara's men were posted. MacNaughtan having dismounted marched with the guide a little in advance of his party. In their route they came to a broad ditch in a swamp called Stair-caillach over which the guide leaped, but MacNaughtan was obliged to make a circuit before he could reach the spot where the guide was. When the party came up they were astonished at the leap which the guide had made. Some of them attempted it but fell short and up to the armpits in mire, and so were with difficulty got out and not a man of them could clear the ditch. They were under the necessity therefore of going round, but were pleased with the idea, that if they could meet the person they were in search of, the guide was so powerful a man that he alone would master him.

"Whilst the party was separated from MacNaughtan and the guide the latter put his hand into that of MacNaughtan, saying 'Now Sir you have by the hand the man you seek.' 'What are you the man?' said MacNaughtan. 'I am,' was the answer. MacNaughtan then called to his people to come for he had seized the man they wanted. Ruara upon this said, 'If that is the case Sir I shall make sure of you, and my men who are at hand (and started up upon being called by MacGregor) will match yours and perhaps prevent any of them from returning to tell the news; and at all rules you shall fall with me.' MacNaughtan was pleased at finding that his son-in-law was at the head of a body of people, and himself so fine a fellow and solemnly promised perpetual friendship saying that their people should in future be as one.   The parties feasted on the ground which they respectively occupied without mixing and MacGregor remained in quiet possession of Ruara and other farms viz Balnacraig, Ruadhrashruth-gearr, Balmeanach, Balchannait, Ballamtull, Ruadhsruthmore and Inverinan now rented at about £1200.

"At one period the whole of Glenlyon belonged to Ian dubh nan Lainn, There were nine Lairds of the name of MacGregor in that quarter of the country.' Two battles. were fought.

"The Clan vic Iver formerly in Glenlyon quarrelled with MacDiarmid, MacIver struck MacDiarmid who complained to Stewart of Gart his foster brother.   MacDiarmid was murdered.

"IV. Gregor MacGregor of Roro (Duncan's eldest son) succeeded and married the daughter of the Laird of Weem, by whom he had issue several sons of whom was Patrick who got possession of Dunan in 1480 and Duncan who got Lerigan about the same time."[1]

The Obituary has the following entries, which partly correspond with the traditional generations :—

"1477. Feb: 17. Death of Duncan Beg MacGregor at Roro.

"1491. March 10: Death of John Duncanson MacGregor at Bellicht (Balloch). He was buried in Inchadin in the north side of the Great Altar.

"1493. August 14; Death of Catherine Cardny, daughter of the Laird of Foss, and widow of the late John Duncanson MacGregor. She was buried in the Church of Dull, before the step of the Great Altar.

"1494. July 24 : Death of Terloch Keir[2] son of Duncan MacGregor he was buried at Dysart.

"1503. Death of Gregor Duncanbegson at Morinch.

"1510 Nov. 28. Death of Gregor Patrickson at Innerchattan.

"1511 Jane 5 Death of Gilbert Duncanson at Roro Vicar of Kilmartin."

The annexed Table has been drawn out to show the earliest authentic

---

[1] The Memoir' of Roro gives as the fifth in line another Gregor, stating that he married a daughter of Sir Colin Campbell by Lady Katherine Ruthven, and that he was beheaded on the stump of an old tree between Taymouth and Kenmore, but although this is popularly believed, it arises out of a confusion with Gregor nam Bassan Gheal, as will be seen farther on.

[2] It is not clear that Terloch Keir's father, Duncan, belonged to Roro.

notices of MacGregor of Roro. The two recorded sons of Ian Cham are placed at the head, and a third brother, Duncan, is added according to the conjecture of Mr MacGregor Stirling. But it may be clearly seen that one generation in addition, at least, is required between an ancestor who lived about 1415 and one who died in 1515, and this is a sufficient reason for rejecting the conjecture that Roro descended from a brother of Gregor Aulin and of John Dhu. The race were known as the "Slios Dhonche," or Tribe of Duncan (whence Mac or Vic Condoquhy corrupted into "V^{c}onche"), and a distinction is made in the Obituary between the sons of Duncan and the sons of Duncan Beg. It is very difficult to bring the traditionary account and the persons therein named to correspond with the ascertained facts; tradition is apt to be imperfect as to dates and to skip generations. We may safely conclude that the first named Gregor of Roro in family history was Gregor Duncanson who died in 1515, but the "Baronage" supposes him to be a son of Gregor Aulin, whereas to match the dates he must have been his grandson, if his descendant, or otherwise his nephew. There is a difficulty in tracing Ian dhu nan Lann who, the traditional account states, was son and successor to Gregor. As this account also states that John Dhu was succeeded by his brother Duncan, and as it is known from the Obituary that there was a Duncan at the time, Father of another generation at Roro, we may suppose that both John Dhu nan bann and this Duncan were brothers of Ewin, son of Gregor Duncanson who is known to have died at Roro in 1511, and who may have been a younger brother of the other two, as it is not stated that he was possessor of Roro.

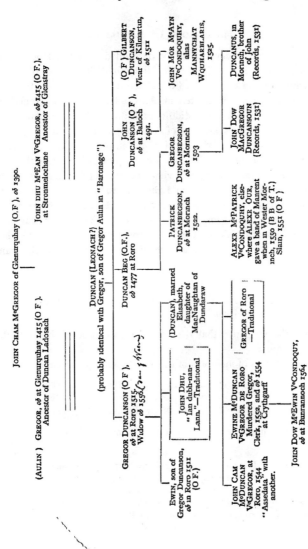

JOHN CHAM MᶜGREGOR of Glenurquhay (O.F.), *ob* 1390.

JOHN DHU MᶜEAN VᶜGREGOR, *ob* 1415 (O.F.),
at Stronmelochane   Ancestor of Glenstray

(AULIN) GREGOR, *ob* at Glenurquhay 1415 (O F.),
Ancestor of Duncan Ladosach

DUNCAN (LEONACH?)

(probably identical with Gregor, son of Gregor Aulin in "Baronage")

DUNCAN BEG (O.F.),
ob 1477 at Roro

JOHN
DUNCANSON (O F),
ob at Balloch
1491.

(O F) GILBERT
DUNCANSON,
Vicar of Kilmartin,
ob 1511

GREGOR DUNCANSON (O F),
ob at Roro 1515,
Widow *ob* 1556

(DUNCAN), married
Elisabeth,
daughter of
MacNaughtan of
Dundaraw

PATRICK
DUNCANBEGSON,
ob at Morinch
1522.

GREGOR
DUNCANBEGSON,
ob at Morinch
1523

JOHN MOR MᶜAYN
VᶜCONDOQUHY,
alias
MANNYCHAT
WQUHARELARIS,
1525.

JOHN DHU,
"Ian dubh-nan-
Lann."—Traditional

ALEXR MᶜPATRICK
VᶜCONDOQUHY, else-
where ALEXR OUR,
gave a band of Maurent
when in Wester Mor-
inch, 1550 (B B of T.)
Slain, 1551 (O F)

JOHN DOW
MACGREGOR
DUNCANSOUN
(Records, 1531)

DUNCANUS, in
Morinch, brother
of John
(Records, 1531)

EWIN, son of
Gregor Duncanson,
ob in Roro 1511
(O F.)

EWINE MᶜDUNCAN
VᶜGREGOR DE RORO
Murdered Gregor,
Clerk, 1552, and *ob* 1554
at Cryhgariff

GREGOR of Roro
—Traditional

JOHN CAM
MᶜDUNCAN
VᶜGREGOR, at
Roro, 1544
"Assedata with
another.

JOHN DOW MᶜEWIN VᶜCONDOQUY,
ob at Bunrannoch 1564

O F., Obituary of Fortingal. MᶜG S., MacGregor Stirling. Names in brackets relate to those whose existence is only shown
by the names of their sons and grandsons. Panel enclosed by a dotted line implies a name added from the Roro Memoir, but not
recorded in Obituary.—(A. G Murray MacGregor, 1896)

MacGregor of Balhaldies.

This family are understood to be descended from the House of Roro. Their appellation in Gaelic is "Mac Ian mhallich," or son of John with the Bushy Eyebrows, and a traditional account of the origin of this name is given in a memoir by Lieutenant Alexander MacGregor, Innerhaddon, formerly in the Royal East Middlesex Militia. It is recounted that the daughter of a certain MacGregor of Ardeonig on Loch Tay, on the murder of her father, by order of one of the Campbell Lairds of Glenurchy, became heiress of the property, and that to protect her rights she resolved to seek a husband. "With this view she set out for Roro to solicit the protection of one of his sons, and the first to whom she had made the proposal refused her suit, but she was not to be easily defeated, and turned to another half-grown lad, saying that perhaps this 'Fear-na-Maileach dubh' (alluding to his black eyebrows) would take her, to which he consented, and to this circumstance his descendants owe the name of Malloch."

The Obituary mentions :—

"1523 Feb: 9. Death of John Malloch McHustone, at Tullicheamin, he was buried in Killin."

From this we gather that the immediate ancestor of the Mallochs was named Hugh.

Farther traces of members of this family will appear later.

MacGregor of Learagan.

The following is from a Memoir by Colonel Hugh MacGregor :—

"I. Duncan Macgregor, younger son of Gregor MacGregor of Roro (No 4) commonly called Donnacha dubh Liomhanach, from his having come from Glenlyon, got possession of Learagan, in Rannoch, from a tribe called clann Tavish, that resided there about the year 1480. His Estate consisted of eleven merks of land, extending from Aldcheardie to the Clachghlas near the east end of Loch Rannoch. His brother Alexander went to Rannoch about the same time, and

Q

after a hard fought battle, with a tribe called Clann- 'il bhuidh (Stewart) defeated them and took possession in Dunan.   His Estate consisted of the Twelve merks of land, by west the river Ericht, the middle division of Slismine, or north side of Loch Rannoch having been then, as well for several generationes before the sons of Roro came to Rannoch, possessed by the MacGregors of Ardlaraich   The descendants of Donnacha-dubh homhanach, occupied Learagan either as Proprietors or as Tenants, from the above mentioned period till 1792 when the present system of sheep farming caused their removal   Duncan married a daughter of McPherson of Noelmore, in Badenoch by whom he had several children and was succeeded by his eldest son Malcolm MacGregor called Callum Glas or the pale faced Malcolm "

Different accounts agree that either Duncan or his son Malcolm was noted as a good sportsman, and one notice states that the lands were obtained from the Earl of Atholl, from satisfaction at MacGregor's activity and address and at the swiftness of his dogs at a hunting which took place in the Glens of Atholl.

MacGregor of Dunan

Lieutenant MacGregor, Innerhaddon's, Memoirs contain the following account of this family ·—

"I. Patrick, who first settled in Dunan in Rannoch and was the founder of this family, was the son of MacGregor of Roro in Glenlyon, who accepted his patrimony, from his father, consisting of a number of cattle, and a few men and set out to seek his fortune, as it was termed, about the year 1480.   He happened to set out at a very fortunate time, for having proceeded only the length of the hill of Gar-Dunan, where he lodged all night with his cattle, a messenger, reached him early next morning from the camp of an adventurer who had lodged all night upon the opposite side of Loch Lydon, to try his hospitality ; and upon learning where they were, he sent their commander a fat cow   Their commander seemed much aston-ished at so unusual a gift, and asked his man who it was that had sent it, they could not tell, and consequently sent back to enquire   The two leaders met and having communicated their views to each other, MacGregor learned that he, who he had entertained, was the son of the Laird of Appin (in Argyleshire) and the head of a party of men intending to take revenge upon the inhabitants of the Braes of Rannoch, called Clann Ian Bhuidhe, and the clan Ian Maileaich, who had but recently offered an affront to the Laird of Appin's men who were passing by. They then agreed to join issue, and that when they had rooted out the inhabitants, they would divide the conquered lands between them. They proceeded, and succeeded in conquering from the west as far as Errocht on the north side of the Loch, and as far as West Camghouran on the south side. MacGregor took possession of his own share and Stewart left a representative and a party of men to occupy his part, and returned to his own country. upon the next succeeding Sabbath, each with his party proceeded to the parish Church of Killiechonnan, which, when they were about to enter, a dispute arose about which should enter first, MacGregor or Stewart's representative, when both drew their swords and MacGregor slew his opponent. Word was immediately dispatched to Stewart to inform him of what had happened, to which he replied, 'That if he were there in person, there might be some cause for disputing MacGregor's precedence, but that he had never authorised his servant to dispute it for him ; that the fellow only met with what he deserved, adding that as they could not agree together, MacGregor might enjoy the whole of it for him ; which was the case, and MacGregor shortly sent, and settled one of his brothers in Learagan, from whom that family are descended and another at Learan from whom Clann-macGeal Callum, are descended.

Reflections may, of course, be made as to the lawlessness and turbulence of these proceedings, but those were times when physical courage and strength of arm, with some address in taking advantage of opportunities, were the only qualities much esteemed, and they knew no other means of gaining a livelihood. Traditions of a similar kind were very graphically told by many in the Highlands up till a few years ago, having been transmitted down by word of mouth with the full intention of neither adding nor taking away from them, although some deviations must have been unavoidable.

MacGregor of Ardlarich.

This family is descended from the House of Glenstray, of which it is believed to be the next representative, failing the direct heirs, but it is supposed that none of the male line of Ardlarich remain in Scotland, and all trace of those abroad are lost.[1]

In the Obituary the death is recorded on the 31st July 1526 of Gregor, son of John MacGregor, alias McEwine McAllaster of Glenstray, as has

---

[1] The family claimed to be very ancient, and even to be the Chief. They were certainly very early settled in Rannoch.

been noticed at the end of Chapter V., page 54. Mr MacGregor Stirling, from a comparison of dates, makes out that this Gregor left a son Allaster, father of Archibald Dhu McCondachie VcAllaster in Ardlarich, mentioned under this name many years later, as will appear in the sequel. A Memoir from Lieutenant Alexander's papers only begins with a Gillespie (Archibald) Ruadh in the sixteenth century.

MacGregor of Glengyle.

The Ancestor of this House is universally supposed to have been the fifth son of Gregor Aulin named Dougal, and that from some remarkable colouring of hair or eyes he was distinguished as Dougal Ciar, which word in Gaelic means dusky, dark brown, or dark grey, and which name became the designation of a very powerful and stirring tribe.

Besides these Perthshire Families, others settled in Aberdeenshire and elsewhere. An old MS. relates very circumstantially a settlement of the Clan in Braemar at Little Inverey, giving the date as far back as 1403, which is certainly too early.

The Gregories of Kinairdie trace their descent from a son of Roro who went to the Boyne in 1500, and married a daughter of the Laird of Finlater, by whom he had a son James surnamed Gregor, who became Chamberlain to Finlater at Woodland, in the parish of Udney. He married Agnes More, sister to William More of Ferryhill, and died in 1584

These brief notices of the origin of the different families are merely given at this place to explain the names which occur in the histories of the subsequent times, and serve as a guide to the identification of some of the individuals mentioned. It is intended to give as full genealogical accounts as possible later on.

Before resuming the general history, an anecdote of one of the ancient Chiefs may be related, which, amidst the sterner features of the times,

shows that the virtue of hospitality and good faith shone brightly. The
following version of this anecdote, which is now well known, was communicated to Sir John MacGregor Murray by the Rev. Dr Joseph
MacIntyre, Minister of Killin in 1800:—

"The Chief was at that time residing on his freehold in Glenorchy: His son
had gone in the shooting season, with a party of young associates, to the Moors
in the Braes of the country: they met with a young gentleman, of the name of
Lamont from Cowal, who attended by a servant was going to Fort William. They
all went to the kind of inn that was in the place, and took a refreshment together;
in the course of which at the close of the day a trifling dispute arose betwixt
Lamont and young MacGregor; Dirks were drawn, and before Friends could
interfere, MacGregor fell wounded, and soon expired beside the table. In the
confusion Lamont escaped, and though pursued, under the cover of night got
securely to the House of MacGregor, the first habitation that met him by the dawn
of the morning. The Chieftain had got up and was standing at the door, 'Save
my life' said the stranger 'for Men are in pursuit of me to take it away.' 'Whoever you are' says MacGregor 'Here you are safe.' Lamont was but just brought
to an inner apartment and introduced to the family, when a loud enquiry was made
at the door if any stranger had entered the house. 'He has' says MacGregor
'And what is your business with him?' 'In a scuffle' cried all the pursuers, 'He
has killed your son, deliver him up, that we may instantly revenge the deed.'
MacGregor's lady and his two daughters filled the house with their cries and
lamentations, 'Be quiet' says the Chief, with his eyes streaming with tears, 'and
let no man presume to touch the youth- for he has MacGregor's word and honour
for his safety and as God lives, he shall be safe and secure whilst in my house.' In
a little, after every kind treatment of Lamont he accompanied him with twelve men
under arms to Inveraray saw him in safety on the other side of Lochfyne took him
by the hand and thus addressed him, 'Lamont, now you are safe: no longer can I,
or will I, protect you; keep out of the way of my Clan. May God forgive and
bless you.' This happened some short time before the severe act of proscription
against the Clan in the year 1633.[1] when to the discredit of Justice a weak
government sacrificed a whole people for the atrocities of a few. MacGregor lost
his property, and was hunted for his life by this iniquitous act: He took shelter in
the house of this very Lamont, noted for his urbanity and his known contrition for
the misfortune of his younger years, and by every act of kindness to his venerable
guest, and some branches of his family in some measure revered the providence
that had thus put it in his power to repay to the family in some measure the loss he
had occasioned them by the death of a son."

[1] The period must have been much earlier, if the Chief still lived in Glenurchay, and it must
have been one of the earlier persecutions when he was hunted for his life.

Chapter XII

DURING the early years of Queen Mary, internal divisions and the dread of English invasions, entirely occupied the Government, therefore little is heard of the Highlands in the Public Records except the mention of a few Chiefs at the Battle of Pinkie.

The Reformation, which attained its recognition in 1560, had little effect amongst the distant mountains, where the usual feuds continued to prevail unchecked till after the return of the young Queen, the Dauphin's widow, from France in August 1561.

Soon afterwards the Queen's attention seems to have been directed to the conflicts in the North, as a series of proclamations shortly appear. The Queen's marriage with Lord Darnley took place on the 27th July 1565. On the 19th June 1566 the young Prince was born, and, on his mother's forced resignation, he was, in 1567, crowned King of Scotland as James VI.

The following year the perplexed Queen took the fatal step of trusting herself to the mercy of her cousin, Queen Elizabeth of England, who caused her, after a lingering captivity, to be executed at Fotheringay Castle in Northamptonshire, 8th Feb. 1587.

It has been related in Chapter IX. that Duncan Ladosach and two of his sons perished in June 1552. This slaughter seems to have dismayed and disorganised the Clan, for several Bands of Manrent with Sir Colin Campbell were soon afterwards made, doubtless with the object of obtaining a temporary respite from persecution.

Band of the McOlcallums from the "Black Book of Taymouth":—

"At the Yle of Loch Tay the thrid day of August 1552. William McOlcallum in Rannocht, Malcum his son, and Donald Roy McOlchallum Glas bindis and oblisses thame thair airis barnis, and posterite to be . . . afald seruantis to Colyne Campbell of Glenurquhay and to his airis maill quhom . . . thai haif electit and chosyn for thair cheiffis and masteris, renunciand McGregour thair auld chief and all utheris in the contra, the authorite alanerlie except. and that because the said Colyne hes deliuerit to thame his letter of maintenians . . and als the saidis personis for thameselffis, thair airis, and successouris gevis thair calpis to the said Colyne and his airis conforme to the use thairof . . and gif it happens the saidis William, Malcum, or Donald to faill in the premissis to pay to the said Colyne and his airis the soume of ane hundreth pundis money within XV days eftir the faill be triiet and maid manifest . . and heirto the foirsaidis personis ar bundin . . . and sworn uoun the holy evangellis . . . presentibus Alexandro Menzies de Rannocht, Colyne Campbell filio Archibaldi Campbell de Glenlyoun, Patricio Campbell et Johnne Leche testibus vocatis.

" Willelmus Ramsaye Notarius."

" 1552. August 4.   Malcum McAynmallicht (son of John Malloch) Donald his brother Duncane McNeill V^cKewin (Ewin) William and Malcum McNeill V^cEwin brothers to the said Duncane, renouncing McGregour their Chief, bind themselves to Colyne Campbell of Glenurquhay giving him their Calpes."—B.B. of T.

" 1552. August 21.   Gregour McGregour son of the deceased Sir James McGregour Dean of Lismore binds himself to the same 'taking thame for his chiefs in place of the Laird McGregour.' "—B.B. of T.

" 1552. Sep. 9.   Donald Beg McAcrom Duncane and William his brothers duelling in the Bray of Weyme bind themselves to the same. 'having overgiven the Laird McGregour and his heirs and successors.' "—B.B. of T.

" 1552. Dec. 21.   Duncan McAindrew in . . . Duncane and Malcum his sons renounce the Laird McGregour and his heirs as their chief and choose the same. Dated before among other witnesses, William McOlcallum McGregour and John McYndoir."—B.B. of T.

From the " Chartulary " :—

" 1552 Nov. 24.   Colin Campbell bought of Finlay McNab of Bowaine the lands (amongst others) of Ardchalzie Easter which had been in the hands of the McNabs for a long time previously.[1]

" 1554. May 9.   'Gregourstone' is mentioned in Charter by Queen Mary to John Creichtoun of Strathurd and Janet Ruthven daughter of William Lord Ruthven, Spouse of the said John, of the Tower, Place and Mains of Strathurd vic: Perthe as is Drumquhar then possessed by John Gregour Cokkar.—Mag. Sig. XXIX, 115.

---

[1] Patrick MacNab of Bowaine gave to his son Finlay and heirs the lands of Bovaine and Ardkelzie Ester at Killin, 1st January 1486-7, for a pair of gloves to be given to the King at Pentecost.—Register of Great Seal.

"1555. May 2. William of Tullibardine 'Plege for William Our McGregor and John McYnkeir (Lan Ciar)' under penalty of a hundred marks each.—Records of High Court of Justiciary.

"1556-7. Feb. 1. Precept of a Charter of Confirmation of a Charter of Sale made by Janet Makgregour heretrix of the lands underwritten with consent of Malcolm McGillcmichaell her spouse, to Colin Campbell of Glenurchay and his heirs male, of all and whole the 8 merk land of Kingart, lying in Stewartry of Strathearn and Shire of Perth.—Privy Seal.

"1557-58. Jan. 31. Preceptum legitimationes Gregorij McGregour et Dugalli McGregour bastadorum filiorum naturalium Domini Jacobi McGregour (Sir James McGregor Dean of Lismore) in communi forma &a apud Edinburgh ultimo Jan.—Privy Seal.

"1557-8 Feb. Menzies of that Ilk on account of the lawless and independent spirit of the ClanGregor in Rannoch (as by him alleged) obtained an exemption from answering for these, under the seal and subscription of Mary of Guise Queen Regent.[1]

"1558. Feb. 8. Death of Malcolm McNeill V^{c}Ewin at Lagfarme in his own house. Pray for the soul of him who did good to God and man. . . . . . . Quhilk summyr Schyr Dougal McGregour byggit (n)ew hous besyd the Kirk of Fortingall, samyn yer Schir Dougall got the sencellari . . . . . Lesmoyr fra Collin Campbell of Glenurchy.—Obituary."

It may have been about this time that a terrible outrage on the Clan Laurane took place. Subsequently, in the year 1604, John McCoul Chere with other McGregors was tried for the slaughter of eighteen house-holders of the Clan Laurane[2] (forty-six years syne or thereby), of which he was acquitted. It has also been alleged that Duncan Ladosach and his son Gregor were concerned in the raid, but as they were killed fifty-two years previous to this trial, the accusation does not coincide with the time supposed. There is a tradition that the immediate cause of provocation was that the McLauranes had cut the mouths of some horses belonging to the McGregors in Glen Dochart.

The McLauranes, who claim to have been settled in Balquhidder since

---

[1] See next page.

[2] A moumental stone was placed in Balquhidder churchyard, 1868, by Daniel McLaurin, Esq., of St John's Wood, London, a descendant of MacLabhrainn of Auchleskin, in memory of those who perished in this unhappy occurrence, with the following inscription, "In Memoriam of the Clan Laurin, anciently the allodian inhabitants of Balquhidder and Strathearn, the Chief of whom in the decrepitude of old age, together with his aged and infirm adherents, their wives and children, the widows of their departed kindred, all were destroyed in the silent midnight hour, by fire and sword by the hands of a banditti of incendiarists from Glendochart. A.D. 1558."

the thirteenth century, exercised a priviledge of being the first to enter the Church of Balquhidder at the Diets of Worship on Sundays. The MᶜGregors shared this precedence, having in the fifteenth century stipulated, it is said, to be allowed to share the right, as a preliminary condition before they effectually assisted the MᶜLauranes in a great fight with the Lenies. This right led eventually to a serious brawl inside the Church in 1532, when the vicar, Sir John MᶜLaurane, was killed. (Taken from "Curious Episodes of Scottish History," by Robert Fittis.)

"1559. March 11. Malcolm MᶜCoule Keir appears as a witness in a Bond by the Clan Laurane dwelling in Balquhidder.

Sir Alexander Menzies having represented to the Queen Regent, Mary of Guise, in 1559, that he could not be answerable for the actions of the MacGregors in Rannoch, he received the following exemption :—

"Letter by Mary of Guise, Queen Regent of Scotland, exempting Alexander Menzies of that Ilk from finding caution for MacGregors his tenants in Rannoch, for seven years. 7th Feb. 1559.

"'Regina.—We understanding that it is not within the power of Alexander Menzes of that Ilk to ansuer for the gud reule of the Clangregour inhabitantis of the Rannoch, and that our chozing the Erle of Ergyle and Coline Campbell of Glenvrquhay hes the seruic of that clann, and that thai will do thare deligens to caus gud reule be kepit be the said clann, and for diuers vther resonable causis and considerationis moving ws, grantis and gevis licence to the said Alexander to set intak and assedatioun all and haill his tuenty-pund land of Rannock liand within the sherefdom of Perth, too the auld tenentis and inhabitantis thairof of the Clangregour for the space of sevin yeris; and will and grantis that he nor his airis sall nocht be haldyn to our derrest dochter, nor ws, to ansuer for thair gud reule during the said sevin yeirs, nor to enter thame to our lawes, our justice airis, nor justice courtis for thair demeritis, nochtwithstanding the generall band maid be the lordis and landit men of the said S . . . . our said derrest dochter and ws there upoun : Anent the quhilkis we dispens with hym be thir presentis a panis contenit thairin. Gevin vnder signet. Subscriuit with our hand at Edinburgh vii day of Fabruarm the zeir ogf God.

"'Marie R.'"

—From the Charter Room of Castle Menzies.—"Red and White Book of Menzies."

From "Chartulary" :—

"1559. March 9. Patrick MᶜConachy VᶜCoull MᶜGregour in Inwirzelly John his brother german, Patrick McAne McGregour in Dalmarky Johne McAne his brother german, and Malcum McCoule Kair McGregour dwelling in Balquihidder, bind themseves to render Colin Campbell faithful service when required, ay and quhill the said Colyne and his airis, stayk thame with sum rowmis or stedingis quhairby they may serve themsel upoune thair awin expensis and to give thame their Calpes.—'Black Book of Taymouth.'

"1560 Feb 16   John McAvyr Alexander McAlester McGregour VcNeill witness.—'Chartulary'

"1561 April 17.   Duncan McCoule Keir a witness at Strathfillan.
    July 4   Gregour McAne and Patrik McOlane witnesses.

"1561. 14 Feb. St Andrews.   Charter of Few-farm of the lands of Dull by David Guthrie, Vicar of Dull and John Wyram, usufructuary thereof, with consent of the Lord James Commendator of St Andrews, and of the Convent 113 in number in favour of John McGrigor.—'Red and White Book of Menzies.'

"1561 Augst 24   Archibald Earl of Argyle addressed a missive from Achallader to Grigor MacGregor son and apparent heir of the late Alexander MacGregor of Glenstray narrating a grant of the superiority of the lands of Glenurchay with the islands called Elanewir and Elanduffeir, Elankilequhyrne and Elan bochtoliff, part of the lands of Auchynna with the island called Elanvoriche part of Kellan, Fernach, Inverynan, Craigbarnory, Sonnochan, Altbane and Allbre-Mnycht lying within his barony of Lochaw which were formerly hereditarily possessed by Colin Campbell and which he had resigned into the Earl's hands as the representative of the King as Superior and which were now granted to Duncan Campbell his son and apparent heir.' Amongst the witnesses is 'Johanne McCondoquhy Roy —Excerpt from the Sheriff under 22d June 1584 in 'Chartulary.' (Translation and abridgement taken from Dr Joseph Anderson's note books.)

"1562 May 21   Allester McEwin Dow VcGregor slain by Patrik McAyn Vyc Olchallum alias McGregor Kyllejiese (Killiehassie) and buried at Foss —Obituary

"1562 Feb. 2   Death of John Dow McCondoquhy VcGregor at Castle of Glenurquhay.

"1562 August 1   Bond by Johnne Dow McCouilaid in Braiklie at Kendlochtollive, Donald Dow Mak Couilaid and Makum McCouill Laid his brothers, to Collein Campbell of Glenurchy giving him their Calpes; signed at the Castle of Glenurquhay before these witnesses Greigour McKein Keeper of the Castle of Glenurquhay, Ewin McKein in Mourlaganmoir and John Makindovin in Portbane.—B. B. of T "

It has been stated in Chapter X. that Sir Colin Campbell had made John McCondoquhy Keeper of the Castle of Glenurquhay in 1550; his son, Gregor MacIan, appears to have obtained the appointment in succession to his father, who died a few months previous to this date.

"Chartulary" :—

"1562-3 Jan. 12. Letter to Coling Campbell of Glenurquhair of the Escheit of Gregour MakGregour of Glenstray alias Laird Makgregour, Duncan MakGregour in Roro, Duncan Makandoy (Ian dhu) elder, Duncan Makandoy younger Patrik Makane McGillichallum glas, Ewin Makgregour chellych, Malcolme Makgregor alias Kendmoir. and Duncan Oig alias Laddossoune[1] for the slaughter of Tearloch (Charlie) Campbell.—Record of Privy Seal.

"1563. (Obituary) . . . . . . Ane gud symmyr and gud harist, pece and rest excep the Lard of Glenurquhay, wyryth (wrath or warreth) aganis the ClanGregor."

Having obtained the escheit of so many of the ClanGregor, Sir Colin Campbell now endeavoured to turn it to the best advantage, and having a lease from Sir Alexander Menzies of part of the Loch Rannoch lands, arranged to sublet them to MacDonald of Keppoch, to get their support against the MacGregors.

Contract between Glenurquhay and Cappycht (Keppoch) :—

"1563. April 25. At Ballocht. It is agreit betuix Colyne Campbell of Glenurquhay on that ane part and Rannald McRannald McConiglas off Cappicht on that uther part in maner following, the said Colyne havand of our Souerane Lady the gift of escheit of the Clangregour now being our Souerane Lady rebellis, of thair takis, rowmis, stedingis, gudis, and geir. And havand of the Lard of Weyme in lifrent the tuelf merkland of Rannoch on the west syde of the watter of Erachtie, to haif sett in assedatioun to the said Rannald his airis maill, and subtenantis of nay hiear degre nor himself . . . . . . witht power to set the saidis landis to subtenantis of lawer degrie nor himself of ony surname (the Clangregour alanerlie except) . . . . . during the gift of the takis of the said Colyne escheit, malis, and deweteis usit and wont conforme to the payment that McGregour suld haif maid to the Lard of Weyme. And efter the furthrinnin of the said Colyne lyfrent and takis, he and his airis sall do thair exact diligence in obtaining of new takis and lyfrent upoun all the

---

[1] Apparently Duncan Laddosach's son; he is not mentioned in the "Baronage."

forsaidis landis, and thairefter mak the said Rannald and his airis tytill thairof .   and the said Colyne and his airis, sall defend the said Rannald his airis and subtenantis in the forsaidis landis . . . .   For the quhilkis the said Rannald oblisses hym and his airis, freindis &a to be leill trew seruantis to the said Colyne &a and the said Rannald sall . . . mak his principal residens thairupoun ay and quhill he may bring the samyn to quietness for the commoun weill of the cuntre and sal nocht suffer ony of the Clangregour to haif entres or intromissiounes of the forsaidis landis .   Atour the said Rannald and his airis forsaidis   . . oblisses thame to . . . persew at thair utermaist power samony of the ClanGregour as ar now our Souerane Lady rebellis and apprehend and bring thame to the said Colyne and his airis to be punesit according to the lawis."

The Macdonalds of Keppoch were not more famed for their docility than the MacGregors, and possibly they found the task of guarding the country uncongenial, for the following year Rannald McCouilglas of Cappicht renounced by contract his right to the 12 merkland of Rannocht.—"Black Book of Taymouth"

"1563 May 6   Contract of manrent and protection between Collyne Campbell of Glenurquhay and Johne Oyg McAne Abricht of Glen cho providing that if he will not instantly serve against the ClanGregour his contract shall be void"

From "Black Book of Taymouth":—

"1563 Nov. 17.   Gregour McGregour of that Ilk obliges himself his kin servantis, and dependants to do all the steid he may to Jhone Stewart
· apparent of the Appin, without exposing himself to hurt at my Lord Ergyle's hand subscribed at Ellan na mayn witnesses Duncan MacGregor of Rorow Ewin McGregour and Duncan McAllaster VcEwin "

Register of the Privy Council of Scotland   Queen Mary.

" Apud Striveling, XXIJ Septembris, anno, etc, (1563)
"The Quenis Majestie, understanding that the Clangregour, being hir Hienes rebellis, and at hir horne for divers horrible attemptatis committit be thame hes nocht onlie massit thameselfis in greit cumpanyis, bot als hes drawin to thaim the maist part of the broken men of the hail cuntre, quhilkis at thair plesour birnis and slayis the pouer lieges of this realme, revis and takis thair gudis, sornis and oppreessis thame in sic sort that thai ar hable to lay waist the haill boundis quhair thai hant, and to bring the samyn to

be inhabitable, without the hastier remeid be providit thairfoir. and knawing that the saidis malefactouris for the maist part hantis and repairis within the boundis following, and that the noblemen underspecifiet quha ar principalis of the boundis undernamit, ar maist hable to expell the saidis evill doaris furth of thair boundis, or ellis gif thai be fundin within the samyn to apprehend and tak thame and bring thame to the Justice or his Deputis to be punist for thair demeritis. Thairfoir ordainis the said noble men to expell and hald the saidis broken men furth of the bondis undernemmit in maner underspecifiet; that is to say, James Erle of Murray, furth of the boundis of Bramar, Badynoch, Lochquhabir, Bra of Murray, Strathnarne, and Stratherne, within the boundis of the Sherefdome of Inverness, Archibald Erle of Argyle, furth of the boundis of Argyle, Lorne, Levinax, and Menteith : Johne Erle of Athole, furth of the boundis of Athole, Strthardail Glensche, and Dunkeld. George Erle of Errole, furth of the boundis of Logiealmont; James Lord Ogilvie furth of the boundis of the Bra of Angus; Patrick Lord Ruthven, furth of the boundis of Strathbarne; David Lord Drummond furth of the boundis of Stratherne; Colyne Campbell of Glenurquhy, furth of the boundis of Braidalbane and Buchquhidder; and Johne Grant of Freuchy, furth of the boundis of Strathspey, Strathawn and Bra of Strathbogie. And to that effect grantis and committis to the saidis noble men and every ane of thame, within the boundis forsaidis, full power speciale mandiment, and charge to pass, serche, and seik the saidis rebellis, malefactouris, and oppressouris quhair evir thai may be apprehendit within the boundis abonespecifiet; and apprehend and tak thame and bring thame to the Justice or his Deputis, to be punist for thair demeritis; and to convocat and gadder oure Soverane Ladies liegis in cumpanyis and armyis; and to persew, follow, and invade the saidis tresspassouris, with fire and suerd and gif thai or any of thaim, happynnis to entir in houssis or strengthis, to lay assaige yhairto, and to raise fyre for recovering of the samyn gif neid be; and ordainis the gentilmen, induellars within the boundis specifiet upoun the command gevin to thame be ony of the saidis noble men, or utherwyise be lettres, assemble thair folkis togidder, and meit the saidis noble men ilkane within the boundis foirsaidis at sic place or places as salbe assignit to thame, and to remaine with the saidis noble men during the space thai salbe commandit. and als gevis power to the saidis noble men gif neid requiris to joine thair cumpanies togidder and pass fordwart in army or armies for persewing of the saidis evill doaris. And gif any of thame happynnis to be slane or mutilat in the persewing or taking, the Quenis Majestie will and granteth that the saidis noble men nor nane of hir Graces lieges being with thame, or ony of thame in cumpany, sall nocht be callit nor accusit thairfoir, nor incur ony skaith or danger thairthrow in thair persone, landis, or gudis in ony wyise in tyme cuming; and ordains, gif neid beis, speciale commissions to be gevin to the saidis noble men and every ane of thame to the effect foirsaid, to be extendit in the maist ample forme, and the Clerkis of Chancellerie, to direct out commissions under the testimonial of the great

seill to every ane of the noble men above specifiet, to the effect foirsaid.' And this
present ordinance sal be sufficient warrand to thame to pass the saidid commissionis
upoun, and siclyke ordainis the Lordis of Counsale to direct out lettres to charge
oure Soverane Ladies liegis to ryise, concur assist and gang fordward with the saidis
noble men in maner foirsaid, for accomplissing of the premissis apprehending or
expelling of the saidis rebellis in maner abone specifiet, And that the samyn may be
the mair suirlie done, ordainis the saidis noble men and baronis to cause in all the
partis foirsaidis, the lieges thairof be gadderit togidder upoun the XX day of
October nixt to cume, but forther delay, and to remain togidder every man within
his boundis limitat as is befoir specifiet for the space of XX dayis next theireafter,
to the effect that the saidis rebellis be expellit or apprehendit in maner abone
mentiantat as thai will answer to the Quenis Majestie thairupoun ; and under all
hiest pane, charge and offence that thai, and ilkane of thame may committ and inrin
againis hir Majestie in that part."

"Apud Edinbrugh, 8 Jan 1563-64
"(The preamble down to the words ' bring the samyn to be inhabitable ' is the
same as the last. The Proclamation continuing)
"The Quenis Majestie . . . . . . the maist part of the cause quhairof, is that
in all partis quhair thai repair and hant, thai ar resett be the inhabitaris and induel-
leris and furnissit with vittallis and uther necessaris and in sik wyise fosterit and
nurissit as gif thai wer the Quenis Majesties trew and faithfull subjects and nevir
had committit cryme or offence in ony tyme bigane ; quhair throw hir Hieness
authorite be the saidis resettoris and furnisseris is sa contempnit that in ane maner
it sal gif occasioun to hir trew lieges, quhilkes nevir myndit to mak ony brek, to
becom manifest contempnaris, sornaris, thevis, oppressouris and rebellis, thinking
thairby to leif idillie and wickethe, and be furnist upoun uther trew mennis gudis.

"For remeid quhairof and stopping of the saidis rebellis to be forther furnissit be
the Quenis Grace liegies in ony tyme cuming the Quenis Hienes givis, grantis and
committis hir full, fre and plane power to hir lovit Coline Campbell of Glenurchy,
to pass serche, &ᵃ (giving him a commission against the resetters during hir
Majesties gude will and pleasure, &ᵃ."

The Earl of Atholl[1] objecting to the rights of search granted to Colin
Campbell among his own tenants &ᵃ, made a protest of which the following was the result:—

"Apud Edinburgh, 10, Jan, 1563-64.
"In presence of the Quenis Majestie and Lordis of hir Secreit Counsale
comperit Johne Erle of Atholl, and maid this offer underspecifiit, that is to say,

[1] John Stewart, 4th Earl of Atholl.

Forasmeikle as Colin Campbell of Glenurquhy hes impetrat ane commissioun of the Quenis Majestie for sercheing, seiking and apprehandeing of certaine of the ClanGregour, and complices to thame, hir Graces Rebellis, and at hir horne, and for inbringing of thame and resettaris of the saidis rebellis to the Justice to be punist for thair contemptioun and inobedience as the said commissioun beris; nochtwithstanding the quhilk, the said Earl, in presence of the Counsale forsaid, obliss him to ansuer for all sik personis duelland, within his boundis, rowmes and possessiojns, quhilkis he sall gif in writ to the said Lard of Glenurquhy, for ony attemptatis committit or to be committit be thame, conforme to the ordinance maid be the Quenis Grace and hir Secreit Counsale thairupoun; the Quenis Majestie with advyse of the saidis Lordis hes thocht ressonable that ane exemptioun be granted to the said Erle, examand all and sindrie men tennentis, fewaris, servantis, vassallis, and occupiers of quhat sumevir landis and rowmes pertaining to him. or of quhome he hes dominioun and cure of, and of quhame qnd quhat landis he sall accept the burding be his said writing, to be gevin to the said Lard of Glenurquhy, that thai and ilk ane of thame, thair boundis landis, and possessionis sal be fre of the said commissioun, or any part thairof, grantit to the said Lard of Glenurquhay; and to the effect of the samyn sall na wyise strek upoune thame selfis, thair bodeis, landis, or gudis in ony wyise; dischargeing alwayis the said Lard of Glenurquhy; and all uther officiaris or liegeis quhatsumevir, to attempt or presume ony thing contrair the saidis Erles landis, rowmes, tennentis and occupyaris thairof quhilkis he sall gif in bill as said is, thair gudis or geir, in ony wyise be vertew of the said commissioun, suspendand the effect thairof, and of thair offices in that part be the same exemptioun."

With the object of starving out the dreaded Clan another proclamation follows :—

"For asmekle as eftir divers slauchteris and utheris haynous and horrible crymes committit be Gregor MᶜGregor alias Lard MᶜGregour[1] Ewine MᶜGregour[2] his brether, Duncan MᶜGregor[3] in Rora Duncane MᶜAnedoy MᶜGregor, Duncan Oyg MᶜGregor,[5] Patrik MᶜAne MᶜHollonglas MᶜColme,[6] Duncane and Patrik MᶜAne M. Hollonglas[6] hes brether, Malcolme Cham M. Candoquhy, Ewine MᶜGillehelichy, Duncane MᶜGillehellich his bruther, Williame MᶜColchollum, Malcolme and George MᶜColchollum his sonnis, and thair complices, to greit

---

[1] Gregor MᶜAllaster MᶜGregor of Glenstray, " Gregor na'm Bassan Gheal."

[2] Ewine, afterwards Tutor of Glenstray.

[3] Roro.

[5] Duncan Oig, probably "Laddosoune," mentioned 12 Jan. 1562-3, or Duncan Makundoy younger.

[6] Family of John MᶜChallum glas, son of Callum glas (pale faced), son of Duncan—a branch of Roro, who left Glenlyon and settled at Learagan-Rannoch.

nowmer of personis; that being callit to underlie the law thairfore, and to find cautioun to that effect in contempt of the Quenis Majestie, hir authorite all ordour and justice, past to the horne, quhairat thai remainit thir twa yeris bigane with the mair. (Proclamation goes on to complain that in spite of the commissions and other measures taken, the Clan are still furnished with necessaries) Thairfore and to the effect that hir liegis may be inexecusable of sik furnessing and mantenance of hir rebellis, hir Grace ordinis lettres to be direct to hir messingeris in that part, chargeing thame to pass to the mercat croces of hir burrois of Perth, ... and utheris places neidfull , and thair be open proclamatonn in hir Hienes name and autorite, command and charge all and sundrie hir liegis, that nane of thame tak upoun hand to ressave, ressett, mantene, nuriss, foster, provide or furniss, the saidis rebellis, or thair complices, in house, meit, drink, clething, armour, wappyn-neis, counsale or uther wayis , &ᵃ (under pain of being 'punist with all rigour at the saidis particular Justice Courts') "

" Apud Perth, 18die mensis Marcii, 1563-64.

"(after a preamble to the same effect as the preceding proclamations this continues) . . .

" For remeid quhairof, her Hienes hes gevin and grantit, and be the tennour heirof gevis and grantis and committis hir ful power generall and speciall command, express bidding, and charge to hir traistie cousingis and counsalouris, Archibale Erle of Ergyle Lord Campbell and Lorne, &ᵃ and Johne, Erle of Atholl Lord of Balveny &ᵃ, to convocat and assembill togidder all and sindry our Soverane Ladies liegis dwell-and within the boundis respective underwritten that is to say, the Erle of Ergyle within the boundis of the Sherefdomes of Ergyle, Tarbert, Dunbartane, Bute, the Stewartrie, Erledom and haill cuntre of Menteith, the landis and cuntreis of Braidalbyne, Buchquhidder, &ᶜ and samekill of the Sherefdome of Striviling as lyis be west Buchquhan ; and the said Erle of Athole within the boundis of Badey-noch, Lochquhabir, Strathspey, Strathowin, Bray of Mar, Strathdone, Bray of Angus, and the haill sherefdome of Perth except Braidalbane, Buchquhidder, and Menteith, or any part of the saidis countreis, sa oft and at quhatsumevir place or places as he sall think convenient, and to pass serche seik, persew, and apprehend the saidis rebellis and malefactouris quhairevir thai can be apprehendit within the boundis abonewritten or farder as occasioun sall occur, to be brocht to the Justice or his Deputis to be punist for thair demeritis, and falying thairof to persew thame untill thai be expellit and put furth of the saidis boundis . . . .

" With power alswa to the said Erle to direct, chargeis, and command mentis, to the inhabitantis of the cuntreis abone written, or quhaisumevir part or place thairof, for convening with him or sik personis as he sal happin to depute, upoun sic warning and at quhatsumevir place he sall think expedient, to pas forwart and to use the direction that salbe thocht maist convenient for resistence or persute of the saidis rebellis , certifeing the personis swa to be warnit and chargeit be the said

Erle or thame havand his power, within the saidis boundis and nocht passand forthwart to the frayis, or quhen the saidis rebellis resortis in thair boundis and schawis nocht thair reddie service, and exact diligence in thai behalfis to the contentation of the said Erle or thame havand his power as said is,—that thai salbe repute and haldin as plane partakeris and assistaries with the saidis rebellis in thair rebellioun, and salbe callit and persewit thairfore at particular dyeties and puneist for the samyn, conforme to the lawis and consuetude of this realme. and forder gewis power to the said Erle to use and exerce all and quhatsumevir uther thingis he sall think expedient for furthsetting of hir Majesties service and authorite in the said commissionn and in all thai doingis hir Hieness promettis to hald hand to him as aperentis hir of hir princelie honour, without ony contradictioun or revocatioun, nochtwithstanding the generalities heirof.'"

On the same day (18. March 1564) another order follows, after shortly recapitulating the commission, it continues :—

"Quhilkis the saidis Erlis can nocht weill and convenientlie execut, without thair actionis, and the actions of all sic personis dwelland within the boundis of thair present charge, as ar necessar for the present service dependand afoir the Lordis of Counsal Sessioun, be continewit, and delayit during the tyme thairof. Thair foir the Quenis Majestie be the avyise of the Lordis of hir Secreit Counsall ordainis all actionis dependand befoir the saidis Lordis of Counsall and Sessioun pertening to the saidis Erlis of Ergyle and Athole or to ony persoun or personis dwelland within the boundis abone specifiit respective quhom thai will testifie be thair writ to the saidis Lordis to be necessar for thair service, and to be actulie thairin and worthy of the privelege of this act to be continewit, supersedit, delayit, and na proces to be had thairin unto the XX day of Maii next to come, discharging the saidis Lordis of all proceeding in ony of the saidis actionis in the menetyme, eftir the sycht of ather of the saidis Erlis writtingis to be direct to thame, testifeand of the actioun and persoun in quhais favouris thai wryte."

In consequence of the complaints made against Sir Colin for the manner in which his commission was executed amongst those who he was supposed to be protecting from the MacGregors, the following band was required :—

"Apud Perth XXIJ Marcii 1563-64. The quhilk day in presence of the Lordis of Secreit Counsall, compeirit Colin Campbell of Glenurquhy, and band and oblist him for himself his kin, friends, assistaris, and partakaris passand with him, or in his name and behalf, for persewt of the Clangregor and utheris, the Quenis Majesties rebellis, that thai nor nane of thame sould sorne or oppress our

Soverane Ladus liegis dwelland within the boundis of Stratherne, or ony utheris
partis of this realme, be ony maner of sort in bodiis or gudis in tyme cuming   And
in caise complaint beis made heireftir to the Quenis Majestie and hir Counsall
upoun his saidis kin friendis, assistaris and partakeris, in that caise he sall entir the
persoun or personis complenit upoun befoir the Justice or his Deputtis at ane
convenient day and place to be appointit thair to, to undirly the law for the
crymes, sornyngis, oppressionis, and offencis to the Quenis Majestie upoun his lyff
and heretage contenit in the complaint, and failying thairof, sall answer himself for
the samyn

"The quhilk day anent the complaint presented to the saidis Lordis of
Secreit Counsall be the Lordis, Baronis, landtsmen, gentilmen and inhabitantis of
Stratherne, desyrand the commissioun gevin and grantit be our Soverane Lady to   ·
Colene Campbell of Glenurquhy anent the sercheing and seking of the Quenis
Majesties rebellis of the surname of the Clangregour, and thair complices, and
towart the arresting and inventure making of thair gudis, to be dischairgeit at
the leist safer as the samyn can or may be extendit towart the inhabitantis of
Stratherne, as the said complaint mair fullelie proportis   The Lordis of Secreit
Counsall in respect of thai ressonis, quhilk wer exponit aganis the samyn be the
said Coleine and for utheris wechty causis and considerationis moving thame selffis,
decernis the said commissioun to haif effect and strenth in tyme cuming and na
wyise to be dischargeit, unto the finall repressing of the rebellion of the saidis
rebellis   Nevirtheless during the tyme of the peisute of thame be the Erlis of
Ergyle and Athole quhome to the Quenis majestie hes grantit commissioun to
that effect, the said Colene sall use his said commissioun, bot onelie upoun thau
personis in quhais houssis he actualie findis the saidis rebellis, or quhairfra thai ar
instantlie for the tyme departit in the sycht of him, or of thame berand his power,
and as for the utheris personis resettaris, supplearis, or intercommunaris with the
saidis rebellis, delatit or suspectit, yea althocht the deed be notour and certane to
the said Colene swa that ony space pas owir betwix the time or the resorting of the
saidis rebellis in thai partis and the cuming of the said Coline, or thame havand his
power to the same,—in that cais the said Colene sall temperat the extremitie of his
said commissioun notand onelie the personis resettaris, and sal use na forder
exccutioun upoun thame unto the tyme he notifie the mater to the Quenis
Majestie & counsall & ressave new and speciall direction of thame in that
behalf &a "

Soon after the arrival of the Macdonalds of Keppoch in Rannoch, they
began to rebuild the dismantled fort or castle of the Isle of Loch Rannoch,
which by order of James V. had been demolished, the aim being to drive
the MacGregors from the lands of Rannoch, and hold their goods under

Glenurchy's warrant. The Queen kindly interfered in favour of the persecuted MacGregors.

Letter from Queen Mary to Colin Campbell of Glenurchy, in reference to the MacGregors of Rannoch, &a, dated at Glentilt, in Atholl :—

"3rd August 1564.—Traist freind we greit yow wele   We remember we disponit to yow the escheitis of certaine personis of the Clangregour, duelland in the Rannoch, and be that way sute ye the entries to thair stedingis; and we ar informit that ye have plasit Makrannald in the sam yn rowmes quhairof the heretage pertenis to James Meingeis the Laird of Weym, and thairof Mackgregour had neuir takkis of him.   We are surlie informit that the said Makrannald is alreddy to big ane hous and strenth within the Ile of Loch Rannoch, and to laubour the grind of the lands adicentpquhilk hous was castin doun and distroyit at command of our fader of guid memory as yourself hes dlaithe done sen syne.   And sen it hes allwayis bene a receptacle and refuge to offendouris we waitt nocht to, quhat effect the biging of it or any streth in the Heland suld serve without our speciall command and that the causis wer of befoir considerit be ws and oir counsale   For to output the Clan-Gregour and impute vther brokun men of the like condition, allwwayis sic as of any continewance werwer neuir permanent in our obedienc we jugeit nocht mete nor expedient to be done.   And thairfoir, our pledour is that ye causs the werk begun in the Ile within the said loch to ceiss, and not that onlie, bot all vther innouatioun quhairof your nychbouris may justelie complene, especiallie the inbringing of strang-eris of vther clannis and cuntres.   Bot lat all thingis rest without alteratioun our returning, and than mete was other at Sanct Johnstoun or Dunde, as ye heir of our dyett, quhair we sall tak sik ordour in this behalf as apertenis to your ressonable contantamemt   Subscriuit with our hand, at the Luncartis in Glentilth, the third day of August 1564.

"Marie R."

—Contemporary Official Copy in Charter Room of Castle Menzies.[1]

"Complaint before the Lords of Council—'Menzies of that Ilk against Campbell of Glenurchy and McRannald of Keppoch for wrongous intrusion on his isle in Loch Rannoch and its fortification, parties cited, and charged to remove from the isle, unless cause be shewen for possession   Fortification and placing of broken men and Highlanders therein prohibited'

"James Menzies of that Ilk recovers the isle of Loch Rannoch, seized from him at Edinburgh, 19th October 1564

"Coline Campbell charged 'to compeir befoir the Quenis Majestie and thair Lordschipis at Edinburgh' on 2nd Nov. 'to heir him be decernit to remove himself, the said Rannald McRannald, and all utheris, his partakaris, and servandis, furth of the said Ile in the said Loch Rannoch, and deliuer the samyn to the said James

[1] "Red and White Book"

Menzies to be usit be him at his plesour thairefter as his heretage'"—Record of Privy Council.

"1564 July 9   Contract of manrent and protection between Archibald Earl of Ergyle, Colyne Campbell of Boquhane Knight, Dugall Campbell of Auchynbrek, James Campbell of Ardinglass, John Campbell of Lochynell, Ewir Campbell of Ardgartney, Colyne Campbell Barbrek Johne Campbell of Inuerlevir, on the one part and Colyne Campbell of Glenurquhay on the other part, against all persons and specially against Gregour McGregour son to the deceased Alexander McGregour of Glenstray his accomplices and assistants, now being our Sovereign Lady's rebels and at her Grace's horn for suppressing and daunting of their uproarious and tyrannical attempts, and pursuing them with all rigour so long as they remain rebels to the Queen and enemies to the said Colyne and his heirs &a   Subscribed by the saids parties at Inueraray."

"1564 Sepber 29   Summons in the name of Queen Mary and under the signet at Edinburgh on the narrative that a complaint had been made by James Menzies of that Ilk, and that whereas he had the lands of Rannoch and forest thereof in few farm heritably, and because Coline Campbell of Glenurquhay, and Ranald McRanald McConilglas, under pretext of a gift of escheat to the said Colin of the goods of the Laird McGrigor the Queen's rebel, and at the horn had intruded themselves wrongously in the Isle of Lochrannoch, and the said James's lands of Rannoch 'be-est the vatter of Erachtie' and were bigging and fortifying the said isle to the trouble of the whole country; the said Ranald and his complices being of the Clanrannald and Clan Chameroun and 'utheris of the maist broken clanns within oure realm.' That the said James Meingeis had complained of this to the Queen at her late being in Atholle in the 'Lunkairtis', where being in her progress she could not take order fors reformation thereof, but wrote to the said Coline to cease from building in the said isle, and bringing in of strangers of other clans and countries, and to meet the Queen on her return, either at St Johnstoun or Dundie where she would take such order as might appertain to his reasonable contentment; nevertheless, they had still continued to fortify the said isle, and that when the Queen had given the said Coline, gratis the gift of the escheat, it was for the expulsion of the ClanGregour and not under pretence of it to fortify the said isle, which strenth had been demolished in her father's time, and again at her command by the said Coline, nor had ever command been given to repair it, or occupy the said James Meingeis lands, to which the Clangregour had no right; far less would it be allowed to place in the same James's lands the Clanrannald and Clan Chameroun, who if once permitted to get possession, would ever claim kindness thereto: That the said Coline had met the

Queen at her home-coming at Perth, and was commanded by our brother James, Earl of Murray, to come to Edinburgh to answer the said complaint which he had failed to do. Summoning the said Coline, therefore, to appear before the Queen and the Lords of her Council within 10 days after warning."—Contemporary Copy in Castle Menzies Charter Room Red and White Book.

"1564. Nov. 3. Weyme contra Glenurquhay—

"The which day anent our Sovereign Ladies Letters purchased by James Menzies of that Ilk Against Coline Campbell of Glenurquhay for the wrongous intrusion of himself and of Rannald McConilglas of Keppach and others in his name in the Isle within the Loch Rannoch pertaining heritably to the said James, and fortification thereof since the Queen's Majesty's inhibition made to the contrary. Delayed till 25. Nov. Defender to summon witnesses to prove his exception."—Record of Secret Council Acta.

"1566. Letter from Queen Mary to the Laird of Weym relative to the Clan-Gregour in Rannoch—

"1566. August 31st. dated at Drymen. Traist Freind, we greit yow weill. We vnderstand that diuerss personis of the Clangregour occupiit and inhabit your landis of the Rannoch, fra the quhilk thay wer eiectit the tyme of thair rebellioun. Now as ye knaw, we have ressauet thame in our peax, and sen thai can not leif without sum rowmes and possesionis, we pray and effectuuslie desire yow to permitt thaim to occupie and manure the same landis and stedingis quhilkis thai had and broukit of you of before, and mak thame ressonable takkis thairvpoun for payment of males and dewiteis, vsit and wont as ye will do ws thankfull plesour.—And further, quhair as ye may feir to be constrenit to ansuer for the saidis personis and thair doyingis, as duelland vpoun your land, be vertew of the generall band, we be thair presentis, exoneris, relevis, and dischargis yow of your said band in that behalf, sa fer as the samyn may extend towert ony personis of the said Clangregour or otheris imputt in your landis be thame ; and will and grantis that ye sall na wis be callit, accusit, or in ony wys persewit thairfoir, nochtwithstanding the said generall band thairfoir, or ony clause thairin contenit or vther lawis or ordinances quhatsumevir, anent the quhilkis we dispens be thir presentis. Gevin vnder our signet and subscriuit with our hand at Drymen, the last day of August 1566.

"To our Traist Freynd the Laird of Weym.

"Marie R."

—From the Castle Menzies Charter Room.

Chapter XIII

James MacGregor, Dean of Lismore and Family

FROM Obituary :—

> "1564 7th Dec. Patrick McAyn VcCouill VcAyn slain by James McGestalcar at Ardewynnek and buried at Inchaddin in the tomb of his Fathers.
>
> "1565. June 11th Slaughter of Gregor son of the Dean of Lismore alias McGregor and Robert McConil VcGregor viz in the afternoon of the Pentcost and the house was burnt and they slain by James McGestalker with his accomplices and buried in their grave in the Choir of Inchadin (Kenmore). A just God judges hidden things and punishes those who do them in the third and fourth generation
>
> "1565 July 27 James McGestalcar VcPhatrik and his accomplices were slain by Gregor McGregor of Stronmelocan with his soldiers at Ardowenec They were wicked and oppressors of the poor and the said malefactors could not be suffered to live upon the earth
>
> "1565. Item ane gud symmer and harist viz sexte fyv yeris—gret hayrschippis in mony partis of Scotland, in Stratherne, in lennox in Glenalmond, in Breadalbane bayth slattyr and oppressyon beand mayd in syndry vdr partis be the Erl of Ergill and McGregor and ther complesis. Siclyk in Strathardill mony men slain be the men of Atholl and the Stuartis of Lorn "

The following passages are taken from the introduction by William Skene, Esq, to "The Dean of Lismore's Book," a selection of ancient gaelic poetry :—

"In the latter part of the fifteenth and beginning of the sixteenth centuries, there dwelt here, the village of Fortingall, a family of the name of Macgregor. They were descended from a vicar of Fortingall, who, at the time when, during the century preceding the Reformation, the Catholic Church was breaking up, and their benefices passing into the hands of laymen, secured for himself and his descendants the vicarage of Fortingall and a lease of the Church Lands

"Of the history of this family we know something from an obituary commenced by one of his descendants, and continued to the year 1579, by the Curate of Fortingall (Fothergill) which is still preserved

" His son (whether legitimate or illegitimate we know not), was Ian Rewych, or John the Grizzled, termed Makgewykar or son of the Vicar.[1]

" His Grandson was Dougall Maol, or Dougall the Bald or Tonsured called patronymically Dougall Johnson, or the son of John. This Dougall Johnson appears in 1511 as a notary public, and dwelt at Tullichmullin, where his wife Katherine, daughter of Donald McClawe, alias Grant, died in 1512. He is twice mentioned in the ' Obituary or Chronicle of Fortingall'; in 1526, as repairing the cross in Inchadin, or the old Church of Kenmore, situated on the north bank of the river Tay, nearly opposite Taymouth Castle; and in 1529, as placing a stone cross in Larkmonemerkyth, the name of a pass among the hills which leads from Inchadin to the south.

" Of Dougall the Bald, the son of John the Grizzled, we have no farther mention ; but of his family we know of two sons, James and Duncan.[2]

" James was a churchman. He appears as a notary-public, an office then held by ecclesiastics, along with his father, in the year 1511, and he early attained to honour and influence, through what channel is unknown ; for in 1514, we find him as Dean of Lismore, an island in Argyllshire, lying between the districts of Lorn and Morven, which was at that time the episcopal seat of the Bishops of Argyll. He was besides Vicar of Fortingall and Firmarius or tenant of the church lands ; and died possessed of those benefices in the year 1551, and was buried in the choir of the old church of Inchadin.

" In 1557, a year after his death, Gregor Macgregor, son of the deceased Sir James Macgregor, Dean of Lismore, as became the head of a small, but independent sept of the MacGregors, and with a due regard to its safety, bound himself to Colin Campbell of Glenurchy and his heirs, ' taking him for his chief in place of the Laird of MacGregor,' and giving him his calp.

" In 1557 Gregor and Dougall MacGregors, natural sons of Sir James Macgregor, receive letters of legitimation ; and in 1574 Dougall MacGregor appears as Chancellor of Lismore.

" It is unnecessary for our purpose to follow the history of this family any further ; suffice it to say, that the two brothers James and Duncan, members of a Clan which though under the ban of the Government and exposed to the grasping aggression of their powerful neighbours, the Campbells of Glenurchy, considered themselves as peculiarly Highland, and had high pretensions as descended from the old celtic monarchs of Scotland—connected with the church, and as such possessing some cultivation of mind and such literary taste as Churchmen at that time had, yet born and reared in the farm house of Tullichmullin, in the secluded vale of

---

[1] 1542, Dec. Death of Katherine Neyn Ayn Neill, wife of Ian Rewych Makgewykar, in Achlie (Auchline).

[2] Duncan McCowle voil vic Eoyne Rewych.

Fortingall, and imbued with that love for old Highland story and cherished fondness for Highland song, which manifests itself so much in many a quiet country Highlander, and which the scenery and associations around them were so well calculated to foster—the one from his high position in the Church of Argyll, having peculiar facilities for collecting the poetry current in the West Highlands— the other though his brother, yet as was not uncommon in those days, his servitor or amanuensis, and himself a poet—and both natives of the Perthshire Highlands —collected and transcribed into a commonplace book, gaelic poetry obtained from all quarters.[1]

"This collection has fortunately been preserved It is, unquestionably, a native compilation made in the central Highlands, upwards of three hundred years ago"

"1564 April 25 at Edinburgh   Edward Reidheugh of Cultebragane became surety for Patrik Duncansoun in Glenlednoch Patrik Johnsoun McGregour there and Patrik his brother That that and ilk ane of thame sall enter thair persones in ward within the Burgh of Perth

"May 25 at Edinburgh Archibald Naper of Merchainstoun became plege and souertye for the entrie of Neill McGregour McInvalycht in Tullichchannane within the lordschip of Dessoyer[2] and Toveir."—Record of Justiciary.

The following is the text of a warrant given by Queen Mary to the avengers of the murder of the son of the Dean of Lismore, which had occurred on the 2nd June 1565:—

"1565 June   The Quenis Majestie understanding that Patrick dounk-anesoun,[3] James McGregour,[4] Malcallum Croy McGregour Pitteny,[5] John Cam McCondoquhy VcGregor in Fortingill,[6] Malcum McGregour in Drum-quharrycht,[7] Patrik Johnsoun McGregour in Glenleidnocht (Innerzaldie),[8] Patrik his breder,[9] John McCondoquhy Mcgregour thair,[9] John dun-cansoun his broder,[9] and Neil McAne wallicht in Tullyctcannan[10] ar under souerities actid in the buikis of Secrete Counsell and adwurnale for keping

---

[1] Such of these poems as relate to MacGregors are given in Chapter VII
[2] Discher or Deasaidh and Toir or Tuagh—side facing Leven and side facing north respectively, of Loch Tay
[3] In Glenleidnoch.—See 25th April 1564, page 92.
[4]—[5]—[6]—Not yet identified
[7] The place is near Aberfeldy.
[8] Also mentioned page 92.
[9] These sons of Duncan were also in Glenleidnoch
[10] Neil, son of John McInvallycht—but on 25th April 1264 he is styled son of Gregor.

of gude rewle and entering agane in certain wardis as thai salbe requirit as the actis maid thairupoun at lenth beris And now laitlie umquhile gregour Denesoun in Stwix ane peciabill trew man quha witht the personis abune written wes under souertie, is cruellie murtherit be certane rebellis for persequwtioun of quhome nane ar mair mete nor the above namit personis having thair neir kinsman slane, quhilkis dar nocht put on armes and persew the tressonabill murthuraris of the said umqle Gregour be reason of thair souerties standand undischargit.   And thairfoir the Quinis Matie ordanis the Justice Clerk and his deputis and the Secretar and his deputis Keparis of the buikis of Secret Counsale to deleit and put forth all actis furth of the saidis buikis or uther of thame be the quhilkis the foirsaidis personis or thair souerties ar in ony wyss restrictit, for hir hieness having sa gude experience of thair gude behaviour the tyme, thinkis nocht expedient to retene thame langer under the Band of Caution. Kepand ther presentis for thair warrant signed Marie R."—Taken from the original in the Books of Adjournal and copied into the "Chartulary."

This Deed, relieving the relations from their obligation to keep the peace and thus authorising them to pursue the murderers, is very remarkable, and is specially noticed by Mr Donald Gregory in his "Historical Sketch."[1] The retribution on the culprits was formally carried out by the acting Chief himself, in the month of July, as recorded on the previous page.

About the same time, however, the following Letter of Fire and Sword was issued against the ClanGregor by the Earl of Argyll :—

"At Dunstafnis the 16. day of June 1565. my Lorde Erle of Ergyle with awyis (advice) of his kin, and friends present for the tyme, commandis that all and sindrie his subjectis, barrones, gentillmen, and tennentis, within his boundais, in cais the Clangregour now being the Quenis rebellis and enemies to the hous of Glenurquhay resort to thair boundis Sall with ane woce concur togidder and rais the schoutt aganis thame, and persew thaim with bayth sword and fyre to ther destructioun, and givis full commissione to every man within our boundis to tak and apprehend the said Clangregour quhairever they may be gotten, and the takeris therof to have their escheit to their awin behuif, certifeing quhaevir contravenis this act or favouris or concelis the said Clangregour in ony sort that we sall persew thaim be extremite of law according to our former act maid theranent.

"And in cais the said Clangregour gett ony refuge or fortificatioune of ony utheris our nychtbouris or cuntremen ewis us, we promise to tak plane pert with the said Lard of Glenurquhay in persute of thame and their fortifearis according to equitie with our haill force and poeer."

---

[1] See Chapter XIV.

T

Glenurquhay, in the ground of great abuses committed by him in the face of his Bond, was later deprived of his commission to search out the Resetters of the ClanGregor.

HENRY AND MARY—DISCHARGE OF GLENURCHY'S COMMISSION.

"1565. August 25   The King and Quenis Majesties understanding that thair wes ane commissioun gevin be hir Hienes of befoir to Colene Campbell of Glenurquhy, Gevand and committand to him full power to pas serche and seik all maner of personis duelland in quhatsumevir partis or places of this realme quhilkis in ony time sould happin to resset ony rebellis and surname of ClanGregour or thair complices or to furneis thame oppinlie, quietlie or be quhatsumevir uther cullour, meit drink cleythis, armour or utheris necessaries and to apprehend and tak thame and send thame to the Justice or his deputtis to underly the law thairfoir as the said commissioun of the dait at Edinburgh the 8. day of Jan. 1563 mair fullelie proportis.   Quhilk Commissioun the said Colene hes not onelie alluterlie (utterly) abusit Bot alsua under cullour thairof hes be himself and uther evill personis his complices, in his name of his causing command, assistance and ratihabitioun , (confirmation) committit. sensyne diverss and sindrie sorningis, oppressionis, heirschippis, spulzies, yea and crewall slauchteris upoun diverss oure saidis soveranis liegis not being rebellis, and thair throw the said commissioun is worthie to be dischargeit and annullit   Quhairfoir oure saidis Soveranis be thir presentis casses (breks, make void) annullis and dischargeis the said commissioun and all points thereof and discernis the samyn to expyre and have no forder strenth in tyme cuming for the causes foirsaid ; and ordainis letteris to be direct heirupoun to mak publicatioun heirof in forme as efferis, sua that nane of thair graces liegis pretend ignorance herein "—Record of Secret Council, Acta, quoted in " Chartulary "

Complaint against the Macgregors by the tenants in Menteith :—

"1555-6. Jan 17   Anent the Complaint presented by Andro Schaw of Knockhill, Will Schaw his sone and apperand heir, James Edmonstoune of Ballintone, James Balfour of Boghall, James Balfour of McCanestoun, Archibald Edmonstoune, Agnes Schaw relict of umquhile Alex. Schaw of Cambusmoir, and divers others their Majesty's tenants and feuars of their proper lands of Menteith are utterly herned, wasted, and destroyed by the ClanGregour and other evil doers And in special the lands belonging to the complainers foresaid where through they are unable and may not pay the feu mails thereof until the time the said lands be occupied, laboured, and manured by tenants as they were of before, Requiring therefore command to be given to the comptroller and Chamberlains to desist and cease from all craving and uptaking of the mails of the said waste lands."—Record of Secret Council Acta.

" 1555-6. March 21. Remission to Earl of Argyle and others for aiding the Duke of Chastelherault . . . . One of the others mentioned is ' Gregor McGregor of Glenstrae.' "—Record of Privy Seal.

Chastelherault's insurrection to oppose the kingly dignity of the Queen's husband being conferred by Royal Proclamation, instead of by Act of Parliament, took place in Sep. 1565.

From " Chartulary " :—

" 1566 June 17. Precept of Remission to John Murray and Andrew Murray for aiding the ClanGregor in their murderous homicides &a.
    "August 31. Menzies of that Ilk on account of the lawless and independant spirit of the ClanGregor in Rannoch as by him pleaded, obtained an exemption from answering for these under the Seal and subscription of Queen Mary."—Record of Secret Council.

Contract between the Earl of Atholl and Glenurquhay and their friends :—

" 1569 May 6. At Ballocht. Thairfoir to be bundin that thai sall tak plane, leill and trew and afald part in persewing invading and suppressing of all sik wickit and ewill personis and specialie the Clangregour quhay daylie usis thame selffis maist horribillie in the forsaidis crymes intolerabill to the leigis of thir boundis next liand unto thame and that nether ane of the saidis parties sall appoint in ony of the said ClanGregour in ony tyme cuming by the avis of utheris ay and quhill thai be brocht under obediens to our Souerane Lord, or ellis bannisit the realme or wrekit within the samyn.
" 1569 Sep. 8. Gift to Alexander Stewart of Pitarreg of the Escheit of . . Malcum beg M^cferlane
        Duncan Abbrache MacGregour [1]
        Gregour Gar McGregour his bruthir [1]
        Patrik McGregour his bruthir alsua [1]
        Gregour McGregour of Glenschra [2]

[1] The three sons of Gregor, eldest son of Duncan Laddosach, the last of these being usually known as Patrick Adholach or Auloch, *i.e.*, brought up in Atholl as was Duncan in Lochaber.
[2] Glenstray.

Malcum Makcoulkeyr zoungar alias McGregour[1]
Gregour McCoulkeir[1]
John McCoulkeir his brethir[1]
Duncan Macphatrik voir[2]
Allaster McRobert voir alias McGregour in Strathyre[3]
Duncan oig McGregour Ardchallie[4]
Duncan McGregour V^cNeill
James McGregour Makkillip in Kallyn
Robert Moyr V^cCaster (Vicalaster) alias McGregour.

now pertaining to oure Souerane Lord be ressoun of escheit throw being of the said personis ordourlie denuncit his Majesteis Rebellis and at the horne for art and part of the slauchter of umquhile Hew Stewart and John Stewart his brother committit in the Landis of Balquhidder in Dec. 1568."—Record of Privy Seal.

Scotland had again had the misfortune of a long regency till the last Regent, the Earl of Morton, was dismissed, and the young King nominally took up the reins of government himself in 1577, at the age of twelve years.

An interval in legislation relating to the Highlands appears after 1665-6 till 1580-1, when King James VI. began a series of minute and watchful legislation against the ClanGregor, with the intention of pacifying the Highlands in general.

[1] Descendants of Dougall Ciar.
[2][3] Not yet identified.
[4] Duncan, younger son of Duncan Laddosach, who here is shown still in Ardchoill, he seems to have kept the distinctive name of "young" through life.

Chapter XIV

CONTINUATION of the "Historical Notices" of Professor Donald Gregory, from Chapter III., page 35 :—

"The ClanGregor had during the reign of James V. become very numerous in Balquhidder, and in the adjacent district of Strathearn, and as may well be supposed were proportionally annoying to the Lowlands next to that great natural boundary by which the Highlands are so strikingly defined. This appears from several passages in the Justiciary Records, and likewise from a deposition made before the Lords of Council on 22nd Dec. 1530, by John Drummond of Inner-peffray, and William Murray of Tullibardine, to the following effect: That Sir John Campbell of Calder, Knight, be authorite, supple and help of the Erle of Ergyle, may cause the ClanGregour to keep gude rewle within thair boundis, siclik as uther pacifeit landis adjacent to them; and that the Kingis liegis may lief in rest and pece for onie skaith to be done be the said ClanGregour, the said Sir John bindand him thairfoir with support of the said Erle as said is.[1] This proceeding was two days after followed by a respite to the ClanGregor from all criminal actions for the space of ten days, with licence to them to appear before the King and Council within that time 'to wirk and mene for thaim of all attemptatts bigane, and to geif plegeis and sufficient securitie for gud rewle in tyme to cum.'[2]

"In making such incursions, the MacGregors did nothing which others of the Highland Clans were not more or less in the habit of doing. But as their depredations were generally committed in the neighbourhood of Perth or Stirling, where the Secret Council often met, and the Sovereign frequently resided, so they became peculiarly the terror of the government, and subject consequently to the operation of measures which from their extreme severity, as well as from the conflicting interests of the great barons employed in putting them into execution, failed in producing the desired effect, and only succeeded in forcing this devoted Clan to further acts of desperation. By this time indeed, many of the MacGregors were under one pretext or another denuded of every lawful means of supporting themselves and their families. Is it therefore to be wondered at that they should have perpetrated frequent spoliations, impelled as they were by the most necessity?

[1] Acta Dominorum Concilii.   [2] *Ibid.*, 4th Dec. 1530.

Such results, however deplorable, flowed naturally and necessarily from the system, alike impolitic and inhuman, pursued with lands alleged to belong to the Crown ; and by which, as we have seen, a numerous tribe was driven from one degree of privation to another, to *struggle for existence* against those who had law, no doubt, as well as power, but hardly justice, on their side

"About the year 1560 arose a deadly feud between the MacGregors on one side and Sir Colin Campbell of Glenurchy on the other   From the representations on the subject to the Secret Council, a Commission of fire and sword was in 1563 issued to sundry noblemen and barons, against the ClanGregor [1] Of this most anomalous production, the precursor of many such in later times, and which, in the preambles, indulge like this in the most unqualified abuse of the unfortunate race against whom they were directed, a prominent feature is the strict manner in which it is directed that the Clan be expelled from all the districts in which they dwelt, or to which they were in the habit of resorting, without specifying, or so much as hinting at, any other district into which they might be received.   The impolitic and remorseless severity of this measure, which could only have been carried into effect by a universal massacre, naturally rendered it abortive   Another commission was accordingly next year (1564) issued to *two* only of the *nine* former commissioners,[2] from which we may infer that the former had not answered it's purpose

"Sir Colin Campbell of Glenurchy had, about the date of the first of these commissions, been individually armed with a separate and additional commission of fire and sword against the *Harbourers* of the ClanGregor, in whatever part of the kingdom [3]—a proof that the Secret Council not only neglected to provide a place to which the ClanGregor might, when ejected from their homes, retire, but absolutely attempted to exclude them from every spot on which they might, on retiring, seek shelter, or even existence   Sir Colin, under colour of his individual commission, perpetrated on the lieges, as appears, atrocities not inferior to those alleged against the ClanGregor ; and in consequence of a regular complaint by the barons and landlords of Strathearn, was, in the following year, threatened with loss of his commission, and in 1565, having been deaf to remonstrance, and persevering in the most intolerable outrages, actually deprived of it

"As Glenurchy had been thus pre-eminent in severity against all whom he chose to suspect of tenderness towards the persecuted ClanGregor, we may fairly presume that his conduct towards the latter was not remarkable for moderation.   In the manuscript history, indeed, of the Campbells of Glenurchy, and in a passage written by order of his son and successor, it is expressly asserted of him that 'he wes ane greit Justiciar all his time, throch the quhilk he sustenit that deidly feid of the Clan-Gregour ane lang space ; and, besides that he causit execut to the death mony notabill lymmaris, he beheidet the Laird of Makgregour himselff, at Kenmor, in presence

---

[1] Record of Secret Council, *ad annum* 1563   [2] The Earls of Argyle and Athol
[3] Record of Secret Council, *ad annum* 1563, and *ibid.* 1564.

of the Erle of Athole, and the Lord Justice Clerk, and sindry other nobill men.'
With the assistance as appears of Macdonald of Keppoch he invaded Rannoch, the
ClanGregor's stronghold. His proceedings, however, on this occasion were formally complained of by the Laird of Weyme; whence we may infer that, in this, as
in other instances, Glenurchy had overleaped the limits of his double and but too
ample commission.

"There occurs in the history of the Clan at this time a singular instance of the
weakness of Government, and of the difficulty of administering the laws in the then
state of the Highlands. A number of the best disposed of the MacGregors had, on
being charged to that effect, given hostages and found security for their good behaviour. While under this obligation one of them lost his life in a private feud
with some neighbouring Highlanders. His kinsmen eager for revenge, but at the
same time deterred by the penalty in the bond from taking it on the spot, applied
to the Sovereign (Queen Mary), and obtained, not the trial of the alleged culprits,
but a warrant to relieve themselves from their obligation to keep the peace, seeing,
as the warrant expresses it, 'that nane ar mair mete for persequutioun of the tressonabill murthouraris of the said umqle Gregor nor the foirnamit persones hauing
thair neir kinsman slane quhilkis dar nocht put on armes and persew the said
murthouraris be ressoun of thair souerteis standand undischargeit.'[1]

"It cannot be surprising that the disorders of the ClanGregor, far from being
suppressed, should under such a government, have increased with each succeeding
year. We find accordingly, that in the year 1566, the tenants and feuars of Menteith presented to the Government a supplication praying to be relieved from payment of their rents and duties, the whole Lordship having, as stated in the complaint,
been laid waste by the ClanGregor.[2]

"That the ClanGregor were in many instances the tools merely of their more
powerful neighbours is highly probably. The celebrated George Buchanan, in a
political pamphlet, printed and circulated in 1571, alluding to the Hamilton
Faction, introduces, as illustrative of this theme, a passage descriptive of the then
known state of society in Scotland. 'Howbeit,' says he, 'the bullerant blude of a
King and a Regent about thair hartis quhairof the lust in thair appetite gevis thame
little rest dayly and hourly making neu provocatioun; yit the small space of rest
quhilk thay haue beside the executioun of thair crewaltie thay spend in devising of
generall unquyetness thro' the haill countrie; for, nocht content of it that thay
thameselffis may steal, bribe, and reave, thay set out ratches on euerie side to gnaw
the pepillis banes, after that thay haue consumit the flesch, and houndis out, ane of
thame the Clan Gregour, another the Grantis and Clanquhattane, another Balcleugh
and Fairnyhirst, another the Johnstounis and Armstrangis.'[3]   The peculiar circum-

[1] Warrant preserved in the Books of Adjournal, dated in June 1565.—See next chapter.
[2] Record of Secret Council, 1566.
[3] Admonitoun direct to the trew Lordis.—Book of Taymouth.

stances, doubtless, in which the ClanGregor had been so long placed in relation to their ancient possessions, must have disposed them to enter with alacrity into every plan, however violent and rapacious, by which they might have the slightest chance to better their condition; and more particularly as, in any event, they had nothing to lose.

"In 1581 an act of the Legislature, reprehensible for it's glaring iniquity, was passed under the title of 'Ane additioun to the Actis maid aganis notorious Theiffis and Sornaris of Clannis.' By this it was made lawful for any individual who might happen to sustain damage from a notorious thief, or from a ruffian insisting to be an inmate of a family, living at its expense, and on the best it could produce, provided the actual delinquent could not be laid hold of, to apprehend and slay the bodies, and arrest the goods of any of the Clan to which the culprit belonged, until satisfaction was made to the injured party by the rest of the said Clan. This act must have been severely felt by the ClanGregor, whose feud with the family of Glenurchy still continued to rage with unabated animosity. About this time accordingly Gregor MacGregor of Glenstray, Laird of MacGregor, was executed by Duncan Campbell, younger, of Glenurchy.

"As there is something singular in the history of the MacGregors of Glenstray, the noticing of a few particulars concerning them may not be irrelevant. Soon after the extinction, whether real or apparent, of the very ancient family of Glenurchy, we find a branch of the ClanGregor holding the small estate of Glenstray, 20 merks old extent, as vassals of the Earl of Argyle. The MacGregors of Glenstray were allied matrimonially to most of the principal families of the name of Campbell; and so long as they continued to hold their lands of the Argyle family, they appear to have flourished, so as to become, in process of time, the most consequential house of their Clan. On the other hand, when the Earl of Argyle had conveyed the superiority of Glenstray to Campbell of Glenurchy, which he did in 1554, these Macgregors shared the wretched fate of the rest of the Clan, as it was obviously the great aim of the Glenurchy family to get rid of every vassal of the name of MacGregor. They refused to enter Gregor MacGregor MacGregor of Glenstray as heir to his father, on the ground possibly of his being a rebel in the eye of the law; and after the death of Gregor, who as formerly mentioned was executed by Campbell, younger, of Glenurchy, they denied the proper feudal investiture to his son Allaster, who in 1590 was legally ejected from the lands of Glenstray, on the assertion that he was merely tenant of these lands against the will of the proprietor as Sir Duncan was pleased to style himself. We see then that this time the leading family of the name of MacGregor was in no better situation than others of the landless Clan.

"In January 1584-5 the Secret Council summoned several of the Highland Chiefs and Barons connected with Perthshire and Argyleshire, and amongst the rest Ewin MacGregor, Tutor of Glenstray, to appear personally before the King and

Council, to answer to such things as should be inquired at them touching the suppression of the Lymmars and broken men of the Highlands, by whom the countries of Lennox, Menteith, Stirlingshire, and Strathearn had, as alleged, been cruelly harassed. What proceedings, if any, were adopted by the Council, does not appear. It is probable that they now, however, commenced the draft of a long act of parliament, vulgarly called 'the General Band,' and which was passed in 1587. By one of the many sections of this voluminous act, it was declared that theft committed by landed men should be reckoned treason, and punished as such. It was farther ordained, that the Captains, Chiefs, and Chieftains of the Clans, both Border and Highland, be noted in a roll, and obliged under pain of fire and sword, to surrender to the King and Council certain pledges or hostages, liable to suffer death if redress of injuries were not made by the persons for whom they lay. We shall presently have occasion to see the attempts made, under the operation of this act, to reduce the ClanGregor to obedience.

"The slaughter of Drummondernoch, Under King's Forrester of Glenartney, said to have been committed in 1589 or 1590, by some of the ClanGregor, induced the Secret Council to grant in 1590 a commission of fire and sword to various noblemen and gentlemen, for pursuit of the whole Clan, of whom nearly 200 are mèntioned nominatim in the commission and which is said to have been executed with extreme severity in the district of Balquhidder especially, and around Lochearn.

"In July 1591 Sir Duncan Campbell of Glenurchy had a commission of fire and sword against the ClanGregor, who are described as being for the most part rebels, and at the horn for divers horrible crimes and offences committed by them ; and also against their harbourers ; with power to convocate the lieges of Breadalbane and the adjacent districts to aid in the execution. The various noblemen and barons of these countries are enjoined under severe penalties to aid Sir Duncan with all power. The King as stated in the commission had been informed of certain bonds of maintenance subsisting between Sir Duncan on the one part, and some of the more leading individuals of the ClanGregor on the other, and between the last mentioned and sundry others of the noblemen, barons, and gentlemen ; and which if suffered to remain in force might, as was thought, hinder the execution of the commission. All such bonds were therefore declared void and null, and Glenurchy strictly prohibited from entering into any engagements of this nature. Six months however, had scarce elapsed when Sir Duncan obtained his Majesty's licence to enter into bonds of friendship with the MacGregors, including an oblivion of all past animosities and authorising him to liberate such of the Clan as were then in his custody, in consequence as may be presumed, of his fidelity in the discharge of his late commission against them. In virtue of the royal licence, a contract was entered into by the principal barons in the Highlands of Perthshire, among others Sir Duncan Campbell on one part, and Allaster Roy MacGregor of

Glenstray, having 26 of the leading persons of the ClanGregor as his sureties, on the other. The parties became bound to abstain from mutual slaughters and depredations; and in any disputes that might arise, to renounce their own jurisdictions, and submit to the commissariat of Dunblane. The youthful Laird of MacGregor soon found to his confusion that he had undertaken a task beyond his strength; nor was it long ere he incurred the usual penalties of the law for non-fulfilment.

"On 1st Feb: 1592-3, Archibald seventh Earl of Argyle, whilst yet in his nonage, had from the King and Council, a commission 'aganis all and sindrie of the wicked ClanGregour and the Stewartis of Balquhidder'; with power to charge them by his precept to appear before him, to find surety, or to enter pledges for the preservation of peace and order, as the Earl should think most expedient. Recusants were given over to the discipline of fire and sword; and Argyle empowered to convocate the lieges within the sheriffdoms of Bute, of Tarbet, and of so much of those of Perth and Stirling as lay within 21 parishes specified, for pursuit of the persons of the ClanGregor and the Balquhidder Stewarts. A proclamation accordingly was issued to all the barons and landed gentlemen within the districts above mentioned, to assist with their whole force; whilst 15 principal householders of the name of Macgregor were ordained to be charged to appear before Argyll as his Majesty's Justice General and Lieutenant in those parts, on a certain and early day, to answer to such things as should be laid to their charge touching their obedience to the laws, under pain of being held 'part-takers' with the 'broken men' of the Clan in all their wicked deeds and punished accordingly. About this time, those barons and gentlemen who had the ClanGregor as tenants, and who in the Records are forensically styled 'landlords of the ClanGregor' forced by the severe enactments of the General Band, which made every landlord answerable for the misdemeanours of his tenants, began to take measures for an universal ejection of the Clan from their possessions; and as far as the forms of law could go, numerous ejectments did in consequence take place,—to such an amount indeed, that when, in July 1596, the Laird of MacGregor appeared personally before the King and Council at Dunfermline, and bound himself for the good behaviour of his Clan, there was as may confidently be affirmed, scarce a single farm occupied by a MacGregor, unless by force, and in defiance of the proprietor. On this occasion the Chief after acknowledging his past offences and expressing his contrition, promised to remain in attendance on the King, as a hostage for the obedience of his tribe. He seems however, to have soon become tired of this unwonted thraldom, where he found himself out of his natural element and to have made his escape to the mountains.

"Situate as this unfortunate Gentleman, and his no less unfortunate Clan, now were, they appeared to Argyle (who although only a youth, had already begun to distinguish himself by that crafty policy which marked the whole of his long and

crooked career) fit instruments for extending his power and influence in the
Highlands and for avenging his private quarrels, as will be illustrated in the
sequel; and it will scarcely be believed that distant tribes under the order of this
nobleman plundered and laid waste the lands occupied by the ClanGregor, in order
no doubt, that the measures of retaliation which the latter were expected to adopt,
might still farther widen the breach between them and the constituted authorities,
and make them more ready to follow the perfidious councils of this arch-dissimulator.
The Laird of MacGregor, however, took the uncommon step of resorting to a Court
of law for redress, being induced to this probably, by the persuasions of his real
friends or by the heavy penalties under which he lay.   He succeeded in obtaining
a sentence of the Court for a large sum of damages; but as may be supposed, it
was easier to obtain the sentence than to put it in execution in a state of society
of which some notion may be formed from the terms of a protest taken by
MacGregor's Counsel in this suit. 'that the Laird of Macgregor and his kyn, wer
the first sen King James 1st his tyme that cam and sought justice.' This assertion
cannot be taken literally but there must evidently have existed good grounds for
making it.

   "In May 1599, the Barons on whose lands any of the Clan resided were
charged to produce before the King and Council on 3d July, each of them the
persons of the name of MacGregor for whom he was bound to answer; and the
Chief and his whole Clan were charged to appear on the same day, 'to underlye
such order as should be taken with them touching the weal and quietness of the
country.' On 25th July 'Offeris for Allaster Makgregour of Glenstray' were in his
name presented to the King by Sir John Murray of Tullibardine, Knight, Sir
Duncan Campbell of Glenurchy Knight, and John Grant of Freuchy (known as the
Laird of Grant).[1]

   "In pursuance of these offers various proceedings took place, in which the
anxiety of the Council to reduce the ClanGregor to obedience without undue
severity is very manifest.   All their good intentions however were secretly frustrated
by Argyle, who undid in the Highlands, what had been done at Court, whilst the
whole blame meanwhile rested upon the unfortunate Laird of MacGregor, who was
charged by the Council with having dishonourably violated his most solemn
engagements.   For proof of this assertion reference is made to the dying
declaration of MacGregor, ... and likewise to a statement made by the
gentlemen who had become his sureties, that the 'default of the not entrie of the
said Allaster with his said pledge, at the peremptour day appointit to that effect,
wes not in thame (the sureties) bot proceidit upoun sum occasionis quhilk intervenit
and fell oute befoir the day of his entrie, quhilkis discourageit and terrifiet him to
keip the first dyet.'

   "At last the King and Council in dispair of reducing the Clan to the obedience

---

[1] These "Offeris" are given in full,—Chapter XXV.

of the laws by the existing plan, constituted the Earl of Argyle his Majesty's Lieutenant and Justice in the whole bounds inhabited by the ClanGregor, and invested him with the most ample powers, extending over as well the harbourers of the MacGregors as the MacGregors themselves; and it was provided that the former should be responsible for the crimes of those of the latter to whom they might give shelter and protection. The commission was to continue in force for a year, and longer if not specially discharged; and the King promised not to show favour or to grant pardon to any of the Macgregors during the continuance of the commission, but to remit them and their suits to the Earl's disposal.

"Under Argyle's administration, the Clan, as might be expected from the policy pursued by that nobleman, became daily more troublesome to the Lowlands, and to such of the proprietors more particularly who had the misfortune to be at feud with Argyll. The Lairds of Buchanan and Luss suffered severely from the incursions of the ClanGregor; and those of Ardkinlass and Ardincaple escaped assassination only by the Laird of MacGregor's refusal to execute in their cases the revolting fiats of the King's Lieutenant. Finally in the spring of 1603 at the instigation of Argyle couched probably in the most imperious terms, MacGregor with his men of Rannoch invaded the Lennox, and fought the celebrated conflict of Glenfrune, opposed by the Colquhouns and their friends and dependants; and having routed these with great carnage, ravaged the whole district, and carried off an immense booty.

"The King and Council, horrified by the intelligence of this hostile inroad, proceeded to take the most severe measures for bringing the offenders to justice. A series of sanguinary enactments against the unhappy ClanGregor was crowned by that of the proscription of the names of Gregor and MacGregor under pain of death, which bears date 3d April 1603.[1] Argyll was the first to turn upon the unfortunate chief, whom, and several gentlemen of his Clan, he betrayed in circumstances peculiarly infamous, and all inquiry into the origin of the raid was studiously stifled to save the Earl. The Declaration however of his victim produced on the trial, and preserved in the original, distinctly charges Argyll with having caused MacGregor not only to violate engagements under which he had come to the King and Council in 1599, as above detailed, but to commit many of the crimes for which he was about to suffer death.[2]

[1] See Excerpts of Record of Secret Council in the Earl of Haddington's Collection, preserved in the Advocates' Library, Edinburgh. The volume or volumes, whence these Excerpts for the years 1603-4-5 were taken, are unfortunately missing.—D. Gregory.

[2] This is evident from there being a packed jury on the trial of the Laird of MacGregor, notwithstanding the notoriety of the crimes charged, and from the indecent haste which mark the whole of the proceedings in Edinburgh; not to mention from Calderwood's History, and other sources, that seven gentlemen of the name of MacGregor were executed along with the Laird of MacGregor without a trial, although, as asserted by the candid historian, "reputed honest for their own parts."—D. Gregory.

" I have thus, in the preceding pages, endeavoured to show that the causes of the proscription of the ClanGregor were closely connected with the impolitic system on which the ancient crown lands were managed ; and that this Clan suffered more severely under that system than others from having lost their early freehold possessions, or at least the greater part of these by forfeiture, as early as the reign of King Robert Bruce, and being thus deprived of that weight in the Councils of a rude nation which uniformly accompanies the possession of extensive land-property.   This view is farther confirmed by a fact that I have lately discovered, that King James V. actually proscribed the Clan Chattan by acts equally severe with those directed by his grandson against the ClanGregor. Wherein consisted the difference between the two Clans?   The answer is obvious. The Captain of the Clan Chattan and several of the chief gentlemen of his tribe, held extensive possessions under the Crown, and were thus in a manner independent of the great families in the neighbourhood.   How different the case was with the ClanGregor we have already seen ; and the fate of the Macdonalds of Glencoe (who were in other respects more favourably situated) is nearly parallel to that of the MacGregors and may be traced to the same causes."

Chapter XV

MacGregor of Glenstray

RETURNING to the MacGregors of Glenstray it was noted in Chapter V.[1] that John of Glenstray died of the hurt of an arrow, and was succeeded by his brother.

VI. Gregor Roy MacGregor of Glenstray, who was never infeofed in this property although bearing the title of it. Archibald Earl of Argyll sold the superiority of the twenty markland of Glenstray to Colin Campbell of Glenurquhay in 1556, and granted the ward and marriage of Gregor MacGregor, heir of the late Allaster, to him.

The "Black Book of Taymouth" contains the following short history :—

"Gregor Roy his (John's) brother succeidit to him The said Gregour Roy mariet the Laird of Glenlyoun's dochter, 'by whom he had' Allaster McGregour and Johne Dow McGregour his brother. the foresaid Gregour wes execute be Colne Campbell of Glenurquhay."

Possibly Sir Colin might have befriended him if he had been willing to give up his own Clan, but Gregor evidently preferred to cast in his lot with his persecuted brethren. His name is found in several of the complaints against the MacGregors, and in 1563 we have seen in a previous page[2] that he endeavoured to "fortify" himself, as it was called, by a treaty of alliance with Stewart of Appin, a family who had also "trokings" with MacGregor of Roro ; but there is no evidence of his having led any great outbreak, and the notices of the Clan in the twenty years succeeding the death of Duncan Ladosach and his son Gregor, also called Roy, not having been specially turbulent, it must be supposed that there were

---

[1] At page 55.   [2] Chapter XII., page 132.

some feuds, the history of which has not been transmitted, or other causes to excite the malignity of Glenurquhay and as it seems the displeasure of the Government. Tradition appears to confound the death of Duncan Ladosach with that of young Glenstray; both deeds were the work of Glenurquhay, but it is apparently to the latter to whom reference is made in the Biography of Sir Colin in the "Black Book": "he beheiddit the laird off McGregour himselff at Kandmoir in presens of the Erle of Atholl, the justice clerk and sundrie other noblemen."

> "In 1569. A commission was given to the Laird of Glenurchy to 'justify' Gregor McGregor of Glenstray, who was accordingly beheaded on the green of Kenmore."—Breadalbane Papers in Report of The Historical Commission.
> "Obituary. 1570 the 7. day of Apryll Gregor McGregor of Glensra heddyt at Balloch."

There have been conflicting theories as to the hero of the beautiful gaelic song "Cumha Ghriogair MhicGhriogair," but from tradition and various circumstances it seems probable that Gregor of Glenstray was the Gregour Roy nam Bassan gheal (of the white hand or palm), and from the "Black Book" his marriage with a daughter of Campbell of Glenlyon has been ascertained. The gaelic words of this old lament are here given with the English translation, both copied from the "Killin Collection of Gaelic Songs" by Charles Stewart, Esq., Tighnduin Killin, which has the following preface giving the Glenlyon tradition of the story :—

> "In the latter half of the sixteenth century lived Duncan Campbell of Glenlyon who was so celebrated for his hospitality that he was known as 'Donnacha Ruadh na Feilach.' His residence was 'Caisteal a Curin-bhan' about two miles above the pass. He had a daughter whom he intended giving in marriage to the Baron of Dall, on the south side of Loch Tay. The daughter was of a different opinion for having met with young Gregor MacGregor of Glenstrae she gave up to him her heart's warmest affections and which he fully returned. In spite of all opposition, she left her father's house, and married him. Duncan was bitterly vexed, and so were the then heads of the eastern Campbells, Sir Colin of Glenurchay and his son 'Black Duncan.' In consequence Gregor and his wife were followed with the most unrelenting enmity. They were often obliged to wander from place to place, taking shelter in caves under rocks, and in thickets of woods. On the night preceding the 7. of April 1570, they had rested under a rock on a hillside above Loch Tay. Next morning after taking such breakfast as in the circumstances they

could compass, the young wife sat herself on the ground, and dandled her young babe in her arms whilst Gregor was fondly playing with it. This endearing episode of pure love and affection was ruthlessly broken in upon. In an instant they were surrounded by a band of their foes, and carried off to Balloch. Gregor was at once condemned to death, and beheaded at Kenmore in presence of Sir Colin; his wife, daughter of the Ruthven, who looked out of an upper window; Black[1]

[2]CUMHA GHRIOGAIR MHICGRIOGAIR.

"Ochan, ochan, ochan, uirigh,
'S goirt mo chridhe a laoigh ;
Ochan, achan, ochani uirigh,
Cha chluinn d' athair ar caoidh.

1 Moch 'sa' mhadain là di-Dòmhnaich
Bha mi 'sùgradh marri 'm ghràdh,
Ach, m' an d' thainig meadhon latha
'S mise bha air mo chradh.

2 Mallach aig maithibh 's aig càirdean,
Rinn mo chràdh air an dòigh ;
Thainig gun fhios air mo ghràdhsa,
'S thug fo smachd e le foill.

3 Na 'm bhiodh da-fhear-dheug d' a chinneach
'S mo Ghriogair air an ceann,
Cha bhiodh mo shuil a sileadh dheur,
No mo leanabh fein gun daimh.

4 Chuir iad a cheann air ploc daraich
Is dhoirt iad 'fhuil mu 'n làr,
Na 'm biodh agamsa sin cupan,
Dh' òlainn di mo shàth.

5 'S truagh nach robh m' athair ann an galar,
Agus Cailein ann am plaigh,
Ged bhiodh nighean an Ruthainaich
Suathadh bhas a' s laimh.

[1] The text is here interrupted to allow the Gaelic song to be opposite the translation.
[2] From the Killin Collection of Gaelic Songs by Charles Stewart of Tighnduin.

Duncan; Atholl the Lord Justice Clerk, and Duncan Campbell, of Glenlyon. Most pitiful of all, the unutterably wretched wife was forced to witness her Husband's execution. Immediately thereafter, with her babe in her arms she was driven forth by her kindred helpless and houseless. The kindness however thus cruelly denied, was abundantly given by others who sorely pitied her sad case. In her great anguish she composed the song that follows, and sung it as a lullaby to her babe :—

LAMENT FOR GRIGOR MACGRIGOR.

(Translation by Charles Stewart.)

"Ochan, ochan, ochan, ooree,
Breaks my heart my own wee dear,
Ochan, ochan, ochan, ooree,
Thy slain father cannot hear.

1 Early on last Sunday morning,
I was joyous with my love ;
Ere that noonday had passed o'er us
I was pierced with sudden grief.

2 Cursed be nobles and my kindred,
Who have sorely stricken me ;
Foul betrayed my own heart's darling,
Seized him fast and laid him low.

3 Were there twelve men of his clanship,
And my Grigor them to lead,
My sad eyes were not thus streaming,
Nor my child so sore bereft.

4 His dear head upon an oak-block,
They have placed, and shed his blood ;
Could I have a cup of that, then
Ah, how deeply could I drink.

5 Oh ! that Colin were plague-smitten,
And my father in sore pain,
Whilst the daughter of the Ruthven,
Rubbed her hands and palms in vain.

X

6 Chuirinn Cailein liath fo ghlasaibh,
  'S 'Donnacha Dubh' an laimh ;
  'S gach Caimbeulach a bha am Bealach
  Gu giulan nan glas-laimh.

7 Rainig mise réidhlein Bhealaich,
  'S cha d' fhuair mi ann tamh.
  Cha d' fhag mi ròinn do m' fhalt gun tarruing,
  No craicionn air mo laimh.

8 'S truagh nach robh mi 'n riochd na h-uiseig
  Spionnadh Ghriogair ann mo lamh,
  'Si chlach ab 'airde anns a chaisteal
  Clach ab 'fhaisg do 'n bhlàr.

9 'S truagh nach robh Fionnlairg na lasair,
  'S Bealach mor na smàl,
  'S Griogair bàn nam basa geala,
  Bhi eadar mo dha laimh.

10 'S ged tha mi gun ubhlan agam,
   'S ubhlan uile aig làch,
   'S ann tha m' ubhal cubhraidh grinn,
   A 's cul a' chinn ri làr.

11 Ged tha mnaithibh chàich aig baile
   Na 'n laidhe 's na cadal seimh,
   'S ann bhios mise aig bruaich mo leapa,
   A bualadh mo dha laimh.

12 'S mor a bannsa bhi aig Griogair,
   Air feadh choille 's fraoich,
   Na bhi aig Baran crion na Dalach,
   An tigh cloich a 's aoil.

13 'S mor bannsa bhi aig Griogair,
   Cur a chruidh do 'n ghleann,
   Na bhi aig Baran crion na Dalach,
   Ag ol air fion 's air leann.

6 Grey haired Colin I would dungeon,
  And 'Black Duncan' make secure,
  Every Campbell within Balloch
  In chained wristlets, I'd make sure.

7 When I reached the plains of Balloch,
  There no resting place I found;
  Not one hair left I untorn,
  Nor my palms one shred upon.

8 Could I fly as does the sky-lark
  I'd tear Grigor from their hands,
  And the highest stone in Balloch
  As the lowest I would lay.

9 Oh, for Finlarig in blazes,
  And proud Balloch steeped in flames.
  Whilst my Grigor, the white palmed one,
  In my arms then rested safe.

10 Though now reft of my own loved one,
   Whilst all others have their own,
   One I had both fragrant, lovely,
   But his head is lowly laid.

11 When the wives of all my kindred
   Are deep wrapt in balmy sleep,
   On my bed I sit sad weeping,
   And my hands I wring in grief.

12 Fain would I be with my Grigor,
   On the heath, or 'mongst the woods.
   Than of Dallach the wee Baron's
   Housed in walls of stone and lime.

13 Fain would I be with my Grigor,
   Driving cows along the glen,
   Than of Dalach the wee Baron's,
   Drinking beer and quaffing wine.

14 'S mor a bannsa bhi aig Griogair,
   Fo brata ruibeach roinn,
   Na bhi aig Baran crion na Dalach,
   Giùlan siòd a 's sroil.

15 Ged biodh cur a 's cathath ann,
   A 's 'latha no seachd sion,'
   Gheibheadh Griogair dhomsa cragan,
   'S an caidlimid fo dhion.

   Ba hu, ba ho, aisrain bhig,
   Cha 'n 'eil thu fathasd ach tlàth,
   'S eagal leam nach tig an latha,
   Gun diol thu d' athair gu bràth."

The compiler of " The Lairds of Glenlyon" records his version of the Glenlyon tradition on the subject of Gregor MacGregor of Glenstrae's marriage to be that her father, Duncan Roy Campbell of Glenlyon, was friendly to Gregor, although probably obliged to follow the lead of his chief, Colin Campbell, at the last. In this work the following prose version of the translation is somewhat closer to the original :—

" On Lammas morn I rejoiced with my love : ere noon my heart was pressed with sorrow.

   "Ochain, ochain, ochain, uiridh,
   Sad my heart my child ·
   Ochain, ochain, ochain, uiridh,
   Thy father hears not our moan.

" Under ban be the nobles and friends who pained me so : who unawares came on my love, and overmastered him by guile.   Ochain &c.

" Had there been twelve of his race, and my Gregor at their head, my eyes would not be dim with tears, nor my child without their father.   Ochain &c.

" They laid his head upon an oaken block . they poured his blood on the ground : oh had I there a cup I would drink of it my fill.

" Oh that my father had been sick, and Colin in the plague, and all the Campbells in Balloch wearing manacles.

" I would have put ' Gray Colin' under lock and ' Black Duncan' in a dungeon, though Ruthven's daughter would be wringing her hands.

" I went to the plains of Balloch, but rest found not there : I tore the hair from my head, the skin from my hands.

14 Fain would I be with my Grigor,
   'Neath a wrapper torn and bare,
   Than of Dalach the wee Baron's,
   Silks and gauzes as my wear,

15 Though it snowed, and though it drifted,
   On a ' day of seven blasts '
   Yet a crag my Grigor found me,
   Where I warmly there could rest.

      Ba hu, ba ho, my own wee dearie,
     Thou art but a little child,
     E'en in manhood, I much fear me,
     You his death can't full redeem."

"Had I the wings of the lark the strength of Gregor in my arms, the highest stone in the castle would have been the one next the ground.

"Oh that Finlarig were wrapped in flames, proud Taymouth lying in ashes, and fair haired Gregor of the white hands in my embrace.

"All others have apples : I have none : my sweet lovely apple has the back of his head to the ground.

"Other men's wives sleep soft in their homes : I stand by the bedside wringing my hands.

"Better follow Gregor through heath and wold, than be with the mean little Baron of Dall[1] in a house of stone and lime.

"Better be with Gregor putting the cattle to the glen, than with the mean little Baron drinking wine and beer.

"Better be with Gregor under sackcloth of hair, than wear silken sheen as the mean Baron's bride.

"Though it snowed and drifted, and was a day of sevenfold storm Gregor would find me a rock, in whose shelter we might lie secure.

     " Ba hu, ba hu, my orphan young,
     For still a tender plant art thou
     And much I fear the day wont come
     When thou shalt earn thy father's fame."

The latter version is much tamer, and the last verse especially seems to miss the widow's longing that her boy should revenge his father's murder.

---

[1] A MacOmie or son of Thomas.

The following letter addressed by Sir Colin Campbell of Glenurquhay
to Gregor McAne, keeper of the Castle of Glenurquhay, only a few months
after the execution of Gregor of Glenstray, shows the old Knight in a very
different light; kind, considerate, and cheerful to a curious degree for a
man who acted as executioner by choice :—

"1570 August 18.   Gregor McAne—I commend me hartilie to yow.   McCallum
Dow hes schawin me quhow the Clangregour hes tain up your geir, and your puir
tenentis geir, the quhil I pray yow tak no thocht of, for albeit I haf na ky to
recompanss yow instantlie, I sall God willinge mak yow and youris suir of rowmis
that sall mak yow mair profeit nor the geir that ye have tint at this tyme, ye beand
ane trew and faythfull seruand to me.   And gif the puir men that wantis geir
duellinge onder yow be trew to yow, tak thame into the place upoun my expenssis,
and gif to thair wyffis and bairniss of my victuall to sustein thame as ye think
expediant.   I pray yow have the place weill provydit with sic furneshing as ye ma
get, and spair nowther my geir nor yat your awin for God leuwinge us our heilthis
we will get geir enewche.   I pray yow and als commandis yow that ye lat nain
within the place but your awin traist seruandis albeit I gaif yow ane command to
resaue sum utheris at my departing, and keip this writing for your warrand; for
albeit the geir be awa and the ground waistit, I keepand that auld houss and
haldand the regis haill as God willinge I sall, ye beand ane faythfull seruand to me,
my bairnis and youris sall leif honorabill in it will God, quhen the plage of God
will leyth upoun tha and thair posteritie out of memorie that molestis me and yow
at this present.   Send word to me gif ye mister men or ony uthir thinge ye wald
have doand with this berar, quha is ane man I credeit and ye ma schaw to him
your mind.   I sall provyid sum scharp boy that can writ and reid to yow schortlie,
and hald ye him on my expenssis sa lang as this induris becaus credeit ma nocht
be gevin to boyis.   The rest to your wisdomn, and to treit yourself weill and be
merrie, and tak no thocht of geir for we will get geir enewche, will God., quha mot
have yow in keepinge.   At Ilanran—youris

"COLIN CAMPBELL."

The severe measures, however, towards the rest of the Clan only
provoked acts of revenge :—

"1570. August 22.   John McConil Dow V^cGeglas V^cKessoch slayn besyd
    Glenfalloch and thirteen of the Lardis of Glenurquhay's men slayn that da
    be Clangregour and thar complessis.   Gud in hawin stance them of ther
    vykytnes.   So be it.

"1571. Nov. 16. Death of Gregor son of the Vicar of Fortingill in the houss of his father and buried in the Church there.

"1572. Sep. 24. Allester McAllester slain and his son ane yonge barne of sewin yer ald callyt Gregor and Duncan brodyr tyl Allester[1] al slain in Stromferna be Patryk Dow McGregor V^cCondoquhy Lawdossyt[2] with his complessis and be the drath ('draucht,' artful scheme) of Allester Gald V^cGregor.[3] The saidis Allster and his son and brodyr zyrdith (buried) in Fortingill.

"1572. Nov. 10. Death of Donald Elder McQuhewin ai Theneff in the house of his son. Donald.

"1572. -3 Jan. 9. Death of Katherine Neyn Allester V^cOlchallum V^cGregor wife of Patrik McQuhewin at Ardtrasgyr, 'in gallocate' (insane?).

"1573. March 30. death of Ronald McGregor V^cCouil in the nordland and buried in the Church of Taldow in Strathdayn.

"1574. Donald Dow McConil V^cQuhewin heddyt at the Kenmore be Collene Campbel of Glenurquhay April 7. and zirdit in Fortingall same day.

   "April 28. Gud Mald N^cAyn Vay in Glenlyon spous till the clerk McNiven and zirdit in Branwo.

   "Death of Ellyssat Neyn Huston V^cEwin spouse of Donald McCondoquhy Voyr at Fortingill.

   "Murder of Patrik[4] Dow McGregor V^cDuncan Lawdossyt at Bofudyr Balquhidder) by Clandowilchair. Oct. 4.

"1576. June 30. Death of Joneta neyn Duncan V^cGregor wife of Donald McQuhewin at Thyneff and buried at fortingill."

This entry ends the last part of Fortingal Obituary.

From " Chartulary " :—

"1571-1. 1. Jan. To a messenger 'Passand of Edinburgh to Stirlin with lettre to summon an assize to Duncane McGregour to be accusit of certain crimes and justifiet at Stirling."—Lord High Treasurer's Books.

---

[1] Their identity not ascertained.

[2] This Patrick was murdered two years later by the Clan Dougal Ciar. Although his patronymics read Patrick, son of Gregor, son of Duncan Ladosach, he is not identical with Patrick Aulach, who was son of Gregor. Two explanations occur, either this Patrick Dow was a natural son of Gregor, or he was his brother, and " McGregor " is merely mentioned as a surname.

[3] Younger brother of Gregor Roy.

[4] See above. 1572, September 24.

Chapter XVI

WE now resume the Baronage Memoir which, although occasionally led into error, has always a valuable connecting thread. We find

"XVII. Duncan eldest son of the Gregor slain in 1552 and grandson of Duncan Ladosach, called Donach Abberach[1] from his having been immediately after his father's murder carried into Lochaber by his mother's friends, as were his two brothers, to Athol and Strathearn, by other relations, in order to save them from the like danger. He was a stout man of a very fine appearance, and soon acquired a reputation over all the Highlands; in so much that Duncan Dubh a Churic, dreading lest this young hero should make his old head answer for the murder of his father and grandfather, and also cut him out of the lands he had acquired by that and the like means from his family and friends. endeavoured by all means to reconcile himself to Duncan Abberach who would certainly have taken that cruel but just revenge; had not Locheil's influence prevailed with him to accept of the offer made by Duncan Dubh, of his father's lands, with those of Corriecharmaig and Tomachrochair, in Glenlochy, as an addition; in consequence of which the two Duncans were sworn to an inviolable friendship in presence of Locheil and several other Chiefs, at a very numerous meeting of the friends of both parties, held for the purpose in the Braes of Glenurchy.[2]

"Duncan Abberach took for his first wife Christian, a daughter of the ancient family of Macdonald of Keppoch, by whom he had a son who died young.

"He married 2dly . . , daughter to Macfarlane of that Ilk descended from the family of the Lennox and by her he had three sons whose descendants are at this day known by the name of Slioch Donachadh Abberach, 'the tribe of Lochaber Duncan.'

"1. Patrick his heir, whose line carried on the representation. See further on.

"2. Robert,[3] a man of a rare martial genius. He laid the plan of attacking the Colquhouns.

"3. Alpin who married and had issue of whom Sir Evan Macgregor of Newhaven."

[1] He was eventually slain at Bentoig 1604.—See Chapter XXVII.
[2] Chapter XII., page 148.
[3] Known afterwards as Robert Abroch.

The first mention of Duncan Abberach on his return from Lochaber is in the record of forfeitures, Sept. 8th, 1569.[1] He soon afterwards found favour with the Earl of Argyle, as appears from the following Bond of Maintenance :—

> " 1573. August 24. . . . Be it kend till all men and sundrie to quhom it efferis we Archibald Erle of Argyle Lord Campbell and Lorne justice and chancellor of Scotland &a, &a. to haif resavit our louittis (lovites) Duncan Abbroche McGregour, Patrik McGregour, Allaster Skorinche (   ) McGregour, Molcollum McGregour, Patrik Awilochi (Aulach) McGregour and Dougal McGregour the saidis Duncanis bredrene, thair airis and offspring in our maintenance. And also in our airis protection and defence in all thair juste and lesum materis aganis all maner of mane. the authorite of Scotland beand exceptit. The saidis Duncane McGregour and the rest, bredern, thair airis and offspring beand leill and trew to us and our airis and to serf us at all tymes we pleis, to chairge thayme to thair powar and alss the foirsaidis, to be of rewl in all tymes cumin, as trew and ciwil subdittis of our souerane the Kingis Maiestie, And giff ony hes to say to thayme for ony thing that sall chance fra this farther to call thame or ony of thame, according to the ordour of law and equal justice sall be ministrat to the use of this realme witht certificatioune gif ony wald intend aganis thame or ony of thayme by the law, that we sall be thair party and nocht thay, seeing thayme aplyable to the lawis. And willis thir presentis to be maid manifest in all placis neidfull Be this subscryvit with our hand at the Carrick the 24. day of Aug. 1573. (signed) Ar: Erall Ergyll And for the mair verificatioune causit affixe our signet hearto, &a The names of thair airis and offspring conteinit in this band and off thameselffis that is presentlie in lyff, Duncan Abbrach McGregour, Robert McGregour his sone, Duncan and . . . . also his sonis ; Allaster Skerrich M^{c}gregour, Dugall and . . . . his sones, Patrik Aulich McGregour, Duncan . . . . also his sones Johne McGregour in Morinche, sone to Patrik Dow and Patrik McGregour brother to the said Johne."—Luss Collection.

This Paper, quoted in the " Chartulary," after Mr MacGregor Stirling's careful investigations among the Luss Papers, corroborates the names Patrick Aulach, and of Duncan's son Robert, as given in the " Baronage " many years before the existence of this Band was known.

[1] Chapter XII., page 147.

From the "Chartulary," 1574, Dec. 28, Glenurquhay's Band upon a non-entry [1]·—

"Be it kend till all men be thir present Lrës Me Colyne Campbell of Glenurquhay, That forsamekle as oure souerane Lord with awise &a (of Earl Morton Regent of the Kingdom) hes gevin and disponit to me, my airis and assigniyes the nonentries, males, fermes, profeitis and dewuties of all and haill the landis of Conry, Roro, Morinche Eister, Morinche Middill and Morinche Wester, Duncrosk, Candknok and Auchmoir with all cottages &a liand in the Barony of Menzies of all zerris (years) and termis bygane sen the deceis of umqle Robert Menzies of that Ilk or any other last lauchfull possour thereof 'Neuitheless to be bundin and obleist to oure Souerane Lord and his said regent that we sall na wayis use the said gift of nonentries bot be awise and contentment of his hienes and his said Regent,' otherwise the said gift salbe of nane avale, force, or effect.—Record of Secret Council

"1574 Dec 28   Charter by Dougall McGregour Chancellor of Lesmoir to Patrick Campbell of the four merk land Auchnacroftie dated at Balloch.—Register Decreets of Court of Session

"1575 Nov 9   Precept for Royal Charter of Confirmation of Feu Charter 'per Dougallum cancellarium Lesmoren' to Patrick Campbell 3d son of Glenurquhay with consent of 'glenurchie'

"1574   'Dougal Makgregour reidare [2] at Fortingill.'
Duncan Makgregor reidare at Killin and Strathfillan

"1575-6 March 24   Gregor McDougall alias McGregour presented to the office of reidare in the Church of Moulin.

"1576   Johnne Clerk als McGrregour Reidare at Ardewnane   Dougall MakGregour reidare at Forthergill —Register of Assignations for the stipends of Ministers, 1574.   Advocates' Library.

"1575 June 25   Advocatis against McGregor and others, George McGregour alias Johnstoun, Johne and George McGregor his sones, Duncan McGregor & Burgesses of Perth to have broken Lawborrowis.[3] delayed till 15 Jan. next

"1576. June 2   Charter and infeftment given to Gregour McGregour alias

---

[1] Sir Alexander Menzies had neglected to be properly "retoured heir" to the lands of Loch Tay, &c , on the death of his father, Sir Robert. No question on the subject was raised till in 1574, sometime after the succession of the next heir, James Menzies, when Glenurchy obtained this "disposition" of the properties mentioned —Explanation taken from the " Red and White Book of Menzies."

[2] Reader.

[3] Letters under the signet binding persons to keep the peace

Johnstoune, burgis of Perth, by Dene Adam Forman Prior of the Charterhouse of Perth. is rescinded by the Court of session in so far as regards the
sunny half of three quarters of St Leonards. Lee.—Decreets of Court of
Session.

"July 3. Precept of Charter Royal of Confirmation of Feu Charter by
Adam Forman Prior of the House 'Vallis Virtutis' (Charter house) near
the Burgh of Perth to George McGregor alias Johnestoune, burgess of the
said burgh of the forty shilling land of the forest of Bynzemoir in the barony
of Glen Dochart and shire of Perth.—Privy Seal.

"1576. Bond by Duncan McGregour V^cCondoquhy Abrach and Patrick
McGregour V^cCondoquhy his brother to Colin Campbell of Clenurquhay
and his heirs giving them their calps."

This confirms the statement in the "Baronage" in reference to the
reconciliation for a time.

"1578. Jan. 30. Gregor McGilquhallum in Glenlednoch Gregor McPhatrick
McCondoquhy yair, John Johnestoune yair, Patrik Johnstoune yair. pledges
for Drummonds.—Record of Justiciary.

"1580. July 28. Precept of (royal) Charter of confirmation of Feu Charter by
George Balfour Commendator of the Priory of Charterhouse of Perth,
to George Makgregor alias Johnestoun of the half of the Charterhouse
yairdies.

"1578. March 11. and again on the 26. Oct. 1580 Gregour McEan Constable
of Glenurquhay witness to a bond.

"Again with the addition of Johne Makgregor his son 1580-81.

"1581. May 4. David Forrester of Logie ofttymes callit to have produceit
our Soverane Lordis lettres dewlie execute aud endorsit; purcheist be Ewir
Campbell of Strachur Forrester of Glenfernate and our Souerane Lordis
advocat to tak suertie of certane persones viz Gregour McIllichallum
McCoule in Glengyle,[1] McCom beg McFarlane, Ewin McCondoquhy Glas
McColchallum queyelecht, & Duncan McGregour in Glen [2] brother to the
Laird of McGregour, Allester Gall [2] McGregour his brother &a &a to
compeir and underlye the law for slaughter of deir, liairt, (grey hen) Hynd,
da, ra, and other wild fowls, with culveringis pistollettis, handbowes, within
the forest of Glenferroch."—Record of Justiciary.

From the "Chartulary" :—

"1581 july 26. Mr John Grahame Justice Deput Mr James Herring Provost
of Methvene oft callit to haif produceit oure Soerane Lordis lettres dewlie

---

[1] Gregor Dhu, third Chieftain of the Dougal Kier Family.
[2] Brothers of Gregor Roy of Glenstray, slain in 1569.

execute and indorsate purchest be Duncane Stewart, Mr James McWattie nerrest kynnisman with ye remanent kyn and friendis of umqule Duncan Stewart M^crobert McWattie, and ye Advocat to tak souertie of Ewin McGregour tutoure of Glenschra, Allester McGregour V^cDonichy V^cAllester, Johne Dow his brother, Patrick Moirwell, Allester Pudreauch McGregour, Malcum MacWolchallum V^cWill, Dougall Denesoune, David and Johne Dow brether, and Duncane. That they should compeir and underlie the law For airt and pairt of ye slaughter of ye said umqule Duncan Stewart committed in Nov. last bypast. And nocht produis ye samyn in manner foursaid wes yairfore amerciat in painis contenit in ye actis of Parliament viz for non productioun yrof upoun ilkane of ye persouns abone writtin in ye pane (rest blank).—Record of Justiciary.

"1580-1. 19. Jan. Holyroodhouse. Complaint of Johne Makintalgart in Bocastell, servant to James Commendator of Sanct Colme, as follows: On the 17, of Nov. last 'Johnne Drummond of Drummondernoch, Johnne Makgruder, sone to James McGruder servand to the Lord Drummond, Alexander Reidoch, servand to the Lard of Cultilbragan, James Reiddoch, servand to William Reiddoch, Malcolme Closach McGrege, servand to the Lard of Calender, Allester McKewin servand to the Lord Drummond and his sone, and tailyeour Makwillie, houshald man to the Lard of Tullebragane, with utheris thair complices, come under silence of nicht to the said Johnnes duelling hous of Bocastell, and perforce rift spulyit and awaytuke ane hundreth pundis of reddie money being in ane kist in his said hous to his utter wrak and herschip; pertening to him and utheris nychtbouris, thre mylk kye and all the said Johnnes insicht and plennessing of his said house. to his utter wrak and herschip; lyke as thairafter thay pat violent handis on the said Johnnes persoun tuke him perforce with thame and detenis and withaldis him in strait prisoun and captivitie.' Charge had been given to the defendants to liberate the complainers within twenty-four hours under pain of rebellion, or else to appear before the Council presenting him or shewing cause to the contrary, and now 'the said Johnne Makintalgart comperand be the said James Commendator of Sanct Colme and the defendants being of tymes callit and not comperand' the order is made peremptory that thay present their prisoner before the Council on the last day of Jan. instant 'that ordour may be taken with him as appertinis,' under the pain of horning and escheat."

The above, from the Register of the Privy Council, is not quoted in the "Chartulary," and only one MacGregor and the McGrudars appear in it, but it gives an instance of the kind of raids that were continually taking place, and Drummondernoch was himself of the party.

The following proclamation was made by the Government :—

"1582. The King had 'laitlie appointed ane Court of justiciary to be halden in the Burgh of Perth for administratioun of justice to all compliners, and appointit alsua certane personis of gude knawlege and experience to compone for remissionis to sic as wer not able to underly the rigours of the justice' but having been informed 'that the inhabitantis of the Highlandis and Brayis within this Schirefdoume, throw the lang troubles that wes amang thame during the disobedience of the Clangregour and utheris broken men of the far Hielandis culd not weill abyde his Hienes lawes, na criminal justice in effect, being halden heir thir 29 yeris bygane,' he had 'condescendit thairfoir to grant thame mercy and pardon for thair bygane offenssis, to the effect that they comperand and being persewit be the compliners, suld find gud secur suritie to satisfie the parties offendid and to abstain from the lyke offenssis in tyme cuming.' Notwithstanding this act of grace 'little special dittay hes been givin up, and nane or verie few complenaris hes offerit thame to persew the personis enterit on pannell sen the begyning of this present justice Court, how sa evir now thay murmour that thay be not redres of thair skaith sustenit.' Now accordingly 'to the effect that thay may ressave justice and guid redres and satisfactioun of thair saidis skaithis bygane, and that the personis, offenders, for feir of thair lyffis and in default of pardoun, sall not lie out and continue in thair former evil doingis to thair utter wrak and utter distructioun,' it is ordered that proclamation be made by a herald macer, or other officer of arms, at the market cross of Perth and elsewhere, 'to command and charge all and quhatsumevir personis compliners quhilkis hed ony special complaintes and dittayes upoun personis already arreistt to this present court of Justiciar that thay present and gif in the same to the justice clerk or his deputis with diligence, and be reddie to follow thai complaintis and to cause summond ane assise aganis the personis offendouris in cais thay sall offer thaymeselffis to enter on pannel in this burgh ay ony tyme betuix . . . and the 1 day of August nix to cum, or in Streviling befoir the fyftene day of the same month, quhair his Majestie hes willit thame to be ressavit in cais thay offer thameselffis to enter betuix . . . and the same said day, and als hes ordainit my Lord Thesaurar and utheis compositouris to grant componitur for remissioun to all maner of personis inhabitants of the saidis Brayis and Hielandis within this schiref-dome, for all offenssis and crymes committit be thame in tymes bygane, thay comperand in judgement and findand gude suretie for satisfactioun of the parties offendit unto and to abstain and forbear from like offences and crymes in tymes cuming."—Register of the Privy Council.

It must be confessed that this reads as a very fair and merciful ordinance, but doubtless the deep sense of injury on the part of the Clan, the
want of space, and means of livelihood, with the numerous temptations of
habit and of the exciting times, forced on the more pacific spirits to renewed
troubles at whatever cost

From "Chartulary" —

"1582 May 20   Precept &a of the feu ferme of the half land of Innerzeldies
to Patrick Makgregour alias Duncane Donaldsoune (*i e.* son of Duncan and
Grandson of Donald) in Innerzeldies and Grizelda Murray his spouse and to
the longest liver in liferent, and to Gregor McGregor son and apparent heir
of the said Patrick and to the heirs male and assigneys of the said Gregor.
Dated at Halyrud Hous —Privy Seal.

"1582 July   Item to ane boy passand of Perth with clois lrès (letters) to the
Lord Drummond, lairds of Buchquhaane, Knockhill, tutour of Menteith,
William Rudoch McGregour and Harie Schaw of Camusmoir.—High
Treasurer's books.

"1582-3. Jan 8.   Anent the actioun and cause persewit be Merline McChewit
seruand to Donald Robertson of Murlgane Ewin oig in Rannoch, &a aganis
Gregour McGillichallum in Glenlyoun and Neill McGregour McGillechallum
his sone tuching the spoiliatioun fra the saidis personis of sindrie gudis and
geir (Defenders do not appear)."—Sheriff Books of Perth

From the "Black Book of Taymouth " —

"Colene Campbell 6th Laird of Glenurquhay   .   ob 1583. aged 84
Memorandum He was ane great justiciar all his tyme throch the quhilk he
susteinit thee deidlie feid of the Clangregour ane lang space.   And besydis
that he caused executt to the death money notable lymnaris, he beheiddit
the laird off McGregour himseff at Kandmoir in presens of the Erle of Atholl,
the justice clerk and sindrie other nobillmen

    "Notwithstanding his tyranny his son and successor proved a still worse
foe to us

"1583 May 15   Ane letter maid to James Lord Doune his aires &a of the
escheit quhilk pertenit of befoir to Duncan Bane McRobb alias McGregour
in Craigrostane and now pertaining to our soverane Lord through being of
the said Duncane Bayne McRobb alias McGregoure, denounced his Maiesties
rebell and put to the horne. at the instance of Lord Doune from whom he
had stolen 'a quhyt meir and ane foill and ane mirkgrey meir' Same date
at Perth   assisa. In a retour of John Murray afterwards 1st Earl of Tulli
bardine, one of the persons quoted is George McGregoure alias Johnestoune

elder burges of Perth. He is named as an arbiter for Edward Pitscottie
apparent of Luncarty Nov. 8. same year.

"1583-4. Feb. 5. Anent the actioun persewit be Robert Menzies of Comrie
aganis Gregour V^{c}Hutcheon in Culdar and Finlay McCondoquhy V^{c}Coneilglas
ther tuching the allegit wrangous detening and withalding of the profeittis of
their ky.—Sheriff Books of Perth.

"1584. April 8. Anent the actioun and caus persewit be James Menzies of that
Ilk heritour of the landis underwritten aganis Duncan McGregour eldest sone
to umqule Johne cam M^{c}condoquhie tuching the violent profeittis of the
fourtie schilling land of Rorow with the pertinentis libellit, acclamit &a.

"1584. May 20. Bond by Dougall Deneson McGregor to Duncane Campbell
of Glenurquhay and his heirs giving them his Calp signed at Ilanran before
witness, Duncan Abrach McGregor."

"1584. June 30. Cause aganis Duncan McGregoure at the instance of Menzies
of that Ilk, Delayed till 25. July. No farther mention in the Sheriff Books
of Perth.

From "Chartulary" :—

"1584-5. Mention of Johne McGregor as one of the executors to the late Colene
Campbell of Glenurquhay.

"1584-5. Jan. Charge on the Laird of Buchanane and utheris For samekle
as the King's Majesty and Lords of his Pryvy Council are creditably informed
that his good and peaceable subjects inhabiting the countries of the Lennox,
Menteith, Struilingschyre, and Stratherne are heavily oppressed by reif,
stouth, sorning, and other crimes, dayly and nightly used upon them by
certain thieves, lymmers, and sorners lately broke loose upon them furth of
the braes of the countries next adjacent, to the heavy trouble of his highness's good subjects. foresaid, and to the high contempt of his Highness
authority and laws, if timeous remeid be not provided, therefore ordain
letters, to be directed charging George Buchanane of that Ilk, Andro
M^{c}farlane of the Arroquair . . . Colquhoun of Luss &a here follows a string
of names of Lairds including the name of Ewin McGregor tutor of Glenstray,
. . . . To compeir before his Majesty and Lords of his Privy Council at
Haliruidhous, or quhair it sall happin him to be for the time, the 28 day of
Jan. instant to answer to such things as shall be inquired of them &a.

"1585. Oct. 4. Item to ane boy passand with clois lr̆es of Striveling to the
Earle of Athoill, the Lord Drummond, the Laird of Glenurquhay, McGregour,
and with lr̆es to be proclamit at Perth for ye airmyie to be convenit at
Crufurd the 22 day of Oct."—Lord High Treasurer's Books.

The object of assembling this army was to resist those of the Scottish lords who had the previous year been exiled forth of the Kingdom for seizing the King's person at Ruthven, 1582, and whose plots the English Queen, having given them an asylum in England, was regarded as favouring.

Three Bonds with Glenurquhay follow in point of date. "Black Book of Taymouth."

"1585. June 25. Bond of friendship by Johnne Earl of Atholl Lord of Balvany, to his cousin and Brother-in-law Duncane Campbell of Glenurquhay. . . . . That if the said James Menzies (of that Ilk) should pursue the said Duncane Campbell or be pursued by him, he would assist the said Duncane Campbell with his whole force ; and that he should give the like assistance against the Clangregour if they should render aid to the said James Menzies.

"1585. July 5. at Balloch. Bond of Gregour Makconaquhie V^cGregor in Roro, Alester McEwin V^cConaquhie there, Gregour Makolchallum in Inverbar in Glenlyoun, Duncane Makgregour his sone in Killdie, and Williame Macgregour son to the said Gregour there, to Duncane Campbell of Glenurquhay showing that their forebears had granted the like bond to the deceased Coleine Campbell of Glenurquhay, and obliging themselves, if it should happen that Makgregour by himself or his accomplices should break upon the said Duncane or his heirs their lands, tennants, and possessions, to renounce him as their Chief and to take part with the said Duncane against him.

"1585. Aug. 3. Gillemorie Makillevollich grants to Duncane Campbell of Glenurquhay and his heirs 'a bairn's part of his geir because the said Duncane has promised to trauel to dress (have recourse to, treat with) with the Earl of Atholl and friendis of umquhile . . . . . slain by the said Gillemorie Makillevollich upone suddantie.' Duncane McIllevollycht brother of the said Gillemorie, Johne Makgregoure lawful sone to Gregour McEan Constable of Glenurquhay and Duncan Makpatrik Vekolchallum witnesses at Ilanran."

From the "Chartulary":—

"1586. June 15. Anent the actioun and cause persewit be William Redheugh of Meigour aganis Johne Comrie of that Ilk, . . . three other Comries, and Patrik McVallycht alias McGregour in Comrie, tuching the allegit wrangous spoliation be thame, ther seruandis and complices fra the said William Ridheugh of ewes and sindrie jowellis, gold, silver, insight plenishing, soumes of money, guidis and geir, furth of his dwelling-house of Garterlume within the sheriffdom of Perth. (Defendants do not appear; 2d July instant appointed for the farther hearing of the cause.)—Sheriff Books of Perth, in which however there is no farther notice of this cause.

"1586. Aug. 8. Letters of Horning recorded at Perth, at the instance of Allane Stewart in Stuikis, Johne Drummond in Drummenerinoche, William Grahame, fear of Callander and Patrik Grahame of Inchbrakie" against

*1 "Gregor[1] McGregour of Glenscheroche, (Allaster of Glenstray).

2 Ewin MacGregor, Tutour thairof, (uncle to Allaster the young Chief).

3 Allester Gauld, his brother, (under Earl of Argyle).

4 Allester pudrech MacGregor (from Balquhidder 'huidder'[2]) under the Laird of Weyme.

5 Dougall sone, (Dougall Denistoun, *i.e.* Dean's son) MacGregor.

6 Donald MacGregor.

7 Allester McCondoquhie McAllester.

8 Johne dow MacGregor his brother. (probably occupier of Camuserachtie beg in Rannoch, page 165).

9 Patrik Duncansoun MacGregor in Innerzaldie.[3] (in Glenleidnoch) under Laird of Tullibardine. The Ammonachs were of this family.

10 Gregor his son.

11 Duncan MacGregor his son in Port of Latherne, (Lochearn).

12 Donald Dow his son in Megor.

13 Duncan Glen MacGregor (brother to the Tutour as appears elsewhere).

14 Johne MacGregor in Dundurn.

15 Duncan Roy his brother.

16 Johne Dow McCondoquhey MacGregor (brother of Allaster McCondoquhie).

17 Donald Dow.

18 John Dow McCallum owir MacGregor (M^cilchallum).

19 Johne Moir MacGregor in Callichra, (M^cilchallum owir).

20 William McGillchallum MacGregor in Letterling (M^cilchallum ower MacGregor).

21 Duncane Bane MacGregor in Stuikinroy, (Duncan Bane McRob under the Laird of Buchannan).

22 John McRob MacGregor in Ruchois.

Those marked thus * executed after Glenfruin.

[1] The word umquhile omitted, as *Gregor* had been killed in 1580.

[2] The term Puderache was applied to inhabitants of Balquhidder, and a stone near the church is still extant under this name. It was a test of strength for young men, who had to lift it on to another stone.

[3] See List 1565, page 144.

23 Gregor McRob MacGregor in Comer.
24 Callum Moir MacGregor (McRob) in Knockheilt
25 Callum Dow (McRob) his brother.
26 Robert Roy (McRob) his brother in Comer
27 John Dow McRob their brother (alsua)
28 Allester McCoule McIllvirum MacGregor in Dessour (or Dischoir from Deasach the side of Loch Tay facing south).
*29 Malcum McCoulquheir (McDougal Keir) in Innerlochie [1] (Balquhidder) under the Laird of Tullibardine.
30 Duncane McCulquheir MacGregor in Drummilliche, son of Malcolm the 2d Chieftain of their House
31 John McCoulquheir MacGregor thair, brother of above.
32 Dougall McCulquheir MacGregor in Glengyle, another brother under the Laird of Buchannan.
33 Gregour McCulquheir MacGregor in Keylecter (Caoletter).
34 Patrik McCulquheir in Strathyre (Strachur), another brother of Duncan in Drummilliche
35 Finlay keir McCulquheir MacGregor in Culgart.
36 Allester MacGregor (M^ceanduy) in Strathphillane.
37 John dow McWilliam M^cilchallum MacGregor.
38 Patrik MacGregor in Cadern, (Cadderine—known as 'our' youngest Brother of the Tutor.)
39 Duncan (McCondochy) Cleroch (clerk) MacGregor
*40 Gregour craginche MacGregor (or in Craiginshache spelt in several ways) (Craigan).
41 Donald our (odhar, dun or sallow) McInleith (M^cillich).
42 Duncan McCondoquhie (or M^cewin) McCondoquhy.
43 Allester his brother
44 John MacGregor in Schadowne.
45 (Ewin MacGregor Jamesoun in Scaderin)
46 Gregour McCondoquhy in Roro (under the Laird of Weyme) Head of House of Roro.
47 Callum croy MacGregor in Candrochie.
48 Malcum glas (pale or grey) MacGregor in Kynaltie.
49 William (M^cilchallum) MacGregor thair.
50 Duncane (M^cilchallum) MacGregor thair
51 Allester MacGregor in Fernan, (Loch Tay) ⎫
52 Williame (McWilliame McNeill) MacGregor ⎬ Under Laird of thair . . . ⎭ Strowan (Robertson).
53 Gregor (McHucheon) MacGregor in Calder

[1] Ancestor of Innerarderan   Those marked thus * executed after Glenfruin.

54 Finla (M^ccondoquhy glas) MacGregor thair.

*55 Duncan (M^callester vreac) MacGregor in Lagfernan (or Langfernan).

56 Callum MacGregor McNeill.

57 Neill his brother.

58 John Dow his brother.

59 John Dow (M^ccondoquhy) cleroche MacGregor.

60 Malcum (bane) MacGregor N^cNeill in Rannoch.

61 Dougal his broder in Roro.

62 Donald gorme M^cinleiche in Rannoch.

63 Gregor M^cillechallum (M^ceanmoyle) in Innervar (in Glenlyon) under the Laird of Glenlyon.

64 Neill dow his son.

65 Gregor McCondoquhy (in Roro), (repetition of No. 46).

66 Callum dow his brother in Glenlochy.

67 John Mauloch (or Manloche) thair brother.

68 Gregor M^cilchallum in Comrie, (in the District of Auchmore in the Barony of Weem).

69 Duncan oig M^ceanduy MacGregor in Glenlochy, ⎫ Under the Laird of

70 Duncan our M^ceanduy thair,   .   .   .   ⎭   Lawers.

71 John dow M^ccondoquhy MacGregor in Roro.

72 Robert beg Clerich MacGregor (or McRobert earlich, 'Tearlach' Charles).

73 Duncan MacGregor in Tullichewne.

74 Duncan MacGregor McWilliame.

75 Callum MacGregor McWilliame in Rannoch, (Kinlachar) under Laird of Weyme.

76 Duncan MacGregor McWilliame his brother.

77 Callum McConnel M^ceane MacGregor.

78 John dow (M^cchallum) in Rannoch.

79 Callum MacGregor McWilliam his brother thair.

80 Allester M^cinnes (M^ceane) MacGregor in Rannoch.

81 Gregor McNeill MacGregor in Candrochth (Candrochitmerk).

82 John MacGregor his sone in Ardquhillarie, (Loch Lubnaig or Ardchoille?).

83 Ewin MacGregor his brother.

84 Allester MacGregor his brother alsua.

85 Allester McRobert (moir) MacGregor in Strathyre and his sons.

86 Walter McAlpie in Lingrathletterling (McAlpine in Lurg at Letterlung).

87 Robert McAlpie (McAlpine) his son in Duchois, (Ruchoiss).

88 Murdo McAlpie (Murdoch McAlpine) his brother.

Those marked thus * executed after Glenfruin.

89 John Bane M^cillechallum glas MacGregor in Rannoch.
90 Gregor ger (often gar from gearr, short) his brother
91 John McNeill (or invill) his brother also
92 Gregor cam (blind of an eye) thair brother's sone.
93 Dougall Danesoun (Denesoun) MacGregor.
94 Donald Denisoun his brother's son
95 Dougall Jamesoun MacGregor
96 William his brother
97 Gregour M^cneill (M^ceanmoyle in Bofrak).
98 Gregour McNeill McInwalliche in Ardewinch, (Ardewnaig).
99 Ewin M^ceanvalliche thair.
100 Callum McCondoquhy Vreak MacGregor.
101 John his brother and
102 Gregor his brother
103 John McConneill M^cinlay in Glenscheray, (Glenstray)
104 Nicoll McGowne in Achtervich '

for different acts of theft, from the complainers.—Register of Hornings Perth, in General Register House, Edinburgh
"1586 Sep. 15. They are released from the horn till 13, Oct"

1586 Aug 13   On this date the Earl of Montrose gets the escheit of Gregor MacGregor of Glenscherache, Glenstray, the word umquhile having been omitted by error before his name, and of all those mentioned in the preceding list, the names being repeated.

The two lists [1] have been collated in the "Chartulary," and again very carefully by the present compiler, and names occurring only in the second list, or other supplementary information taken from other lists, &c, are added in brackets

From the "Chartulary".—

"1587 May 31   Duncane Bayn McGregour in Craigrostan and Duncane M^cillechallum McGregor in Boquidder are mentioned along with a number. of Grahams and Buchanans —Record of Justiciary
"June 28   Anent the actioun persewit be Duncan Campbell of Glenurquhie and William Moncreiff of that Ilk, aganis Gregor McHutcheon in Culdar

¹ To the ordinary reader these lists repeated on several occasions, must seem dull and dry but to the student of the Clan's history they are full of interest, as making mention of individuals of the various families known to have existed.

tuiching thair releiff of the soume of fyve hundretht merkis at the hendis of
ane nobill lord francis Erle of Erroll. (defender does not appear;) July 12.
assigned for a further hearing of the case.

"July 1. Anent the actioun persewit be James Campbell of Laweris taxman
of the landis underwritten, againis Duncan M^cgregour, Dougal McGregour
his sone, Gregour McCainroy, and Malcom M^cinroy his brother, zoung
Duncan M^cindowie and Gregour beg M^cgregour pretentit occupiars of merk
land of Duncrosk mylne and mylne landis therof witht the pertinentis lyand
within Glenlochy and shrefdom of perth. Tuching the removal of thame.
(Defenders not appearing are decerned to remove, una cum expensis, salua
taxatione judices.)

"July 5. Anent the actioun persewit be Gregoure M^chutcheoune in Culdar
aganis Duncan McKewin McCondochie in Croftgarrow and Allester
McGregour clerich in Croftlevin Tuiching his relieff of cautionrie lybellit
speciallie anent the soume of money of fyve hundretht merkis acclaimit.
(Defender absent.)"

The above three cases are quoted from the Sheriff Books of Perth.

"Dec. 12. same year Ewin McGregour Tutour of Glenschew witness to a
contract between commissioners of the Earl of Huntly and the assigny of
Margaret Douglas Countess of Menteith.—Record of Deeds Edinburgh.

"1587-8. Feb. 19. Contract betwixt Walter Cunningham and Archibald
McGregour in Dunfin, heir to umquhile John McGregour piper, indueller
within the Burgh of Edinburgh.

"Feb. 29. Contract between Archibald McGregour in Little Drumfing, and
Walter Cunningham recorded in the Books of Council and Session 1 March
following.—Privy Seal.

"Feb. 14. Anent the actioun of transferens persewit be Johne Campbell of
Laweris aganis Marion McGregour relict executrix and succeedant in the
of umquhile M^cinroy her spous.

"Feb. 24. Marion McGregour decerned to flit.

"1588. July 6. Duncan McGregour (resident in Perth) a juror in an inquest
of Marion McEwin as heiress of several lands in the Barony of Strowan in
Atholl.

"July 6. Anent the actioun and cause persewit be Donald Robertson of
Strowan aganis (amongst others) Allester Pudrach alias MacGregour
pretendit occupiar of part of the landis of Innercharney, William Neill
Vic Ewin pretentit occupiar of ane pairt of the bordlandis and haif of the
mylnne of Ferny, Allester McGregour clerych pretentit occupiar of the
landis of Croftualzen, lying within the barony of Strowan. anent the
removing of them from the lands.—Sheriff Books of Perth.

"July 7. Anent the action of removing persewit be John Schaw heritable proprietor of the toun and lands underwritten aganis Patrik McGregour alias galliocht (Alech or Aulich, *i e.* Atholl) pretentit occupiar of the toun and lands of Cornechrombie, with the pertinentis, tuyching the removing of him. (Defender not appearing is decerned to remove)—Sheriff Books of Perth.

"1588-9. Feb. 21. Anent the actioun persewit be Robert Menzies of Comrie takisman of the landis underwritten aganis Gregour McNeill VicEwin, Donald McAchon (Hutcheon?) and Donald Mcewin roy in Wester Kynnaldie anent the removing of them fra the landis (Defenders not appearing are decerned to remove)—Perth

"1589 July 4. The Bishop of the Isles a procurator in the Court of Session of Patrik McGregour in Mekle Caddirly and John our McPhadeun.—Reg. of Decreets

"July 16 Anent the actioun persewit be James Commendator of Inchaffray aganis Duncan McPharik alias McGregour, Neyne Phatrik Stewart relict of umquhile James Stewart, Duncan McVallich, Duncan slaoch McGregour anent the removing fra the landis (apparently in Balquhidder). Decerned to remove.

"Aug 13 Anent the action persewit be Donald Robertson of Strowan aganis Duncan McAllester VcAllester VcGregour, Marion Stewart, Donald McCondoquhy, Findley McAllester, Allester Jamesoun and Donald Jamesoun and McAllester Jamesoun and the removing of them. Decerned to flit.

"August 20. Anent the actioun persewit be Donald Robersoun of Strowan lyfrenter of the landis underwritten aganis Neill McCondoquhy and John bean Vichallum Vcewin VcGregour pretentit occupiars of the lands of Midfernay "—Sheriff Books of Perth

The following traditionary tale is taken from the "Lairds of Glenlyon"[1]:—

"1590. Colin the 3d of the Campbell Lairds of Glenlyon, had married (2dly) a sister of the Laird of Lawers who was very active in persecuting the Clan-Gregor. Colin was invited to join his relative in this oppression but he declined, and 'threatened death to any who injured a MacGregor within his bounds.' To mark his contempt he invited all the MacGregors in his neighbourhood to a great feast that he prepared for them. But there was a traitor in the camp · his wife had sent secret information to her brother Lawers and pointed out how, at one fell swoop, he could destroy so many

---

[1] By Mr Duncan Campbell, formerly of Fortingal and now of Inverness. Privately printed for Sir Donald Currie of Garth and Glenlyon.

enemies. As dinner was not served up as soon as Colin wished it, he sent his henchman to ask the cause of the delay. The lady forgetting herself replied quickly: 'I expect my brother.' The reply was announced in the hall; and the McGregors, thinking they had been entrapped, rushed out, deaf to all Colin could say. It was time: Lawers was crossing the ford below the Castle, before they gained the hill side. Colin was disgraced on his own hearth by his nearest friends."

Chapter XVII

General Band

A T this time the troubles in the Highlands, and also on the Borders, becoming source of disturbance to the nation and a constant anxiety to the Government, very stringent enactments were made, and, as they bore heavily on the future misfortunes of the Clan, it is desirable to quote them in full.

"Acts of Scottish Parliament   King James VI Julij 1587.

(Known as The General Band)

Caution suld be found for Land-lords and utheris.

"THAT ALL Landis-lordis and Baillies of the landes, on the Bordours and in the Hie-landes, quhair broken men hes dwelt, or presently dwellis, contained in ane Roll, ratified in the end of this present Act of Parliament, sall be charged to finde sufficient Caution and sovertie (surety) Landed-men in the In-country, to the contentment of our Soveraine Lord, and his privy Councill Betwixt . . . . and the first day of October, nixt to cum ; Or within fifteen days after the charge, upon conditiouns following, under the paine of rebellion ; And gif they failzie, the said day being by-past, to put them to the Horne ; that is to say, gif ony of their men, tennentes, servandes, and indwellers upon their landes, rowmes, steadingses and possessiones, or within their Baillieries, committis ony maisterful reife thieft, or receipt of thieft, depredationes, open and avowed fire-rasing, upon deadlie feeds (feuds) protected and mainteined be their Maisters ; That the Landis-lordes, and Baillies, upon quhais Landes and in quhais jurisdiction they dwell sall bring and present the persons compleined upon before Our Soveraine Lordis Justice, or his deputes to abide tryall, and underlye the law for the same, upon fifteen dayes warning, to be maid them lauchfully ; and failzeing therof, that the saidis Landis-lordes and Baillies be debt-bound, to satisfie the party skaithed, and to refound, content and pay to them their heirschippes and skaithes of their awin proper guddes and landes, according to the availl and quantity tane fra the compleiners, quhilk sall be modified be aith of the parties hurt, ather before the Lordes of Councell and Session, or the Justice, and his deputes, quhair upon execution sall passe, baith against the principalles and soverties, in forme as effeiris. Providing alwaies, that the landis-lordes. quha hes ther landes lyand in far Hie-landes or Bordours, they making residence themselves in the Inlands, and their tennentes, and inhabitantes of their landes, being of Clannes, or dependars on Chieftaines, and Captaines of the Clannes, quhom the Landis-lordis ar na waies able to command, but only gettes their mailles of them, and na uther service nor obedience sall na wayes be subject to this Act, but in the manner following, viz They sall be halden to direct their Precepts of warning, obtenine decretes against their Tennentis, and immediately after their denunciation, that the saides Landes-lordes, raise letters, be delivrance of the secreit Councell, and charge the Chieftaines and Captaines of the Clannes, on quhom their tennentis dependis and obeyes, to take and apprehend the disobedient tennentis, and present them to the Justice, under pain of rebellion; &a.

"ITEM. Although sum of the Lordes of the ground never uses to make residence in the partes, throw the quhilkis thieves resorts, in their passing to steal and reive, and return therefra; zit sall they be bounden to their Baillies and tennentes, to make their arreistmentes, and stay and make publication of the same; gif it be in their power, or cummis to their Knawledge; or utherwaies, to be halden and oblished for redress, as gif they dwelt upon the landes themselves. And that the chiefs of the Clanes in the boundes quhair broken men dwellis, throw the quhilkis limmers and broken men. repairis in their passing to steall and reive or returning therefra, sall be bound to make the like stay, arreistment, and publication, as the Landes-lordes, or Baillies, and be subject to the like redres and action criminall and civill, in case of their failzie or negligence. And because sindrie immediat tennentes to Our Soveraine Lord, hes disponed their landes to uthers, halden of themselves; In that case, it sall be sufficient for the Over-Lord, to enter and present his tenant and vassall, for answering or his sub-tennent; and the Landis-lord, to have his reliefe upon his tennents there-anent, as accordis."

"King James VI. July 11. and 29. 1587.

"(97). The Chiefe of all Clannes sall find pledges.

"It is alsua statute and ordained, that the Captaines, Chieffes and Chieftaines of all Clannes, alsweill on the Hieland as on the Bordoures, and the principallis of the Branches of the saides Clannes, to be specially noted in ane Roll ratified and insert in this present parliament; Quhilkes Clannes dwellis upon the landes of diverse Landes-lordes and dependis upon the directions of the saidis Captaines, Chiefes, and Chieftaines (be pretence of bloud or place of their dwelling) althought against the will oftimes of the Lord of their ground, be charged in like manner, and answer the paine abone written; to enter sik persones pleges, as sall be nominate be the Kings Majesties letters to be direct to them, upon fifteen daies before his Hieness and his secreit Councell, at the dayes to be appointed, to be placed as his Hienes sall think convenient, for keeping of gude rule in time cuming according to the conditions abone written, quhair unto the Landes-lordes and Baillies, are subject; under the paine of execution of the saidis pleges to the death in case of transgressions and nocht redresse maid be the persones offending for quhom the saidis pleges lyes. And that the saidis pleges sall be relieved quarterly with utheris of the same Clan or branche, to be specially named, as may be after the beginning of this ordeur. Also one and all Clannes, Chieftaines, and Branches of Clannes, refusand to enter their pleges at the day; and maner contained in the charge, to be directed to that effect; to be esteemed publick enemies to God, the King and all his trewe and faithful subjectes, and to be persewed with fire and sword, quhair ever they be apprehended, without crime, paine or danger, to be incurred be the doers there-throw. And that compt (count) be tane anis in the zeir, at the first day of November, quhat persoes pleged for, ar dead, and quhat zoung men sprung up in their race and Clanne, able to offend. And quhair complaint is maid upon ony person pleged for the principal of the Clanne or Branche, to be charged to present the offenders before the King or his Councell, or before the Justice and his deputes, to under-lie the law for the same."

"King James VI. 29. July 1587.

"(96). All men borne in the Hielandes and Bordoures to return to the places quhair they were borne.

"Item. That all sik notorious thieves, as were born in Liddisdaill Eskdaill, Annandale and the landis sum-time called debaitable, or in the landis of the Hie-landis that has long continued in-obedient, sall be removed out of the In-land, quhair they ar planted, and presentlie dwellin or haunts, to the parts quhair they were borne; Except their Land-lordes quhair they presently dwell, will become soverty for them, to make them answerable to the Law, as Low-land and obedient men, under the paines contained in the Acts of Parliament.

"(97). Anent the register of pleges and uthers.

"Item. It is statute and ordained for furtherance of, and quieting of the in-obedient Bordours and Hie-landes; That a buik be maid containing the names of the pleges entered, and to be entered, for gude rule and of the haill persones for quhom they lye and be quhom the pleges suld be relieved ; As alsua that a register be maid of the haill Parochiners of the landes inhabited be thieves and disobedient persones, in the Hie-landes and Bordours The names of the Landis-lordis and townes in every Parochin and of the haill men, inhabitantis therof past the age of sexteene zeires ; quha ar Landis-lordes or Baillies of every land or town ; or of quhat Clanne or branch the saidis inhabitantis ar. And that the name of ony person that hes entered on the broken landes, after the removing of ony uther inobedient person therefra, be sent to the keeper of the said register within twelve days nixt after his first entry.

"(100). Divers sureties being maid sall be vailzieable, and the ane stoppis not the uther.

"Item. It is declared statute and ordained that the surety maid be the Landis-lordis and Baillies sall not be prejudicial nor stop the suretie maid be the Chieftaines, and principalles of Clannes. Nor be the contrair the surety maid be them to the Landis-lordes and Baillies."

The following Rolls were appended to the Act of Parliament :—

"The Roll of the Landislordis and Baillies of landis in the Hielandis and Isles, quhair brokin men hes duelt and presentlie duellis, 1587.

LANDISLORDIS AND BAILLIES.

The Duke of Lennox.

The Laird of Buchanane.

The Laird of McFarlane of the Arroquhar.

The Laird of Luss. (Colquhoun.)

The Laird McCawla of Ardincaple.

The Laird of Marchinstoun. (Napier of Merchistoun and Edinbellie holding lands in Menteith and Lennox inherited from his ancestress a coheiress of Patrick de Menteth of Rusky.)

The Laird of Glennegyis. (Haldane of Gleneagles descended from the other coheiress of Menteth of Rusky.)

The Erle of Glencarne. (Highland possessions unknown.)

The Laird of Drumquhassill. (Cunningham held the Islands of Loch-lomond).

The Laird of Kilcreuch. (In the Lennox, Galbraith.)

The Tutour of Menteith. (George Graham.)

The Laird of Knockhill. (Shaw of do. in Menteith.)

Hary Schaw of Cambusmoir.

The Laird of Kippanross. (Stirling.)

The Laird of Burley. (Balfour, superior, if not proprietor of the lands of Mochaster in Menteith.)

The Laird of Keir. (Stirling.)

The Master of Levingstoun. (Family possessed lands of Callander and Corriechrombie in Menteith.)

The Lord of Down. (Father of the ' Bonny Earl of Moray.')

The Lord Drummond.

The Laird of Tullibardin. (Sir John Murray, who possessed lands in Balquhidder.)

The Laird of Glenorquhy. (Sir Duncan Campbell.)

The Laird of Laweris. (Sir John Campbell.)

The Laird of Weyme. (James Menzies of that Ilk.)

The Abbot of Inchaffray. (James Drummond, Commendator of Inchaffray and Laird of Innerpeffry, created 1609 Lord Maderty.)

Coline Campbell of Ardbeich. (Brother of Glenurchy, on Lochearn.)

The Laird of Glenlyoun. (Campbell.)

The Erle of Athoill. (5th, of the Stewart of Innermeath line.)

The Laird of Grantullie. (Sir Thomas Stewart lands in Strathtay.)

The Laird of Strowane-Robertsone. (In Atholl.)

The Laird of Strowane-Murray. (In Strathearn. The daughter of the then proprietor John Murray married Eoin dubh MacGregor brother to Allester of Glenstray.)

The Laird of Wester Wemyss. (Said to have had the superiority of Kinnaird selling the property to Stewart of Rosyth.)

The Laird of Abbotishall. (Supposed Scott, a family in Fife.)

The Laird of Teling. (Sir David Maxwell, Forfarshire.)

The Laird of Inchmartine. (Ogilvie.)

The Laird of Purie-Fothringhame. (A proprietor in the Brae of Angus.)

The Laird of Moncreiffe. (William Moncreiffe of that Ilk proprietor for several centuries of Culdares and Tenaiffis in Breadalbane which he sold to Sir Duncan Campbell of Glenurchy.)

The Laird of Balleachane. (Stewart of Ballechin in Atholl, formerly styled of Stuiks.)

The Barroun of Fandowie. (In Atholl. James Macduff, alias Ferguson.)

The Erle of Erroll. (Possessed Logyalmond.)

The Erle of Gowrie. (James Ruthven, possessed lands in Strathardill and Strathbrane.)

The Laird of Cultibragane. (Alex. Ridheuch, Lands in Glenleidnoch in Strathearn.)

The Lord Ogilvy (of Airly).

The Laird of Clovay. (Ogilvy of Clova, in the brae of Angus.)

The Laird of Fintray. (Sir David Graham Knight in Forfarshire.)

The Laird of Edyell ; (Sir David Lindsay of Glenesk in Forfarshire.)

The Erle of Mar. (Proprietor of Braemar, &a.)

The Master of Elphingstoun. (The family appear to have possessed Corgarff in Banffshire, Kildrummy, &a.)

The Erle of Huntlie. (Lord of Badenoch and Lochaber.)

The Master of Forbes. (Highland estates on the Don, Aberdeenshire.)

The Laird of Grant.

Makintosche (of Dunauchton, Captain of the Clanchattan.)

The Lord and Tutour of Lovat. (Simon 8th Lord and Thomas Fraser of Knockie and Strichen, his uncle and guardian.)

Cheisholme of Cummer (or Comer.)

The Larde of Glengarry. (Proprietor also in right of his Grandmother of half the lands of Lochalsh, Lochcarron and Lochbroom.)

Makanyie. (Mackenzie of Kintail possessing the other half of the above lands.)

The Laird of Fowlis. (Munro.)

The Laird of Balnagown. (Ross.)

The Tutour of Cromartie. (Urquhart of Craigfintray, guardian to Sir Thomas Urquhart.)

The Erle of Suthirland.

The Laird of Duffus. (Sutherland.)

James Innes of Touchis.

The erle of Caithnes.

The Erle Merschall.

The Lord Oliphant. (Possessed Berrydale in Caithness.)

The Laird of Boquhowy. (Mowat of Boquhally, Caithness-shire.)

The laird of Dunnibeyth. (Sinclair of Dunbeath in Caithness.)

Macky of Far. (Father of first Lord Reay.)

Torquill McCloyd of Cogoych. (Son of Macleod of Lewis.)

The Laird of Garloch. (Mackenzie.)

Makgillichallum of Raarsay. (Malcolm Macleod.)

McCloid of the Harrich. (Harris.)

McKynnoun of Strathodell. (Mackinnon of Strathwardill in Skye.)

McCleud of the Lewes.

McNeill of Barray.

McKane of Ardnamurchan. (Macian of the family of the isles.)

Allane McKane of Ilandterum.
The Laird of Knoydert. (Alexander McRanald.)
McClane of Dowart. (McLean.)
The Lard of Ardgowir. (McLean of Ardgour.)
Johnne Stewart of the Appin.
McCoull of Lorne. (Dougal Macdougal of Dunolly.)
McCoull of Roray. (Allan Macdougal of Roray.)
The Laird of Lochynnell. (Campbell of Lochnell.)
The Laird of Caddell. (Campbell of Calder, often called thus.)
The Laird of Skermourlie for Rauchry. (Montgomerie of Skelmorlie
    appears to have had the small island of Rachry, coast of Antrim.)
McCondoquhy of Innerraw. (Dougal McConachy Campbell of Inveraw.)
Angus McConeill of Dunyveg and Glennis (?).
The Laird of Lowlip. (Alex. Macallaster of Loupe in Kintyre.)
The Schiref of Bute. (John Stewart.)
The Laird of Camys. (Hector Bannatyne of Kames.)
Erle of Ergile.
Laird of Auchinbrek. (Campbell.)
The Laird of Ardkinglass. (Campbell.)
McNauchtane. (Malcolm Macnaughtane of Dunderaw.)
McLauchlane. (Arch. Maclauchlane of Stralauchlan or of that Ilk.)
The Laird of Lawmont (of Inveryne or of that Ilk.)
The Laird of Perbrak. (Campbell of Barbrek.)
The Laird of Duntrune. (Campbell.)
Constable of Dundy. Laird of Glastry. (Sir James Scrymgeour of Dudope
    and of Glasry, in Ayrshire.)
The Laird of Elanegreg. (Campbell.)
The Laird of Otter. (Campbell.)
The Laird of Coll (Maclean.)
MakClayne of Lochbuy.
McFee of Collowsay. (Murdoch Macfee of Colonsay.)
The Lord Hamiltoun. (For the Isle of Arran.)"

"The Roll of the Clannis (in the Hielandis and Isles) that hes Capitanes, Chieffis,
and Chiftanes quhome on thay depend, oft tymes aganis the willis of thair
Landislordis: and of sum speciale personis of branchis of the saidis Clannes.
1587.

Buchananis.
McFerlanis, Arroquhar.
McKnabbis.

Grahmes of Menteth.
Stewartis of Buchquhidder.
Clangregour.
Clanlawren.
Campbellis of Lochnell.
Campbell of Innerraw.
Clandowill of Lorne.
Stewartis of Lorne, or of Appin.
Clane McKane of Avricht. (The Clan Eoin or Macdonalds of Glencoe,
    whose chief was patronomycally styled ' MacEoin Abrach.')
Stewartis of Athoill and pairties adiacent.
Menyessis, in Athoill and Apnadull.
Clan McThomas in Glensche.
Fergussonis.
Spaldingis.
Makintoscheis, in Athoill.
Clancamroun.
Clanrannald, in Lochquhaber. (Macdonalds of Keppoch.)
Clanrannald of Knoydert, Modert, and Glengaray.
Clenlewid of the Lewis.
Clanlewyd of Harray.
Clanneill.
Clankynnoun.
Clan Ieane. (The Clan Eoin of Ardnamurchan.)
Clanquhattan.
Grantis.
Frasseris.
Clankanye. (Kenzie.)
Clanandreis. (The Rosses.)
Monrois.
Murrayis, in Suthirland."

Both these Rolls have, for convenience, been taken from " The Transactions of the Iona Club, 1839, and the notes condensed from those of the
editor, Donald Gregory, Esq.

It may be remarked that in the latter half of the sixteenth century, of
which we are now treating, scarcely a Clan was at peace. The Earls of
Sutherland, Caithness, and Huntly; the Murrays, MacKenzies, Gunns,

Clan Chattan, and Gordons in the North and East were perpetually at war—bloodshed, fire, and even poison figure in their history. The MacDonalds, MacLeans, MacLeods, and MacNeills kept the West in fierce conflict Such was the normal state of the country, and on the Southern Border matters were not much better. Some remedy was absolutely necessary The scheme of the Government was very ingeniously contrived, though perhaps too fussy and minute to be easily workable By it theft was made treasonable, a strong measure, as loyalty to the Sovereign had never been questioned in the Highlands Frequent reference is made in subsequent years to this Act, known as the "General Band." It did not work a speedy pacification, but in the instance of the ClanGregor, more especially, actual existence was made impossible, except by fighting for it, as few could dare to shelter them under such precarious conditions.

Although other Clans were equally turbulent, none suffered eventually as severely. Mr Donald Gregory believed the chief cause of this to have been the circumstance that, unlike the Clan Chattan for instance, the ClanGregor had no extensive possessions under the Crown which could render them independent of the great families around It may be added that of their neighbours, Campbell of Glenurchy was ever ready to profit by their misfortunes, and Campbell of Argyle to make a cat's paw of them. for his own purposes Nothing but the brave and elastic spirit inherited from our ancestors, and the power of endurance learnt in the school of adversity, could have saved us from entire annihilation, such as some of our neighbours desired for us

Two characteristic MacGregor songs from the "Killin Collection" seem to belong to about this period, and may therefore fitly follow here .—

NA TULAICHEAN (REEL OF TULLOCH).

"The following incident occurred in the latter part of the sixteenth or early part of the seventeenth century A John MacGrigor, usually known as Iain Dubh Gearr of the Ruaru branch of that Clan, was at Killin attending St Fillan's market

('Feill Fhaolain'), which is held there in January. He was set upon in Street-house[1] by eight men; but being very powerful and a splendid swordsman, he either killed or seriously wounded the whole of them. Upon this he fled to Strathspey, where he married a young lady named Isabel Anderson. Twelve men and a superior in command were sent after to take him either dead or alive. He was slumbering in a barn when intelligence was privately brought him that they had arrived and were near at hand. His first impulse was to fly, but being strongly persuaded by Isabel, he resolved on fighting it out. They had a gun and a pistol, with plenty of ammunition, and as John fired at his pursuers through crevices in the wall, Isabel, who stood behind him, loaded. The result was that in a very short time the whole thirteen were severely wounded, whereupon John sallied forth and cut off their heads. Isabel gave him a draught of beer which he quaffed; and seizing her round the waist they improvised and danced those reel-steps which have ever since been so popular.[2] The words were also improvised and sung as a mouth-tune, but the music must have been old.

"John, it is said, afterwards became a peaceable and prosperous man; and it has been satisfactorily shown that the celebrated Doctors Gregory who did so much to establish the fame of the Edinburgh Medical School were descendants of his. Before settling down, however, there is reason to believe that he 'raised' some successful 'creachs' in Breadalbane. There can be no doubt about his period, as his name appears in the Record of Privy Seal, of date 15th May 1586."

[1] The local name for Killin Hotel.
[2] Probably few who gaily dance this merry reel know anything of the grim tale of its origin. Iain Dubh Gearr's name does not appear in the list of August 1586. Although it may read strange, yet after the intense strain of defending himself and his wife against such overpowering odds, that the excitement and reaction should culminate in violent exercise is not improbable.

Na Tulaichean.

"Bu Ghriogaireach darireadh
A Ruadh-shruth 'an Gleann-liomhunn.
A rinn an ceòl 'tha riomhach,
Ris canar leinn na Thulaichean.

  Chorus—O Thulaichean gu Bhealaichean,
     'S 'o Bhealaichean ;
     'S mur faigh sinn leann 's na Thulaichean,
     Gu 'n ol sinn uisg e Bhealaichean.

B' ann an Tigh-na-Sràide
Athug iad ionnsuidh bhàis air ;
'S mur bitheadh e ro làidir,
Bha ochdnar nàmh ro mhurrach air.
    O Thulaichean, &a.

Ach labhair Ian-Dubh-Geàrr riubh ;
'Bha mi ann 's a' cheàrdaich,
'S cha chrom mi sios mo cheann duibh,
Ged thionndadh sibh uile rium.'
    O Thulaichean, &c.

'N sin bhuail iad uil' air comhladh ;
'S ged 'bha Ian Dubh na onar ;
Cha b' ann da m' buannachd tòiseach,
Bha fuil mu shròin na h-uille fir.
    O Thulaichean, &a.

'S 'n uair thaisg e suas a gheur-lann,
'S a dh' ioc e mheud 's a dh' eigh e,
Gu 'n tug e 'n sin Srath Spé air
'S bha té ann a chuir furan air.
    O Thulaichan, &a.

Chuir iad cuideachd làidir,
Ann déigh Iain Duibh Mhic Phàdruic ;
'S 'n uair shaoil leo e 'bhi 'n sàs ac'
'S e bas bh' air a chumadh dhoíbh.
    O Thulaichean, &a.

REEL OF TULLOCH.

"From Ruaru in Glenlyon
A true MacGrigor scion,
Made music which we own the chief,
And which we call the Tullechin.

> *Chorus*—From Tullechin to Ballechin
> From Ballechin to Tullechin;
> If beer we don't in Tullechin
> We'll water get in Ballechin.

In Streethouse at Feill Fhaolan
On him they made an onset dead
And were he not most manly brave,
Eight sturdy men had mastered him.
> From Tullechin, &a.

Then Black John spake up hurriedly :
' I'm just come from the armoury
And will not down my head coward-bend,
Though all of you should grapple me.'
> From Tullechin, &a.

On this they all fell foul of him ;
And though alone he stoutly faced ;
'Twas not advantage that they won
For down their cheeks poured bloody drops.
> From Tullechin, &a.

Then having sheathed his good broadsword
On shewing what his manhood could,
He to Strathspey his steps betook
And there a maiden welcomed him.
> From Tullechin, &a.

Against Black John MacPhatrick
Was sent a stout and goodly band,
But when they thought that him they'd caught
'Twas death that shaped their destiny.
> From Tullechin, &a.

Oir thàinig fios an uaighneas,
Do 'n t-shabhal 's e na shuain ann .
'Tog ort, Iain Duibh, 's bidh gluasadh,
'S thoir as cho luath 's a 's urra dhuit.'
          O Thulaichean, &a.

'S e thuirt a leannan ceutach ;
'A ghaoil, cuir ort,' 's bidh treunmhor ;
Is dhuit bi thidh mise feumail,
Oir bidh mi gu d' chuideachadh.
          O Thulaichean, &a.

'Thoir uidhean dhomh gu sùrdail,
Is lionaidh mi gu dlùth dhuit,
'N sin cumsa 'ghraidh, do chùl rium,
'S do shùil air na h-uile fear.'
          O Thulaichean, &a.

Sheall e cia lion bh' ann diu,
Mu 'n rachadh e gu 'n ionnsuidh ;
Bha dà-fhear-dheug 'us ceannard.
Co teann air 's a b' urra iad.
          O Thulaichean, &a.

Chum e riu a bhòtach,
'S bha Isabail 'g a chònadh ;
Cha do thàr iad gus an eòlas,
'S ann leòn e gu h-ullamh iad.
          O Thulaichean, &a.

Gheàrr e leum gu h-eatrom,
Gu 'n ionnsuidh, agus fraoch air,
Cha d' ag e ceann air h-aon diu,
Thoirt sgeul air an turas ud.
          O Thulaichean, &a.

'Mo bheannachd air an t-shealgair ;
Ann ad chuirinn earbsa ;
'S tu rinn an gniomh neo-chearbach,
'S tu dhearbh a bhi urramach.'
          O Thulaichean, &a.

To Black John 'midst his slumberings,
A message came in urgent haste :
' Be up Black John bestir you quick,
And take you off right speedily.'
From Tullechin, &a.

Then said his darling Isabel
' Be up and quit you valiantly
A helpmate true I'll make to you
In your sore straits to succour you.'
From Tullechin, &a.

' Your ammunition hand me quick
I'll load for him I fondly like,
As you with back straight turned on me
Your eye keep towards the enemy.'
From Tullechin, &a.

Ere Black John raised his battle shout
His eye he o'er the foe keen glanced,
Twelve men with one to lead them on
He found were closing fast on him.
From Tullechin, &a.

His musket then he aimed at them
Whilst Is'bel pressed each charge fast down ;
And ere their fears to danger woke
Sore wounded was each one of them.
From Tullechin, &a,

Then out he leaped with nimble bound
And with fierce wrath fierce kindling him,
No head he left on body then
To tell of their sad tragedy.
From Tullechin, &a.

' My blessings on my sportsman good ;
To him I will entrust my life ;
You there in strife a hero stood
And did a deed of mightihood.'
From Tullechin, &a.

Thuirt Iain Dubh 's e tionndadh :
'O n' rinn mi 'n gniomh bha shannt orm ;
Ghaoil grad thoir deoch do 'n leann domh,
'S gu 'n danns mi na Thulaichean.'
       O Thulaichean, &a.

'B' e 'n t' aighear 'us an t-aoibhneas,
'N am cruinneach re cheile,
'N uair chluinneadhmid na teudan
Ga 'n gleusadh do na Thulaichean.'
       O Thulaichean, &a.

'N a' mrbithinn mar bu ghnàth leam,
'S MacAilpein a bhi làimh rium,
Bu bhinn leam bhi ga eisdeachd
'N uair thàireadh air na Thulaichean.'
       O Thulaichean, &a."

Oran Chlann-Ghriogair. (Glenorchy MacGregor's Song.)

"This song was composed by a MacGregor woman who was married in Glenorchy. It dates back probably to the early part of the 17th century when the persecution against this unhappy clan raged so fiercely. It points to a time when guns were not unknown, but when bows and arrows were still in use. The circumstances which called it forth arose out of these troubles. A party of them flying from their foes having taken shelter in her husband's house were suddenly informed that their pursuers were close at hand and in full view of the front of the house. The housewife with great presence of mind instantly rushed out and

Oran Chlann-Ghriogair.

Mi am shuidhe 'n so 'm ònar,
Air còmhnard an rathaid ;
Dh'fheuch am faic mi fear fuadain
'Tigh'n Chruachan a' cheathaich.
'Bheir dhomh sgeul air Clann Ghriogair
No fios cionn a ghabh iad,
'S iad bu chuideachd a dhomhsa
Didomhnuich so chaidh.

Says Black John turning towards his bride :
'Since I did what I meant to do ;
Give me a drink of beer to quaff,
And we will dance the Tullechin.'
            From Tullechin, &a.

'In meets for joy and happiness,
What mirth and gladness fills our hearts
Whene'er we hear the strings attuned
For giving us the Tullechin.
            From Tullechin, &a.

'Were I where my desire is set
MacAlpin sitting by my side
With what delight I'd hear him play
The King of tunes the Tullechin.'
            From Tullechin, &a."

sitting herself by the roadside commenced singing this song.   The other party
stopped to listen and thus allowed time for the MacGregors to escape by the back
of the house.

"The language is highly metaphorical ; but not so much so as to prevent our
unravelling the meaning.   A party of MacGrigors called Dark-blue Stags were
startled by their enemies at the riverside and chased to the Glen of Mists.   One
of their number a kinsman of the songstress, by whom he is designated the
'Graceful Bird' was murdered by them.   The arrow wound she speaks of having
received is evidently not a physical wound at all, but the pain of mind she experienced in consequence.   Reciting this to the murderers, she could not possibly even
with all the protection which her womanhood gave her use plainer language."

GLENORCHY MACGRIGOR'S SONG.

All alone I am seated
By the side of the highway
Watching for some coming wanderer
From Ben Cruachan the misty.
My hope is he can give me
Some sure news of ClanGrigor.
With whom spent I last Sunday
In kinship and greeting.

Cha d'fhuair mi d'an sgeul,
Ach iad bhi'n dé air na sraithibh,
Thall 's a bhos mu Loch-fine,
Ma 's fior mo luchd-bratha
Ann an Clachan-an-Diseart
'G òl fìon air na maithibh,
Bha Griogair mór, ruadh ann
Lamh chruaidh air chul claidhimh.

Agus Griogair mór, meadhrach
Ceann-feadhn ar luchd-tighe,
Mhic an fhir á Srath-Arduil,
Bhiodh na bàird ort a tathaich.
Bheireadh greis air a chlarsaich
'S air an taileasg gu aighear,
'S a sheinneadh an fhidheal
'Chuireadh fiughair fo mhnathan

S ann a rinn sibh 'n t-sithionn anmoch
Anns a' ghleann am bi'n ceathach,
Dh'fhag sibh an t-Eoin boidhaech
Air a' mhointich 'na laidhe.
Na stairsnich air feithe,
'N déigh a reubadh le claidheamh,
'S ann a thog sibh greigh dhù-ghorm
Bho luban na h-abhann.

Ann am bothan na dige,
Ghabh sibh dion air an rathad,
Far an d'fhag sibh mo bhiodag
Agus criosd mo bhuilg-shaighead.
Gur i saighead na h-araich
So tharmaich am leathar,
Chaidh saighead am shliasaid
Crann fiar air dhroch shnai theadh.

Gu'n seachnadh Righ nan Dul sibh
Bho fhudar caol neimhe
Bho shradagan teine
Bho pheileir 's bho shaighead.

No news has since reached me
Of how they are faring,
Save, yestreen, that they wandered
Up and down through the Strath-glades.
At Lochfyne they were heard of
If true be my story;
At Clachan Diseart they were drinking
Goodly wine with the Chieftains.

There was 'mongst them red Grigor
Truest hand behind broadsword
And big Gregor the light-hearted,
Of our horsemen the leader.
Son of him from Strathardle
On whom bards would be calling
For a lilt on harp tuneful,
Then awhile at backgammon.

He could play a strain cheerysome
On the violin so sweetly
As would fill the fair maidens
With joy and with gladness.
Late at even you were hunting
In the glen where the mist wreathes.
There on the top of the moss-bog,
A grand bird you left lying.

Stretched out on the soft bog,
There he lay as you sped him,
With claymore cruelly tearing
His comeliest person.
From the loop where the stream bends,
You the dark-blue stags startled;
In the bothy by the dyke's side
You took shelter in passing.

There left you my true dirk,
With the belt of my quiver;
'Twas the arrow of slaughter
That piercéd my body.

2 C

Bho sgian na roinn' caoile
'S bho fhaobhar caol claidhimh,
'S ann bha bhuidheann gun còmhradh
Di-domhnuich 'm braigh bhaile.

'S cha dean mi gair eibhinn
'N am éiridh no laidhe,
'S beag an t-iognadh dhomh fein sud
'S mi an deigh mo luchd-tighe.
'S beag an t-iognadh dhomh fein sud
'S mi an deigh mo luchd-tighe,
'S mi'm shuidhe'n so 'm onar
Air comhnard an rathaid.

Through my thigh went that arrow,
And wounded me sorely ;
Whose shaft was but ill-trimmed,
Both crooked and tearing.

May the God of all Nature
Thou preserve from grained powder
From the sharp flashes flaming,
From bullet and arrows.
O'er my face then shall henceforth
No laugh flit in dimples
Nor smile of heart gladness
At morn or night-fall.

Chapter XVIII

Death of Drummondernoch

WE now come to the darkest page of our history, the murder of John Drummond of Drummondernoch; a crime which we would fain believe to have been perpetrated by men of another name. Of this deed there are several different accounts which agree in attaching the blame to the ClanGregor   The following is taken from the " Black Book of Taymouth " —

"Bond to pursue the Clan McGregour for the murder of Johne Drummond of Drumnevenocht

"Be it kend to all men. Us undirsubscryveris undirstaning be mony actis maid nocht onlie be the Kingis Maisties progenitouris bot alsa be his Maiesties self baith in Parliament and privie Counsel anent the daylie morthouris slauchteris herschipis and thiftis committit be clannis of hieland men upoun the inhabitantes of the laiche cuntreis speciallie be the clan of McGregouris   Lyke as laithe the said Clan of McGregour in the moneth of Sep last bipast, maist creuallie slew and murtherit Johne Drummond of Drumnevenocht in Glenarkney being under thair doubil assurance, the ane grantit be my Lord Huntlie in thair name to my Lord of Montroiss assuring that he and al his and in special the said Johne Drummond suld be unharmit in body and geir ay and quhil the said assurance sud be upgiffin and dischargit on to my Lord of Montroiss be the said Erle of Huntlie, quhilk onavyss ves na done afoir the said slauchter nor yit sensyne, the uther assurance to my Lord of Inchaffray and all his kin, friendis and surname upone the Monunday befoir the said slauchter, sua that nather of the foresaid assurances ves than outrun; the said Johne being directit be his Chief at his Maiesties commandment for getting of vennisoune to have send to Edinburght to his Maiestie's marriage, the said Clan cuttit and oftuik his heid, and thairefter convenand the rest of that clan, and setting doun the heid befoir thame, thairby causing thame authoreiss the said creual murthour, lykas thai have done, mening thairby to continew the lyke or greter gif thai be not preventit. . . . We undersubscryvand beand sua tender of bluid allyance and nychtbouris being sua of thereft of our frinedis tennentis and seruandis slane, murtherit and herreit be the said clan of befoir. and of mind to revenge the said creuel murthour and bluid of the said Johne Drummond, hes bundin ilkane of us to tak trev and efald pairt togidder for perseuing of the said clan and committaris of the said murthour quhairevir thai may be apprehendit, and gif thai sall happin to frequent or invaid ony ane of us ve all sall repair and hald our forces to the partie invadit, and ve bind us upone our honour and lautie that nane of us sall appoint or aggre witht the said clan bot the advyss of the rest of the subscryveris. In vitness quhairof we have subscryirt this present with our handis at Mugdoge, Inispeffre and Drummen and Balloche the 20, 23, & 30 days of Oct. 1589. befoir thir vitness Robert Grahame of Auchinclocht, William Drummond of Pitcairnis."

     " DRUMMOND   JOHNE Erle of Montroiss
     " DUNCANE CAMPBELL of Glenurquhay   Inchaffray."

" The Erle of Montroiss binds himself to raise 30 men, my Lord Drummond and his friends 40, and the Laird of Glenurquhay three score to perschew the said clan for revenge of Johne Drummondis slawchter. 24. Dec. 1589."

The Record contained in the Register of the Privy Council is more detailed and gives a full list of those of the Clan who were proscribed, which is here copied for genealogical studies :—

     " 1589-90. Feb. 4. At Edinburgh.

" The Lords of secret Council being creditably informed of the cruel and mischievous proceeding of the wicked ClanGregor, so long continuing in blood, slaughters, herships manifest reiffs, and stouths, committed upon his highness peacable and good subjects, inhabiting the countries next the Braes of the highlands these many years bygone, but specially how after the cruel murder of umqle John Drummond his Majesty's proper Tenant and one of his Foresters of Glenartney committed upon the   day of   last by past, by certain of the said Clan, by the counsel and determination of the whole, avowing to defend the authors there of whoever would pursue for revenge of the same, when the said John was occupied in seeking of venison to his Highness at command of Patrick Lord Drummond, Stewart of Stratherne and principal Forester of Glenartney The Queen his Majesties dearest spouse being then shortly looked for to arrive in this realm. Like as after the murder committed the authors thereof cut off the said umqule John Drummond's head and carried the same to the Laird of MacGregor who, and the whole surname of MacGregors purposely convened upon the next Sunday thereafter at the Church of Balquhidder where they caused the said umqule Johns head to be presented to them and there avowing the said mursder to have been committed by their common counsel and determination laid their hands upon the pow, and in eithnick (heathenish) and barbarous manner swore to defend the authors of the said murder, in most proud contempt of our sovereign Lord and his authority and in evil example to other wicked limmers to do the like if this shall be suffered to remain unpunished, Therefore Ordain commissions to be made and expede under our Sovereign Lords Signet in due form making constituting and ordaining George Earl of Huntly, Lord Gordon and Badenoch, Colin Earl of Argyle Lord Campbell and Lorne, John Earl of Athole Lord of Balveny, John Earl of Montrose Lord Graham, Patrick Lord Drummond, James Commendator of Inscheafftray, Archibald Campbell of Lochnell, Duncan Campbell of Glenurchy, John Campbell of Cadell (Calder) James Campbell of Ardkinglass, Lauchlan Macintosh of Dunnauchtan, Sir John Murray of Tullibardine Knight; George Buchanan of that Ilk and Andrew Macfarlane of Arrochar, our Sovereign Lord's Justices in that part to the effect underwritten, Giving Granting and Committing to them conjunctly and severally full power special command and authority to pass, search for seek take and apprehend

1 Allaster MacGregor of Glenstra,
2 John dhu MacGregor his brother, (killed at Glenfruin),
3 Dulechay (*i.e.*, Dougal chaich, or Dougal of the mist)[1] MacGregor,
4 Duncan Macgregor his brother,
5 John dhu macneill Marfarlane,
6 Ewin Macfarlane,
7 Patrick ower MacGregor (in Cadderine—paternal uncle (youngest) of Glenstray, No. 38 of 1586),
8 Duncan Glen MacGregor (paternal uncle of Glenstra, 13 of 1586),
7 Alexander Pudrach MacGregor (from Balquhidder) under the Laird of Weyme (4 of 1586),
8 Alexander galt MacGregor (paternal uncle of Glenstra, 3 of 1586),
9 Patrick Duncanson in Overzaldie, (Innerzaldie, 9 of 1586),
10 Gregor (his son),
11 Duncan his son in Port of Latherne (11 of 1586),
12 Donald dhu (his son) in Megor (12 of 1586),
13 Finla, his son,
14 Patrick Johnstoun MacGregor in Dalm-kland (Dalmarglan),
15 Patrick Ammonach (of Glenalmond) his brother, (died before 1598),
16 John,
17 Duncan,
18 and Gregor Macphatricks his sons,
19 John Johnston MacGregor, in Balenacoule,
20 Duncan Macallaster in Dundurne (15 (?)—1586),
21 John Macallaster his brother there (16 (?)—1586),
22 John MacAllaster his brother in Ballenacoule,

---

[1] Of the Dougal Kier or Ciar tribe, the name sounding alike.

23 ⌠Gregor Macilchallum V^{c}Gregor in Comrie,
24 ⌡Callum MacGregor his brother in Blairinroga,
25 Duncan slaach MacGregor in Morell,
26 Gregor Cam MacGregor in Donnyra (Duneira),
27 Gregor Macconachy moir in Finglen,
28 William Maceane V^{c}Donald in Clern,
29 William ower MacGregor in Tullichattill,
30 Allaster macconachy moir in Glen Torchan,
31 Allaster macneill in Tullibenacher,
32 ⌠Allaster macphatrick beg in Carraglen,
33 ⌡Thomas Macphatrick his brother there,
34 John dhu MacAllaster in Callander,
35 ⌠John dhu macconachy V^{c}Allaster in Rannoch,
36 ⌡Donald dhu,
37 ⌡and Archibald dhu his brothers,
38 Gregor macean V^{c}Connachy,
39 Neill MacGregor,
40 Allaster MacGregor,
41 ⌠Dougal Chaich MacGregor (mentioned previously),
42 ⌡Duncan dhu his brother (ditto),
43 ⌠Duncan ower MacGregor in Duncrosk,
44 ⌡Dougal his son,
45 Gregor beg MacGregor,
46 Gregor macanroy there,
47 Dougal maceanduy in Candkirk,
48 John macconachy V^{c}eanduy in Rannoch,
49 Duncan macallaster in Fernay,
50 ⌠John dhu,
51 ⌡and Allaster his brother,
52 Neill macconachy,
53 ⌠William macneill (52 (?)—1586),
54 ⌡Malcolm his brother,
55 ⌡Neill macneill his brother,
56 John bane MacGregor in Fernay,
57 Allaster MacGregor Cleroch there,
58 Duncan macewin in Creichgarrow, Grandson of Duncan VI. of Roro,
59 Gregor Machutcheon his son in Couldar,
60 Duncan Maceancham in Tullichmullen,
61 ⌠Gregor macconachy in Rorow, (Head of the tribe of Roro),
62 ⌡John dhu his brother,
63 ⌡Allaster macewin there, brother of Duncan (58),
64 ⌡Duncan Macconchy clerich there,

65 ⎧Gregor Macilchallum in Glenlyon,
66 ⎪Duncan,
67 ⎨Neill,
68 ⎩and William his sons,
69 ⎧John Macgregor Jameson in Apindull,
70 ⎨William,
71 ⎩Dougal his brothers,
72 Gregor Maceanmoyle (Maol, bald, tonsured) in Bofrak, (97—1586),
73 ⎧Gregor Macneill V^cInvallich in Ardewnaig, (98—1856),
74 ⎪Ewin Maccanvallich there, (99—1586),
75 ⎨John Roy Maceanvallich there,
76 ⎪Duncan Macinvallich in Comrie,
77 ⎩Donald Maceanvallich his brother, (the Mallochs),
78 Allaster Birrach Macewinmoir,
79 ⎧Malcolm Macdougalchere, in Balquhidder, (ancestor of Innerardaren,
   ⎪   29—1586),
80 ⎪Dougal Maccoulchere in Glengyll,
81 ⎨Duncan macphatrick V^cCoulchere,
82 ⎪John his brother,
83 ⎪Patrick,
84 ⎪and Gregor his brothers,
85 ⎩John Macgregor V^cCoulchere,
86 Duncan bane macrob V^cearlach in Stukenroy, (21—1586),
87 John Macrob MacGregor in Ruchoise, (22—1586),
88 Gregor macrob MacGregor, in Comir, (Foot of Benlomond, on north-
       east, 23—1586),
89 ⎧Callum McCallum moir MacGregor, kurkhelich (Knockheilt, 24—
   ⎪   1586),
90 ⎨Callum dhu his brother, (25—1586),
91 ⎪Robert Roy his brother in Comrie, (26—1856),
92 ⎩John dhu Macrob their brother, (27—1586),
93 Allaster Maccoul V^cGregor in Dishoir, (north side of Loch Tay, 28—
       1586),
94 Malcolm MacGregor there, (29—1586),
95 Duncan (30—1586),
96 John MacGregor in Drumnauchtie,
97 Finla Keir MacGregor in Colcarrach, (Culgart, 35—1586),
98 Allaster MacGregor in Strathfillan, (36—1586),
99 John dhu Macilchallum V^cGregor, (39—1586),
100 Patrick MacGregor V^cilchallum,
101 Duncan Clerach MacGregor, (39—1586),

102 Gregor Craginslach MacGregor, (40—1586),
103 Donald ower macean clerach, (41—1586, McInleith?),
104 Malcolm Glas MacGregor in Kinnadie, (48—1586),
105 Dougal Denestoun MacGregor (93—1586),
106 Donald maccoule V^ceandane,
107 Malcolm MacGregor V^cNeill in Rannoch,
108 Dougal his brother,
109 John beg clerach,
110 Duncan MacGregor in Tullichew, (Tullichewne 73—1586),
111 John dhu macwilliam V^cIlchallum,
112 Duncan MacGregor McWilliam, (74—1586),
113 Callum McWilliam MacGregor in Rannoch, (77—1586),
114 Duncan McWilliam his brother, (75—1586),
115 Callum V^cNeill V^cEwin V^cGregor, (76—1586),
116 Malcolm MacGregor V^cWilliam (79 (?)—1586),
117 Allaster macinnes in Rannoch, (80—1586),
118 Gregor macneill V^cGregor, Candochaach (Candrochitmirk), (81—1586),
119 ⌠John his son Ardchalzie, (or Ardquhillerie?), (82—1586),
120 ⌡Ewin MacGregor, (83—1586),
121 ⌊and Allaster MacGregor, his brothers, (84—1586),
122 Allaster macrob in Strathyre, (85—1586),
123 Walter Macalpine in little Gaikie, (86—1586),
124 Robert Macalpine his son, (87—1586),
125 Murdoch Macalpine his brother, (88—1586),
126 ⌠John bane macilchallum glas in Rannoch, (89—1586),
127 ⎮Gregor Ger his brother, (90—1586),
128 ⌡John m^cneill his brother also, (91—1586),
129 ⎮Gregor bane[1] their brother's son, (92—1586, where he is called 'Cam'
    ⌊ instead of bane),
130 Patrick MacGregor in Cadderlie, (38 again?—1586),
131 Ewin erenoch MacGregor,
132 Patrick maceanroy MacGregor in Dundurn,
133 Neill macdonachie V^cNeill,
134 Gregor his brother,
135 Gregor MacGregor als Colbanach,
136 ⌠Malcolm macean v^cconachy son to umquhile John Duncanson in Meltie,
137 ⎨Duncan,
138 ⌊and John dhu his brothers,
139 Patrick MacGregor in Callendar,

[1] Noted, it is said, for fleetness of foot.

2 D

and all others of the said ClanGregor or their Assisters culpable of the said
odious murder, or of theft, reset, of theft, herships, and sorning wherever they may
be, apprehended, to put and hold them in ward, and to the knowledge of an assize,
or assises for the said crimes, and, as they salbe found culpable, or innocent to
minister justice upon them conform to the laws, and consuetude of this realm and
for that effect to sett, begin, affirm, hold, and continue Courts of Justiciary in
whatever parts, or places, to cause suits be called, to fine those absent, and to
punish tresspassers, to make create substitute, and ordain Deputes under them
with clerks, servants, Dempsters, and all other officers and members of Court
needful, for whom they shall be holden to answer, To summon warn chuse and
cause to be sworne Assises one or more of the best and worthiest persons dwelling
within Stratherne, Menteith, Atholl, Lenox, and four halfs about, least suspected
and that best knows the verity of the said matter, each person under the pain of
forty pounds ; To apply the escheits of the persons convicted, and to be justified to
the dead, the one half to his Highness Treasurer or Treasurer Depute, and the
other half of the same to the takers and apprehenders own use for their labour ;
and if any of the persons abovewritten or others assisting them refuse to be taken,
and fly to strengths and houses to pursue and besiege them with fire and sword,
raise fire, and use all force and warlike engines, for recovering thereof And if any
of them shall be hurt, slain, or mutilated, or any destruction of houses and goods
take place, Decerning and declaring that the same shall be imputed for no crime
or offence to the said commissioners, nor they nor none of them shall be called or
accused criminally or civilly in any manner of way, in time coming Discharging
and exonerating them of the same for ever by these presents, and that the said
Commission be extended in the best form with all clauses needful and for the
space of three years after the same to endure."—Rec. Sec. Con. Acta Vol., from
1587 to 1589.

The following Complaint appears in the Register of Hornings, Perth :—

"1590. April 4.   Complaint at the instance of Levingstoun with the bairnis and
remanent friendis of Johne Drummond of Drummenerinoch upon Alester
MacGregour of Glenstra, John Dow MacGregour his brother (here follows a
recapitulation of the list of names which has been previously given) charging
them with coming to the number of four hundred persons, setting upon the
said John Drummond (being direct be Patrick Lord Drummond to our park
and forestis, for slaying of weansone to have been sent to our palice of
Halieruidhous for preparation to have been made for the quene our darrest
spouse cuming to our realm than luikit for) and there schamefullie and
cruellie and unmercifullie slew and murdered him, cuttit off his hand after
the said murder and caried the same to the Laird MacGregor quha with the

haill persons above written purposelie convened upon the next Sunday thereafter at the Kirk of Balquhidder where they causit the said Johne's hand be presented to them and allowed that the said murder was done by their common consent and counsel, laid their hands upon the samye and swore to defend the authors thereof against all that would see the revenge thereof."

In the above document it must be observed that the "hand" of the murdered man is mentioned instead of the "head," an important difference in refutation of the Ardvorlich legend.

The Princess of Denmark sailed for Scotland in August 1589, when the ship was beaten back by storms. The King eventually embarked on the 22nd October to fetch his bride; the royal marriage took place on the 23rd November, the winter was spent in Denmark, and the royal pair landed at Leith on the 1st May 1590.

From the "Chartulary":—

"1590. April 7. James Commendator of Inchaffray,[1] brother of Lord Drummond was by the High Court of Justiciary at Edinburgh called to produce letters at the instance of the Kin and friends of the late John Drummond of Drummondernoch to be surety of a considerable number of the individuals of the ClanGregor who had been denounced nominatim by the Secret Council 4. Feb. preceding, viz Patrik Duncanson in Overzeldie, Gregour Duncan Donald Dow, Finlay and Duncan his sones, Duncane McAllaster in Dundurne John McAllaster his brother yair, Gregour Cam McGregour in Doura, Gregour McCondoquhie Vayne in Finglene William McEwin VcDonald in Clwnye (Cluny) William our McGregour in Tulliechettill, Allaster McPatrik beig in Farne Glen, Thomas McPhatrik his brother, Dougall McCoullicheir in Glengyle, Malcum McDougallcheir in Balquhidder, Allester McRobb in Strathyre   his sones Gregour McGregour alias Cattanach, Malcum McEwin VcConquhill sone to umquhile Johne Duncansoun in Mevie, Duncan his brother, John Dow his brother; That they sall compeir for the slaughter of the said umqle John Drummond."—Record of Justiciary.

The foregoing papers give a very circumstantial account of the murder, although without any details, and lay it to the charge of some of the

[1] On Aug. 31, 1590, the Commendator was "unlawit" fined in the pains contenit in Act of Parliament for nocht production thairof upoun ilk ane of the persones abone written in the pane of fourtie pounds.

ClanGregor. The tradition handed down in Balquhidder, however, is that the real perpetrators of the deed were the McIans of Ardnamurchan, and there does not appear to be any proof of the painful addition of the alleged brutality at Ardvorlich, which, even in those rough days, would have been surely looked upon with horror.

When "The Legend of Montrose" was first published with the ghastly tale related by Sir Walter Scott in the introduction, Sir John MacGregor Murray was much concerned at this accusation against the Clan, and took much trouble to collect evidence on the other side.

The following letter gives the Ardvorlich tradition in full :—

" Letter from William Stewart of Ardvorlich to Sir John MacGregor Murray dated Ardvorlich 13. Dec : 1812.

" With regard to the story of the murder of Drummond of Drummondiarnach, an account of which I sent to Mr Scott I am sorry I did not retain a copy otherwise would have sent it to you, The story is briefly this so far as I have been told by my Father and several old men in this neighbourhood, Drummondiarnach was Steward Depute of the Stewartry of Strathearne under his cousin the then Lord Drummond. Some little time before the accession of James VI. to the Crown of England, he had been active in apprehending two or three McGregors of a tribe in the Braes of Balquhidder called ' Clan Duie a cheadnich' who had been committing depredations upon some part of the estate of Perth. and causing them to be executed at Crieff; some time thereafter Drummondiarnach was surprised by a party of these McGregors in the forest of Glenartney and in revenge for the death of their kinsmen they murdered him and carried off his head. After committing the deed they came down to this place ; at that time Alexander Stewart of Ardvorlich one of my ancestors was married to Margaret Drummond a sister of Drummondiarnach's, they came into the house, the mistress having set some cold meat before them upon her going out of the room, at her return she was surprised to see her brother's bloody head upon the table and they by way of diversion desiring him to eat, for many a hearty meal had been made at that table. The poor woman in a state of distraction immediately left the room and it was said she never halted till she went to the spot where her brother was killed. Many legendary stories were told of her wildness and associating with the deer for several months, but the fact was she was secured by her husband and friends, and gradually recovered her reason and lived many years after. Immediately after this happened an express was sent to Drummond Castle ; soon after letters of fire and sword were obtained against the MacGregors ; Drummond of Invermay, a younger brother of Drummondiarnach was sent up with a strong party here, assisted by a party from the Earl of Montrose, they were likewise joined by another party here; they went up the Braes of Balquhidder and upon the field below Invernenty it was said they killed thirtyseven of them. Some time thereafter the proprietor here seized twelve of them, carried them to the east end of Lochearn and hanged them upon an oak tree which grew upon a spot that has been pointed out to me. This I was told extirpated the whole of that race and I have repeatedly heard from several McGregors in this country that these were the only McGregors implicated in that murder for which they suffered so severely. I see by a copy of the letters of fire and sword which are inserted in a late publication that this happened in 1589, and that Drummondiarnach was at the time employed in killing venison for the nuptials of King James VI. with Ann of Denmark."

Sir John afterwards obtained depositions from old inhabitants of the district, which are here given, and followed by two letters from impartial correspondents, written at the period when the tradition was brought to light.

Depositions regarding the Tradition of the Slaughter of Drummond Earnach, Forrester of Glenarthy in the reign of King James VI.

"Kirktown of Balquhidder 26. May 1815.

"Alexander Macnab Residing at Lochearnhead aged sixty-nine years, having been called to make oath with regard to the above slaughter, and being accordingly sworn and examined Depones That he was acquainted with one John Carmichael in Leaks in Breadalbane, who died about forty-four years ago, at the age of eighty. That several years before the death of the said John Carmichael, who was the Deponent's father's neighbour in the same Farm the Deponent heard him repeatedly give the following account of the above mentioned slaughter, viz That two young Lads of the MacIans or MacDonalds of Glencoe having gone to the Forest of Glenartney, of which the said Drummond Earnach was Forrester frightened the Deer from the Forest, and were met by the Forrester who, as a punishment cut a piece off their ears. . That having gone home and complained of the injury done to them, it awoke the anger of their Clan, who in consequence assembled and sent a party of their number down to the said Forrest, where having met with the said Forrester and a servant, the servant ran away and the MacIans cut off the Forrester's head. That having done so, they carried the head to the house of Ardvorlich, the Lady of which was sister to the Forrester so slaughtered. That she set meat before them on the table, and having occasion to go out of the room to get some drink to give them, they placed her brothers head on the table; and one of them was in the act of holding a Caiper[1] to the head saying as she entered "Eat that, you are welcome." That she instantly lost her judgment, left the house, and went

[1] Kebbuch-cheese.

to the hill, where according to the tradition she remained for some time amongst the Deer until her Husband found her one night in a hut and took her home next morning. That according to the same tradition a poor woman of Glencoe a Druidess, threw a spell over the Forrester which deprived him of the power of seeing an enemy : owing to which spell he would not believe his servant when he informed him that he saw the MacIans approaching and advised him to fly when he saw danger. That when Ardvorlich's Lady was brought back she had a stone in her hand, which is called the Red Stone, but which the deponent who had seen it thought resembled a chrystal. and he knows that people from a distance are still in the practice of coming to Ardvorlich and taking away water in bottles for the cure of their cattle, after the same being stirred about with the stone to which there was a chain attached, And being interrogated whether he had not heard that the above slaughter was imputed to the Macgregors Depones that he heard so only lately having heard of old what he has already deponed to. And being asked what impression that late report made upon him? Depones that he considers it to be a lie, never having heard of any enemity between the Drummonds and the Macgregors but on the contrary that they were in friendship. That the Deponent also heard the foregoing tradition from other people, and particularly about thirty years ago from John MacGregor who resided at Meovey in the parish of Comrie, and who died about four years ago aged nearly 100. That he has heard of the McIans and some of the Glengarry MacDonalds headed by Glengarry's Brother whose title was Achuanie, having plundered Breadalbane and of the MacEans having once plundered Glenlyon, which was the cause of the enemity between the Campbells and the Glencoe people. And being asked if ever he heard of the Forresters head having been brought to the Kirktown of Balquhidder and tossed about by the Macgregors, Depones that he never did and that it was impossible that he ever could have heard it as he had never heard the murder imputed to the MacGregors, excepting very lately as before mentioned, and if such a remarkable circumstance had happened he thinks the tradition could not have passed away. And being asked if he had ever heard of seventeen or any other number of Macgregors being hanged upon one tree in Balquhidder? Depones that he never heard of such a report, and considers it highly increditable that if such a circumstance had happened, the tradition could have died away, and all this is truth as he shall answer to God."

        "signed ALEX : M^cNAB
            Jo, Coldstream J P."

"Robert MacGregor in Middle Achtow one of the Elders of the Parish of Balquhidder aged sventy four, being solemnly sworn and examined on oath Depones that he is the sixth generation of Macgregors who have lived in Achtow.

That his father was born in 1701 and lived to the age of 77, That the invariable report from his infancy with regard to the slaughter of Drummond Earnach the Forester of Glenartney, which the Deponent had from his father and many others was that it was committed by the MacIans or MacDonalds of Glencoe That it was in consequence of an injury done by the Forrester to some of the Clan Ian, a party of whom came down for the purpose of putting him to death. And being examined with regard to the other particulars in the preceding Deposition and afterwards having heard the same read over to him Depones and concurs with regard to the servant running off from the Forrester when the MacIans approached : of his head being cut off and carried to Ardvorlich : of the Forrester's sister the landlady entertaining them : of the caiper being put to the head in her sight ; of her going to the hill distracted when she saw her brother's head ; of her being taken back by her husband, and of the spell or witchcraft which prevented the Forrester from seeing his enemies ; Depones that the preceding tradition is more familiar to the Deponent from the circumstance, that his great grandfather by his father's side was a son of the daughter of the Lady Ardvorlich who was distracted and ran off to the hill as before mentioned, and who was sister of the Forrester so put to death. Depones That he never heard of the report of the murder being imputed to the Macgregors till questioned respecting this his deposition. And which report he believes to be false having always heard that the Drummonds and Macgregors lived in a friendly way. That he has often heard that the MacIans of Glenco were in the practice of coming down and subsisting themselves by plunder in this and the neighbouring parts of the country. And being asked if he ever heard of seventeen or any other number of Macgregors being hanged on one tree in Balquhidder Depones that he never heard of such report and he thinks it improbable from never having heard of it. And all this truth as I shall answer to God."

" ROBERT MacGREGOR   JO. Coldstream J.P."

Traditional account of the murder of Drummond Earnach :—

" Balquhidder 16. Dec. 1813.

"During the time that Drummond Earnach was Forrester in Glenartna two young boys named Johnstons or Clan Eoin Glencoe having gone to that place for the purpose of hunting the Deers, Drummond Earnach upon seeing them took hold of them and clipped their ears desiring them to go home, when they reached home they told what had happened to them to their friends, who being so enraged that they swore they would be revenged upon him for treating them so roughly. They immediately dispatched an old wife who went under the name of a witch to bewitch Drummond Earnach. She goes to his sister who being Lady of Ardvorlich at that time and says to her, that if she would compliment well, she would give her a piece of cloth, which being sewed to her brother's coat he would never see his enemy. The lady thinking that the old wife meant that her brother never would have an enemy, gave her some thing and accordingly the piece cloth was sewn to his coat, and shortly after this a band of Clann Eoin's friends went to Glenartna there to lay wait for Drummond Earnach, and as soon as they saw him they ran towards him his servant seeing them coming warned his master, and made off himself, Drummond Earnach not seeing any, would not follow his servant, he was seized and his head cut off."

The ghastly tale of the head having been placed on the table at Ardvorlich as related by Sir Walter Scott is repeated, adding that the lady was for a week in the forests among the deer, but was found and brought home; her child was born directly afterwards, and became a Major in the army.

The deposition is thus certified—

" We Alexander McNab, Lochearnhead and Robert McGregor Auchtow Balquhidder do affirm that we heard the above circumstances told by the people after mentioned all of them to the same purpose, Alex: McNab heard it from one John Carmichael Glen Dochart who died about forty years ago—from John McGregor Meovie east end of Lochearn where he died above three years ago and was about 98 years of age also from Lieutenant Stewart Perthshire Militia; Robert McGregor from his father Hugh McGregor."

" signed
      " Alexr McNab.
      " Robert MacGregor."

" Manse of Balquhidder, 19 June 1817.

" Robert MacGregor an elder of the Parish of Balquhidder in which his Grand-Father & Great grandfather were also elders in presence of the Rev. Alexander MacGregor Minister of the said Parish, states that since he emitted his affidavit relative to the murder of Drummond Earnach which had been unjustly ascribed to persons of the name of MacGregor he has been informed by several Natives of Lochaber that Allister MacDhuil, Paternal Brother of MacDonald of Keppoch, having conceived the design of seizing on Keppoch's lands in the minority of his three sons, went to the house of Keppoch on the pretence of visiting his nephews, on their return from school, that Alister MacDhuil was accompanied by his six sons that the servants of the family were in the fields cutting down corn, and the Boys left in the house; that their uncle and his sons taking advantage of this circumstance put the boys to death that Ian Lom a celebrated Bard, and a friend of the young men had charge of the family, and was superintending the Shearers at harvest work; that having observed Alister MacDhuil and his sons going through the motion of taking leave of the boys at the door and sometime after the departure of these men, thinking it strange that the boys did not come to see the people at work, Ian Lom went to look after them and was horrorstruck at finding them murdered that Alister MacDhuil and his sons immediately left their country under a consciousness of the criminality of this atrocious murder that they skulked seven years in different parts of the neighbouring countries, and haunted a considerable part of that time in Perthshire and particularly near the forest of Glenartney where they were in the habit of making free with the deer; that the present Mr Stewart of Ardvorlich had informed the Declarent, that these men had built a hut in Finglen the most eastern farm of his estate very near the forest where they principally resided for two years; that the Forrester Drummone Earanach having cropped the ears of these sons of Alister McDhuil or of some of that tribe as a punishment for their trespasses in the forest, his own murder was the consequence of their revenge as the Declarent verily believes; that Alister MacDhuil and his sons having afterwards returned to their own country were apprehended, and their heads thrown into a well not far from the house of Glengarry, called to this day Tobar nan ceann, or the Well of the heads, That the Declarent was credibly informed that there is a tribe of MacDonalds called Clann Dhuil; another styled Clan Fhionla and that several other tribes of MacDonalds have family patronymics; that the imputation of this murder falsely made against the Macgregors was founded on no better grounds than the circumstance of a tribe of that Clan being called Clan Duil; whereas there are many tribes in the Highlands of other subnames bearing the patronimic of Clann Duil."

" ROBERT MACGREGOR."

The above declaration emitted and signed in presence of Alexander MacGregor, Min. of Balquhidder.

Letter from Duncan Stewart of Glenbuckie to the Rev. Alexander MacGregor, minister of Balquhidder:—

"5. August 1820.
" Rev. dear Sir,

"From having read the 'Legend of Montrose,' containing allusions to the Children of the Mist (McGregors) as being the perpetrators of that horrid deed mentioned therein, I am led to suppose that the author who often blends truth and fiction together, has had an erroneous accout of an antient but true story handed down in the upper parts of Perth and Argyleshire from father to son, upon which he founded this part of his narrative. If my memory is correct, the story ran thus:—The MacIans of Glencoe being upon an excursion to the Lowlands, as then not uncommon, being disappointed on their expedition, of course much in want of food, in passing through the King's forrest in Perthshire killed a hart or deer, the keepers with the principal, Drummond ernach as leader, apprehended the MacIans and sent them home with bloody ears, having literally cropped them, such insult being more than death was not to be forgiven, The Clan of course rushed from their mountains seized upon the unfortunate Drummond, cut off his head, came to his sister's house who ignorant of the deed and by way of Peace offering entertained them and who upon her return to the guest chamber, observed her brother's head upon the table with bread and cheese in the mouth. The consequence to the poor woman was distraction running wild with the animals of the forrest as hinted in the Legend.

"All the share the children of the Mist or McGregors had in these horrid trans- actions was perhaps over stretched hospitality in screening the MacIans till they could make their escape to their own (for those days) impregnable mountains. Having heard of late a good deal of conversation of this affair I think it right that Sir John should be informed of what was currently said of it in my younger days, My sister who is much better versed in highland story than I am joins in regard with

"Dear Sir Your faithful & obd.

"DUN. STEWART."

Letter from the Rev. Alexander Irvine, minister of Little Dunkeld, well known for his acquaintance with all Highland subjects, to Captain Donald MacGregor, 96 Reg. of Foot, Ayr, afterwards proprietor of Balnald Strathardle, Perthshire :—

"Dunkeld 12. July 1815.

"With regard to the murder of Drummond Erinach by a few MacGregors it is a made up story to answer the purpose intended, that is to deprive them of all their lands. He was murdered by the Johnsons or MacIans of Ardnamurchan, a sept of the MacDonalds who even as far down as the 1752. regularly laid the country under contribution. Being three years minister in their country, I had every opportunity of knowing the history of this roving tribe. It is well known that they came to hunt in the forest of Sechallin, Ben Douran, Cruach, and others. Walter Scott took the story as he found it and unfortunately gave celebrity to a falsehood. I have written the history of the ClanGregor as a part of my account of the Scotch Clans in which I have endeavoured to do justice to a long oppressed though noble and generous race. If a party of the MacGregors should have in a hunting match killed a rival it would not surprise any one acquainted with the history of the age; such things happened every day, but it is enough for ClanGregor to bear their own burdens."

The foregoing depositions are in themselves interesting, whatever weight they may be allowed to carry.

The Chief at the time of the transaction was Allaster Roy, son of the Gregor Roy who was so ruthlessly murdered by old Sir Colin Campbell, under colour of judicial execution in 1570. A sense of terrible injustice, the knowledge that his Clan could do no right in the eyes of their cruel enemies and traducers, must have most deeply goaded him if (?) he took the desperate resolution of accepting for himself and his followers the full responsibility of the foul deed, by whomsoever it might have been done. With the following extract from a poem on the subject, this painful chapter may be fitly closed :—

QUOTATION FROM A POEM BY SIR ALEXANDER BOSWELL, PRINTED IN 1811, BUT NOT PUBLISHED.

" And pausing on the banner gazed :
Then cried in scorn his finger raised,
' This was the boon of Scotland's King,'
And with a quick and angry fling,
Tossing the pageant screen away,
The dead man's head before him lay,
Unmoved he scann'd the visage o'er
The clotted locks were dark with gore
The features with convulsion grim
The eyes contorted, sunk and dim,
But unappalled, in angry mood,
With lowering brow unmoved he stood,
Upon the head his bared right hand
He laid, the other grasped his brand :
Then kneeling, cried, ' To Heaven I swear
This deed of death I own, and share ;
As truly, fully mine, as though
This my right hand had dealt the blow ;
Come then on, our foemen, one come all ;
If to revenge this caitiff's fall
One blade is bared, one bow is drawn,
Mine everlasting peace I pawn
To claim from them or claim from him,
In retribution, limb for limb.
In sudden fray, or open strife,
This steel shall render life for life.'

He ceased ; and at his beckoning nod,
The clansmen to the altar trod ;

And not a whisper breathed around,
And nought was heard of mortal sound,
Save for the clanking arms they bore
That rattled on the marble floor.
And each as he approached in haste,
Upon the scalp his right hand placed;
With livid lip and gathered brow
Each uttered in turn the vow
Fierce Malcolm watch'd the passing scene,
And searched them through with glances keen;
Then dashed a teardrop from his eye;
Unbid it came—he knew not why.
Exulting high, he towering stood;
'Kinsmen,' he cried, 'of Alpin's blood
And worthy of Clan Alpin's name,
Unstained by cowardice or shame,
E'en do, spare nocht, in time of ill
Shall be Clan Alpin's legend still.'"

Chapter XIX

Proclamation against the Clan Gregor

FROM the Register of the Privy Council :—

" 1590. July 13th.

"The King & Council understanding that the ClanGregor being for the maist pairt denunceit his Hienes rebellis and at the Horne for divers horribill crymes and offensis. have of late 'convocate thame selffis togidder in greit cumpanyis, and associat and drawin onto thame the broken men of sindry cuntreis, quha at thair pleasour hes maist cruellie and tressonablie rasit fyre, brynt, slayne, and hereit his Hienes gude subjectis, reft and takin thair gudis, and utherwayis opprest thame in sic sort as thair landis and boundis ar altogedder laid waist, and sindry baronis, gentilmen and uthris compellit to leif thar huossis, to thair utter wrak, and greit contempt of his Majestie, and his authoritie and hurt of the commonweil of theis realme, uttering herewithall a disdayne as it wer to his Majestie and all that professis his obedience, be counterfaitting of his princelie power, making of unlauchfull vowes, gevand proude and disdainfull specheis, and using of sindry uther tressonabill and extraordinar deidis in maist barbarous and ethnik manner, as thair wer nayther God nor man to controll and repres this thair contemptuous and insolent forme of doeing :' and his Majestie having 'eftir consultatioun had theiranent with certain nobill men, baronis and utheris inhabitantis of the cuntreis maist ewest to the saidis rebellis,' and with advice of his council 'thocht meit and concludit that the same rebellis, thair resettaries, assistaris and partakeris salbe persewit with fyre and sword and all kind of extremitie, ay and Quhill they be reduceit' to that effect full power and commissioun of justiciary has been given to Sir Duncan Campbell of Glenurchy 'to do exerce and use that in the premississ and for executioun thairof is necessarlie requirit to be dune' with full indemnity for him and his auxillaries in such proceedings. But 'because it is understood to his Majestie that thair is sum bandis of mantenance and friendschip standing betuix the said Sir Duncane Campbell and sum of the

principallas of the said ClanGregour, as alsua betuix thame and sindry
utheris nobillmen baronis and gentilmen of the cuntre, quhilkis gif thay
salbe sufferit to stand and have effect may grietlie hurt and prejudidige the
execution of this present commission,' the present act discharges all the
said bandis, and ordains the said Sir Duncane not to band with the said
rebellis in time cuming,   Proclamation hereof is to be made at the market
crosses and all the lieges within the said boundis and especiallie Johnne
Earl of Montrois Johnne Earl of Menteith, Johnne Murray of Tullibardin,
George Buchannane of that Ilk Andro McFarlane of Arrochair, and the
Barons and gentilmen of sic pairtis of Ergyle as are maist ewest thar unto
'are to assist the said Duncane in the execution of this present commission,
under the penalty of being held as art and part with the rebels.   Further
George Earl of Huntly, Arch : Earl of Ergyle, Johnne Campbell of Cadder,
James Campbell of Ardkinglas his curators, Johnne Earl of Atholl,
Lauchlane McIntoshe of Dunnaughtane, and Johnne Grant of Freuchie
are commanded to find sureties within 15 days after being charged, that they
and each of them 'sall concur, and fortifie and assist the said Sir Duncane'
also under the pain of being reputed art and part with the said Clan."

From the " Chartulary " :—

" 1590. Aug. 1. Decreet Sir Duncan Campbell of Glenurquhay in virtue of
his infeftment and Sasine against Alexander Roy MacGregor (Allester
MacGregor of Glenstray) Donald MacIntyre and John Mcapersone (Macpherson) occupiers of Stronmelochan, Patrick MacGregor VcDonald occupier
of Tullich, John dhu MacGregor and Neill MacGregor his brother, occupiers
of Dowletter, Patrick MacGregor occupier of Castellan, and Patrick Oure
MacGregor occupier of Derdoniche : Defenders decerned in absence to flit
and remove."—Gen. Reg. Decreets of the Court of Session. Vol cxxv. fol. 216.

Allaster Roy MacGregor (VII.), eldest son of Gregor Roy nam Basan
Geal, by his wife the daughter of Campbell of Glenlyon, must have been
very young at the time of his father's death in 1570.   Ewin MacGregor,
" Tutour of Glenstray," is frequently mentioned in public documents, and
as late as 1581 he was given the first place on the list ; the distinctive title
of Tutour was even afterwards always attached to his name.   Another
surviving brother of Gregor Roy's, often in the Records, was Duncan na
Glen.

Allaster McGregour VcDonache VcAllester (who had one brother,[1] John

---

[1] From the traditional account of Gregor Roy's wife having only one child at the time of her
husband's murder (see song believed to have been composed by her, page 161), it is supposed that
the second son was posthumous.

dhu na Luarach, coat of mail,) appears to have been one of the best and most capable leaders the Clan ever had ; brave in action and generously willing to share every peril of his people, he was truly an ideal Chief. The action he felt compelled to take in accepting the responsibility for the Drummondernoch murder proved, however, very unfortunate for the Clan, raising the whole power of even the least vindictive landlords against the MacGregors, and forming the ground of very severe enactments which speedily followed.

From the Register of the Privy Council :—

" 1590. August 24.

"Caution by Johnne Grant of Freuchy as principal, and Patrik of Rothirmurchus, as surety for him, that he will fortify and assist Sir Duncane Campbell of Glenurquhy in the execution of his commission for pursuit of the ClanGregor rising with his whole force for pursuit.

" 1590. August 29th.

" Duncan McPhatrik Mculcheir [1] in Innerand, John Mculcheir there, relaxed from the horn for being art and part in the above crime on finding caution to appear before the Justice Clerk and his deputes.—Register of Hornings. Perth.

" 1590. August 31st.

"James Commendator of Inchaffray called to produce letters at the instance of the kin and friends of umqle : John Drummond of Drummaneri-noch To take surety of

Patrik Duncansoun MacGregor,

Gregor, Duncan, Donald, and Finla his sons,

Malcum MacCoulcheir,

Dougal his brother in Glengyle,

Gregor and Duncan McPhatrik MacCoulcheir,

William oure MacGregor,

William McEane MacConneil,

Alex : McPhatrik Roy Gregor McConnochie voir,

Duncan slaich MacGregor,

Gregor son to Allaster Scorach MacGregor,

Mcincoll alias Conoch Ion no MacGregor,

Gregor McEan VcConnochie,

John Dow MacGregor in Callender,

[1] MacDougal Ciar.

Gregor Cam MacGregor in Mavie,[1]
Patrik his brother there,
Duncan MacGregor there,
Duncan MacGregor under James Chisholm,
John MacGregor his brother there,
Patrik Murray,
Gregor McEan MacGregor Capitan of Glenurquhar, and
John MacGregor VcNeill,

for slaughter of said John Drummond."—Record of High Court of Justiciary

" 1590 2 Nov Holyroodhouse.

"Complaint by Sir Duncane Campbell of Glenurquhy as follows · The execution of the commission granted to him for pursuit and punishment of the ClanGregor is greatly retarded by the reset of the said rebels at all times within the countries of Ergylle & Atholl 'be the ouersicht allowance and permissioun of the curatoris of the Erll of Ergyle and of the speciall baronis and gentilmen of the cuntrey of Atholl quhairupoun the saidis ClanGregor ar encourageit to committ all kynd of mischieff and slauchter upoun the said complainar and his friendis, assistaries, with him in the executioun of the said commissioun ' There had been such reset of them in the county of Ergyle, where they were pursued by the complainer in July last 'and now laithe in the moneth of August they have shamfullee murdreist and slane ane man of the Laird of Laweris, three men of the Laird of Glenlyon, and ane boy of the said complenaries awne, besydis the barbarous hocheing of ky and oxen, soirning and wraking of the landis of Auchnafree, pertaining to the said Laird of Laweris. Eftir the Quhilk murthour the said complenair haveing directit ane cumpany of his speciall friendis and utheris in the begynning of August last to the boundis of Rannoch, for apprehensioun of ane noumer of the said ClanGregor denunceit rebellis and at the Horne the said ClanGregor being advertissit of thair cuming fled with thair wyffis, bairnis and guidis to the cuntrey of Athoill and to the place of Blair, being the said Erllis principall duelling house quhair they wer noucht onlie reset by the baronis and gentilmen of the cuntry, bot the same baronis and gentilmen, assisted with 23 personis of the said ClanGregor maist cruellie invadit and persuit the said complenaris saidis friendis with all kynd of extremitie and assayit fortifeis, interteinis and sufferis the said ClanGregor to remane within the said cuntrey, quhairthrow the executioun of the said commissioun is altogidder frustrate ' Charge had been duly given to underlie pain of Rebellion to Johnne Stewart Neillsoun in the Foss, Johnne Stewart McAndro there, George Leslie Bailie of Athole, Stewart of Bonscuid, Robert

----
[1] "Mevie," Duneira.

Stewart in Fascastell, (Fincastle?), Alexander McIntoshe in Terreney, Duncane Robertson in Strowan, Robert Stewart McAndrew in Fos, Johnne Stewart and Neil Stewart, Johnne Stewart, McAndrewois son. Alexander Robertson apparent of Fascalyie, Johnne and Alexander Menziessis his brothers to appear personally and also to present the following rebels before the Council, that order may be taken with them according to the general band. viz Allaster Pudrach McGregor, Donald Dow McConoquhy McAllaster, Gregour McGregor in Roro, Johnne Dow his brother, Johnne Dow McConnaquhy VcAllaster, Malcallum McGillechallum VcWilliam, Johnne Dow McCallum VcWilliam alias McGregouris and now not appearing ordained to be denounced."

But a change came over the state of matters, and the astute Sir Duncan got apparently a hint to underlie the law himself.

On the 14th December of the same year, James Stewart of Stikkis became cautioner and surety for the Atholl Barons to compeir before the King's Majesty and Lords of Secret Council. Accordingly—

" 1590. Dec. 17.

"The which day Sir Duncan Campbell of Glenurchy Knight as Principal and James Commendator of Inchaffray and John Campbell of Caddell as cautioners and sureties for him became acted and obliged conjunctly and severally that the said Sir Duncan for himself and all that he is bound to answer for by the laws and General Band shall keep the King's peace; and in no ways invade pursue or oppress any of his Highness subjectis otherwise than by order of law and justice under the pain of 20,000 merks; and also that the said Sir Duncan shall make his men tenants and servants answerable to justice."

" 1590. Dec. 18th.

"The which day the King's Majesty with advice of the Lords of Secret Council grants and gives licence to Sir Duncan Campbell of Glenurchy Knight to contract, Bond, enter in friendship and reconciliation of all bypast quarrels, deadly feuds controversies, and debates standing between him and his friends, assisters and dependers on the one part, and the surname of Clangregor their friends assisters and dependers on the other part, and to the effect that the said friendship and reconciliation may be the more perfect Grants and consents also that such persons as the said Sir Duncan has presently in his custody, retention or keeping being friends, assisters, and dependers upon the said ClanGregor be put to liberty and freedom and suffered to pass where they please &a &a, Dispensation to Glenurchy from any acts of Parliament or Secret Council in the contrary."

2 F

" 1590-1. Feb. 1st & 2nd.

"Contract betwixt Johne Erll of Montroise, Erll of Menteith Lords Drummond and Livingstone, Campbells &a on the one part and Allaster Roy McGregour of Glenstray &a, (among others Duncane Aberoche in Corroquharnik) on the other part registered in the commissary Books of Dunblane 12 Oct. 159- Parties ar bound not to commit slaughter upon forthocht felony, upon others nor yet upon suddantie, nor theft &a to renounce their own jurisdictions and submit them to the jurisdiction of the said Commissariat."—Register of Hornings, Perth

" 1591-2. Jan. 4th

"James &a Of our special grace and favour We have remitted to our lovites Allaster of Glenstray

John Dhu McGregor his brother
Duncan McGregor na Glen (his uncle vide page   )
Allaster Pudrach MacGregor (from Balquhidder)
Allaster Galt MacGregor
Dougal Chay MacGregor (Chaithe ?)
Duncan his brother
Gregor Macconochy in Rora,
John dhu Macconnachy VcAllaster in Rannoch
Donald dhu his brother
John dhu McWilliam
Duncan MacAllaster VcAllaster in Ferrye (Fernan)
Duncan bane McRob
Gregor MacGregor in Craiginschathe
Patrick McGregor in Cadderling,

and all their friends kinsmen, servants, dependers, and partakers the cruel slaughter of umqle· John Drummond of Drummenerinoch committed by them in the month of   1589. and any other criminal actions committed by them against John Earl of Montrose, Patrick Lord Drummond, Sir Duncan Campbell of Glenurchy Knight and James Commendator of Inschaffray, and their friends &a from the date of the said murder."

It seems a curious illustration of the times that so dreadful a murder should have been so easily passed over within about fifteen months from the date of its committal, unless a doubt existed as to the real perpetrators of it.

All seemed now peaceable, but there could not be room for the old and new inhabitants of the land. A small dispute in the meantime, illustrates this

"1591. May 10th.

"Anent the actioun persewit be Colene Campbell Arbeyth aganis Patrik Johnstoun alias McGrigour Patrik Amenocht and John Mcewin, Anent the removing of them from the four merk land of Kingarth (The first and third of the defenders not appearing are decerned to remove.) Patrik Amenocht appearing personally denied the competency of the Sheriff of Perth & depute Because that Duncan Patersoun alias McGregour his guidsir Deit heritably Rentalit in the landis libellit to our souerane lord And the said Patrik as Air, at the leist aperand Air, to his said umquhile guidsir, as succeeding to him hes brukit the saidis landis thir diverss zeiris bygane And payit the few malles & Dewties to the comptrolleris his collectouris, And therfour be the prevelege of the said rentall and daylie practis observit in faouris of all kyndlie possessouris of landis haulden of his Majestie & therefore newayis aucht to be removed, protesting the former being discussit to sy forder As he may of the laes and therupon askit actis.

"The pursuer answered that the first part of the pretended allegation ought to be repelled, as not specifying that the said Patrik Amenocht is dewlie infeft, and sesit, be rentale or otherwayes in the landis libellit nor of any part thereof nor that he is air to any of his predecessors, or hes geissin rycht proceeding from them, quha ver dewlie infeft & sesit, in the saidis landis nor any other sufficient titill to bruik the samyn. And as to the alledgit pretendit rentale gif ony wes grantit to his umqyhill guidsir the samyn expyrit be his deceaiss. Attour the saidis landis wer lawfullie set in few ferme be our Souerane lordis Darest mother to umquhill Colin Campbell of Glenurquhie the said perseweris father fra quham the perseweris rycht proceidis, quha during his lyftyme and sensyne the persewer be him self, his tenentis, and seruandis hes been in possessioun of the landis, to be setting and reseting therof. At the leist vptaking and ressauing of the mailles & dewties of the samyn fra the said Patrik Amenocht thir dierss & sundrie zeiris bygane quha throw is acknowledgit and allowit the persewer to be undoublet proprietor of the landis libellit. &a &a &a.

"After various continuations of the diet, the defender (Patrik Amenocht) is decerned to remove."—Sheriff Books of Perth.

MacGregor of Ardinconnal.

We have alluded in Chapter XI. to MacGregor of Ardinconnal in Dumbartonshire, where the family were settled as early as 1429. But after bringing its history down to 1544, all subsequent notices about this house have been omitted, both to avoid still further complicating the tangled thread of the General History, and also, with a view of now presenting the family in a consecutive manner, to serve as an introduction to the future troubles with the Colquhouns, which it has been stated had probably their origin in this outlying branch of the MacGregors, whose quarrels the Clan was of course bound to support.

From the "Chartulary".—

"1545. July 27   The four merk land of Laggarie belonging in property to Patrik McGregour, and holding of the Earl of Lennox, and the 6 merk land of Ardinconnell, belonging to the Laird of Ardinconnell, are thus mentioned in a Charter of Queen Mary of the above, apprysing the' Earl's estates for the damage done in his late rebellion, to James Stewart of Cardonald " 4. Jan 1543-4 Reg. Mag Sig xxx 22   (By the laird of Ardinconnell is obviously meant the person to whom that property was assigned under redemption by MacGregor of Ardinconnel)

"1559-60. Jan. 17.   At Rossdhu 'Instrumentum pro Johanne procutore et de nomine Patricii McGregor de Laggarie sui Patris.'   Present Colin Campbell of Ardkinlass James Colquhoun of Garscube 'magistro' John Wood, Robert Campbell of Craignow 'domino' Ninian Galt 'capellano' and Robert Colquhoun son of Malcolm.   The said day Johnne procurator treulie constitute to Patrik McGregour of Laggarie his fader, past to the presence of Johnne Colquhoun of Luss, Patrik Colquhoun of Ardinconnel and ct, Umphra Colquhoun sonne and apparent air to ye said Patrik and wernit' them all thre personnallie apprehendit, to compeir at the parishe kirk of Dunbertane and yer upon the Altr of Sanct Sebastiansis situat within ye same to reseiff fra ye said Patrik McGregor or his lawful procurator ye soume of 500 merks upon Witsundaye next coming for lauchful redemption of ye VIII merk land of Ardinconnell in forme and tenor of ye reversion made yrupon "—Record of the Burgh of Dunbarton

"1561-2 Jan 2 &   Summons before the Court of Session at the instance of Patrik McGregor of Legery for himself, and as sone and air to umquhill Patrik MacGregor of Legerie his fader agains Johnne Colquhoun of Luss and others, pretendit possessors of the VIII merk land of Erdinconnall, for resignation of said lands in Makgregour's favour as now redeemed by him Delayed till 1 March."—Reg of Decreets of Court of Session

"1563. March 16   John Colquhoun of Luss alleged that his father John Colquhoun of Luss, had had of Patrik MacGregor of Legerie an infeftment in the lands of Ardinconnel 'lang befor the dait of the said reversion' New Term viz 10 May next assigned to MacGregor

"1563. July 6.   Colquhoun of Luss decerned to warrand, acquyet, and defend to Patrik McGregour of Legarie the lands of Ardinconnell, in which Colquhoun's Grandfather had been infeft by umqle Patrik McGregour under reversion of 400 merks. Nov. 29. Said Decreet suspendit by Colquhoun until the princepal action and cause of redemption depending before the Lords be first discussit and ane Decreet comdampnator or absolvitor given.

"1564. June 22. The lands of Ardinconnell decerned to be lawfully redeemed by Patrik McGregor of Lagary who had consigned 500 merks in the Church of Dumbarton, Colquhouns, Buchanan, and Donaldstoun having refusit the ressait thereof and culd not aggre yrupon."—Decreets, Court of Session.

"1564. Sep. 8. Patrik Colquhoun of Ardinconnell, grants a receipt to Patrik McGregor of Lagarie for 500 merks in redemption of Ardinconnell, at the same time resigning these lands into the hands of John Colquhoun of Luss in favour of the said Patrik McGregor. Of the same date. Patrik Colquhoun protests that this resignation was made 'be compulsion' in obedience to a Decreet of the Lords of Council and it should not prejudice his claim of warrandice against John Colquhoun of Luss. Accordingly infeftment was given in Ardinconnal, on 6. Nov. following, to Patrik McGregor in liferent and to his son John in fee. Another son Archibald is witness."—Record of the Burgh of Dumbarton.

"1573. Oct. 6. John, son of Patrik McGregour was retoured heir of his father Patrik McGregor in Ardinconnal."—Retours in General Register House, Edinburgh.

"From the Records of the Burgh of Dumbarton it appears that John MacGregor of Ardinconnall married Christian Denzelstoun and that he had three sons Alexander his son and heir who appears in Record 1612. as Alexander Stewart of Lagary John, and Gregor.[1]

"1575. June 25. John McGregor of 'Ardounconzie' (Ardinconnall) against Omphra Colquhoun of Ballermye. John McGregor is infeft in said lands lying in the parochin of Rosneth. Colquhoun and others though warned, refused to leave ther 2 merk land of the wester half of the said lands of Ardinconnall. Decerned to remove."—Decreets of Court of Session.

"1578. John MacGregor of Ardinconnell entered into a contract with Humphrey Colquhoun of Ballermickmore, That his son and heir apparent shall marry Marion daughter of the said Humphrey and that the said Humphrey's eldest son John shall marry Janet daughter of the said John."—Record of Dumbarton.

"1578. May 7. Decreet in favour of John MacGregor of Ardinconnal 25 June 1575. is suspended, Colquhoun of Ballermick and John Schearer having found security to remove.

[1] See 1602 and 1619.

"1580   Several Infeftments of annual rents this year to which John
MacGregor, Christian Danzelstoun his spouse, and John 'puer' are
parties "—Dumbarton.

"1581 April 11   Mald Neikgregour, sister of John MacGregour of Laggarie
married John Denzelstoun brother of Robert Denzelstoun in Tullichewin
Her tocher was 100 lib and 100 merks "—Paper in possession of Dennis-
toune of Colgrain.

"1585 May 1   The double contract of intended marriages between the
children of John MacGregor and Ballermickmore discharged by consent of
parties "—Record of Burgh of Dumbarton

"1590 Sep 29   'Denunce Buquhannanis'

"Anent our Sovereign Lord's Letters raised at the instance of Allan
Macaulay of Durlyne, the Father, with the remanent kin and friends of
umqle. Walter MacAulay, Duncan MacAulay son also to the said Allan,
John dhu MacGregor in Ardinconnell, James Colquhoun son to Robert
Colquhoun in Port, —— MacAulay Servitor to Robert Colquhoun of
Ballernie John Miller younger in Drumfeing and —— MacGibbon son to
Malcolm MacGibbon in Port complaining of Thos Buchanan in Blairlosk
Sheriff depute of Dunbarton and a number of Buchanans &a &a for
attacking the complainers on the 1st of August last in the Highway and
Street of Dunbarton where they struck, hurt, and wounded the said Duncan
MacAulay in his head through the harn (brain) pan therof, the said John
dhu MacGregor behind his shoulderblade, wherethro' his lights and entrail
might be seen, the said James Colquhoun in his wamb, the said ——
MacAulay in his shoulder, the said John Miller in his right (?) and has
mutilated him thereof, and the said —— MacGibbon in his head and slew
the said Walter MacAulay   Defenders not appearing are put to the Horn."
—Record of Secret Council

"1590 Oct. 6th at Edinburgh

"Intran Thos Buchanan of Blairlosk John Buchanan his son John
Buchanan Burgess of Dunbartan, Duncan Buchanan of Bracherne, Will:
Buchanan in Boccurich, Walter Buchanan his brother, Walter Buchanan in
Bollatt, Mungo Buchanan in Tullichewen, Andro McArthoure in Kirk-
michell, John Buchanan in Drumfad John Buchanan in Auchmedin, &
James Buchanan in Fenwick, charged with the slaughter of umqle Walter
MacAulay sone to Allane McAulay of Dowarlin Sir George Buchanan of
that ilk, Thos Buchanan of Drummakill and John Stirling of Gloratt
became caution for the accused that they shall appear before the Justice or
his deputes at Edinburgh the 21st of Dec· next to underlie the law for the
said slaughter."—Record of High Court of Justiciary

"1590-1. March 1st. (To which day the case had been deferred.)

"Trial in the High Court of Justiciary of the alleged slayers of Walter McAllay sone to Allane M^ccaley of dowarlin and certain Buchanans before-named. The cautioners are fined for not having produced Blairlosk and Bracherne, The pursewers asserted that the deceased was killed by a shot; and that a pistol was fired by Bracherne."

"1591. May 27. Band of Manrent. MacGregor and MacAulay.

"Be it known to all men by these present letters, Us Alexander MacGregor of Glenstray on the one part and Aulay MacAulay of Ardin-caple on the other part, understanding ourselves and our name to be MacAlpins of Old. and to be our just and true surname whereof we are all come, and the said Alexander to be the eldest brother and his predecessors for the which cause I the said Alexander, taking burden upon me for my surname and friends, to fortify maintain and assist the said Aulay MacAulay his kin and friends in all their honest actions against whatsoever person or persons the Kings Majesty being only excepted. And siclike I the said Aulay MacAulay of Ardincaple taking burden upon me for my kin and friends to fortify assist and partake with the said Alexander and his friends, as come of his house, to the utmost of our power against whatsoever person or persons the kings Majesty being only excepted. And further when or what time it shall happen the said Alexander to have a weighty or honest cause requisite to have the advice of his kinsmen, and special friends, come of his house, I the said Aulay as branch of his house shall be ready to come where it shall happen him to have to do, to give counsel and assistance after my power and siclike I the said Alexander Bind and oblige myself when it shall happen the said Aulay to have to do, if it is requisite to have the counsell and assistance of the said Alexander and his friends, that he shall be ready to assist the said Aulay and come to him where it shall happen him to have to do, as coming of his house; Providing always that the said Alexander and his predecessors be the eldest brother, the said Aulay is to have his own liberty of the name of MacAulay as Chief, and to uplift his Calpe as before, And the said Aulay grants him to give to the said Alexander a Calpe at his decease in sign and token, he doing therefore as becomes to the principal of his house. And we the said parties Bind and oblige ourselves each to the other by the faith and truth in our bodies and under the pain of perjury and defamation, at Ardincaple the 27. day of May the year of God 1591. Before thes witnesses

Duncan Campbell of Ardintenny
Alexander MacGregour of Ballemenoch,
Duncan Tosach of Pittenne
Matthew MacAulay of Stuck

Aulay MacAulay in Durlyne
Alexander McAulay sone to the said Awlay
Duncan Bayne McRob (McGregour in Stuknaroy)
with utheris

Signed

Awlay McAwlay of Ardincapill
Alexander McGregour of Glenstre
Duncan Tosach of Pittene Witness
Matthew McAwley of Stuk witness
Alexander McAulay witness."

Transumpt of Bond in General Register House

Abridged from the "Chartulary".—

"1591 July 21st. At Edinburgh.

"Suspension William Buchanane in Bucreuch Makend mention That
quhair throw occasioun of the late troubles, and variance which fell out
betwix certain of the name of Buchanane and the Laird of Ardincaple his
kyn and friends qyhair sum slaughter and spoliatioun of gudis hes chancit
The said Laird hes consauit ane deidlie hatrend and malice aganis the said
complenar, and hes sutit (sought?) and daylie seikis all indirect meanis to
troubill him And first the complainer having been found innocent before
the Justice 'The said Laird finding himself disappointit at that tyme of his
intentioun He intendis now under the pretext and cullour of justice and of
his Majesties powar and authoritie To sorne, herey, and wrak the said
complenars haill landis and possessiouns, And to mell and intromet with
his gudis and geir' &a 'proceeding on this point by ane act of parliament
(Nov 1581,) For executioun of the quhilk act the said Laird of Ardincapill'
&a 'Bot alsua hes associat unto himself and brocht within the cuntrie the
Lard Makgregour and ane greit noumer of his Clan all thevis, broken men
& soirn aris Be quhais assistance he intendis now to put to executioun his
preconsauet hatrend and malice aganis the said complenar' &a &a Thairfore it is nawayis equitable that he because he is of the name of Buchannane
sould be burdynet or troublit for the misbehaviour of the broken men of the
cuntrie &a." (McAulay's letters suspended till he shall produce them to the
Council)

1592 July. Sir Humphrey Colquhoun of Luss was besieged in his
castle of Bunachrea by the MacFarlanes, when the castle was burning Sir
Humphrey perished in the flames as it would seem. No mention is made
in the "Chartulary" that any MacGregors were concerned in this affair of

which the facts are traced by two entries in the Records of The Privy Council several years later charging certain MacFarlanes with the crime. In the work, "The Chiefs of Colquhoun," to which reference has already been made,[1] the following account of the event is given from traditions current in the Colquhoun country. But it must be remembered that amidst the complaints so freely made against the ClanGregor none on this subject are to be found in public Records.

After alluding to the recent band with Ardincaple Sir William Fraser continues :—

"From these connexions and alliances of the ClanGregor, it is easy to see how they might be brought into collision with the Colquhouns, and how the growing hatred between them might ripen into a standing feud. The Colquhouns were at enemity with the Earl of Argyll, as well as with the ClanGregor; and it was the uniform polity of the Earls of Argyll to have the MacGregors always about them in such force as to enable them at will to annoy their neighbours, and to take summary vengeance on their personal enemies. 'That the Colquhouns and the MacGregors were in a manner constituted enemies to each other from the position in which the MacGregors were placed by these bonds and alliances, is confirmed by actual fact; for in the very next year after the bond made between Macaulay of Ardincaple and the MacGregors the latter[2] strengthened by the Macfarlanes, came into collision with the Colquhouns. In July 1592, a body of the Macfarlanes and the MacGregors descending from the mountains, committed extensive depredations upon the fertile lands of Luss, which were now ripening for the harvest. to repel the aggressors, Sir Humphrey collected together a number of his vassals, and was joined by several neighbouring landed proprietors. The hostile parties met, and a sanguinary conflict which lasted till nightfall ensued. Sir Humphrey's assailants were more than a match for him and he was forced to retreat. He betook himself to his castle of Bannachra, a stronghold which had been erected by the Colquhouns at the foot of the northside of the hill of Bennibuie, at the south end of the parish of Luss. But here the Knight did not find the shelter he expected. A party of the Macfarlanes and Macgregors pursued him and laid siege to his castle. One of the servants who attended the Knight was of the same surname as himself. He had been tampered with by the assailants of his master and he treacherously made him their victim The servant, while conducting his master to his room up a winding stair of the castle made him, by preconcert, a mark for the arrow of the clan who pursued him, by throwing the glare of a paper torch upon his person when opposite a loophole. This afforded a ready aim to the besiegers whose best

[1] By the friendly permission of the author.
[2] No proof of this statement that the MacGregors were in this raid is adduced.

2 G

bowmen watched for the opportunity. A winged arrow darted from its string with a steady aim, pierced the unhappy knight to the heart, and he fell dead on the spot The fatal loophole is still pointed out but the stair, like its unfortunate Lord, has crumbled into dust'[1]

"Traditions regarding these lawless proceedings still linger in the district around the ruins of Bannachra The memory of the traitor servant is still held in odium, and his descendants are known to this day as the 'Traitor Colquhouns' While it is plain how Sir Humphrey was assassinated, it is unknown by whose hand the deadly arrow was actually shot.[1]

A contemporary chronicler in a work "Diary of Robert Birrell Burgess of Edinburgh" charges a younger brother with having been executed for murdering "the Laird of Lusse," but there is no other evidence in support of it. Sir Humphrey was only 27 at the time of his death He was himself "at the Horn" for non-appearance to answer for the slaughter of William Brisbane of Barnishill.

From the "Chartulary".—

"1593. May 3　Exemption to the Lairds of Luss and Ardincaple, Anent our Sovereign Lords letters raised at the instance of Alexander Colquhoun of Luss, and Alan (Aulay McAulay of Ardincaple evidently reconciled to Luss) making mention that where Robert Galbraith of Culcreugh by the special devise and Counsell of George Buchanan of that Ilk has lately purchased a commission of Justiciary from his Majesty for purduit of the ClanGregor their resetters and assisters, with fire and sword, ． ．which commission the said Robert has not purchased upon an intention to attempt anything against the ClanGregor but under collour thereof to extend their hatred against the said complainers, with all extremit and under pretence of searching and seeking of the MacGregors to assiege their houses, &a. In consequence of this complaint Culchreuchs commission is taken from him

"1593. May 8.　Alexander Colquhoun of Luss besides finding caution conforme to the General Bond (i e. Act of Parliament 1587) Binds himself and others not to intercommune with any of the names of Buchanan, MacGregor, or MacFarlane Robert Galbraith eventually comes under a similar Bond on the 20. May "

Without direct evidence against the Luss Tradition that the MacGregors were art and part with the Macfarlanes in the Raid of Bentoig, the above excerpts do not agree with the tone of rancour that might have been expected had there been a Blood Feud.

[1] Chiefs of Colquhoun, vol i., pages 157 and 158.

Chapter XX

FROM the "Chartulary" :—

"1592. Oct. 22. at Perth. Edward Reidheuch (or Riddoch) and Beatrix
  Drummond his spouse, against Alexander McGregour of Glenstra Principal
  and Chief man of the surname of McGregouris, Johne Dow McGregour his
  bruther, Johne dow McGregour McEwin, and certain Comries and utheris
  quha daylie and continuallie boistes and menaises the saidis complenars
  intending to accumpane themselves with the haill surname of Macgregouris
  and Comries and cum down in the cuntrie and wrak the saidis complenaris
  (who had been ejected from the 20 shilling land of Tullibanchar) the saidis
  personis, speciallie the Laird of MacGregour being outlaws, men quha, thir
  mony yeiris bigane hes wrakit the haill law cuntrie, and committit mony
  slauchteris and heirschippis upoun the induellaris thairof, neither feiring God
  nor regarding our lawes as is evident to the Lordis of our Counsale and haill
  cuntrie."—Register of Hornings, Perth.

"Nov. 7. At Perth. Horning proceeding on a Decreet obtained before the
  Court of Session by Sir John Murray of Tullibardin Knicht 13. June last,
  Decerning and ordaining Duncan McPhatrik McCoullcheir, and Johne
  McGillechallum, to remove from his land of Innernantie, lying in the
  Lordship of Balquhidder and Sheriffdom of Perth. Witnesses to the
  execution of the Charge, Donald McInteir Balquhidder and Gregor
  McGregour alias Gun, in Dalveich. and Johne Dow McGillemichel in
  Lewin."—Register of Hornings, Perth.

"Nov. 15. Duncane McPhatrik McCoullcheir McGregour having been denounced rebel for not obeying the above charge. Sir John obtains a gift
  of his Escheit. under the Privy Seal."

About this time a list of the principal men of the ClanGregor belonging
to the three chief houses was made out, apparently by order of the Government, in compliance, doubtless, with the scheme laid down in the General
Band of 1587. An original list has been preserved as a State paper, which

was formerly in the Collections of Lord Hopetoun, and is now in the British Museum. Mr MacGregor Stirling copied this document (which he states had been discovered in a "private collection") more than sixty years ago, in one of his MS genealogical volumes[1] with the following remark :—

"It is a formal schedule, which bears that it was handed by the Clerk of the Register to Sir John Murray (afterwards 1st Earl of Tullibardine) for revision and correction   Sir John deletes some of the names, and supplies others   The name of Duncan Abroch had been omitted and is added by Sir John Murray under the House of Gregor McEan but he did not correct the patronymics of Duncan Glen the uncle of Allaster of Glenstray   The first list in the letter is genealogical, while in the second the individuals are arranged without regard to descent "

Letter (precise date not known[2]) from Sir Alexander Hay, Clerk of the Secret Council, to Sir John Murray of Tullibardine, Kt. :—

"Endorsed 'To the lard of Tullibardin anent Hielandis'
     Also 'To the Rgt honoll the Lard of Tullibardin this
                    Anent the Clangregour.

I may not omit to thank zou maist humblie for zour advertisement   And nixt to pray zou zit again to louke thir names, and notand twa to be chargeit to enter for everie branche of thir first thre rankis to deleet the remanent. for I am pntlie (presently) directand away the Lrz (letters) and to gar this berair mend quhir thair is ony wrang spelling or wanting of stylis.

For the lardis   1 Johne dow McGregour brother to the Lard McGregor
awin gang   2. Duncane Glen McGregour[3] V^cGregour McEwne
                  3. Donald dow McCondoquhy V^cAlister in Rannoch

*1 John Dow, brother of Glenstray
*2 Duncan na Glen na Phanan, uncle of Glenstray (repeated in 2nd list).
  3. Donald Dow McCondoquhy V^cAlister, probably of the Ardlarich family —See No 8

[1] Mr MacGregor Stirling makes special reference to this List in the "Memoir of the House of Glenstray," which forms one of his small genealogical volumes   In 1889, the same paper was copied in the British Museum, and sent to Lady Helen MacGregor of MacGregor by Mr Robert Armstrong, a gentleman much interested in historical researches, but who knew nothing of Mr MacGregor Stirling's previous reference to it.

[2] Reference is made to the Three Houses in an "Offer" by Glenstray, dated July 1599.—See chapter xxii

[3] Properly D Glen McAllaster V^cEane V^cEwine
The numbers are here added to connect such names as appear in both lists.
         * These obtained a remission, 4th June 1592.

For the gang	4.	Gregour McCondoquhy in Rora

For the gang   4. Gregour McCondoquhy in Rora
and hous of   5 Gregour McNeill in Ardewnych
Roro   6. John dow McCondoquhy bruther to Duncan McCondoquhy
   7. William McGregour McGillechallum M^canevoill ,
   8. Johne dow McCondoquhy Keir McAlister in Rannoch

For the hous   9 Gregour McAne in Brakley in Glenuraquhy
and gang of   10. Gregour greginshawch McGregour
Gregour McAne   11. Duncan abrach McGregour in Correcharmich under Glenurquhy
   12. Duncane bane McRob in Stukaneroy

The names of the principallis houshalderis of the ClanGregor

   2. Duncane a Glen McGregour in Fairna under the Erll of Ergyle
   13 Alester gald McGregour in   under the Erll of Ergyle
   14 Alester Pudrayt McGregour   under the lard of Weyme
   15. Malcolme McCoulkeir McGregour in   under the lard of Tullibardin
   16. Dougall McCoulkeir McGregour in Glengyle under the lard of Buchannan

*4. Roro (repeated in 2nd list) In a MS history (to be given later) he is called VII of Roro.

5 Gregour McNeill in Ardeonaig Twenty pound land at an early period in the possession of the old Earls of Lennox, the western half devolved later on Elizabeth, daughter of Sir Murdoch Menteith, wife of Napier of Murchiston As the Gregour McNeill in 2nd list was also under the Laird of Murchiston, he was probably identical with No 5 Ardeonaig was afterwards held by a family of MacGregors till the end of the 17th century, when it fell to the Campbells of Edinchip, and eventually to the Campbells of Breadalbane.—Taken from the "Lairds of Loch Tay Side" (repeated in 2nd list).

*6 John dow, brother to Gregor No. V , who is known to have had a brother John, mentioned in list 1589 They were sons of Duncan, and may have had a brother Duncan also

7. This William's last name is McAne (or Ian) Moyl (bald), therefore he was probably related to No 20. Also probably occupied Stuenochane-Rannoch —See page 242

8 John dow McCondoquhy Vic Alister occupied the 6 merk land of Ardlarich in Rannoch, the addition "Keir" may have been an error ; it is, however, remarkable that he is here placed with Roro, whereas the Ardlanch family are believed to have branched off from Glenstray.

9. Gregour McAne (Brackley in Glenurchay had by this time devolved on a cadet of Duncan Ladosach's family) Gregor was Captain of the Castle of Glenurchay, under Sir Colin, 1570.

*10. Gregour, Greginshawch, i.e , Craiginshache or Craggan. There was a lard called Craggan on Aldeonaig.

11. Duncan Abrach had obtained Corriecharmaig in the Braes of Glenurchy from Glenurchay by the mediation of Locheil ("Baronage") (repeated in 2nd list)

*12. Duncan Bane McRob McGregor in Stukenroy (repeated in 2nd list, also in Craigrostan, 1583).

*13. Alester Galt, brother of Duncan na Glen and uncle of Glenstray.

*14. Alester Pudrayt (Pudrach from Balquhidder) Although here mentioned as under the Laird of Weyme (Chief of Menzies) he is mentioned, July 29th, 1595, as under Stewart of Grandtully.

15. Of the Dougal Ciar family, in Innerlochie in Balquhidder (or Innerlochlarg)
16.   Do.

17 Paterk McCondoquhy McGregor in Glenleidnoch under the lard of Tullibardin

18 Duncane ower McAneduy McGregor in   under the Lard of Lawers.

19 William Oig McNeill McGregor in Fairny under the lard of Strowan

5 Gregour McNeill McGregor in Ardelbuyct under the Lard of Merchiston

20 Gregour McAne movll McGregor in Innervar under the Lard of Glenlyoun

21 Patrik McGregour in Cawderly in Glencorff under the Lard of Caddell

22 Paterk Amonach McGregor in Kingart under Colin Campbell of Ardbeycht

4 Gregour McCondoquhy McGregor in Roro in Glenlyoun under the Lard of Weyme

12 Duncane bane McRob McGregor in Stukenroy under the Lard of Buchannane

11. Duncane Abroche McGregour in Corrie Charnaig under Glenurquhy
yours to command with service

(Signed)   A. HAY"

From the " Chartulary " :—

"Commission to the Earl of Argyle against the ClanGregor and the
" Stewarts of Balquhidder.

" 1592-3 Feb. 1. Forsamekle as it is understand to the Kingis Majesty and Lordis of his Secreit Counsale, That the wicked ClanGregor, the Stewartis of Baquhidder, and divers uthers brokin men of the hielandis, being dividit in severall cumpanys have continewit this lang tyme bigane as thay do yit, in committing of murthouris, slauchteris, manifest reiffis, stouthis, soirnings, heirshippis, and oppressiounis upon his hienes peceable and gude subjectis inhabitantis of the cuntreyis ewest the brayis of sum pairties of the lawlandis nixt adjacent to the saidis hielandis, to the grite offens of God, contempt of his Majestie and his authoritie and utter wrak of mony honest householderis, quhais landis and rowmes presentlie lyis waist, unoccuput, to the grite hurt alsua of the commounwele, For remeid quhairof, His Majestie hes gevin and grantit and be thir presentis gevis and grantis, his hienes full power, and

17. One of the Innerzeldie family

18 Duncan Our in Glenlochy (or Duncrook).

19 William oig McNeill McGregor in Fernen under Strowan Robertson (Boirland, Fernochie and Mid Fernochie

20 Gregour McAne Moyll McGillechallum McGregor.—See No 7.

*21 Patrick McGregor in Canderly in Glencorff (or Cadderling).

22 " Amonach" from Glen Almond—but Kingart was under Colin Campbell of Arbeyth. See page 227.

commissioun, Expres bidding, and charge, To his Rycht traist Cousing Archibald Erll of Ergyle Lord Campbell and Lorne, his Hienes Justice Generall, All and sindrie personis of the surename of the McGregour and the Stewarts of Baquhidder, thair assistaris, and pairt-takeris to charge be his precept, and compeir befoir him at sic dayis as he pleis appoint, To find souritie, or to enter plegeis, as he sall think maist expedient for observatioun of his hienes peace, and quietnes, and gude reule in the cuntrey and that thay sall be ansuerabill to Justice, conforme to the lawis and actis of parliament undir the pane of rebellioun · The personis disobeyand to caus denunce at the horne, And thereftir to convocat his hienes liegis in weirlike maner within the boundis of the Schireffdomis of Dunbarton, and Perth as lyis within the parrochynnis of Fothergill, McLagan, Inchechaddin, Ardewniche, Killin, Straphillane, Cumry, Tullikettle, Strowane, Monyward and Monzie, the Porte Callenteich, Kilmahing, Lany, Aberfull, Luss, Drymmen and Inchecalzeoch; Requiring alwayes the aduice and concurrence of Ludovick Duke of Lennox and John Earl of Athoill, in persute of the personis of the said ClanGregour duelland, or hantand, within the boundis of thair commissionsis or Regalitie Dunbartane, Perth, and Stewartries of Stratherne and Menteith, and to pas serche seik and tak the saidis rebellis quhairevir thay may be apprehendit, and to putt thame to ane assise and minister justice upoun theme or utherwayes to bring and present thame befoir the Justice or his Deputis in the Tolbuith of Edinburgh, to the effect justice may be execute upoun thame for thair demeritis conforme to the lawis of this realme, Courte, or Courtis of Justiciarie, als oft as neid beis within the saidis boundis, or ony pairt thairof, to sett, begin affix, hald, and als oft as neid beis to continew &a &a (as in Commissioun of Fire and Sword 4 Feb 1589-90) And ordainis lettres to be direct to mak full publicatioun heirof at all placeis neidfull quhairthrow nane pretend ignorance of the samyn, And to command and charge all and sindrie the Baronis and Lairdis of Glenurquhy, Ardkinglass, Laweris, Glenlyoun, Coline Campbell of Arbeyth and all uthiris Baronis, Landit men, Gentilmen and utheris his Hienes liegis quhatsomevir within the saidis boundis conteinit in this commissioun, actual duellaris thairin, to ryse, concur, repair to the said Archibald Erll of Ergyle or his saidis deputis at sic pairties, placeis, and at sic tymes, and to remane and pas fordwart alsoft, and with samony dayis victuallis, and provisioun as thay salbe advuertisit and warnit be the said Erllis proclamatiounis or missive lettres at all tymes and occasiouns, for persute and reduceing to his Hienes obedience of the saidis ClanGregor, the Stewarts of Baquhidder and utheris foirsaidis; and on nawayis to absent thameselffis, shift, excuse or delay upon ony cullour or pretens to the hindrance of his Majesties service and quieting of his estate and cuntrey, undir the pane of tinsale

(loss) of lyfe, landis and guidis.   And the said Commissioun for the space
of three monethis to enduir "—Record of Secret Coun.

"Eodem die.
" Charge against certain Principal men of the ClanGregor to appear before
"the Earl of Argyle at Stirling

"Forasmekle as oure Soverane Lord is certanelie advuerteist of the present
disordouris, heirshippis, soirningis and oppressiounis daylie committit be the Clan
Gregour in contempt of his Hienes auctoritie, and to the grite trouble and inquiet-
ing of the peceable and guid subjectis of the cuntreyis adjacent quhilk is liklie to
draw on forder Inconvenient giff tymous remeid be not providit ; Thairfoir ordanis
Lettres to be direct to command and charge . . .   . . ."

The List is the same as that of the " Principallis houshalderis " in the
document sent to the Laird of Tullibardine as given on previous page,
excepting 8, viz · Nos. 1, 3, 6, 7, 8, 9, 10, 14.

" To compeir personallie befoir the Erll of Ergyll his Hienes Justice General
and Lieutenant in that part, at Struiling the   day of Feb instant to answer to
sic thingis as sall be layed to thair charge concerning thair obediens to his Hienes
and his auctoritie and gude reule of the cuntrey under the pane of Rebelhoun &a
and with certificatioun &a And as thay salbe halden mantenaris and pairt-takaries
with the broken men of the said Clan in thair rebellioun and wicked deidis, and
punist for the same with all rigour in example of utheris."—Record of Secret
Council—(Acta).

Various transactions with regard to Allaster MacGregor of Glenstray
about this time are somewhat complicated.

From the " Chartulary " .—

"1590 Aug. 1   Decreet from the Court of Session obtained by Sir Duncan
          Campbell of Glenurquhy in virtue of his infeftment and sasine against
          Alexander Roy Macgregor, Donald MacIntyre and John Macpersone
          Occupiers of Stronmelochan, Patrick McGregor VcDonald occupier of
          Tullich, John dow McGregor and Neill his brother, occupiers of Dowletter,
          Patrick McGregor occupier of Castellan, and Patrick ower MacGregor
          occupier of Derndoniche, charging them to flit and remove from said lands.
          Decerned against them in absence   N B The above lands are all parts of
          the 20 shilling lands of Glenstray on which neither Allaster MacGregor nor
          his father Gregor had been feudally invested.   Hence it was possible to
          eject MacGregor and his subtenants from them

" 1594-5. March 17.   Act in favour the Laird of Glenurquhy.   Complaint by Sir Duncan Campbell, apparently with the view of obtaining exoneration from being answerable (according to the regulations of the General Band) for Allaster MacGregor who was still at his Majesty's Horn ' not having removed fra the said Sir Duncan's Landis of Stronmeloquhan and thair pertinentis) and becaus he remanit at the said proces of horne as he dois zit unrelaxt, and in the meantime still possest and occupiet the said Sir Duncanis Landis be violence aganis his will, as he dois yit Notwithstanding that he be his proceeding aganis the said Alexander in maner foirsaid hes followit oute the ordour prescrivit be his Majestie and his Esteatis be the lait Act of parliament maid anent the removing of broken men fra landis quha ar not ansuerable, nor sall not find cautioun to be ansuerable to Justice for relief of thair landislordis and Maisteris ', the said Duncan had presented a previous supplication to his Highness and the said Lords in Feb last craving that by Act of Council they would declare that neither he nor the cautioners lately found by him should be answerable for the said Alexander.   Although his desire had been found reasonable, yet, because the said letters were not then produced to verify the premisses the giving out of the said Declarator had been suspended till the letters should be produced   This having been done by Sir Duncan it is decerned and declared, that the said petitioner and his cautioners shall not be answerable for the said Alexander in time coming

" 1595. May.   Item payit to George Johnstoun Messenger passand with letteris to charge Archibald Erle of Ergyle, Schir Duncan Campbell of Glenurquhy Knight Johne Murray of Tullibardine Knicht and others to entir and present certane of the McGregouris and uthir broken men of the Hielandis specifiet in the said letters.

" 1595 May 24   Alexander Menzies of that Ilk obtained a Decreet in the Court of Session proceeding on the Act of parliament (the General Band) against Alexander McGregour of Glenstray pretendit tenant and occupier of the 32 merk land of Rannoch be himself and subtennentis underwritten viz

Rannoch MacGregors

Alester (bereicht) McGregour McEwin voir,
Duncan McEwin voir McGregour,
John McConeill Kinneis (V^cInnes),
occupearis of the 2 merk land of Downan
Alester McGregor, Malcolme McWilliam, and Finlay McWilliame,
occupiers of the 4 merk land of Kinclachar (for Malcolm see No 75 Letters of Horning, Perth, 1586, page 179)

2 H

John (McGregor) M^cV^cEaneduy, and John McGillevie,
Occupearis of the 40 shilling land of Camuserachtie moir.
   John McWilliame and
   Malcolme McWilliame,
occupearis of the 40 shilling land of Camuserachtie beg;
   Ewin dow, occupear of the Miln and Milne Croft of Ardlariche,
   John dow McCondochie V^cAllester,
occupear of the 6 merk land of Ardlariche
   John McPhatrik V^cGregour,
occupear of the 2 merk land of Kilconan
   Patrik and John Garris, Donald Glas and Gregour McPhatrik,
occupearis of the 40 shilling land of Leran
   Alester McKinnes alis Robertsone (see No. 80, Horning, Perth, 1586,
      page 125),
   Duncan McKinneis his brother, and
   Duncan McEwin V^cCondochie,
occupearis of the 6 merk lands of Aulich.
   Malcolme McCallum glas,
   John McCalium his sone, and
   John bane McCallum glas (see No 89, Horning, Perth, p 125),
occupearis of the 40 shilling land of Leragan.

Decerning and ordaining him and his said subtenants to flit and remove
from the lands above mentioned . on this decreet Menzies raised letters of
horning by which they were charged to the above effect and the letters
of horning were recorded on the 7. June 1595."—Decreets of Session and
Register of Hornings, Perth.

"Eodem die.

" Alexander Menzies of that Ilk obtained a similar Decreet against
   John Jamesone McGregour,
pretentit Tenant and occupier of the 40 shilling land of Drumdewane and
Kynnald and the 20 shilling land of Doulmane.
   John dow McWilliame,
occupear of the 23/4d land of Kyndrochie
   Williame McGregour V^cIlchallum,
occupear of the half merk land of Stuenochane (or Endlochane).
   Ewin McCondochie, occupear of the half merk land of Glendoran.

Decerning and ordaining as in the preceding entry.   Letters of Horning
raised and recorded as above."—Decreets of Session as above, and Register
of Hornings, Perth.

"1595. June   Item payıt to Patrık M^ccomısche Messenger passand of Edinburgh wıth lettreıs to charge James Lord of Doun and Herıe Stewart hıs
tutour, to compeır personalıe befoır the Lordıs of Secreıt Counsall the 24 of
thıs ınstant, and to entır and present befoır thame Johne McGregour of
Ardveıllarıe, (Ardchullerıe? on Loch Lubnaıgsıde)   To underly sıc ordour
as sall be prescrıvıt for keıpıng of peace and guıd reull ın the cuntrey, undır
pane of rebellıoun "—Lord hıgh Treasures accts
"June 20.   Ane Respıte maıd to Patrık McGregour in Corequhrombıe,
Alıster McKessane ın Leny, Gılchrıst M^cKınturnour ın Drumardoch John
M^cGıllespıck ın Leny, Eure Angussoun ın Tombay, and to ılk ane of thame,
for resettıng suppleıng and ıntercommunıng wıth the rebellıous men of the
surname or clan of ClanGregoure and utherıs broken men of the Hıelandıs
fugıtıves and dısobedeıent to hıs Hıenes and hıs lawıs, contraır the actes
of Parlıament and gude order taken be hıs Majestıe thaıranent "—Prıvy
Seal.

The above Patrık ıs supposed to be Patrick Aldoch, brother of Duncan
Abroch

"June 21   Anent the actıoun persewıt be Robert Robertsoun herıtabıll
proprıetar of the Landıs and barronıe of Strowane and Fernocht aganıs
Johne dow M^callaster, Allester M^callester, Duncane McAllester wıct Allester,
Neıll M^cwıllıame, neıll M^ccondıch, Wıllıame M^cneıll, Allester McGregour
vıct clerıch, Allester M^ccane Roy, Anent the removıng of thame fra the
landıs lıbellıt   Compeırıt the sıad persewer personalhe wıtht Wıllıame
Robertsone hıs procurator, And the saıd Neıll M^cWıllıame comperand be
Wıllıam McNeıll,[1] And the saıd Wıllıame comperand personalıe for hımself,
Allester McGregour clerıche and Allester M^ceane roy and Neıll M^condıch
comperand personalhe be them selffıs And the saıd Johne dow McAllester,
Allester McAllester, and Duncane McAllester vıc Allester nocht comperand
&a.   The Sherıff deput foırsaıd decernes the defendarıs to flıtt and Remove
conforme to the Sherıffıs precept and tytıllıs producıt Becaus thaı comperıt
nocht to shaw ony ressonabıll caus ın the contrar quhy the samyn suld
nocht be doıne, una cum expesıs lıtıgatıonıs

"The saıd Allester McAne Roy comperand personalıe Under pro-
testatıone for all and sundrıe hıs just and lawful defensıs to be proponıt
and allegıtt tyme and place as accordıs and allegıt he aucht nocht to be
decernıt to Remowe becaus he hes ane lyferent rıcht of all and haıll the
xx shıllıng landıs of Cultalaskyne for all the dayes of hıs lyfetyme sett to
hım be Donald Robertsoun than off Strowane &a And for verıfyıng thaıroff

[1] No 19, page 238.

produceit the said tak subscryvit be the said Donald Robertsoun of Strowane of the daitt At Strone in Fernan the sewintt day of Appryll 1589. (The pursuer alledged that the granter of the tak had no power, being himself only a liferenter, to give any tak beyond his own lifetime) The Sheriff deput foirsaid takis to adwysett upoun the former alledgances (till 28. instant) and assigns the said day to pronounce the interloquitur and absolvitt the personis folowing witht consent of parte fra the vairning lybellit becaus the said Williame M^cneill personallie comperand producett ane tak "

"List of persons on the lands of Strowane Robertson 1595 and names of their tacks

Williame McNeill,
7 merk land of Boirland and 'hauff' of the milne and multur of Fernochie and of the 1 merk land of mid Fernoche
Allester McGregour clerich,
3 merk land of Croftnailzeane
Neill M^ccondoquhie,
in Middle Fernan

"The above, tennentis and occupearis of the saidis landis haulden be them of Robert Robertsoun of Strowane thair maister heretour of the samyn land within the barony of Fernan and Sherifdome of Pertht And of their awin frie motive Willis untreatit or compellit as thai declarit Actit and oblisc them their Airis succesouris executouris and assignayis in the Sheriff buikis of Pertht ilk ane respective for their awin pairtis That thai and ilk ane of them During thair occupatioun of the saidis landis sall be obedient to our Souerane lordis lawis for seeing the end of oppressioun, thift resetting of thift, heirschippis, slchter, or ony uther crymes quhairby the said Robert Robertsone of Strowane thair maister and landislord mey be trublit or persewit for be quhatsoevir persone and forder sall do their dewtifull behauiour and dewite in all respectis to the said Robert Robertsone of Strowane thair maister his airis and successouris At the handis of our Souerane lord and lykwayis at the handis of all and quhatsumevir pairteis that sall happin heireftir to be intrest Damnfeit or skaythit in thair Defaultis of all inconvenientis that the said Robertsoun or his foirsaidis or the persewaris sall happin to be insthe callit for and sustenit as thair landislord or Maister be vertu of the generall Band or act of parliament and conforme thairto in all pyntis quhair upoun the said Robert Robertsone of Strowane askit actis and instruments   William McNeill in fernay witht &a."—Sheriff Books of Perth.

The above action at law is interesting, as shewing the working of the heavy responsibility which landlords incurred by the enactments of the General Bond, which obliged even those proprietors who might be on friendly terms with their MacGregor tenants to protect themselves by giving them notice to remove. And, at the same time, the policy of the Crown in selling letters and commissions against the ClanCregor naturally had an effect the reverse of pacific on the country in general. There were numerous small encounters; no honest calling was left open for the Clansmen, and, being from their adventurous nature always ready for a fray, their services were gladly secured for other people's quarrels or skirmishes.

> "1595. June 8   Robert Robertsone of Strowane aad his curators obtain Decreet from the Court of Session charging John Dow, Duncan and Allaster McAllaster alias McGregours, to flit and remove from his lands of Stronfernan, Lagfernan, and Vindevoir in Barony of Fernan
> "(Jan. 18 1596-7.   Letters of Homing at Perth enforced their removal)
> "1595. July 12.   Sir Duncan Campbell of Glenurquhy obtained a Decreet in the Court of Session against Gregour McEane, pretendit Tennent of the Lands of Boquheillies and Kincrakin; Duncan McGregor pretendit Tennent of the lands of Arthie; and Gregour McGregour pretendit Tennent of the lands of Moiris; Decerned to flit and remove from the lands abovementioned "—Decreets of Court of Session
> "July 29.   Stewart of Grantyllie obtained a Decreet in the Court of Session against Allester Makgregour alias Puddrache pretendit Tennent of Ardcaskard, and Duncan McGregour alias McEan cham pretendit Tennent of the Lands of Tullichvoulin. Decerned to flit and remove from said lands."

The following letter from King James VI. to McIntosh was copied from the original in the archives of Moy by Sir John MacGregor Murray. It shows the anger which possessed the mind of the King—a feeling which had been kindled, and doubtless carefully nurtured, by those whose interest it was to get rid of the Clan and enjoy their escheats :—

> "1596 March 30. James R. Richt traist friend we greet you hairtlie well. Haveing hard be report of the late preiffe gevin be you of your willing disposition to our service in prosequiting of that wicked race of MacGregour we haif thocht meit hereby to signifie unto you that we accompt the same

as màist acceptable plesour and service done unto us and will not omitt to
regaird the same as it deserves, and becaus we ar to gif you oute of oure
awin mouthe sum forder directioun thairanent, It is oure will that upon the
sicht hereof ye repaire hither with all haist and at your arriving we sall
impair oure full mynde, and heirwithall we haif thocht expedient that ye
befoir your arriving hither sall caus execute to the death Duncan McEan
caim lately tane be you in your last raid aganis the ClanGregour, and caus
his heid to be transported hither to the effect the same may be affixt in sum
public place to the terror of uther malefactouris, and comitt you to God
From Halyrud hous the penult day of March in the yeir 1696."

"(signed)   JAMES VI."

(The correct month is supplied by a Latin MS in the Advocates'
Library, Edinburgh, which makes mention of the 'very polite letter' sent to
McIntosh. The royal mandate was not, however, carried into execution, as
Duncan was alive eight years later.)

"1596 July 15   The quhilk day compeirit Alexander Maister of Elphinstoun
and produceit our Soverane Lordis Lettres dewlie execute and endorsat
purchest by himselff, Alex Elphinstoune Broyr to Alex· Lord Elphinstoune
&a &a to charge Archibald Erll of Ergyll as principall, Sir James Seytoune
of Tulliebodie Knight James Schaw of Sauchie &a as cautiouneris and
sovereteis conjunctlie and severallie for ye said Erll of Ergyll actit in ye
buckis of Secreit Counsall to enter and present

> John Dow McGregour broyr to the laird of McGregour,
> Johnne Dow McEwin McGregour's sone,
> Johnne Dow Campbell McCondoquhy tutour of Inueraw,
> Duncan Campbell his sone,
> Patrik McCondoquhie broyr to ye said Johne Dow,
> Lauchlane Campbell his broyr sone,
> Archibald and Duncan Campbells sones to Alexander Storach (Skorach)
> Patrick McGregour sone to Patrik Dow McGregour, and
> James McGregour sone to Duncan Glene,

Mentenents and seruands to ye said Archibald Erll of Ergyll to underlie the
law for certain heirschipis committit aganis the complemaris foirsaidis "—
Extract of Record of Justiciary

"Bond by the Laird of MacGregor for the good behaviour of himself
and his Clan

"1596. July 17   At Dunfermline.   The Quhilk day in presens of the Kingis
Majestie and Lordis of Secrete Counsale, In maist humble maner com-

peirit Alester Macgregoure of Glenstra acknowledging his offenses and
dissobedience bypast quhairof he maist ernistlie repentit, and actit and
obleist himself as Chief of his Clan and name That he and his said Clan
and name and all sic personis as he is obleist to answer for be the lawis of
this realme, Actis of Parliament and General Band Sall keip his Hienes
peice quyetnes and gude rewle in the cuntrie and nawyse invaid, trouble nor
oppress his Hienes Subjectis by ordour of law; And that he and thay sall
be ansuerable to his Majestie and to justice, and sall satisfie and redres thair
skaithis and attemptatis conforme to the saidis lawis, actis and Band, And
for the better satisfaction of the premisses, the said Alester becumes Plege
and sall remane in his Hienes cumpany and house, and nawyse eschaip
eschew, nor pas hame without his Hienes license and Lettre subscrivit be
his Majestie and his counsale, undir the pane to be puneist at his Majesteis
plessour in his persoun, landis guidis and geir, And alsua the said Alester
gaif his ayth of fidelitie to his Hienes and that he suld not knaw his hurt
nor skaithe but suld revele the same to his Majestie; and to do all uther
that as His Hienes Houshaldman, he aucht to do, as he suld ansuer to
God upon the salvatioun of his saule."—Rec. Sec. Council Acta penes
Insularum et Marchiarum ordinem.

" 1566 July 24. Precept of a Remission[1] to Allaster McGregour of Glenstray
and all persons of his surname of McGregour, and their friends, kin, men-
tenants servants and Dependers, for being art and part of the cruel murder
and slaughter of umple John Drummond of Drummenerenoch, committed
by the said Alexander and his foresaid Clan in the month of Jan 1589. and
for all other committed by the said Alexander or by any of his surname of
McGregour."—Privy Seal lxviij 199

N.B. A previous and equally complete remission had been granted on
the 4 Jan. 1591-2.

" 1596 October   John Campbell of Ardkinglas made a complaint that his
wife whilst travelling peacebly home was set upon by a 'number of men
'armed with weapons at the special sending and hounding of the Earl of
Argyle and carried off her horses and those of her servants &a and compellit every one of them to scourge utheris with belts and brydillis, in maist
cruell maner' And 'forceit the said Dame Jane to returne back again on
her feit.' Several MacGregors are enumerated in this affair in which another
MacGregor one of the complainers servants was taken away captive and
carried to 'the place of Inueraree' where he was kept for three or four days "
" Nov. 19. Letters of Horning recorded at Perth. Because by contract dated

---

[1] This Remission, of course, implies that the Chief and Clan were implicated in the Murder of
Drummondernach, but it does not prove the truth of the accusation

1 & 2. Feb. 1590 they became bound not to commit slaughter or felony (see contract of that date) and 'Albeit it be of verity that Johnne McGregour brother german to the said Allester McGregour of Glenstray Johnne Dow McEwin V^cGregour and Donald Dow McAllester with their accomplices stole from Graham of Fintrie, yet Allaster Roy McGregour and his Cautioners refuse to apprehend them."—Reg. of Hornings, Perth.

It must have been very strange to the turbulent Chief to be toned down into a docile courtier in the "company" of King James, though it was a merciful chance for him had it been possible for his Clan to have remained at peace. But doubtless neither opportunities nor wily tempters were wanting to allure them onwards to break the very insecure truce.

Chapter XXI

1596 to 1598

FROM the "Chartulary" :—

" 1596-7. Robert Campbell second son of Sir Duncan Campbell of Glenurquhy
had a letter of gift dated March 12. of this year under the Privy Seal granting to him the life rent &a of the Lands of Glenfalloch which pertained
formerly to Ure Campbell of Strachur and Charles Campbell his son and
fell to the King because the Father and son were denounced rebels for non-
payment of their Part of the taxation of £100,000 granted to his Majestie
for the baptism of Prince Henry, effeiring to their £6 land of Glenfalloch.
In consequence of this transaction the following Decreet was given.

" 1597. July 28. Robert Campbell of Glenfalloch son to Sir Duncan Campbell
of Glenurquhy obtained Decreet against Ewin Campbell of Straquhir and
Charles Campbell his son pretending rights to the lands of Glenfalloch with
their Tennents as follows.

" The saidis Ewir and Charles Campbell pretendand right to the saidis
Landis of Glenfalloch and utheris,

Archibald McEwir,

pretendit occupear of the Ile of Lochdochart with the merk land thairof; and
uther 2 merk land of Innerhary.

Duncan Glen (McGregor),

3 merk land of Innerchaganymoir and Innerchaganybeg ;

John McGillechreist VcEwir,

merk land of Innerardoran ;

Gregour McPhdrik McCoulkeir,

20 shilling merk land of Kyleter beg and Corarby ;

Neill Mcgregour and Neill McGillechallum,

20 shilling land of Clachanbretane,

(Two McFarlanes follow),

Duncan Abroch alias McGregour,

5 merk land of Ardchalzie (Ardchoille Wester).

2 I

"They had been decerned to remove at Whitsunday 'Notwithstanding quhairof the foirsaidis personis hes continewallie sen the said feist occupiet the foirsaidis landis with the pertinentis and as yit will nocht remove, desist, and ceiss thairfra to the effect foirsaid, without they be compellit.

"Letters of Horning were recorded at Perth July 1599 from which it appears that the Defenders refused to remove and were accordingly denounced as rebels —Reg of Hornings Perth

"1597-8 Jan and May   The caus of Strowane Robertson against some of his MacGregor tenants in Fernan is continued but at last disappears.

"1598 May 23   Comperit (at Edinburgh) Thomas Steven in Bannachan and presented our soerane lordis letteris dewlie execute and indorsate purcheist be him, for chargeing of James Erll of Glencairne as Landislord to enter Johne McGregour in Comer and George Buchanane of that Ilk to entir Malcolme McGregour in Glengyle   It is decreed that the above are men-Tenants to the Earl, or Buchanane and the matter is referred to the oaths of the Defenders —Record of Justiciary

"1598 May 25   Decreet in the Court of Session at the instance of one Oswald against Gregor McGregor in Glenleidnoch son of umqle Patrik Ammonoch McGregour (in Kingart) in Glenleidnoch for payment of six oxen —Decreets of Session

"1598 June 8   Decreet McGregouris agt McLeans at Edinburgh

"At Edinburgh Comperit Malcolme McWilliame in Kinclachar,
Finlay McWilliam thair,
Donald dow McEane V^cGregour in Downan,
John McConneill V^cInnes thair,
John McConnochie V^ceanduy in Camuserach,
Donald McCondochie oyar thair,
John dow M^cilchallum in Camiserach beg,
and Donald M^cconnochie V^cWilliam thair and presendit oure Soerane Lordis Lettreis dewlie execute purcheist be thame against certain McLeans who were charged to appear to answer for certain heirships. The McLeans were fined for the value of the stock carried off from the lands of the Macgregors   In reference to this action on the same day 'Comperit William Murray (in the High Court of Justiciary) and tuik instruments that he alledged that the Laird of McGregor and his kin were ye first sen King James I, that cum and sucht justice' meaning probably that they thus reframed from taking the law into their own hands as was usual

"The same day The Justice Depute decernit and ordainit Sir Lauchlan McLean of Dowart as landislord and Chieftain of Clan, with others, McLeans, 'To content and pay to the said Finlay McWilliam in Kinclachar a fine for stock and geir carried off.'

"1598. July 8. Anent the actioun and caus peresewit be James Commendator of Inchaffray, Laird of Innerpeffrie Heritour of the Landis and utheris under-written aganis Duncan McGregour, Margaret Stewart Relict of Alexander Pudrych, Duncan McGregour his sone, Allester McGregour, Malcolm McCoullcheir, Helen McGregour Relict of umqle Robert Stewart (Decree of removal Lands not specified).—Sheriff Books of Perth.

"July 19. Lord Drummond against his tenants Malcum McCulcheir, Callum closs (glas?) McGregour and John Smythe in Blairvoir.
    Duncan McGregour,
part of 4 merk land of Mewy called the Straid.
Ordered to flit. but tak produced from Lord Drummond of the 4 merk land of Dalchirlay and not decerned to remove.

"October 21. Anent the actioun and caus persewit be Sir John Murray of Tullibardin Knicht, heritour of the Landis underwritten Aganis John dow McGregour brother german to Allester McGregour of Glenstrae pretendit occupair of the five merk land of Glenbaich and 2½ merk land of Mekill Stronvair, lyand within the Lordship of Balquhidder (Defender not appearing decerned to flit).

"1598. Horning at the instance of Sir Duncan Lindsay of Edzell against Menzies &a, John dow McEwin McGregour, Donald Darriche houshald servand to Allester McGregour of that Ilk. Allester McGregour in Fernane servitor to Robertson of Strowane, John dow McEwin McGregour both (boch? deaf), William McEwin VcGilleecheliche in Rannoche,
McGregour of that Ilk, John Oig his brother, Johne McCondochie VcAnedowie McGregour in Rannoche &a for theft and oppression.—Hornings Perth."

From the "Red and White Book of Menzies":—

"Holyrood House, 25. Jan. 1599. Complaint by Alexander Menzies of Weyme, as follows: In the month .... last Donald Menzies, a 'commoun and notorious theiff and lymmer, and a declarit rebell and fugitive' had been apprehended by complainer in the actual committing of theft and warded within his place of Weyme 'quhill the commoditie of his tryale had bene offerit.' In these circumstances Johnne Dow McWilliame alias McGregour a copartiner with him in all his thifteous deidis, being informed of the danger quhairin he was had 'for preventing and disappointing of his tryale, coulle at night, 'accompanied with a nowmer of his rebellious com-pliceis, all thevis sornaris and lymmeris' to the place of Weyme, and 'be some secreit practize and policie, he surprisit and tuke the place, dang up the durris of the prisone quhairin the said Donald lay for the tyme and fred him out of warde.' Both of them had passed to Sir John Murray of

Tullibardin, knight, 'be quhome thay wer ressett, and his bene intertenyit sensyne, as thai ar yit with him as his household men and servandis, and are specialie acknawlegeit be him as twa ordinaris of his household and familie.' Moreover the said Donald having committed sundro stouths upon the Laird of Edzell, the complainer, as alleged Chief and Chieftain of the Clan is called upon to enter him before the King and Council. Wherefor it is necessary that letters be executed against the Laird of Tullibardin, as well for the entry· of the said Donald as for that of Johnne to underlie trial for their demerits; The complainer and Sir John Murray appearing personally the King with advice of the Council assoilzie the Defender from the entry of the said Donald simpliciter in time coming but ordains him to enter the said Johnne Dow before the Council upon the 22. day of Feb. next under pain of horning, because the said Sir Johnne has confessed that the said Johnne Dow was in his house after the day of the charge given to him for his entry viz 17. Jan instant and had remained with him a certain time thereafter 'and sua it lay in his poware and possibilitie to have enterit him as required '—Reg of Privy Council."

From the "Chartulary" —

"1599. May   Item payit to Patrik McComeiss, Messenger passand of Edinburgh with lettres to charge

> Duncane Campbell of Glenurquhay Knight,
> Johne Campbell of Caddel (Calder),
> Johne Campbell of Lawers,
> Robert Robertson of Strowane,
> Sir Thomas Stewart of Garntullie Knicht,
> Alexander Menzies of Weyme,
> Colene Campbell of Glenlyoun,
> James Haldane of Glenageis,
> James Commendator of Incheafray,
> James, (mistake for Patrick) Lord Drummond,
> Sir Jhone Murray of Tullibardin Knicht,
> David Grahame of   ,
> Dame Margaret Douglas, Countess of Argyle,
> Alexander (Campbell) Bishop of Brechin,
> Coline Campbell of Lundie,   .

To enter and present everie ane of thame the particular persons of the Clan of McGregour for quhome thay ar obleist to ansuer as maisteris and Landis-lordis speciallie designit to thame in the saidis lettreis, the thrid day of July nixt to underlie sic ordour as sall be tane with thame tuiching the weill and quietnes of the cuntrie; And alsua with Lettreis to be publeist at the Marcat Croce of Perth chargeing Allester McGregour of Glenstraa, and remanent haill persones of that mischievous Clan to compeir personalie; as alsua the said Alester as thair Capitane, Chief, and Chiftane To enter and present the samen personis befoir his Majestie and Counsall the thrid day of July nixt to cum, To underlie sic ordour as sall be tane with thame tuiching the reduceing of thame to obedience.

"Item payit to ane boy passand of Edinburgh with clois lettreis to the Commendatour of Incheafray, the Lairdis of Glenurchy and Glensraa.

"Item to James Purdie Messingir passand of Edinburgh with Lettreis to charge

> Ludowick Duik of Lennox,
> James Erle of Glencairne,
> Alexander Lord Levingstone,
> Sir Archibald Naper of Edinbellie Knicht,
> Jhone Naper his sone,
> James Chisholme of Cromlix,
> William Schaw of Knockhill, and
> Alexander Schaw of Cambusnoir,

As maisteris and Landislordis of the particular persones of the Clan of McGregour speciallie designit in the said lettreis (&a as above) and alsua with Lettreis to be publeist at the croces of Striveling and Dunbartane chargeing the Laird of McGregour and his haill Clan in manner as is befoir writtin.—Lord High Treasurer's Books.

"1599. June 9. Robertson of Strowan against his tennents; mention made of Malcolm McWilliam McGregour in Blairfettie.—Sheriff Books of Perth.

"June 13. Tullibardine against his tennents, John McCoulle, Malcolm McCoulle, Duncan McPhatrik McCoulle, Johne McEane McGregour, Gregour McConeill, and John Galt McGregour (defenders not appearing are decerned to flit Lands not specified).—Sheriff Books of Perth.

"June 20. Removing; Glenurquhay against McGregouris.

> Patick McQuene in Eister Tenneiffis (Duneaves),
> Alester McGregour clerich,
> Allester McEwine V^cGregour,
> Neill McGregour V^cHucheoun,
> Duncane McEwin V^cGregour,
> Allester McEwin V^cGregour,
> Gregour M^chutcheoun,

Gregour McEwin,
Duncan Abroch,
Allester Scorach his brother,
Gregour M^{c}eane, and
Allester McGregour his sonne,
Neill McGregour,
Gregour McPhatrick,
Duncane McPhatrick ammonach (Glen Almond),
Gregour McPhatrick ammonacht, and
Patrick dallach McGregour,

pretendit tennents and occupears of the landis lybellit. (Decreet against Defenders in absence).—Sheriff Books of Perth.

"Same date   Anent the actioun and caus persewit be Sir Thomas Stewart of Garnetullie Knicht, Takisman of the Landis and Baronie of Forthergill (Fortingall) with the fortalice and place of Garth and office of the Forestrie of Schehallion, Aganis

Duncane M^{c}eane chame V^{c}Gregour,
Janet Stewart, Relict of umquhile Allester Puderach V^{c}Gregour,

and others (defenders not appearing are decerned to remove).—Sheriff Books of Perth.

" 1599. July 14.   Removing Laird of Weyme against McGregouris
        "Johne McGregour and his subtennentis pretendit occupearis of the
20 shilling Land of Drumdewane,
20 shilling land of Dalmayne,
20 shilling land of Kirkland of Dull with the milne thairof,
20 shilling land of Kynnaill, all lyand within the Sherifdom of Perth
(Decreet of Removal in absence) —Sheriff Books, Perth

" 1599 July 24   Offeris for Allester McGregour of Glensray presentit to his Majeste and Lordis of Secreit Counsale in name of the said Allester be Sir Johne Murray of Tullybardine Knt, Sir Duncane Campbell of Glenurquhay Knicht, and Johone Grant of Freuchie at Edinburgh
        "Because it is impossible to the sais Allester to get inlande Cautioun upoun the conditiounes of the General Band conforme to the Act of Parliament; In respect nather is he responsale of the sowmes quhairupoun the cautioun is found, and that no Inlandis man will be cautoun for him, in respect of the bypast enormities of his Clan; Thairfor it is offert that the said Alexander for satisfactoun of his Majesties honour sall cum in his Hienes will for ony offence committit be himself. And that he sall deliver to his Majestie Three Plegeis of the sex to be nominat be his Majestie oute

of the Thrie Housses [1] of that Clan (viz the houses of Glensrae, of Roro and of Gregor McEane) his Majestie nameand twa for everie houss, Johne dow McGregour (Glenstray's brother) alwayes exceptit To be placeit quhair his Majestie and his Counsall sall appoint to remaine as plegeis for the guid reule and obedience of the haill Clan and name of McGregour in tyme cumeing; and for sic of the said Clan and name as beis disobedient he sall outher entir thame to his Hienes or to Justice or ellis use justice upoun thame himselff he havand his Majesteis Commissioun to that effect.[2] Attoure we obleiss oure selffis to present oure selffis befoir his Majestie and his Counsale upoun the 28. of this instant and gif ane resolute ansuer to his Majestie and his Counsall anent the dew performance of thir offeris in everie point.

Tullibardin
Duncan Campbell

Signed   off Glenvrquhay
Jhone Grant
off Freuchy

Original in General Register House, Edinburgh.

"1599. Aug. 2. At Falkland Bond by the Laird of McGregour for his Clan.

"The quhilk day Allaster McGregour of Glenstray compeirand personallie in presence of the Lordis off Secreit Counsale, Tuke upoun him the haill personis of the name of McGregour and promeist to be ansuerabill for thame be making of thame furth cumand to Justice for all the attemptis to be committit be thame heireftir ay and untill he in presence of the saidis Lordis lat thame under utheris Landislordis and qualifie sufficientlie that they duell under utheris Landislordis; At quhilk tyme he to be na forder burdynit with samony as he layis aff him, bot for relieff of the Landislordis according to the Act of Parliament.

"1599. Aug. 2. (same day as the preceding Bond)

"Cautioun for Makgregour.

"Quhilk day James Commendator of Incheaffray and Sir Jhone Murray Knicht become actit and obleist as Cautioneris conjunctlie and severalie for Allester McGregour of Glenstrae, That the said Allester sall compeir personalie and present and entir with him befoir the Lordis of Secreitt Counsale at Edinburgh upon the 4. day of Sep. nixt ane of the plegeis

---

[1] Enumerated chapter iv., page 161.

[2] If Glenstray had solemly taken upon himself the guilt of the murder of Drummond of Drummondernoch it seems improbable that the King would entrust him with a commission and accept his offer of caution.—Ed.

specifeit and contenit in his awne offeris to remaine and be placeit quhair
his Hienes sall appoint under the pane of 10,000 merkis.—Record of
Secret Council Acta.

" August.   A number of the Landlords of the ClanGregor previously mentioned
and in addition George Graham of Boquhapple) had letters charging them
to appear before the Council to find bail for making all persons of the name
of MacGregor dwelling upon their lands answerable to justice under the
pain of Rebellion —Lord High Treasyrers Books.

"Sep 6   The entrie of Makgregour prorogat untill the 15 Nov. nixt. "[1]

Although at this time the King and Council do not seem to have
wished to press hardly on the Clan, and evidently had a respect, and
perhaps regard, for MacGregor of Glenstray, yet the severe laws which had
been devised against Highlanders who were unquiet (for in this respect the
General Band threatened them all) fell with great weight on the Mac-
Gregors   The laws requiring superiors and landlords to be personally
answerable for those living on their lands forced even friendly neighbours,
such as we must esteem Sir John Murray of Tullibardine and James
Drummond the Commendator of Inchaffray, to prosecute the prescribed
race, and drive them from one refuge to another till they had not a single
resource left, and under such circumstances it was not surprising that their
hand should be against every man, and that even the best efforts of their
Chief should fail.

In the introduction to the sixth volume of the Register of the Privy
Council of Scotland which has been published, the following remarks
occur :—

" Other entries bring out the ominous fact that of all the Highland clans
the Macgregors were now the objects of most unremitting attention on the
part of the Government. While other more distant Clans were lawless
enough, the lawlessness of the MacGregors of the LochLomond country,
whether from their comparative nearness or for other reasons exposing them
to special dislike, was the most heard of, in the privy Records, and while
we have but glimpses of Makenzie of Kintail, or Macleod of Dunvegan, or
some other of the greater chiefs as moving about in their distant parts of the
map, hardly to be reached by Government commands , or missives, the
poor Chief of the transgressors is kept constantly in our sight walking

[1] *Vide* next page.

hither and thither over his more accessible tract of territory, pursued by summons to appear, or to give securities for his men.

"1599 Sept 6. at Edinburgh   The entry of Macgregour prorogat   The which day the Lords of Secret Council with consent of James Commendator of Inchaffray and Sir John Murray of Tullibardin Knight Prorogate the Entry of Allaster MacGregor of Glenstray before his Majesty and his Council, conform to the Act whereby they became Cautioners to that effect, until the 15th day of Nov next to come   Like as they are content and consent to stand obliged for the Entry of the said Allaster before his Majesty and his Council upon the said 15th day of Nov next to come under the pain of 10,000 merks specified in the said Act.

"Protectioun in favour of the Commendator of Inchaffray, The which day Sir John Murray of Tullibardine entered and presented before the Lords of Secret Council John dhu Macewne as pledge for Allaster MacGregor of Glenstray specified and contained in the said Allaster's own offers conform to the Act whereby the said Sir John and James Commendator of Inchaffray became acted for the entry of the said pledge   Whereupon the said James Commendator of Inchaffray asked instruments and protested that he might be relieved of all further entry of the said pledge Which protestation the Lords admitted.

Tullibardin's Band for entry of John dhu.

"The which day John dhu Macewne[1] as pledge for Allaster MacGregor of Glenstray being entered and presented before the Lords of Secret Council by Sir John Murray of Tullibardin Knight, conform to the Act whereby he and James Commendator of Inchaffray became acted to that effect, the said Lords have delivered the said John dhu macewne back again to the said Sir John to be of new entered again before the said Lords upon the day appointed for the entry of Allaster MacGregor of Glenstray   Therefor the said Sir John Murray of Tullibardin Knight in presence of the said Lords of Secret Council acted and obliged himself to re-enter and present the said John dhu macewne before his Majesty and his Council upon the 15th day of Nov. next to come, under the pain of 5000 merks —Reg Sec · Con · Acta.   Vol 1598 to 1601.

"Oct   Item payit to Robert Elder messenger passand of Edinburgh to charge the various landlords to certain of the Macfarlanes and McGregouris, to enter and present everie ane of thame respective the particular persons, thair men and tennenis, as is mentioned.

"Dec 5   Alexander Menzies of Weyme denounced rebel and put to the horn

---

[1] Son of the late Tutour of Glenstray and cousin germane to Allaster

at the instance of Mr John Moncreiffe, advocate (in absence) for not producing before the Council 'his men servants and proper dependers, Donald McGregour alias Donald Dorie in .   and Donald Menzies.'

" Dec 17. Decree that 'from the 1 of Jan. next the beginning of the year shall be reckoned instead of from the 25th of March.' The King and Council 'being willing that thair salbe na disuniformiti betuix his Majestie his realme and leigis and otheris nichtbour cuntreyis in this particular.'

" Dec. 19 Comperit Mr Donald Campbell (in the Court of Justiciary and produceit oure soverane Lordis Lettres dewlie execute and indorsate purcheist be

"Allaster McGregour as Chief and near Kynnesman to umquhile Patrik McGregour in Cadderlie. John Hay of Urchaye as broy^r with the kin and friends of umqle Willm Hay and siclike John McConeill V^cintailzeour sone to umqle Donald M^cintailzeour in Barglas and Donald McGilleis as father to vmqle Dowgall McGilleis to tak souertie of William McIntoshe of Esseich, Duncan McIntoshe son to Lachlan McIntoshe of Dunnachtan and others who had been 'denunceit rebels' and put to the horn, for not compeiring to underlie the law for the slauchter of the saidis umquhile persons

" 1600. Jan. 29. at Holyroodhouse Forasmekill as James Commendator of Incheafray and Sir Johne Murray of Tullibardin Knicht, (recapitulation of their obligations in regard to Glenstray and John dow McEwine,) 'Quhilk's actis being called upon the said day of Nov.[1] last and continuit fra tyme to tyme thairefter unto this 29, day of Januare instant upoun the saisis cautiouneris awin sute and promeis, maid and renewit be thame fra tyme to thime for the entrie of the said Allester and his said pledge, ... and the saidis cautioneris being of new callit upon . . . and not compeirand nor yet the said Allester and his pledge foirsaid being entrit and presentit be thame nor nane in thair names &a &a ' Follows Decreet of Council against Inchcaffray and Tullibardin conjunctly and severally for 10,000 merks for not presenting Glenstray and against Tullibardin singly for 5000 merks for not presenting John dow McEwine.—Rec : Sec Con · Acta .

" Proclamation against the Resetters of the McGregoris Goods.

" 1600. Jan 31 At Holyrood Forsamekle as the wicked and unhappie race of the ClanGregour continewing sa lang in blude, thift, reif, sorning, and oppressioun sa frequentlie committit upoun the peaceable and gude subjectis of the incuntrey, to the utter wrak, miserie, and undoing of grite nowmers

---

[1] Mention is made in this Act that on the first occasions (2nd August and 6th September) "the said Allaster was visited with infirmity and sickness so that he was not able to travel."

of honnest and substantious houshalderis, and laying waist of divers weill
plenished roumes, to the offence and displesur of God, and contempt of his
Hienes and his lawis; and his Majestie finding thame alwayis bent to follow
the unhappie course of thair awne pervers nature and inclinatioun eftir that
his Hienes haad delt and travellit be fair and gentill meanis to have broucht
thame under sum obedience; and Allester McGregour of Glenstray thair
cheif and ringleidar haveing maist undewtifullie and unhonnestlie violat his
promeis maid to the gentilmen quha interponit thair bandis for him to his
Majestie, and thairby professing and avowing himsell and his unhappie race
to be outlawis and figitives, and enemies to all dewtiful and gude subjectis:
his Majestie thairfoir is resolved to persew and prosequate thame with all
rigour and extremitie, according to thair deservingis.   Bot becaus the bipast
conforte and countenance quhilk thay have fund amangis thair landislordis
and uthar cuntrey people at sik tymes as be his Hienes aucttoritie thay have
been heirtofoir persewit, in resetting, huirding, and keiping of thair guidis
and making of bloikis and barganis with thame hes encourageit thame at
everic occasioun to brek lowse, and to some, herrey, and wrak his Hienes
subjectis quhair as gif sic unlawfull resett and huirding if thair guidis were
denyet and refused unto thame, sum redress micht be gottin of the stouthis,
and reiffis committit be thame.   His Hienes thairfoir with advice of his
Counsall, hes avowed to punishe with all rigour and extremetie all sic
personis as heireftir sall gif ony sic unlawful resett, to the saidis lymmaris,
thair guidis, or geir; and to the effect nane pretend ignorance heirof,
ordainis letters to be direct to command, charge and inhibite all and sindrie
maisteris and landislordis of the McGregouris and all utheris his Hienes
subjectis quhatsumevir be oppin proclamatioun in all places neidfull, that
nane of thame presume nor take upon hand at ony tyme heireftir to resett,
huird or keip ony of the guidis, or gier pertening to quhatsumevir personis
of the name of McGregour, thair followaris, and pairttakeris, nor to mak
bloikis nor bargainis with thame, thairanent, privatelie nor publicklie in
mercat or utherwayis, certifeing thame that failyeis, or dois in the contrar,
that thay salbe repute, haldin, and estemit, as arte and pairttakeris, and
allowaris of thame in all thair wicked deeddis, and salbe persewit and punist
thairfoir with all rigour and extremitie, to the terrour of utheris.

"Discharge to Tullibardin of MacGregor.

"1600. Feb. 17.   The quhilk day Sir Johnne Murray of Tullibardin Kt.
aveing enterit and presentit befoir the Kingis Majestie, Allaster McGregour
of Glenstrae conforme to ane act quhairby he and James Commendator of
Incheafray became cautioneris to that effect, his Majesty hes grantit the

resett of the said Allaster and exoneris and relevis the said Sir Johne of all forder keiping of him.

"Same day. Petition by Tullibardine and Inchaffray to be relieved of the penalties imposed upon them the previous month 'Alwayis thay have now enterit and presentit to his Majestie the said Allaster quha is presentlie in his Hienes warde to be tane ordour with be his Majestie as his Hienes sall think maist meit and expedient for the wele and quietnes of the cuntrey; And seeing the default of the not entrie of the said Allaster with his said Pledge at the peremptour day appointit to that effect wes not in the saidis Complenaris, bot proceidit upoun sum occasiounis quhilkis intervenit and fell oute befoir the day of his entrie quhilkis discourageit and terrifiet him to keep the first dyet And that now they have usit thair diligence and be thair moyane and travellis hes brocht in the said Allaster and deliverit him to his Majestie with quhome the like ordour may now be takne as micht have been at the first dyett; and that nathing hes intervenit nor fallin oute in this tyme of delay to the hurt or prejudice of his Majestie's gude subjectis Humbly desire &a &a." Decreet rescinded (of Jan. 29) by the Council.

"March 4. John galt Makgregor in Cannoquhan is denounced rebel and put to the horne for not appearing before the Council to have been delivered to the justice or his Deputes, to stand his trial for the alledged carrying off of nine oxen and five kye from the Lands of Maidlinis, belonging to Willia n Pitalloch in Maidlinis and Walter Kynnaird there, committed on the 24. Feb. 1594-5.

"March 6. Certain Landlords of the ClanGregor (*i.e*, those on whose lands the MacGregors were living) compeared with Allaster McGregor of Glenstray and 'thay being burdynit with suirties and plegeis for halding and retening the said Clan under obedience and for redress of pairties skaithit, it wes complenit be the saidis Landislordis that ane of the speciall causes quhilk procurit the misreule and disobedience of that Clan wes the resett and conforte quhilk thay fand of thair said Chief and amangis the Landislordis thameselffis, seeing every ane of thame for the maist pairt resett the men and tennentis of utheris quhan thai wer persewit be thair maisteris or quhan thai had committit ony wicked or ill deidis. Be the unlauchfull resett and mantenance sa frequentlie gevin unto thame, not onlie ar they encourageit to continow in all kynd of misreule and to misknaw thair landlordis, bot the saidis landislordis ar maid unable to answer for thame.' It was ordained that whoever of the Landlords resett or protected the tennants of others should be equally answerable for these persons as if they belonged to their own ground.

"On the same day. the same persons having compeared 'and a catalogue

having been maid of certane speciall househaldaris duelland under the
Landislordis and of sum utheris quhome the said Allaster had taken upoun
himselff; yit his Majestie understanding that thair wilbe a nowmer of that
Clan quha hes na certane residence nor duelling and can not be laid upoun
landislordis being left lowse and na certane ansuer maid for thame may
commit grite trouble and unquitie,' . . . . it is found and declared
that 'the said Allaster oucht and sould be ansuerble for the haill personis of
the name of McGregour quhome he hes not layed upoun Landislordis, and
the pledgis to be enterit for him aucht and sould ly alsweill for the gude
reule and obedience of thame as of the speciall personis quhome the said
Allaster hes tane upoun him.'

"The same day and compearance of same persons. First those landlords who
had not yet found caution for their MacGregor tenants were enjoined to do
so forthwith. 'And because the said Allaster cannot get cautioun conforme
to the General Band That Thairfoir Plegeis be tane for the gude reule and
obedience of sic as he ansueris for And for this effect, that thair be tuelff
personis gevin to him in tickett of quhome he sall mak chois of thrie to be
pledgeis for the first quarter, and thai to be quarterlie relevit with uthir thrie
of the tuelff Pledgeis. and that the saidis thrie Pledgeis be committit to the
custodie and keipeing of the Lord Drummond, the Laird of Tullibardin and
the Laird of Glenurquhay viz to everie ane of thame ane quha sal be haldin
be this present act to assuir thair keiping and not eschaiping under the pane
to be accountabill and ansuerabill to his Majesteis Subjectis for the haill
skaithis quhilkis thay may sustene of ony of the persons for quhome the
saidis plegeis lyis; and in the mean tyme quhill the entrie of the saidis
plegeis that the said Allaster be still detenit in warde within the castell of
Edinburgh, or utherwise fred and relevit upoun sic conditiounes as his
Majestie and Counsall sall think meit and expedient.'—Record of Secret
Council.

"1600. March 31. Precept of Remission in favour of Malcolm and Duncan
MacGregors brothers, servants of Patrick Lord Drummond for the slaughter
of umquhile Duncan McCleriche.

"April 16. The quhilk day in presence of the Kingis Majestie and Lordis of
Secret Counsall compeirit personallie Patrik Murray sone to Sir Johne
Murray of Tullibardine Knicht, as procurator for his father and enterit and
presentit Johne M^ceanduy in Rannoche and Ewne McAllaster Pudrach tua
of the plegeis specifiet and contenit in the tickett delivered to Allaster
McGregour of Glenstra conforme to the act quhairby the said Sir Johne
became cautioner and souertie to that effect upoun the 11th day of March
last Lyke as the said Patrick in name of his said fader Declairit that his
said fader had delyverit Johne McFatrick V^ceane, the thrid of the saidis

plegeis to Sir Duncane Campbell of Glenurquhay Kt quha presentlie hes
him in his custodie and keiping. In respect of the quhilk exehibitioun of
the saidis twa plegeis and delyverie of the uther plege to the said Sir
Duncane his Majestie and Counsall Declaris the act foirsaid . . quhairby
the said Sir Johne Murray became cautioner for the entrie of the saidis
thrie plegeis to be satisfeit and obeyit and exoneris and discharges him
thairof be thir presentis —R S C   Ewne McAllaster is delivered to John
Earl of Montrose Chancellor to be kept by him and John Mceanduy is
delivered to the said Patrick Murray to be convoyed to Patrick Lord
Drummond to whose custody he is appointed.

"1600. April 30.   His Majesty had been informed that Patrick Murray notwithstanding his faithful promises had not delivered John McEanduy to
Lord Drummond, 'so that not onlie has the said Patrik violated promise,
but occasion is given to the ClanGregor to continue thair accustamat trade
of evill doing, Sir John Murray is charged to deliver the said pledge to Lord
Drummond within three days under pain of rebellion'

"August 12   At Holyroodhouse.   At the late ordours takin with the Landislordis and Chiftane of the MacGregouris for retening of that haill Clan
undir obedience, Allaster McGregour of Glenstra Chief and Chieftain of
the said Clan tuke upon him certane personis for quhome he wuld be
ansuerable, and for the gude rule and quietnes to be keipit be thame the
personis following viz

> Johne dow McEwne,
> Duncane McEwne,
> John Mcfatrik VcEane,
> Gregour McGregour VcEan,
> Patrik gar Mcilchallum glas in Rannoch,
> John McEanduy in Rannoch, the eldest brother,
> Ewne McAllaster pudrach, and
> John McPatrik oig,

wer delyverit to him in tickett, of the quhilkis he wes ordanit to entir thrie
as plegeis, and thrie to be quarterlie relevit with utheris thrie of the remanent
personis sua that alwyse his Majestie micht be suir of thrie of thame, conforme to the quhilk in the moneth of Aprile last the said Ewne McAllaster
pudrach wes entrit and deliverit to Johne Erll of Montrose Chancellair, the
said John Mceanduy in Rannoch wes delivered to Patrik Lord Drummond
and the said John Mcfatrick VcEane wes delyverit to Sir Duncane Campbell
of Glenurquhay, ... Quhilkis personis haveing now lyne ane haill
quarter of ane yeir Necessair it is that thai be relevit be the entrie of the
uthir thrie of the remanent personis foirsaidis, and tharfoir ordainis Lettreis

to be direct charging Allaster of Glenstra, to enter present and delyver uthir thrie plegeis of the personis speciallie abone written 'to the same custodians as before, who are charged' to ressave the saidis plegeis within thrie houris eftir thay be presentit unto thame and to keip and detain thame &a and efter the ressett of the saidis plegeis to putt the plegeis presentlie lyand with thame to libertie and suffer thame pas quhair thay pleis, as they will ansuer to his Majestie at thair higher charge.

"1600. Dec. 5th, at Perth. Allister McGregor schieff and chiftane of the said clane tuik upone him certane personis of the name of McGregor for whom hie wald be answerable And for the gude rewll and quietnes to be keipit be thame the personis following viz

Johne Dow McEwin,[1]
Duncane McEwin,
Johne McPhatrik V^cEane,
Gregor McGregor V^cEane,
Patrick Gar McIllchael McGlass in Rannauche,
Ewin McAllaster Pudrache, the eldest brother,
and John McPatrick og,

are delivered to him in ticket off the quhilkis he is ordainit to enter thrie to be quarterlie relewit withe vthers thrie of the remanent personis sua that alwayis we might be suir of thrie of thame conforme to the quhilk in the moneth of Aprile last the said Ewin McAllaster Pudrache was enterit and delivered to Johne Erll of Montrois chancelair The said Ewin M^ceanduy in Rannauche was enterit and delivered to Patrik Lord Drummond, and the said Johne McPhatrik V^cEane was deliverit to Sir Duncan Campbell of Glenurquhay, Quhilkis plegis haveing layne now one haill quarter of ane zeir Necessar it is that thay be relievit be the entrie of vther thrie of the remanent personis forsaidis. Our will is Heirfoir &a.

"Allaster Galt McGregor, fathair brothair to the Laird, witness.
"Duncan McAllaster quhiddrache V^cGregor witness (Pudrach).

—Register of Hornings, Perth, in General Register House."

[1] See on previous page, same list, August 12.

Chapter XXII

1600. King James VI. XV. November 1600

A CT anent removing and extinguishing of deadly feud :—

"Our Soveraigne Lord and haill estates of parliament presently convened for removing of the present feuds that abounds within the Realme Finds it meet and expedient that the parties be charged to compeir before his Highness and secret Council at sik days as shal be thought expedient to submit to tua or three friends on either side or to subscrive ane submissioun formed and sent by his Majesty to them to be subscrived. Whilkis friends by their acceptatioun shall be bound either to decerne within the space of thretty days after they have accepted, or else to agree at their first meeting, on ane oversman wha shall decerne within that space, whilk if they cannot do, they shall within the foresaid thretty days report the ground and cause of their disagreement to his Majesty and sik specials of his council as his Highness shall find least partial and suspect (Whaes Majesty by the advice of the Estates here present is declared to be overs-man in the matter) And failying that the friends arbitrators either decerne, or report not, within the foresaid space after their acceptation everie one of them by this authority of this present act to incur the pain of one thousand pounds to be employed to his Majesty's use. And because all feuds are ane of thir three natures, namely that there is either slaughter upon neither side or slaughter upon ane side only or else slaughter upon both sides the parties in the first may be commanded to agree, due satisfaction being offered and performed at the sight of friends and overs-man in manner foresaid Where there is slaughter upon both sides his Majesty may by rigour and equality of justice, compell them to agree, due satisfaction being made on either side according to the quality of the offence and persons offended; where the slaughter is only on one side the party grieved cannot refuse in reason to submit in manner foresaid all quarrell he can beare to any person innocent, Justice being made patent to him against the guilty specially he being ordained by this present Act to persew nane uther but the guilty and that by the Law. And the party so peresewed not to beare quarrel for it, but to defend in lawful manner. And that all quarrels shall cease against ilk as shall be lawfully persewed in this forme either by their conviction or execution by law or otherwise by their clenging and agreement that all persons of perfitt age, and within the countrie and having entries to persew any parties for crimes capitall shall within forty dayes after the publishing of this present Act at the head burgh of the shire where the persewer dwells raise and cause execute their letter in the said matter and insist in the persuit thereof with certification to sik as failzies that their action shall perish, expire, and be extinct The daid persewer shall be compelled to submit his action in manner above specified reserving alwaies to his Majesty his action as accords with the law. Provyding that if the said persewer satisfie the ordinance of this present act and be delayed either by ane continuation of the diet by warrand of the Prince or by the dilatour defences proponed by the pannell for eliding of the final tryell of the persuit In that case the prescription nawise to run against the persewer, having done his possible diligence in maner foresaid And because the guiltines of crymes consists not only in the persons of the actual committers thereof, but also in the authors, causers and mivers of the samin to be committed wha are art part and gilty of the said fact where na publict knawledge nor certane tryell is had, His Majesty and Estaitis nowyse willing that neither the authors nor actours of sik heinous crymes escape the dew punishment through obscurity and laik of publik knawledge thereof Declares that the parties offended doing thier diligence as said is against the actual and knawn committers of the said crymes and satisfying this Act anent their reconciliation with all other persons shall in nowyse be prejudged of their action competent against sik persons of whaes giltiness they shall hereafter get knawledge provyding that they shall bear no fead against the said suspect persons whill first after sufficient information obtained they raise their letters for summonding of the saids parties to underlye the law and either make them fugitive or otherwyse obteine ther persute decided. And further the prescription of this present act shall in nowyse militate aginst any party whaes actions are already submitted to ane langer day, nor is prescribed in this act Provyding that the party doe his diligence in maner above written within fourty days after the expiring of the said submission And to the intent that justice be na occasion to breed farther trouble every party shall come to the town accompanied allanerlie with twentyfour persons where bath they and thir company shall keepe their ludging to the hour of cause. At the quhilk first the ane and then the other shall be brought out by the town (guard?) in Armes accompanied from their ludging to the bar with the number presrived to their rank by act of parliament. The contravene whereof if he be persewer shall tyne his persute in tyme comming and if he be defender he shall be denounced rebell as presumed guilty, and refusing lawful triall. And for staying all deadly feads in tyme cumming it shall not be lawful to the persewer to invade, persew, bear fead, or quarrel against any friend of the offender innocent or not accused and convict of the cryme under the pain of tynsell of his action and persute against the guilty and to be compelled to submit with the

2 L

offenders self Reserving alwyse to his Majesty his action against him for the cryme Lyke as the friends of the gilty person being convict of the cryme and fugitive from the law, shall not bear quarel for his persute be law neither maintein, supplie nor reset him under the paines conteined in the act against resetters of fugitives and rebels. And in case any of the friends of the guilty persons reset him in contempt of the present act and others his Highness Lawes, the partie grieved, assisted with his Highnes Advocat, shall onely persew the resetters by ordour of law without convocation or fead, grudge, or quarrell to be borne against him therefore otherwise under the paine of tynsel of his said lawful action in all tyme comming. And to this ordour before specified the haill nobilitie and estaites here present have given their consent and approbatioun and sworne to conforme them thereto in all feads whilkis shall fall out in tyme comming. And this present Act nowyse to militat in sik cases where the party offender is denunced rebell or shall happen hereafter to be fugitive and put to the horne, for slaughter or other odious capital crymes, during the tyme of their rebellion. And to the intent these present articles may have the better effect and be the mair willingly embraced by his Majesty's haill subjects, his Highnes of his proper motive and gracious inclination to justice, quyetness and well of his people, solemnly declared and faithfully promissed in presence of the saidis estaits that for slaughter and other odious crymes to be hereafter committed his Heighness shall grant no respit, remissioun, pardon, nor oversight at any tymes efter, albeit the parties transact and agree themselves, till these inveterate and damnable customes of the saids heynous crymes be rooted out and altogether suppressed ; whilkes articles above written in the haill heads and poijnts of the samyne our Soveragne Lord and Estaites foresaid presently convened, ratifies, approves and confirms and ordains the samine to have the strength, force and effect of ane law in all tyme comming &a.

1601 March 3. at Holyroodhouse, Commission of Lieutennandrie against the ClanGregor.

"Forasmekle as the Kingis Majestie and Counsall haveing tane grit panis and travellis thir divers yeiris bigane for reduceing of the wicked and unhappie race of the ClanGregour quha sa lang hes continuet in bluid, thift, reif and oppositioun to the obedience of his Majestie and his lawis and to a peceable and civile forme of leving : In end Allaster McGregour of Glenstray Chief and Ringleidar of that Clan was moved to cum in and to mak an offer of the entrie of thrie plegeis quarterlie for the guid reule and obedience of himselff, and all sic as be the law and his awin bandis he is ansuerable for, and tua onlie of the saidis Plegeis being enterit for the first quarter, And his Majestie expectand a constant continuance of the said Allaster in his promeist obedience, Notwithstanding it is of a treuth that he following the perverse counsall and inclinatioun of his wickit and misreulie Clan hes

failzeit in the entrie of the plegeis for the second quarter and is thairfoir
ordourlie denouncet and registrat at the horne, and hes remanet thairat this
lang tyme bigane, as he dois yit unrelaxt, Intending thirby as appeiris to
oversie and wink at all the insolencies and attemptatis of the disorderit
thevis and lymmaris for quhome he aucht to ansuer,   And his Majestie
being careful to have the saidis insolent lymmaris repressit and reduceit to
obedience and his Majestie's gude subjectis redressit of thair skaithis, And
acknawledging the gude inclinatioun of his rycht traist Cusing and Coun-
sallor Archibald Erll of Ergyll Lord Campbell and Lorne, to justice and to
do his Hienes service,   Thairfoir his Majestie hes maid and constitute and
be the tennour heirof makis and constitutis the said Erll his Majesteis
Lieutennent and Justice in that pairt to the effect following, Gevand Grantand
and committand to him, his Hienes' full power and commissioun, expres
bidding and charge, To direct preceptis and Lettreis in his awin name for
chargeing of the haill personis of the name of McGregour severallie or
togidder to compeir befoir him quhen and quhairevir he sall appoint
alsweill for randering of thair obedience and making of suirte for thair
guid behaviour as for redress of complenaris, and undirlying of the lawis
under the pane of Horning ;   The disobeyaris to denunce to the horne, and
eftir thair said denunciatioun to prosequte thame as fugitives and outlawis
with fyre and suord and to burne thair housses and to follow and
persew thame quhairevir they sall flie for eschewing of apprehensioun,
and to asseig all housses and strengthis quhilkis thay sall tak for thair saif
gaird ; Rais fyre and use all force and Ingyne quhilk can be had for
recoverie thairof and apprehending of the saidis fugitives and lymnaris
being thairintill ; As alsua to chairge thair maisteris and Landislordis,
To entir and present thame befoir him at sic tymes and places as he sall
pleis to appoint conforme to the General Band, Lieutennent and Justice
Courtis aganis the said ClanGregour sa oft as the said Liutennent will
think expedient. to sett, begin, affix hald and continue ; Suittis to mak
be callit ; absentis to amerciat ; Trespassouris to punische ; unlawis,
amerchiamentis and eschaittis of the saidis Courtis, to ask, lift and raiss
and for the same, giff neid beis, to poynd and distreinzie ; all and sindrie
personis of the ClanGregour, suspect and dilaitit of thift, Murthour,
Slauchter, Fyre-raising, Sorning, oppin and maisterful oppressioun and
uther odious crymes, to serche, seik, tak and apprehend, commit to waird
and put to the knawledge of ane assyse ; And as thay sal happin to be
foundin culpable or innocent, to caus Justice to be ministrat upoun thame
conforme to the lawis of this realme ; Assysouris (Jurors) neidfull to this,
effect ilk persone under the paine of fourty pundis to summond, wairne,
cheis, (choose) and caus to be sworne, Deputis under him with clerkis,

servandis, dempstaris and uther officeris and numberis of Courte neidfull to mak creat substitute and ordane; for quhome he salbe haldin to ansuer; The escheit, gudis of sa mony of the ClanGregour as sall be denunceit Rebellis and put to the horne, or as sal be convict and execute to the deid be vertew of this commissioun, to intromett and uplift, and for the same, gif neid beis to poynd, and distrenzie, and to the said Lieutennentis awin use for his labouris to apply; Quhilkis Escheitis his Majestie and Counsell be the tennour heirof Gevis, Grantis and Disponis to the said Lieutennent; And generallie all and sindrie uther thingis to do, exerce and use, quhilkis for executioun of this commissioun is requisite and necessar, firme and stabill halding and for to hald, all and quhatsumevir thingis sal be lauchfullie done herein; And becaus the resett and comfort quhilk fugitives and lymmeris sa frequentlie gettis among thair friendis and acquentance is not onlie an encouragement to thame to continew in thair evill doingis, bot alsua and grit hinder to the ordiner courss of Justice, Thairfoir his Majestie and Lordis of his Secrete Counsall, Declaris Statutis and ordanis, That quhatsumevir personis sall happin to resett supplie and interteny ony of the said ClanGregouris, thair wyffis, Bairnis, and geir, eftir they be denunceit Rebellis and declarit fugitives and dew internatioun maid thairof at the mercat croce of the Schyre; That the same personis sal be halden culpable and giltie of the halii bigane offensses committit be the personis quhome thay sall resett, and sal be haldin ansuerable to the saic Lieutennent for ony offence to be committit be thame thaireftir; And forder his Majestie nawyse willing that the executioun of this commissioun sall be onywyse frustrat or disappointit be ony favour or pardoun to be grantit be his Majestie to ony of the ClanGregouris heireftir; Therfoir his Majestie in presence of his Counsall promeist that his Hienes sall grant na favour nor oversicht to ony of thame during the tyme of this present Commissioun, bot shall remitt thame and thair suittis to the said Lieutennent, And for the executioun of this commissioun ordainis lettries to be direct, chargeing all and sindrie his Majesties liegeis and subjectis within the boundis of Athoill, Lennox, Menteith, Strathearne, Ergyle and Tarbert that thai and everie ane of thame Ryse, concur, fortefie, and asaist the said Lieutennent within the boundis of the Schirefdome quhair thay duell in the persute of the said ClanGregour, and executioun of this commissioun, at sic tymes as the said Lieutennent sall repaire within the boundis foirsaidis and sall wairne and chairg thame to this effect be his awin Proclamatioun or particular missives under the pane of horning; And that this present Commissioun ressave executioun for redres of complenaris fra the moneth of August anno 1596, and induir heireftir for the space of ane zeir nixt to cum eftir the dait heirof

and forder ay and quhill the same be speciallie dischargit be his Majestie.—
Sec: Con: Rec: Acta."

Perhaps no Statute Book contains a more singular regulation, giving
the power of life and death into the hands of Argyll and even guarding
against the possibility of Royal mercy.   Moreover, it is made retrospective,
although fortunately excluding the murder of Drummonderinach, the
remission for which was dated July 1596, a month before the limit of
former complaints.

> "1601 March 3. Act against the Resetters of the MacGregors goods nearly
> similar to the latter part of the Proclamation of Jan. 31. 1600 and proceeding
> on the narrative of the Commission of Lieutennency of this date.—Rec. Sec.
> Coun. Acta."

From the "Chartulary":—

> "Bond given by the ClanGregor to the Earl of Argyle as
> King's Lieutennent.

> "1601. April 22. At Striuiling.   The quhilk Day Alexander McGregour of
> Glenstra compeirand personallie in presence of ane nobill and potent Lord
> Archibald Erle of Ergyle, Lord Campbell and Lorne, Justice Generall of
> Scotland, his Majesties Lieutennent in that pairt; Band and obleist and
> tuik upoun him, to be ansuerabill for the haill personis of the surname of
> McGregour be making of thame to be furthcummand to Justice for all
> Thiftis, Soirningis, and oppressiounis, depradatiounis, wrangis, and attemptis
> to be committit be thame, or ony of thame, heireftir and in tyme comeing
> except for sa mony of the surname as he sall qualifie to have maisteris, and
> Landislordis, in presence of the Lordis of Counsall, the said Lieutennent,
> or any uther his Hienes Lieutennent for the tyme; and that he hes na resett,
> mantenance or defence of thay quhome he layis upoun the saidis Landis-
> lordis and Maisteris; at quhilk tyme the said Alexander to be na forder
> burdynit for thay, that he justlie puttis aff him, be qualificatioun foirsaid,
> conforme to the Actis of Counsall sett down thairanent And for the better
> performance heirof the said Alexander sall enter in pledge to the said noble
> Lord

>> John dow McCondochy V^cAllaster
>> Patrik gar M^cilchallum glas and
>> Finlay McWilliame

> sua sone as he may possible, and himself with

>> Malcolme McDougall Keir, and
>> Duncane McPatrik V^cDowgall Keir

> To remane and abyde in wairde ay and quhill he entir the saidis thrie

Plegeis, or ellis John dow McGregour his brother with uther twa responsabill
men of his kin and surname, and the saidis thrie plegeis, or ony of thame,
being deceissit or execute, or fred, be the said Alexander, he sall entir and
present utheris in thair placeis at the requisitioun of the saidis Lordis of
Counsall or Lieutennent for the tyme; Makand continuallie without inter-
vall thrie of his surname to remain as plegeis and speciallie thrie of the
personis following.

> John dhu McEwne (second son of Ewne the 'Tutour'),
> Duncan McEwne, his brother,
> Johne dow M^cilfadrik V^cRobert,
> Robert Abroch McGregour (son of Duncan Abroch),
> Patrik McEanduy in Rannoch,
> Archibald McCondochy V^cAllaster,
> Gregour Skorocht, and
> Duncane M^cfadrik,

or ony uther of his surname for the quhilkis he aucht to be ansuerable, at
the nominatioun of the saidis Lordis &a . . . . under the tinsall of his
landis, and heretage to be renunceit to the said noble Lord ipso facto for
ever, or ellis put and qualefie the same to be mentennentis to utheris maisteris and Landislordis without his mantenance and defence.   Concerning
redres of biganes &a (same as in preceding act) The said Alexander
McGregour is ordainit and fullie heirto consentis That he or ellis the said
John dow his brother sall remane in wairde, quhill redres and satisfactioun
be maid be him and they of his awin surname and utheris for quhome he is
obleist be law to be ansuerable to mak payment as the law, constitutioun,
and pratiques of the cuntrey requyris ; The clames and dittayis to be gevin
in befoir the thrid day of May nixt to come, and the tuelft day of the said
moneth assignit to the pairties defendaries, to compeir and ansuer as the
said Alex : sall be wairnit to that effect ; withoute prejudice of the contract
maid betwixt the Erle of Montrois, Patrik Lord Drummond, Sir Duncane
Campbell of Glenurquhay Knicht on the ane pairt, and the said Alexander,
as it beiris (1 & 2. Feb. 1590-1) As alsua the personis following, Principallis,
and maist speciallis, of the race and name of MacGregour, ar ordainit of
thair awne voluntar, quha be thir presentis ar become bundin, and obleist
to be ansuerable for thair raices and housses respective for observing guid
reull in tyme comeing towardis his Hienes liegis, and for the redres of faultis
the space of yeiris bigane contenit in the said noble Lordis commissioun as
alsua for all uther thair men Tennentis and servantis as law will, viz.

1. Gregour McEwine V^cGregour (eldest son of Ewine the Tutour)
be the assistance and concurrence of the said noble Lord (Argyle) and the
said Alexander McGregour of Glenstra, sall be ansuerable for himself and

for all discendit, and to discend of umquhile Ewne McGregour (Tutour of Glenstra, see Jan. 1584-5), his fader;

 2. Duncane na Glen MacGregour of Phanean, Paternal uncle of Glenstray,

for his sones and raice to come of him,

 3. Allaster galt MacGregour, Paternal uncle of Glenstray,

for his sones liberall (natural?) and raice cum and to come of him,

 4. Duncane McAllaster pudryche, (Pudrach)

for himself and all come and to come of umquhile Allaster pudryche his father;

 5. Johne Dhu McGregour,
  brother to the said Allaster for himself, his bairnis and raice to
  come of him;

 6. Gregour McNeill,

 7. Williame McNeill,

 8. Duncane McEanekaine (cham)

 9. Allaster McEwne,

 10. Johne dow McAllaster,

 11. Williame McGregour V^cGillechallum,

 12. Johne dow McGregour, Rora,

 13. Duncane McEwne V^cAllaster,

 14. Duncane McGregour V^cWilliam in Rannoch,

 15. Duncane M^cinvalloch,

 16. Johne dow McCondochy V^cGregour in Innervar,

 17. Johne McGregour V^cNeill,

for thameselffis, and conjunction for slegh (sliochd) and raice to come of umquhile Duncane Lienoch (Roro),

 18. Johne McGregour V^cEane V^cGregour,

 19. Allaster, Charleis, and Gregour, brether, for thameselffis, hous, and
  raice cum and to come of umquhile Johne McGregour, and
  Gregour, thair Guidsir and father.

 22. Duncane abroch, and

 23. Patrick aldoch McGregouris

for thameselffis and all discendit and to discend of umquhile Duncan Latois, (Ladosach) thair predecessour.

 24. Johnne M^cfadrik ammonach, (Glen Almond)

 25. Gregour M^cphadrick ammonoch,

 26. Johne dow McGregour McPhadrick of Innerzeldie,

 27. Duncane McAllaster in Dundurne,

 28. Duncane McPhadrick V^ccondoquhy,

 29. Allaster McCondochy voir,

for thameselffis and conjunctim for thair haill raice cum and to come of umquhile Patrik Chaoldich,

 30. Malcolme McDowgall keir,
 31. Duncane McPhadrik V^cDowgall Keir,
 32. Johne M^cilkeir
 33. Dougall M^cilkeir,
 34. Malcolme oig McGregour V^cDowgall Keir

for the raice and hous present and to come of the Clan Dowgall Keir ;

 35. Allaster McRobert voir,

for himself and his sones and all discendit and to discend of him

 36. James McGregour in Drumphin, for himself his bairnis and all cum
  or to come of him.

" Quhilkis Bandis and Obleisment sall be interpret and extendit towardis the airis and successouris of the said Alexander McGregour and all utheris obligantis foirsaidis respective without prejudice and not annulling the Bandis and oblisingis of thair Maisteris and Landislordis respective, as alsua without prejudice of the said Alexanderis Band gevin for himself and all utheris for quhome he man be ansuerabill be the law, Sua that everie ane of the saidis Bandis have thair awin force and effect in full integretie as thay beir at the instanceis of all pairties pretendand enteres thairintill, all fraud and gyll secludit ; In witness heirof the presentis written be Johne Hog we have subscrivet with oure handis and followis day, zeir and place foirsaidis, Befoir thir witnesses.

 David Commendator of Dryburgh,
 James Commendator of Incheafray
 Sir Duncane Campbell of Glenurquhay Knicht,
 Sir Archibald Stirling of Keir Knicht
 Sir William Menteith of Kerss Knicht
 James Campbell Fear of Laweris,
 James Leytoun of Tullibody,
 James Kinross of Kippanross.

Sic Subscribitur, Allaster McGregour of Glenstra abonewrittin with my hand tuiching the notaries pen underwrittin becaus I can not wryte.

" May 12. personallie compeirit

 Malcolme McGregour in Glengyle,
 Malcolme McDowilkeir,
 Duncane McPhatrik V^cdowilkeir,
 Gregour Neilsoun,
 Johne dow McGregour Ammonoch,
 Johne McGregour V^cEane V^cGregour

in presence of Archibald Erle of Ergyll and subscrivit the Act abonewritten

with thair handis led at the pen of the Notar underwrittin, in presence of
. . . . same witnesses as before with the addition of Sir William
Kerss knicht and James Seytoun of Tullibody. The Bond was eventually
recorded June 28. 1602. in the Books of Council.

"Note in 'Chartulary.' Out of the 36 Principal men of the ClanGregour
proposed to be parties to the Bond along with Allaster McGregor of Glenstra
only six actually sign it, and that three weeks after him. Argyle appears to
have had the Bond in his possession for upwards of a year without being
able to procure any additional signatures to it.

"1601. June 26. Marie McGregour relict of umquhile Johne Tosheoch son of
Duncane Tosheoch in Pittenzie is mentioned at this time in the Register of
Hornings for Perth."

The necessary result of the invitation to bring forward old complaints
against the Clan appears in numerous complaints as well as notices to
quit.

"1601. July 5. Garntullie as tacksman of Fortigall obtains decreet of removal
against Janet Stewart relict of umqle Allaster Pudrache MacGregor, Duncan
McEane cham alias McGregor in Tulliechwillen (Lands of Balnacraig) and
others.

"1601. July 25. Strowan Robertson against his tenants same as on 21. Jan.
1597-8 and June 9. 1599; and also John dow McAllester V^cGregour
William McNeill compeired personally; and Neill McWilliam, John dow
M^callaster. Malcolm McWilliame McGregour and Duncan his sone compeirand by procurators. Diet continued.

"July 25. Strowane Robertson against his tenants. William McNeill V^cEwin
McGregour, in Boirland of Fernan and half milne of Strowane Fernan.
Umquhile Neill McCondoquhie land of Fernan, Alexander McGregour
cleriche, land of Croftnallin, Neill McWilliam McNeill Wester Fernan,
Duncan McAllaster McGregour land of Tunivoir, Malcolm McGregour sone
to the said umquhile Neill McDonquhie Gregour, and several others compeired personally. They were all styled 'pretendit occupiers.'

"July 25. With regard to Strowane Robertsone's tenants, William McNeill
made various allegations stating ' That of the lands from which he is
charged to remove' The said William and his predecessors hes been in
possessioune thrie hundredth yeiris or thairby as native and kyndlie titularis
and possessouris therof.

"Oct. 10. At Brechin. Remissioun to the Laird of Glenurquhay.

"James &a. Whereas we understanding the great enemity which has
subsisted from early times (ab antico) between the Laird of Glenurquhay

2 M

and the surname of MacGregor; in the course of which many and various herschips, slaughters, and oppressiouns have been committed by both parties and surnames, and their complices against the others, And that our lovite Sir Duncan Campbell present Laird of Glenurquhay Knicht was frequentlie forced to seek remeid by force and the strong hand; Therefore &a Remission in the usual form to Sir Duncan and four of his friends for the tresonable burning of the houses of Bar in Glenurchy occupied by McGregour.—Privy Seal lxxij, 162.

" 1601. Nov. 10. Compliant Glenurquhay &a against certain MacGregors.

"Anent our Soverane Lordis Lettreis raised at the instance of Sir Duncan Campbell Knicht Superiour and Heritable Proprietor of the landis underwrittin, and Donald McInnes in the Lands of Tennent to the said Sir Duncane in the samyn landis for his enteres, makand mentioun, That quhir the said Donald and his servandis haveing in the monethis of September last bipast and October instant Schorne and Wyne his cornis quhilkis grew this present yeir upoun the ground of the landis of and they being transportand and away leidand the same cornis off the saidis landis to the saidis Donaldis Barne and Barneyaird; It is of treuthe that

> John dow McGregour V^cPatrick (in Innerzeldies, see Ap. 1601),
> Duncan McPhatrick (his father's brother),
> Gregour Ammonoch (in Kingart),
> Johne, brother to the said Gregour,
> Duncane dow McEwin V^cEane,
> Patrik McEwin V^cEane his brother,

with utheris their Complices, haveing schaken aff all reverence and dewtifull obedience thay should have, and beir to his Hienes lawis, all bodin in feir of weir (arrayed in warlike fashion) with haberschois, Poleaixis Tua handit suordis, and other weaponis invasive and haquebuts and pistols prohibete to be worne be act of Parliament; came upoun the said complenaris tennent and 'broke down his wains and cars, and threatened to murder him if he mede any resistance.'

" Nov. Item payed by command and direction of his Majesty for the expenses made upon the expeding of the Remissioun granted to the Laird of Glenurquhay and his servants, and of a gift of discharge of all unlaws and penalties incurred by Glenurquhay, £49, 2s. 4d. (Scots).—Lord High Treasurer's Accounts.

" 1601. Dec. 10th. The Earl of Argyle denounced rebel for not producing before the Council Allaster Macean oig of Glencoe to whom he is master and landlord, and for whom he ought to be answerable As also John Galt MacGregor whom he has at least had in his custody and keeping, &a &a

" 1602. Jan. 31st The King undertook to assist Queen Elizabeth of England with a levy of 'Hieland men' to repress a rebellion in Ireland and directed a levy 'of thir men upoun sic of his Majesties subjects within the Hielandis as ar of maist power to furnis yame.' In this levy The Laird of Mac-Gregour is set down for 50 men

" 1602. 19th June

"Alexander Colquhoun of Luss having apprehended 'Robert McGregor sone to Duncane Abrach MacGregor and with his awne hand put him to liberty' is charged to produce the said Robert And Letters were sent directing Luss accordingly.

" 1602.

"Complaint by Alex. Stewart of Dalguis that, about 6 years ago, Johne Dow McGregour, brother of the laird of McGregor or at least his servants stole out of the 'Mucht of Strabrane' (Strathbran) 16 head of horses & mares, worth 20 merks each,—' To the takin the said Johnne McGregour being in his own cradak in a rowme that he haldis of the Laird of Tullibardine, in Balquhidder, sent owt his men and tuke the said hors fra the said compliners sone, and sic uthers his servandis that wer thair that followit the said hors '[1]

" 1602. June 28th.

"The Band executed between the Earl of Argyll and the ClanGregor in April 1601 is put before the King and Council at Perth, and ordered to be registered Promise was also made for the Earl of Argyll 'that whenever the said Earl should be required by his Majesty and Council, to enter and produce the persons underwritten or any three of them viz John dow McEwne, Duncan McEwne his brother, John Dhu McIlphadrick VcRobert, Robert Abroch MacGregor, Duncan McInduy in Ranoch, Archibald McCondochy VcAllaster, Gregor Scorach and Duncan Mcfadrick.

" 1602. July. The Earl of Argyll is desired to produce John Galt McGregor.

" 1602. July 13th.

"Anent letters raised at the instance Menzies of Weem explaining that he is not able to make certain of the ClanGregor and uthers dwelling in Rora answerable because 'Quhilkes persones albeit they duell within the boundis of Rora zit thay are nowther mentennentis nor seruandis to the said com-plenar and pass not maill nor dewtie to him nor nawayis aknawledges him but thay are substakismen to Duncan McGregor sone to umqle Gregor McCondochy his tennent and were input and placit by (without) the said complenars knawledge, consent, permission & allowance be him and be

[1] The sentence does not run very clearly, but it is taken from the original account

William McNeill in Farnan, Duncane McAllaster there and Duncane M^ceane
cam in Forthergill tutor to the said (Duncan McGregor) And seeing the
said complenar is not able to mak them answerable Ressoun and equitie
cravis that he sould have the relief of the said tutor be quhome the saidis
personis complenit upon wer enterit in his saidis landis and thay sould be
enterit and presentit befoir his majesty and the saidis Lordes the said day
be thair maisteris and landislordis for order to be taken with theme anent the
said complenars relieff and the billis layed upoun him And anent the
Charge gevin to Robertsoun of Strowane maister and landislord to the saidis
Williame McNeill Duncane McAllaster &a (who were in Fernan) Robertson
of Strowan for being oft times callit and not compeiring or presenting the
men, is denounced Rebel.

"Strowan is also charged to present to the Council Alester MacGregor
Cleriche, to answer to a complaint by Watson in Arntullie. Various
complaints follow.

" 1602. June or July.

"Anent the complaint given in by Patrick Scott in Glennilmet in the
bishoprick of Dunkeld upon Duncan McEachanie MacGregor, in Tulloch-
moline in Fartirchill servant to the laird of Garntullie for stealing with his
complices, broken men of his friendship at his command 4 Cows and
an ox in 1600 and 3 wedders 3 years old, was challenged selling one of the
cows at Andermas fair, Garntullie decerned to redress the above.

A note by Mr MacGregor Stirling states that this Duncan is the person
mentioned as having been taken prisoner by MacIntosh in King James VI.
letter of 30th March 1596-7 ; whilst in the entry of 13th July 1602, he is
stated to be ' tutour ' of MacGregor of Rora.

" 1602. July 17th.

"Alexander McGregor was infeft in the lands of Lagarie in the Dukedom
of Lennox and Shire of Dumbarton on a precept of Clare Constat as heir of
his father John MacGregor of Ardinconnell.   His brother Gregor Mac-
Gregor was a witness to the infeftment.—Record of the Burgh of Dumbarton.

" 1602. August 3d.   At Falkland.

"Complaint of Andrew Ramsay at Mill of Innerqueich, theft of Cattle by
Alaster McAlaster and John Dow McEwen McGregor and others from the
lands of Corb and Drycurie in the forest of Alyth.

" 1602. August 6th.   At Falkland.

"Earl of Argyle denounced, eight different entries for not producing
before the Council Donald M^ceane dowy McAllaster in Glencoans, McCon-

dochy V^{c}ean roy, Ewne McAllaster Pudrach, John dow McEwne MacGregor, McCondochy of Inneraw and Duncan McEwne MacGregor.

"1602. Earl of Argyle charged to present John Galt MacGregor and all the remaining persons of the ClanGregor for whom he has become answerable on 24th Nov.

"1602. Nov. 25th. At Holyroodhouse.

"Colquhoun of Luss against the Earl of Argyle, for proving that the Earl is answerable for certain persons ;

> Allaster MacGregor of Glenstray,
> John Dhu his brother,
> Duncan Glen of Fernan,
> Gregor son to the said Duncan,
> Patrick also his son,
> Allaster Galt in Culquhirrilan,
> Patrick and Duncan his sons,
> Patrick in Caldernot and his sons,
> John Dhu and Duncan,
> Duncan McOtter dow in the Otter,
> Gregor McEwne in Moirninche,
> John dow McEwne his brother,
> Duncan McEwene   do.,
> Allaster McAllaster vreik,
> Gregor McCoull,
> Duncan Ger his brother,
> Duncans McEwene his brother,
> Callum MacGregor V^{c}ulcheir (Dow),
> Dougal roy MacGregor, vagabond,
> Allaster McCondochy M^{c}eane dowy V^{c}Gregor householdman to the
>   Laird of MacGregor,
> Neill M^{c}eane duy V^{c}Ewne,
> Duncan McEwene V^{c}illevoill,
> Donald McEwine,
> John dow lean McPhadrick V^{c}culcher,
> Challum McNeill vane MacGregor,

All men tenants and servants to Archibald Earl of Argyll dwelling upon his land and are such persons as by the laws of this realme acts of Parliament and General Band he will be held to answer for. Therefore ordain letters to be direct to summon such witnesses as the said Laird of Luss intends to use for proving of the said matter To compeir personally the said day to bear leal and soothfast witnessing in the said matter, under the pain of rebellion &a.   And the said Laird of Luss compeiring personally and the said Archibald Earl of Argyll compeiring by Mr George Arskin his procurator are warned hereof apud Acta.

" 1602 Nov.

"Item to Patrik M^comeis messenger passing from Edinburgh with letters to charge Archibald Earl of Argyll to compeir personally before the Council the 16th day of Dec. next to answer to such things as shall be inquired of him touching his lying at await for the laird of Ardincapill upoun set purpose to have slain him."

From the published Register of Privy Council [1] :—

" 1602.   The Earl of Argyll had become bound in 20,000 merks that he and those for whom he is answerable should observe good rule in the country and satisfy parties skaithed, Since then the Earl had obtained a commission of lieutenancy against the ClanGregour dated in March 1601, & still undischarged, empowering him to take surety of the Clan for their good behaviour in future.   In accordance with this commission he had convened before him at Stirling the Laird of McGregor, and all the principals of the branches of that name, and thus having them 'all undir his power'; either took or should have taken ample surety from them, Yet though the said commission is in full force, the said ClanGregour 'has bene and ar als insolent and of als wicked and inhappie a dispositioun as they wer at ony time preceiding, and hes committit not onlie oppin and avowit heirschippis and depredationis upoun fair daylicht upoun divers of his Heynes guid subjectis, as namely upoun the Laird of Luss and Buchannane bot alsua they commit daylie prevey stouthis and robberies in all pairtis quhair they may find the commoditie of thair pray.' . . . For example (several cases follow,) . . . John Galt McGregour having been apprehended by the said Earl as his Majesty's lieutenant, the said Earl was required to enter him before the King and Council; but although he made sundry promises to his Majesty to enter the said Johne yet he has not only failed to do so 'bot to the forder contempt of his Heynes' has set him at liberty.   The King and his Council decern the said principal and his sureties to have incurred the penalty of 20,000 merks and ordain letters of Horning &a."

[1] An abridgment of a paper in the "Chartulary."   Mention is made of Allaster Galt MacGregor, Duncan Glen MacGregor, and Patrick MacGregor, all brothers, and father's brothers to Allaster MacGregor of Glenstrae; also of Catternach MacGregor in Lorne, and sundry others, all men tenants and servants to the said Earl of Argyle.

Chapter XXIII

Battle of Glenfruin

FROM the " Baronage," continued from Chapter XVI. :—

"XVI. Alexander MacGregor of that Ilk, a man of determined and martial spirit. He fought the memorable battle of Glenfroon, against the Colquhouns, Buchannans, Græmes, *anno* 1602.

"We have hereto subjoined a full account of this affair, faithfully translated from a Latin history of the family of Sutherland, written by Mr Alexander Ross, Professor in the University of Aberdeen, *anno* 1631 : by which it plainly appears how grossly this unfortunate Clan have been represented and abused."

Although the differences are but slight, it may be better here to give the published version of Sir Robert Gordon's history, which is very nearly similar.[1]

"Extract from the 'Genealogical History of the Erldom of Sutherland from its origen to the year of God 1630.' written by Sir Robert Gordon of Gordonstoun, Baronet with a continuation to the year 1651. published from the Original Manuscript. Edinburgh 1818. Folio pages 244-247 :—

"In lent, the yeir of God 1602., ther happened a great tumult and combustion in the west of Scotland, betuein the Laird of Lus (Chieff of the surname of Colquhoun, and Alexander Mackgregor (Chieftane of the ClanGregar). Ther had ben formerlie some rancour among them, for divers mutuall harships and wrongs done on either syd ; first by Luss his freinds, against some of the Clangregar, and then by John Mackgregar (the brother of the forsaid Alexander Mackregar) against the Laird of Luss, his dependers and tennents. And now Alexander McGregar

---

[1] A MS. Note in the Family Edition of Douglas's "Baronage," probably by Mr MacGregor Stirling, adds Mr Ross, who seems to have freely, and with some slight variations, translated into Latin Sir Robert Gordon of Gordanstoun's "History of the Earldom of Sutherland," written the year before, *i.e.* 1630. Other accounts are added in Appendix.

(being accompanied with 200 of his kin and freinds) came from the Rannoch into the Lennox, to the Laird of Lus his owne bounds, with a resolution to tak away these dissensions and jarrs by the mediation of freinds. In this meantyme the Laird of Luss doth assemble all his pertakers and dependers, with the Buchannans and others, to the number of 300 horsemen and 500 foott; intending that iff the issue of their meitting did not answer his expectation, he might inclose the enemies within his cuntrey, and so overthrow them. Bot the Clangregar being vpon their guard, it happened otherwise; for presentlie after that the meitting dissoued, the Laird of Luss, thinking to tak his enemies at vnawars, persued them hastylie and eagerlye at Glen-Freon. Mackgregar had his company pairted in tuo; the most pairt he led himselff, the rest he committed to the charge of and conduct of his brother John, who drew a compas about, and invaded the Laird of Luss his company when they least expected. The combat wes foughten with great courage; In end, the Clangregar prevailed, chased ther enemies, killed divers gentlemen, and some burgesses of the toun of Dumbarton, with 200 others and took divers prisoners. Of the Clangregar (which is almost a wonder) tuo onlie wes slain; John Mackgregar (the brother of Alexander) and another; but divers of them wer hurt.

"The report of this combat and victorie came to the king's ears at Edinburgh, where elevin score bloodie shirts[1] (of those that were slain in that skirmish) were presented to his Mātie, who wes therupon exceedingly incensed against the Clangregar, having none about the King to plead their cause, which proved hurtfull to them, almost to the rwyne of thet famelie and surname; for the King afterward caused proclaime them rebells, directed commissions and lettres of intercomuning against them, forbidding any of his leiges to harbor them. At last he imployed the Earl of Argyle and the Campbells against them, who pursued them divers tymes; and at Bentoik[2] where Robert Campbell (the Laird of Glen Vrquhie his sone) accompanied with some of the Clanchamron, Clanab, and Clanronald, to the number of tuo hundred chosen men, faught against thriescore of the Clangregar; in which conflict tuo of the Clangregar wer slain, to witt, Duncan Aberigh (one of the Chieftanes) and his sone Duncan. Seaven gentlemen of the Campbells syd were killed ther, though they seemed to have the victorie. So after much slaughter, many skirmishes, and divers slights vsed against the Clangregar, in end they subdued them, by the death of many of them and ther followers, and no lesse (iff not farr greater) slaughter of the Campbells. Then commissions wer sent thorow the Kingdome, for fyning the recepters and harbourers of the Clangregar, and for punishing such as did intercommoun with them; all which fynes wer given

---

[1] See further on. It appears to be conclusively shown that there were two conflicts between the MacGregors and Colquhouns, with an interval of two months between them, and it was after the first, called the Raid of Glenfinlas, that this incident took place.—Ed.

[2] See later, in 1611.

by his Mâtie to the Earle of Argyle, and converted to his vse and benefit, as a recompense of that service.

"After many severall changes of fortune, Alexander Mackgregar rendered himselff to the Earle of Argyle, vpon condition that he wold suffer him to goe saiflie into England to King James, to let his Matie know the true state of their bussines from the beginning; and in pledge of his returne agane to the Earle of Argyle, he gave him threttie of the cheifest men, and of best reputation among the Clangregar, to remain in Argyle his custodie till his return from England. Mackgregar wes no sooner at Bervick, vpon his journey to London bot, he wes brought back again to Edinburgh by the Earle of Argyle, and ther, by his meanes, execute, together with the thretty pledges befor mentioned , whereby he thought not onlie to pacefie all these broills, bot also to extinguish vtterlie the name of Clangregar , yit he wes deceaved, for now agane the Clangregar are come almost to their former vigor, and Argyle reaped small credet by this service."

The notes in the "Baronage" may still serve as a comment on the foregoing.

"Though this account differs greatly from Mr George Crawfurd's history of the family of Colquhoun , yet whether that account written by an impartial author, within less than 30 years after the affair happened, when the whole transaction was fresh in everybody's memory, or that written above 100 years thereafter, when many of the facts must have been forgotten, deserves most to be believed, is submitted to the judgment of our readers "

Traditional account of one of the incidents which led to the Battle of Glenfruin —

"Before Marshal Wade paved the way for carriers and stage-coaches, the Highlanders received all their little necessaries and luxuries through the hands of pedlars, who made regular visits to one or other of the large towns, and brought back in their packs the articles chiefly in demand at home The pedlars as a class, were of great importance to the whole community, and Highland faith and hospitality guaranteed to them security and good reception wherever they went. Two pedlars of the McGregors of Dunan, in the Braes of Rannoch, were benighted while on the way home from Glasgow, on the property of Sir Humphrey Colquhoun of Luss. They asked hospitality which was refused This churlishness was owing to the quarrels of the Colquhouns with their neighbours, the McGregors of Glengyle , but the Colquhouns in setting limits to the hospitality asked, so far violated the conventional and hereditary code of Highland morality, that the pedlars deemed themselves justified in taking what was refused They kindled a fire in an unoccupied sheiling-house, and taking a wedder from the fold, killed it and feasted on its carcase.

2 N

Unluckily for them, the wedder was the most marked animal in the fold.   It was black all but the tail, which was white.   In the morning, the shepherds missed at once ' Mult dubh an earbhail ghil '—the black wedder with the white tail.   The pedlars were at once suspected, pursued, captured, brought back, and hanged without delay.   The MᶜGregors could not tamely pass over such an affront. Alastair of Glenstrae Chief of the Clan with about 300 men left Rannoch in the beginning of the year 1602 and encamped on the Colquhoun Marches.   He proposed an accommodation, on condition that the Colquhouns acknowledged their fault and made reparation to the friends of the deceased by paying the blood ' eric.'   Sir Humphrey . . . . . . scorned the offers of peace."—From the " Lairds of Glenlyon," pages 20-21.

The other side of the conflict now claims attention, and it will be easiest found in the " Chiefs of Colquhoun." [1]

First in point of chronology it may be well to take the following excerpt :—

"Among the Luss papers there are lists of articles stolen by the MacGregors from the Colquhouns in the year 1594, and in other years previous to 1600 and these lists show how much the Colquhouns had suffered from the MacGregors. But in 1602, the MacGregors made more formidable inroads into the lands of Luss, spreading consternation among the inhabitants.   Complaints were made against them by the Laird of Luss to King James, upon which his Majesty dispensing with the provisions of an Act of Parliament, forbidding the carrying of arms, granted permission to him and his tenants to wear various kinds of offensive weapons.   The royal letter granting him this liberty is in the following terms :—

        " ' Rex,
        " ' We vnderstanding that sindrie of the disorderit thevis and lymmares of the Clangregour, with utheris thair complices, dalie makis incursionis vpon, and within the boundis and landis pertening to Alexander Colquhoun of Luss, steillis, reiffis, and away takis, diuers great heirschippis fra him and his tenentis lykas they tak greater bauldnes to continew in thair said stouth and reaff, becaus they ar enarmit with all kynd of prohibite and forbidden wapynnis.   Thairfoir and for the better defence of the Laird of Lus, and his saidis tennentis, guidis, and geir, fra the persute of the saidis thevis and broken men, to have gevin, and granted, and be the tennour heirof gevis, and grantis, licence, and libertie, to the said Alexander Colquhoun of Lus, his houshald men, and seruandis and sic as sall accompany him, not onlie to beir, weir, and schuitt with hagbuttis and pistolettis, in the following

<hr>

[1] Sir William Fraser, K.C.B. and D.C.L., the distinguished author of this valuable work, has given a very cordial assent to the Editor's wish to take advantage of it for quotations.

and persute of the saidis thevis, and lymmeris, quilk is lauchtfull be the Act of Parliament, bot also to beir and weir the same hagbuittis and pistolettis in any pairt aboue the water of Leaven, and at the said Lairdis place of Dunglas and lands of Colquhoun and, for the watcheing and keiping of thair awne guidis, without any crime, skaythe, pane, or danger to be incurrit be thame thairthrou, in thair personis, landis, or guidis, be any maner of way, in tyme cuming, notwithstanding any our actis, statutis, or proclamationis maid in the contrair thairanent, and painis thairin contenit, we dispense be thir presentis. gevin vnder our signet and subsciuit with our hand, at Hamiltoun the first day of September, and of our reigne the xxxvi. zeir, 1602.   JAMES R.'

"The right to carry arms thus granted to the Laird of Luss and his retainers, so far from inspiring the MacGregors with terror seems rather to have inflamed their resentment against the Colquhouns and proved, there is reason to fear, the immediate occasion of the disastrous conflict at Glenfinlas and Glenfruin which followed.

"The Laird of Luss made a complaint in Nov. 1602 if not earlier against the Earl of Argyle, as the King's lieutenant in the bounds of the Clangregour, for permitting them and others to commit outrages upon him and his tenants.   The Lord High Treasurer and the King's Advocate had before 30. Nov. that year, prosecuted Argyll for certain alleged atrocities of that Clan, of which the only one specified is said to have been committed 'on the lairds of Luss and Buchannan.' Argyll and his sureties in the bond which as King's lieutenant he had given to the government, not having appeared before the Council in obedience to the summons issued against them, were fined in terms of the bond ; but he was assoilzied from the charge brought against him by Colquhoun, the latter having failed to prove it.

"The first of the raids referred to between the MacGregors and the Colquhouns took place on the 7. December 1602. at Glenfinlas a glen about two miles to the west of Rossdhu, and three to the north of Glenfruin, to which it runs parallel, namely in a north-westerly or a south-easterly direction.

"The raid was headed by Duncan Makewin Macgregor, tutour of Glenstray.[1] Accompanied with about eighty persons to quote from a contemporary Luss paper, by way of oppressions and reif, he came to the dwelling houses and steadings of many tenants, broke up their doors, and not only took their whole inside plenishing out of their houses, but also took and reft from them three hundred cows, one hundred horses and mares, four hundred sheep, and four hundred goats. Among the tenants despoiled were John Maccaslane of Caldenoth and John Leich of Cullichippen, besides various tenants in Edintagert, Glenmacairne, Auchintullich,

---

[1] Ewin MacGregor, Tutour of Glenstray, died before 1601. After his death, Duncan McEwin, his third son, was sometime later styled the Tutor of Glenstray.—Ed.

Finlas. Tomboy Midros &a. The houses plundered amounted to forty-five (another Luss paper states ' above fourscore ').

" Another of the Luss papers entitled 'Memorandum for Duncan MacKinturnour, elder in Luss. records that in the month of Dec. 1602 years, at the herschip of Glenfinlas, two months before the day of Glenfruin, Duncan Mackewin Macgregor and his accomplices to the number of fourscore persons most cruelly reft, spoilzeit and away took from the said Duncane Mackinturnour, forth of his xxs land of Glenmakearne, twenty-five cows, and thirty sheep, the property of the said Duncan.

" Various lists of the names of the accomplices of the Macgregors are preserved among the Luss papers. These accomplices were chiefly persons of the name of MacGregor, under the Earl of Argyll and also under the Lairds of Tullibardin, Strowan Robertson, &a. The resetters of the plundered articles were chiefly about Lochgoylhead, Strachur, Ardkinlas, and Appin.

" At the fray of Glenfinlas, besides the depredations committed two of the Colquhoun people were killed, one of them a household servant of the Laird of Colquhoun and the other a webster. Under the date of 12. Aug. 1603 Neill Macgregor was ' delated and accused of being airt and pairt of the slauchter of umqle Patrik Layng and of vmquile John Reid wobster, servandis to the Laird of Luss committit in Dec. last and also of stealing.'

" Alexander Colquhoun of Luss as we have already seen, before this raid complained to the Privy Council, against the Earl of Argyll, for not repressing the ClanGregor. Having then failed to obtain any redress from the Council, he was advised by some of his friends after the conflict at Glenfinlas, to appear before the King, who was at Stirling, to complain of the depradations and cruel murders committed by the MacGregors, and to give the greater effect to his complaint, to take along with him a number of women carrying the bloody shirts of their murdered or wounded husbands and sons. The idea of this tragical demonstration was suggested to him by Semple of Fulwood and William Stewart, Captain of Dumbarton Castle, as we learn from the following letter, written to him by Thomas Fallisdaill, burgess of Dumbarton, only a few days after the conflict :—

" ' Rycht honorable Sir, my dewtie with service remembrit, plas zour ma(stership) the Lard of Fullewod and the Capitane thinkis best zour ma : adres to zour self, wyth als mony bludie sarks, as ather ar deid, or hurt of zour men, togitter wyth als mony vemen, to present thame to his Maiestie in Stirling, and to zour ma : to be thair vpone Tysday nixt, for thai ar bayth to ryd thair vpone tysday, quha will assist zow at thair power. The meistest tyme is now becauss of the French Imbaissadour that is with his Maistie. The rest of thair opinioun, I sall cum wpe the morne, vpone zour ma : aduertisment. . . . . Me Lord Duik is also in Stirling, quhome the Laird of Fullvad and the Capitane wald fain zow agreit with presentlie, and lat actionis of law rest ower   Sua I end, committing zour ma . for ewer to the Lord   Dumbartane, this Sunday, the xix of dec 1602.

"' zour ma(stership) awen for ewer,

"'' Thomas Fallusdaill, Burges of Dunbertane.

" ' To the Rycht honorable Alexander Colquhoun of Luss, in haist, this vretting.'

" Thus advised, Alexander Colquhoun of Luss went on the 21 of the same month, to the King, at Stirling, accompanied by a number of females, the relatives of the parties who had been killed or wounded at Glenfinlas, each carrying the bloody shirt of her killed or wounded relative, to implore his Majesty to avenge the wrongs done to them   The scene produced a strong sensation in the mind of the King, who was extremely susceptible to the impression of tragic spectacles. His sympathy was excited towards the sufferers , and his resentment was roused against the Macgregors, on whom he vowed to take vengeance   As the speediest means of redress, he granted a commission of lieutenancy to Alexander Colquhoun of Luss, investing him with power to repress crimes of the description from which he had suffered, and to apprehend the perpetrators

"This commission granted to their enemy, appears to have roused the lawless rage of the Macgregors, who rose in strong force to defy the Laird of Luss , and Glenfruin, with its disastrous and sanguinary defeat of the Colquhouns, and its ultimate terrible consequences to the victorious clan themselves was the result Sir Robert Gordon, in his history of the Earls of Sutherland, mistakes the conflict of Glenfinlas [1] for the more serious one of Glenfruin which took place shortly after.

. . Sir Walter Scott founding on this (Gordon's) as his authority improves upon it by the addition of various circumstances which, however, are purely fictitious. 'The widows of the slain,' says he, 'to the number of eleven score, in deep mourning, riding upon white palfreys, and each bearing her husband's bloody shirt on a spear, appeared at Stirling, in presence of a monarch peculiarly accessible to such sights of fear and sorrow, to demand vengeance for the death of their husbands, upon those by whom they had been made desolate' The bloody shirt scene was after the raid at Glenfinlas, and as only a few (two) were killed on that occasion, though a great number might be wounded, Sir Robert Gordon and after him Sir Walter Scott, exaggerates what actually took place   The scene was not repeated after the more sanguinary conflict at Glenfruin, though then it would have been a spectacle much more impressive from the far greater number who were killed and wounded.

" It has been asserted by some writers that, in the beginning of the year 1603, the MacGregors and the Colquhouns made friendly propositions to hold a con-

[1] Sir William Fraser gives positive proof of the two separate conflicts and of the display of shirts taking place after the first of the two.

ference with the view of terminating their animosities, while at the same time each determined should the result of a meeting be unsuccessful, to have recourse to instant measures of hostility. Sir Robert Gordon . . . . represents the matter more favourably for the Macgregors. (Here follows a short quotation from Sir Robert Gordon from the departure of Alexander Macgregor of Rannoch, the Laird of Luss persewing them at Glenfruin.) Sir Robert Gordon was contemporary, but he is here incorrect in various of his statements, as can be proved from authentic documents of the period. No evidence whatever exists of the conference referred to having been either held or intended. From the position of the two parties, it is hardly possible that any such conference could have been thought of, far less held. The Macgregors were more in the position of rebels, whilst Colquhoun was invested with a commission from the King to apprehend and punish them for their crimes. and the whole circumstances of the case, so far from affording any ground to believe that, at the close of the alleged conference, the Laird of Luss treacherously attacked the MacGregors, render it far more probable that he himself was entrapped by them while proceeding through the Glen in execution of his commission.[1]

"That the Macgregors were, in the present instance, the aggressors is the conclusion, to which we are led from the statements made in the indictment of Allaster Macgregor, in which he was accused of having deliberately planned the destruction of the Colquhouns and their allies, the extirpation of their name, the plunder of their lands, and of having for the purpose of carrying out these plans, invaded Alexander Colquhoun's lands with numerous armed men; all of which was proved against him by a jury of most respectable gentlemen.[2] Similar statements are contained in the indictments of others who were tried for the same crime, and in many acts and proclamations against the clan. If the correctness of the statement of the Government may be disputed, it is to be observed that its truthfulness is strongly confirmed by the declaration made by Allaster Macgregor before his execution.

"That some desperate attack upon the Colquhouns was at this time contemplated by the Macgregors appears to have been the feeling prevalent throughout the Lennox. The order issued by the town Council of Dumbarton, that the burgesses should be provided with armour, and be ready to present the same at the muster, plainly indicates the apprehensions entertained in that burgh, that

---

[1] The whole of the last paragraph is, of course, only a matter of conjecture on the part of the learned Baronet ; but if Luss was proceeding down the Glen on the errand of capturing the MacGregors by armed force, could he be said to be entrapped when his victims turned the tables upon him? It is very doubtful whether Glenstray was aware that the Laird of Luss had the King's Commission.

[2] The gentlemen of the jury were undoubtedly highly respectable, but not all of them impartial. A list of them will be found in chapter xxvi.

danger was impending, and that it was necessary to be prepared for resisting some dreaded foe, who was doubtless the ClanGregor.

"1603 Jan 8   It is ordained that all burgesses within the burgh be sufficientlie furnissit with armor, and that sik persones as the baillies and counsall think fitt sall be furnissit with hagbuttis, that they haif the samyn with the furnitear thairto, utheris quha sall be appointit, to haif jak, speir, and steilbonnat, that thay be furnissit with the samyn, and that the baillies and counsall on the xxi of this instant, mak ane cathelok of the saidis personis namis with thair armor, and thay be chargeit to haif the said armor redey, and to present thame with the samyn at muster and this to remaine in all tymes under the pane of ten pundis, the ane half to the baillie, the uthir to the use of the burgh.   Item that ilk merchand or craftisman, keipand baith haif ane halbart within the samyn under the pane of five pundis   Item, that na burges be maid heirefter without production of his armor at his creatioun, and that he sweir the samyn is his own

"How well founded these apprehensions were was proved by the event. Allaster Macgregor of Glenstra, at the head of a large body of the ClanGregor, with the addition of a considerable number of confederates from the clans of Cameron and Anverich, armed with hagbuts, pistols, murrions, mailcoats, pow-aixes two-handed swords, bows, darlochs, and other weapons, advanced into the territory of Luss.   At that time there was no turnpike on Lochlongside, the present Lochlong road having since been made, it is supposed by the Duke of Argyll, and therefore formerly called 'The Duke's road.'   There was however a tract or path of some kind along the side of Lochlong and this may have been the way by which the Macgregors came to Glenfruin.   To repel the invader, the Laird of Luss hastily collected a considerable force of men, whom, under a royal commission, he had raised for the protection of the district, and for the punishment of the Macgregors.

"The parties encountered each other on the 7. of Feb. 1603. at Glenfruin, at a spot, according to tradition, situated upon the farm of Strone, or Auchengaich, near the sources of the Fruin.   The name Glenfruin which means the 'glen of sorrow' well accords with the sanguinary scene which on this occasion it witnessed, but it did not from thence derive its name.   In charters of the lands of Luss, of a date previous to the battle, mention is made of Frevne.   It forms a verdant valley, of considerable length, some of it under cultivation with a deep loamy soil, nearly half a mile in breadth between hills barren of trees and shrubs, with the exception of here and there a thorn or mountain ash, but whose sides, especially to the north of the glen, are covered with beautiful green pasturage for sheep, instead of the brown heather of the olden times.   The spot on which the bloody conflict took place is still pointed out by tradition, which preserves fresh the memory of what has rendered it so memorable, ... What the numbers were on each side has not been exactly ascertained.   The Macgregors have been estimated by some at

300 foot; by others at 400, and there can be no doubt that this clan could without difficulty, muster at least that number, when they had some great purpose to accomplish such as their taking vengeance on their enemy the Laird of Luss would doubtless be accounted. The forces of Colquhoun of Luss have been also variously estimated, some probably by exaggeration making them 300 horse and 500 foot. That he would succeed in raising in his own district including the town of Dumbarton, so large an army is extremely doubtful. The ground on which the conflict took place was very unfavourable, both for the horse and foot of the Colquhouns, especially the former. Surprise has been expressed that the Laird of Luss should have risked a conflict with the enemy in such a position, but having been entrapped [1] he was placed in circumstances which gave him no choice. The Macgregors assembled in Glenfruin in two divisions, one of them at the head of the glen, and the other in ambuscade near the farm of Strone, at a hollow or ravine called the Crate. The Colquhouns came into Glenfruin from the Luss side, through the Glen of Auchengaich, which is opposite Strone, probably by Glen Luss and Glen Mackurin. Alexander Colquhoun pushed on his forces, in order to get through the Glen before encountering the Macgregors; but aware of his approach, Allaster Macgregor, the Captain of the Clan, also pushed forward one division of his forces, and entered at the head of the glen, in time to prevent his enemy from emerging from the upper end of the glen, whilst his brother, John Macgregor, with the division of his clan which lay in ambuscade by a detour, took the rear of the Colquhouns, which prevented their retreat down the glen without fighting their way through that section of the Macgregors who had got in their rear. The success of the stratagem by which the Colquhouns were thus placed between two fires seems to be the only way of accounting for the terrible slaughter of the Colquhouns and the much less loss of the Macgregors.

"Allaster Macgregor, at the head of his division furiously charged the Laird of Luss and his men. For a time the Colquhouns bravely maintained the contest. An old weaver, resident in Strome, who took part with the Colquhouns is said to have been one of the best fighters on that day. He is said to have killed with his own hand a good many of the Macgregors which confutes the story that they suffered so little at Glenfruin that though many of them were wounded, not more than two of them, during the whole battle were killed, which of course was impossible in such a conflict. But in the unfavourable circumstances in which they had to fight, the Colquhouns soon became unable to maintain their ground, and

---

[1] This word does not seem applicable to the conflict. Luss was in his own territory and, we are told, seeking the MacGregors to seize or otherwise punish them. Luss must have known every inch of the ground, and the whole of the country people must have been on his side and could act scouts for him. By a " Ruse de Guerre " and superior tactics, Glenstray's force was divided into two divisions, and succeeded in hemming in the Colquhouns between them, but Luss can hardly have been taken altogether unawares.—Ed.

falling into a moss at the farm of Auchengaich, they were thrown into disorder, and being now at the mercy of the Macgregors, who taking advantage of the confusion killed many of them, they made a hasty and disorderly retreat, which proved even more disastrous than the conflict, for they had to force their way through the men led by John Macgregor, whilst they were pursued behind by Allaster, who, reuniting the two divisions of his army continued the pursuit. But even in the flight there were instances of intrepidity on the part of the Colquhouns One of them when pressed hard by some of the Macgregors as he fled from the scene of battle, on reaching the Coinach, a black, deep whirling pool or linn of the water of Finlas in Shantron Glen, with steep, almost perpendicular banks, on both sides, rising to a height of at least 120 feet above the pool at the bottom, where the rays of the sun never penetrate, and where the sky is scarcely ever visible overhead, by a desperate effort at once jumped the frightful chasm. None of the Macgregors ventured to follow him by making the perilous leap The Colquhoun immediately turned round, drew an arrow from his quiver, and shot the nearest of his pursuers as he stood perplexed and baffled on the opposite brink, and then made his escape without further molestation. Whoever fell into the hands of the victors even defenceless women and children, were remorselessly put to death The Chief of the Colquhouns was chased to the very door of the Castle of Rossdhu, whose loopholed walls, six feet in thickness, afforded a secure refuge, and his horse, while leaping over a fall or gully not far from Rossdhu, was killed under him by a Macgregor. The ruins of the castle are still to be seen near the present more modern mansion In the flight the Laird of Bucklyvie was killed by the Macgregors at the farm of Ballemenoch or Middle Kilbride, at the eastern entrance of Glenfruin, and the small rivulet, which is a tributary to the Fruin, is called Buchlyvie's Burn to this day from the Laird's having been killed there."

We deem it unnecessary to quote any passages from Chalmers "Caledonia," because the same information is to be found elsewhere, and that author evinces throughout, what appears to be a personal spite against the Clan.

. "From the Chartulary" :—

"Conflict of Glenfruin.

"1603. Feb. 18 In a summons by Alexander Colquhoun of Luss against Sir Duncan Campbell of Glenurchy as cautioner for certain of the aggressors of Glenfruin, the following narrative of the battle occurs
  "Vpoun the aucht day of Feb instant (the Clangregor) with thair disorderit complices thevis sornaris and lymmaries of thair clan, friendship and assistance, all bodin in feir of weir with halberchois, powaixis, twa handit

suordis bowis and arrowis and vtharis waponis invasive, and with hagbuttis
and pistoletis prohibite to be worn be the lawis of our realme and actis of
parliament come upon fair daylicht within the landis of the barony of Luss
Kilbryde and Finnart pertening to the said complenaris freindis and tenantis
thair wyfis and bairnis duelland vpon the saidis landis to the nowmer of
sevinscoir personis or therby. and brunt and distroyit the said complenaris
haill cornis wictuellis barnis and girnellis cattell and guidis being within the
saidis houssis and herreit the saidis haill landis and reft and away tuke furth
thirof sax hundreth heid of ky pryce of the pice overhead xx merkis ane
thousand scheip price of the pice overheid i shillings ane thousand gait price
of the pice xl shillings and hundred hors and meiris pryce of the pice our
heid xxxlib.—Luss Col."

Chapter XXIV

Conflict of Glenfruin

THE world-wide celebrity of the writings of Sir Walter Scott, whose sympathetic mind caught the fire of Highland adventure and was able to reflect it back into the hearts of thousands who never saw the scenes, or knew the Highland people, has led to implicit belief in all that he has narrated, although it was his avowed purpose to mix romance with history, and the congenial materials which he wove into his brilliant pages were derived from various informants and mingled sources. Sir Walter's account of the Battle of Glenfruin as given in the introduction to "Rob Roy" must ever be interesting, and therefore it is here copied verbatim.

"Other occasions frequently occurred, in which the MacGregors testified contempt for the laws, from which they had often experienced severity, but never protection. Though they were gradually deprived of their possessions, and of all ordinary means of procuring subsistence, they could not nevertheless, be supposed likely to starve of famine while they had the means of taking from strangers what they considered as rightfully their own. Hence they became versed in predatory forays, and accustomed to bloodshed. Their passions were eager, and with a little management on the part of some of their most powerful neighbours, they could easily be hounded out, to use an expressive Scotch phrase, to commit violence, of which the wily instigators took the advantage, and left the ignorant MacGregors an undivided portion of blame and punishment. This policy of pushing on the fierce Clans of the Highlands and Borders to break the peace of the country, is accounted by the historian one of the most dangerous practices of his own period, in which the MacGregors were considered as ready agents.

"Notwithstanding these severe denunciations, which were acted upon in the same spirit in which they were conceived, some of the Clan still possessed property, and the Chief of the name in 1592, is designed Allaster MacGregor of Glenstrae. He is said to have been a brave and active man; but from the tenor of his confession at his death, appears to have been engaged in many and desperate feuds, one of which finally proved fatal to himself and many of his followers. This was the celebrated conflict at Glenfruin, near the south-western extremity of Loch Lomond, in the vicinity of which the MacGregors continued to exercise much authority by the ' coir a glaive,' [1] or right of the strongest, which we have already mentioned.

"There had been a long and bloody feud betwixt the MacGregors and the Laird of Luss, head of the family of Colquhoun, a powerful race on the lower part of Loch Lomond. The MacGregors' tradition affirms that the quarrel began on a very trifling subject. Two of the MacGregors being benighted, asked shelter in a house belonging to a dependent of the Colquhouns, and were refused. They then retreated to an outhouse, took a wedder from the fold, killed it and supped off the carcase, for which it is said they offered payment to the proprietor. The Laird of Luss seized on the offenders, and, by the summary process which feudal barons had then at their command, had them both condemned and executed. [2] The MacGregors verify this account of the feud by appealing to a proverb current amongst them, execrating the hour (Mult dhu an Carbail [3] ghil) that 'the black wedder with the white tail' was ever lambed. To avenge this quarrel the Laird of MacGregor assembled his clan, to the number of three or four hundred men, and marched towards Luss from the banks of Loch Long, by a pass called Raid (Ruidh) na Gael or the Highlandman's pass.

"Sir Humphrey Colquhoun received early notice of this incursion, and collected a strong force, more than twice the number of that of the invaders. He had with him the gentlemen of the name of Buchanan, with the Grahams, and other gentry of the Lennox, and a party of the citizens of Dumbarton, under command of Tobias Smollett, a magistrate or bailie of that town and ancestor of the celebrated author.

"The parties met in the valley of Glenfruin, which signifies Glen of sorrow—a name that seemed to anticipate the event of the day, which, fatal to the conquered party, was at least equally so to the victors, the 'babe unborn' of the Clan Alpine having reason to repent it. The MacGregors somewhat discouraged by the sight of a force much superior to their own, were cheered on to the attack by a seer, or second-sighted person, who professed that he saw the shrouds of the dead wrapt around their principal opponents. The clan charged with great fury on the front of the enemy, while John MacGregor, with a strong party, made an unexpected

---

[1] Right of the Sword.

[2] This tradition, given more fully in the previous chapter, page 281, appears extremely probable, in addition to the other circumstances as to Argyle (see page 321). There was no ancient feud with the Colquhouns, and even after the conflict, on the MacGregor side, there was no feeling of old grudge.

[3] This word, meaning tail in Gaelic, should be "earball," the first letter has evidently slipped into "c" through reprints.

attack on the flank. A great part of the Colquhoun's force consisted in cavalry, which could not act in the boggy ground They were said to have disputed the field manfully, but were at length completely routed, and a merciless slaughter was exercised on the fugitives, of whom betwixt two and three hundred fell on the field and in the pursuit. If the MacGregors lost, as is averred, only two men slain in action, they had slight provocation for an indiscriminate massacre. It is said that their fury extended itself to a party of students for clerical orders, who had imprudently come to see the battle. Some doubt is thrown on this fact from the indictment against the chief of the ClanGregor being silent on the subject, as is the historian Johnston, and a Professor Ross, who wrote an account of the battle twenty-nine years after it was fought. It is however constantly averred by the tradition of the country, and a stone where the deed was done is called 'Leck a Mhinisteir,' the Minister or clerk's flag stone The MacGregors impute this cruel action to the ferocity of a single man of their tribe, renowned for size and strength, called Dugald, Ciar Mhor,[1] or the great mouse-coloured Man He was MacGregor's foster brother, and the Chief committed the youths to his charge, with directions to keep them safely till the affray was over. Whether fearful of their escape or incensed by some sarcasms which they threw at his tribe, or whether out of mere thirst of blood, this savage, while the other MacGregors were engaged in pursuit, poniarded his helpless and defenceless prisoners When the Chieftain, on his return demanded where the youths were, the Ciar Mhor drew out his bloody dirk, saying in Gaelic, 'Ask that, and God save me.' The latter words allude to the exclamation which his victims used when he was murdering them. It would seem therefore that this horrible part of the story is founded on fact, though the number of the youths so slain is probably exaggerated in Lowland accounts The common people say that the blood of the Ciar Mhor's victims can never be washed off the stone. When MacGregor learnt their fate, he expressed the utmost horror at the deed, and upbraided his foster-brother with having done that which would occasion the destruction of him and his Clan The homicide was the ancestor of Rob Roy,[2] and the tribe from which he was descended. He lies buried at the church of Fortingal, where his sepulchre, covered with a large stone, is still shown, and where his great strength and courage are the theme of many traditions.

"MacGregor's brother was one of the very few of the tribe who were slain. He was buried near the field of battle, and the place is marked by a rude stone called the Grey Stone of MacGregor

"Sir Humphrey[3] Colquhoun, well mounted, escaped for the time to the castle

---

[1] The name is confused with that of a distant ancestor; the MacGregors do not acknowledge that such a deed was done, and do not impute it to anyone of the Clan.

[2] This statement is also erroneous.

[3] See next page for correction of this name and statement.

of Banochar, or Benechra. It proved no sure defence however, for he was shortly after murdered in a vault of the castle,—the family annals say by the MacGregors, though other accounts charge the deed upon the MacFarlanes."

"Note by Sir Walter Scott.—The above is the account which I find in a manuscript history of the clan MacGregor, of which I was indulged with a perusal by Donald MacGregor, Esq.[1] late Major of the 33rd Regiment, where great pains have been taken to collect traditions and written documents concerning the family. But an ancient and constant tradition, preserved among the inhabitants of the country, and particularly those of the clan MacFarlane, relieves Dugald Ciar Mhor of the guilt of murdering the youths, and lays the blame on a certain Donald or Duncan Lean, who performed the act of cruelty, with the assistance of a gillie who attended him, named Charlioch or Charlie. They say that the homicides dared not again join their clan, but that they resided in a wild and solitary state as outlaws, in an unfrequented part of the MacFarlane's territory. Here they lived for some time undisturbed, till they committed an act of brutal violence on two defenceless women, a mother and daughter of the MacFarlane clan. In revenge for this atrocity, the MacFarlanes hunted them down, and shot them. It is said that the younger ruffian, Charlioch, might have escaped, being remarkably swift of foot. But his crime became his punishment, for the female whom he had outraged had defended herself desperately, and had stabbed him with his own dirk on the thigh. He was lame from the wound, and the more easily overtaken and killed. I incline to think that this last is the true edition of the story, and that the guilt was transferred to Dougal Ciar Mhor as a man of higher name, or it is possible these subordinate persons had only executed his orders."—Introduction to "Rob Roy," 1829.

The preceding account of the Battle of Glenfruin by Sir Walter Scott falls into the error of dates to be found in the article on Colquhoun in Douglas's "Baronage,"[2] which is understood to have been written by Crawford, the Peerage writer, and was apparently taken from a MS. History in the Colquhoun family. It has been shown from the "Chiefs of Colquhoun," that while Sir Humphrey met his death in the Castle of Bannachra, by a raid of Macfarlanes only, so far as can be proved, in

---

[1] Who afterwards purchased Balnald in Strathardle; the MS. History perused by Sir Walter Scott, we are informed by Alex. MacGregor, Esq., Crosshill, Glasgow (grand-nephew of Major Donald), has been lost. It is supposed that the tradition as to the students may have been collected whilst Major Donald was quartered at Roseneath in 1824.

[2] In the article on MacGregor in Douglas's "Baronage," explanation is made that Humphrey, Laird of Luss, was not murdered after Glenfruin—Buchannan stating that [he was "killed in Benechra Castle by the Macfarlanes, through influence of a certain nobleman whom Luss had disobliged." See also chapter xx., pages 233-4.

1592, it was in the time of his brother and successor, Alexander, that the conflict of Glenfruin took place on the 7th Feb. 1603, and it also appears that the display of shirts to excite the King's indignation followed the smaller raid of Glenfinlas of the 7th Dec. 1603. The picturesque account of the procession of the widows, mention is only made of two men slain, is given by Sir Walter after the recital of the alleged affair of the murder of the students, with these few words preceding it :—

"This battle of Glenfruin, and the severity which the victors exercised in the pursuit, was reported to King James VI. in a manner most unfavourable to the ClanGregor, whose general character being that of lawless though brave men, could not much avail them in such a case. That James might fully understand the extent of the slaughter, the widows of the slain, &a." [1]

We have now to consider more particularly the accusation of the murder of the defenceless students. Sir Walter quotes an account from traditional sources, collected by the late Major Donald MacGregor of Balnald. Sir William Fraser repeats this, and adds a few particulars :—

"On the memorable day of the conflict of Glenfruin, according to the tradition of the country, a number of youths who, from mere curiosity had come from the Grammar School of Dumbarton to witness the battle that was expected to take place, were massacred in cold blood by one of the Clan Macgregor. The boys came along the ridge of the high hills on the south side of the Fruin called the Highland road ; and they were shut up for safety in a hut or barn, to the west of the battle on Greenfield Moor, under the charge of a Highlander, who, on seeing the MacGregors successful, stabbed them with his dirk one by one as they came out of this place of shelter. The site of the barn is still pointed out at a spot called Lach na faul, or Lagnagaul, 'hollow of the Lowlander.' . . . . . . It is worthy of notice that this atrocious massacre forms no part of the charges in the indictment of any of the MacGregors who were tried before the High Court of Justiciary on account of the raid of Glenfruin, or 'The field and murder of Lennox,' as that conflict is sometimes called. But some colour of truth seems to be given to the tradition by an act of Privy Council 5. Jan. 1609. in which Allan Oig McIntnach,[2] in Glencoe, is accused of having, while with the ClanGregor in Glenfruin, 'with his awne hand murdered without pity the number of fourtie poor persons who were naked and without armour.'

[1] See page 285, where this account is given from the quotation in "Chiefs of Colquhoun."
[2] A misspelling for "Mac an Tuagh," "Son of the Axe."

"Sir William also quotes in a footnote 'The barn of Blairvadden in the dukedom of Lennox was burnt by the Macgregors in Feb. 1603 as appears from the records of the Privy Seal 28 July 1612. and 21 Dec. 1613.' In the Records there is no allusion to any persons having been killed or even injured on that occasion. Sir William adds the following remark 'Nor do the MacGregors deny that the story is founded on fact; but they affirm that the Clan as a body execrated the crime, and they impute it to the ferocity of one of their tribe, Dugald Ciar mhor, &a &a.' "

The original Dougal Ciar died many years before the date of Glenfruin, though one of his descendants at that time bore the name of Dougal, with the patronymic belonging to his house, Dougal McCoulcheir, but there is no evidence against him. We cannot assent to the statement that Mac-Gregors do not deny the story. On the contrary, it may be confidently asserted that there is no proof, or even probability, that any MacGregor was concerned in the deed. Turning to the "Baronage" under the article of MacGregor we may see what Sir John MacGregor Murray's views were on the subject :—

"It has been industriously reported, that one Cameron, a servant of Mac-Gregor's had murdered a number of boys the sons of gentlemen of distinction, who were on their way to the school of Dumbarton, or had come to see the fight; the following reasons may be sufficient to discredit these reports :—

"1. That we had few or no very young scholars in these days, they were generally young men from 15 to 25. and of course capable of bearing arms.

"2. Glenfruin, about six miles in length lies beyond large mountains, at a distance of several miles from, and far off any road leading to Dumbarton; and as the fight was at the farthest end of the Glen, which was then entirely wild and uninhabited so it is totally incredible that the scholars should have been there accidentally or that any boys, much less the sons of gentlemen of distinction, should walk so many miles to school, across such hills.

"3. Professor Ross, who wrote an accurate account of the battle in the course of the history of another family, about 29 years after it was fought, when the truth or falsity of the report must have been well known, does not mention such; nor does Mr Johnston, who about 20 years after Mr Ross, wrote a detail of the battle, and who as he was employed to traduce the Mac-Gregors, Macdonalds, and Macleans, and write the eulogiums of their enemies, would not have omitted a circumstance which if true would have afforded him such a field of declamation against this Clan; nor is there any such cruelty even hinted at in the preamble or any other part of the Act of Parliament afterwards made against them.

"4 Since neither Mr Ross nor Mr Johnstone mention it, it is clear no such report prevailed in those days and therefore it was trumped up of a later date to serve certain purposes of the enemies of the MacGregors, or if there were any scholars they must have been such as had followed their friends as volunteers to the battle and shared the fate of the day"

It may be readily granted that local traditions have usually some grains of truth, although names of personages are apt to get mixed up with personal prejudices in their transmission from past generations It seems probable that a calamity happened to some unarmed persons after the fight, whether by the hand of a McLean, a Cameron, a McIntuagh, or a MacGregor remains undecided, but the latter, for reasons already stated as to the readiness with which guilt would have been attached to one of the Clan on their trial, is most improbable. Whoever may have been the criminal (if such there were) the act was that of a single individual apart from any clan [1]

Whilst regretting such carnage, as there may have been in the eagerness of pursuit, in days when quarter was seldom asked or given and the victors were of an excitable race, peculiarly liable to the "madness of battle" (as it was called), yet MacGregors cannot read of the conflict without just pride in the admirable generalship of the two Glenstray brothers, and in the valour of the Clan which carried the day against such great odds.

Allaster MacGregor of Glenstray had a holding in Rannoch, and it was from thence that he started for the Colquhoun country. Dwelling on the Sliosmin side of Loch Rannoch (*i e*, the north side under Menzies of Menzies, the Laird of Weem), he probably first crossed the Gaur Water by the Ferry called Tighnalinne, a little above the head of the Loch, thence across the hill by Lairig Mheachdainn (an old Gaelic word for twigs or branches) to near Pubil, towards the head of Glenlyon, thence by a pass called Lairig nan Lunn [2] to Glenlochay, striking that glen about

---

[1] See chapter XXVIII , where the apprehension of Alan Mac an Tuagh on the 3rd January 1609 is recorded.

[2] "Lunn" means the poles or staves on which a coffin is borne.

eight miles above Killin, thence up that glen to near its head and across the ridge to Strathfillan at Crianlarich, down Glenfalloch to the head of Loch Lomond, and from Tarbet on Loch Lomond through the Pass of Arrochar to Loch Long.[1]   Glenstray had allies in the McFarlanes of Arroquhar, and we know from the indictment against his own clansmen, the tribe of Dougal Ciar, that they (whose dwelling was in Balquhidder) convoyed him to "the syd of Lochloun," from whence by Gairlochhead he would strike off Strone in Glenfruin. The march must have occupied several of the cold, misty days of February. The wives and bairns doubtless watched these "pretty men" all starting in their warlike array, and many an anxious heart must have been left amongst their womenkind, although trained to courage and endurance. Happily, however, they could not foresee the calamities which victory was to bring upon them. In whatever light the case may appear in these days when the power and justice of law are established, and when all things work comfortably for the nation at large, yet when the ClanGregor sallied forth in strength that wintry morning, whether for an intended conference or for mortal combat, it was under a deep sense of wrong done to them and of bitter persecution. Few, if any, of these warriors returned, and worse times than any yet experienced in their struggling existence, were to follow the ill-starred success of their arms.

[1] Assistance in tracing the probable route has been kindly given by Mr John Robertson, Old Blair, Blair Atholl, himself a Rannoch man.

Chapter XXV

Letters and Charges following Glenfruin

FROM the "Chartulary" :—

"1603. Feb. Messengers sent with letters charging the Sheriffs of Perth and Stirling and their deputes, the Steward of Monteith, and the Laird of Glenurquhay to convocate, and assemble the haill inhabitants within their bounds and commandment, in arms, and to keep thair saidis bounds from the invasion of the ClanGregor under the pain to be repute as airt and pairt takers with them in all thair wicked deeds.

"Letters also to charge Mr George Lindsay minister at Kilmahew, James (Dennistoun) of Cowgrane, William Nobill of Ardardane, &a and Johne Bunteine appeirand of Ardoch to compeir before the Council the 8. day of March next to testify what they knew anent the slaying of such as were commanded to resist the MacGregors.

"Letters also to charge the Lairds of Glenurquhy, Tullibardin, Lords Drummond, Incheafray, Lawers, Strowane, Wemye, Glenlyoun, Glennageis, Garnetullie, Abercainy, baroun of Bordland, barroun of Combrie, John Stewart of Fossa, and Murray of Auchtertyre, to compeir personally before the Council the 19, day of March next, And to bring, present and enter certain particular persons of the MacGregors, their men, and tenants, to answer for the late barbarous and horrible murder committed by them, in the Lennox, And with letters to be published at the market crosses of Perth charging the Laird of MacGregor, and the remanent of his race, to compeir personally before the Council the 29. day of March next to come; To answer for the late horrible and monstrous barbarity used by them in the Lennox And with Lettres to be published at the said market cross, inhibiting all our sovereign lord's lieges, that none of them resett, supply, nor show comfort to any of the MacGregors, or resett their goods, and to inhibit the transporting of any of them to the Isles.

"Letters also to charge the Duke of Lennox, the Earls of Argyle, Mar, Glencarne, Linlithgow, the Lairds of Buchannane, Luss, Ardkinglas, Glenageis, Keir, Merchinstoun, Kirkhill, Cambusmoir, Sir James Chisholme, and David Grahame, as masters and landlords to certain particular persons of the MacGregors, to enter and present them before the Council the 29. day of Marche next to answer for their barbarity under the pain of rebellion. And with letters to be published at the market crosses of Dumbarton, Stirling, and Inverara, charging the Laird of MacGregor and the Remanent of his clan to compeir the said day to answer for their said barbarity under the pain of rebellion And with Letters to be published at the said market crosses inhibiting the resett of the said persons of their goods.

"1603. Feb 10. Protection in favour of Robert Campbell 'son of Sir Duncan Campbell of Glenurquhy Knicht' prosecuted by Donald Menteith of Carquhine as having charge in his father's absence of his men tenants &a to. produce Gregour Ammonach in Glenlednoch to answer for stealing 3 cows and 2 oxen, aucht zeir syne ; Pursuer not appearing Campbell protests that he is not answerable and Protest admitted.

"March. Letters to charge John Earll of Atholl to enter his person in ward within the castle of Blackness within four days after the charge, under the pain of rebellion, And with letters to charge all and sundry our sovereign Lords lieges dwelling in the bounds of the Earldom of Atholl and Braes of Angus That they address themselves with one months provision to convene and meet at the head of Loch Rannoch upon the 6. of April next And there concur with the remanent forces appointed for pursuit of the barbarous ClanGregor or else that they send out three score men well provided with a Captain and commander over them ; under pain of tinsall of life, lands, &a Also Letters to the Duke of Lennox the Earl of Argyll and Laird of Glenurchy.

"1603. March 17. At Edinburgh. Aulay Mᶜaulay of Ardincaple and his sureties were ordered to compear to answer for 'ressett, supplie, and inter-cowmoning,' with Glenstray and his brother and for not 'rising ye fray' and following the MacGregors 'in yair incoming in ye cuntrey of ye Lennox.' The same day the said Aulay MᶜCuallay caution for relief of Allaster MᶜGregor of Lagarie."

The volumes of the Register of the Privy Council belonging to this period have unfortunately been lost for many years, but the following entry from the published edition of the Register explains best all that is known about an Act against the ClanGregor which was now formulated.

"1603. April 3. To . . . . Sunday has been ascribed, ... the famous Act of Council proscribing the Clan Macgregor and abolishing their very name, Though from the loss of the volumes of the Register of Council carrying affairs from Feb. 1603 to August 1606, the official copy of this famous Act has not been preserved, there can be no doubt as to its date, inasmuch as it is cited thus in the preamble to a subsequent Act of Parliament relating to the MacGregors in 1617 :—'Oure Soverane

Lord and Esttaittis of this present parliament remembering how that
his sacred Majestye being verie justlie moved with a haterent and de-
testatioun of the barbarous murtheris and insolencies committit be ther
Clangregoure upoun his Majestiyes peciable and goode subjectis of the
Lennox at Glenfrone in the moneth of Feb. 1603. and how that the
bair and simple name of MacGregour maid that haill Clane to presume
of their power, force, and strengthe, and did encourage thame, without
reverence of the law or fear of punischement, to go fordward in thair
iniquities : Upoune the consideratioun quhairof his Majestie with advyse
of the Lordis of his Secreit Counsall, maid dyvers actis and ordinances
aganis thame speciallie one Act upoun the 3. day of Aprill 1603, whereby it
wes ordainit that the name of McGregoure sulde be altogidder abolisched,
and that the haill persounes of that Clan suld renunce thair name and tak
thame sum uther name, and that they nor nane of thair posteritie suld call
thame selffis Gregour or McGregoure thair efter, under the payne of deade '
&a.—Acts of Parl. of Scot. iv. 550) It is clear, therefore, that on that same
Sunday on which King James took his farewell, of the Edinburgh
people, in the Church of St Giles, there must have been a Council meeting
at which he left this parting thunderbolt, against the unfortunate MacGregors."

" 1603. April. Item paid by command of his Highness to Robert Lyle servitor to
the Earl of Argyle for inbringing of three notorious thieves of the name of
the barbarous ClanGregor £333 . 6 . 8.—Treasurer's books
  "Item to George Mathow messenger passing from Edinburgh to the market
cross of Perth charging Allaster MacGregor of Glenstra and the remanent of
that unhappy Clan to compeir personally before the Council the 19. day of
April instant to be answerable to the laws and to renounce their names
under the pain of rebellion.—*Ibid.*
  "The Chronicle of Perth 9. April 1603, states that the proclamation was
read there and then.—MS , Advocates' Lib. Edin.
" Letters to be proclaimed at the market crosses of Stirling and Dumbarton
  "Item to the officer of Justiciary for summoning an assize to four Mac-
Gregors who were justified to the deid.
" April 29   Extract from a letter from the Lord Fyvie to the King (shewing
the feelings in regard to all Highlanders) Zour Majestie will onderstand be
zour Counsalls letter the estait and proceedings with Macgregors Gif all the
greate hieland Clannes war at the like point, I wald (think?) it ane great
ease and weill to this common weill and to zour Majesties guid subjects heir.
—Balfour's Collections, Advocates' Lib Edin
" April 13   Sasine John McGregor of Innerzaldie son of Gregor McGregor of
Innerzaldie, 4 merkland of Innerzaldie on precept from chancery   Sasine

. Barbara Drummond spouse to the said John in the said lands.—Register of Sasines Particular, Perth.

"April 28. In the Court of the Justiciary of our supreme Lord the King held in the Pretorium of Edinburgh by Mr William Hairt entered 'Allaster McKie Gilchrist Kittoch alias Makilmoylie, M^cinroyer, Fynlaw dow M^colean, delaitit of certane poyntis of thift, and for coming to ye Lairdis of Lussis boundis in companie with the Laird of McGregour and airt and pairt of the murthour and reif committit thairon in Feb. last' Allaster McKie for stealing sheep &a the others for being art and part 'with the Laird of McGregour and his complices in the crewal murthour and slauchter of diverss of the Laird of Lusses freindis in the monethe of Feb. last to the number of seven scoir persones,' are all convicted and sentenced to be hanged on the Burrow muire.—Record of Justiciary.

"May. Item paid by command and direction of the Lords of Council to Robert and Colene Campbells for inbringing and presenting of three MacGregors who were thereafter executed to the deid for their demerits. £200.

    "Item to the officers of Justiciary for summoning of an assize to Three MacGregors that were execute to the deid.

    "Also close Letters to the Lairds of Bachananne, Luss, Glenurchy, and Tullibardin.—Treasurer's Books.

"May 20. Court of Justiciary &a Enter Gillespie M^cdonald McInnes Dow, Donald McClerich alias Stewart, Johnne McConneil McCondochie servants to the said Gillespie. Dilaitit of certain poyntis of thift and soirning and of airt and pairt of the slauchter of the Laird of Lusses friendis and assisters to ye number of 140 persones. Sentenced to be hanged on the Castle Hill.

"1603. May 18. Letter, Secret Council to the King in England.

    "According to that commissioun quhilk was direct anent the taking ordour with the ClanGregour We haif ressavit alreddie aucht pledges And the uther four ar expectit for within thrie or four dayis, To remane heir in waird, upone the perell of thair awin lyfis, To ansuer for the dew perform-ance of all offeris ; zour hienes salbe assuirit that the qualitie of the pledgeis thameselffis will procure ane necessitie of the forderance of that wark, the prosequuting quhairof is nocht to ressave ony Lang Delay seing be theise gentlemene quha ar commowneris, thair is allenarlie aucht owlkis crawit (weeks craved) betuix and the Ischew quhairof it is undertakin that all that is promessit salbe performit. We mentionat of befoir to zour Maiestie Anent the transporting of sa mony of that Clan that ar appointit for banischment, that ane schip micht be sent hither, We mon maist humblie renew our switc seing all theise quha ar to depart In quhilk numer the Laird hinself is ane, Ar to be in redines heir, reddy to embark agane witsontide, Being onable of thameselffis to defray thair chargis, furness thameselffis of victualle, or pay thair fraucht. Siclyke it will pleis zour Majestie to knaw &a &a (about others) zour Majesties humble and obedient subjectis and servitouris

> Jn Prestoun Rokburne (?)
> Montrois
> Elphingstoun
> Fyvie

—Original in General Register House, Edinburgh."

The above shows that the King was not so incensed against the Clan and the Chief as to be unwilling to consent to their banishment from the realm instead of their death, and to this alternative Glenstray alludes in his last declaration. Those whose signatures appear were apparently not enemical to the Clan, but other counsels must have prevailed later with the King.

"June. Letters to charge Johnne McNauchtane of Dundarrow, Colene Campbell of Straquhir, Neill Campbell of Drumyn, Johnne Campbell of Ardkinlas, Duncane Campbell Capitane of Carrick, John Robert and Dougal Campbells, sons to the Bailhe of Rossneth, Campbell Auchinwilling, Arthour, and Dowgall Campbells, brothers to Straquhir, Evin Dow Campbell of Corry, Johnne McEdward, Donald oig, and Duncane McNeill in Blythegolsyde, To compeir personally before the Council the 5. day of July next to answer upon the 'aird'[1] and the assistance given by them to the Laird of MacGregor and his villanous race, under the pain of rebellion and to charge certain witnesses to verify this their fact and deid.—Treasurer's Books.

"Item to the officers of Justiciary for summoning of an assize to one MacGregor who slew the constabill of Dundees man.

"July 5. Court of Justiciary &a enter 'Gillemichel Mchischok' servant to umquhile John dow McGregor, Nicoll McPharie Roy McGregour Dilaitit of being at the Field of Lennox. &a. To be hanged on the Castle hill.

"July 7. The Secret Council offered besides pardon of offences, 500 merks to any of the ClanGregor who should kill a denounced rebell.

"Benefits of the proclamation granted to ane Mackgregor for slaughter of ane rebell

"1603. July 7. John dow McEwin McGregor for the slaughter of David Ross McWilliam and William Ross McWilliam his brother, sought the benefit of the proclamation made against the said David and William, to wit remissioun

---

[1] Oath.

of all his bypast crimes and 500 merks which was granted to him by act of Council."

It is difficult to decide which act was the most criminal—the purchase of life and liberty at the cost of blood or the offer dangled out as a bait by the Government.

"July. Item paid by special command and ordinance of the Secret Council to Archibald Cunninghame, Mr Porter of the Castle of Edinburgh for the entertainment of certain pledges of the Clangregor. As the warrant of the Lords of Council with the particular compt bears £99.13.4.—Lord High Treasurer's books.

"July 12 At Edinburgh. The quhilk day Johnne Boyll of Kelburne and Normand Innes of Knockdarne Became plegeis and souerties conjunctlie and severallie for Duncane Campbell capitane of Carrick, and Ewin Campbell of Dargache That they sall compeir &a the 3 day of the next Justice air of the sheriffdom of Ergyle or soner upoun xv dayis warning To underly the law for the wilfull and contemptuous resetting, suppleing, and furneissing with meit, drink, and herbrie of Allaster McGregor of Glenstra or ony utheris of his unhappie raise and associattis quha wer Laitlie within the Lennox committit upoun the aucht day of Feb last and fostering of the said Alexander and ye persones foirsaid, diverss and sindrie tymes, within thair houses efter ye said barbarous murther; And namely in the monethis of Feb, Marche, Apryll, May, and Junij respective or sum dayis yrof and furneissing of ye said persounis in yr necessetees and keiping with thame frequent trysting and meitingis Alswell be nicht as day and ressauving of ye guidis and gear within thair landis that war reft, and away tane be ye saidis thevis, furth of the Lennox, the tyme foirsaid, under the paines following, That is to say For the said Duncane Campbell capitane of Carrick under the pane of thre thousand merkis, And for the said Ewin Campbell twa thousand merkis

"And siclyke That yai nor nane of thame sall ressett, supplie, furneiss, or keip trysting wilfullie or contemptuouslie (with the saide persones nor ressett the guidis nor gear quhilkis war reft or away taen &a This caution taken out at command of the Lords of Secreit Council

"July Item paid by ordinance of the said Lords to Andro Ross for inbringing and presenting to the Council Duncane (name of Johne Dow scored out) MacGregor of Angrie; as the warrant of Council with the said Androis acquittance, upon the resset thereof produced upon compt bears

"Letters to charge George MacGregor burgess of Perth, George McPatrik, Archibald, George and John MacGregors and Dougall MacGregor dwelling in Perth to compeir personallie before the Council the 26. of this instant resolved to change and alter their surnames of MacGregor and to take them to another famous and honest surname.—Treasurer's Books.

"Letters to the Market crosses of Stirling and Dumbarton And thereat charging all our Sovereign Lord's lieges within the bounds foirsaid to be in readiness to resist all invasion that may be expected at the hands of the MacGregors and for that cause that good watches be kept at all places convenient.

"1603. July. Same letters to be proclaimed at the market cross of Perth.

"Letters to charge Sir Johnne Murray of Tullibardin Knight to compeir and present with him Neill M‹Allaster . . . . . MacGregor personally before the Council the 4, of August next To the effect he may be made answerable to justice conform to the Law of this realme.

"July 14. Court of Justiciary &a 'John M‹Gregor at the kirk of Comrie' Dilaitit for being in company with Allaster M‹Gregour of Glenstra and his complices at the Field of Lennox aganis the Laird of Luse and his freindis and airt and pairt of the slauchteris, thiftis and robberies committit be thame &a Item for the slauchter of John M‹Arber committit in Junij last. The assyse in ane voce fyles John M‹Gregour of the crymes foirsaidis; Called in the Indictment Johnne dow M‹eane valich M‹gregour, 'To be tane to the Castlehill, and thair, his heid to be stricken fra his body.'

"August 4. Archibald Dalzell son lawful to Robert Dalzell of that Ilk presents to the Secret Council a petition stating that owing to some 'misreports maid be Nicoll Dalzell of Dalzell Milne' &a for not compeiring before the Council, the petitioner had been put to the Horn, and to obtene the King's benevolence had adventured his person and 'apprehendit ane of the speciall of the name of M‹Gregor callit Neill Makgregor pudrenois,[1] quha wes delyuerit in roll, to my Lord Chancellor be his men' and was ready to deliver the said Neill M‹Gregor to the Justice to be executed, and to do further acts 'aganis the name of M‹Gregor and rest of that Clan &a He was disabled by being in the situation of 'his Hienes rebell' and therefore praying that he might be allowed to appear before the Council to produce the said M‹Gregor. Petition granted. Original in General Register House."

Thus, by the base but ingenious device of the Executive, every man who was himself a felon, had the strongest inducement to serve the Government as executioner of the MacGregors, whose faults, whatever they might be, had now incurred the penalty of every man's hand being stirred up against them. And yet, seeing the numerous instances of ressett and kindness nobly shewn to them in spite of the imminent risk of so doing; it is evident that they must have had qualities which secured the strong attachment of their friends.

[1] Pudrach.

"August 12. Court of Justiciary. Dougall McGregour, Neill McGregour pudrach, Dilaitit of airt and pairt of the slauchter of four men that assistit the Laird of Luise at the field of ye Lennox committit in the moneth of Feb. last. Neill is dilaitit of airt and pairt of the slauchteris of umqle Patrik Layng and John Reid wobster (weaver) servants to Luss, and of the stealing of 'tuelf scoir of guidis furth of Lussis boundis in Lennox committit in Dec. last. Both are sentenced to be hanged on the Burrow muir.'

"August 20. Ane (royal) Letter maid to David Grahame servitour to the erle of Montrois his aires &a of the gift of the eschete of all guidis geir &a quhilkis pertenit of before to Duncane McGregour alias McInvalliche and now Drummond and now pertening to our soverane Lord throw being of the said Duncane ordourlie denuncit rebell and put to the horne at the instance of David Grahame, vicar of Comrie for not payment to him of £200.—Reg. of Privy Seal, vol. lxxiv. fol. 81.

"1603. August 25. Intromissioun with the MacGregors goods that were at Glenfrune.

"Act in favour of the Gentlemen of the Lennox being a supersedere to them for all pursuit criminal or civil for any of their intromission with the goods and gear of the ClanGregor who are guilty of the murder of Glenfrune. (MSS. notes taken by the first Earl of Haddington from the missing volume of the Record of the Privy Council, in Advocates' Library, Edin.) On the application of the 'gentlemen of the Lennox' the secret Council 'grantis thame ane supercedere fra all persute criminal or civill moved or to be moved aganis thame for thair intromissioune with the clangregouris geir, quha ar culpabill, and guiltie of the attempt cometit within the Lennox, during the tyme, that the commissioune grantit aganis the said Clangregor. And licentiatis the saidis complenaris to adjoyne to thame selffis sum brokene men for persyte of that wicked Race for quhome the saidis complenaris sal be ansuerable.'—Luss Coll.

"Sep. 14. Letter from the Presbytery of Stirling addressed To our speciall gude Lordis The Lordis of his Majesteis secret Counsell.

". . . . It may pleis zour llo. That the miserablle esteat of this province, and pairt of the cuntree within the bounds qrof we bear the charge, in the ministrie, hes movit and constrainit us in conscience to mak humblie sute to yr Lops : for present remeid for the cryis of the oppressit aboundis daylie, for raising of fyr, slauchter, Taking of men captives, Murthering of thame being tane captive without pitie makand yair pastyme yrof, Reaffis, heirschippis, spulzeis and uther manifest enormities and oppressionis, Committit within thir bounds be the broken men in the hielands especiallie be the ClanGregour, and sic uthers Clanes of thair inbringing, qrthrow the gentillmen of the cuntrie quha ar not able to withstand thair powar ar compellit for feir of thair tirany to laive thair duellings and flee to burghis for refuge and saiftie : and the pure ar exponit as ane pray to yr crueltie ; Sua that of our deutie, we cannot be silent in sua great a desolatione. In consideration qrof, We have tane occasione, to direct thir presents, to your llordschippis, To quhome, the cair of the defenss of the innocent, and oppressit, belangis now in the absence of his Matie · our Soverane. Re questing and exhorting zour LLs : in ye name of the eternall God, to quhome zr lls man give a rekoning ane day to tak su spedy order, for repressing of sic manifest enormities and oppressionis that God's pepill may leive peciablie, and quyethe at zour handis and as ye will be answerable to his Divine Maiestie, and have zour Lo awin soullis fre frome the giltines of the inocent blud that is sua neidleshe shed   The particular Complentis that has cui and ar to cui in befor zour llo : Will mak this matter mair manifest. Thus expecting redres of the miseries from zor llo. We commend zr lo to the blessing and protectioun of ye eternall   From our Presbytrie ef Stirling 14 Sep. 1603   zr lo. maist humble &a, The Brethren of the Presbyterie of Stirling.

.   A. LEVINGSTONE moderator
JAMES DUNCANSONE clerk.

—(Original of Letter in General Register House Edinburgh)

" 1603 September   Letters to charge George Marquis of Hunthe, Johnne Earl of Atholl, Patrik Lord Drummond, Sir Duncane Campbell of Glenurquhy Knight, Sir John Murray of Tullibardin, Mr John Moncreiff Sheriff depute of Perth, Lauchlane McIntosch of Dunnachtane, Angus McIntosche of Tarvat, James McIntosche of Gask, Johne Grant of Freuchie Alexander McRonald of Glengarray and Allane McConneill duy, to compeir personally before the Council the 20 day of this instant , To underly such order and direction as shall be prescribed and enjoined to them anent the pursuit of the ClanGregor conforme to first inclusion (conclusion) had thereanent under the pain of rebellion.

"Letters also to charge Archibald Earl of Argyle, Hary Stewart commendator of St Colme, —— Campbell of Lundy, Alexander Colquhoun of Luss, Aulay McAulay of Ardincabill and Robert Galbraith of Kilchreuch to compeir before the Council the 20 day of this instant to the effect and for the cause above specified.

"October. Letters to be proclaimed at the market crosses of Stirling and Dumbarton charging all his Highness's lieges dwelling nearest (ewest) and subject to the incursions of the Clangregor that they live on their own guard, keep watch and be ready at all occasions to defend themselves from their pursuit.

"Letters also to charge the Lairds of Tullibardin, Grant, and Strowane to exhibite and produce before the council the 25 of this instant each of them that . . son of umqle John Dow McGregor, which they have in keeping, respectively, to be taken order with as shall seem most expedient to the Council under the pain of rebellion —Treasurer's Books "

The following is from the "Annals" written by Sir James Balfour, Lyon King of Arms, who lived in this reign, and died in 1657 —

"The 2. of October this zeire the notorious thief and rebell Allaster McGregor Laird of Glenstrae quho had escaped the Laird of Arkinlesse handes was taken by Archibald Earle of Argyle, quho (befor he would zeild) had promised to him to conevoy him saue out of Scotts ground, to performe which promisse, he caused some servants conwey him to Berwicke, and besouthe it some myelles, and bring him back againe to Edinburgh quher he was hangit with maney of his kinred the 20 day of January in the following zeire, 1604 "

In a Diary written by Robert Birrel, quoted with Pitcairne's observations in next chapter, the 2nd Oct was the day of the capture by Ardkinlas; and the 4th Jan, the following year, the date of the recapture, &a, it seems probable, from the minuteness of Birrel's Diary, that the dates he gives may be the most correct.

Returning to the "Chiefs of Colquhoun,"[1] we find much useful information and instructive commentary ·—

"The melancholy fate of the Colquhouns excited very general commiseration. But the results were more disastrous to the victors than to the vanquished The resentment of the Government was intensely inflamed against the ClanGregor, whose lawless deeds, ruthless as they may have been before, had culminated in the terrific scenes enacted at Glenfruin. The measures of the Government against them were very severe, contemplating nothing less than the extermination of the clan.

"To the Earl of Argyle, who was the King's Lieutenant in the part of the country inhabited by the Macgregors, chiefly was committed the task of executing the severe enactments made against them. Indignant complaints were made against Aulay Macaulay of Ardincaple, who though he had formally joined with the Laird of Luss against Galbraith of Culcreugh, was charged with having reset and intercommuned with the MacGregors at Glenfruin, which would certainly have been only to act in conformity with the bond of clanship, into which he had

[1] "Chiefs of Colquhoun," vol. i., page 203.

entered with Allaster Macgregor.[1] Against Macaulay the Earl of Argyle now directed the weight of his official authority.

"On 17. March 1603.[2] John Stewart of Ardmolice, Sheriff of Bute, became surety for Aulay Macaulay of Ardincaple, that he would compear before his Majesty's justice, or his deputies, in the Tolbooth of Edinburgh, on the 17 day of May following, to underlie the law for reset and intercommuning with Ewin Macgregour, (Allaster) Macgregour of Glenstra, the deceased John Dow Macgregour his brother, and others of the Macgregours, and for 'not rysing the fray and following the thre saidis Macgregours commoun thevis and soirnaris, in thair incumming in the cuntrey of the Lennox, and steilling of leill menis guidis, and for inbringing of the saidis thevis and rebells, and also for airt and pairt with them in the incumming vpoune the Laird of Lussis lands, and for airt and part with the saidis Macgregouris in steiling fra the Laird of Luss, and his kyn and friendis and tennentis, of certane nolt, scheip,' etc.

"But M^caulay escaped by a summary suppression of all investigation. Shielded by the Duke of Lennox, and being in the Duke's train, which was to accompany King James VI. on his way to England, to take possession of the English Throne vacant by the death of Queen Elizabeth, his Majesty issued a warrant at Berwick, 7. April 1603. to the Justice General and his deputies, commanding them to desert the dyet ' against Macaulay, as he was altogedder frie and innocent of the allegit crymes laid to his charge.' The Justice, accordingly, on the 17. of May 1603, when this warrant was presented in the Justiciary Court by a servant of the Duke of Lennox, deserted the diet. Many others were less mercifully dealt with."

After the Conflict of Glenfruin. (Chiefs of Colquhoun, *continued*).

" Before any judicial inquiry had been made on the 3. of April 1603, only two days before King James VI. left Scotland for England . . . . . . an Act of Privy Council was passed by which the name of Gregor or MacGregor was for ever abolished. All of this surname were commanded under the penalty of death to change it for another, and the same penalty was denounced against those who should give food or shelter to any of the clan. All who had been at the conflict of Glenfruin, and at the spoliation and burning of the Lands of the Laird of Luss and other lands, were also prohibited under the penalty of death from carrying any weapon except a pointless knife to eat their meat. Such a commencement did not augur well for the impartial administration of Justice, much less for the exercise of clemency to this clan. This was followed by the execution of many of those who had taken part in the sanguinary conflict of Glenfruin, some at the Burrowmure of Edinburgh, others at the castle Hill, and others

---

[1] 27th May 1591. See page 231.

[2] Full transcript of these transactions relating to Aulay MacAulay given in "Chartulary," but not quoted in these Memoirs, because they do not relate to MacGregors.

at the public Cross; and by other measures which bore the impress rather of vengeance than of calm judicial procedure. . . . . Thus cast beyond the pale of the Royal mercy, except on the most dishonourable conditions, the clan were driven to desperation, and thinking only of retaliation, broke forth into new outrages. After the conflict at Glenfruin, the MacGregors lost no time in selling and distributing the plunder which they had carried off, and this they did chiefly in Argyllshire. Some facts in reference to this subject we learn from the depositions made 20 July before Alexander Colquhoun of Luss, in the presence of a notary, by Donald Makglaschane in Baichybaine, officer, tenant, and servant to Sir John Campbell of Ardkinglas. He confessed that he himself had bought three cows, at the head of Lochfyne, from two of the most noted actors in these deeds of spoliation, and slaughter, three or four days, after they were perpetrated. He also confessed that he knew many of the tenants of the Laird of Ardkinglas, for whom that laird was responsible, who had bought from other of Allaster Macgregor's men, cows, horses, and other spoil. and who had entertained some of the same party.

"Some of the Campbells who were said to have been the secret allies of the Macgregors, having reset them after the battle of Glenfruin, and having been receivers of their stolen property, the Government now resolved to proceed against them. . . . . . . 'Commissions had been given by the Government to the gentlemen of the Lennox empowering them to seize the property as well as to pursue the persons of the ClanGregor. But this clan as 'the gentlemen of Lennox' describe them being 'in all their wicked actiounes maist subtil and craftie' with the view of defeating the object of these commissions distributed their goods among some of their friends, and moved them to take action before the Lords of secret Council against those invested with such commissions for their wrongous intromissiones with the said goods, ...'"

This was the object of the "supercedere" granted to the petitioners as mentioned at page 306.

"Towards the end of 1603. Alexander Colquhoun and his men apprehended three of the ClanGregour,—Gregor Cruiginche Macgregor, John dow Macrob Macgregour, and Allaster Macewne Macgregor. On 24. Nov. he compeared before the Lords of the Secret Council at Stirling, presented these prisoners before them, and craved that he might be exonered and relieved of them. Their Lordships granted the prayer of his petition and having taken them of his hands, delivered them to the magistrates of the Burgh of Stirling.

"In the trials which took place from the 20. May 1603. to 2. March 1604. thirty-five of the Macgregors were convicted, and only one acquitted. In most or all of these instances the sentence of death, as we learn from Birrel's Diary, was carried into effect.

"Allaster MacGregor, the Chief of the Clan, did not fall into the hands of the

Government till nearly a year after the battle of Glenfruin   He had been almost entrapped by Campbell of Arkinglas, Sheriff of Argyllshire, who, with the intention of arresting him, and sending him to the Earl of Argyll, had invited him to a friendly banquet in his house, which was situated on a small island in a loch, and who there made him a prisoner, and put him in a boat, guarded by five men , but Macgregor seeing that he was betrayed, made his escape by a deed of romantic daring, having leapt out of the boat into the water, and swam to the shore in safety   He was less successful in eluding Archibald Earl of Argyll "

After relating the circumstances regarding Argyll's treatment of Glenstray as given from several authorities in Pitcairne's " Criminal Trials," Sir William Fraser continues:—

" He arrived in Edinburgh on the evening of the 18. Jan. 1604   Only two days after his trial, and that of four of his clan, Patrik Aldoche Macgregour, William Macneill his servant, Duncan Pudrache Macgregour, and Allaster Macgregour Macean, took place before the High Court of Justiciary for the crime of treason, in their having attacked the Laird of Luss whilst armed with a royal commission to resist the 'cruel enterprises' of the ClanGregor.' . . . . . ' Having been found guilty Allaster MacGregor and his four accomplices were sentenced to be hanged at the Cross of Edinburgh, on the same day. . . . . . .' Effect was also given to the forfeiture of their lands, heritages &a.

" The heads of Allaster and of his associate, Patrick Aldoch Macgregor, were by order of the Government, sent to Dumbarton to be placed on the tolbooth of that burgh, the chief town of the district where the crimes for which they were executed had been committed. On 13 Feb 1604 the Town Council of Dumbarton concludit and ordainit that the Laird of Macgregor's heid, with Patrik Auldochy his heid, be put up on the Tolbuith, on the maist convenient place the Baillies and Counsall thinkis guid —Dumbarton Town Council Records.

" On the 19. of Jan. the day before his execution, Allaster Macgregor made a declaration or confession, which if entitled to credit, would throw light on the causes which led to the conflict of Glenfruin, as well as explain other matters connected with the family feuds of that period   In this confession he distinctly throws the whole blame of the outrages committed by the Macgregors against the Colquhouns upon the Earll of Argyll, and accuses that Earll of having instigated him to commit other slaughters and depredations. But as observed before, declarations which so seriously criminated the Earll of Argyll are not entitled, in the circumstances, to implicit credit for Allaster was doubtless much exasperated against the Earl, by whom he had been captured and delivered as a prisoner to the Government."

Reverting to an earlier page of " The Chiefs of Colquhoun," the following passage relates to the same subject.

"If the declaration or confession made by Allaster MacGregor before his execution is true, Argyll, instead of repressing the ClanGregor, made use of the power which, as the King's Lieutenant, he had acquired over them to stimulate them to various acts of aggression against Colquhoun of Luss and others, who were his personal enemies.   Founding mainly on the dying declaration of the Laird of Macgregor, Pitcairn, in his 'Criminal Trials,' says, 'It is to this crafty and perfidious system of the Earl therefore, that we must solely trace the feud between the Colquhouns and the Macgregors, which proved in the end so hurtful to both, a result no doubt all along contemplated by this powerful nobleman.'

"We do not however agree with Pitcairne in founding so much on Macgregor's dying declaration.   The feeling of Macgregor against Argyll must in the circumstances have been intensely strong, as his words plainly indicate, and though in the presence of death, the motive to speak only the truth was powerful, yet our knowledge of human nature suggests caution in giving implicit credit even to his dying declaration; and its main features are certainly not confirmed, as Pitcairne asserts, by the Records of the Privy Council.   The Laird of Macgregor's testimony, therefore, in the circumstances, unsupported by that of other credible witnesses, is not a sufficient ground on which to impeach Argyll."

Another passage has also to be here quoted.

"The statement made by Mr Pitcairne in his 'Criminal Trials,' that the Macgregors and the Colquhouns at Glenfruin 'were in a manner equally armed with the royal authority' is quite unfounded.   The Laird of Luss was indeed then acting under a commission from the King to apprehend the ClanGregor, but to speak of the 'Laird of Macgregor as marching to invade the Lennox under the paramount authority of the King's Lieutenant,' Argyll, is a gratuitous assertion. Whatever the friends of the Macgregors may say as to Argyll's secretly encouraging the Macgregors to attack the Colquhouns, it is certain that he had no power to arm them with authority for that purpose, and there is no evidence that he formally did so.   To place the two parties nearly on a footing of equality as to the right of meeting in hostile array for trial of strength, is a view entirely erroneous. The Macgregors were rebels, and the Colquhouns were armed with royal authority to suppress their outrages."

A few remarks on the preceding observations must here be made.   In the next chapter, Pitcairne's article on the trial of Allaster MacGregor of Glenstray and of the conflict of Glenfruin are given in full, where the points to which Sir William Fraser raises objections can be studied carefully.

The opinion that the Colquhouns had the Royal sanction for taking up arms, and that their adversaries had not this authority, may be willingly conceded. In fairness to the Colquhouns, it may be noticed that there is no evidence that they purchased letters of fire and sword against their foes, as was so often the case, legalising violence and bloodshed by money. Their claim was, therefore, all the stronger, and consisted of two grants of authority: the first a Royal letter, sanctioning their opposing the MacGregors "without any crime," date Sep. 1602; the other a formal Commission of Lieutenantcy, given to Alexander Colquhoun of Luss, in Dec. 1602. We may consider that this Commission was obtained by an artifice in regard to the parade of shirts, but this does not affect the fact of the Royal authority, on which much stress is laid in the subsequent trials. The view taken by Mr Pitcairne, however, can be understood if its grounds are analysed.

The Commission given by the King to the Earl of Argyle against the ClanGregor, March 3, 1601, expressly annulled the Sovereign's own power to forgive any MacGregor, or to make terms with one of the name. This Commission was thus such a complete and absolute delegation of the Royal authority that if Argyle, as the King's Lieutenant in special charge of the MacGregors, had openly convened them to invade the Colquhouns, the curious anomaly of both opponents being armed with the Royal authority, as Mr Pitcairne conceived, might have actually occurred. But such overt acts were no part of Argyle's policy.

With regard to the last Declaration of Glenstray, it is impossible for one of the ClanGregor to feel strictly impartial. To us it is a legacy, the truth of which is a matter of painfully deep, and we may believe inherited, conviction. However presumptuous it may be to attempt to break a lance with the learned and courteous knight who has adopted the side of the Chiefs of Colquhoun, but who has evinced much delicacy and forbearance in treating of our combats with them, loyal duty to our heroic Chief must disregard any "skaith" risked in his defence.

Endeavouring to unravel the arguments advanced in the attempt to vindicate Archibald, second Earl of Argyle, by discrediting Glenstray's testimony, it must be remarked that Pitcairne, who had made criminal trials his special study and is recognised as a most competent authority

on the subject, has collected excellent illustrations from nearly contemporary histories which relate the manner in which Glenstray was
conveyed across the Border and brought back again.[1] This act of
treachery is in conformity with the dying Chief's accusations against
Argyle. Glenstray was no ordinary culprit, whose word was known to
be unreliable; he had been befriended by the Laird of Tullibardine and
the Commendator of Inchaffray, two landlords who appear to have borne
a high character—there is no special bitterness in the Chief's last Declaration; it reads sad, sober, and earnest. But in so hurried a trial, with
several of the jury personally incensed against Glenstray, and warned
beforehand to bring in a true bill, his Declaration apparently received no
attention. It is highly improbable that he could have been acquitted
after the events of Glenfruin, especially as the fact of Luss having had a
Royal Commission was fully recognised as adding to the offence, but the
circumstances of the Declaration having been disregarded and hushed up
by his adversaries is no argument against its truth. Nor was any contemporary refutation made, so far as is known.

Against Argyle there are certain suspicious probabilities. It is true
that, whilst suffering from the ill-will and greed of their Glenurchay
neighbour, the MacGregors had received some protection from the Earls
of Argyle, but the enormous power with which this very young man was
invested enabled him most easily to force those dependent on him, to
carry out his behests whatever they might be, and Argyle had enemies
who it was to his interest either to put out of the way or reduce to submission. The same complaint of double-dealing and of stirring up the
Clans against each other was repeated a few years later, in the case of the
MacDonalds and others.[2] We cannot hold Argyle guiltless of the charges
brought against him by Glenstray.

[1] J. Hill Burton, in his "Narratives from Criminal Trials in Scotland," referring to Glenstray's
trial, simply states that he does not believe the narrative of Glenstray having been taken across
the Border, &c. His disbelief in the last Declaration naturally corresponds with this summary
judgment.

[2] Gregory's "History of the Islands and Isles," &c.

Chapter XXVI

Conflict of Glenfruin, 1603

THE following excerpts are from the collection of "Celebrated Trials in Scotland," with critical and historical remarks by Hugo Arnot, Esq., Advocate, 1812 :—

"Alister Macgregor of Glenstra, Laird of Macgregor, for slaughtering the Laird of Luss's friends and plundering his lands.

"1604. This trial, and the subsequent proceedings relating to the ClanGregor, afford the most characteristic evidence of the barbarous state of the Highlands in those times, of the lawless manners of the people, and despicable imbecility of the executive arm. The crimes with which the prisoner was charged resemble more the outrage and desolation of war than the guilt of a felon. He was accused of having conspired the destruction of the name of Colquhoun, its friends and allies, and the plunder of the lands of Luss; of having, on the 7. of Feb. preceding, invaded the lands of Sir Alexander Colquhoun of Luss with a body of 400 men, composed partly of his own Clan and of the Clan Cameron, and of lawless thieves and robbers, equipped in arms, and drawn up on the field of Lennox in battle array; of having fought with Sir Alexander, who, being authorised by a warrant from the Privy Council, had convocated his friends to resist this lawless host; of having killed about 140 of Sir Alexander's men, most of them in cold blood, after they were made prisoners; of having carried off 80 horses, 600 cows, and 800 sheep; and of burning houses, cornyards, &c.

"A jury of landed gentlemen of most respectable family sat upon the prisoner. . . . . One of these persons indeed, Thomas Fallasdaill,[1] burgess of Dumbarton, ought to have been kept far aloof from this jury. He was the special confident and adviser of the Laird of Luss; and it was in consequence of his suggestion that the Laird made the parade before his Majesty at Stirling, with the bloody shirts, stained with the gore of his followers. The jury unanimously convicted the prisoner, who,

---

[1] It appears from the indictment of Glenstray that David Fallasdaill, Burgess, and two sons, Thomas and James, were slain at Glenfruin—all probably near relations of the Juror. In the Assize of March 1, 1604, against five MacGregors, besides Thomas Fallasdaill on the Jury, there was John Sempell of Foulwird, the Laird who had joined in advising the display of shirts, whilst William Semphill was "tane away captive."

in consequence of the verdict, was condemned to be hanged and quartered at the Cross of Edinburgh, his limbs to be stuck up in the chief towns, and his whole estate, heritable and moveable, to be forfeited. Four of the Laird of MacGregor's followers, who stood trial along with him, were convicted and condemned to the same punishment, eleven on the 17. Feb. and six on the 1. March, and many pages of the criminal record are engrossed with the trials of the MacGregors. It became the object of national attention to break this lawless confederacy, of which the object was pointed revenge and indiscriminate plunder, supported by uniform contempt of the laws and resistance to the magistrates."

The whole subject of the Conflict of Glenfruin has such deep interest for everyone of the ClanGregor that it is desirable to give here in full the article upon it in the records of Criminal Trials by Robert Pitcairne.

("Mr Williame Hairt, Justice-Depute.)

" 'Field of the Lennox, or Conflict of Glenfruine—Slaughter of the Colquhouns —Stoutreif—Treason—Fire-Raising, &a.'

" The proscription and the cruel and systematic persecution of the ClanGregor, for a long series of years, although, in the abstract, a subject familiar to every reader of Scottish History, has hitherto been very imperfectly explained. The Criminal Records, and the Acts of the Privy Council, throw much light on all the branches of this extraordinary event. To save the necessity of future repetition, it appears to the Editor to be necessary, at the outset of these proceedings, to give a very brief sketch of the circumstances which led to the Field of the Lennox—or 'the Raid' or 'Conflict of Glenfruin'; and of those events which ultimately terminated in the Execution of the Laird of Macgregor, and of many others of his name. All the future oppression and persecution of the race of the Macgregors ostensibly take their rise from this conflict.

" The ClanGregor which, from whatever causes, had been for some time looked upon as an unruly tribe, was, for some years previous to 1603, placed under the control of Archibald (seventh) Earl of Argyle, who, as King's Lieutenant in the 'Bounds of the ClanGregor,' was invested with very extensive powers, and who, by his acceptance of the office, was made answerable for all excesses committed by this Clan. In these circumstances, it might be supposed that it was Argyle's interest, as it certainly was his duty, to have done all in his power to retain the ClanGregor in obedience to the laws ; but, on the contrary, it appears that from the time he first, as King's Lieutenant, acquired the complete control of the MacGregors, the principal use he made of his power, was artfully to stir up the Clan to various acts of aggression and hostility against his own personal enemies, of whom it is known Colquhoun of Luss was one. It is to this crafty and perfidious system of the Earl, therefore, that we must solely trace the feud between the

Colquhouns and Macgregors, which proved, in the end, so hurtful to both; a result, no doubt, all along contemplated by this powerful but treacherous Nobleman. But it is unnecessary to enlarge on this point, as the Dying Declaration of the Laird of Macgregor places in a very clear light the cruel and deceitful policy pursued by Argyle, and which was too frequently resorted to by others, in those days, for quieting the Highlands It may be remarked, that this interesting document, besides undoubtedly bearing internal evidence of truth, is corroborated, in almost every detail of it, by the Public Records.

" It is also to be remarked, as particularly worthy of notice, that at the period of this fatal conflict, both of the contending parties were, in a manner, equally armed with the Royal authority, the Laird of Luss having raised his forces under a commission, emanating from the King himself, while the Laird of MacGregor marched to invade the Lennox, under the paramount authority of the King's Lieutenant."[1]

It is unnecessary to quote the repetition of refutation of the alleged murder of Sir Humphrey, which error has been sufficiently cleared up already.

"The popular accounts of this transaction charge the MacGregors with two atrocities committed after the battle, ... and the Slaughter of a number of defenceless boys from the Grammar School or College of Dumbarton, who, from curiosity, came to see the fight, and had by Colquhoun's orders, been put into a barn for safety; where, on the success of the Highlanders, they were said to have been murdered. . . . . . It is enough to state that this circumstance forms no point of any of the Dittays against those of the MacGregors who were tried for their share of the battle, although every criminal act which could be possibly adduced against each of them is carefully inserted in their Indictments Such an atrocious fact could not have escaped the notice of all his Majesty's Advocates, for such a length of time—and there was no lack of informers. It is thought that this massacre is alluded to in the Records of the Privy Council, Jan. 5. 1609, where it is stated that 'Allan Oig M°Intach, in Glenco,' when aiding the ClanGregor at Glenfruin, 'with his awne hand, murdered without pity, the number of forty poor persons, who were naked and without armour.' "

According to Pitcairne's usual plan, some passages from contemporary MSS. are appended in illustration of the facts.

"1604 Jan 20. Allaster M°Gregour of Glenstra, Patrik Aldoche[2] M°Gregour, Williame M°Neill his seruand, Duncane Pudrache M°Gregour and Allaster M°Gregour M°Kean[3]

---

[1] *Vide* previous Chapter. [2] Younger brother of Duncan Abroch.

[3] Younger son of Gregor of Brackly—he was second cousin of Patrick Aldoch in the male line.

Dilatit, accusit, and persewit, at the instance of Sir Thomas Hammiltoun of Momkland, knycht, aduocate to our souerane Lord, &a off the crymes following : Forsamekill as thay and ilk ane of thame accumpaneit with umqle Johnne Dow, brother to the said Allaster McGregour of Glenstra, and vtheris thair kin, friendis and of thair counsall, haifing concludit the distructioune of Alexander Colquhoune of Luse, his kyn, freindis and alya, and the haill surname of the Balquhannanis, and to herrie thair landis ; thay convenit to thameselffis the Clanhamrone, the Clanan-verich, and dyuerse vtheris brokin men and soirneris, to the number of foure hundreth men, or thairby, all bodin feir of weir, with hagbuttis, pistolettis, murrionis, mailzie-cottis, pow-aixes, tua-handit-swoirdis, bowis, darloches, and vtheris wappones, invasiue, incontraire the tennour of the Actis of Parliament : And for the perform-ance of thair wicked conclusioune, vpon the sevint day of Februare last bypast come fordward, in arrayit battell, to the Landis of Glenfrwne, pertening to the Laird of Luse ; quhair the said Laird of Luse. accumpaneit with certane of his freindis, war convenit, be vertew of our Soerane lordis Commissioun, to resist the saidis persones crewall interpryses ; and thair set vpone him, his kyn and freindis, and crewallie invaidit thame for thair slauchteris, schamefullie, crewallie and bar-baruslie murdreist and slew Peter Naper of Kilmahew ; Johnne Buchannane of Buchlyvie ; Tobias Smallet, bailzie of Dumbarten ; Dauid Fallesdaill, burges thair ; Thomas and James Fallesdaillis his sones ; Walter Colquhoun of Barnehill ; Johne Colquhoun fear thairof ; Adam and Johne Colquhounes sones to the Laird of Camp-stradden ; Johne Colquhoun of Dalmure, and dyueris persones our souerane lordis leigis, to the number of sevin scoir personis or thairby ; the maist pairt of thame being taen captiues be the saidis McGregouris befoir thai pat violent handis in thame, and crewallie slew thame.   And tressonabillie tuik Williame Sempill and dyueris vtheris, our souerane lordis frie legis, and convoyit thame away captiue with thame, and be way of maisterfull Stouthreif staw, reft and away-tuik sax hundreth ky and oxin, aucht hundreth scheip and gait, fourteen scoir of horse and meiris, with the haill plenissing, guidis, and geir, aff the fourscoir pund land of Luse ; and at the samyn tyme, tressonabillie raisit ffyre in the houssis and barne-zairdis thairof, brunt, waistit and distroyit the samyn, with the coirnis being thairin.   And the foirsaidis personis and ilk ane of thame ar airt and pairt of the saidis crewall, horrible and tressonabill crymes ; the lyk quhairof was nevir committit within this realme ; Com-mitting thairby manifest Tressone, in hie and manifest contempt of our souerane lord, his hienes auctorite and lawis.

" ASSISA.

Sir Thomas Stewart of Garnetullie,	Moyses Wallace burges of Edr.
Colene Campbell younger of Glenorchie,	Sir Robert Creychtoune of Clwny Knicht,
Alexander Menzies of Weyme,	Robert Robertsoun of Faskeil,

Robert Robertsoun of Strowane,	Thomas Fallasdaill burges of Dumbartene,
Johne Naper fiear of Merchinstoune,	Johne Herring of Lethendie,
Johne Blair younger of that Ilk,	William Stewart, Capitane of Dumbartene,
Johne Grahame of Knockdoliane,	Harie Drummond of Blair,
	Johne Blair elder of that Ilk.

"For verificatioun quhairof, the said. Sir Thomas Hammiltoun of Monkland, aduocat, produceit the saidis persones Depositionis and Confessiones, maid be thame in presens of dyuerse lordis of his hienes Secreit Counsall and Sessioun, subscryuit with thair handis. The Aduocat askit instrumentis, 1. Of the sweiring of the Assyse, and protestit for Wilfull errour aganis thame, in cais thay acquit. 2. Of the sweiring of the Dittay be the Laird of Luse. 3. Of the productioune of the pannellis Depositiones to the Assyse.

"Verdict. The Assyse, all in ane voce, be the mouth of Johne Blair elder of that Ilk. ffand pronuncet and declarit the saidis Allaster McGregour of Glenstra, &a to be fylet, culpable and convict of the crymes aboue specifeit.

"Sentence. And thairfoir, the Justice-depute, ffinding the saidis crymes to be tressonabill, be the mouth of James Hendersoun dempstar of Court, Ordainit the saidis persones to be tane to the mercat-croce of Edinburgh, and thair to be hangit vpone ane gibbet quhill thay be deid; and thairefter thair heidis, legis, airmes and remanent pairtis of thair bodeis to be quarterit and put vpone publict places, and thair haill landis, heritageis, annuel rentis, takis, steidingis, rowmes, possessiones, coires, cattell, guidis, geir, and sowmes of money pertening to thame, to be fforfaltit, escheit and inbrocht to our souerane lordis vse, as convict of the saidis tressonabill crymes.

"Footnote.[1] The matter is thus noticed by Birrel and Fleming. 'The 9. of Feb. (1603) the Laird of MacGregour. with fourhunder of his name and factioune, enterit the Lennox, quhair he maid spulzie and slauchter, to the nwmber of 60 honest men, besyid wemen and bearnis. He spareit nane quhair he come.'—Birrel's Diary. '(April 9.) Proclamatioun sumonding all the McGregouris to compere and wnderly the law for the slauchter of the Laird of Luss and men of Dumbartane.'—Fleming's MS. Chronicle.

"Documents illustrative of 'The Field of the Lennox or Conflict of Glenfrune' and of the Proceedings against the Laird of MacGregor and his Clan.

"I. Extract from Calderwood's MS. Church History, Advocates' Library, vol. v. p. 677—

"'Upon the 8. of Feb. a great company of somers and broken Highland men of the Clane of Mackgrigore, the number of 400 men, came down to Lennox to reave and spoyle. The people of the country convened to make impediment. There were slaine of the country people, specially of the surname of Colquhoun, to the number of fourscore persons or thereby ; of which number were landed men of good rank. The Laird of Luce himself, Chief of the Colquhouns, escaped narrowly They carried away 1000 head of cattell, besides other insight and plenishing It was reported, that that was done at the instigation of the Duke of Lennox his lady, seeking the wrack of the Laird of Luce, who held of the King and not of the Duke '

"II Extract from MS History of Scotland, Anon Advocates' Library, A 4 35—

"'Now on the 2. day of Oct. (1603) the Laird of Arkinles takis in hand to the Erll of Argyill, to tak the Laird of MacGregour, and callis him to ane bankatt in his hous, quhilk hous stuid within ane Loche ; and thair takis him prissoner to send him to Argyll. And putting him in ane boitt, with fywe menne with him by thame that eowit the boitt; he seing him selff betreiffit, gettis his handis lowse ; and striking him our burd that was narrest him he lowpis in the watter, and out-sowmis to the land. And so escheappis wntene (untaken) for the presentt. Now the Erll Argyill, perseaffing that he was eschappit, he sendis to him ; desiring him to cum to him, that he mycht confer with him, wnder promeis to let him gang frie gif thay culd nocht agne. Wpoun the quhilk, the Laird Macgregour come to him, and at his cuming was well ressauit the Erll, quha schew him, that he was commandit be the King to bring him in ; bot he had no doubt bot his Majesty wald, at his requeist pardoun his offence, and he- suld with all diligense, send tua Gentill menne to Ingland with him, and suld with all diligense follow him selff. Wpoun the quhilk fair promeissis he was content ; and come with the Erll of Argyll to Edinburgh, quhair, on the 10 day he was be the Gaird conwoyit to Berwick, within Inglis grund, and syne brocht back to Edinburgh. And on the 20 day he was hangit at the Corse, with tenne of his kin and friendis hangit with him to the gritt discredeit of the Erll Argyill, quha wes the doare of the samin.'

"III Extract from Robert Birrel's Diary, MS Advocates' Library (p 138)—

"'The 2 of Oct (1603) Allester McGregour of Glainstre tane be the Laird of Arkynles, bot scapit agine, bot efter, taken be the Earle of Argyill the 4 of Jan and brocht to Edinburche the 9 of Jan. 1604 with 18 mae of his freindis, McGregouris. He wes convoyit to Berwick be the Gaird conforme to the Earlis promese for he promesit to put him out of Scottis grund. Swa he keipit ane Hieland-manis promes, in respect he sent the Gaird to convoy him out of Scottis grund Bot thai wer not directit to pairt with him, bot to fetche him bak agane. The 18 of Januar, at evine, he come agane to Edinburghe, and vpone the 20 day, he wes hangit at the Croce, and ij (eleven) of his freindis and name vpone the gallous, Himselff, being chieff, he wes hangit his awin hicht abone the rest of hes freindis '

"IV. Extract from Calderwood's MS. Church History—

"'Upon the 18 of Januar, Mackgregore was conveyed be the guard who attended upon the Counsell to Berwick, because Argyle promised to him, when he rendered himself, that he sould be caried to Ingland : But post was appointed to meet him to caus bring them back againe which was done. Immediately, upon the 20 of Januar, he, and sundrie of his Clane were hanged in Edinburgh. Sevine of thair number came in, long before, as pleadges for performance of certaine conditions, which were to be filled by their Chief; but they were hanged with the rest, without the knowledge of ane Assyse. They were young men, and reputed honest for their own parts. The Laird of Makgrigore was hanged a pinne above the rest. A young man called James Hope, beholding the execution, fell down, and power was taken from half of his body. When he was carried to ane house, he cryed, that "one of the Highland men had shott him with ane arrow." "He died upon the sabbath day after." [1]

"Footnote. Fleming in his Chronicle (MS. Advocates' Library) thus records the event. The Laird of McGregour hangit at Edinburgh and xj of his unhappie kin. They hang all nicht on the gallous. This almost unexampled act of perfidy, on the part of Argyle the King's Lieutenant, and the Justice General of Scotland, gives a lamentable picture of those unhappy times ; and it would appear that the government seemed to think it no discredit to take advantage of such an infamous breach of trust.

"V. The Laird of McGregours Declaratioun, produceit the tyme of conviction.

" 'I, Allester Magrigour of Glenstra, Confesse heir before God, that I have bein persuadit, movit and intysit, as I am presentlie accusit and trublit for ; alse gif I had usit counsall or command of the man that hes Intysit me, I wald have done and committit sindrie heich Murthouris mair ; ffor trewlie, sen I was first his Majesteis man, I culd never be at ane eise, by my Lord of Argylls falshete and inventiones ; for he causit McClaine and Glenchamrowne commit herschip and slauchter in my rium of Rennoche,[1] the quhilk causit my pure men therefter to bege and steill : Also, therefter, he moweit my brother and sum of my freindis to commit baith herschip and slauchter upoune the Laird of Luss : Also he persuadit myselfe, with message to weir aganis the Laird of Boauhanene, quhilk I did refuise ; for the quhilk I was contenowalie bostit (threatencd) that he sould be my unfriend ; and quhen I did refuise his desire in that point, then intysit me with uther messingeris, as be the Laird of M^cknachtane and utheris of my freindis, to weir and truble the Laird of Luss ; quhilk I behuffit to do for his fals boutgaittis (roundabout ways) Then quhen he saw I was at ane strait he cawsit me trow he was my guid freind ; bot I did persave he was slaw therin ; Then I made my moyan to pleis his Majestie and Lords of Counsall, baith of service and obedience, to puneische faultouris and to saif innosent men ; and quhen Argyll was maid foresein (informed) thereof, he intysit me to stay and start fra thay conditions, causing me to understand

---

[1] Glenurchy introduced Keppoch and others into the Isle of Loch Ranoch 1564, but no such act on the part of the Earl of Argyle appears on record.—Ed.

that I was dissavit; bot with fair wordis to put me in ane snair, that he mycht gett the lands of Kintyre in feyell (fee feu-farm) fra his Majestie, begane to putt at me and my kin, The quhilk Argyll inventit, maist schamefullie, and persuadit the Laird of Ardkinlaiss to dissave me, quha was the man I did maist trest into, bot God did releif me in the mean tyme to libertie maist narrowlie. Neuertheless, Argyll maid the oppin bruit (report) that Ardkinlaiss did all that by falsheid, by his Knawlege quhilk he did intyse me, with oft and sindrie messages, that he wald mak my peace and saif my lyfe and landis only to puneis certane faltouris of my kin, and my innosent freindis to renunce thair surname, and to leif peaseablie. Vpone the quhilk conditioune he was suorne be ane ayth to his freindis, and they suorne to me; and als I haif his warrand and handwrytt therevpon. The promeis gif they be honestlie keipit, I let God be the Juge. And at our meting in oure awin chalmer, he vas suorne to me in witnes of his awin freind. Attour, I confess befor God that he did all his craftie diligence to intyse me to slay and destroy the Laird Ardinkaippill, McKallay, for ony ganes kyndness or freidschip that he mycht do or gif me. The quhilk I did refuis, in respect of my faithfull promeis maid to Mckallay of befor Also he did all the diligence he culd to mowe me to slay the Laird of Ardkyndlas, in lykmaner, bot I neuer grantit therto, Throw the quhilk he did invy me grettumly. And now, seing God and man seis it is greidenes of warldlie geir quhilkis causis him to putt at me and my kin, and not the weill of the realme, nor to pacifie the samyn, nor to his Majesties honour, bot to putt down innosent men, to cause pure bairnes and infantis bege, and pure wemen to perisch for hunger, quhen thay ar hereit of thair geir, The quhilk, I pray God that this faltis lycht not vpon his Majestie heirefter, nor vpon his successione. Quherfor I wald beseik God that his Majestie knew the weratie, that at this hour I wald be content to tak baneisment, with all my kin that was at the Laird of Lussis slaucgter, and all utheris of thame that ony falt can be laid to thair charge; And his majestie of his mercie, to lat pure innosent men and young bairnes pass to libertie, and to lerne to leiff as innocent men; The quhilk I wald fulfill, bot ony kynd of faill, quhilk wald be mair to the will of God, and his Majesties honour, nor the greidie cruell forme that is devysit, only for leuf of geir, haueing nether respect to God nor honestie.'

"Footnote The Original of the very interesting paper now given, is preserved in the General Register House, and is in the hand of the then Clerk of Secret Council, James Primrose It is marked as 'Presentit be Mr Williame Hairt' (of Livilands), as an article of evidence of his guilt at his trial. Glenstray had surrendered to Argyll, on condition of his being permitted to go to England, by which the former meant that he should visit the English Court and have, if possible, access to the King. It was obviously Argyll's policy to prevent this, but that he might fulfil his promise, he sent him under a strong escort of troops, to beyond the river Tweed, at Berwick, where the soldiers wheeling to the right about, made Mac-

Gregor retrace his steps. He was two days only in Edinburgh, after his return from England, when he was executed.—See Sir James Balfour's Annals.

"In the Lord Treasurer's Books of Scotland, Nov. 1602, is the following entry: 'Item to Patrik M^comeis, messinger, passand of Edinburgh with lettres to charge Archibald Earle of Argyle to compeir personallie befoir the Counsall, the xvi day of Dec. nixt, to ansuer to sic thingis as salbe inquirit at him, tuiching his lying at await for the Laird of Ardincapill, vpon set purpois to have slane him.' Pitcairne next alludes to the Bond of Clanship between Glenstray and MacAulay of 1591 as on page 231, regarding which he adds: 'This instrument had as would seem, been discovered by the Government, and led to the suspicion that MacAulay had aided Glenstray in the feud of Glenfruin. MacAulay seems to have escaped death, by being under the protection of the Duke of Lennox, and forming one of his train or "tail" in the King's journey to England, to take possession of the English Throne.'

"Field of Glenfrune—Murder—Fire-raising, &a.

"1604. Feb. 17. Johnne Dow McEwin McGregour, Patrik McIlvarnoch his man, Duncan M^cinham McGregour, Duncan McAllester Vrek, Allester McEwin V^cCondochie, Johnne M^cean V^cGregour, Ewin M^ccondochie clerich, Johnne Ammonoche McGregour, Duncan Beg McGregour V^cCoull chere, Gregour McNicoll in Dalveich, Johnne Dow M^ccondochie V^cEwin.

Dilatit of certane crymes of Murthour, Thift, Soirning; and for being at the ffeild of Glenfrune, in companie with vmquhile Allaster of Glenstra, his kyn and freindis; and of the Slauchteris, ffyre raising, Reiff and Herschippis committit in the moneth of ffeb.

"1603 yeiris, aganis the Laird of Luse, his freindis and pairtakeris, viz.

"1. Johnne Dow McEwin McGregour,[1] for his intercommuning with umqle Allaster McGregour of Glenstra, vmqle Patrik Aulauch McGregour and utheris thair complices, quha war at the tressonabill burning of Robert Wattersones barne of Kallechoit, and at the steilling of the Laird of Merchinstounes oxin; committit in Sep. last. Item of airt and pairt of the thiftuous steilling, furth of Andro Allan's house in Kippine, of fyve ky; committit in Oct. last. Item for airt and pairt of the slauchter of vmqle Johnne Drummond in Drony of Cowgask; committit in Aug. last. Item for airt and pairt of the steilling of ane milk zow (ewe) fra Patrik McBoricht, furth of his duelling hous of Glenmawak: committit in Sep. last. And siclyk, of cowmone Thift and cowmon resett of thift.

"Patrik M^ckilvarnoch, servand to the said Johnne Dow, of airt and pairt of the haill crymes aboue writtin; as being in companie with his said maister thairat.

"2. Duncan M^cinham (M^cean cham) V^cGregour, ffor airt and pairt of the thiftuous steilling fra Eduard Reidoche of fyve horse and meiris; committit in the moneth of . . . . . Im Vc fourscoir and fourtene yeiris (1594). Item of airt and

[1] Second son of Ewin, Tutor of Glenstray.

pairt of the thiftuous steilling fra Allaster M^ccondochie Vic James Robiesone, in Callewin, of ten horsis and meiris; committit in the moneth of . . . yeiris.

" 3. Duncane McAllaster Vrek in Farne, ffor airt and pairt of the thiftious steilling furth of the Laird of Strowane's crandoche of his haill insichtworth Imlib. Item for the airt and pairt of the slauchter of vmqle Donald Dereiff. Item for the airt and pairt of the thiftious steilling furth of the landis of Downance in Menteith, of fourtie ky, tuelf horsis; committit 1588. And for intercowmoning with the Laird of McGregour; And for cowmone thift and cowmone resset of thift.

" 4. Ewin McCondochie Clerich. ffor his tressonabill intercowmoning with vmqle the Laird of McGregour, and geving him supplie and comforte.

" 5. Johnne Ammonache McGregour in Kingart, ffor airt and pairt of the thiftious steilling if sax scheip furth of Schandballie; committit aucht yeir syne or thairby. Item for cowmone Thift and cowmone resset of thift.

" 6. Allaster M^cewin V^ccondochie, in Couldar, ffor airt and pairt of the heirschip of the Downance in Menteith; and of the slauchteris then committit; and speciallie of the slauchter of vmple Andro Grahame.

" 7. Gregour McNeill alias Cownache, ffor airt and pairt of the crewall murthour and slachter of vmqle the ffidler M^ckillope, within his awin hous in Dalvey; committit at Andersmes, 1602. Item ffor the thiftious ressetting and tressonabill intercowmoning (of vmqle the Laird of McGregour?) efter he wes discharget be proclamatioun.

" 8. Johnne McKean V^cGregour, in Glenogill vnder Tawie barne, ffor the crewall murthour, slauchter and drowning of M^ckillopis wyfe that duelt in Glenartnay, being in company with vmqle Patrik Aulach committit in harvest last. Item for resset of the brokin men of the McGregouris, within his duelling-hous, and tressonabill intercowmoning with thame aganis his hienes Proclamatioune.

" 9. Duncan Beg McGregour V^cCoull Chere, ffor airt and pairt of the crewall Murthour and slauchter of sevin scoir persones slain at Glenfrwne; and heischip than committit thairin, in the moneth of Feb. 1603. Item for cowmone thift and ressett of thift; And for the tressonabill intercowmoning with vmqle the Laird of McGregour, eftir he was discharget be proclamatioune.

" ASSISA.

Mr Moreis Drummond of Culcherie,	Thomas Fallasdaill in Ardoche,
James Spreull ffiear of Cowden,	Dauid Muschet of Orcheardheid,
Colene Campbell of Aberuchill,	Johnne Buchannane of Ibert,
Mungo Lyndsay of Ballull,	Jacobi Edmestoun of Newtoun,
Robert Naper of Blakzairdis,	Johnne Naper of Kilmahew,
Mungo Buchannane in Tulliechewin,	Dauid Drummond in Drymen,
James Dennystoune of Cowgrane,	Johnne Muschet at the mylne of Tor,

Harrie Mitchell in Darra.

The Aduocat askit instrumentis of the sweiring of the Assyse; of Johnne Dowis Declaratioune, that Patrik M^cilvarnoch his man hes bene with him this tua yeir bygane, and is pairtaker of all his factis The Aduocat, for verifeing the poyntis of Dittay, producet the Kingis Proclamatioune, Actis of Secreit Counsall, contenit in the buik of Secreit Counsall produceit, and askit instrumentis thairvpoune, And protestit for wilfull Errour aganis the Assyse in caise thai acquit.

"Verdict The Assysis, be the mouth of Dauit Drummond, chancellor ffand pronunceit, and declairit the siadis persones to be fylet, culpable and convict of the perticular poyntis of Dittay aboue written

"Sentence. The Justice-depute decernit and adjuget the said John Dow (McEwin) &a to be tane to the mercait-croce of Edinburgh, and thair to be hangit vpoun ane gibbet quhill thai be deid, and all thir moveabill guidis to be escheit and inbrocht to our souerane's Lordis vse, as convict of the saidis crymes.

"Footnote 'The 18 of Feb 1604 9 of the name of MacGregor hangit quho had lain lang in the Tolbuith '—Birrel

"Field of Glenfrune—Slaughter of the Colquhouns &a.

"1604 March 1. Neill McGregour in Meirie (Mewie)[1] Patrik Gair McGregour,[2] Donald Roy McGregour, Duncane McGregour, Donald Graffiche[3] McCadanich.

"Dilatit, accusit and persewit for being in company with vmqle Allaster McGregour of Glenstra and his complices, at the ffield of Glenfrwne, and of airt and pairt of the slauchter of sevin scoir persones, being all freindis, servandis assisteris and pairtackeris with the Laird of luse at the said ffield, and of the heirsch-ippis thair committit be the said Laird of McGregour and his complices, And of the tressonabill raising of fyre and burning of dyuerse houssis, within the boundis foirsaid, committit in the moneth of Feb 1603 And siclyk,[1] for intercowmoning with the said Laird of McGregour and personis foirsaidis, his complices, that war at the said slaughter and heirschip, sen the committing thairof. And als, the said Patrik Gair McGregour being indyttit and accuset for the hounding out of his thre sones to the said ffeild, and murthouris and slauchters than committit vpone the said Laird of Lussis freindis, And of Airt and pairt, red, counsall, foirknawledge assistance and ratihabitioune of the said murthouris and heirschippis; And siclyke, for the ressett and intercowmoning with the Laird of McGregour and his complices that war at Glenfrune, and resetting of thame with the bludie hand, sen the tyme foirsaid of the said heirschip and slauchteris.

---

[1] Duneira.   [2] Of the Roro family   [3] Grassaiche.

"ASSISA

Mungo Lyndsay of Ballull,	Thomas Naper of Barnekynrayne
Johnne Buchannane burges of Dumbarten,	Johnne Naper of Kilmahew,
George Buchannane in Ladrische	Johnne Sempill of Foulword
Thomas Fallasdaille burgess of Dumbarton,	Robert Buchannane in Kippen
Constene Moirtoun,	Robert Buchannane Waltersoune
Hew Glen of Lynthillis,	Dougall Mᶜfarlane in Murnagane
Johnne Buntene of Ardoche,	Walter Blair of Fynnech

Dauid Hadden (Haldene) Tutour of Glennageis.

"Verdict   The said Assye, all in ane voce, be the mouth of the said Robert Buchananne Waltersoune, ffand, pronuncet and declairit the saidis fyve persones to be ffylet, culpable and convict of the haill crymes aboue specifeit.

"Sentence And thairfoir, the Justice-depute, be the mouth of Robert Scott, dempster of Court, decernit and ordanit the saidis persones to be tane to the gallouse of the Burrow-mure of Edinburghe, and thairupone to be hangit quhill they be deid, and thair haill moveable guidis to be escheit and inbrocht to his hienes vse, as convict of the saidis crymes.

"Theft—Resett of Laird of MacGregor—Field of Glenfrune, &a

"1604.   March 2   Malcolme MᶜCoull clench (Chere, i e Ciar)[1] in Innerlochlarg, Duncan Mᶜfadrik VᶜCoull Chere,[2] in Innerlochlarg, vnder the Laird of Tullibardin, Johnne MᶜCoull Chere, in the Bray of Balquhidder, and Neill MᶜWilliame VᶜNeill

"Dilaitit of certane poyntis of Thift, and for intercowmoning with vmqle the Laird of MᶜGregour, sen the Raid of Glenfrune, viz

"1   Malcolme MᶜCoull Cleriche (Chere) ffor airt and pairt, and being on the grundis at the crewall Slauchter of vqle Hew Stewart serveand to my Lord of Atholle, committit threttie yeir syne or thairby.   Item for Airt and pairt of the slauchter of vqle Patrik MᶜGregour in Glenbokie; committit in the moneth of Sep. 1596.   Item for geving of counsall to vqle the Laird of Makgregour, his kyn and freindis, to pas fordward aganis the Laird of Luse to Glenfrune and for convoying the said Laird of MᶜGregour agaitward (on the way or gait) to the syd of Lochloun. afoir the ffeild, And for airt and pairt of the slauchteris and heirschippis committit at Glenfrune be the said Laird of MᶜGregour and his complices, in the moneth of Feb 1603   Item, for the tressonabill Intercowmoning with the said Laird of MᶜGregour, and Ressett of him and his freindis and pairtakeris that war at the ffield of Glenfrune, and geving of thame herbrie, help and supplie, in meit, drink, and bedding, wittinglie and willinglie, at dyuerse tymes, sen thai war denuncet our

[1] Second son of Malcolm chieftain of his tribe, and ancestor of Innerardaran.
[2] Son of Patrick Roy MᶜCoull Ciar in Strathyre

souerane lordis rebellis and declairit tratouris, and sen his Majesties Proclamatioune, inhibeiting all our souerane lordis leigis to intercowmone, ressett or gif
countenance or schaw fauour to the saidis rebellis.

"2. Duncan M^cfadrik V^cCoull cheir, ffor airt and pairt of the slauchter of the said
Patrik McGregour; committit in Sep. 1576. Item for geving of counsall to the
Laird of MacGregour to pas fordward to the ffeild of Glenfrune aganis the Laird of
Luse and convoying him to the syde of Lochloune, agaitward, to the said ffeild.
Item for wilfull Intercowmoning and geving of counsall to the Laird of McGregoure,
and convening with him at dyuerse meittingis and conventiounes, had and keipit be
him and his freindis, sen thai war denuncet his Maiesteis rebellis, for the murthour,
slauchteris and heirschipis committit be thame at the said ffeild of Glenfrune,
incontrair to his Majesties proclamatioune.

"3. Neill McWilhame V^cNeill, ffor the tressonabill Intercowmoning with the
Laird of McGregour, his kin and freindis that war at the murthour and heirschipis
in Glenfrune, and ressett of thame within his hous, and geving meit and drink to
thame wittinglie and willinglie at dyuerse tymes sen thai war denuncet rebellis, &a.

"4. And siclyk, Johnne McCoull Cheire, ffor airt and pairt of the crewall
Murthour and Burning of auchtene houshalderis of the Clanlawren, their wyves and
bairnis; committit fourtie sax yeir syne or thairby, Item off airt and pairt of the
Slauchter of vqle Hew Stewart, servand to my Lord of Athole, committit threttie
yeir syne or thairby,[1] And in taking pairt with the ClanGregouris at the heirschip,
committit the tyme foirsaid aganis the Tutour of Bofrak. Item for Intercowmoning
with the Laird of McGregour and his complices that war at the ffeild of Glenfrune,
sen thair denunciatioune; and geving of conforte, supplie and freindschip to thame,
contrair the tennour of the Proclamatioune Item, for cowmone Thift, cowmone
ressett of thift, outputing and inputing of thift fra land to land, fra cuntrey (to
cuntrey), baith of auld and new.

"Verdict The Assyse, be the mouth of Mungo Lynsay of Ballull, chancellor,
ffand, pronuncet and declarit the saidis Malcolme, Duncan and Neill to be fyllit,
culpable and convict of the haill crymes and poyntis of Dittay aboue writtin; And
the said Johnne McCoull Cheire to be clenc, innocent and acquit of the saidis
crymes

"Sentence. And thairfoir the said Justice-depute, be the mouth of Robert
Scott, dempstar of Court, decernit and ordaint the saidis Malcolme McCoull and
Duncane McFadrik to be tane to the gibbet at the mercat croce of Edinburghe,
and thair to be hangit quhill thay be deid, and all thair moveabill guidis to be
escheit and inbrocht to his Maiesteis vse, as convict of the said crymes."

From the "Black Book of Taymouth":—

"Item the said Sir Duncane (died 1631) in *anno* 1603 and 1604. hade great

[1] Of which he was acquitted. See Chapter xii. He was brother of Malcolm McCoull

wearis with the Clangregoris at quhat tyme thay brunt to him the barronie of Monzie, the barronie of Cowledair and Tinnaiff, the tuelf pund land of Achalladar, the skaith quhairof extendit to ane hundreth thowsand markis; for the quhilkis hanous and intollerabill factis eightene of the principallis of the Clangregour wer tane to Edinburghe, and ther wer hangit and quarterit; quhais names eftir followis—

> Alester Roy McGregour of Glenschray (quho wes hung on ane pyn about
>   ane eln heichar nor the rest),
> Gregor McEwin V^cGregour in Moirinche,*
> Johne Dow McEwin his brother (tried on 17th Feb),
> Duncane McAllester Pudriche in Achatue,
> William oig McNeill in Fernay,
> Duncane V^cAllester in Fernay,*
> Duncane McGregour V^cNeille in Ardewnak,*
> Gregour McGregour V^cCondochie in Roro,*
> Allester McOndochie V^cCleriche in Glengowlendie,*
> Allester McEwin V^cCondochie in Critgarrow (tried 17th Feb).
> Malcolme McCoulgeir in Balquhidder (tried 2nd March),
> Duncane McGillepatrik V^cCoulgeir thair (tried 2nd March),
> Johne McCane V^cGregour in Glenogill (tried 17th Feb.),
> Patrick Allachie McGregor in Corriechrankie,
> Allester McGregor V^cCane in Braiklie,
> Gregor McNicoll in Ardbeiche (tried 17th Feb),
> Malcolm Oig V^cOlchallume Oig V^cDulcheir in Balquhidder,*
> Patrik McPatrik Ammonache in Glenleidnek (tried on 17th Feb)

Besydis thir foirsaidis that wer hangit at the mercat cros of Edinburghe, thair wes sundrie otheris hangit thair and in other places, quhais names wes superfluous to wrett."

The names marked with a * do not appear in the trials recorded in the previous pages, and may have been executed without trial Several names appear later than the 20th January, and, therefore, they could not be those executed the same day as Glenstray.

LIST OF MACGREGORS EXECUTED EARLY IN 1604, ACCORDING
TO PRECEDING PAGES.

1604.   January 20—Five persons executed.

ALLASTER ROY MACGREGOR OF GLENSTRAY, seventh of his line,
Captain and Chief of the ClanGregor.

PATRICK ALDOCH (AOLADH) MACGREGOR, in Corriechrambie,
younger brother of Duncan Abroch and grandson of Duncan
Laddosach.

WILLIAM (OIG) MᶜNEILL his servant, in Fernan, Loch Tay, son of
No. 52.[1]

DUNCAN PUDRACHE MᶜGREGOUR, in Achtoo, Balquhidder, son
of No. 4.

ALLASTER MACGREGOR MᶜKEAN (MᶜANE), younger son of Gregor
MacGregor of Brackly.   He was second cousin of Patrick
Aoladh.[2]

1604.   February 18—Eleven persons executed.

JOHN DOW MᶜEWIN, second son of Ewin MacGregor, Tutor of
Glenstray, No. 2.

DUNCAN MᶜEAN CHAM VᶜGREGOUR, Tutor of Roro.

DUNCAN VᶜALLASTER VREK, in Fernan, No. 55.

EWIN MᶜCONDOCHIE CLERICH, in Glengowlendie, probably son
of No. 39

JOHN AMMONACHE, in Kingart, probably son of Patrick Ammonach.

ALLASTER MᶜEWIN VᶜCONDOCHIE, in Couldar (or in Critgarrows),
probably No. 43.

GREGOUR MᶜNEILL ALIAS COWNACHE, probably No. 81.

JOHN MᶜKEAN (MᶜANE) MACGREGOR, in Glen Ogle.

[1] The numbers refer to List of 1586, Chapter xvi.

[2] There appear to have been more MacGregors executed at the same time as Glenstray, but
without trial.   The "Black Book of Taymouth" mentions some names not tried till later, and
other names which do not appear on the Trials.

DUNCAN BEG M^cGREGOR V^cCOULL CHERE.
ALLESTER M^cEWIN V^cCONDOCHIE, No. 43.
JOHN DOW M^cCONDOCHIE V^cEWIN, probably No. 71.[1]

1604.   March 1—Five persons executed.

NEILL MACGREGOR, in Mewie (Duneira).
Patrick Gair MacGregor.
Donald Roy MacGregor.
Duncan MacGregor.
Donald Grassaiche McCadanach.

1604.   March 2—Four persons executed.

Malcolm McCoull Clerich (Chere), in Innerlochlarig, No. 29.
Duncan M^cfadrich McCoul Chere, in Innerlochlarig, under the
    Laird of Tullibardine.
John McCoull Chere, in the Brae of Balquhidder.
Neill McWilliam V^cNeill, son or brother of No. 52.

---

[1] Eleven MacGregors are stated to have been entered and all condemned to death, see page 338.
Birrel only mentions nine executed on the 18th Feb , page 325

Chapter XXVII

Genealogical

ATTENTION must now again be turned to the Genealogy. The narrative in the "Baronage" at the period after the executions consequent on Glenfruin falls into a very regretable error, asserting that the immediate successor of Glenstray was his illegitimate son. No such person appears in the "Records," and Ian dhu nan Lurach, Glenstray's brother, left three lawful sons, of whom Gregor, the eldest, eventually succeeded as *de facto* Chief. The source of this serious mistake cannot now be discovered, but the circumstances giving rise to it must have been very credibly related, before Sir John MacGregor Murray could have adopted such a statement.

For the better refutation of the error, the words of the "Baronage" are here quoted :—

"Alexander Laird of MacGregor . . . . . leaving no lawful issue and his brother John being killed at Glenfruin unmarried,[1] the succession of this most ancient family jure sanguinis, most undoubtedly devolved upon Gregor, heir male in a direct line of John Laird of Macgregor No. 12. of these memoirs of whom afterwards. Soon after Alexander's death there was a meeting in the old church of Strathfillan, where in Gregor's absence the tribe called ' Sliochd dhiul chier ' set up a Chief of their own in usurpation of his right ; of which Gregor who was a very fine darling fellow having intelligence ; hastened to the meeting and carried with him Gregor, a natural son of the last laird, a man of martial fire who had been bred in his family and was married to his (Gregor's) only daughter. Upon entering the Church he found the new elected Chief placed in a chair resembling a throne, above the rest ; to him he immediately made up and throwing him under his feet, placed his son-in-law in the chair without any person daring to oppose, and he was thereafter acknowledged Chief by the whole Clan except by his brothers-in-law when they came of age."

As most Highland traditions are founded on fact, it is probable that

[1] This is an error—see next page.

such a scene may have taken place; although it does not match the ascertained circumstances at this time; the period, the actors, and even the alleged cause, may all have been different, and no one is likely now to be able to cast any light upon it [1]

John dhu nan Lurag, or " Black John of the Mail-coat," mentioned in the list of the chief houses of the Clan as " Johnne dhu McGregor, brother to the Laird McGregour," was a leading man in every fray   It is stated in the complaint made by Dalguise, 1602 (page 275), that " The said Johnne McGregour being in his own cradak in a rowme that he haldis of the Laird of Tullibardine," &a   This was the house or castle of Innis Gregor at the eastern end of Loch Voil, said to have been fortified on the land side by a fosse and drawbridge, and on the other three sides washed by the lake   The following account is from a memorandum taken down from the words of John Fergusson, a native of Stronvar, aged 60, in 1817, by the Rev. Alexander MacGregor, minister of Balquhidder, in reply to questions written out by Sir John MacGregor Murray :—

"Innis MhicGhrioghair on Loch Voil also called ' Geata 'n tuim bhain ' belonged to John Dhu MacGregor who chased the Colquhouns at Glenfruin   There was a space between the island and the shore in the end of last century about six yards wide which space was filled up in 1762   It is said that a drawbridge connected the island with the mainland and the pillars of it could still be seen the end of the 18th century.   John Fergusson ' remembers to have seen an old building there composed of lime and stone, and as it were a gentleman's House and place of defence.'   It was 14 feet broad 60 feet in length within walls.   He thinks the walls were 3 feet thick, he does not recollect how high the building was   He did not see any vault or arched room in it   The stones were afterwards used in filling up the intervening space between the island and the shore and in 1817 some were taken to surround the Innis with a dyke " [2]

At the conflict of Glenfruin John dhu was "killed by an arrow aimed by a stripling named McLintock, who succeeded in hitting him through the neck joint of his mail."

[1] John Dhu's sons being young at the time of his brother's decease, some confusion may then have arisen   In the " Black Book of Taymouth " it is stated that Allaster Roy "left no children bot ane dochter "   This daughter may have been concerned in the dispute

[2] In corroboration of the tradition of Innis Gregor it is stated that John dubh occupied the 2½ merkland of Mekill Stronvar (exactly opposite this island on Loch Voil) as also the five merkland of Glenbaich (on Loch Earn side).—See Chapter xxi. 1598, Oct 21.

The following lines are from an old memorandum amongst the Edinchip papers :—

" By MacGregor's Bard at ye Battle of Glenfroon on seeing Lindsay of Bosville fall on the side of the Colquhouns.

> " Tierna bhun olla, 'scris olla mi chlai
> B'chiar dun toll a hoana
> 'm foll moana na lai."

" By Colquhoun's Bard on seeing John, brother of the Laird of MacGregor fall by the hands of McLintoch.

> " Stappi hug u'n tante orst bhic an Landarig og
> Thug Ian duh nan Lurich lot,
> mac ur bhic Gregoir voir."

The spelling of the above is not very intelligible, but the correct reading is conjectured to be as follows :—

> " Tighearna Bhunolla,
> 'Cris olla mi chliaheamh
> Bu chiar dubh fuil a' choin
> Am poll-moine na laidh."

> " 's tapaidh thug thu'n tionndadh ort,
> Mhic an Leanndaig oig
> Thuit Iain dubh nan Luireach,
> Mac ur Mhic Ghriogair mhoir."

which may be thus translated :—

> " Lord of Bunolla
> And a woollen belt about his sword,
> Dark was the black blood of a dog,
> In a peat hag lying."

> " Quickly you gave a turn
> Young McLintoch
> You gave a wound to Black John of the coat of mail
> The fresh son of MacGregor."

John dhu MacGregor, according to the " Black Book of Taymouth," married a daughter of John Murray of Strowan, by whom he left three sons.

1. Gregor, who appears to have been in the custody of Sir John Murray of Tullibardin after his father's death, and on whom devolved the succession to his uncle Allaster of Glenstray.

2. Patrick, of whom the Laird of Grant had charge.

3. Ewin, for whom John Murray of Strowan, his maternal grandfather, was answerable.[1]

The death of Glenstray did not suffice to appease the wrath of those who desired the extermination of the ClanGregor. The "Baronage" gives a fair abstract of the general condition of affairs in the time of the above Gregor

"This Clan continued to be cruelly harassed through means of Argyle the Earl of Montrose chancellor,   and of George Buchanan,[2] Lord Privy Seal, who had much of the king's ear, and bore an ill will towards the MacGregors.

"To such a height of ferocity were matters carried, that a price being set upon the heads of the Clan by the Privy Council two of their enemies who had shared considerably of their estates, got blood hounds with which they hunted them, devouring and mangling them wherever they were found.

"But not only Glenurchy and the rest of that name employed themselves in this persecution, but all the Lords and Chiefs from the west to the north seas were enjoined to assist them ; so that it would have been impossible for one of them to escape had all their neighbours been spirited with the same zeal with those who had private views to their estates and possessions."

Alan, Chief of the Camerons, being then under a state of outlawry and prescription for joining the Marquis of Huntly against the

"earl of Murray his estate became a prey to the neighbouring chiefs Argyle had made "himself master of the twenty pound land of Lochiel which Alan endeavoured to "recover the conditions were submitted to his Majesty, and Clanranald employed to "negotiate for Alan but the King would not hearken to any proposals of being "reconciled to Lochiel, unless he would enter into an indenture with the Earl of "Argyle his lieutenant, and the Earl of Dunbar, Lord High Treasurer for extir-"pating the MacGregors, to which Alan having accordingly agreed his Majesty "was so well pleased with his compliance, that he wrote him a letter with his own "hand, in which after mentioning the conditions and ratifying the indenture "against the MacGregors, he orders him faithfully and diligently to prosecute the "same, until the final end thereof, in such form as you shall receive directions from "the Earl of Argyll our Lieutenant.

"Pursuant to which there happened a fierce battle in the braes of Lochaber "between a body of the Camerons and Macdonalds, and the MacGregors seconded "by their allies, the Macphersons, in which the former were totally routed with

---

[1] See supra.

[2] John Buchannan, Baron of Bucklyvie, was killed at Glenfruin.

" considerable loss. And though Locheil and the other chiefs who had been in
" perpetual friendship with the MacGregors, soon penetrated into the interested
" designs of their principal enemies, and instead of distressing, protected them
" from their violence, yet so keen and powerful were the conductors of their de-
" struction, that a very severe act was made against them in the succeeding reign,
" upon a narrative of the diction of those in possession of almost all their estates,
" whereby their name was proscribed, and all persons at liberty to mutilate or slay
" them, without being liable to law therefor nay encouraged to it by promise of
" their 'moveables, goods, and gear.'

" This barbarous law which is on record, made no distinction of age or sex, or
" character; five of their principal enemies, who had been raised upon their ruin,
" were for form's sake appointed their judges while all persons were encouraged at
" short hand, to murder the MacGregors, whether greyhaired sires of many years,
" or the little babes who knew not how to offend; whether women or children;
" whether priests or laymen; whether rich or poor; whether innocent or guilty
" and all this says the Act 'for the timeous preventing the disorder and oppressions
" that may fall out by the said name and Clan of MacGregor and their followers.'

" In this situation the MacGregors continued till the solemn league and cove-
" nant came into play, which as their principal enemies were deeply interested in,
" afforded them some respite. They were much courted to join the confederacy,
" upon promises of future friendship but as rebellion against Majesty had ever been
" detestable to them and as they believed that the present purposes once served
" the future friendship of the foederati would at best be lukewarm they declared
" 'That as they bore the crown upon the point of their swords, they could not fail
" to use the latter in support of the former.'"

1604. April. It appears from a subsequent trial in the Court of
Justiciary seven years later that it was in this month a skirmish took place
in which Duncan Abroch lost his life. The following account of the
occurrence is from the " Black Book of Taymouth " :—

" Attoure Robert Campbell second son of the said Sir Duncan (Campbell of
Glenurchy), persewing ane great number of thame throch the countrie, in end over-
tuk thame at Benetoeg[1] in the Brae of Glenurquhay, quhair he slew Duncane
Abroch McGregour with his sone Gregore in Ardchyllie, Dougall McGregour
McCoulcheir in Glengyle with his son Duncane, Charlis McGregour V^cEane in
Braiklie quha wer principallis in that band, with tuentie otheris of thair complissis
slain in the chais."

In the subsequent Record of Assize, given fully in 1611, it is noted
that certain MacGregors were present

[1] A hill (2712 ft.) two miles N.-W. of Loch Tulla, Glenorchy, Argyleshire.

" At the fecht or skirmische of Bintoiche in ye moneth of Apryle 1604, and Dougall M᷎cGregour Clerache M᷎cGregour " was accused " for ye crewall slaughter of umqle Gregour sone to umqle Duncane Abroche M᷎cGregour be schuteing of him with ane arrow behind his back committit in August 1604."

In Sir Robert Gordon's history of the Earldom of Sutherland, quoted previously for his account of the conflict of Glenfruin, the following notice of the fight at Bintoig (or Ranefroy) appears :—

" The King caused proclaim them (the MacGregors) rebells, directed commission and lettres of intercommuning against them forbidding any of his lieges to harbor them. At last he employed the Earle of Argyle and the Campbells, who pursued them divers times ; and at Bintoig wher Robert Campbell (The Laird of Glenurquhie his sone) accompanied with some of the ClanChameron, Clanab, and Clanronald to the number of two hundred chosen men fought against thriescore (about one third the number of their opponents) of the ClanGregor in which conflict tuo of the ClanGregor were slain, to wit Duncan Aberigh (one of the chieftanes) and his son Duncan.[1] Seaven gentlemen of the Campbell syd wer killed, though they seemed to have the victorie. So after much slaughter, many skirmishes and divers slights used against the Clangregor in end they subdued them by the death of many of them and their followers and no lesse if not far greater slaughter of the Campbells."

From the " Chartulary " :—

" Duncan Abroche of Ardchoille [2] grandson of Duncan Ladosach had fled to Lochaber after the deaths of his father and Grandfather in 1552 he gave a Bond 1576, he is not named in the list of persons denounced after the death of Drummondcarnach (Feb. 4 1589), but his name appears Feb. 1 1592, as living at Corriechairmich part of the lands included in those of Ardchoille, and he was one of sixteen principal persons of the ClanGregor cited to appear personally before the Council at Stirling ; again he and his brother Patrick are mentioned as ' Duncan Abroch and Patrick Aldoch M᷎cGregors ' proposed parties in a bond by Allaster M᷎cGregor of Glenstray to the Earl of Argyll as King's Lieutenant in the bounds of the ClanGregor 22. April 1601. and are stated, as about to be bound ' for themselffis and all descending or to descend of umqle Duncan Latois thair predecessor.'

---

[1] In the previous account of the skirmish of Bentoig from the " Black Book of Taymouth," the name of the son of Duncan Abberach, slain with him, is mentioned as Gregor, and in the subsequent trial of a person for shooting a son of Duncan's in the back, the name is also given as that of Gregor, but as the month of August is there mentioned, it is possible that one son perished at Bintoig and another a few months later by the shooting of an arrow. Duncan had a son by his first wife whose name is not mentioned in the " Baronage," and who died young, but his other sons must have been of mature age in 1604, as Robert had a command at Glenfruin.   [2] See page 168.

This bond however they did not sign. Patrick Aldóch perished with Glenstray, Jan. 1604."[1]

Returning to the "Baronage," mention has been already made[2] of Robert, 2nd son of Duncan Abberach XVII., a man of a rare martial genius. He laid the plan of attacking the Colquhouns in battle. The command of a division was given to Robert, to whose gallant conduct much of the success of that victorious though unlucky day is attributed, and his sword is actually preserved to this day.[3] His subsequent career is very interesting as it appears in the notices in State Records. Eventually, after a final submission in 1624, he was released from prison, August 1626, and delivered to Sir Donald McKy, Knight, to serve in the wars abroad under the charge of Count Mansfield, after which time nothing more is known of "Robin Abroch."

From the "Chartulary":—

"1604. Feb. 10. Ane (royall) Lre : maid to James Murray[4] fear of Strowane his aires and assignaries of the gift of the eschete of all guidis geir &a ; quhilkis pertenit of before to vmqle : Johnne Dow M^cgregour broyer germane to vmqle : Alester M^cgregour of Glenstrae the tyme of his deceis. And now pertening to our Soverane Lord—thrw being of the said vmqle, Johnne Dow M^cgregour ordourly denuncit rebell—for not finding cautioun and souirtie of his Mr and landlordis gif he ony had that war sufficient. And for failżing yairof vyer responsall personis that ha and all sic personis yat ar oblist to ansuer for be ye lawis of yis realme, actis of Parliament, and general Band sould keip his Maj, peax, gude reul and quyetnes And sould not invaid, truble, oppres, nor persew his hienes subiectis in yair persones, landis, &a.—Register of the Privy Seal.

"In this month messengers were sent with 'Letters from the Council' to the 'Erle of Argyle and Laird of Glenurquhay' also to persons in the Stewartrie of Stratherne and erldome of Athole to compeir befoir oure Souerane Lord Justice and his deputiis in the tolbuith of Edinburgh the 17. day of Feb. instant to pas upoun

---

[1] It is a significant fact in confirmation of the claim of the MacIan Family to the seniority that the War Cry should be taken from their possession Ardchoille.—Chartulary.

[2] Chapter xvi., page 168.

[3] This sword is in the possession of Sir Malcolm MacGregor of MacGregor having been handed down with the utmost care. It is mentioned in a letter from Colonel Evan Macgregor Murray (Sir John MacGregor Murray's father) as "Old Duncan Ladosach." The tradition is that it was borne at Glenfruin, when it appears to have been used by Robert Abroch, and a letter from Duncan MacGregor of MacGregor to his nephew, implies that "Duncan Abberigh" was not himself in action at Glenfruin.

[4] Brother of John Dhu MacGregor's wife. See page 333.

2 U

the assyes of certane of the M^{c}gregour. also to persons within the Stewartrie of Monteith and ye bounds of Lennox accordingly.

" 1604. Feb. 17. In the Court of Justiciary of our Supreme Lord the King, held in the Judgement Hall of Edinburgh 17 Feb. 1504. by Mr William Hairt of Adielands (misnomer for Levilands).—Justiciary Depute."

Entered 11 MacGregors who were all condemned to death. See Chapter xxvi., pages 323 and 329.

" 1604. March. A payment made by command of the Secreit Counsall for the apprehension and 'presenting befoir yame of Dowle Oig McGregor quha yairefter was execute to ye deid.'—Treasurer's Books.

"Item to Robert Elder messenger passing from Edinburgh and with Letters to charge the said McIntosche (viz. Lauchlane McIntosche of Dunnachtan) to exhibit before the said Lords of Secret Counsel the day foresid (10. April) of certane McGregors quha ar reteirit with their wifes, bairns, and guids to rest within his bounds and likewise to exhibit certain others of his own broken men to underlie such order as shall be prescribed to them at their coming under the pain of rebellion.—Treasurer's Books.

" 1604. April 17. Heiring the treacherie of ye tyrranus persones of ye name of Clangregor and fyreing of the toun (of Dumbarton) be yame Thairfore it is statut and ordanet yt the town be devydit in aught pairts and ilk aucht pt to vacht ane nycht The vaches to be arranit and placeit nytly by ye quartare Mrs chosen be the Baillies And quha keeps nocht vache according to ye Baillies ordinance to wit giff he be at hame himself And in his absence ane sufficient man, to pay fourties. for his diisbedience and the saym to be payit to the vacheis And yt the Baillies chies aucht quartare masters. Item yt na dwellers in this town ressave ony strangers puir or rich wiout making the Baillies forsein under the paine of fourties the two pts to the town the third to the Baillies.

" 1604. April. Letters charging Alex. Colquhoun of Luss, Buchanane of that ilk Aulay McAulay of Ardincaple, Robert Galbraith of Culcreuch   Sempill of Foulwode, The Laird of McFarlane and Andrew Dow McFarlane of Gartavertane and all others barons and landed gentlemen within the bounds of Lennox to convene and meet within the burgh of Dunbarten and agree upon the setting out of their watches and the form and manner of their entertainment and to set out the said watches betwix   and the sixth day of April instant under the pain of Rebellion. —Treasurer's Books.

" Item to   messenger passing from Edinburgh with letters to be proclaimed at the market crosses of Stirling, Dunbartane, Perth, and Stewartries of Stratherne, and Menteith charging all our Sovereign Lords Lieges within the said bounds to raise the shout and fray upon the MacGregors whenever they happen to repair within their bounds And to rise, hunt, follow and pursue them forbearing to grant them any support under the pain to be repute pairt takers with them And with letters.

"1604. June. Item to David Lindsay keiper of the Tolbooth of Edinburgh at the commandment of the Lords of Council for entertaining of eleven pledges of the McGregors from the 10, day of May to the 1, day of July to the space of fiftyone days every one of them having in the day 13 shillings and 4 pence of allowance Inde £374.—Treasurer's Books.

"1604. July 13. The Baillies and Council of Dunbretan 'concludit and ordanit that the Laird of MacGregor's heid wy Patrik Aulddy his heid be put up in the Tolbuith on the maist convenient place the Baillies and Council thinks gud.'"

Strange custom of the times, when men were so familiar with bloodshed and its ghastly emblems, these gentle citizens probably thought themselves less barbarous than Glenstra when driven to take upon him "MacAlpin's" fearful vow.

"1604. August 3 at Perth. Alexander Buchannane [1] in Strathyre, Robert M^ccoll, Johne Malcolme, and Patrik Buchannane, his sons, That whereas according to our Acts of Parliament made against the Clangregour anent the changing of their names The said complainers have presented themselves. Renounced their former names of MacGregor and have found sufficient and responsible cautionrie &a.—Hornings of Perth, General Register House, Edinburgh.

"August 31. Act anent the benefit for taking of MacGregors extended in favour of Camstradden.

"Anent the Supplication presented to the Lords of Secret Council by John Colquhoun [2] fear of Cumstrodden making mention that whereas eftir the horrible and detestable murther committed be the wicked and unhappy Clangregor upon his Majesties good subjects of the Lennox His Highness and Lords of his Secret Council resolved altogether to extirpate and root out that infamous race and for the better effectuating thereof Acts and Proclamations were published promising a free pardon and remission to whatsomever person or persons who should take, slay, or present to Justice ane of the said Limmers As in the said Acts published over all parts of this Kingdom at more length is contained And considering thereby the sincerity of his Majesties haste to have these infamous limmers punished, and

---

[1] See No. 85, List of 1586, Allaster McRobert (Moir) MacGregor in Strathyre, and his sons.

[2] Although Cumstrodden captured two MacGregors, and claimed a reward for the same, few of the Colquhouns kept up the enmity, which shews that the quarrel could only have been of recent origin, and Sir John MacGregor Murray makes the following remarks in private MS.:—"To the honour of the family of Colquhoun it may be said that, far from participating in or countenancing the subsequent oppressions of the MacGregors, carried on by interested neighbours, the Colquhouns naturally did not possess themselves of any of their lands, but actually protected many of the Clan, and some of the most respectable tenants on the Estate of Colquhoun at this day are MacGregors under the name of Colquhoun, assumed for protection and retained from gratitude."

being moved therewithall to give his Majesty proof of his affection to his Majesty's service in that errand the said complainer to the great peril and hazard of his life resolved to pursue them with his whole force and after many skirmishes and onsets had at sundry times with diverss of them at last he made an onsett on umquhill Gregor Cragniche McGregor,[1] Duncane M^{c}ilchallum [2] and certain others of the most common and notorious thieves of all that name. And after a long and dangerous conflict had with them with the loss of the blood of certain of the complainers' servants he apprehended them, committed them toward, within the which the said Duncane barbarously stabbed himself whose head with the said Gregor Cragniche he presented to the said Lords of Secret Council at Stirling who was executed to the deid as he worthily merited, and seeing in this particular the said Complainer for a testimony of his affection to do his Majesty's service has hazarded his life and presented the said persons as said is, the benefit of the said Act ought to be extended to him and in his favours Humbly desiring therefore that he might have an act of council past and expede in his favour in manner and to the effect following &a.—Haddington's MS. Collections in Advocate's Library, Edinburgh.

"August 29. Andro Ramsay at the milne of Innerqueich against Argyle to present Allaster McAllaster McGregor and Johne McEwin McGregor for theft.— Register of Hornings."

In the Comptroller's account for the year is the following entry :—

"Item for the wagis of certain horse hyrit to carry XVI of the McGregouris fra Linlithquew to Edinburgh within the tyme of this compt."

"Letter from the King to the Earl of Montrose 1604 Oct : 3.

"To our right trustie and wellbelouit counsellour the erle of Montroiss chancellour and remanent erlis lordis and vther of our counsale of estait in the kingdome of Scotland.

"Marginal title ' Makgregouris, Erle of Argyle's rewarde.'

"(Dated) From our honour of Hamptonn the thrid of October 1604.

"As for the McGregours we signified our pleasure that the Earl of Argyle should either prosecute the service according to the first condition, Like as we are willing that he should be assured of the reward appointed, or else that he should put matters under assurance till Martinmas, betwix and which time by advice of the Commissioners and such others of the Council as are here we shall certify our mind concerning the said Earl's last petition, we would be glad that he should end the service and enjoy his reward for so is his meaning, that freely and honourably he should have it, but if we be frustrated and the country wrackit, we will be compelled to deal otherwise with him than we should wish his behaviour should procure."

---

[1] No. 40, List of 1586.　　　　　　　[2] Probably No. 50.

This letter from the King to the Scottish Council in Record of Council was copied into the Earl of Haddington's Collections.

"1604. Oct. 29. Horning Apud Perth, Pursuers, Tenants of Sir David Lindsay of Edzell. against Findlay McLauchlan V^cComes in . . . . . Ewin Dow McCondoquhie in Camescherachlie, Allaster McEan Dowie Rannoche, Donald McInnesche McInroy in Glentrone (Glentrumie) in Badzenoch Makgillipatrik M^cinneshin Crathly (Crathie) in Rannoche Johnne Tarlachsoun McLauchlan, servitor to James Glass & John McAllaster Gregour servitor to Duncan McGregour . . . . Johne McLauchlan McComes tenant to the said James Glass McFindlay McRobert tenant to the Laird of Grant Johne McCondochie Toundowie in Rannoche all ' brokin heilland men' for theft."—Register of Hornings for the shire of Perth.

It may here be mentioned that a tradition exists that Stewart, Earl of Londonderry, is descended from the ClanGregor. Sir John MacGregor Murray remarks :—

" MacGregor of Ardnaconnell is said not to have been in the Battle (Glenfruin), but he found it difficult to maintain his estate in peace, and being in the habit of intimate friendship with his neighbour, MacAulay of MacAulay, who had an estate in Ireland called Bally Law, he exchanged it with MacGregor of Ardnaconnell, who went to Ireland, where he assumed the name of Stewart, and the belief in the country is that he was the ancestor of the family of Londonderry."

The well-known and beautiful song, " MacGregor of Roro," is said to have been composed about this time, and is here given from " The Killin Collection of Gaelic Songs," by (late) Charles Stewart, Tigh 'n Duin, Killin.

After the fight at Glenfruin, when the Chief and fifteen of the principal men of the Clan were executed, amongst the number was " Gregour MacGregour McIndochie in Roro." " On the sad news reaching Glenlyon this lament was composed, but by whom is not known."

MacGriogair 'o Ruaru.

1 Tha mulad, tha mulad,
    Tha mulad, ga'm lionadh ;
 Tha mulad bochd, truadh orm
    Nach dual domh chaoidh dhìreadh.

2 Mu Mhac-Griogair a Ruaru,
    D' am bu dual bhi 'n Gleann-Liobhunn,
 Mu Mhac-Griogair n'am bratach
    Dha 'm butar tarach pioban.

3 Ga'm bu shuaicheantas giubhas
    Ri bruthach ga 'dhir eadh,
 Crann caol air dheadh locradh,
    'S ite dhosrach an fhir-eoin.

4 Crann caol air dheadh shnai theadh,
    Cuid do dh' aighear mhic Righe ;
 Ann an laimh dheadh Mhic Mhuirich,
    Ga 'chumail reidh direach.

5 Ge do bhuail e mìmba-looch, g
    Gu m' ghearan cha bhi mi ;
 Ge do dhean iad orm-eu-coir,
    A thi féin co 'ni dhioladh.

6 'S luchd a ghabhail mo leithsgeil,
    Anns a chaibeil so shios uam ;
 Luchd a sheasamh mo chorach
    Is e mo leòn iad bhi-dhi orm.

7 Mo chomh-dhaltan gaolach,
    An leaba chaol 's an ceann iosal ;
 Ann an leinne chaoil anairt,
    Gun bhannan gun siod' oirr'.

8 'S nach d' iarr sibh ga fuaigheal
    Mnaithean uaisle na tire,
 Ort a bheirinse comhairle
    Na 'n gabhadh tu dhiom e.

Lament

MacGregor of Roro.[1]

1 There is sorrow, deep sorrow,
　　Heavy sorrow down-weighs me ;
　Sorrow long dark forlorn,
　　Whence nothing can raise me.

2 Yea my heart is filled with sorrow,
　　Deep sorrow undying
　For MacGrigor of Roro
　　Whose home is Glenlyon.

　For the bannered MacGrigor
　　So bravely who bore him,
　With the roar of the war-pipe
　　Loud thundering before him.

3 His emblem the pine tree
　　On mountain-side swinging ;
　His trim tapered arrows
　　The true bird was winging.

4 Trim shafts that a king's son
　　Might glory in bearing ;
　From MacMurdoch's strong hand
　　Home they sped, how unerring.

5 Now I will not complain
　　Though a coward should smite ;
　Should they wrong and outrage,
　　Oh heaven who shall right me ?

6 'Tis my pain they are not here
　　Whom living nought ailed me :
　East in yon chapel lie
　　The true hearts that ne'er failed me.

7 Their fair heads are low,
　　My dear foster brothers ;
　Them the scant linen shroud
　　In strait bed barely covers,

8 Linen shroud with no bands
　　Nor silk tassels made ready,
　Nor sewed by the fingers
　　Of nobly born lady.

[1] The beautiful old air is given in appendix.

9 Nuair a theid thu'n tigh-osda
   Na òl ann ach aon deoch ;
  Gabh do dhrama na dèsheasamh,
   'Us bi freasd' lach mu d' dhaoineadh.

10 Na dean diuthadh mu d' shoitheadh,
   Gabh an ladar no 'n taoman ;
  Dean am faoghar do' gheamhradh,
   'S dean an semhradh do 'n fhaoiltich.

11 Dean do leaba 's na creagaibh
   'Us na caidil ach aotrom ;
  Ge h-aineamh an fheorag,
   Gheabhar seòl air a faodainn.

12 Ge h-aineamh an fheorag,
   Gheabhar seol air an faodainn ;
  Ge h-uasal an t-sheobhag
   Is tric a ghabhar le foill i.

13 Tha mulad, tha mulad,
   Tha mulad ga m' lionadh ;
  Tha mulad bochd truadh orm
   Nach dual domh chaoidh dhireadh.

9 Now a rede I would rede thee,
 And thereon well think thou;
When thou goest to the hostel
 But a single cup drink thou.

10 Stand and drink;—of the men
 That are round thee be wary;
Be it bale-dish or ladle
 Drink it down nothing chary.

11 Make winter as autumn
 The wolf days as summer;
Thy bed be the bare rock,
 And light be thy slumber.

12 For though scarce be the squirrel,
 There's a way got to find her;
Though proud be the falcon
 There are deft hands can bind her.

13 There is sorrow, deep sorrow,
 Heavy sorrow down weighs me;
Sorrow long dark, forlorn,
 Whence nothing can raise me.

Chapter XXVIII

FROM the "Chartulary":—

"1605. March. Item be commandement of the Lords of counsall to David Lindsay Keeper of the Tolbuith of Edinburgh for the entertainment of the pledges of the McGregors fra the 1. day of July 1604 to ye day of yr execntioun.

"1605. April 19. The Secret Council ordain that 'whoever' should present to it any of 'the McGregouris quik (alive) or failing thereof his heid' shall have a nineteen year lease of all 'Lands roumes and possessions belonging to the said McGregouris' or else a compensation 'for their kindness' to be paid by the Landlord at the modification of the Council.

"In a letter dated April 20, from the Earl of Dunfermling to the King mention is made 'And has tayne some resolutounes with my lord Ergyll concerning the persute of the McGregouris, whilkes hiull proceedinges I haiff written mair particularlye to my Lord of Berwick.

"Sep. 30. Horning Buchanans [1] in Strathyre against Allaster McCondoche vic fatrik in Strathyre Duncan and John McKirrist vic Condochie his sonis, Allaster sone to umqle Walter Stewart yair, Patrik cowle McGregour yair, molestation and oppression.—Register of Hornings, Perth.

"1606. Dec. 23. at Edinburgh. Sederunt Commissionair, Chancellair Cassilis, Kinghorne, Ochiltree, Roxburgh, Blantyre, Bishop of Dunkeld Aduocat, Collector Bruntlland, Quhittinghame, foisterhait Sir George Douglas, Clerk of Register. Anent the Clangregour Forasmuch as albeit the course which was taen for exterminioun of the wicked and theivish race of the ClanGregour, has been mitigated and some oversight and permission granted unto them to live in the country and to enjoy the breath of their natural air upon hope that they moved with a hatred and detestation of their former evil life should have conformed themselves to his Majesty's obedience and studied by their good and peaceable behaviour, to have buried and put in oblivion their former misrule and insolence. Nevertheless the Lords of Secret Council are surely informed that the said MacGregor has begun to renew their former misdemeanours not only by committing of Stouths, reiffs, sorning, and oppressions upon his Majesty's peaceable good subjects but by ravishing and forcing of women and other odious and detestable villainies not

[1] Probably the family of MacGregors who had adopted this name. See page 339.

worthy to be heard of in a Country, subject to a Prince who is armed with power
and force sufficient to repress and extirpate such an infamous byke of insolent
lymmers and to the effect that the truth of these informations may be the
better known and some solid and good course tane for remedy of these evils
and preventing the farther growth of the insolence of these lymmers. Necessary it
is that the noblemen, barons, and gentlemen of the bounds next adjacent to such
lymmers be heard and such overtures as they can make, and give in, anent
this mater be considered and embraced accordingly for which purpose ordains
letters to be direct chairging Johnne Earl of Tullibardine, James Lord Ogilvie of
Airly, James Lord Inchaffray, Sir Duncan Campbell of Glenurquhy &a. &a. to compeir personally before the Lords of Secret Council upon the 13. day of Jan. next to
give their best advice and opinion how the misrule and insolence of the said
lymmers may be suppressed and the country freed of their farther trouble, under
the pain of rebellion."

It has been already observed[1] that from the 28th February 1603 to the 7th
August 1606, two entire folio volumes of the original minutes of the Privy
Council are missing, having disappeared, according to Professor Masson's
Introduction to the now published Register, "before the middle of the last
century." In the publication mentioned, all other information as to the
period missed out has been most carefully gathered together, but it is
satisfactory to find how well Mr MacGregor Stirling had anticipated these
labours as far back as sixty years ago. Any excerpts taken from Professor Masson's Collections instead of from Mr MacGregor Stirling's MS.
will be acknowledged as so quoted.

"1605. The Earl of Ergyle has charged . . . . . McLarrane to appear before
the Council this day, viz, 27. June instant, to answer for his resetting the following
and others of the ClanGregour upon   day of   in his own house in Blar-
quharry, viz. Duncan Phadrik Aldoch,[2] Patrik McGregor his brother, Johnne
McEanes in Glenogill and Braggane McGildoych, and also for passing with them
to the dwelling house of . . . . McGillip[3] in . . . . and taking away the whole
goods in the said house. The Earl not appearing, McLarrane being present,
protests that he shall not be held to answer for them till again warned; and the
Lords admit the protest.—Masson.

"1606. This year was in Scotland remarkable for a general pestilence both in
town and country. All the Judicatories of the Kingdom were deserted except the
Secret Council which met at intervals for a day at most, 'to keipe' as stated by the

---

[1] *Vide* page 300.   [2] Son of Patrick Aulach.
[3] The Fiddler, McKillipe in Dalney (Glenartney?) *vide* page 324.

Lord Chancellor Earl of Dunfermline to his Majesty 'some face and countenance of order and government.'

"1607. Jan 7. Letter from the Earl of Dunfermline to the King 'In the Hielandis the McGregours affairses lyis owir partlie be the seasoun of the year, and pairtly be mylord of Ergyle's absence, whom we looke daylie for.'

"1606. Sep. 10. At the Doune of Menteith the tenth day of Sep. The quhilk day in presence of ane noble and potent Lord Archibald Erlle of Ergylle Lord Campbell and Lorne, &a. his Majesties Lieutenant and commissionair over the Clangraigour constitute be act of secrite counsalle to chairge thaim be his awine precept to compeir befoir him quhen and quhair he sall appoint with power to grant respettis, and remissiounis to samony of the said surname of McGregour as will renunce thair awin surnamis and find caution to be ansuerable and obedient to his Majestis and his Hynes lawis in tymes coming for paccfeing of the heylandis and pairtis next adjacent thairto conforme to the tenour of the Act of Parliament haldin in July 1683. as the said act of Secrete counsalle of the date At Perth the 11 July 1606 zeirs instant mair fullie proportis Personalie compeirit the personis vnderwritten descendit of the race and surname of McGrigour; Thay ar to say

Archibald McDonche VcAllester and tuke upoun (him) selff the surname of
        Stewart,
and siklike personallie compeirit

Gregour McPatrik . . . . . . the surname of Dougall
Allaster McEwne VcGrigour . . . . . . the surname of Stewart,
Callum McGrigour Dow . . . . . . the surname of Dougall
Neil McGrigour VcEane VcGrigour . . . . . . Grant
Gregour McGrigour Dow bruthir to the said Callum . . . . . . Dougall
Johnne Dow McGrigour VcEane . . . . . . Grant
Duncan McRobert . . . . . . Dougall
Duncane Mcpatrik Vcean in Cadderlie . . . . . . Grant
Johne Mcdougallowir . . . . . . Dougall
Johne Dow Mcdonche bain Vcrob Vcgrigour . . . . . . Cunynghame
Dougall Chaiche . . . . . . Dougall
Allaster Mcdonche bain . . . . . . Cuningham
Johne McWilliam McGregour . . . . . . Dougall
Duncane na glen McGrigour tuke to him the surname of . . . . . .
Patrik Mcdonche na glen tuke to him the surname of . . . . . .

And all the foirsaidis personis sweir that in all tymes comming that they sall call themselfis and thair bairnis efter the surrnamis respective abone written and use the samyn in all their doingis vnder the paine of deid to be execute upoun thame without favour or any of thame incaice thay failzie in the premissis. And siklyk the said Erle of Ergylie voluntarilie become actit, and obleist as cautioner and suirtie for the personis vnder written vnder the pecuniall panes efter specifeit viz. for the saidis

Archibald McDonche	Gregour McPatrik
Callum McGrigour	Duncane McRobert
Patrik McPatrik Abdoche (Aldoche?)	Duncane na Glen.

vnder the pane of 500 merkis and for the saidis

Allaster McEwin	Neill McGrigour
Johne Dow	Duncane McPatrik
Johne Dow Mcdonche bain	Dougall Chaiche
Allaster Mcdonche bane	Patrik Mcdonche na Glen

vnder the pane of thrie hundredth merkis and for the saidis

Grigour McGrigour   Callum Bain McGrigour our

vnder the pane of twa hundreth merkis and for the said Johne McDougall vnder the pane and hundreth merkis all Scottis money That the saidis personis and everie ane of them sall in all tymes coming behave themselffis as dewtifull and obedyent subiecties to our Souerane Lord and that themselffis and all sik personis as thay are obleist to ansuer for be the lawis of this realme and general Band sall observe and keip our Souerane Lordis peace guid reule and quietnes in the cuntrey and nawyse trouble, invaid, molest, nor opres his heynes subiectis by ordour of law and justice vndir the pecuniall panes abone written to be payit to the saidis principallis and cautionaries bot for ane failzie or ane contraventoun allenarlie conforme to the concurrence, sence, and meining of the said act of Secret Counsall. And the saidis personis having interchangeit and renuncit thair surnames and now callit thame selffis eftir the surnames abone written, band and obleist them frie relief and skaithles keip, the said Erll yair cautionair of ye premiss and of all yhat may result yairvpoun And for the mair faithfull observing of the premiss the saidis principall and cautionair ar content and consentis that thir pnts (pointis) be actit and regrat (registered) in the buikis of our Souerane Lordis secrete counsale and sheff (Sheriff) buikis of Ergyle alternative ad perpetuam rei memorium to have the strenth of ane Decree of the saidis Lordis and Sheriff be interponing thair aucteis rexus heirto with all exellc necessary to follow heirvpoun in forme sa effeiris and the horning to be vpoun ane simple chairge of ten days allenarlie and for registratioun heirof constitutis &a thair pro : coiunctlie seuerallie In witness of ye qlk thingis written to Mr James Kirk Shēf Depute foirsaid Before thir witnes

Johne Erll of Tullibardin
Harie Stewart of Sanctcolme
Alexander Schaw of Cambsmoir
James Dog fear of Dunrobin
Willm; Stirling of Achyll.—Luss Papers."

This paper is quoted verbatim by Mr MacGregor Stirling as above.

The different sums under which different men were bound is remarkable.

Sir William Fraser in the " Chiefs of Colquhoun " alludes to an Act of the Secret Council dated at Perth, 11th July 1606, by which Archibald Earl of Argyle was appointed

"To charge them by his own precept to appear before him when and where he should appoint with power to grant respites and remissions in favour of such of them as would renounce their own surnames, and find caution to be   and obedient to his majesty's laws in time coming."

Allusion is then made to the meeting at Downe of Menteith, but it is not given at length.

From Register of the Privy Council, by Dr Masson :—

"Privy Council Papers. 1607 (?).

"His Majestie at the first advertisment of McGregouris apprehensioun maid promise to give the Erle of Ergyle ane worthie reward, to remayne heretablie with him and his aires heirafter. Seing now nocht only is the said McGregour apprehendit and delyverit, bot the greite pairt of all that clan and the best and choicest men of thame, quha micht haif bein maist fearit, ar at commandiment, na doubt his Majestie wilbe moveit to continew that his resolutioun, and augment the rewaird rather than impaire the same in onyway, respect being had that, in procureing of this wark, the said Erle of Ergyle hes not only bein driven to intollerable toyll and payne in his awin persoun, bot also hes bestowit huge and greit sowmes of money, als weill in levieing of men as in particuler rewairdes to sum persones to effectuat this turne.

" The mater demandit is the gift of the landis of Kintyre ; quhairin it wald be rememberit how small or na proffeitt thay evir importeit to the King, his Majestie often tymes being driven to put the cuntrey to greitar chairges in the space of thrie or four yeir for getting in of the rent thairof, quhilk is nocht greit, than mycht haif doubled the pryce and utter valew of the haill land.

" The dispositioun of it to the Erle of Ergyle will embark him in actioun aganis the Clan Donald, being the strangest piller of all the broken hieland men, quha nevir in any aige wer civill, bot hes bein the scoolmaisteris and fosteraris of all barbaritie, savaignes, and crueltye,—hes evir from the beginning bein addictit nocht only to rebellioun within this continent land and the iles, bot evir wer assisteris of the northerne Irische people, dwelling in Ireland, in all thair rebellionis. Now, this nobleman in actioun of blude being enterit with the said Clan Donald, nocht only will he procuire thair ruitteing out and utter suppressing, bot upoun that same respect will evir be ane feir to those in the northe of Ireland to rebell, haveing ane enemye lyand sa neir to thame ; quha, besydes that dewty, quhilk as ane nobleman and his Majesties subject he is bund unto, will, upoun his former embarking aganis the said Clan Donald, preis be all meanis to supres thair doingis. Quhairin the difficultye may be considerit quhilk the said Erll of Ergyle will haif in the removeing of that mischevous Clan, quhais actionis deservis na les than thair utter extirpatioun and ruiting out, thay being of nowmeries sa mony and of sa greit freyndschip that hardlye without greit bluide this turne may be effectuat ; and, sa lang as the said Clan Donald remaynes unremoveit furth of the saidis landis, his Majestie nor na utheris sal half any proffeit, and the uncivilitie and barbaritie sall continew nocht only thair bot in the Iles.

"The Erle of Ergyle himself had the foirfaltour of thir same landis of Kintyree, the iles of Ilay, Jura, Coloula, Sunward, and Ardwa, all offerit unto him for
m[1]
ten   erkis, the saidis landis of Kintyre skairse ansuering to the fyifte pairt of the haill ather in valew or yeirlie proffeit, sua that the present demandit rewaird is baith meane and ressonable,—the landis of Kintyire being mair proper in his persoun than in the persone of any uther subject, be ressoun he is heretabill Justice, Colonell, and Chamberlane, and his Lordshipis predicessouris had heretabill infeftment of the landis thameselffis disponeit by King James the Fourth of worthie memorye."

"1. There is no date to this paper, nor any indication who was the writer. Evidently, however, it is written in the interest of the Earl of Argyle, urging the Earl's claims on his Majesty for some reward for his services against the ClanGregor ; &, as the suggested reward,—an infeftment of the Earl in the Lordship of Kintyre,—did not come till 30th. May 1607 (see Ratification of the infeftment by the Parliament of 1617 : Acta Parl. Scot. iv. 559-560), the present paper must have been written before that date. It may even have been written in some year earlier than 1607 ; for the opening paragraph might be read as implying that the apprehension of the chief of the MacGregors and the crushing of his clan were rather recent events in the writer's mind. It may have taken time and argument to bring about the desired result."

1607, in July, King James VI. granted to the Earl of Argyll[2] and his heirs part of the lands and lordship of Kintyre in reward for his services against the ClanGregor. The following royal letter addressed to David Murray, Lord Scone, his Majesty's Comptroller, is given in " The Chiefs of Colquhoun " from the original in the Argyll Charter Chest :—

---

[1] The "m" is above the line, as in the original.
[2] For the Earl's claims, see previous page.

"JAMES R.

" Dauid Lord of Scoone, our Comptrollare, we great yow wele : Forasmeikle as, in consideratioun and recompance of the goode and noble seruice done to ws be our richt trusty and weilbeloued cousing and counsallour, Archibald Erll of Argyle, Lord Campbell and Lorne, against that insolent and weikit race of the ClanGregour notorious lymneris and malefactouris, specialie in the inbringing of the Larde of Macgregour, and a nowmer of the principallis of that name, quhilkis wer worthilie executed for their transgressionis, and for reducing of a goode nowmer of vthers of that Clan and thair associattis, to our obedience, we ar gratiuslie pleased to bestow vpoun our said cousing sameikle of our landis and lordship of Kintyre, as will amount in yearlie rent to twentie chalder of victuall, heretabillie to him and his airis, togidder with the sowme of twentie thowsand merkis Scottis money, to be payit to him at Martimes nixt. . . . . . .

" Gevin at our Courte in Whytehall, the nyntein of July 1607.

" DUMBARE."

From the " Chartulary " :—

" 1607. May.   In May the order prohibiting all his Majesty's subjects except the guards, to wear guns and pistols was put in execution under penalty of imprisonment and fines.—Balfour's ' Annals,' ii. 21.

" 1607. August 11.   The parliament decreed to the Earl of Argyle the twenty chalders of victual of the few farms of Kintyre according to the above letter from the King.—Mr MacGregor Stirling.

" 1609. Jan. 5. at Edinburgh.   Charge against the Earl of Tullibardin.

" Forasmuch as the Lords of Secret Council are informed that John Earl of Tullibardin has lately taken and apprehended Allan oig McIntnach in Glenco a common and notorious thief, murderer, sorner and oppressor who was one of the principal and personal executors of that most odious, barbarous and detestable butchery and slaughter committed by the ClanGregor upon his Majesty's good subjects at Glenfrone, and with his own hand he murdered and slew without pity or compassion the number of forty poor persons who were naked and without armour, and in the whole course and progress of his bypast life he has so exercised himself in theft, murder, reif and oppression as he is most unworthy to be suffered to breathe the air of this country, and therefor the Earl of Tullibardin, in regard of his own honour and credit, and for discharge of his duty to the King's Majesty, ought and should enter and put the said Allane before the said Lords, To the effect order may be taken with him for his trial and punishment as appertains, for which purpose Ordain letters to be direct charging the said Earl as 'haueair' of the said Allane in his custody and keeping ; at the least who had him, and in that respect ought and should be answerable for him, To bring, put and exhibit him before the said Lords upon the   day of   to the effect, order may be taken with him for his trial and punishment, as appertains under the pain of rebellion &a or else to show a cause why &a with certification.—Record of Secret Council."

The above accusation of a person called Allan oig McIntnach [1] (there is no proof of his having been a MacGregor), as having killed forty people without armour, is the nearest judicial mention of the alleged slaughter of young school boys at Glenfruin, but, even in this document, it does not appear to have been a solid or well grounded endictment, and may be now dismissed.

" 1609. Nov. 1. The samyn day Harie Grahame. of Meadowlandes ofttymes callit as cautioner and souertie for reporting letters (at the instance of Craigs, &a) To take souertie of Allaster Bowie M^cgregour —— McIntyre domestick servitour to —— Abroch McGregor of —— and —— M^ccaische ahochie in Drunkie for theft."

From the "Chiefs of Colquhoun."

" By the severe laws that had been enacted against the Macgregors, and from the rigour with which these laws were executed, the proscribed Clan were infuriated and driven to desperation. Placed beyond the pale of the protection of law, they often fiercely retaliated the wrongs which they believed had been done on them, on those who were empowered to punish them, by fire and sword. Against the Laird of Luss, who was invested with such a commission, they were exasperated to the uttermost, and they continued to harass the inhabitants of the Lennox keeping them in constant terror." [2]

In a letter to King James VI. in the year 1609, Alexander Colquhoun renewed his complaints of the aggressions and spoliations which the Macgregors still committed on himself and his tenantry.

" Most Gracious Soveraigne,

" May it pleas your most sacred Maiestie I hhaif ofttymes compleaned of the insolence and heavye oppressioune committit vpoun me, my tennentis, and landis be the Clangregour, And haif bene forced to be silent this tyme bygaine, Hopeing that some tyme thair sould beine ane end thairof Bot now finding my selfe disapoynted and thame entered to thair former coursses Haif tane occasioun to acquent zour sacred Maiestie thairwith, beseiking zour Maiestie to haif pitie and compasssioun vpoun ws zour Maiestie's obedient subiectis and remanent pwire pepille quha sufferis, and to provyd tymous remeid thairin, and that zour Maiestie may be the better informed in the particularis I haif acquent zour Maiestie's

---

[1] M^can Tuagh of the axe. See page 295.   [2] Vol. i. page 214.

Secretare thairin To quhois sufficiency referring the rest. And craving pardoune for importuneing zour Maiestie I leive in all humanitie in zour Maiestie's most sacred handis.

"Zour sacred Maiesties most humble and obedient subiect,
"ALEXANDER COLQUHOUN, of Luss."

"Rosdo, the 13 day of Nov. 1609."

The version of the letter above given is taken from the "Chartulary" where it is entitled "Original of Letter preserved in Advocates' Library, Edinburgh, in Sir James Balfour's Collections"; it differs very slightly in spelling from the copy given by Sir William Fraser from the "Luss Papers."

"Influenced by these and similar complaints, the Privy Council continued to adopt other severe measures against the ClanGregor. Formerly, this clan when pursued betook themselves to the Lochs of Loch Long, Loch Goil, and Loch Lomond, and having the means of transportation to and from these Lochs, they found themselves secure, and defied the might of their enemies. The Lords of the Privy Council anticipated that now when the means of punishing them were put into active operation, the MacGregors according to their wonted manner would seek shelter in these lochs and would thus frustrate the measures of the Government against them. They therefore on 6 Sept. 1610[1] ordained that by public proclamation all his Majesty's subjects who were owners of the boats and skows upon these lochs, should be prohibited from carrying any of the ClanGregor, their wives, bairns, servants, or goods over for them, upon any pretence whatsoever, under the pain of being reputed and punished with all rigour as favourers and assisters of the said Clan in all their criminal enterprises."[2]

From the "Chartulary" :—

A Series of Proclamations and Edicts were made at this time.

"1610. April. Horning Patrick Sqwar in Cumbuswallace against 'Patrick M°Gregour sone to umquhile Patrick Aldech M°Gregoure' and two others his servandis rebellis persones with their complices.—Leny Papers in 'Chartulary.'

"May 15, at Edinburgh. Letters mentioned at the instance of Patrick Squyer in Cambuswallace against patrik M°Gregour sone to umqle Patrik Aldoche M°Gregour Neill Bowie M°Gregour M°incaind and John Caldoche his servants (for theft).—Record of Justiciary.

"1610. June. In Juneii this zeire, his Maiestie intendit to have imployed the Master of Tullibardin against the Clangregor; bot he hauing drawin vpe suche ane extraordinarey draught of a commissioune, that rather or his Maiestie should condescend to suche a one, the Lordes of his priuey counsaill, by ther letters, humbly

---

[1] See chapter xxix.   [2] Chiefs of Colquhoun, vol. i, page 215.

intretted the King to take some other course against them, then to give way to that wich might alienat the hearts of his best subiects, and wrong his awen royall authority so muche.—Balfour's 'Annals of Scotland,' 1435."

It may be from this inferred that the proposals of the Master of Tullibardine were counter to those of the Earl of Argyll.

" 1610. August 14 at Edinburgh. Sederunt

Chancellair	President	Kilsyith
Thesaurair	Justice clerk	Bruntyland
Perth	Clerk of regr.	Sir Johnne Arnott,
Lotheane	Aduocate,	

" Commissions against the Clangregour.

" Forasmuch as the wicked and rebellious thieves and limmers callet the Clan-Gregour who so long have continued in blood, theft, murder, sorning and oppression to the wrack, misery and undoing of a great number of his Majestie's poor subjects not contenting themselves to live under the obedience of his Majesty and his laws when now the whole remaining Clans as well of the Highlands as of the Isles are become answerable and obedient, but preferring their bygone wicked and unhappy trade of evil doing, to civility and obedience of the law and being divers tymes dealt with to have forsaken their former lewd doings and to have embraced a peaceable and quiet form of living They do notwithstanding continue in all kind of impiety and wickedness, and have amassed themselves together awaiting times and occasions to prosecute their detestable and thievish doings against his Majesty's poor people where they may be masters and commanders highly to his Majesty's offence and disregard of his Majesty's authority, and his Majesty and Lords of secret Council having resolved to pursue this infamous ' byke ' of lawless limmers with fire and sword, and by the force of his Majesty's royal authority to reduce them to obedience, And understanding the good and willing disposition of the persons underwritten to do his Majesty service, and to employ their own persons and their friends in the pursuit and prosecution of the said limmers Therefore the said Lords ordain commissions to be past under his Majesty's signet to the persons particularly underwritten within the bounds following, viz. to William Lord Tullibardin, Sir Duncan Campbell of Glenurquhay &a &a (a long list of the commissioners and their districts follows but may be here omitted).
. . . . . . Giving, granting and committing to the Commissioners particularly above written within the bounds particularly above specified full power, commission and authority, express bidding and charge To convocate his Majesty's lieges in Arms and to pass, search, seek, hunt, follow and pursue all and whatsomever persons of the ClanGregor, their followers, assisters and partakers wherever they may be apprehended and to prosecute them with fire and sword and to take them and put them to his Majesty's privy Council to be taken order with

and punished for their offences conforme to the laws of this Realm And if it so happen the said ClanGregor their assisters and partakers for eschewing of apprehension, to flee to strengths and houses, with power to the said commissioners to follow and pursue them, besiege the said strengthes and houses, raise fire, and use all kind of force and warlike engine that can be had for wynning and recovery thereof, and apprehension of the said limmers being there intill, and if in pursuit of the said limmers they refusing to be taken or besieging of the said strengths or houses, it shall happen the said limmers or any of their assisters and partakers, or any being in company with them and assisting them, or within the said strengths and houses, to be hurt, slain, or mutilated, or any other inconvenient whatsoever to follow, the said Lords decern and declare that the same shall not be imputed as crime nor offence to the said commissioners nor persons assisting them to the execution of this commission nor that they nor none of them shall be called or accused therefore criminally nor civilly by any manner of way in time coming notwithstanding whatsoever, acts, statutes, or constitutions made to the contrary whereanent the said Lords dispense by these presents . . . . with power also to the said commissioners and persons assisting them in the execution of this commission To beir, weir, and use hacquebuts and pistoletts in the execution of the said commission. And generally to do use and exerce all and sundry other thaing which for executing of the said commission are requisite and necessary, firm and stable, holding and for to hald all and whatsoever things shall be lawfully done herein charging hereby his Majesty's lieges and subjects to reverence, acknowledge, and obey, concur, fortify, and assist the said commissioners in all and everything tending to the execution of the commission as they and each of them will answer upon their obedience at their highest peril.

"Proclamation for assisting the Commissioners against the ClanGregor.

"Forasmuch as the King's majesty by the power and force of his Royal authority has now reduced to a perfect and settled obedience the whole Isles of this kingdom and continent next adjacent The principals and chieftains of the whole Isles and continent are come to his Majesty's Council and have found good surety for their obedience hereafter so that now no part of the heylands is rebellious but so much as is possessed by that infamous byke of barborous and detestable lymmars called the ClanGregor who being void of the fear of God and of that due obedience which they owed to his Majesty and preferring their bygane thievish and unhappy trade of theft, reiff sorning and oppression to the fear of punishment which his Majesty in his justice has resolved to inflict upon them and contemning his Majesty's lenity and long patience in suffering them to run headlong so long, in all kind of impiety They do yet continue in their wicked deeds, have ammassed themselves in companies taking their advantage of every occasion to trouble, wraik, and oppress their neighbours where they may be masters and his Majesty and Lords of secret council resolving no longer to bear with the rebellion and contempt of their rebellious and detestable lymmers but in his wrath and justice by power and force to reduce them to conformity, has for this effect given order and commission to the Sheriff of Perth and Stewarts of Stratharne and Manteith and their deputes every one of them in their bounds and to . . . . to pursue the said thieves limmars with fire and sword and all kind of rigour and extremity and never to leave off the pursuit of them until they be reduced to obedience As in the commissions granted to them respectively thereupon at length is contained. In the execution whereof necessary it is that they be well and substantiously accompanied with the power and force of his Majesty's peaceable and good subjects dwelling within the bounds of their commissions for which purpose the Lords of secret Council ordain letters to be directed charging all and sundry his Majesty's lieges and subjects dwelling within the bounds of the Sheriffdoms of Stewartries and cuntreys respectively abone written by open proclamation at the market crosses of the head boroughs of the same That they and every one of them well armed in their most substantial and warlike manner prepare themselves and be in readiness to rise, concur, fortify, and assist the said commissioners in all and everything tending to the execution of this commission and for this effect To convene and meet them at such days, times, and places and with so many days victuals and provisions as they shall be advertised by their proclamations, missive letters or otherwise and to follow their direction in everything according as they shall be commanded in the execution of this commission as they and every one of them will answer &a &a," the usual clauses at the end.

" Proclamation that none resett the ClanGregour.

" Forasmuch as the King's Majesty by the power and force of his royal authority having now reduced to a perfect and settled obedience the whole Isles of this kingdom, and continent next adjacent The inhabitants whereof being void of the fear and Knowledge of God and of that due reverence which they ought to have carried to their Sovereign Prince, and consequently exercising themselves in blood, theft, reiff and oppression are now most happily brought to a reasonable conformity both in the one and in the other, and chieftains and principals of them are come to his Majesty's council and have found good surety for their obedience hereafter So that no part of the Highlands is rebellious and disobedient but so much as is possessed by that infamous byke of barbarous and detestable thieves and lymmars called the ClanGregour who some years ago having felt the weight of his Majesty's heavy wrath and displeasure against them by the apprehension and execution to the deid of a great many of the principal ringleaders of that infamous society and it being thought that the remanent who were spared at that time should have 'preissit' by their peaceable and quiet behaviour to have averted his Majesty's displeasure against them that thereby they might have been suffered to have lived in the country in the

rank and condition of lawfull and lawbiding subjects, Nevertheless such is the perverse and wicked disposition of that barbarous and wicked society that being careless of the vengeance taken upon the rest of their fellows and preferring their
unhappy trade of theft, reiff, and murder, sorning, and oppression to the fear of
punishment which his Majesty in his justice has resolved to inflict upon them,
They have continued and do yet continue in their evil doings taking their advantage of every occasion to trouble, wrack, and oppress their neighbours where they
may be masters whereunto they are the rather encouraged by the unworthy
behaviour of a great many of the barons and gentlemen of the country who not
only most unlawfully are assured and under bands of friendship with the said
thieves, but by their connivance and oversight, they have free passage through
their bounds, and country in their theftuous deeds, and are resett, supplied, protected and maintained by them, as if they were lawful subjects, highly to his
Majesty's offence, and to the shame and discredit of those who are assured with
them, and who are their protectors and resetters. And his Majesty and the said
Lords finding it a discredit to the country that a handful of miserable caitifs shall
be suffered longer to have continuance within the country Or that any lawful
subjects shall be under assurance with them Therefore ordain letters to be directed
To command, charge and inhibit all and sundry his Majesty's lieges and subjects
of what estate, degree, quality, or condition soever they be, by open proclamation
at all places needful, That none of them presume nor take upon hand to resett,
or supply any of the ClanGregor, their wives, children or servants, nor to intercommune with them, nor yet to resett, hoard, or keep their goods or geir, or to
'bloke' or bargain with them thereanent, nor keep trysts, conventions, nor
meetings with them under the pain to be reputed hald and esteemed as art and
parttakers with them, in all their theftuous and wicked deeds, and to be pursued
and punished for the same with all rigour and extremity to the terror of others,
And the same to command and charge all and sundry his Majesty's lieges and
subjects who are under assurance or bands of friendship with the said thieves and
lymmars, To renounce and discharge the same bands and assurances, and to enter
into no such fellowship, or society, with them hereafter, but to repute and hold
them as traitors to God, their prince, and country, and accordingly to pursue them
with their whole power and forces, Certifying them who shall stand and continue
under the said assurances, and bands of friendship, with the said lymmars after the
publication hereof that they shall be repute, holden, and esteemed as guilty with
them in all their evil deeds, and shall be punished therefore accordingly.—Record
of Secret Council Acta."

The above proclamations show, indeed, that war with the small
"handful" of the doomed Clan who survived, was to be waged without
respite. The Chiefs of the two principal Houses had fallen, together with

many of the other most valiant and experienced leaders, but the spirit of
a brave race remained unbroken, and still struck terror into their enemies.
Evidently there were many friends who, whether from sympathy with
their courage, or from timidity, still gave them shelter and countenance,
which secret favour alone can explain their having contrived to subsist,
when every way of living honestly was denied them.

Chapter XXIX

Proclamations against Transporting the ClanGregor over Lochs

FROM the "Chartulary":—

"1610. August. Item to William Cuningham Messenger passing from Edinburgh with letters to charge Patrik Home of Argate and Thomas Grahame of Bowtoun cautioners for John Dow McGregor V^cEane V^cGregor John Buchannane of that ilk, cautioner for Alex. McGregor in Strathyre Robert McColl; John, Malcolm and Patrik McGregour his sons To exhibit them before the Council the penult day of August instant And to charge the said McGregours by open proclamation at the market Crosses of Stirling and Dunbarton To compeir the said day and underlie such order as shall be taken with them for their obedience £6.

"Item to Robert Elder messenger passing from Edinburgh with letters to charge James Earl of Athole, son of Earl of Tullibardin, James Lord Maddertie, Alex. Meinzies of Weyme, James Campbell of Lawers, Mr William Murray of Auchtertyre, John Grahame of Balgowne, John Stewart of Foss cautioners for the surname of McGregours to exhibit them before the Council the penult day of August to underlie &a conforme to their acts of cautionerie made thereanent &a.

"Item to a boy passing from Edinburgh with a close letter to the Laird of Buchannane.

"Item to do with letters and commissions concerning the McGregors To the Earls of Montrois, Perth, Tullibardin, The Sherif of Perth, the Laird of Glenurquhy, Grantully, Balleachan, Weyme, Glenlyoun, Lawers, Sir William Stewart, and Donald Farquharson, &a.

"Item to a boy passing from Edinburgh with close letters and commissions concerning the McGregours, To the Earls of Murray, Monteith, Linlythgow, Lord St Colme, The Lairds of Lundie, Keir, Auchinbrek, Ardinglas, and Muschet, £8.

"Item to a boy passing from Edinburgh with close letters and commissions concerning the McGregours To the Lord of Blantyre, the Lairds of Luss, Buchannane, Foulwede, John M^cfarlane, fear of Arroquhair, £4, 4s.

"Item to a boy passing from Edinburgh with close letters to the Lords Forbes and Elphingstoun, the Laird of Aberzeldie, Pitsligo, Dunn, Lessmoir, Grant, Caddell and Angus Williamson, and with a proclamation to be published at the market Cross of Innerness, concerning the McGregors, &c.—Lord High Treasurer's Books."

Next follow two proclamations on the subject of forbidding the transport of any of the Clan across the numerous Lochs which intersected their country, and to which allusion has been made in an extract from the "Chiefs of Colquhoun."[1] If, turning from the dry record of legal entries, the Highland country scene with living figures can be pictured, the hasty arrival on the shore, of the fugitives whether armed men or aged decrepid "bodachs," anxious women and young children, all eager to be ferried across to escape from cruel enemies, rowed over by the strong arms of trusty friends, and hastening to find a brief shelter on the opposite shore till driven forth again, deep must be the sympathy of their descendants. Thus runs the proclamation to stop these means of temporary respite :—

"1610. Sep. 6. at Edinburgh. Proclamation that nane transport the Clangregor over Loichlung and other Lochs.

"Forasmuch as the King's Majesty having given order and direction for pursuit of the rebellious and barbarous thieves and lymmers called the Clangregor by whom the peaceable subjects of the in-country are heavily oppressed, troubled, and wracked and the execution of the service being now in hands and some good and happy success expected in that errand, it is very likely that the said thieves according to their wonted manner when as formerly they wer pursued, shall have their recourse to the Lochs of Lochlung, Lochegyll and Loich Lowmound, and thir having the commodity to be transported to and from the said Lochs they will frustrate and disappoint the intended service against them, Therefore the Lords of Secret Council ordain Letters to be directed to command, charge, and inhibit all and sundry his Majesty's lieges and subjects, owners of the boats, and scoutts, upon the said lochs that none of them presume, nor take upon hand, to transport any of the ClanGregor, their wives, children, servants or goods, over the said Lochs upon whatsoever colour, or pretence, under pane to be repute, holden, and esteemed as favourers, assisters, art and part takers with the said ClanGregor in all their thievish and wicked deeds, and to be pursued and punished therefor with all rigour in example to others, and farther to command and charge the masters and owners of the said boats and scouts, To find caution and surety acted in the

[1] Page 355.

2 Z

books of Secret Council That they shall not transport any of the ClanGregor their wives, children, servants or goods over the said Lochs each of them under the pain of 500 merks and that they find the said surety in manner foresaid within six days next, after they be charged thereto which six days being bypast and the said surety not being found In that case the said Lords give power and commission to his Majesty's commissioners within the bounds of the Sherrifdom of Dumbarton, To intromitt with the said boats and scouts and to remove them off the said Lochs and to keep them off the same so long as the service against the ClanGregor is in hands.

"Proclamation for concurring with the commissioners against the ClanGregor.

"Forasmuch as the King's Majesty and Lords of Secret Council having past and expede certain commissions to some special barons and gentlemen in the Lennox for the pursuit of the wicked and rebellious thieves and lymmers called the ClanGregor, by whom the peaceable and good subjects within the Lennox are heavily oppressed, troubled, and wrakit, and proclamations being past and lawfully executed for charging of the inhabitants within the Sherrifdome of Dumbarton, to concur with his Majesty's commissioners in the execution of his Majesty's service, against the said lymmers, The said inhabitants do notwithstanding refuse all concurrence and assistance with his Majesty's commissioners so that the execution of his Majesty's service is like to be frustrated and disappointed unless remedy be provided, Therefore the Lords of Secret Council have declared and by these presents declare and ordain that the escheits of all and sundry persons within the bounds of the Sherrifdome of Dumbartane who shall refuse to give their concurrence and assistance to his Majesty's commissioners foresaid in the execution of his Majesty's service against the ClanGregor shall be gifted and disponed to the said commissioners and they shall have warrand, commission, and authority from the said Lords to meddle and intromit therewith and to dispone thereupon at their pleasure and ordain letters of publication to be directed there upon whairthro none pretend ignorance of the same—Record of Secret Council Acta."

On the 24th August the same year, a commission, worded very much the same as those of the 14th of August, was given to John, Earl of Atholl, and John, Earl of Tullibardin, to pursew the ClanGregor with fire and sword.

"1610. Item to the Laird of Lawers for undertaking of service against the MacGregors. His acquitance upon the receipt thereof bears £1200.—Lord High Treasurer's Books.

"1610. Sep. 24. Charge anent the Houses of Garth, Glenlyoun and Balquhidder.

"Forasmuch as for the better fartherance of the King's Majesty's service against the ClanGregour necessary it is the houses of Garth, Glenlyoun and Balquhidder, be made patent and ready to Allan Cameroune of Lochyell and Alexander McRannald of Gargavach two of his Majestys commissioners specially directed and employed in that service, for the resett of them, their viuers, and servants at all such times as they shall have occasion to repair to the said houses during the time that the service foresaid is in hands Therefore ordain letters to be directed charging Johnne Erll of Tullibardin . . . . . . Campbell of Glenlyoun, Sir William Stewart Knt. and all others havears, keepers, and detainers of said houses To make the same houses patent and ready for receiving of the said commissioners, their servants, and vivers, at all such times as they shall have occasion to be resett within the same, during the time of that service, as the persons foresaid, keepers of the said houses, will answer to his Majesty and his Council at their highest peril and under the pain to be repute holden and esteemed as favourers, assisters, and partakers, with the said Clan-Gregour in all their evil deeds and to be pursued and punished for the same with all rigour and extremity, in example of others.—Record of Council Acta."

The task of hunting down the MacGregors, had, it appears, been entrusted to Cameron of Locheil and Clanranald. The traditions on which the narrative in the " Baronage " was based, agree with this fact now proved by the " Records," and the " Baronage " adds that the two war-like Clans who accepted the commission in a short time " penetrated into the interested designs of their enemies and again befriended the ClanGregor." Two points may here be remarked. In the preceding century different noblemen or chiefs took out " Letters " of fire and sword, for which privilege they were willing to pay a contribution into the State exchequer, but in the reign of King James VI. commissions were given by the government to certain noblemen and others, and large sums were paid to them as a reward for services which formerly were considered in the light of an agreeable foray ; the second point is that Clans from a distance were chosen for the duty, and although the heads of the great Campbell houses were the constant and mortal enemies of the ClanGregor and the chief inheritors of any spoils that could be got from them, yet the Campbell clansmen were seldom, if ever, brought into conflict with the Mac-Gregors, as their battles appear to have been fought by other Clans.

" 1610. Sep. 24. Charge against Highlandmen.

"Forasmuch as Allane Cameroun of Lochyell and Allaster McRannald of

Gargavaich being employed and directed in his Majesty's service against the Clan-
Gregor, and they having desired the persons underwritten, They are to say &a who
are their own friends, servants and dependers To join, concurr assist and pass
forward with them in that service The said persons most undutifully have refused
their concurrence and assistance, in his Majesty's service foresaid, testifying thereby
that they are favourers of the said ClanGregor and doing what in them lies to
frustrate and disappoint the course intended against them for reducing of them to
his Majesty's obedience, to the offence and contempt of our Sovereign Lord
and misregard of his Majesty's authority, and Laws. Therefore the Lords of Secret
Council ordain letters to be directed charging persons above written to compeir personally before the said Lords upon   day of   To answer to the premises
and to underlye such punishment as shall be enjoined to them for the same, under
the pain of rebellion, &a with certification.— Record of Council Acta.

   " 1610. Sep. 24.   Charge against the resetters of the ClanGregor.

   " Forasmuch as the King's Majesty in his just wrath and indignation against the
unhappy race of the ClanGregor having given order and direction for the pursuit of
them with all kind of hostility and reducing of them to his Majesty's obedience, and
for the better furtherance and execution of this service, having by public proclamation prohibited and discharged all his Majesty's subjects in any ways to resett,
supply, and assist the ClanGregour or to resett, hoard and conceal their goods,
Notwithstanding it is of truth that the persons underwritten they are to say, &a have
at divers and sundry times since the publishing of this proclamation resett certain of
the ClanGregor, their wives, bairns, and goods, have supplied them with victuals,
armour, and other necessaries comfortable to them, and thereby have encouraged
them to continue in their rebellion in contempt of our Sovereign Lord and misregard of his Majesty's authority. Therefore letters to be directed charging the
persons particularly above written to compeir personally before the said Lords &a.
—Record of Secret Council Acta.

   " 1610. Oct. 4:   At Edinburgh.

   " Proclamation for concurring with the Commissioners against the ClanGregor.

   " Forasmuch as the Lords of Secret Council having past and expede certain
commissions to Walter Lord Blantyre, Alexander Colhoun of Luss,
Buchannane of that Ilk, Sir James Edmestoune of Duntreithe ——— Sempill of
Foulwode and Johne M'farlane of Arroquhair, making them conjunctly and
severally his Majesty's Justices and commissioners within the Sherrifdome of Dumbartane for the pursuit of the barborous thieves and lymmars called the Clan-
Gregour. Necessary it is for the better execution of the said commission and
furtherence of his Majesty's service, that the said commissioners have the concurrence and assistance of the inhabitants within the parishes of Inchecalloch
Drummen, Killearn, Balfrone, Fintry, Strablane, Campsie, and Baddernoch, for
which purpose ordain letters &a.

"1610. Oct. Item to the Laird of McRonald, for himself and Allane McIldowie, And to McColl clapen,[1] appointed by his Majesty's direction to attend upon them for putting in execution his grace service in the Highlands as his Majesty's warrant bears £3566.—Lord High Treasurer's Books.

"In Nov. 1610. several close letters were sent from Court to Allan McIldowie the Laird of McRonald and to various Lairds in Athole and elsewhere.

"Letter from the Chancellor ——— to the Laird of Airntully 1611."

From the introduction to Vol. ix. of "The Register of the Privy Council of Scotland," edited by David Masson, LL.D., some appropriate passages may now be quoted.

"All the while that the Hebrides, and the fringe of Mainland coast most immediately connected with them, were being managed in the manner described, a dreadful business had been separately going on in that nearer and more inland portion of the main Highlands which stretches from the northern shores of Loch Long and Loch Lomond over the wild junctions of Stirlingshire and Dumbartonshire with Perthshire and Argyleshire. This was the continued or renewed Persecution of the ClanGregor. It is a sickening story, forming the matter of a larger series of entries in this volume than any other single subject. For many years already, as many previous volumes have shown, this Clan of the Macgregors had been the object of the most vehement hatred of the central Government, and the one doomed and unpardonable Clan in all the Highlands. 'The wicked and unhapie race of the ClanGregour, quha sa lang hes continewit in bluid, thif reif, and oppressioun' is a recurring phrase against them in proclamations and other publick documents of the years when James was King of Scotland only. The culmination of vengeance against them however, had been in April 1603, the very month of the King's departure from Scotland into England. It was in that month that, in consequence of a new and crowning offence of the Macgregors in the preceding February, in that Battle of Glenfruin fought by them against the Colquhouns of Luss, the Buchanans, and others, which figures in the criminal records as the Massacre of Glenfruin, there was passed the tremendous Act of the Scottish Council proscribing the Clan utterly, and decreeing under pain of death, the disuse of the very name of Macgregor by all persons of the Clan. Of this Act, describable from it's date as literally James's parting gift to Scotland, and the chief agent in the execution of which was the Earl of Argyle, the effects may be traced in various incidents of the immediately subsequent years, one of them being the hanging and quartering at the Market Cross of Edinburgh, on the 20 Jan. 1604, of Alexander MacGregor of Glenstrae, the Chief of the Clan, and eleven of his principal kinsmen and retainers. Naturally, however, it was impossible to carry out such an Act thoroughly and from 1604 onwards there had been a comparative lull in the proceedings against the

[1] Clephane.

Macgregors. A lull only, for now the King having set himself in earnest to the
enterprise of the complete subjugation of the Highlands and Islands, the Macgregors were again remembered. One would have thought that, by tolerably wise
management, such as Bishop Knox had applied to the Western Islands, it might
have been easy by this time to bring within terms of judicious mercy the few scores
of families that constituted the remains of the broken and nameless Clan. This
was not the course that suited the policy of those days, or the interests of those
concerned. The course actually adopted was one with which Bishop Knox, if one
judges him rightly, would have refused to have anything to do. There was to be a
war of absolute extermination against the Macgregors root and branch. The campaign was opened in August 1610. From that date to the end of our volume the
horrible business may be chronologised as follows :—

"A Series of Proclamations.

"Proclamation of August 1610.[1] (Comment) In other words they were to be
put beyond the pale of society and hunted down as mere vermin.

"Sep. and Oct. Evidence that the Commission is having some effect, the Macgregor hunting having begun, and the clan being in flight hither and thither, but
especially towards their old haunts of Loch Long, Loch Goil and Loch Lomond.
Orders for preventing them having the use of the boats or ferries on these Lochs.
Some captive MacGregors in the hands of the authorities in Edinburgh. Evidence at
the same time that the lieges in some parts of the Macgregor-infested region are in sympathy with the fugitives or at least very backward in assisting in the pursuit of them.

"Nov. 1610—Jan. 1611. Macgregor-hunting apparently over for the season.

"Jan. and Feb. 1611. Great signs of renewed activity against the Macgregors,
who have now turned at bay and are showing fight. In the course of January, if
not before, they had shut themselves up in the island of Loch Katrine 'whilk thay
haif fortifeit with men, victuall, poulder, bullett, and uther weirlyke furnitour,
intending to keepe the same as ane place of weare and defence.' Accordingly on
the 31st of that month, the Council having gone to Stirling to concert the necessary measures, there is a cluster of resolutions. A number of the Commissioners,
who are personally present, are instructed and undertake, 'to go to the feildis and
to enter in actioun and bloode' within the next fourteen days, the service to be at
their own charges for a month from that date ; after which they are to be assisted,
if needful, with 100 men at his Majesty's charges. The hope being that 'thir
woulffis and thevis' may now be destroyed at one effort 'in thair awne den and
hoill' there is order for all the lieges between sixteen and sixty years of age, within
certain specified bounds to be at the head of Lochlomond well armed on the 12.
of Feb. thence to carry all required boats to Loch Katrine for use in the intended
siege,—two pieces of ordnance one afterwards finds, to be sent from Stirling Castle

[1] See page 355, &c.

for the same purpose. By way of precaution in case the siege should fail and the Macgregors escape, letters were sent to nobles and lairds within whose bounds the fugitives were likely to pass. Accompanying these aggressive measures however there were proofs that the Council knew that the extreme severities against the Macgregors were becoming more and more unpopular. Not only had there to be warning to 'a grite many of the baronis and gentlemen' not to continue their favour to the clan; but there was a redefinition or modification of his Majesty's policy against the clan to meet squeamish objections. His Majesty 'in his accustomat dispositioun to clemencie and mercye' would distinguish between the poorer wretches of the clan and their chiefs or ringleaders. Six of these chiefs and ringleaders were therefore named, viz.

Duncan McEwan Macgregor called the Laird or Tutor.[1]
Robert Abroch Macgregor
John Dow McAllaster Macgregor,
Callum Macgregor of Coull,
Delchay Macgregor (Dougald Cheir) and his brother
McRobert Macgregor.

with a promise of a reward of £1000 to anyone that should slay anyone of these, and of a reward of at least 100 merks for the head of any inferior Macgregor; while anyone of the clan that desired to separate from the rest and come to his Majesty's peace might earn his pardon by bringing in the head of any other Macgregor of the same rank as himself. So matters stood on the 31 Jan. and, with the exception that on the 12 Feb. one wretched Highlander of another clan delivered 'ane McGregouris heid' to the Council in Edinburgh and got 100 merks for it, we have to pass to the end of Feb. for further information, Then it appears that the projected expedition to Loch Katrine had entirely collapsed, and that the Macgregors had got clear away from their island fastness on that loch, without 'so muche as any mynt or show of persute.' Eight of the commissioners with the Earl of Tullibardine at their head were consequently under rebuke.

"March 1611. No special entry in the Macgregor business."

The other entries and notices do not differ materially from those elsewhere recorded.

Jan 14. 1614. After alluding to the submission of Robert Abroch, Dr Masson remarks

"That even after this desertion of the Macgregors by their latest captain there was some unsubdued remnant of them wandering about somewhere or at least that the dangerous Macgregor spirit was not regarded as extinct among the broken and dispersed fragments of the clan is proved by the Act of Council, 26 Jan. 1613.

[1] 3rd son of Ewin, the uncle and tutor of Alastair of Glenstray. This Duncan is also called Douglas of Moirinche and is sometimes mentioned as the Laird of Macgregor.

"The persecution of the Macgregors it will be seen was not yet over. It was to continue for years yet to come. No need to anticipate what the 'Records' of these years may have to tell, but even at this point one cannot avoid remarking how intimately this persecution of the Macgregors, like so many other Highland trans-actions, is inwound with the history and traditions of the great house of Argyle. Five and twenty years hence when Charles I. was on the throne that Archibald Campbell 7th Earl of Argyle who was now so active against the Macgregors was to be living in London as a mild old Roman Catholick gentleman who had been for a while in the Spanish service abroad, and had been sequestrated from his Scottish estate and honours on account of his change of religion ; and one wonders whether in those later and more pensive days of his life, spectres of the butchered Macgregors of 1610-13 and of their wives with the key-mark branded on their faces, ever came to his bedside.

"1611. Jan 31. At Stirling.

"Act against the ClanGregor.

"The which day in presence of the Lords of Secret Council compeired per-sonally Johnne Earl of Tullibardin, William Lord Murray his son, Hary Lord Sanctcolme, Sir Duncane Campbell of Glenurquhy, Knt. Alexander Colhoun of Luss, Sir George Buquhannane of that Ilk, James Campbell of Laweris, and Andro M'farlane of Arroquhair and undertook the service against the ClanGregor, and promised to go to the field, and to enter in actioun and blood with them, betwix . . . . and the 13. day of Feb. next. and to prosecute the service for a month thereafter upon their own charges, and after that the King's Majesty's to bear the charges of one hundred men to assist them and they to bear the charges and expenses of another hundred men till the service be ended, and that they shall do some notable service against the ClanGregour before his Majesty be burdened with any charges in this service.

"For the better furtherance of the which service Alexander Earl of Linlithgow and James Earl of Perth, promised either of them to furnish fifteen men well armed at their own charges, which shall join in action at the first with his Majesty's said commissioners, and assist them for the space of the said first month, and there-after his Majesty to bear the one half of their charges, and the said two Earls the other half of their charges.

"The which day compeired personally . . . . Campbell of Lundy[1] for the country of Argyle, and Alexander Menyeis of Weyme, Sir James Stewart of Balleachane and John Stewart Neilson for the country of Athoill and promised to guard the said countrys, and to keep the MacGregours furth thereof.

"The Lords ordain a missive to be written to the Marquis of Huntly to set out watches and people to guard Badyenauch that the MacGregors have no resett there.

---

[1] Lawers ?

and that another letter be written to the Laird of Grant. to keep his bounds free of them.

"The Lords ordain a missive to be written to Duncane Campbell Captain of Carrick to remove the whole boats out of Lochlung and Lochgoyll to the effect the ClanGregour have no passage by these Lochs.

"Forasmuch as this rebellion and proud contempt of his Majesty's royall authority professed and avowed by the rebellious thieves and lymmars called the ClanGregour, who so long have continued in committing of blood, theft, reiff and oppression upon the King's Majesty's peaceable and good subjects, having most justly procured his Majesty's heavy wrath and indignation, and the force and severity of his royall power to be executed against them which his Majesty has resolved to prosecute till they be reduced to obedience, yet his Majesty in his accustomed disposition to clemency and mercy being well willing to show favour to such of them who by some notable service shall give proof and testimony of the hatred and detestation which they have of the wicked doings of that unhappy race, and aill be content to live hereafter under the obedience of his Majesty's laws, his Majesty knowing perfectly that a great many of them who are now imbarked in that rebellious society and fellowship have rather been induced thereunto by the cruelty of the Chieftains and ringleaders of the same society than by any disposition and inclination of their own Therefore the Lords of Secret Council have promised and by these presents promise That whatsoever person or persons of the name of MacGregor, who shall slay any person or persons of the same name being of as good rank and quality as himself and shall prove the same slaughter before the said Lords—That every such person slayer of a MacGregor of the rank and quality foresaid shall have a free pardon and remission for all his bygone faults, he finding surety to be answerable and obedient to the laws in time coming And suchlike that whatsomever other person or persons will slay any of the particular persons underwritten They are to say.

"Duncane M^cewne McGregour now callit the Laird[1] (he was Tutor of Gregor the eldest son of John McGregor nan Luarag.)

Robert Abroch McGregor

Johne Dow McAllester[2]

Callum McGregor of Coull (a clerical error for V^cCoull viz Malcolm McGregor in Glengyle.)

Duelchay McGregor (Dougal ciar) and

McRobert his brother (?)

or any others of the rest of that race, that every such person slayer of any of the persons presently above written or any other of that race shall have a reward in money presently paid and delivered unto them according to the quality of the person to be slain, and the least sum shall be a hundred merks and for the

[1] See page 367.   [2] See note page 375.

Chieftains and ringleaders of these McGregors a thousand pounds apiece and that letters be directed to make publication by open proclamation at the market crosses of Dumbartane, Striveling, Doune in Menteith, Glasgu. and Auchterardour.

"Forasmuch as one of the chief and principal causes which has procured the proud and avowed rebellion and disobedience of the wicked thieves and lymmars of the ClanGregour against his Majesty and his authority, now at this time when as the haill corners of his Majesty's dominions by the power and force of his Majesty's royal authority are reduced to obedience has proceeded and doth proceed from the unworthy behaviour of a great many of the barons and gentlemen of the country, who not only grant them free passage through their bounds and countrys in their thievish deeds, but reset, supply, protect, and maintain them as if they were lawful subjects highly to his Majesty's offence and to the shame and discredit of the same resetters and seeing there is some course now taken whereby these infamous lymmers may be reduced to the acknowledging of their iniquities, and to the conformity, and obedience of his Majesty's laws wherein some good success is constantly expected, if the reset and protection of them be refused and forborne his Majesty in his just wrath having resolved to punish the said protectors and resetters without all favour and mercy.   Therefore the Lords of Secret Council ordain letters to be directed charging officers of arms to pass to the market crosses of Stirling, Dumbarton, Glasgu, Perth, Auchtirardour, Downe in Menteith and other places needful and there by open proclamation to command, charge, and inhibit all and sundry his Majesty's lieges, and subjects of what estate quality or degree soever they may be that none of them presume or take upon hand to resett supply or intercomoun with the said ClanGregour, their wives or bairns nor to keep conventions, trysts nor meetings with them nor to reset or hold their goods, or geir or to make blokes or bargains with them thereanent, under the pain to be repute, holden and esteemed as part-takers with them in all their wicked deeds and certifying them that fail and do the contrary that not only shall they be pursued and punished therefor in their persons with all rigour and extremity but they their persons, lands, and goods shall be proclaimed free to his Majesty's commissioners who are employed in service against the ClanGregour to be pursued by them with fire and sword as if they were of the race of the MacGregours themselves.

"Forasmuch as the wicked and rebellious thieves and lymmars called the ClanGregor who so long have continued in committing all kind of iniquity and barbarity upon his Majesty's peaceable and good subjects in all parts where they may be masters and commanders being now despairing and out of all hope to receive our favour or mercy seeing their own guilty consciences bear them testimony and record that their detestable and barbarous conversation has so far exceeded the limits of grace and favour that nothing can be expected, but his Majesty's just wrath to be prosecuted against them with all severity.   They have now amassed themselves together in the Islae of Lochkitterine[1] which they have fortified with men, victual, poulder, bullet and other warlike furniture intending to keep the same as a place of war and defence for withstanding and resisting of his Majesty's forces appointed to pursue them and seeing there is now some solid and substantious course and order set down how these wolves and thieves may be pursued within their own den and hole by the force and power of some of his Majesty's faithful and well affected subjects, who freely have undertaken the service, and will prosecute the same without any private respect, or consideration, in so far as the execution of this service, that the haill boats and birlings being upon Loch Lowmond be transported from the said loch to the loch foresaid of Lochkitterine, whereby the forces appointed for the pursuit of the said wolves, and thieves may be transported in to the said Isle which can not goodly be done but by the presence and assistance of a great number of people Therefore ordain letters to be direct to command and charge all and sundry his Majesty's lieges, and subjects, betwix sixty and sixteen years within the bounds of the Sherrifdom of Dumbarton, Stewartry of Menteith and six parishes of the Lennox within the Sherrifdom of Stirling by open proclamation at the market crosses of Dumbarton, Stirling, and Downe in Menteith, That they and every one of thae, weele bodin in feir of weir for their own defence, and surety convene, and meet at the head of Lochlowmond upon the 13. day of Feb. now approaching and to transport and carry from the said loch the haill boats and birlings being upon the same, to the said Loch of Lochketterine whereby his Majesty's forces appointed for pursuit and hunting of the said wolves, and thieves may be transported in to the Isle within the said Loch under the pain (tinsel) of loss of life, lands and goods.—Record of Council Acta."

The difficulty of transporting all the boats from Loch Lomond must have been great. The route was probably from Inversnaid by Stronaclachadh and the end of Loch Arklet; and, as there could only be a rough drove road, the portage of the boats must have been effected with much labour.

"1611. Jan. 31. The quhilk day Johne Erll of Tullibardin band and oblist himselff to mak furthe comeand and ansuerable to his Majesties laws, all and whatsomever persons that presently ar duelling, or herefter shall duell vpoun his landis, and to enter them before the Council when required.—Record of Secret Council Acta.

[1] "Ilanvernock, as it is elsewhere in the Records denominated, being a small island opposite to Portnellan, near the northern shore and western extremity of the lake."—Mr MacGregor Stirling in "Chartulary." Messrs Johnston, Geographers, in reply to inquiries, February 1897, state that no trace of the position of Ilanvarnoch, or "Eilean varnoch," can now be found, and the name does not appear on any map. Possibly it may have been identical with the Ellen's Isle of Sir Walter Scott, as it is larger than the other islands and better suited for defence.—Ed.

"1611. Feb. 5. From the Council to the commissioners aganis the Clan-Gregour.

"After oure verie hairtlie commendations. It is not unknowen to you how that the Kingis Maiestie our awne moist gratious Souerane hes had a speciall cair and regaird thir diuerss yeiris bigane That this proud and avowed rebellioun and dissobedience of the infamous thievis and lymmairis of the Clangregour may be suppressit and thay reducit to obedience, And althocht his Maiestie amangis vtheris his Maiesties imploymentis layed a pairt of the burddyne of this service vpoun his Maiesteis trustie counsallour the Erll of Dumbar whome it hes pleased God now to call to his mercie frome this mortall lyff, zet the deceis of that nobleman hes not maid his Maiestie forgetfull of this seruice, bot sensyne his Maiestie hes speciallie recommendit this same seruice vnto ws that the same may be prosequited and followed oute with all suche diligence and possibiliteis as goodlie may be, with assurance that whatever be worde or write hes bene promeist vnto you that same salbe performit and satisfeit. And thairfore these ar to requeist and desyre you and euerie one of you to go fordwart with your haill pouir and forceis in the prosequition of this seruice and let not the deceis of this man mak ony impressioun in your hairtis That his Maiestie will outher be forgetfull or cairles of this seruice bot that his Maiestie will not onlie hald hand to sie the seruice go fordwart bot will verie narrowlie examine the particular chairge and behaviour of euerie man in this seruice, and accordinglie will remember theme And so recommending the matter to your consideratiouns, as that which most neirlie tuitces his Majesty in honour, and estate. we commit you to God. From Edinburgh your verie good freindis Alexander Cancellarius, Mar, Glencairn, Perth, Lothiane, Blantyre.— Record of Secret Council; Royal and other Letters.

"1611. Feb. 9. Warrant to Buquhannane.

"Quhairas Sir George Buquhannane of that Ilk hes vndertane some service aganis the wicked and rebellious thievis and lymmaris of the ClanGregour in the executioun of the which seruice it being verie necessarie that the said Sir George be assistit with his haill kin and friendis whairever and vpoun whose landis and possessiounis they do duell Thairfoir the Lords of Secreit Counsall gevis and grantis libertie and licence to the said Sir George to convocat and assemble his haill kin and friendis for thair assistance and furtherance to be gevin to him in the executioun of the said seruice commanding likewayis his saidis kin and friendis to rise, concur, fortiefie and assist the said Sir George with thair haill power and forceis in the executioun of his Majesteis said seruice aganis the ClanGregour for the which they sall incur no skaithe nor danger in thair personis, nor goodis Excroning and releving thame of all pane and cryme that may be imputt to thame thairthrew for euer.

"1611. Feb. 5. The whilk day a warrand wes subscryvit to Sir Johnne Arnott to mak payment to the Erll of Perth of the soume of fyve hundreth merkis advanceit be him to Allane McEanduy[1] for the furtherance of his Majesteis service agauns the ClanGregour and ane uther warrand wes subscryvit for delyverie of ane hundreth merkis to the Laird of Lundy[2] for the heid of Gregour Ammonach.

"1611. Feb 19. at Edinburgh. Charge against the Undertakers of the service against the ClanGregour.

"Forasmuch as Johnne Earl of Tullibardin, William Lord Murray his son, Harie Sancolme, Sir Duncane Campbell of Glenurquhy, Alexander Colhoun of Luss, Sir George Buquhannane of that Ilk James Campbell of Lundy and Mcfarlane of Arroquhar, compeiring personally before the Lords of Privy Council upon the last day of Jan. now bygone They undertook his Majesty's service against the ClanGregor and promised to go to the field and to have entered in action and blood, with them betwix the 13 day of this instant Feb. and to have prosecuted that service thereafter with their whole power and forces in manner specified in the acts made thereanent and although the said 13 day be now bygone Nevertheless there is no thing as yet done in that service but the same is altogether frustrated and the ClanGregor who were enclosed within an Isle an great hope had and promises made that they should not have got forth therof until the service had begun, against them in the Isle, are now escaped and got out and not so much as ane mynt or show of pursuit intended against them, but the undertakers, every one in their several discourses doing what in them lies, to vindicate themselves from all imputation of sloth, negligence, or neglect of duty in that point highly to his Majesty's offence and fostering of the lymmers in their rebellion and wicked deeds Therefore letters to be directed charging the said undertakers to compeir before the said Lords upon the last day of Feb. instant To answer to the premisses and to give account to the said Lords of the form and manner of their proceeding in the said service and upon what occasion the same service is frustrated and disappointed under the pain of rebellion and putting of them to the horn with certification to them should they fail that Letters shall be directed simpliciter to put them thereto.—Record of Council."

The following revolting entry refers evidently to the campaign of the previous autumn under Clan Ranald :—

"1611 Feb. Item by warrant and direction of his Highness Council to Allane McIldowie's servant who brought three heads of the MacGregors and presenting the same before the Council. As the same warrant produced upon compt bears £66, 13s. 4d.

"Amongst other warrants for service done . . .

"Item by warrant and direction of his Majesty's Council to James Campbell of Lawers for the slaughter of Gregor Amononche McGregor. As the same warrant with the said James acquittance produced upon compt bears £66, 13s 4d

---

[1] Locheil. [2] Clerical error for "Lawers."

"Also in Feb. of this year sums to messengers passing with the letters and proclamations lately given.

"1611. Feb. the last at Edinburgh.

"Glenurquhyis promise anent the entry of Gregor McEane and Duncane M^cincaird.

"The which day Sir Duncane Campbell of Glenurquhy Knt. compeiring personally before the Lords of Secret Council he took upon him and promised to enter Gregor McGregor M^ceane and Duncane M^cincaid before the said Lords upon the 14. day of March next to come As he will answer the contrary at his peril.

"Anent the Commissioners aginst the ClanGregor.

"(The first part is almost an exact recapitulation of the former charge on Feb. 19. but continues.)

"And all the said persons compeiring personally and the excuses and defences propounded by them wherefore the said service took not effect being at length heard and considered by the Lords of Secret Council and they ripely advised therewith.   The Lords of Secret Council find and declare that the persons particularly abovewritten and every one of them have failed in the execution of the charge, and service foresaid undertaken by them against the ClanGregour and that they have not fulfilled the same conform to their promises made thereanent and the said Lords Reserve the farther deliberation of what shall be enjoined unto them for their said failure to another occasion, ordaining them in the mean time, to address themselves home and to keep their own bounds so that the ClanGregor have no resett, protection, comfort nor maintenance within the same.—Record of Secret Council."

The "Black Book of Taymouth" gives a fuller account of what took place on Loch Katerine :—

"The King his Maiestie hering of the great rebellioun and oppressioun praxtisit be the Clangregour of new againe in anno 1610 sent from England the Erle of Dounbar for taking order with theme and for settling of peace in thee helandis as he hade done in the Southe borderis of befoir.   And amangis otheris noble and gentle men the said Sir Duncane was burdenit to pursue the said Clangregour for ruitting out of thair posteritie and name.   Thairefter the Earle of Dounbar reterit himselff back to the Kingis Maiestie And in the month of Februar anno 1611. the Clangregour being straitlie pursued, they tuke thame selffis to the Ile callit Ilanvernak in Menteith.   Quhairupon the Secret Consell imployed the said Sir Duncane and otheris gentlemen in the countreis about, to besiege them Quhilk being begun, the seige wes haistelie dissolvit throch ane vehement storme of snow.   The said Sir Duncane his folkis reteiring thairfra,

Robert Campbell his secund sone, hering of sum oppressioun done be a number of thame in the said Sir Duncane his landis, tuke thre of thair principallis, and in the taking ane wes slaine the other twa wer sent to Edinburghe. About this tyme the Erll of Dounbar departit this lyffe, upon the occasioun of whois deith the King his Maiestie chargit be severll commissions the Erle of Argyle and the said Sir Duncane and thair freindis to pursue the Clangregour. Quhairupon the Counsell appointed ane meeting to be in Edinburgh of all thair landlordis, quhair the said Sir Duncane being amangis the rest directit out of Edinburch for attending on the countrie, his sone Robert and Johne Campbell sone to the Laird of Lawiris, quha slew the maist speciall man and proud lymmer of thame, callit Johne Dow McAllester[1] in Stronferna, and with him Allester McGorne. Immediatlie thairefter, the said Sir Duncane abyding in Edinburch with the rest of his sones and friendis, attending on the Secret Consell, the Clangregour burnt the hundreth markland of Glenurquhay, the twentie pund land of Glenfalloch, the ten-lib · land of Mochaster in Monteith, the twentie pund land of Abirnquhill perteining to Colene Campbell of Laweris brother, the eighteen marklandis of Cowldaris and Finnaves , and in the Cosche of Glenurquhay they slew fourtie great mearis and thair followaris, with ane fair cursour sent to the said Duncane from the Prince out of Londoun   And fra that furth the Clangregour held thame selff togidder to the number of VI or VII. scoir men, till the said Sir Duncane eftir his returning from Edinburch directit furth his sone Robert accompaneit with Colene Campbell of Abirruquhil to persue thame, quho followit thame straithe throch Balquhidder, Monteith, and Lennox, and drave thame to the forrest of Beinbuidh in Ergyle, quhair they slew Patrik McGregour sone to Duncane in Glen, and tuke Neill McGregour bastard to Gregor McEane, with otheris fyve, quhom they hangit at the Cosche quhair they slew the mearis, and from that chaissit thame straithe to the month that lyis betuix Rannoch and Badenoch, that from that tyme furth thay wer so scattered that thay newir mett agane abone the number off ten or tuelff. And from the month of Maii in the said zeir, the service wes followit furth be the said Erle of Ergyle and Sir Duncane and thair friendis, induring the quhilk tyme thrie wes tane and slane be the said Sir Duncane his sones and servandis to the number of sixtene of the said ClanGregour."

A tradition relates that one of the besiegers was lighting a fire on the shore, when Callum Oig McGregor V^cCoull shot him dead with a long barrel, and called out so as to be heard across the water " Thugadh thall a chrom na geredh "—" take care you dirty crook." As the Gaelic crom signifying crook literally is used for shoemaker, of which trade the defunct

[1] John Dow McAllester breac, nephew of Gregor MacGregor of Roro.

was, Callum was supposed by the daunted besiegers to be a Conjuror, against whom they could no longer carry on the war."

This tradition was reported by Donald MacGregor, a native of Strathfillan, schoolmaster in the parish of Luss, and learned in Gaelic tradition. He knew nothing when he told the story, of either the "Record of Council" or the "Book of Taymouth."

Some modern verses appear on the margin of the "Chartulary" relating to this tradition and to the epitaphs given to the Clan in the proclamations.

From the "Chartulary," referring to the siege of the MacGregors in Ilanvernoch, Feb. 1611.

> "In fair Loch Ketrin's farther Isle
> Yclep'd by Council 'den and hole'
> The Wolves kept holiday awhile,
> Devouring what 'twas said they stole.
> To snare them here vast schemes were tried;
> Each stratagem the horde defied,
>   And hunters kept at bay.
> Some say a kindly fall of snow
> Bade these the hopeless sport forego,
>   And give the brutes the play.
> But others that the Second Sight
> Had given them such a panic fright
> No longer tarry here they might,
> But ere tomorrow's peeping light,
>   Should homeward hie away.

"1611. Feb. John Campbell brother to the Laird of Lawers, slew, this month, John Dhu McAllaster MacGregor of Stronferna for whose head as for those of several others, the Council had 31. Jan. offered £1000. It was not till the 24. May following that he forwarded his head to the Council. He claimed as reward not that above alluded to, but in terms of an act of council 19. April 1605. a 19 year lease of his lands, or compensation at sight of the Council. This tribunal after formally consulting his Majesty and being told (3. June)[1] that he left them to their direction in regard to the execution of laws which they themselves had framed and of the interpretation of which they were the best judges, ordered 19. Dec. 1611 the superior of the lands of Stronferna, viz. Robertson of Strowan, to pay Campbell a compensation, and that the wife, children, servants and tenants of the late John Dhu MacGregor of Stronferna be instantly ejected."[2]

---

[1] Chapter xxxv.   [2] Chapter xxxiv.

Chapter XXX

Continued Trials of sundry MacGregors

FROM the "Chartulary":—

"1611. March 2. Court of Justiciary. Mr Alexander Coluill, Justice Depute.

Entered

Johnne McEwin in Kilbryde

Archibald McIlvoyll McLowrin

Donald M^cinowie in Glencho

Duncane Caird McGregor

Patrik M^ceandow McGregor

Allaster Bowie McGregor clerache

Dougall McGregor Clerache McGregor

Duncane McNeill McGregor

Donald M^ceandich McGregor tane bak agane to waird and nocht put to ane assise.

Dilaitit accuset and persewit be Mr Robert Foullis substitute to Sir Thomas Hamiltoun of Bynnie Knt Advocate to our Souerane lord for his hienes intereis, of the crymes respective following viz   The said Johne McEwin for airt and pairt of the thiftious steilling of tuelf scheip fra ye Barrone McCaslane furth of his landis of Innerthonoling ; committit in the moneth of August last by past, 1610 zeiris, Item for the thiftious steilling of tua gait (Goats) and ane scheip fra Adame Colquhoun in Poirt furth of the landis of Banvie in the moneth of Dec. Jvvj and sax (1566) zeiris Item for airt and pairt of ye steilling of ane pair of Pleuch irnes fra William Myller in Schennekillis furth of the Lands of Schennekeillis in ye moneth of Aprryle Ivvj and aucht zeiris (1568.) Item for commoun thift and commoun re-sett of thift inputing and outputing of thift &a And of daylie intercowmoning and keiping cumpanie with the McGregouris assisting and taking pairt with thame in all thair thiftious deidis, heirschipis, robries and oppressiounes, this thre or four zeir bygane.

" The saidis Archibald McIlvoyll McLowen and Donald McInnowie servandis to Allester and Allane M^cindowie in Glencho for airt and pairt of the tressounabill raiseing of fyre about Johnne Stewartis hous in the Camerone in the Lennox in ye moneth of Dec. last bypast assageing of Duncane, James and umqle Johnne Stewartis yawintill And for airt and pairt of the slauchter of ye said umqle Johnne Stwart at ye tyme foirsaid.

"The said Duncane Caird McGregor for cowmone thift and resset of thift, outputing and inputing of thift &a And for daylie Intercowmoning and keiping of trystes and consultationis with the McGregors assisting and taking pairt with thame in all and sindrie thair thiftis, reiffis, and oppressionis committit be yame this thre zeir bygane.

"The said Patrik McEan Dowie McGregour for being in company with the McGregouris at the fecht or skirmisch of Bintoiche[1] in ye moneth of Apryle Jvvj and four zeiris and for airt and pairt of the tressonable raising of fyre burning of the Castell of Achallader and of tuentie houssis in Glenlochie and for the crewall slauchter of fourscore kye at ye said fecht. And siclike for airt and pairt of the slauchter of umqle Patrik Dow McNab and ane servand of ye Laird Glenvrquhies namit McLayne baith slane in ye said fecht of Bintoich And for cowmon thift intercowmuning &a. the said Allaster Bowie McGregour for cowmone thift and commone resset of thift outputing and inputing of thift fra land to land fra cuntrie to cuntrie And for Intercowmoning and keiping daylie trystis and conventionis with the McGregouris and taking plane pairt with thame in all yair and thiftious deidis thir diuerse zeiris bygane.

"The said Dougall McGregour Clerache McGregour for ye crewall slachter of umqle Gregour McGregour sone to umqle Duncane Abroche McGregour be schuteing of him with ane arrow behind his bak committit in August Jvj and four zeiris 1604 Item for intercowmoning &a The said Duncane McNeill McGregour for cowmone thift, intercowmoning &a.

"The said Johnne McAndro for airt and pairt of the burning of Johnne Stewartis hous and slauchter of the said umqle Johnne Stewart committit in the same moneth of Dec. 1610 at ye least for keiping companie with the saidis Archibald McIlvoill McLaurin and Duncane M^cinnowie and ye remanent of yair complices quha cam furth of Glencho to ye doing of ye saidis crymes."

There follows a list of the persons on the assise.

"The Assyse be ye mouth of ye said Thomas Fallasdaill chanceler fand, pronunceit, and declairit the saidis (repetition of names) to be fylit culpable and convict of seuerall crymes respective abone written contenit in zair dittayis And ye said Dougall McGregour Clerache to be fylit culpable and convict of airt and pairt of the slauchter of ye said Gregour McGregour committit be ye said Dougall he being within the age tuelf zeiris for ye time.

"And siclyke fand, pronunceit, and declarit ye said Johnne McAndro to be clene, innocent, and acquit of ye burning of ye said Johnne Stewart's hous &a.

[1] See Chapter xxvii., page 336.

"Dome —for the quhilk cause ye said justice be ye mouth of Alex Kenneddie dempster of Court decernit and ordainit ye saidis

Johnne McEwin
Duncane Caird McGregour
Patrik McIndow McGregour
Allaster Bowie McGregour and
Duncane McNeill McGregour

to be tane to ye Borrowmuir of Edin and yair in ye ordinar place of executioun to be hangit quhill thay be deid and all zair landis heritages, guidis, geir, moveable and unmoveabil, &a to be forfaltit and escheit to our Souerane lordis use as convict of ye saidis crymes And superceidis the pronunceing of Dome upon the vyer thre quhill be advisit with the Lords of Secret Council yairanent And ordainit yame to be tane bak againe to yair prissone.—Record of High Court of Justiciary

"1611 March. Item by warrant and direction of his Highness Council to Sir Alex. Colhoun of Luss Knicht in name of his friends who slew three Makgregouris, As the same warrant together with his acquittance produced upon compt bears, £200

"Item to the MacGregours that were kept in the tolbooth of Edinburgh every week the space of ten weeks before they were executed one dozen of bread at 16 shillings the dozen, £8

"Item to the officers of Justiciary for sommoning of an assise of the Macgregours and some of the Gang of Glencoe, £1. o 10 "

NOTE —The Glencoe prisoners were evidently in no way connected with the MacGregors, but only summoned in one assise for convenience. One of them was acquitted, and the two others returned to prison, as also one of the MacGregors, viz , Dougall McGregour Clerache McGregor. His trial is altogether curious   If he killed his young clansman intentionally, however guilty he might be morally and in the eyes of disinterested persons, yet he had done the Government a service thereby. Possibly they intended to recognise this, and therefore reprieved him, but there is no explanation of why they felt called upon to prosecute him, except the tender age of his victim, as from the point of view of the Council young Gregor was a "wolf."[1]   Another MacGregor, Donald McEandich, was taken back from the assise.

"1611. April   Item to George Matho messenger passing from Edinburgh with letters to charge Sir Duncane Campbell of Glenurquhy to bring and exhibit before the Council Gregor McEane upon the 10. day of May next to come to the effect he

[1] See proclamation of 31st Jan. 1611, page 264

may be tried and punished for his offences conform to the laws of this realm,
£6. 13½.—Lord High Treasurer's Books.

"1611. April 11. At Roystoun. From his Ma: anent Gregor MᶜEane.
'Right trustie and weilbelouit cosines and councellouris we greet you weele ; wheras
it hes bene complenit to ws by Robert Buquhannane seruand to James Buquhannane gent of our butterie That one Gregor MᶜEane not onlie spoyled his fader of
all his goodis but allsua cruellie murdereist him. It is thairfoir our plaisour (seeing
the said Gregor is now apprehendit by the Laird of Glenurquhy) that you cause the
said Laird exhibit him befoir you and that you cause sich order to be tane with him
as his behauiour in former tyme in this and the lyke caiss do deserue whiche
assuring ourselff you will see performed we bid you fareweele. from our Courte at
Roystoun the 11 day of Aprile 1611.'—Record of Secret Council.—Royal Letters.

"1611. Aprile 29.   At Greenwich.

"From his Ma : anent the Erll of Ergyll.

" ' Right traist cosine and counsellour and weilbelouit Counsellour we greete you
weele, The oppin and avowed rebellioun of that barbarous race of the name
of MᶜGregour is growne to suche hicht as we ar resolued by thair examplarie
punishment to terrifie vtheris our evil disposit subiectis to committ the lyke insolencyis heireftir ; we haif had conference with our cosine the Erll of Ergyll beirair
heirof for the caus to whome we haif given power and commissioun to persew these
rebellis with fire and swerd, and becaus in the prosequiting of this oure seruice thair
will be mony thingis fall oute wherin oure authoritie must be joyned with his
forceis and wherein he must be assisted with your aduice and counsell we will
heirfoir eirnistlie desire you that, at all occasionis as he sait haif to do ayther to come
or send vnto you give him that assistance aduice and counsell as sallbe most fitting
for effectuating of this seruice to our honnour and the quiting of the cuntrey. and
becaus the saidis MᶜGregouris ressaueth (receiveth) grite comforte by thair wyffis
who leving peceablie without trouble and possessing thair goodis not onlie suppleis
all thair wantis and necessities bot furneist thame with dew intelligence making
thame thairby the moir able to continew in thair rebellioun and to prevent all
occasiounis of thair over thraw as lykewayes thair childrene being mony in number
are lyke in few yeiris to be als grite if not a griter pest and trouble to our cuntrey
nor these present rebellis ar, we will lykewayis desire you to confer with oure said
cosine and aduise vpoun the best meanes for preventing of these two euillis, whairin
yf you find ony difficultyis or impediment Latt vs be acquentit thairwith that we may
deliberat vpoun the best meanes for remedying thairof You must heirwith haif
a speciall cair that these cuntrys nixt adiacent to the pairtis wher these MᶜGregouris
haif thair ordinarye delling and residence to be so gairdit and watcheit as they haif
no ressett nor comfort thairin And so expecting your cairfull accomplishment of the
premiss we bid you heartilie fairweele. frome our Courte at Greewiche the 29.
of Aprile 1611.'

"1611 April 29   Commission to the Earl of Argyle to pass upon the Clan-Gregour

"James &a Forasmuch as the open and avowed rebellion of that barbarous race of the name of McGregor is grown to so great a height as shaking off all fear of God and reverence of us and our authoritie thay become every day more insolent for remeid whereof and by their exemplary punishment to imprint fear in the hearts of all others our evil disposed subjects we have given power and commission to Archd : Erll of Ergyll and James Campbell of Lawers

"Commission to the Earl of Ergyll against the ClanGregour James &a Forasmuch as ever since we were of perfect years and able in our own person to govern the kingdoms committed by God to our charge and government   Our chief care (next our duty to his Holy Majesty) hath been to maintain justice and govern the same in peace, and quietness, and rather by lenity than using the rigour of our authority To draw all our subjects to live in a peaceable form under the government of a just Prince.   Ever preferring mercy and pardon where the same was humbly suited of us (upon assurance given by the suitors of their conformity to our laws and living as peaceable subjects in time thereafter) to the rigour of our laws, and not using the last remeid where the first was not suited in time convenient, As by example of the middle shyres of our kingdom and farthest remote parts of our Isles is evidently known, the inhabitants thereof now live in as great security without oppression or trouble as our subjects of any other parts of our kingdoms do to their unspeakable comfort ; yet notwithstanding of all these premises that most unhappy and barbarous race of the name of McGregor having shaken off all fear of God and reverence to us and our authority have not only neglected that good occasion, in suiting and obtaining of our pardon for their bygane misbehaviour but as if there were not a God to punish them nor a Sovereign Prince to put his decree in execution And, as if they only, of all our subjects were able to make good against us and withstand our authority , they still persist in their most barbarous and wicked life to the great harm and impoverishing of many honest men for remeid whereof and to give example to all others our subjects to continue in our obedience and not to presume upon the impunity of the said McGregors to lead the like wicked life as they do, We are resolved to lay mercy aside and by justice and the sword to root and extirpate all of that race, their assisters, and partakers that shall be found rebellious and disobedient to us and our authority And that this our determination may be put in full execution we have made speciall choice of the Earl of Argyle "

Next follows an iniquitous proclamation, which must leave an indelible blot on its authors

"1611. April 29. Licence and commission to the Earl to heir the offers of the ClanGregour

"For mitigating of the rigour of our other commission given to our said cousing

We licence and permit him to hear the offers of such of the said MacGregors as shall submit themselves in our mercy and to receive them to our obedience upon the conditions following viz that he shall humbly sute our pardon, shall before obtaining thereof enter in action and blood against any of that race and name being our declared rebels, hunt, follow and pursue them with fire and sword and never leave off the pursuit of some of them till they be reduced to our obedience or rooted out of our kingdom, and that he shall likewise either deliver to our said cousing or to the Lords of our privy Council the person or head of a McGregor of as good rank, quality and action as himsel and find caution.—Record of Council.—Commissions.

"1611. April 29. Proclamation to the Laird of Glenurquhy and such as shall be employed by him for the taking of ClanGregour, narrating the former commission to Erle of Argyle.

"For better effectuating of which service we have appointed Sir Duncan Campbell of Glenurquhy Knight to attend upon and assist our said cousin 'Attoure we have taken the said Sir Duncane Campbell and all such persons as shall assist him under our special protection, defence, supply, maintenance, and safeguard to be uncalled, troubled, or pursued criminally nor civilly.'"

In May of this year Glenurquhy burned the houses and lands of Dewletter and the Castle of Glenstray, as appears from a pardon for these acts granted in 1621 and 1627.

"1611. May 24. The head of John Dhu McAllaster McGregour of Stronferna was sent to the Council by John Campbell brother of Lawers.[1]

"1611. May 24. at Edinburgh.   Certain Acts concerning the ClanGregor.

"Forasmuch as the King's Majesty having made and constituted Archibald Earl of Argyle his Majesty's Lieutenant Justice and commissiones for the pursuit of the rebellious thieves and Lymmers called the ClanGregour And his Majesty and Lords of Secret Council being willing to assist the said Lieutenant in everything which may further and advance the service, and considering that in the prosecution thereof he will oftimes have occasion to have sundry companies of men upon the fields who must have their entertainment, and victuals in the countries where they shall happen to encamp, therefore his Majesty and the Lords of Secret Council allow that the said Lieutenant and the Captains and commanders of his camp and Host shall take vivers for themselves and their companies in the parts and countries where they shall encamp, upon the prices following viz the mairt for twenty merks, the boll of meal, for four pounds, the sheep or wedder for two merks, the stone of cheese for 24 shillings and ordain them to make present payment of the prices foresaid when they take up the said vivers and that they take no more at one time, than may serve them for meat allanerlie for the space of 48 hours and that they take not their hiall vivers and furnishing from one man but proportionally from all

---

[1] *Vide* the quotation from the "Black Book of Taymouth," page 375.

the neighbours of the bounds and parts where they shall camp in, and according to the necessity of the service and state of the country and bounds where they shall encamp. The Lords ordain that the resetters of the ClanGregour, their wives and bairns shall be called before his Majesty's council for their resetts since the proclamation in the month of —— last and their trial to be according to the form and order of the Council

"The Lords remit the order taking with the wives and children of the ClanGregour to the Lieutenant himself—— The Lords of Secret Council ordain letters to be directed charging the Sherrif of the Shires where the wives and children of the ClanGregour have their residence as also their landlords to render and deliver them to the Lieutenant within three days under the pain of horning and they being delivered to the Lieutenant ordain him to transport them to such parts as he shall think meet and to mark the wives with a key upon the face and if they shall withdraw themselves from the places whereunto they shall be transported the Lords ordain the resetters of them to be called before the Council

"Forasmuch as one of the chief causes which has encouraged the rebellious thieves and lymmers of the ClanGregour to continue in their thievish doings has been the comfort and supply which they have found in sundry parts of the incountry from which they are well provided and furnished with poulder, bullet, and armour and whereas they dare not come themselves to buy armour the same is bought to their use by other Highlandmen, to the great hindrance of his Majesty's service Therefore the Lords of Secret Council ordain letters to be directed To command charge and inhibit all and sundry his Majesty's lieges and subjects within the burrows of Perth, Stirling, Glasgow, Dumbarton and Inverness by open proclamation at the Market Crosses of the said burrows that none of them presume nor take upon hand to sell any kind of armour to any highlandmen but by the knowledge and advice of such special persons, within every one of the said burrows, as shall be appointit to that effect by his Majesty's Lieutenant, to the effect it may be clearly known and understood that the said armour is not to the use nor behoof of the said ClanGregour As they will answer upon the contrary at their highest peril.

"The Lords of Secret Council for the better furtherance of his Majesty's service against the ClanGregour give power and commission to Archibald Earl of Ergyll his Majesty's Lieutenant, Justice, and Commissioner against the ClanGregour to charge such persons within the Sheriffdom of Perth whom in his honour and conscience he shall think to be favourers, resetters, or assisters of the ClanGregor to transport themselves to the Sheriffdoms of Fife, Stirling or Forfar and to remain there for the space of two months

"The Lords ordain a missive to be written to Sir Johnne Moncreiffe to cause the house of Garthe be delivered to the Lieutenant. The Lords ordain Sir Duncane Campbell of Glenurquhy Knight who was personally present to deliver Allaster McGorrie presently being in his hands, to the Lieutenant.

" Forasmuch as for the better furtherance and execution of his Majesty's service against the ClanGregour it is very necessary that the houses of Innerdouglas pertaining to ———— McFarlane of ———— and the house of Fatlipps pertaining to Malcome McFarlane of ———— be delivered to his Majesty's Lieutenant to be kept by him for such space as he shall have that service in hands ; therefore ordain letters to be directed charging the said ———— McFarlane and all others, havears, keepers, and detainers of the said place and house of Innerdouglas and the said Malcolme McFarlane and all others, havears, keepers, and detainers of the said place and house of Fatlipps, to render and deliver the said place and house to the said Lieutenant or any in his name having his power to receive the same, and to remove themselves and their servants forth thereof within six hours next after the Charge under the pain of rebellion &a And if they fail &a to denounue. &a.

" Forasmuch as the King's Majesty having now resolved upon some good and substantious order and course for pursuit of the rebellious thieves and limmers of the ClanGregor and reducing of them to his Majesty's obedience, and the forces destined for this service being now to enter to work, and to prosecute, hunt, and follow and pursue the said limmers with fire and sword and all other extremity It is therefore very necessary and expedient that all his Majesty's good subjects in the countries and bounds next adjacent to the ClanGregor be upon their guard as well for keeping of their own bounds free of them, as to follow and pursue them as they come there ; For which purpose ordain letters to be directed to command and charge the Sheriffs, Stewards and Baillies and all noblemen, barons and gentlemen and others his Majesty's subjects in the bounds and parts where the said thieves and lymmers shall happen to resort and repair To cause diligent attendance to be given that they have no resset, comfort, protection nor maintenance, within their bounds, and if they shall happen to come there for eschewing of apprehension That they immediately rise in arms follow and pursue the said thieves and lymmers, raise the hue and cry and never leave off the pursuit of them until they be off their bounds and countries.   As they will answer upon the contrary at their highest peril.

" 1611. May 25.   The Lords of Secret Council ordain and command Sir Duncan Campbell of Glenurquhy Knight, James Campbell of Lawers, Allane Cameroune of Lochyell, and Alexander McDonald of Gargavache to deliver unto Archibald Earl of Ergyll his Majesty's Lieutenant in his Highness's service against the ClanGregour all such persons of the said Clan as they have already taken prisoners or shall hereafter take prisoners during the time of the said service For the which these presents or the extract thereof subscribed by the Clerk of his Majesty's Privy Council shall be unto them a sufficient warrant.—Record of Secret Council, Acta.

" May 25.   The Council had already been taking measures to levy money from such landlords as had ' MacGregors dwelling within their bounds, or whose grounds were laid waste by them, in return for their efforts to extirpate them which the Government seem to have more at heart than the Landlords.' On 25. these landlords being convened as now asserted by the Council, before the commissioners of the Highlands had promised to give his Majesty £60 for every merk land the second year after his Majesty should have rid them of the oppression of Clan-Gregour. From a subsequent minute of Council however (July 1613.) it appears that the number of landlords present, out of at least sixteen of the best rank and quality of these was five only and that of these Glenurquhy as one, protested against the transaction. The reluctance indeed of the landlords to go along with this measure will be illustrated in the sequel "

Of the Landlords of the ClanGregor at this time the subjoined list is made from a comparison of the "Record of Council," and the Treasurer's Books (July 1613).

"Earls of Argyll, Murray, Linlithgow, Monteith, Master of Tullibardin, Lord of Madertie, Sir George Buchanan of that ilk, Sir Duncan Campbell of Glenurquhy, Sir Archibald Stirling of Keir, John Napier of Merchiston, James Reidheuch of Cultebraggane, Alexander Menzies of Weyme, Robert Robertson of Strowane, Duncan Campbell of Glenlyon, James Campbell of Lawers, John Campbell his brother, Mr James Shaw of Knockhill, Alex. Shaw of Cambusmoir, Thomas Graham of Boquhapple, Duncan Menzies.

"May 25. A motion was made in the Council for relieving the country of the wives and bairns of the ClanGregor."—Haddington Collection, Vol. 1., page 217

Probably it was the "Overture" given in "The Chiefs of Colquhoun," viz :—

"Ane speciall Owertour for transplanting the bairnis of Clangregour.

"Item First, the haill bairnis that is past xii zeir auld to be sent to Irland be zour Lordships warren, to sic settilmen as zour Lordships thinkis meitest that duellis thair, be quhais advysis thair names to be chengit, and to be maid hirdis, and thair to remane vnder the paine of deid.

"As anent these that ar within tuell zeir auld, that thai be zour Lordships warren be transplantit be south the watteris of Forth and Clyd, conforme to his Majestie's will, to the Justices of Peace of these boundis, at thair nixt grate meitting, quhilk is the first Tuysday of Feb. And be thair advyssis to be placeit and sustenit in townis and parochines, and thair namis chengit, and thair to remane vnder the pane of ded, with power to the saidis justiceis of Peace to giff and allow ane fyne to evirilk ane of thame, for the help of thair sustentatioun, and quhen thai come to the age of xii zeris, that they be transplantit to Irland [1]

[1] Copy of "Overture" at Rossdhu—"Chiefs of Colquhoun," vol 1., p. 217.

3 C

"May 1611. Remission for fyreraising and for all other crymes, to McRobert McGregor Grahame.—Privy Seal LXXX. 250.

"1611. May 25. A report was made to the Council that the escheats of the ClanGregor and the fines of their resetters had, by his Majesty been given to the Earl of Argyll.—Haddington's Collections.

"May 25. The resetters of the ClanGregour ordained to be pursued and punished.

"Power given to the Earl of Argyll to command such McGregouris as has found caution, and renounced their names, to transport themselves on this side of Tay if he find it expedient . . . Granted that he shall charge the Sherrifs and Landlords of the Highlands and Brae countries to set out watches and to prepare forces to hold the ClanGregor furth of their bounds, and to pursue them if they come within the same.

"May 26. Johnne Dow M^callester's head sent in be Johne Campbell brother to Laweris.—Haddington Collections.

"1611. Item to the Laird of Lawers for his service against the McGregouris at command and direction of the Council, £1000.

"Several messages to various lairds paid for.

"May 28. The whilk day the Earl of Argyle's commission against the Clan-Gregor was presently read, allowed and subscribed with some other letters and warrants concerning the ClanGregor.—Record of Secret Council Sederunt Book.

"June —. Item by warrant of the Council to Duncan Makfarlane in recompense of the hurt which his brother received in the pursuit of John Dow Eane McGregour as the said warrant in his acquittance produced bears, £66.15.4.—Lord High Treasurer's Books.

"1611. June 5. at Greenwich.

"From his Majesty anent the ClanGregour.

"'Right Trusty and well beloved Cousins and counsellors we greet you well. Wheras we find that upon the slaughter of John Dow McAllaster some suit is made for payment of that price imposed by our Council at Stirling, upon every head of the ClanGregour but particularly of a greater rate of money upon some specials of mark and note among them, of which this John Dow McAllaster was one, we have therein thought meet to refer the interpretation of your own act wholly unto your-selves who first made the same, and as no doubt you can best deliver what was the true meaning and intent at the time of the making thereof, so we wish that you should accordingly proceed and accomplish the condition of it unto whomsoever you shall hold the same to be justly due, and in like sort should give unto every one who shall make an unlawful demand their dispatch and a direct refuse, so far as in reason they cannot justly challenge any thing which you, who were makers of the act can best determine. And so we bid you fairwell. From our Court at Greenwich the 3. of June 1611.'—Record of Council.—Royal Letters.

"July 6.   Commission against Gregor McGregor V^cEane

"Sir Duncane Campbell has taken and apprehended Gregor McGregor V^cEane a common and notorious thief murderer sorner, and oppressour and presently has him in his hands, and keeping.   Commission to Glenurquhy to hold a Court and try him.

"July 16.   The Marquis of Huntlie presented a supplication setting forth that he was 'confynit within his plais of Strathbogie and some certane bounds thereabout' and that for many years he had not been able to visit his countries on license to the great disadvantage of his property   'And now as the saidis Lordis knowis his Maiesteis seruice aganis the ClanGregour is in handis and it is verie likelie that these lymmaris for thair safetie will withdraw themselffis to the said Marques boundis foresaidis whaur without all question thay will find comforte, resett, and protectioun yf he go not thair to impede and stay the same, humbly desyring thairfoir the saidis Lordis to grant and gif vnto him Libertie and License to ressort and repair to the countreis of Badyienauche, Lochquhabir, and Innerness, for the necessair caussis foirsaidis,' &a.   He obtains leave from the 1. August to 20. Sep. and no longer.

"July 17.   William Buchanan nephew and heir presumptive ot William Buchanan of Drumakill and William Buchanan iu Blairnamboyd got from the Earl of Argyll a licence to treat with the ClanGregor from 17 to 25 July.

"August 5   At Salisbury.   From his Majesty anent McConnell duy and McRannald

"'Right trusty Cousin and Counsellor and right trusty and well beloved Councellors we greet you heartily well.   we wrote unto you before to have caused the receivers of our rents of that our kingdom deliver to Allane McConwildwy or the bearer hereof the Laird of McRannald so much money as should amount to one month's pay for fourscore men, and that for prosecuting our service against the ClanGregour and understanding by the bearer that this money was never as yet suited by you and that the sum will amount (at 10 shillings a day for every man) to one hundred pounds sterling our will and pleasure is, that as soon as you shall receive advertisement from the Earl of Ergyll that the said Allane and the Bearer with their forces are gone to the fields and entered in our service against the Clan-Gregour you shall immediately thereafter cause the officers of receipt in that our kingdom pay unto the bearer for himself, and his neighbour Allane, the said one hundred Pounds sterling for which these presents shall be your sufficient warrant. And so we bid you heartily farewell   From our Court at Salisbury the 3 of August 1611.   Sic subscribitur,

'JAMES R.'

"August 16.   Complaint by (Sir Alexander) Menzies of Weyme, as follows. The Lords of Secret Council have at the instance of William Rattray of Rynnagullane, Johnne Tailyeour in Corb, and Johne Beg there, decerned horning against complainer for not entering before the Council Allaster Menzies in Apnadow, rebel as being his man. Now Archibald Earl of Argyle, having been employed by his Highness in the pursuit of the ClanGregour, and having 'the haill cuntrey people of the Hielandis undir his chairge in that present service' compliner and all his men are and must continue during that service on the fields under the said Earl so that he cannot without great prejudice to that service compeir to the effect forsaid. Farther by an act of Council it is ordained that during the time of that service the persons engaged therein shall be free from all compearing before any judicatory of this kingdom. If the complainer had not been burdened with this service he would have willingly compeared and shown why he should not be urged with the entry of the said Allaster in respect that the said Allaster is not his man but is servant to the Earl of Argyll and at present with the Earl in the fields against the ClanGregour. Still complainer has fund caution in 1000 merks to enter the said Allaster if it is found that he ought to do so. On these grounds the said horning ought to be suspended. The Lords do suspend the letters of horning, because the said Allaster is in his Majesty's service against the ClanGregour. as has been verified by a letter sent to the complainer from the Earl of Argyle.—Dr Masson.

"1611. Sep. Complaint by Ronnald McDonald, apparent of Gargavach as follows. Complainer and Allaster McRonnald of Gargavach, his Father and Allane Camroun of Lochyell having been called to his Majesty's service against the ClanGregour had 'for testificatioun of thar willing obedience, to the hazard of thair lyveis and quhat ellis thay haif,' undertaken the service with the resolution to prosequte it to the uttermost of theair possibilities 'Accordingly Camroun and the complainer having sent out some spies against the ClanGregour had learned that Robert Abroche and 22 principal ringleaders of the Clan were in Badyenoch and had the protection there of the whole Clan Chattane and Clan Fersane, Thereupon complainer with his friends repaired in all haste to Badyenoch on 22 of July last 'to have maid ane onset upone the ClanGregour.' The Clan Chattane and Clan Fersane however hearing of their arrival at the head of Badyenoch rose all in arms to the number of 300 men, under the charge of William McIntosche son of the late Laird McIntosche &a   and came to the place where the complainer and his company were and not only stayed them from going farther into the country for pursuit of the ClanGregour but demanded of them how they dared come there against the ClanGregour who were friends of theirs and whom they would protect against all deadly, without respect of his Majesty. Although complainer had then 'objectit unto thame' the directioun he had from his Majesty and the Council for pursuit of the ClanGregor defenders took 12 of his men and these they yet detain prisoners. They would not have failed to slay complainer himself if night had not come on permitting his escape. Charge had been given to certain McFersanes and McIntosches (enumerated) to answer this day under pain of rebellion and now the defenders appearing the Lords find the complaint proven against three who are to be committed to ward in the tolbooth of Edinburgh.—Dr Masson "

In reference to the part taken by Locheill and Clan Ranald in pursuit of the MacGregors, a passage in Gregory's " Highlands and Isles " has an incidental remark as follows :—In 1611

" The Clanchameron and the Clanranald of Lochaber under their respective Chiefs Allan Cameron of Lochiel and Alexander M°Ranald of Keppoch, instead of waging war with each other or with the captain of the Clanchattan, were employed to assist the Earl of Argyle in suppressing of the ClanGregor. Several gentlemen of the families of Locheil and Keppoch refused however to engage on this service, which indeed if carried into effect with good will by the Highland Clans employed would have speedily ended in the utter ruin of the name of MacGregor " [1]

1611. Sep. Robert Abroch had his headquarters near the Laird of Grant's house of Ballachastel.

From the " Chartulary " :—

" 1611. Nov. 19. at Edinburgh. Anent the ClanGregour

" The which day the missive letter and articles respectively underwritten sent from his Majesty were presented to the Lords of Secret Council and in open audience read of the tenour follows.

" ' Right trusty and well beloved cousin and Counsellor we greet you well, we send you now home the Earl of Argyle to make en end according to his promise of that service, which he has already begun. The specialities whereof we have caused to be set down in articles which we have thought good herewith to send unto you, As for the service itself We are thus resolved, that as the connivance at those and the like malefactors might justly be accounted a great iniquity, so the utter extirpation of them and all and every one in particular, would be a work too troublesome, And therefore we have thought good on some to execute justice, and the rest to take to mercy And as we will not have our justice satisfied with the meanest and basest persons, so we would have special choice made of the most notorious malefactors to be an example thereof in this present business for which effect we would have you crave the advice as well of the said Earl of Argyle as of the gentlemen and others next inhabiting unto them, and who have been most endamaged by them by whose information ye may likewise learn what particular persons are most fit to be taken to mercy and which not. As concerning all satisfaction to be made to the persons particularly interested by such as shall be taken to mercy, as it will be a matter altogether impossible, so we must in that point prefer the general

[1] Gregory's " Highlands and Isles," page 341, where a note is added : " Many of the Clan Chattane also, particularly the Macphersons, assisted to protect the ClanGregor at this time."

benefit of the quietness of the whole country to the private interest of any one man, or some few others damnified, yet will we that those who are any way able to make any satisfaction shall according to their power make present restitution and for the rest let their good behaviour in time coming be accepted in part of payment, for if we should go about to exact the extremity both would the performance of that service require longer time and be more troublesome to the said Earl and also be more chargeable to us in recompensing the same, yet do we not mean to set you down an absolute rule herein upon either side, but leave it to your discretion so to temper this business as all occasions of complaint for non restitution may be taken away, so far as may be and yet no impossibility to be thrust upon the offender which may hinder the conclusion of so good a work, But to the intent that an assured peace (and not as it were a truce be obtained, for putting over of an imminent storm) may ensue, one point is carefully to be considered and diligently executed which is, the transplanting of such as shall be taken to mercy and of the wives and children of those who are or shall be killed or executed, (for except they be transplanted out of those places wherein they have had their continual residence according as was done unto the Grahams of Eske we see not how any perfect quietness of the country may be expected.) which point, how it may be best performed ye are likewise to consult with their aforesaid neighbours whose opinions being heard ye are to give such order therein as ye and they shall think most fit and most easy to be followed And all these premises recommending to your special consideration We bid you farewell from our Court at Roystoun.

'the 23 day of October 1611.'

"1611. Nov. Some particuler headis of his Majesteis will and pleasour concerning the ordour takeing with the McGregouris.

"First that my Lord of Argyle give in a roll to the Counsall of all the McGregouris that are killed by him or his, of those that ar takin and in presone and of those that ar come in will, and of those that ar yitt rebellis and lyis out and that my lord leave the copy of this roll with my Lord Fentoun.

"His Majesty is pleasit of that nomber of the McGregouris whiche come in will to grant unto my Lord of Argyle some three or four of thair lyves and a remissioun : off the whiche nomber Duncane Makewin alias Duncane the Tutour to be one, in regaird that he wes chief of thame and breker of the societie : providing alwise that thay find sufficient caution and suretie to the Counsell for observing of the laweris in tyme to come, and that these suretyis be answerable for ony wrong thay do heireftir.

"For the rest of these that ar come in will, if ony of thame haif killed a McGregour als good as himselff (or) two thrie or four of thame which in comparisone may be equal unto him, and assuredlie knowne to be his deid, his Majestie is pleasit he haif a remissioun, with the uther thrie or four whiche his Majestie hes grantit to the Erll of Argyll ; providing lykwise that thay find sufficient surety for keeping good ordour in tyme comeing and such surytcis as sall content the Counsell. And for such as ar come in will and done no service by killing of the McGregouris nor cannot find sufficient suretie that then the law to haif his dew course, and no favour at all to be shown

" For suche as ar yitt rebelslis and outlawis after the Counsell he considered of the roll presentit unto thame by my Lord Argyle that ther be no pardoun grantit unto any nor takin in will except he present a better head at least ane as goode als his awne or such two thrie or more as salbe enjoyned to him by the Counsall. And for Robert Abroche who is now Chief of thame that ar presently out that he be not pardoned unless he bring at least halff a dusone of thair headis.

"To such of the McGregouris that ar pardoned and hes goodis and geir sufficient to mak restitutioun to the poorest sorte and that to be done at the sight and discretion of the Counsall to those that hes most neid of it and whair thair is no guidis nor geir thair is none to be haid.

"That the Counsall advise upon some satled ordour with these that find caution ather be transplantatioun or utherwise as salbe thought best

" For the young children and wyffis that thair be proclamatioun maid to produce theme or utherwise the resetaris to be guyltie of the crymes committed be the childrenes parentis and that the Counsal 1611 Nov be informatioun of my Lord of Argyle and utheris of the cuntrey people learne to know of thame all, and thairefter to dispose of thame so as they sall think best for repressing such a generatioun that thay never come to such a head or insolence again.—Dr Masson.

" His Majesty ordains that the Council take trial of the resetters and so many of them as shall be found guilty by the means and information of Mylord of Argyle shall be fined accordingly which fine his Majesty is pleased to bestow upon MyLord of Argyle to enable him the better to serve his Majesty.

"The conditions of the caution to be founden by the McGregouris who are to be received in favour

" That they shall be answerable and obedient subjects to our Sovereign and his laws That they shall satisfy and redress all parties who shall sustain harm or skaith of them hereafter and for bygane wrongs that they shall make redress so far as they have geir, That they shall not assist nor take part with the ClanGregor, resett them, their wives, bairns nor goods nor keep conventions, trysts nor meetings with them, by word nor write ' That they shall remain and keep ward within the Sherrifdom of Fife or any other part besouth the waters of Forth and shall not resort, nor repair, benorth the said water, and last that they shall compeir personally before his Majesty's Council so oft as they or their cautioners shall be charged to that effect. upon ten days warning under such pecunial sums as shall be modified by his Majesty's Council to be paid to his Majesty, in case they fail in any part of the premisses besides the satisfaction and redress of the parties skaithed —Record of Secret Council.

,

"1611. Nov. 21. Commission for trying the Resetters of the ClanGregour.

"Forasmuch as albeit the resett of the rebellious thieves and lymmers of the ClanGregour, their wives, bairns, goods and geir has been prohibited and discharged by many good acts and proclamations made, and published heretofore; nevertheless the chief and principal cause which has procured and still procures their continuance in rebellion and which has frustrated and disappointed the effectual execution of his Majesty's service against them doth proceed from the resett, supply, protection, and maintenance which they find among great numbers of people as well inhabiting the countries and bounds next adjacent unto them as in some parts of the country, who in outward show and appearance falsely pretending to be unfriends to the said limmers do notwithstanding covertly and obscurely not only supply all their necessities and wants but resett them in their houses, and take their goods and geir in keeping to their own use, and behoof, so that at all times when these fugitive limmers and thieves are pursued, or an course intended against them for reducing of them to obedience, their resetts and starting holes are so sure and certain unto them, as the most part of the courses intended against them have proven fruitless, highly to the offence and contempt of his Majesty and fostering of the said thieves in their insolencies; and whereas bypast experience in the like case gives clear evidence that nothing is more forcible against traitors, rebels, and fugitives than to cut them short of their resetts, and starting holes, cannot be goodly done, but by exemplary punishment to be inflicted upon the Resetters, Thairfore, &a."

Thus in the autumn of the year when such comprehensive plans were laid for the utter extirpation of the race, the King and Council confess that their efforts were mostly fruitless, and this circumstance explains the comparative clemency of the first part of the proclamation of the 19th November with the object of sparing the Commissioner further trouble, and the authorities greater expense.

"1611. Dec. 13. Charges against the Earl of Tullibardine for exhibition of the Laird of MacGregour being in his hands." "Charges against Allane McEanduy for exhibition of Patrick Aldoche and others."—Record of Secret Council Sederunt Book.

"1611. Nov. 21. Certain Gentlemen appointed in each Sheriffdom 'to appoint and sett courts to be halden be thame within the boundis respective at suche tymes dayis and placeis as thay sall think meet and to call and convene before thame all such persons as hes resett ony of the ClanGregour, thair wyffis, bairnis, or goodis sen the first day of August 1610. or who sall resett thame during the tyme of this commissioun (the nemes of quhilkis resettaris with the names of the personaris resett, thay sall rassave fro his Majesteis Lieutennent against the ClanGregour) and to examine try and demand tharupoun the sams resett and gyf thay grant the same, to putt thair depositiorus formerlie in wreatt and gyf thay deny the same, to ressave probatioun and witness aganis thame and to report the depositionis of the witnesses˜with the confessiounis of the pairties offendaries dewlie and authenticallie written and ˏcloseit unto the saidis Lordis to the effect the saidis Lordis may accordinglie pronunce and gif forth sentence against thame.   As alsua that the saidis commissionaris report unto the saidis Lordis the estate and conditioun of the personis who sall grant or aganis whom the resett salbe proven, and what thay ar valiant in landis or goodis and whenas the said commissionaris sall find the said resett to be cleir and manifest outher be confession of the party or deposition of witnes that then thay sal take sure cautioun of the offendouris that thay sal satisfie the decreet and sentence to˙ be pronunceit againist thame be the saidis Lordis and in case of thair refusal to find this cautioun that the saidis commissionaris committ thame to waird and hald thame thairin ay and quhill otherwise his Majesty's Lieutennant aganis the ClanGregour report unto the saidis commissionaris his warrand beiring that he hes ressaved satisfactioun of the offendour or is to employ thame aganis the ClanGregor —Dr Masson

"1611 Edinburgh Dec. 6.   Complaint by Johnne Campbell brother of James Campbell of Lawers as follows.

"The Lords of the Secret Council having upon 19 April 1605 resolved that the 'work of the exterminatioun of that wicked and unhappie and infamous race of lawless lymmaris, callit the Macgregour should be followed out against them till they had been 'alluterlie extirpat and rooted out' had declared 'verie solemnelie' by an Act of Council that whoever should apprehend and enter before them any of the name of McGregor 'quick or dead' should receive a nineteen years tack of all such lands as belonged to the person presented or were possessed by them, or else 'ane contentatioun and satisfaction for thair kyndnes to be payit be the landis-lord at the arbitriement of the Counsale' provided that the person receiving the tack should find cautioun to answer to the laws and to pay the old maill to the landlord, and also that at the expiry of the said tack the tacksman should vacate the said lands to the landlord and claim no kidness to the same thereafter   Now the complainer to the great hazard of his life had 'maid ane onset on the late Johnne Dow McAllaster McGregour in Stronfarnoch a chief rungleader of that Clan, slain him and presented his head accordingly but albeit the said Johnne was kindly tenant of the lands of Stronfarnoche, held by him of Robert Robertsoun of Strowane at the time of his slaughter, and albeit the said Robert, according to the 'said Act ought to deliver to the complainer a nineteen years tack of the said lands, yet he 'proudlie refuses' to do so   Both parties agreed to submit this matter to the Arbitration of Archibald Earl of Argyle and Sir Alexander Hay secretary to his Majesty, who promised to give their judgement by the 20. instant.

"1611. Dec. 19   The matter in dispute having been submitted to the appointed

3 D

arbiters with Alexander Earl of Dunfermlyne as oversman they had awarded to Campbell a certain sum in silver to be paid by Robertsoun in full discharge of his claim. As in these circumstances it is reasonable that the Laird of Strowane be possessed with his said lands, and that the relict and bairns of the said Johnne Dow be removed therefrom 'as personis unworthie to brook ony benefit within his Majesteis kingdome' the Lords declare that it shall be lawful to enter in possession of the said lands without any process of law, and to remove the said widow and her goods furth thereof without incurring any action of ejection, intrusion, spuilyie or wrongous intromission.—Dr Masson.

" 1611. Dec.   Item to George Matho messenger passing from Edinburgh with letters to charge John Earl of Tullibardine To bring and exhibit Gregor MᶜGregor now called the Laird and son to umqle John Dow MᶜGregor [1] personally before the Council the 9. of Jan. next, to the effect order may be taken with him for his obedience as accords under the pain of rebellion. And likewise passing with Letters to the Market Crosses of Stirling and Perth and there be open proclamation, charged Duncane, Patrik, and Gregor MᶜGregors sons to Patrik Aldoch, Dougall MᶜCoull oig in Glenbotha, Johne MᶜEwine MᶜGregor and John Dow MᶜPhatrik vy, To compeir personally As also charged Allane MᶜIndowie of Lochquhaber who promised to be answerable for them To bring produce ane exhibit before the Council the said persons the 9. day of Jan. next to the effect order may be taken with them for their obedience. under the pain of rebellion, £8.

" Item to a post passing from Edinburgh with close Letters to Allane MᶜIndowie of Lochquhaber and with a copy of the charge for exhibition of the said MᶜGregors for whom he promised to be answerable, £6. 13. 4.

" 1611. Dec. 20.   Appeared personally before the Council ' Duncane MᶜEwin MᶜGregor sometime called the Tutor, and renounced his name of MᶜGregour taking that of Dowglas when Argyle became his surety, that he should appear on 15 days warning under penalty of 3000 marks. The Tutor who is elsewhere styled ' of Moirinche' had as appears from his Majesty's letter 23rd. Oct. surrendered some weeks at least before this.

" Dec. 24. Contract John Napier of Merchistoune on the one part and James Campbell of Lawers, Colin Campbell of Aberuchill and John Campbell of Ardewnane by which the three Campbells named became bound that ' in case the said John Napier or any of his tenants in Menteith and Lennox shall be troubled by any of the name of MᶜGregour or any other ' Hieland Brokin Men' they will aid in redressing the wrongs sustained, and the said Johnne Napeir becomes bound to aid the other in their lawful affairs.—Archives of Lord Napier, communicated by Mark Napier, Esq., Adv.

" 1611. Dec. 14.   Letter from the Council to Allan MacEanduy.

" You remember that quhen you procureit the protectioun and over sicht to

_____
[1] " Nan Lurach " Brother of Allaster of Glenstray.

Duncane, Patrik and Gregour McGregouris sones to Patrik Aldoch, Dougall McCoull Og in Glenlocha Johnne McEane McGregour and Johnne Dow McPatrik Vy. that you promeist to be ansuerable for thame and that they sould do some service worthie of his Majesties favour. And now thair being some course in handis for reduceing of that clan to obedience and a catalogue being maid of the haill personis of that name who ar ansuerable and who rebellis and disobedient we haif rankit and nomberit thir personis amongs thame who are lauchfull and answerable subjects and we will so repute and esteem thame yf be thir awne folyis they reject not the present favour offerit to thame and thairfoir these ar to desire to caus thir personis gif thair appeirance heir before the Counsall upoun the 9. day of June nixt to come to the effect thay may renunce thair names and find cautioun conforme to the rest who ar to be ressavit and hes bene alreddy ressavit into favour. yf thay sall neglect and contempte the present occasioun and comp not we will be constrayned for awne exoneratioun at his Majesteis handis to declair thame fugitives and according to give ordour for persute of thame but we hoip that they will be moir careful of thair awne weill and will not draw ony neidless trauble upon thame. &a."

Chapter XXXI

Proclamations, Commissions, &c.

F ROM the "Chartulary":—

"1612. Jan. 9. Letters direct to denounce the Erle of Tullibardin and some MᶜGregours.

"Same date. At Edinburgh. Act against certain MᶜGregours.

"Anent our Sovereign Lord's Letters direct, making mention for so much as Allane MᶜEanduy of Lochaber upon promise and condition made by him for Duncane, Patrik and Gregor MᶜGregours sons to Patrik Aldoche, Dowgall MᶜCoull oig in Glenbatha, John MᶜEane MᶜGregour and John Dow MᶜPhatrik vy, that they should do some notable service to his Majesty meriting his Majesty's gracious favour he procured a protection unto them assuring them to be untroubled or pursued by those who were employed in commission against the ClanGregour and containing some other favour and condition unto them Likeas he promised to be answerable for them in the meantime and seeing there are some courses now in hand for settling of the ClanGregour and reducing of them to obedience, Necessary it is, that the said persons give likewise their obedience whereby others by their example may be moved to do the like, And anent the Charge geiven &a which being called and the said &a not compeiring, the Lords of Secret Council have declared and by the tenour hereof declare all and whatsomever protection, favour, condition, and promise made to the said persons to be null and of none avail in time coming. And ordain the same persons to be reputed, held, and esteemed as rebels, traitors and fugitives from his Majesty's Laws and accordingly to be pursued with fire and sword with all rigour and extremity Like as also the said Lords ordain letters to be directed to the officers of arms charging them to pass and denounce the said Duncane, Patrik, and Gregor MᶜGregouris sons to the said Aldoche, Dougall MᶜCoull oig in Glenbotha, John MᶜEan MᶜGregour, and John Dow MᶜPhatrik vy, his Majesty's rebels and put them to his Majesty's horn and to escheat and inbring all their moveable goods to his Majesty's use for their contemption.

"Jan. 10   A latin Remission to the McEan duys for various crimes in recognition of their service against the ClanGregour

"January.   Commissioners of Council had this month met at Doune in Menteith and passed several acts for fining the resetters of the ClanGregor.   Two Resetters viz Gilbert Graham in Glaschoil and Walter McLauchlan in Blarvoyach had produced Graham of Duchray and Graham younger of Duchray sureties for payment of their fines.

"Feb 4   The Earl of Argyle judging it reasonable that the above sureties should be relieved issued an order on the principals.—Precept of Poynding, The Earle of Argyle against Gilbert Graham and Walter McLauchlane   Original in Gartmore Collection

"Feb 6   At Edinburgh   Another Act anent the fining of the Resetting of the ClanGregour differing very slightly from those already quoted

"Feb. 12.   Alexander Livingstoun of Westquarter became cautioner for 'Duncane and Allaster Livingstounes, sons to umqle Patrik Aldoch MacGregor.'

"1612. Feb.   Item to George Matho Messenger passand with letters to the Mercate Crois of Perth To denounce Patrick and Gregor MacGregor sons to Patrik Aldoch, Dougall McCoull oig in Glenbotha, Johne McEwne McGregor, Johne Dow McPhatrick vy, our Soverane Lordis Rebels —Lordis High Treasurer's Books

"1612   Alexander Stewart of Laggarie is debtor in the testament of Agnes McKean.—Commissary Books of Glasgow   That Alexander Stewart was properly Alexander MacGregor there can be little doubt.   Alexander MacGregor had been infeft in Laggarie on a precept of Clare Constat as heir to his father John MacGregor in 1602.—Record of the Burgh of Dumbarton 1602, as cited under that year.   He had, of course, taken the protective name of Stewart under the operation of the Act of Secret Council April 3. 1603, abolishing the surname of MacGregor.—See 10th Dec. 1603, where mention of him under both surnames.

"1612. Feb 25.   Although Allan Cameron of Lochyell and Allaster McDonald of Gargavach who have been employed by his Majesty against the ClanGregour &a hed expected that their kin and friends would have joined them with their forces for prosecuting that service yet . . . certein of the Camerons and two McDonalds enumerated, said persones having been formerly assissters of the said Allan and Allaster in all their private affairs 'but now being offendit with thame becaus thay have randent thair obedience to his Majestie and tane upoun thame the executioun of some of his Majestie's directionis aganis the Clangregour and some uther brokin men of the Heylandis' and being 'loath that ony suche course sould tak effect in thair personis, bot that rather the saidis Allane and Allaster McDonald sould have followit the wickit and unhappie trade of the rebellious Lymmaris of the Heylandis and Illis that thairby thay micht have been the more able undir thair patrocinie and protectioun to have continewit thair iniquitie and wickedness fra the quhilk

thay feir now to be reclaimed be thame' have not only refused to assist the said
commissioners in his Majesty's service but avowedly oppose them, declaring themselves to be friends of the ClanGregour and of all broken men so that the execution
of the said service is frustrated. Charge had been given to the said defenders to
answer and none of them now appearing they are all of them to be denounced
rebels.

"1612. March. At this time a skirmish took place between the Earl of Perth
at the Head of a considerable force composed partly of MacGregors who had taken
the name of Drummond and a body of MacGregors at Tomzarloch, the latter
having occupied some houses were dislodged by means of fire applied, when five
were captured and six killed. The killed were John Dow MacGregor, Donald
Gramich MacGregor V^cCulchere, John McPhatrik Nadidin MacGregor V^cCulchere,
Gregor McEan V^cEan MacGregor Elensisens (Gillespie ?) MacGregor. The Earl's
force is thus specified in a pardon issued to them early in 1614, as appears from
Mag. Sig. quoted at the proper date.

"John Earl of Perth (2. Earl) John Master of Madertie James Drummond his
brother Sir Alexander Drummond of Carnock Knight, Alexander brother of Mr
William Drummond of Hawthornden, James Drummond of Millness, David
Drummond chamberlain of Drymen, Thomas Drummond of Drummowhence, x
John Drummond of Innerzeldie, x James Drummond his brother, x Duncan
Drummond late of Kincart beg, x Duncan Drummond in Pitluir, x Duncan
Drummond in Wester Dundorne, James Drummond officer, Patrick Drummond
in Dalmarklawis,* John Drummond in Auchinskelloch,* Duncan Drummond in
Mawia, James Drummond in Balliclone, Patrick Drummond in Williamsoune, x
John Drummond in Wester Dundorne, Alexander Stewart in Port, Alexander
Reidheugh,* David Malloch, John Drummond of Drummondearnoch, Patrick
Drummond forester of Glenartney,* John McCoruther, James Drummond of
Pitzalloun,* Malcolm McAndrew in Dundorn, James Stewart late in Torry,*
James Menzies in Mewis William McNiven in Glen Artney,* John McCoruther in
Blairtown, James Dow in Glenkishon.

Mr MacGregor has marked with a cross those who he considers were
MacGregors, adding that more might have been, and several others, who
seem probable, are now marked with a star.

"1612. March 6. To the Erle of Argyle. After our very hairtie commen-
dationis to your good lordschip Thair hes bene ane petitioune exhibite unto us
be the Erlle of linlithgow his tennentis of Calindar in Menteathe and Corychromby
craiving that they might be exoncrit fra that commissioune grauntit for trying of
the resaittis whiche the ClanGregor hes had in Monteithe and they alledgit many
ressonis quhairfoir the exemptioune sould be granntit quhilkis althocht in appeirance
thay seemed to be verrie ressonable for graunting of the said exemptioun yitt becaus

the preparatine therof micht carye a verrye greit preiudice to that service, whiche your lordschip hes in handis, we have been sparing in granting of the said exemptioun alwayes ane thocht meet herrby to requist your lordschip to haue a speciall cair and regaird that all your proceidingis in this busines be well warranted be law, custume, and pratique of the cuntry and nouther the compleneris nor no utheris his Majesties subiectis be trublit unnessarlie witht seuerall dyettis and courtis bot at thair first citatioun & appeirance in judgement thay may be tane ordour with and dismissed, and no just caus of grief and complaint ministrat unto theme, so that it may evidentlie appeir and be known to all men that the speciall cast and proiect of this commissioune is for triall of the saidis resaittis, ouir that under the pretext thairof no vther thing is pretendit we doubt (not) bot your lordschip in your awin honorabill dispositione to equitie and iustice will more con-siderablie and respectiuellie behaue yourself in that errand, nor can we aduise your lordschip to do, and so wischeing your lordschip a progress & happy succes in that seruice and recommending your lordschip to Godis protectioune we rest for ever your lordschippis verrye louing and good friendis Signed.

"A cancellarius Glasgow, Jo Prestoun, Balfour, R Cokburne Alexander Hay J. Cokburne Sr J Hamiltouns clericus registri Edinburghe —From a copy in the Earl of Haddington's Collections in the General Register House

" 1612. April 15 Commission against Patrick Dow MacGregor.

"James &c Forasmuch as it is understood to us and lords of our privy Council that Patrick MacGregour McCotter and John McConochie V^cEan duy McGregour two of the most notable thieves, and limmers of the ClanGregour are lately taken and apprehended by the Earl of Perth Commission given to John Master of Madderue, and others to try them —Record of Secret Council, Commissions.

" May 8. Alexander Earl of Linlithgow, Alexander Livingstone of Belstane and James Carmichael of Pottishaw became sureties to the Council for Patrick Livingstone, son of the late Patrick Aldoch.

"May 8 At Edinburgh. In the Court of Justiciary of our serene Lord the King held in the Judgment Hall of Edinburgh by Mr William Heart.

" Entered,—Dougall McGregor alias Dougall McCondochie.

Callum McGregor called McAllesterstone.

Duncane McCarlich Culzanie McGregour.

Dilatit for being in company with the Laird of MacGregour and his complices at the raid and field of Glenfrune, in the month of Feb 1603. and for being in company with the Laird of McGregour [1] at the burning of Barnehall [2] pertaining to Colin Campbell of Lawers, where they slew nine men and three bairns, Robert Abroch MacGregor and John M^cfadrik being there with them in company.

"June 2. Precept of Remission to Patrick, Alexander and Duncan formerly called MacGregors, now Levingstounes, sons of the late Patrick Aldoch, McGregour

---

[1] Probably the "Tutor" Duncan McEwin MacGregour.   [2] Aberuchill.

in Chorychorumbie for art and part in the burning of the houses and outsteads of
the lands of Glenlochie belonging to Sir Duncan Campbell of Glenurchy, knight,
committed by them in the month (of April) in the year of our Lord one thousand
six hundred (and four) and for all other crimes, &a.—Privy Seal, 81-24."

Note by Mr MacGregor Stirling. The blanks in this record are supplied
by that of the Justiciary, 28th June 1612, which mentions the burning of
Glenlochy to have taken place in April 1604, which it will be recollected
was a few months only after the father of the three individuals above mentioned had been executed by the verdict of a Jury of whom Colin
Campbell, younger of Glenurquhy, was one.

"June 18. Letter from William Buchannan of Drummikill to his 'loving
Uncle' William Buchanan in Drummikill:—

"'Loving uncle and best friend, I haif ressaved ane direction from the Erle of
Argyll his Majesties commissioner to travel with Callum[1] Gregour to bring him to his
Majesties peace and service, Thairfoir I will desyre zow to tak the panis to travell
with sik as ze know that hes credeit off Callum to bring him privilie to sum quiet
place quhair I and ze may confer with him thairanent, at lynth quhilk sall tend
to his weill and I sall schaw zow at meting my credeit in this bissines swa that
ze, nor nane uther quhome ze send to him, misters? to fear or take ony scrupill, for
I haif ane sufficient warrand And sua to zour diligens herein and aduertisement
I rest zouris brothersone, William Buchannan of Drummikill.'—From the Kirk of
Bonnell.—Original of Letter in General Register House, Edinburgh.

"1612. July 23. Allaster McConnochy VcAllaster in Ardlarich (who seems to
have been of the three or four classed with Glenstray's Tutor in his Majesty's letter
to the Council 23. Oct.) formally in the presence of the Council took the name of
Menzies, when the Earl of Argyll was his surety under penalty of 1000 merks.—
Record of Secret Council. Fines.

"July 24. Next day Alexander Balfour of Currie became surety for Donald and
John Balfours sons of the late Patrick Aldoch McGregor.—Records of Secret
Council. Fines 1619.

"July 16. At Edinburgh The quhilk day Alexander Levingstoune fear of West
Quarter, became plege and souertie for Allaster and Duncane Levingstounes
in callendrech of Menteith in sumtyme of ye surname of McGregour That thay sall
compeir &c the 31. instant and underly the law for the allegit airt and pt, of the
slaughter of Robert McPatrick oig in Strathyre &a.—Record of Justiciary Book of
Cautions.

"Argyll rendered an accompt of his office to the Council this month when
seventy of the ClanGregor rested upon him.

[1] " Malcolm oig McGregor VcDougall Keir" Chieftain of his House, see page 272.

"July 28. Commission to Glenurquhie to try Johnne Dow McGregor in Dowletter son to Gregor McEane Patrick and . . . McGregours sons to the said John Dow presently in his custody —Record of Secret Council

"July 28. In the Court of Justiciary of our Sovereign Lord the King held in the Judgement Hall of Edinburgh 28. July 1612 by Mr William Heart of Prestoun Justiciary. Entered

Gregor beg McGregor son to umquhile Gregor M^ceane

Gregor McAllaster galt,[1]

John M^cindreiche—(Johne Dow McInleith as appears farther down in same),

John Dow M^cgille phadrick V^crobert,

Allaster M^callaster V^ccoule,

Patrick McGregor Craiginsche,

Duncane McCoule cheir,

Patrick roy McGregor son to John McPhadrick in Ranache,

Gregor M^ceane V^ccoule cheir,

Johnne Dow moir McGregor in Rora,

"Dilaitit of certain crimes of theft, slaughter, burning

" . . . . The which day (recapitulation of the above names) Being all presented upon pannel dilaitit and accused and pursued by dittay at the instance of Sir William Oliphant of Newtoun knicht advocate, to our Sovereign Lord, for his Highness interest, of the crimes respectively following, viz (the first four names) for art and part of the treasonable raising of fire, burning and destroying of the haill houses and biggings of Glenlochie and Achallater, and for the slaughter of .

McColeane bowman to the Laird of Glenurquhie with divers uyeris persons to the number of eight persons, burning of three young bairns, daughters to Johnn McKishock and for stealing of six score cows and oxen furth of Glenlyoun committed in April 1604. And such like the said (enumerating the next five on the list) being indicted and accused for art and part of the burning and destroying of the haill houses and biggings upon the forty merk land of Aberuchill pertaining to Colene Campbell and for the slaughter of Duncane Webst, John Seatoune, Patrick Stabache, John McGilhevorich, burning of the three daughters of John McKishack, stealing and away taking of eighteen score of cows, six score piece of horse, eight score sheep and goats, pertaining to the said Colene and likewise for burning of the mill of Bolquhaster with the haill houses and biggings upon the grounds and lands of Carne Doune and Dillater pertaining to Robert Campbell of Glenfalloche and of his haill houses and biggings upon his lands of Airdcane, Knochane committed by them in the month of June 1611. Item the said Gregor McGregor beg, for . . the slaughter of umquhile Solomon Lany alias Buchanane committed at the Kirk of Kilmaheug twenty years ago, or thereby, Item the said John Dow

[1] Youngest son of Allaster Galt

3 E

M^cgillephadrick for . . . . of the stealing and away taking furth of Glenfynles of a great heirschip of cows and oxen pertaining to the Laird of Luss and his tenants, and slaughter of umquhile John Reid wobster and Patrick Lang servant to the Laird of Luss committed upon the said lands of Glenfinles in the month of December 1602. And siclike the said John Dow moir McGregor in Rora for stealing and away taking of a great number of goods pertaining to mylord Ogilvie furth of Glenylay And sicklike for taking and keeping of the island called Island varnach against his Majesty's commissioner and hiring and oppressing of the whole tenants and inhabitants of the country about, taking and inbringing of the haill guids and bestiall to the number of eight score cows and oxen, eighteen score sheep and goats which were eaten and slain by them within the said island.   Item the haill forenamed persons indicted and accused for common theft, common reset of theft, common sorning, and oppressing of his Majesty's peaceable subjects and for intercommuning with the rest of the surname of McGregours fugitives and at the horn and furnishing of them with meat, drink, and money and keeping of trysts, councils, and gatherings with them contrary to the tenour of his Majesty's procla-mations, were all put to the knowledge of an assize of the persons following " . . . After the usual formalities of the assise the Court was re-entered   Where the said David Drummond Chancellor in name of the said Assyse all in one voice exponed, pronounced, and declared the said persons on pannel in respect of their own con-fession to be filled culpable and convicted of the crimes respectively above speci-fied, contained in the dittay for the which cause the Justice by the mouth of Alex. Kennedy dempster decerned and ordained the said ten persons to be taken to the burrough muir of Edinburgh and there to be executed &a. — Record of High Court of Justiciary.

"July 28.   Precept of Remission on account of the broken state of the Highlands to Duncan McRobert McGregour now called Grahame for the treasonable raising of fire and burning of the barn of Blair-vadden lying within the Dukedom of Lennox in Feb. 1603. as also for the treasonable raising of fire and burning of the places and house of Aberughill belonging to Colin Campbell of Aberughill in the month of   and for all other crimes.—Privy Seal.

"July.   Item to Archibald Armstrong for his pains in attending his Majesty's service in the Highlands with larg doggis against the ClanGregor, £100.—Lord High Treasurer's Books.

"July 30.   Lord St Colme gave power to William Buchanan of Drumakill ' To trait and deill with Callum McGregor ' till 15. August.—Gen. Register House.

"1612. August 21.   Commission for trying the Resetters of the ClanGregor. Same preamble as on Nov. 21. 1611.—Record of Council.

"Sep. 11.   For wearing hagbutts &a Johnne Stewart in Strangarvalt, Walter Patrick and Duncane Stewartis his brothers, Andro McFarlane in Letter, Duncane McFarlane his brother, William Buchanan in Glengyle, Johnne Grahame son to

Alexander Grahame in Craigvohtie, Andro Grahame his brother, Robert McClarrane in Balquhidder, McClairrane his son there, Donald McCallum there, Gregour McGregour McCoulle and Duncan Fergussoun in Strathyre.—Record of Council.

"The Secret Council wrote to the King that the Earl of Argyle had exhibited eleven individuals of the ClanGregour resting upon him at the former account and who had changed their names and found caution.

"1612 Sep 18 Pleis zour sacred Maiestie The Erll of Ergyle compeiring this day befoir zour Maiesties Counsaill he exhibite elleven of that nomber of the Clan-Gregr resting upoun him be his formair accompt who he changeit thair names and found caution conform to the ordoure He hes a warrand grantit to him for his repair towards zour Maiestie according to zour pleasour and directioun signifeit unto us be zour Maiesteis letrs of the 7. of this instant and he hes nominat the Laird of Lundy his bruther to have a care of the prosequutioun of that service till his returne, who hes undertane the chairge with promisses to do his endeavour to bring the same to some settled perfectioun. We haif had sundrie conferences anent the bairnes of the ClanGregour and hes consultis and advysit heirupoun with the Landlordis whose aduice and opinioun is, that that string sall not be tutcheit nor no motioun maid thairof quhil the service now in handis agains the men be first settled. and brocht to ane end at whiche tyme the executioun of everie suche course as salbe then resolved upoun agains the bairnis may with the lesse difficultie be effecheat This is all that hes been done with him at this meeting so with oure heartie prayers unto God recommending zoure Maiestie to Godis divyne protectioun we rest zour Maiestie's most humble and obedient subiectis and servitouris.—Al. Cancells. Alex. Hay of Edinburgh Original of letter, in Sir James Balfour's Collections in Advocates' Library, Edinburgh.

"Sep 18. Argyll nominated his brother Coline Campbell of Lundie to have charge of the ClanGregour as above He declared that quhairas the Kingis Maiestie was graciouslie pleasit that he sould repair to court for some necessar occasionis of his advis and he being loath that in the tyme of his absence his Maiesties service aganis the ClanGregour sould be neglectit Thairfoir &a Lundie being present accepted the charge "

From the " Register of the Privy Council," edited by Dr Masson.

"1612 Oct. 5. Letter from the Council to the Commissioners against the ClanGregour. We have ressavit from the Lord of Scone four of the Clan-gregour who wer laitlie tane be Duncane the Tutour and we undirstand by a letter sent unto the said Lord that Duncane hes apprehendit and tane Patrik Aldoche and his bruther Duncan Wherein we acknowledge that the Tutour hes weill begun in that service and we do look that he will continew not onlie by a present deliverie of these tua now in his handis to the effect that thay may be exhibite heir befoir the Counsale bot lykewise that he will prosequute that service undirtane be him to the uttermost and quhat promeis and conditioun hes bene maid to him he may confidentlie expect the performance of the same."

From the " Chartulary " :—

"Nov. 24. The Erll of Ergyll contra Wm. McIntosch Anent our Souerane lordis lettres raisit at the instance of Archibald Erll of Ergyll his Maiesties Lieutenant Justice and commissionair aganis the Clangregor Makand mentioun That quhair Duncane M^ceane V^ceaneduy McGregor in Rannach ane common and notorious thief being taen and apprehendit at the said Erlls directioun be Williame M^cintosche of Bordland, Neuertheles the said Williame hes not deleurit to the said Lieutenant the said Duncane, bot keipes him still in his handis of purpois, and intentioun as the said Erll is informed, to put him to libertie.—Secret Council.

"Nov. 22. Patrick Drummond in Darmaglen (Dalmarkland) and Duncane Drummond McAllaster in Dundurne are fined each in £5 for shooting with guns. and killing Roebucks. by the Justices of the Peace in Perthshire.

" 1612. Dec. 10. Argyll complained to the Council of Duncan McQuorquordale brother of Duncane McQuorquordale of Phantillare and John Dow McQuorquordale suspected guilty of the slaughter of Glenfrune &a and having their haunt in the bounds of Argyll.—Secret Council.

"Dec. 11. At Edinburgh the 9. Duncan McCorcodell of Fantelands became plege and souertie for Lauchlane McCorcodale Notter his brother That he sall compeir the 16. day of Merche next to come and underly the law for ye allegit being in cumpanie wt umqle Allaster McGregor of Glenstrae and his complices at ye raid of Glenfrune. under the pane &a.—Record of Justiciary.

" 1612. Dec. 12. Lauchlane McQuorquordill brother to Duncane McQuorquordill of Phantellene and Johnne Dow McQuorquordill charged for resett and assistance to the ClanGregour.

"Dec. 22. The Council fined twenty-nine individuals who by the report of the Commissioner for trying them for intercourse with ClanGregour, had been convicted on their judicial confession.

*John Dow M^ccan V^cphatrick brother to the goodman of Tullochgorme,
*Ewin Grant in Turk,
*John M^ccondochy in Gartbeg,
*Andro Shaw in Glenscharnoch,
*John McWilliam V^ceane in Tulloch,
 Patrick oig M^cthome Grant in Rimor.
*William beg M^ceane V^cangus in Dill of Abernethy,
 Angus McWilliam in Inneresche in Badzenoch,
 John Dow in Innerhaven,
 Donald McAllaster Roy in Foness,

Those thus marked * were, on the 3rd June 1613, put to the horn.

Allaster Dow McConneil reach in Trombeg,
William Smart, burges of Tayne,
*Alexander Murray sometime MacGregor in Ardclathie,
Alexander Murray his sone,
*William Gau in Rothiemoune,
*William M^cfinla M^cdonche in Drum,
*Duncan Grant in Ledach,
John Ross of Holme,
John Grant of Glenmoriston,
Archibald Grant his brother,
*James M^cconneill voir in Dalvert,
Donald Campbell of Duntrune,
Gillespie McClauchlan V^colchollum of Ashacha,
Duncan Stewart of Innernathavil,
John Abroch of Glenwan,
Duncan Ochoather Leyt in Donoleyt beg,
Duncan McPhadrick V^cnichol in Bowlindowich,
Duncan M^cean V^cewin V^cdougall in Millich,
John Stewart of Ardsell.

These are ordered to pay within ten days Certain were 3. June the following year put to the horn.—Record of Secret Council."

Those thus marked * were, on the 3rd June 1613, put to the horn.

Chapter XXXII

Remission to Robert Abroch

FROM the " Chartulary " :—

" 1613. Jan 12. The quhilk day it is thocht meet and expedient be the Lordis of secreit Counsaill That ane remissioun salbe past and exped to Robert Abroche [1] McGregour conforme to his Majesties directioun send to the Lord Chancellor to that effect the said Robert first renunceing his name, and finding caution for his deutifull behaviour, redres of pairtyis to be harmed and skaithit be him, for his personall compeirance quhen he salbe callit and that he sall not resett, supplie, intercomoun, assist, nor tak part with the ClanGregour.—Record of Secret Council.

" Jan. 14. Letter Sir Thomas Hamilton of Byres to the King.[2]

" 'The counsall ressaved your Majesties letter concerning Robin Abroches remissioun and protection which upon hope of your Majesties gracious permission they have delayed to performe, till be thair direction to me; your Majestie may be informed be my letter, that Robin Abroch is reported to have beine the most bluidie, and violent murthourar and oppressour of all that damned race and maist terrible to all the honest men of the cuntrie who now ressaving favour above all utheris of his kin, being dispensed from compeirance before the Counsall, to mensweare his name, and from finding caution for his compeirance before the Counsall, whanever he salbe chairged under competent paynes, which hes beine the ordour prescryved to all the rest of that Clan without exception. The favour grantit to him gevis him louse renzeis, discourages these who stand in feir of his barborous oppression, and may move other brokin men to stand out till they get the lyk conditions, and perhaps tempt some who stand alreddie bound to the peace, to lope furth whill thay obteane the lyke freedom, and immunitie, from all ordour, and obedience. And thairfore the Counsall most humble craives your Majestie may allow thame to urge Robin Abroch to observe the common ordour prescryved to all utheris of his Clan, and obeyed inviolable be such as obteaned

---

[1] Second surviving son of Duncan Abroch. See chapters xvi. and xxvii.

[2] It appears from this correspondence that Robert Abroch had appealed direct to the King instead of through the Council, who were, therefore, the more incensed against Robert.

remissions. Bot if your Majestie be resolved to the contrare, upon signification of your determined pleasour they will most reddelie obey your royal commandments, and do intend for present saiftie to grant him ane protection, whill the 15 day of May. providing he forbeare to repair to the Schirifdoms of Dumbarten, Stirling, Perth and Invernes Thairfore I most humbie beseik your Majestie to returne the signification of your good pleasour so sone as convenientlie may be in thir purposes. &a.'—MS. in Sir James Balfour's Collections, Advocates' Library, Edinburgh

"Jan. 14. His Majesties missive concerning Robert Abroch wes presented and red in counsell Bot becaus he culd not find caution for his dewtifull behaviour in tyme cuming, and for his remaining furth of the boundis, quhair formarlie he committit his insolencies, the Counsell hes superseidit the expeiding of his remission till the knawledge of his Majesties pleasour, And in the mein tyme thay have grantit unto him ane protectioun, to be untroubled quhill the XV day of man next with promeis that he sall not hant within the boundis abonewritten quhill that day, and that he sall compeir befoir the Counsell gif he sall happin to be dischairgit afoir that day The Laird of Lundie brother to the Erll of Argyll being to repair to Court, to confer with his brother anent the service of the ClanGregour as he pretendis, he hes nominat the Laird of Lawers to have the charge of that service till his returne, and upoun Lawers acceptatioun of the charge, Lundie is to have a licence for his upcuming —Balfour's Collections.

" 1613. Jan 21. Proclamation in favour of Robert Abroche

"James &a To all and sundry 'Forasmuch as Robert Abroche McGregour being moved with a hatred and detestation of the wicked and unhappy trade of life, of the rebellious thieves and limmers called the ClanGregour, and being most desirous to become our lawful subject, and to live hereafter in the rank and condition of a humble and obedient subject, he has for this effect, not only entered in action against the said limmers and brought in some of the specials of them who have worthily suffered death, but with that he has come in to our court, and offered to employ his person in whatsoever our services, as well against the ClanGregour as others.'

"Received into favour on finding caution and taken under special protection, defence, supply, maintenance and safeguard 21 Jan 1613.

"Jan 26. Proclamation that none of the ClanGregour wear armour.

" 'Forasmuch as some of the ClanGregour who are guilty of that detestable, barbarous, and cruel butcherie, and slaughter committed upon our Sovereign Lord's peaceable and good subjects at Glenfrune and of the fire raisings, herships, and depredations committed since upon Sir Duncan Campbell of Glenurquhy, Alexander Colquhoun of Luss, and Coline Campbell of Aberurquhill, taking new breath and courage unto them, upon a foolish conceit and apprehension conceived by them that the courses intended, and in hands for reducing of that Clan to obedience were become void and frustrated They have begun to flock together in companies armed with swords, targes, bows, darlochs, harquebuts, pistoletts and other weapons invasive, and they go athwart the country sorning, oppressing, quarrelling, and injuring his Majesty's good subjects, in all parts where they may be masters, and commanders and their pride and insolency is come to this height, that they are become careless, of whatsoever courses are undertaken for reducing of them to obedience, so that if some strict order be not taken with them whereby they may be retained, and held under obedience and fear of the law, the estate and condition of his Majesty's subjects dwelling ewest unto them will become as hard and worse nor at any time heretofore. Therefore the King's Majesty with advice of the Lords of the secret Council has statuted and ordained That no person or persons whatsomever of the ClanGregour who are guilty of the cruel and detestable crime foresaid committed at Glenfroone, and of the fireraisings, murders, slaughters, herschips, and depredations committed since upon the said Sir Duncane Campbell of Glenurquhy, Alexander Colquhoun of Luss, And Coline Campbell of Aberurquhill, shall at any time after the publication hereof, bear or wear any kind of armour except ane pointless knife, to cut their meat, under the pain of death, to be executed upon the person, or persons whatsomever, who shall violate and contravene this present act, and ordinance, and ordain letters to be directed to make publication hereof &a by open proclamation at the market crosses of Perth, Stirling, Dumbarton Inverness and other places needful, in order that none pretend ignorance of the same and to command and charge all Sheriffs, Stewards, Justices of the Peace, Provosts and Baillies within burgh, and other judges, magistrates and officers whatsoever to take and apprehend all such persons of the ClanGregour who are guilty of the crimes abovewritten whom they shall find to bear or wear any kind of armour except a pointless knife, as said is, and to bring, present and exhibit to his Majesty's justice, to the effect the said punishment of death may be executed upon them as the said Sherrifs &a will answer upon their obedience.—Record of Secret Council.'

"1613. Feb. 2. Letter Campbell of Glenurchy to the King.

"'Please your excellent Majesty Your Highness's letters in favour of Robert Abroche MacGregour now calling himself Ramsay I have received. Whereby I am willing to repossess him in whatsoever lands he hath right unto without trouble or plea in law. It is of truth that he did possess certain lands belonging to me without any right or title to them at all yea so far against my consent, that with remembrance of my very great loss I shall repent I had such a tenant. And when he, as one of the chief and special ringleaders of his viporous clan, did not content themselves to wrong me by the most barborous oppressing of my tenants, but had also overrun a great part of three or four Sherriffdoms. Then the general grief of so many dutiful subjects made the exterminion of this damnable race of people to be resolved upon, as most expedient, and necessary for your Majesty's peace, and obedience, and the surety of your Majesty's dutiful subjects dwelling in these parts, which work, since it took beginning, hath been ever chargeable to your Majesty, painful to the country, and with my particular very great hurt, and skaith. Having had besides many former losses, within less than these eighteen months, two hundred merkland wasted, and spoiled by that Clan, conducted by that same man now recommended My tenants, their wives and young children unmercifully murdered, and such of them as escaped the sword, in regard their houses were all burned, being left in the open air, both the aged, and younger sort were killed with cold. It may perhaps by some be supposed that this service is, at some good point, But when all both noblemen, barons, and gentlemen who have most interest in this work were convened, then it was among them resolved, and by them to your Majesty's Council proposed and there also allowed of, That without transplantation of this Clan no quietness to these bounds, could be expected, so as this man's repossession to any lands which by strong hand he held formerly without any right at all Implys a direct ranversing of whatever, was intended for the good of that service, the particular harm and inconvenience whereof being unfelt, no doubt to those who have been so earnest solicitors in the behalf of this man. So are they as far mistaken in their undertaking for his good behaviour, in time coming In regard there is no doubt at all, but when he finds himself of new, strengthened with a fresh growth of this unhappy weed (whereof there be of male kind, some sixteen score of new arising) like enough he will put who promises in his behalf, to a personal action for their relief. And because hard experience has made me more sensible, than others, and my duty to your Majesty doth enforce me to conceal nothing of my knowledge herein, I have presumed to acquaint your Highness with the truth Assuring your Majesty on my credit, that if the ringleaders of this Clan shall have the liberty to dwell, and reside in their former possessions, this undercotting wood,[1] shall be found hereafter more incurable. Always for my own part having life and whole estate ever ready at your Majesty's disposing, I most humbly take my leave praying God Almighty to continue long your Highness' prosperous, and happy reign and rests your Majesty's most humble and most obedient servitor,

"'Duncan Campbell of Glenurquhay

"'Edinburgh, Feb. 2 1613.'—Balfour's Collections

"1613. Feb. 24. Duncan MacGregor in Cambserich renounced the lands of Roro to Duncan Menzies of Comrie.

"March 10. Extract from original Missive from James VI to the Privy Council.

"Right Trusty &a —— Whereas James Campbell of Lawers hath been a suitor to us for an inheritable infeftment of the lands of Morven (being a part of our property not yet set in feu to any) and forasmuch as the said James hath done us so

---

[1] ? Wound.

3 F

good service against that wicked race of the ClanGregour as we think him worthy of a greater recompense &a &a. The King orders the signature to be passed without any composition and that Lawers is to pay no rent for ——— years after entry, on account of the trouble he would have with the barbarous people dwelling on the lands.—Original in General Register House.

"March 11. At Thetfoord. Our farther will and pleasure is, that ye dispose their (the resetters) escheits upon easy composition to the Erll of Ergyll or if ye shall otherwise dispose upon the same in favour of any other person, that ye first see the Erll satisfied of the sums wherein the said resetters have been or shall be fined.—Record of Council.

"April 13.   HIGHLANDS.

"Memorial concerning the Highlands by information sent from his Majesty by Archibald Campbell.

"Archibald declares that in his brother the Laird of Lawer's name he has undertaken to his Majesty that the MacGregor's bairns shall be put in such obedient subjects' hands as shall be answerable for them, and make them forth-coming whenever his majesty or the Council shall call for them. That when any complaint shall be made in Council or any good subject shall dilait any violent oppression to be committed in the Highlands by any masterful outlaw, That upon any advertisement thereof to his Majesty, If he shall please to send a secret warrant or direction to the Laird of Lawers, or his brother for pursuit, and apprehension of the said rebell, they shall pursue him, and do their faithful endeavours to bring him in, either dead, or quick, Providing the direction be kept secret and not divulged to the Council or others. That the Laird of Lawers and his brother shall meet the Laird of Grant in Sanct Johnestoun within seven or eight days and appoint with him the best means of their concurrence, in the pursuit of the rebells of the ClanGregour. Archibald has promised to the Laird of Grant in his Majesty's name and the Earl of Argyll's that if he slay or take Allaster Makallaster or do any other notable service by himself, or his friends, he shall be worthily recompensed, and find favour for a part of the oversights committed by him, or some of his friends, in favouring the ClanGregour. Grant has promised to serve so faithfully in the particular against the ClanGregour or any other his Majesty's rebels, as hopes to diserve both thanks, and benefit, and has willed me to advertise (him ?) of his Majesty's pleasure and promised to write to me of his proceedings.—General Register House.

"April 28. Sir Thomas Hamilton to John Murray of Lochmaben.

"' Archibald Campbell's letters will inform yow of the estate of the service aganis the ClanGregour bothe young and old and of his brother's mention how to prosecute that which rests to be done thairintill, The signatour which his Majestie signed to Lawers is stayed be ane latter warrand, sent from his Majestie. No man will be so foolish as to aduyse his Majestie how to recompense Lawers, which his

Majesty can better consider, nor we can propose, Bot it may be trewlie affirmed that (he) hes faithfullie served, and proffitablie, with great paynes and losse, whairof no dowt his Majestie will graciouslie consider '—Letter in Advocates' Library.

"April 28.   An act appointing and nominating some commissioners to modify and set down the fines upon the resetters of the ClanGregor

"Same Date.   The Commission is past conforme to his Majesty's direction for hearing, and discussing of the suspensions to be granted upon the fines of the resetters of the ClanGregouris, and the Lords of Session are discharged of all granting of any such suspensions   The Laird of Lundy who has the charge and burden of the service against the Clangregour, in the absence of the Earl of Argyll, his brother, having desired of the Council that they would assign him a day for giving of an accompt of the proceedings in that service since the last accompt made by the Earl The Council has assigned unto him the 15 day of June next and has written to the landlords of the ClanGregour to keep that day for hearing of the said accompt made —Minutes of Secret Council in Balfour's Collection.

"May 9   Decreet against certain resetters of the Clangregour.

"May 14   Archibald Campbell to the King.

" 'Pleis your Majesty ressave a certaine accompt of your Majestie's command to me. According to your Majesties directioun I brocht the Laird of Grant befoir mylord Secretar and schew him your sacred Maies Pleasour, quha promeist to amend his bypast neglygens Lykeways Sr theare ar to the number of tuelff of the rebells of the Mᶜgregoris, teakin be my brother the Laird of Lauenis sen your Matie derectit me home   And the 15 of Jun nixt is appointit to the landislordis to be present before your Mateis Counsell heir   That the Erle of Argyll and sicke utheris as your Maie· hes concredit that service to, may make their dischearge   For Sr there is not above fourtie outlawis at the writing heirof   And I hope in God theare sall be few or nane wearie schorthe.   Lykwayis as your sacred Maie commandit my brother he hes maid fast the most peart of the young ones of yat unhopie clan quhich Sr in good faith is more troublesum to him than all the rest of the service Pleis your Matie· thairfore to aduertis gif it be your Maties pleasour that the lyke course be teaken with the young ones of those that ar cum in and fund caution ·   As your Matie hes commandit to be teakin with those quha hes been execute and slaine ; or gif your Matie will have them quha ar cautioun for thair childering. Praying your Matie most humblie that any directioun your Matie sall be pleasit to send heiranent, that my brother may be maid first acquentit thairwith lest it suld impead your Maties good intensioun Sr I dout not bot your Matie. is sufficientlie informed of the great peace and quyatnes of the heilandes of this your Matie's kingdom for the better continowans quhairof if it be your Maties pleasour your Matie shall have ane good overtour maid into your Matie quhich sall teake no monies out of your Matie's kofferis, and quhairwith your Mateis subiectis sall be weill pleasit.   So humblie creaving your Mties pardone for this my boldness with all humilitie I kiss your

Maties hand.   Your Majesties most humell and obedient seruant Archibald Camp-bell.'—Balfour's Collection.

"May.   Item to ane post passand of Edin. wt clois lttrs to the Erlis of Murray, Perth, Tullibardin, Lord Murry Mr of Tullibardin, lairds of Glenurquhay, Lawers, Weymes, Strowan Robertson Garntully Balleachan Luss, Buchannan, McFarlane.

"1613. May 19. at Edinburgh.   Act against the resetters of the Clangregour.

"And thairfoir the said Lords have decerned adjudged and fined the said persons particularly underwritten and every one of them in the sums of money. viz

> Duncan Dow McAngus in Dalchrosk,
> Johnne McJohnne Dow vig (bhig) there,
> Johnne or McCondoquhy oig in Tullichrosk,
> Johnne McInnes V^ceanduy in Leshintullie,
> Bane M^cean in Dalquhossane,
> Johnne M^cconnochy dony there,
> Johnne roy the baron of Fandowy's brother,
> Allester M^cvoreis there, Tarlich M^cean oig,
> Duncan Dow McCondochy Dow oig there, Allaster Stewart Temper,
> Johnne Dow M^ceanhassik in Kinloche,
> Dougald gair M^ccleriche there, Donald McGowie his sone,
> George M^cean V^cRoberteis sone,
> Donald McCaddell in Duncastell, Allaster McThomas McJohnne McRobert
>   there,
> Johnne Stewart son to Allaster Stewart in Drumquhene,
> Allaster McJohnne McRobert there.

The amount of each fine ranges from 100 merks to 500 ; in some cases the groups of names pay 400 merks between them.   From the patriarchal style of the names, the resetters appear to have belonged to the persecuted Clan themselves.

"June 3.   The Erll of Ergyll contra the Laird of Grant.   Anent our soverane lordis lttres raist at the instance of Archibald Earll of Ergyll commissionar aganis the ClanGregor Makand mentioun That quhair upon the tent, and threttene day of Aprile, last bypast John Dow M^ceane V^cPatrick bruther to the goodman of Tullichgorme soone (Ewin) Grant in Cure (Turk [1]) Andro Schaw in Glencairnich Johnne McCondochie in Gartenbeg Johnne McWilliam V^cEane in Tulliche, William beg V^cEan V^cAngus in Dell, Archibald Grant bruther to Johnne Grant of Glenmorriston, Alexander Murray sumtyme callit McGregor in Ardclache, Alexander Murray his son, Duncan Grant in Lettoche, William Gow in Rothmerne, and William McFinlay V^cCondochie in Drum, wer orderlie denuncit rebellis for not payment of fynes for resetting the ClanGregour.—Record of Secret Council.

[1] As appears Record of December 1612.

"June 8. Copy from original missive regarding the ClanGregor

"'JAMES R.

"'Right trusty and right well beloved cousin and counsellor we greet you well. Our right trusty and well beloved cousin the Earl of Argyle now going into that our kingdom to give an account of the service against the MacGregors which we think now almost at an end, we have thought good hereby to signify until you that we are well pleased that at the accompt of the said service our aforesaid cousin shall be charged, with none other but of the surname of MacGregor, seeing for them only and none other his commission was given And seeing that such of them as are already brought in and have found caution for their good behaviour may think themselves free if they survive their cautioners, and so take occasion to return to their former trade of life, for avoiding of that inconvenience, we think it expedient, that you call before you all such as became cautioners for any of the said MacGregors and cause them bind and oblige their Heirs and successors as well as themselves, and because this case is as yet singular in the person of Gregor McCoule chere, it is our pleasure, that you cause him find new caution for his good behaviour, or else commit him to ward. And whereas we are informed that one Gregor McPatrick being brought in at the time of the incoming of Robert Abroch was delivered to the Earl of Perth and by him to the Master of Madderty we see no reason (if the said information be true) that the Earl of Argyll should be further charged with him, but you should cause the said Earl of Perth and Master of Maderty, be answerable for him in all time coming. And all these particularities commending to your special consideration we bid you farewell At our Manor of Greenwich, 8 June 1613.'—Register House.

"June 18. The Erll of Ergyll came heir this day in the efternoone he is to meet the morne with the landislordis of the ClanGregouris and to confer and ressone with thame anent that service whiche he hes in handis aganis the Clangregouris and upoun Fryday or Mononday nixt he is to gif his accompt how far is proceidit, in that service, sen the last accompt maid be him in the monethe of July bygane.

"June 19. A Report made by the Erle of Argyll anent the ClanGregor.

"June 22 at Edinburgh In the Court of Justiciary of our sovereign Lord the King held in the judgement Hall of Edinburgh by Mr W. Heart.

Entered
Duncane McPatrick Mcgregor,
Alexander cass McGregor,
Johnne Dow McCondochie vayne McRob,
Patrick Roy McCoulcheir,
Ewin crowbache McGregor,
Johnne McNeill Corroche,

Dilaitit of art and part of divers points of theft, slaughter, burning, and oppression contained in these dittays."

(The names of the Assyse follow, and after another recapitulation of the names of the prisoners, the dittay continues) :—

"The said Duncane M⁣ᶜPatrick M⁣ᶜGregor for being in company with Gregor M⁣ᶜCondochie vayne at the burning of the Castle of Achallader and lands of Glenlocht, and for being at the field of Benvek where umquhile Patrick Dow M⁣ᶜNab, Donald Campbell oig son to Johnne Campbell and divers others to the number of seventeen persons were slain, and for art and part of the slaughter of umquhile Allane M⁣ᶜDougall servant to the Laird of M⁣ᶜCoule.

"The said Allaster Cass M⁣ᶜGregor for the cruel slauchter of umqle Neill M⁣ᶜWeyane chopman, by striking him in the belly with his own knife whereof he died.   Item for common sorning theft, and oppression the said John Dow M⁣ᶜCondochie vayne for being at the field of Glenfinlas, and of art and part of the herschip, reft, and taen away of the said lands pertaining to the Laird of Luss and his tenants Item for art and part of the stealing of certain cows and horses pertaining to Walter Stirling of Ballaghan furth of the parochine of Campsie, Item for being in company with the rest of the ClanGregor at the burning of Aberuchle, and hership brought furth therof, as also for art and part of the slaughter of umqle John M⁣ᶜGillop a fidler under my lord of Tulliebairne, and for common theft and sorning.

"The said Patrick Roy M⁣ᶜCoule chere,[1] for being in company with Duncane M⁣ᶜEwine M⁣ᶜGregor called the Tutor at the burning of Aberuckle where seven men were slain, three children were burnt, twenty score of cows and oxen were stolen, reft, and away taken, and for common theft sorning and oppression.

"The said Ewin Crowbach M⁣ᶜGregor for art and part taking of the stealing of a mare from Robert M⁣ᶜLaren and for art and part of the stealing of two horses from M⁣ᶜInnarich in Cregan, And for breaking of a poor man's house in Kynaldie, taking of the said poor man, and binding up his eyes, and stealing and away taking of the whole insicht plenishing of the said house, and for stealing of a cow from Donald M⁣ᶜConeill vayne, furth of John Stewart Neilson's lands.

"The said Neill Corroche for being in company with the said Duncane M⁣ᶜEwen M⁣ᶜGregor called the Tutor at the burning of Aberurckle and slaughter, and herschip above written committed by them, and for assisting and taking part with the rebells and fugitives that took in the isle called Ileandevernache and in taking in to the said isle of eight score cows, and oxen, eighteen score sheep and goats, stolen, reft and away taken from the inhabitants of the country about, and such like for art and part of the stealing of five cows from James Chisholme in Dundrwne. And for common theft, sorning and oppression as at length is contained in their several dittays above specified, were all six put to the knowledge of an assise of the

---

[1] No. 34 List of 1586 ; he was 6th son of Malcolm, 2nd Chieftain of his House.

persons foresaid." Recapitulation of the names of the jurors. Who "after re-entering the Court, by the mouth of their chancellor, found, pronounced, and declared the said six persons upon pannel, by reason of their own confessions, made in presence of the most part of the said assise, to be filed, culpable, and convicted of the whole crimes above rehearsed, for the which cause the justice by the mouth of John Dow dempster of Court ordained them and each of them to be taken to the burrow moor of Edinburgh there to be executed &a and all their moveable goods to be escheat and inbrought to our Sovereign Lord's use —Record of High Court of Justiciary

"June 22 Ane Act anent the intertenying of the bairnis of the ClanGregour being in the Laird of Lawer's handis, Ordaining ten merkis to be payit by every landislord for everie mark land pertening to thame formarlie possest be the ClanGregour for intertenying of the saidis bairnis for the monethes of Junii and Julii And ordains the landislordis who ar in this toun to consigne the soume foirsaid in the hands of the clerk of Counsell with certificatioun to thame who sall pas away without paying the said soume that they salbe compellit to mak payment of the double.—Record of Secret Council.

"June 24. There have been three meetings kept with the Erll of Ergyle anent the ClanGregour, at the first meeting which was upon the 19 of this instant, he make an accompt of that roll of 70 persons, resting upon him at his last accompt made in the month of July 1612, of this number he exhibited six notable male-factors who were all executed upon the 22 of this instant, and one of them at his execution confessed the slaying of twelve men with his hand at Glenfrone He gave an account of five other notable limmers slain in this service since the last accompt, and one hanged at Striveling and he reduced the rest of the foresaid number of 70 to 28 persons or thereby, of whom there is only two notable limmers and chieftains to wit Allaster McAllaster wreck[1] and Duncan McEanduy, the rest as the landlords have confessed, are but base followers of the other two chieftains The Council have held them still upon the Earl until he exhibit them or make them answerable.

"At the second meeting upon the 22 of this instant his Majesty's missive anent the boys and young ones was presented and read, and the Laird of Lawenis confessed that he had in his hands threescore and ten of them being the sons of these who have been executed and slain in this service, or are presently outlaws There was a long dispute and reasoning first among the Council themselves and then with the landlords how these young ones might be entertained, and kept in the lowlands, conform to the tenour of his Majesty's missive, but there were so many difficulties proposed, and found out in that matter, as made that point of the service not likely to take effect, that way. It was proposed to the landlords that seeing this service which has been so troublesome and chargeable to his Majesty concerned

[1] Breac, freckled.

principally them, and that the well, and benefit thereof only redounded to them, that therefore they ought to take some burden, in this point anent the boys, and either find out the means how they might be put to crafts, as prentices in burrow towns, or then entertained some other way, and the landlords being earnestly dealt with to make some overtures anent this matter, they flatly refused to take any burden therein, seeming by the conjectures of their discourse, that the burden of that point of the service should be upon his Majesty and the country, The Council perceiving that they could not draw the landlords to any reasonable terms in this point, and the Laird of Lawers being very earnest to have the boys taken off his hands, seeing the entertaining of them, and their keepers which completed the number of one hundred persons was very chargeable unto him, the Council then laid to the land-lords charge that they would take the keeping of the boys only until his Majesty's will and pleasure were returned, what further course should be taken with them, which they likewise refused, whereupon they being removed, and the Council having at length reasoned upon that point, it was found that in reason, the landlords ought to have the burden of this matter, and therefore it was resolved that Lawers should still keep the boys, until Lammas, betwixt and which time, the farther knowledge of his Majesty's pleasure was expected. And that the landlords should make payment every one of them of the sum of ten merks for every merkland pertaining unto them formerly possessed by the ClanGregour and that for the charges and entertainment of the boys, during the months of June and July. And they were ordained to consign that sum in the hands of the Clerk of Council to have been delivered by him to Lawers, and the double of this sum was enjoyned to those who disobeyed. This being intimated to the landlords, and they finding no means to eschew the same, they craved two days leisure to be advised whether they would embrace that condition or make some other overture how the turn might be done which was granted.

"At the third meeting upon the 24 of this instant the landlords being of new heard anent the boys, they agreed to take the keeping of them until Lambmes and that they should be distributed among them according to their merklands, allotting a boy to every four merkland. The Council accepted the condition, and has ordained them, to send and receive the boys from the Laird of Lawers, betwix and the first of July with this certification to the disobeyers, that they shall be compelled to pay to Lawers twenty merks for every one of their merklands formerly possessed by the ClanGregour.

"The Landlords did earnestly urge the transplantation of the whole name of the ClanGregour, man, wife, and bairn. This was thought a matter not only of difficulty but of great rigour, and extremity to transplant men, and families, who had renounced their names, and found caution to be lawful, and answerable subjects, and it was likewise thought against reason, to remove them from the places of their present abode, and to settle them in any peaceable part of the incountry, among honest and lawful subjects, and their cautioners did likewise, propone their impossibility to answer for them if they were transplanted.

"It was demanded of the landlords if they would be content that the whole cautioners of the ClanGregour should be discharged upon that condition of transplantation, but they gave no direct answer to that proposition.

"It was demanded of them, whether or not, they had their lands now peaceable and free of the ClanGregour They all granted, that they had their lands free and peaceable of the ClanGregour.

"Because the meetings and assemblies of these of the ClanGregour who have renounced their names, was thought to be suspicious, and might give matter of new trouble, proclamations are directed discharging all such meetings of the ClanGregour, in any number exceeding four persons and they are likewise discharged to wear any armour but a pointless knife to cut their meat.

"Anent that sum promised by the landlords[1] to be given to his Majesty for making of their lands peaceable because the whole number were not here, whom that matter concerned, they are all ordained to be charged to the 22 of July next to hear and see them decerned to make payment of that sum.—Original Minutes of Secret Council in Sir James Balfour's Collections, Advocates' Library.

"June 26. Act anent the distribution of the bairns of the ClanGregor, charge against the Landlords of the ClanGregour anent that sum promised to his Majesty by them for making their lands peaceable." (The Laird of Lawers promised to deliver John dow McGregor's son to the Laird of Glenurquhy who promised to send him to this Burgh)

"Proclamation that none of the ClanGregour who have renounced their names keep meeting in any number exceeding four persons

"The Laird of Buquhannane acted himself to enter the two sons of young Malcolm McCoull McGregour, whenever he shall be charged.—Record of Secret Council

"June. Item to the officers of Justiciary for summoning an assise to certain of the MacGregors who were executed to the death, £1 6 8.

"Item to Robert Scott messenger, passing from Edinburgh with letters to charge Alexander Earl of Linlithgow, Alexander Levingstoun of Belstane and James Carmichaell of Pottischaw as cautioners for Patrick and John Levingstonis alias McGregours and Alex Levingstoun of Westquarter as cautioner for Duncan and Allaster Levingstounis sons to Patrick Aldoch To bring and exhibit the said persons for whom they become caution and present them before the Council upon the 15. day of July. next to come. to the effect new, sufficient and responsable cautioners may be found by them, upon the conditions to the said persons, should

---

[1] This sum, as appears from an "Act," dated July 29, was a separate contribution to the King himself, and had nothing to do with the "entertainment of the Bairns"

they fail in the entry of the said persons That they shall be decerned to have incurred the pain of 500 merks for every one of them, £6. 13. 4,

"Item to James Fyrie messenger passing from Edinburgh with letters to charge James Drummond of Pitzalloun to bring and exhibit Alex. Drummond alias McGregour son to umquhile John dow McAllaster McGregour before the Council the 15. day of July next under the pain of 500 merks conform to his act of cautionery with certification, £5.—Lord High Treasurer's Books."

Chapter XXXIII

Fines, &c.

FROM the "Chartulary":—

"1613. July 3. The which day Sir Duncane Campbell of Glenurquhie Knight, directed, and sent here to this burgh . . . . McGregour son to umqle Johnne Dow McGregour, who was delivered to the provost of Edinburgh and by him directed and sent with his own man to the Tolbooth of Edinburgh.

"1613. July 8. An Act whereby the Earl of Ergyll yielded to give unto his Majesty £22. 10. out of every hundred pounds which he shall receive of the fines of the resetters of the Clangregour.

"Charges ordained to be directed against the landlords of the Clan who have not taken the bairns of the ClanGregour off the Laird of Lawers' hands, for payment to him of 22 merks out of every one of their merklands possest formerly by the ClanGregour.—Record of Secret Council.

"July. Names of Sederunt. Act anent the fynes of the Clangregour. The quhilk day in presence of the Lordis of Secreit Counsaill compeirit personallie Archibald Earl of Ergyll his Majesties Lieutenant and Justice against the Clangregour, and donatour to the haill fynes whairin the persone or personis quhatsumevir, resettaris, and intercommanaris with the ClanGregour ar or salle decernit, and adjudged for thair resett, supplie, and intercommoning with thame. And maid ane free and willing offer to his Majestie of the soume of tuenti pundis 10 shillings, out of every hundreth pundis of the saidis fynes quhilkis ar alreddy or heirefter salbe discernit againis the saidis resettaris, suppliearis, and intercommonaris, with the said ClanGregour. Sua that his Maiesteis Thesaurair and officiaris in his Maiesties name may freelie and peaceablie intromitt thairwith at thair pleasour. And he promised to be comptable to his Maiesties Thesauerair and ressavearis, for the said soume of £22. 10. oute of everie hundreth pundis of the saidis fynes alreddy intromettit with be him or quhilkis heireftir salbe intromettit with be him.

"July 4. An Act anent the fining of some resetters of the ClanGregour.

"July 15. The Earl of Linlithgow anent Patrick Aldoch's son. The which day in presence of the Lords of Secret Council compeired personally Alexander Earl of Linlithgow and James Carmichael of Pottieschaw and of their own consents took the first day of Oct. next to come, for the entry, and exhibition before the said Lords, of Duncane, Patrick, and Alexander Levingstonis sons to umqle Patrik Aldoche and John Levingstouns sons to umqle Johnne McGregour in Glenoglill, for obedience of the letters and charges executed against them for this effect.—Record of Secret Council.

"July 22. Act anent the payment of the fynes of the resetters of the Clan-Gregour.—Record of Secret Council.

"July 27. Charge for exhibition of Johnne Gromach McGregour ane common and notorious thief apprehended by Johnne Gordoun of Buckie tane off his hand be Colene Campbell of Clunes. who laid him upon Charles Robertson in Athoill. —Record of Secret Council.

"July. Item to George Mathew messenger, passing from Edinburgh with Letters to charge James Earl of Murray, James Lord Madartie William Lord Murray Mr of Tullibardin, Sr Duncan Campbell of Glenurquhy, Alexander Menzies of Weymes, James Campbell of Lawers —— Campbell of Glenlyoun Johnne Campbell of Caddell —— Robertson of Strowan Duncan Menzies brother to the Laird of Weyme and John Campbell Brother to the Laird of Lawers.   To compeir personally before the Council the 22 day of June instant, to hear and see them, and every one of them decerned to make payment to our Sovereign lord's Thesauerers Depute of the sum of £60 for every merkland pertaining to them which was possest by the Clangregour at the term of Whitsunday 1610, or else to show a cause why the same should not be done, with certification &a and with letters to be published at the Market Crosses of Perth and Forfar discharging all meetings, and conventions of the McGregours, above four persons, under the pain of rebellion. £12.   Similar Charges to Earls of Argyll, Linlithgow, Monteith, Lairds of Luss, Buchannan, Keir, Shaw of Cambusmoir, Shaw of Knockhill, Graham of Boquhappil, and Naper of Merchiston, and similar proclamations as to MacGregours, at Stirling and at Dumbarton.   And such like passing with letters to be published at the Market Cross of Inverness. discharging the assemblies and meetings of the ClanGregour in any number exceeding four persons allernallie, under the pain of death. £13.6.8.—Lord High Treasurer's Books.

"July 29. Act in favour of the Landislords of the ClanGregour.   Anent our Sovereign Lords letters making mention for as much as (at) a meeting and conference betwix the Lords of Privy Council and some of the Landlords of the ClanGregour upon the 28. day of May 1611 there was a free and willing offer made to his Majesty by the landlords of the sum of three score pounds out of every merkland pertaining to them, which was possest by the ClanGregour at the feast and term of Whitsunday. 1610.   And anent the charge given to the landlords of the ClanGregour underwritten They ar to say. Archibald Earl of Argyll, James Earl of Murray Alexander Earl of Linlithgow, William Master of Tullibardine, James Lord of Madderty, Alexander Colquhoun Luss, —— Buquhannane of that Ilk Johnne Merchiston, James Reidheugh of Cultibragane, Alexander Menzies of Weyme, Sir Duncan Campbell of Glenurquhie Duncane Campbell of Glenlyoune, Robertsoune of Strowane James Campbell of Lawers Johnne Campbell his brother, Sir Archibald Stirling of Keir Mr James Shaw of Knockhill Alexander Shaw of Cambusmoir, William Earl of Menteith, and Thomas Graham of Boquhappell, and Duncan Menzies, to have compeired personally before the Lords of Secret Council at a certain day bygone, to have heard and seen them, and every one of them, decerned to make payment to his Majesty's thesauerer and officers in his Highness' name, of three score pounds for every merkland pertaining to them, which was possessed by the ClanGregour at the same term of Whitsunday 1610 or else to have shown a reasonable cause why the same should not be done with certification &a Appearance made for a number of the said landlords. The note forsaid, bearing the offer made by the landlords, in the matter above written, produced by the said Lord Advocate, for instructing of the libel being read, heard, seen, and considered The Lords of Secret Council find, and declare, that the note foresaid containing the offer abovewritten can no ways astrict, or oblige the said landlords in payment of the sum above specified, because of the whole number of the Landlords above written, there were only six of the meaner sort that made the said offer and of these six, the Laird of Glenurquhy who was principal, made his offer conditionally, and with a protestation, which did in effect liberate him of his promise, and further the note foresaid wanted certain solemnities requisite in an act obligatory. and therefore assoilzies the said landlords from this pursuit.

"1613. August 3. Sundry persons Dilaitit of certayne crimes specified and amongst others 'of the crewall slaughter and hocheing of threttie heid of ky, oxen, and vther bestiall,' pertaining to Mr William Campbell of Breachlie, his tenentis 25 May last and for art and part of slaughter of 'fourtie heid of guidis,' within the Forrest of Leonache committit upoun the Mononday befoir St Colmmess last. As also the said Johnne McFindla McGuibin, off airt and pairt of the slaughtir of umqule McGreggie Roy in Budyet with ane durke committit be him a tua zeir syne or yairby And for being in company with Robert Abroche McGregour, his kyn, freindis, Thevis and soriers, by the space of ane moneth in duerse yair, wikit and theftious deidis —Assisa

"August 13. The same day the Laird of Grant sent out a company of men to have taken Duncan McVeanduy who having in his company five McGregours, is beset by Grant's men, he and four of his men escape, the fifth being a poor fellow, and given by the Landlords to be thresher in a barn, is hurt and taken. Duncane himself fled to the Earl of Enzie with whom he is presently in company.—Balfour's Collections

"August 25. Charge against the Landislordis of the ClanGregour. Forasmuch as the Landlords of the ClanGregour being so heavily oppressed with that wicked and unhappy generation of the Clangregour as divers of them would willingly have given the one half of the lands possest by the said limmers, for assurance of the other, His Majesty to his exceeding great pains, charges, and expenses, caused take such pains for rooting out of that accursed race as now the haill rooms formerly possessed by them are in the peaceable possession of the Landlords without fear or trouble of the ClanGregour. The consideration whereof moved the said landlords to make a free and willing offer to his Majesty of a certain contribution and sum of money to be paid out of the lands possessed by the ClanGregour; most unthankfully and undutifully they have gone back from that which willingly they had offered Therefore ordains letters to be directed charging" (recapitulation of the names of the Landlords with little variation) "To compeir personally before the said Lords upon the 16. day of Nov. next to come to hear and see his Majesty's will and pleasure concerning the course which his Majesty intends to prosecute and follow out against the ClanGregour hereafter. Intimated to them under the pain of rebellion.

"Sep. 10.

" 'JAMES REX.

" ' Right Trusty, wee grete yow well Understanding that Allaster McAllaster McGregour is apprehended by the Laird of Graunte and Duncane vickeanduy by the Lord Gordon Wee have thought good by these presents to will and require you to send for the said Allester and Duncan and committ them to safe custodie suffering none to have access unto thame without speciall license from yourselves till you shall be advertised of our further pleasur concerning them which not doubting but with all expedition you will do, We bid you farewell at our castle at (Windsor) the tenth of Sep. 1613.'—General Register House, Edinburgh.

"Sep. 15. According to his Majesty's direction charges are directed against the Laird of Grant, his wife, brother, and other keepers of Allaster McAllaster McGregour for delivery of him to one of the guard who is directed to receive him and bring him here and the Erll of Murray is appointed to send three or four men to assist and guard in bringing of the said McAllaster here. The Council has written to the Erll of Enyee to send Duncane V^ceanduy here and at their coming, they will be kept conform to his Majesty's direction.—Balfour's Collections.

"1613. Sep. Item to messenger passand with lettres to charge the Landlords before specified To compeir personallie befoir the counsall the 20 day of Nov. to heir and see his Majesteis will and pleisour concerning the course quhilk he intendis to prosequute aganis the Clangregour, heireftir intimat, and declarit, to them to the effect thay pretend na ignorence. under the pane of rebellioun.—High Treasurer's Books,

"Same date. Act of Secret Council, against the resetters of the Clan, about 150 are fined.

"End of Sep. 'Off the haill names of Clangregour delyverit in a booke to the Erll of Ergyle of whom he wes ordainit to gif ane accompt, thair is bot aboute tuentie persones resting upoun him, of whom Allaster McAllaster and Duncane Mceanduy, being the principallis, Allaster McAllaster is depairted this lyffe laithe, in the Laird of Grantis house, and Duncane Mceanduy being in the Erll of Enyee's handis the counsall hes written to the Erll to exhibit him. The rest of thir McGregouris is bot unworthie poore miserable bodyis.

"Charge to all the landlords to appear on the 15 Nov. as before.

"Nov. 18. The Landlords of the ClanGregour being summoned to the 16 day of this instant, anent that contribution promised for making of their lands peaceable, a number of them compeiring, the rest being absent They who compeired, except the few number, who at the first consented to the payment of the said contribution, refused altogether to contribute to that errand alledging that the consent of a small number of their neighbours could on no ways bind or oblige them, and the Laird of Glenurquhy in respect he had done service himself against the Clangregour, and had sustained great losses and skaith by them, he stood by his first protestation made against the payment of the said contribution, and although remonstrance was made unto them of the pains his Majesty had taken by his officers, and ministers in that errand, the great charges which his Majesty had sustained, therthrough, and the good effect and success flowing from his Majesty's travels (travails?) to the ease, comfort, and relief of the landlords, and freething of them from the oppression of that race, yet they could nowise be induced to consent to the said contribution, whereupon the Council continued them to this 17. day of Nov. and in the mean-time thay were privately dealt with, to give unto his Majesty satisfaction, but no entreaty could move them to yield, And they being this day of new brought before the council and at length heard some of the council, were of opinion, that the consent given by some of the landlords ought, and should bind, and oblige the whole remanent, because the action for the which the contribution was craved was common to all and they were all conjunct partakers of the benefit of that service The most part of the council, were of opinion that the consent of a small party could nowise engage nor bind the rest, and so by a plurality of votes it was resolved in this, the absentees in respect of noncompeirance to defend, and these who con-sented or decerned to pay, the dissenters are dismissed without an answer. It was objected by some of these who consented that the service was not yet ended, and that the causes for which the contribution was granted, were not fully accomplished, the council has appointed unto them Tuesday next to give in the particulars in writing, and the Earl of Argyll to answer thereunto Some course will be taken with the bairns of the ClanGregour at this next meeting with the landlords.—Balfour's Collections

"1613. Nov. 24.   The Lords ordain the landlords of the ClanGregour to convene the morne in the laiche toun counsalhous of Edinburgh, and there to make a
catalogue, and roll of the haill bairns of the Clangregour presently in hand, making
special mention of their ranks, age, qualities, and whose sons they are, and in whose
keeping they presently remain, and to report the roll upon Thursday to the Council
with their opinion what farther is to be done anent the service of the Clangregour committed to the trust of the Earl of Ergyll.[1]—Record of Secret Council.

"Commission to Mr James Kirk for trying of the resetters of the Clangregour
within Ergyll and Tarbett.—*Ibid.*

"Nov. 26.   Letter Sir Thomas Hamilton to the King.

"'Most Sacred Souerane.

"'These days bygone your Majesties council have dealt with some of the Mak-
gregours landlords, who being summoned, compeired before them the (rest being
absent) To give their advice anent the order to be taken with the rebells children,
wherein the care of these landlords appeared to be rather to disburden themselves
and the highlands of these children, and to have them transported and kept besouth
Forth and Clyde, nor to propose any overture for the general good of the kingdom
which the Council has not allowed because, the landlords being the men most interested in the extirpation of the Clangregour, in respect of the relief of their
dangers, and daily troubles, and making their lands formerly possessed by these
rebells peaceable, and profitable to themselves, they had neither bestowed travels,
nor charges in their pursuit, but left all the burden upon your Majesty, and being
now pressed to pay their contribution which some of them had long ago promised
these would have revoked their promises, and the rest being absent, and not having
given their express consent, thought that no lawful decreet could be given by the
council, to compel them to pay.   And albeit they allege that if the bairns rise to
men, they may be of number and power, to renew the trouble of the country, yet it
is found by particular examination, that there is not ten of these children above the
age of five years, And the landlords confess that if order were taken with ten or
twelve, who are the sons of chieftains, the whole remnant of that number are so base
and beggarly, that they will never be able to make trouble.   The council finding the
landlords so unwilling to pay their contribution, think it fittest, to leave the charge
of the bairns upon them until they consent to some such overture, as may secure
the country from their future rebellion.   And because the small number of mean
landlords, who at first consented to pay the contribution, complain of their double
burden of contribution, and entertering the children, the council has thought to
supersede the exaction of that contribution, until some more solid order be taken
with the bairns.   Suspicion is conceived that Glenurchic, Lawers or some other
landlords may by their letters, or otherwise inform your Majesty, that it is necessary
that the bairns be transplanted to the lowland, which course the council is not likely

---

[1] This Roll would be extremely interesting, but no traces of it can be found.

to allow Therefore eschewing your Majesty's trouble by their importunity it appears fit that the matter be remitted to the council but if your Majesty conclude anything to the contrary, I shall ever yield that obedience, and employ such diligence in accomplishing your Majesty's directions, which my faithful duty and your Majesty's gracious favours, does strictly require. So praying God to grant your Majesty long life constant health prosperity and contentment rest &a &a '

"1613 Nov 30. An act anent the bairns of the Clangregour and an act anent the compt by the Erll of Ergyll

"Charge against the Erll of Perth and Lord Madertie for exhibition of Robert Abroche and Charges against the Laird of Grant for exhibition of the Clangregour being in his hands   Charges against the Erll of Enyee for exhibition of McGregour being in his hands   An Act relieving the landlords of all payment of the contribution in respect the burden of the bairns is laid upon them

"Same date. There have been divers meetings with the Erle of Ergyl and the landlords of the Clangregour, anent this last accompt, made by the Erle upon the accomplishment of that service, and what course was most fit and expedient to be taken with the bairns who were apprehended by the Laird of Lawers, And the landlords were deeply sworn to declare the truth of that, which rested in the accomplishment of the service. And this being the appointed day for making of the accompts, and for hearing of the objections proposed by the landlords against the same, the Erll gave in a roll containing the names of these who rested upon him at his last accompt, made in the June last, being thirty persons in number or thereby This number he has reduced to twelve persons who are to be declared fugitives, and outlaws, and accordingly to be prosecuted with fire and sword, and proclamations are to be directed against the resetters of them, besides this number there are two persons and one in the Erle of Enyees hands against whom charges are directed for their exhibition, and charges are to be directed against the Erle of Perth and the Lord Madertie for the exhibition of Robert Abroche and Gregor Gar McPhadrick V^{c}Conneil who as yet have not found caution nor given their obedience.

"There have been divers conferences anent the bairns, and sundry overtures have been proposed to the landlords thereanent whereunto they could not agree, so that the first course which was agreed upon in the month of June last, anent the distribution of the bairns among the landlords, according to the proportion of their merklands was thought meet to be followed out. The small number of landlords who consented to the contribution of £60 out of the merkland, finding that this course anent the distribution of the bairns, among the haill landlords, brought a double trouble upon them, making them subject both to the payment of the contribution, and to the entertainment of the bairns, wheras they who dissented from the contribution, being the greatest number, and of the best rank, were only subject to the entertainment of the bairns. They therefore not only protested

3 H

against the payment of the contribution unless they were free of the bairns, but with that they made offer to receive the bairns, with condition to be free of the contribution. The council having advised upon this proposition, and finding that with reason, they could lay no burden of the bairns upon those, who consented to the contribution, seeing their consent was conditional to be free of all farther trouble and burden of that race, and considering therewithal, that they were but a small number who consented, and that their parts of the contribution were of little avail, they therefore thought meet to take hold of this proposition, and offer, and proposed the same to the haill landlords who were present, who have consented thereunto, upon these conditions To wit, that the bairns shall be equally distributed among them according to the proportion of their merklands, that they shall be subject to keep them furthcoming and answerable, whenever they shall be called for, until they be of the age of 18 years, at which time they shall exhibit them to the council to be then taken order with as shall be thought meet under such a pecunial pain as shall be agreed upon, answerable to the rank and quality of every bairn, if the bairn shall happen to escape from his keepers, the resetter of the bairn, shall not only be held to relieve the landlord who had the keeping of him, of all pain and danger that he may incur through his escaping, but likewise shall be subject to such an arbitral censure, and punishment, as the council shall inflict upon them. The bairn so escaping, being within 14 years of age, shall be scourged and burnt on the cheek for the first escape, and for the next escape shall be hanged, and if he be past the age of 14 years, he shall be hanged for the first escape, and proclamations are to be directed and published therupon.

"The clerk of Register, and the lord Kilsyth are to meet with the landlords, and by their advice to make a catalogue and roll of the haill bairns, and accordingly to make a distribution of them and to set a sum upon every bairn according to the which sum the keepers shall be answerable for them. The first question proposed by the landlords, upon the point of accomplishment of the service, was the decease of some of the cautioners for the Clangregour, whereby they are of opinion, that the cautioner being dead the party for whom caution was found was free, In this point they received satisfaction in respect of an act of parliament bearing that all cautioners taken for the good rule and quietness of the Highlands and the borders, shall oblige the heirs of the cautioners as well, as the cautioner himself. The next point proposed by them was against insufficiency of some two or three of the cautioners, In this point they were satisfied by directions given for renewing of these cautions. Thirdly they objected against the Erle of Ergyll, as not being a good caution, to this it was answered that the Erle was the best cautioner they could get seeing he was answerable and obedient to the law, and more able to relieve (reduce?) these for whom he was caution, under obedience, than any other cautioner was. Fourthly they urged transplantation of all those who have found caution, this was thought most unreasonable, as being a mean to break them all loose, and to bring their cautioners in trouble and danger, seeing the most part of their cautioners have them on their own lands, and would not have been caution for them if they had known of any such motion anent their transplantation.—Balfour's Collections.

"Dec. 1. The which day in presence of the Lords Kilsyth and Clerk of Register, who were appointed to take up a catalogue and roll of the bairns of the Clangregour, compeired personally the lairds of Glenurquhie elder and younger, Buchannan, Weyme, Lawares, and Makfarlane Duncan Meanyees of Comrie, and Robert Campbell of Glenfalloch and gave their solemn oaths to give up according to their knowledge a true roll of the haill bairns of the Clangregour who are presently outlaws, or have been slain or executed or departed this life as outlaws, and according to their oath they made a list and roll of the said bairns, and divided them in three ranks, to wit, the bairns of chieftains, the bairns of under chieftains, and the bairns of the inferior sort, being in number fourscore or thereby the oldest of them not past thirteen years of age, and the most part about eight, six, and four years old. The bairns are to be distributed among the landlords according to the proportion of their lands, the extent whereof was likewise given up, by the persons foresaid upon their oath of verity the pain enjoined to the landlords for keeping and presenting of every bairn of a chieftain £200 for every bairn of an under chieftain £100 and for every bairn of meaner sort £40 The havears and keepers of such bairns as come not in the Laird of Laweris hands are by proclamation commanded to keep them, under the pain foresaid.

"Such persons of the Clangregour as were omitted out of the book and roll given to the Erll of Ergyle by the landlords, are to be inserted in the fugitive roll, and accordingly are to be prosecuted, and pursued, because they lie out, and have never offered their obedience —Balfour's Collections

"1613. Dec 2. The Marquis of Huntly being written for, for giving his opinion anent the form of proceeding against Allane Makeanduy, excusing himself, by reason he was somewhat diseased Committee appointed 9. Dec —Balfour's Collections

"Same date. The Lords assign the 15 day of May next to Johnne Gordoune of Buckie for exhibition of Johnne Gromach McGregour.—Record of Secret Council

"Dec 21 James &a Whereas of our special grace, and mercy and for pacifying the rebellious provinces of the Irish in our kingdom of Scotland, we have forgiven our lovit Duncane Dowglas formerly surnamed McGregour of Morinsche, now Tutor of Glenstra, the displeasure of our mind, royal opinion (sectam regiam) and all process which we had either intended, or may intend, or might in any way intend, for the treasonable burning of the Barn of Blairwaddane lying within the Dukedom of Lennox, committed by the said Duncan in the month of February 1603 and for all other crimes.—Record of Privy Seal."

Chapter XXXIV

Trials, &c.

FROM the "Chartulary" :—

" 1614. Jan.   Item to Walter Smith messenger passing with letters to charge
the Earl of Enzie, and John Grant of Freuquhte to compeir personally before the
Council the 16 day of Feb. next, the said Earl to bring, present, and exhibit with
him Duncan M^{c}eandowy and the said Laird of Grant to exhibit John dow
McGregor Neill massot : (?) McGregour and Allaster Reoch McGregour, to the
effect order may be taken with their rebellion, and conformity to the laws, under
the pain of rebellion and putting of the said Earl and Laird to the horn.   And such
like passing with letters to be published at the market cross of Innerness, Inhibiting the resett, supply or intercommuning, with certain of the McGregours that are
declared fugitives and outlaws   And likewise passing with letters to be published
at the said market cross of Innerness charging whatsumever persons, havears of
certain of the bairns of McGregours, who are kept obscure, and quiet, to exhibit
them to the Lords of Privy Council within the space of a month after the publication
hereof, to the effect, order may be taken with them, for their obedience to the laws,
under the pain to be answerable as well to his Majesty as to parties grieved by
them.

"Item to William Cathro messenger, passing from Edinburgh with letters to
charge the Erle of Perth, James Lord Madertie and Mr : of Madertie to compeir,
bring, present, and exhibit Robert Abroch McGregour and Gregor gair V^{c}Patrik
Coull before the Lords of Secret Council the 17 day of Feb. next to the effect,
order may be taken with them for their obedience, as accords, under the pain of
rebellion and putting of the said Erle of Perth, Lord Madertie, and his son, to the
horn.   And such like passing with the said proclamations, the one concerning the
fugitives of the McGregours, the other concerning certain of the obscured (*sic*) boys
of the McGregours, to be published at the market cross of Perth.

" Item to John Ramsay messenger passing with these two proclamations to
be published at the market crosses of Striveling and Dumbartane Jan. 13. John
Earl of Mar (by his bond dated at Stirling and 'Alloway' 5. and 9. Jan. instant,
became pledge and surety for ' Johnne M^{c}farlane now of Arroquhar' that he
should compeir before the Justiciary of the sheriffdom where he dwells, to underly

the law for the attack on the house of Banachrea in June 1602. Also 'for being in company with umqle Allaster McGregour of Glenstra, his kyn, and freinds at ye field of Glenfrone Feb. 1603 &a.'

"Feb. 17. This day being appointed to the Erle of Perth, and Lord of Madertie, and his son, for the exhibition of Robert Abroch McGregour and Gregor Gair, and to the Erle of Enzie for exhibition of Duncan M^ceandowy, and to the Laird of Grant, for exhibition of some three or four of the ClanGregour being in his hands, The Lord of Madertie compeired for himself, and his son, and the Erle of Perth compeired by David Drummond his servant, and the laird of Grant was excused in respect of his sickness, and continued till Tuesday next   It was alleged by the Laird of Madertie, that he could take no burden for Robert Abroch, because the Vicount of Haidingtoun had taken a dealing for him, and would find caution to make him furth coming and answerable. And for Gregor gair, it was alleged that he was in Ireland, And so there was no necessity of finding caution for him   To this, it was answered by the Laird of Lundie in name of the Erle of Ergyle, that the said Robert Abroche and Gregor Gair were taken by the Erle of Perth, the Lord of Madertie, and the Master his son, and that they were a long time in their company, and that promise was made in their names to the Council to make them answerable, and forth coming And in this respect it was craved that the Erll of Ergyll might be exonerated, and freed of them The Council being loath to quiet the Erll of Ergyll until first they found some other lawful debtor to make them answerable, they have assigned unto the Erll of Ergyll, the 22 of this instant, for proving that the Erll of Perth, the Lord of Madertie, and his son ought to be answerable for the said Robert Abroch and Gregor Gair

"The Erll of Enzie compeired by the gudeman of Buckie, who alleged that the Erll could not, with his honour nor credit, exhibit Duncan M^ceanduy, without a condition and surety for his life. Because he, at the special request and desire, of the Erll of Ergyle took the said Duncan, and made promise to him that he should be in no danger of his life. The council thought this no lawful excuse, for the Erll of Enzie, and have ordained letters to be directed to denounce him rebel, for non exhibition of the said Duncan, and have ordained the denunciation to be superceded until the 10. March.—Balfour's Collections

"Feb. 22. The Laird of Grant compeiring before the council, granted that he had John roy McGregour, son to Duncan M^cean chame, and has acted himself to exhibit him, upon the first council day, of April. This John Roy is that same man for whom there was so much contestation in his Majesty's presence between the Laird of Grant and Archibald Campbell servitor to the Erll of Ergyle, he has likewise granted two other McGregours, and has taken the 10 of March for their exhibition.—Balfour's Collections.

"Feb 23. Letter Argyll to the King

"'Please your Majesty I have been this long time busy in finding the certainty of Grant's guiltiness, for the receipt of one of the Clangregour, (whom he denied in your Majesty's presence, as the copy of the article set down before your Highness will testify) and having accused him before your Majesty's council he is now forced to confess the having of him at divers times, but thinks to free himself of that crime, by procuring your Majesty's pardon to that rebel, which I most humbly entreat your Majesty not to yield to, until such time as the Laird of Grant suffer his trial, in the rest of the articles, agreed upon in your Majesty's presence, which I shall go about, with all reasonable diligence, so reposing on your Majesty's gracious favour in this I rest. Your Majesty's most humble and obedient subject Argyll. Leith, Feb. 23. 1614.'—Balfour's Collections.

"March 12. Ane letter to Gawin Colquhoun in Port, of the escheit of umqle Allaster McGregour M^{c}kean, and speciallie the contractis bandis &a granted be Sr Johnne Campbell of Ardkinglas knight, Johne Graham alias McGregour McKean, to the said umqle Alaster McGreigor, concerning the lands of Auchindowaane, annual rent of £100 from lands of Innerranich miln thereof, and piece of land callit Borriklie, in the King's hands thro' forfeiture, and execution of the said Allaster.—Register of Privy Seal.

"April 1614. April 2. The Remission of John Murray formerly (alias) called Gregour McGregour.

"James, by the grace of God, King of Great Britain, France, and Ireland, &a Defender of the Faith. To all his good subjects, to whom these present letters shall come, greeting. Wot ye, that whereas of our special grace, favour, and mercy, we have forgiven and by the tenour of these presents, forgive John Murray formerly called Gregour McGregour V^{c}Coule chere, in lie[1] bray of Balquhidder, All displeasure of our mind, Royal opinion, and all prosecution, which we either intend against him, or may in any way in future have, for art and part of the traitorous burning, and manslaughter, committed at the house and lands of Aberroughle, And for art and part of the depradation and spoiliation of goods in the said house and lands belonging to Colin Campbell brother german of Sir James Campbell of Lawers Kt and for every action and crime, civil as well as criminal, which may follow hereupon or be competent against the said John.

"1614. June 23. Robert Abroche McGregour appeared before the council and formerly declared that he had renounced the surname of McGregour and taken that of Ramsay. The council ordained Sir George Ramsay (elder brother of Viscount Haddington, and afterwards by creation Lord Ramsay of Dalhousie) to be his surety under penalty of 1000 merks.—Record of Secret Council, Treasurer's Books.

"July 28. The 24. day of August next is appointed to the Erle of Ergyle for making of his last accompt, of the service against the Clangregour. and the haill landlords are written for, to be here that day.—Balfour's Collections.

[1] Appears to come from the French plural definite article "les."

"August 24. Commission for trying the resetters of the Clangregour. Forasmuch as albeit the reset of the rebellious thieves and limmers of the Clangregour, their wives, bairns, goods, and geir, has been prohibited, and discharged by many acts, and proclamations made, and published heretofore; Nevertheless the chief and principal cause which has procured, and still procures, their continuance in rebellion, and which has frustrated, and disappointed the effectual execution, of his Majesty's service, against them, doth proceed from the reset, supply, protection, and maintenance, which they find among great number of people, as well inhabiting the countries, and bounds next adjacent unto them, as in some other parts of the country, who in outward show and appearance falsely pretending to be unfriends, to the said limmers, do notwithstanding covertly, and obscurely, not only supply all their necessities, and wants, but reset them in their houses, and take their goods, and geir in keiping, to their own use and behoof, so that at all times, when these fugitive limmers are pursued, or any course intended against them, for reducing of them to obedience, their resets, and starting holes, are so sure and certain unto them, as the most part of the courses intended against them, have proved fruitless, highly to the offence, and contempt of his Majesty, and fostering of the said limmers in their insolencies. And whereas bypast experience in the like cases gives clear evidence, that nothing is more forcible, against traitorous rebels and fugitives than to cut them short of their resets, and startingholes, which cannot be well done but by exemplary punishment, to be inflicted upon the resetters; Therefore the King's Majesty with advice of his Majesty's Secret Council, has resolved no longer to overlook that proud contempt of his Majesty's authority in resetting of the said limmers. . . . but to use some exemplary punishment, upon them to the terror of others, to commit the like hereafter And because the probation and trial of their resets, must be by witnesses. And his Majesty and Lords of his Secret Council being loath to weary his Majesty's subjects, and to draw them to charges and expenses, in coming here to bear witness, in that matter, seeing the probation may be as well led, and deduced, in the particular Sheriffdoms, where the resetters and witnesses dwell. Therefore &a.

"Commissions appointed in the shires of Argyll and Bute

"August 24 The Erle of Ergyle and the whole landlords of the Clangregour being written for, to be here this day, to hear the last accompt made by the Erle of Ergyll, of his proceedings in that commission granted to him, against the Clangregour, and to declare their opinion if the service be accomplished, and what farther rests to be done thereintill, the said Erll of Ergyle, and almost the whole landlords compeired this day in the forenoon, and his Majesty's letter sent down for this business, being read in their hearing, the same was delivered to the landlords, with that catalogue and roll of the names of the Clangregour which was delivered to the Erle of Ergyle, at his acceptation of the service upon him, and in the afternoon to report their opinion what they (thought) anent the accomplishment of the service. In the afternoon they compeired, and first verbally declared that they could say nothing, but that the Earle of Ergyle had very worthlie behaved, and carried himself in that service. But anent the accomplishing of that service, they gave in some articles in writing, whereby they alleged that the service was not accomplished, that the condition of that service, was to have rooted out that whole race, and name, secondly that none of them should have got remission, nor been admitted to change their names, but such as had done service against their own Clan, Thirdly that some of the cautioners were not sufficient, and last, that those who had found caution, were guilty of the break and violation of sundry acts of council, made against them. To this it was answered by the Erle of Ergyle that he never accepted that service, upon condition to extirpate and root out that whole name, because it was impossible to be performed, and his Majesty did never lay such a matter to his charge, next that none had got remission, but had done service worthy of remission, and that the whole number exceeded not eight persons, and touching those who had changed their names and had found caution, the Erle alleged that no such service was to be laid to their charge, Because they craved no pardon nor favour, but found caution to be answerable, as well for bygones as times to come, upon these points he and the landlords contested, and it was farther alleged by the landlords, that the most part of them who had found caution, were guilty of capital crimes. They being at length heard hereupon they are continued till the morn, and the landlords are ordained to condescend in particular, upon those who are guilty of these crimes. And upon the names of the cautioners who are not sufficient, to the effect order may be taken therewith, as accords.

"The Erle of Ergyle and the landlords being of new heard, the landlords proposed sundry demands, first that the whole Clangregour should be transplanted, which was thought unreasonable, and not agreeable to the course of justice, nor well, of the service, Next that the Erll should not be freed of the service, until first some proof were had, of the obedience of those who are under caution. This point was thought reasonable, and the landlords are ordained to charge such as have offended, to appear at several diets, between and the last of February.

"The number of outlaws is reduced to eleven persons, and remissions are ordained to be exped, to fourteen persons, who have done service and whose service was qualified, in presence of the landlords.—Balfour's Collections.

"August. Letters sent to the landlords, and Item to a post passing in great haste to William Middilmest constable of Dumbarton.—Treasurer's Books.

"Dec. 9. Letter Dumfermline to . . . . .

"'I had John Dow McAllaster, the greatest limmer and brokin man in all the north, and his brother both put out, and the ane execute in this toun, the other with tua of his marrowis, burnt in ane house, because thay would not rander; for this I gave thrie thousand marks, ane other, McGillieworike, I had brought into this toun and execute,'—Balfour's Collections.

"1615. The Lords appoint to the landlords of the ClanGregour any time betwix and the last day of June for charging of the ClanGregour to compeir before them to render them their obedience.—Record of Secret Council.

"Feb. 14. At Edinburgh. The lords Commissioners appointed for managing his Majesty's rents with advice of Sir Gideon Murray of Elibank knight their depute Ratify and approve a Decreet Arbitral pronounced by arbiters chosen by Argyle and Johnne Grant of Freuchie whereby the latter is decerned to pay 16,000 merks in satisfaction of all such sums of money, as the said Johne Grant his friends and tenants are fined, for their resett, supply, and intercomuning with the ClanGregor

"The same lords on the same occasion approved of an agreement by which Rory McKenzie Tutor of Kintail, Rory McKenzie of Redcastle and Mr John McKenzie of Dingwell had paid 6000 merks instead of 12,000 in which these had been fined for intercourse with the outlawed Clan and of an agreement by which John Ross of Holme paid 600 merks instead of 1000 being his fine for the same offence. They also approved of all other agreements by which the favour shewn to the resetters of the said Clan, reduces the fines to not above a fifth of the sums adjudged, so far as his Majesty's share is concerned. They resolved that the same indulgence be extended to all who complain of the fines being too high ; of whom were a number.—Balfour's Collections "

There are in the Treasurer's Books many notices of close letters to various individuals who, as appears from this and other public Records, were about this time employed to put the ClanGregor down. The rebellions in the Isles in 1615, and the year following, engrossed almost exclusively the attention of the Secret Council :—

"Nov. 26 at Edinburgh. Johnne Buchquhannan of that Ilk and Sir George Muschet of Burne bank became sureties for certain Buchannans and others to compeir on the 6 Dec and 'underly the lawis for airt and pairt of the slauchter of umqle Allaster Livingstoun in Corriecrombie '"

The "Black Book of Taymouth" gives some details of the events of this year, which seem closely connected with the various negotiations which have been already recorded in the last few years Sir Duncan Campbell of Glenurchy and the Earl of Argyll seem, one as much as the other, to have done their utmost, both by force and guile, to ruin the whole Clan, for which Argyle and his brothers had the best opportunities by their access to the King, but Argyle was more lenient in some instances than those known as the "Landlords of the Clan." Amidst the cruel edicts and persecution of the children, the generous courage of the resetters stands out in bright relief against the surrounding blackness :—

"Item in the monethe of October anno 1615. the Laird of Lawers past up to Londoun and desyrit of his Maiestie thai he wald wreit to the Counsall desyring the Counsall to send for the landislordis of the Clangregour that they wald grant ane contributioun of fyiftie pund out of the merkland, and his Maiestie wald find ane way that naine of the ClanGregour sould troubill aney of thair landis nor posses thame, bot that the landislordis sould bruik thame paceablie, for Laweris luit his Maiestie to understand that, gif his Hines wald grant him that contributioun, that he sould get all theis turnis satled. quhairin trewlie Laweris haid nather pouer nor moyen to do it. The counsall wreit for the landislordis, sic as the Erle of Linlithgow the Laird of Glenurchay the Laird of Weyme, Alexander Shaw of Cambusmoir and Knockhill. The rest of the Landislordis came not. The Chancellare inquyrit of thame that wes present, gif they wald grant to the contributioun, quhilkis all zeildit to, saifand Glenurquhay, quha said he wald not grant thair to, seeing his Maiestie haid burdnit him to concur withe the Erle of Argyle in persewing of the Clangregor, becaus he knew he wald get moir skaithe be the Clangregour nor all the Landislordis wald. Heireftir the Counsall wreit for the landislordis, and desyrit tham to pey the contrabutioun, and his Maiesties will was that it sould be givin to the laird of Laweris. Glenurquhay refuisit be reassoun that he nevir zeildit to the contrabutioun and the rest of the landislordis that wes absent the first counsall day that the contrabutioun wes grantit, refuisit the contrabutioun in lyke maner Sua the Laird of Laweris wes disapointit of the contrabution. Glenurquhay quarrellit the laird of Laweres and his breithrene that he sould haive tain sic interpryses in hand by his advyse, for to perturb the laird of Glenurquhay's landis seeing that he wes the laird of Glenurquhay's wassell, and kinsman cum of his hous, and als his sister's sone, and that quhen Laweres house wald haive wraikitt in Laweris father's tyme, the laird of Glenurquhay tuik in his mother, his breithrein, and sisteris in his hous, and saivit the hous of Laweris fra rowein and wraik.

"Item in the moneth of December 1615. the Laird of Laweris socht ane suit of the Counsaill for enterteineing of thrie or four scoir of the bairnis of the Clangregor, and desyrit the Counsall to burdein the landislordis with the sowme of 2000 merkis in the moneth thairfoir. The laird of Glenurquhay desyrit the Laird of Laweris and his brethrin not to truble him with that suit, seeing that they knew he had gottin moir skaithe of the Clangregour nor all the subiectis of the kingdome, and that he had done moir service to his Maiestie nor all the rest in oppressing of the Clangregour. Laweris refuisit that Glenurquhay sould haiv aney curtassie, bot that he sould pey as the rest did, for the enterteinement of the bearnis of the Clangregour . For the quhilk refuisall Glenurquhay mett with the landislordis, sic as the Erle of Tullibardin, the Erle of Linlithgow, the Erle of Perth, My lord of Madertie, and the rest of the landislordis, and they tuk the burding upone thameselffis for ane space, to enterteineing the bairnis quhairby Laweris wes disappointit of his tua thousand merkis

"Item, thairefter the Erle of Argyle gatt of his Maiestie the fynns of the receptaris of the Clangregour, and the Laird of Laweris and his Breitherein for the tyme beand, daylie waitaris on upoun the Erle of Argyle gat the fourth pairt of the fynnis to thame selffis Glenurquhay desyrit the Laird of Laweris and his breithereine that his tennentis sould not be trublit in the fynnis, seand that he and his tennentis haid maid moir service to his Maiestie on the Clangregour, nor all the rest of the subjectis in Scotland, and haid gottin moir skaithe be thame nor thame all, and that it wes no reassoun that his men sould be fynned, seinge his countray wes heallie brint, and sindrie of his tennentis slaine in that service Lawens and his breithereine ansueris wes that they wald grant no courtassie to Glenurquhay, quhairupone Glenurquhay postit up to Londoun to his Maiestie quhair the Erle of Argyle wes for the present and declareit to his Maiestie how that his tennantis notwithstanding of their good service, and great skaithe, wes pressed to be fynned, quhilk his Maiestie declarit wes no reassoun, and sua wreit doun to the Counsall, desyring (that none) of Glenurquhy's tennentis or seruentis sould be trublit with oney of the foirsaid fynnis To conclude the hous of Lawens hes bein verie ungraitfull to the hous of Glenurquhay at all other tymes "

Thus the chief persecutors fell out amongst themselves

From the "Chartulary".—

"1616. April Item to ane poist passand of Edinburgh for convoying ye man yt wes directit to ye Marques of Huntlie withe ane lurg dog and with cloiss ltres to ye said Marques and Lord Gordoun. £6. 13 8. Item to ane Ione[1] chenzie to the said dog 40 shillijg —Lord High Treasurer's Books."

1617 May 17 The Scottish Parliament met at Edinburgh on occasion of the first and the only visit which King James VI made to his more ancient Kingdom of Scotland after his accession to the English Crown — Parliamentary Record.

"June 28 Continuation of the Scottish Parliament which at this date made the following Act 'anent the ClanGregour.'

"Our Soveraine Lord and estates of this present Parliament Remembering how that his sacred Majesty being very justly moved with a hatred and detestation of the barbarous murders and insolencys committed by the Clangregoure upon his

---

[1] Iron chain.

Majestie's peaceable and good subjects of the Lennox at Glenfrone in the month of February 1603. And how that the 'bare and simple name of McGregoure maid that haill Clane to presume of their power, force and strength' and did encourage them without reverence of the Laws or fear of punishment to go forward in their Iniquities upon the consideration whereof His Majesty with advice of (his) Secret Council made divers Acts and ordinances against them especially one Act upon the 3. day of April 1603. whereby it was ordained that the name of McGregoure should be altogether abolished. And that the haill persons of that Clan should renounce their name and take them some other name. And that they, nor none of their posterity, should call themselves Gregor or McGregour hereafter under the pain of death." Recapitulation of other Acts after which the present Act continues : "And his Majesty and the said estates acknowledging the said Acts having been made upon very good respect and consideration for the peace and quietness of the country, And therewithal considering that divers of that Clan, who renounced their names and found caution for their good behaviour are departed this life, And that great numbers of their children are now rising up and approaching to the years of majority who if they shall take again the name of McGregoure renounced by their parents upon solemn oath the number of that Clan in few years, will be as great, as any time heretofore. Therefore His Majesty with advice of his said estates, ratifies, allows, and approves the Acts above written, of the tenour and dates foresaid, in all and sundry points, clauses, and articles contained thereintill, and conform thereto Declares, statutes, and ordains that if any person or persons of the said Clan who have already renounced their names, or shall hereafter renounce, or change their names, or if any of their bairns, and posterity shall at any time hereafter Assume or take to themselves the name of Gregoure or McGregoure, or if any of them shall keep trysts, conventions, and meetings, with any person or persons calling, and avowing themselves to be McGregoures, That every such person or persons assuming, and taking to themselves, the said name, and who shall keep the said trysts, conventions, and meetings shall incur the pain of death, which pain shall be executed upon them without favour, for which purpose his Majesty, with advice of his said estates, ordains and commands the Sherrifs, Stewards, Bailzies of regality, Justices of peace, and their deputes, within their several bounds, where any of the persons contravening this present Act. and remains to take, and apprehend them, and committ them to sure ward therein to remain upon their own expenses ay and order, and direction be given for their punishment as accords."

1617. In the same Parliament of King James VI. at Edinburgh another Act was passed connected with Highland customs.

"June 28. Anent discharging of Caulpes.

"Our Soveraigne Lord, and estates, understanding and considering the great

hurt and skaith which his Majesties Lieges have sustained these many years bygone
by the Chiefs of Clans within the Highlands and Isles of this kingdome by the
unlawful taking from them, their children, and executors, after their decease, under
the name of caulpes of their best aught, whether it be ox, mear, horse, or cow,
alledgeing their predecessors to have been in possession thereof for maintaining
and defending of them against their enemies and evil willers of old and not only
the said Chiefs of Clans will be content to uplift his Caulpe, but also three or four
more, every one of them will alleadge better right then other and every one of
them after ane other will uptake the same until four or five several caulpes will be
taken from one person howbeit never ane of the said Clans have right thereto, or
to the lands which the persons occupies, wherefra the caulpes are uplifted And so
severe are they that every ane of them after ane other will pull their horses and
oxen out of their Plowes and Harrows, in the very time of their greatest businesse
and labours so that many of his Majesties subjects which of old were enriched
with sufficient store of goods and Bestial and thereby made his Highness and
others having right, thankful payment of their mails, kaines and dueties indebted
by them yearly to his Majesty and others having right, are now by the extortion of
the said Chiefs of Clans and others claiming right to the saids caulpes, and by
unlawful raising and uplifting thereof become dessauperate and unable to pay his
Majestie and others having good right their just dueties, And seeing there was an
Act made heretofore in favour of the inhabitants of Galloway by his Highnesse
predecessour King James IV of worthy memory in his second parliament and
eighteenth act or chapter thereof discharging the saids Caulpes and uptaking
thereof in all timming coming under the pain of punishment as rebells and be ane
point of dittay against them in the Justice Aire.   Therefore our said Soveraigne
Lord with advice of the estates of this present parliament statutes and ordains that
in no time coming none of his Highnesse Lieges presume nor take in hand to
intromet with nor uplift the saids Caulpes within any part of this Kingdome under
the pain aforesaid."

From the "Chartulary":—

"1618. Feb. Item to George Stewart messenger passing from Edinburgh to
charge Archibald Earl of Argyle being at Glasgow to compeir personally before the
Council and to bring, present, and exhibit with him, Duncan M{c}Ewn M{c}Grigor
called the Tutor now called Duncan Douglas and Archibald M{c}Connoquhie
V{c}Allaster in Ardlariche now called Archibald Menzies upon the last day of March
next to come to the effect the said Lords may know their obedience, certifying the
said Earl as cautioner for their entry, that if he exhibit them not that he shall be
decerned to incur the pain of 3000 merks for Duncan and one thousand merks for
the other. Item to James Law Snawdoun herauld, passing with letters to charge

George Lord Gordoun as cautioner for Duncane McEanduy in Rannache to bring, present, and exhibit him before the Council, the 26. day of March next to the effect he may renounce his name under the pain of 1000 merks certifying the said Lord should he fail that he shall be decerned to have incurred the said pain.

"March.   Similar Letter sent to George Ramsay brother to Viscount of Haddingtoun to exhibit Robert Abroche McGregour now called Robert Ramsay the last day of March under pain of 1000 merks.

"1618.   Archibald 7. Earl of Argyle who had so zealously persecuted the Clan-Gregour, and received the fines against their resetters, in the course of this year, left Scotland for Spain and entered the service of the King of Spain having become a Roman Catholick and distinguished himself in the wars between Spain and Holland.—Taken from Douglas's Peerage.

"April. A messenger sent to charge William McEwin VcGillichelich in Ardlarich, John Dow in Trinafour his brother, and a number of other persons to the number of eightyseven common and notorious slayaris of deir and rae.—Lord High Treasurer's Books."

From the "Chartulary":—

"June 4.   Amongst a number fined for wearing of hagbuttis and pistolettis and the slaughter of wildfowls, and venisoune occur the names of several persons believed to be MacGregors.   Of these

> Donald McEane VcPatrik in Leargoun
> Duncan and Johne McEwill VcCondoquhys in Direcamss
> Finlay McCondoquhy Hermitt in Roray.
> Calum Clas alias McGregor in Lergan.
> Grigour McCane VcCondoquhy there
> Allester McAllester VcJames in Aulich
> Malcolm McNeill in Fernay.
> Donald McPhatrik Vcaclerich, Edinkeip
> Johnne McGregour VcNeill in Edinkeip
> Grigor Roy in Leargane
> Archibald McCondoquhy VcAllaster in Ardlarich
> Johne Oig Mcfrankeine servitor to the Clandaindoney VcAllaster in Downane
> Calum croch in Findart
> Johne McPhatik geir and his son Johne Dow McAchaincasich in Carie
>   and . . .
> . . . McAchaincasich his sone Calum ower, and Patrik McGregour in
>   Findart
> Johne ower McGillechreist VcInvoir in Camscherachtie

all under pretext and colour of thair recreatioun.—Secret Council.

"June 9 at Edinburgh   The Kingis Advocat against the Erll of Ergyll and Sir George Ramsay.

"Anent our sovereign Lords letters raised at the instance Sir Will. Oliphant of Newtoun Knt. his Majesty's Advocate for his Highness' interest making mention that wherein the course and order taken by his Majesty, and the Lords of secret Council, for settling of the Clangregour under obedience, it was ordained that they should not only renounce their names, but find caution to be answerable to his Majesty, and his laws, and to find caution for their compeirance before the said Lords so oft as they should be charged to that effect   According whereunto Duncane McEwin McGregour sometime called the Tutor renounced his name of McGregour and took to himself the name of Duncane Douglas upon the 20 day of Dec. 1611 years   And Archibald Earle of Argyll became caution acted in the books of Privy Council for his obedience, and his compeirance, before the said lords upon a fifteen days warning, under the pain of 3000 merks.   And upon the 23 day of July 1612. years Archibald McConnoquhy VcAllaster in Ardlarich under the Laird of Weyme renounced the name of McGregour and took to him the name of Achibald Menzies and the said Earl of Argyll became caution &a.   And upon the 23 day of June 1614 years, Robert Abroche McGregour renounced his name and took to him the name of Robert Ramsay, and Sir George Ramsay brother to the Viscount of Haddingtoun, became caution &a.   Said cautioners fined for not presenting them.—Record of Secret Council

"1618. July 24   Another set of people accused of wearing arms and of shooting wildfowl.   Among them

> Donald McPhaul Vcaclerach in Edinampull
> Johne Grahame alias McGregour there
> Callum bayne McGregour in Ardlarich, Grigor Roy his brother
> Angus McCondoquhy mic in Ardlarich
> John McEwin VcEwin in Rannoch
> Grigour McEane veill VcGillechallum there
> Johne McEane dowig there
> McConneill VcEane roy chamchorrane
> Archibald McCondoquhy VcAllaster alias McGregour in Rannoch.

"Nov. 4.   Charter by John Drummond of Innerzeldies to John Campbell of Ardewnaig, of certain lands in the Stewartry of Strathearn, proceeding upon a contract between Drummond with consent of his spouse Anna Murray on one part, and the said John Campbell on the other.   These lands had been acquired by John Drummond from John Comrie of that ilk.

"Nov. 26   Instrument of resignation by John Drummond of Innerzeldies formerly McGregour, proprietor of one half the said lands and by James Murray of Strowan proprietor of the other half, in favour of John Campbell of Ardewnaig &a."

Chapter XXXV

1619

FROM the "Chartulary":—

"1619. Feb. 25. Malcolme McGregor V^cdougall alias Stewart in Auchnaharde in Glenfinglas and Duncane McGregor V^cdowgall alias Buchanan in Portnellan in Glengyll are witnesses in a sasine of Sir Duncan Campbell of Glenurqyhy.

"July 29. at Edinburgh. Alexander Livingstoun of Westquarter became cautioner 1612. for Duncane and Allester Livingstonis sons[1] to umqle Patrik Aldocht McGregour and with James Carmichael of Pottieschaw same year caution for Patrik Livingstoun son of the said Patrik Aldocht and Alexander Balfour of Torrie, caution for Donald and Johne Balfouris, sons to the said Patrik Aldocht 1614. Sir George Ramsay KT. caution for Robert Ramsay sometime called Robert Abrocht McGreour; said sureties summoned (the Lords being informed that said persons are broken louse and are going athort the country, especially in the bounds of the Lennox.) with Sir Lauchlane McIntosch to whom said Robert Ramsay has been sensyne and is yet household man, and servant This Sir Lauchlane denies. Westquarter alledgeit that the said Allaster Livingstoun is dead, and that the said Duncane Livingstoun is man tennent to Sir Donald Gorm of Slait. Carmichael promises to search for and present Patrik Livingstoun : Balfour of Torrie does not compeir nor Sir George Ramsay nor the parties for whom they are bound and denounced.—Record of Secret Council.

"Same day. Several of the persons who were accused of wearing arms and 'schooteing wildfowl' are fined amongst them are mentioned as McGregors.

 Malcolme Stewart alias McGregor in Pitchirrell

 Donald Stewart alias McGregor his son

 Gregour McCondoquhy V^cEan in Lerrane

 Duncan McGregour V^cCondoquhy in Camseroche beg

 John dow his brother.

"1619. Item to messenger passing to charge Robert Ramsay (Abroch) and the five sons of Patrik Aldoch to compeir personally also to charge Sir Robert (George)

---

[1] Duncan, Allester, and Patrick, sons of Patrick Aolach, had adopted the name of Livingston, and his other two sons, Donald and John, the name of Balfour.

Ramsay as cautioner for the said Robert Abroche and Sir Lauchlane M'intosche to whom the said Robert is household man (denied) to present him before the Council upon the 29. instant.   Item to another messenger with the said letters to be proclaimed at the market cross of Perth and to charge the said Robert Abroch at the dwelling house of his wife within the bounds of Atholl &a.

" 1619. July.   Messengers to cautioners for the sons of umquhile Patrick Aldoch dispatched in several directions.

" 1619. Nov. 30.   Johnne Stewart in Murlagane, son to Alexander Stewart in
        Drumquhenie
 Donald Stewart son to the said Alexander
 Patrik Dow M°Condoquhy Roy in Innervik
 Johnne M°Gilliechallum V°Eane in Lergane
 Alexander M°Allaster V°Innes in Awliche
 James Campbell in Ardlarich
 Martine Stewart alias M°Gregour in Pitchirrell
 Donald Stewart alias M°Gregour his son
 Callum Bayne in Lergane
 Gregor Roy there
 Angus M°Indowigs V°Condochienuik in Ardlarich
 Gregour M°Condoquhie V°Ean in Lerrane
 Archibald M°Condochie V°Allaster in Ardlarich
 Duncane M°Gregour V°Condoquie in Camseroche beg
 Johnne Dow his brother

"These names appear with others in a charge of carrying weapons.—Register of Privy Council, Vol. xii. (Dr Masson).

" 1620. Feb. 17.   Orders for apprehension of Padrick M°Gregour alias Livingstoun Callum M°Gregour and Donald Roy M°Gregour brothers to the said Patrick Patrik M°Gregour son to the deceased Patrick Dow M°Gregour—Duncan M°Gregour his brother for alleged slaughter of John Buchannane.—Register of Privy Council (Dr Masson).

" 1620. June 29.   Letter from James VI to the Lord of Scone regarding John Murray properly Gregor M°Gregor afterwards known as John Murray [1] of Glenstrae or Gregor M°Gregor of Glenstrae.

" ' JAMES R.

" ' Righte trustie and right beloued cosen, and counsellour Wee greete you well, whereas wee have understood by the petition of one Johne Murray, the sone of umquhile John Dow M°Gregour that Sir Duncane Campbell gave him a bande to enter him to the lands of Glenstra, and Strathmallachan, provided that he could gette our royall consente, and becaus we are in goode hope, that the young man

 [1] His grandfather was Murray of Strowan, and Sir John Murray of Tullibardine was answerable for him, see page 333, hence he was sometimes called John Murray.—Ed.

shall prove serviceable to us, and his contrie, wee are well pleased that yee calle unto you the said Sir Duncane, and use your best means for bringing him, and the said John Murray to a final agreement so as upoun soume reasonable conditions, ye may enter him in possession of the said lands. And not doubting of your best endeavours herein, we bid you farewell. Given at our manor of Greenwich the penult day of June 1620.'—Copied from the Original in the collections of the Mar Family, by Willm. MacGregor Stirling.

"1621. August 29. Certain articles given in to the Lords of Secret Council for preventing of the apparent trouble like to be raised by the Clangregour, to the disturbance of his Majesties peace and the disquieting of the country.

"Whereas there is a new breed and generation of this Clan risen up which daily increases in number, and force, and are begun to have their meetings, and go in troops athort the country, armed with all offensive weapons, and some of the ringleaders of them, who once gave their obedience, and found caution are broken loose, and have committed sundry disorders in the country as namely upon the Duke of Lennox and the Laird of Craigrostan That therefore the former act made against such of the Clangregour as were at Glenfroone and at the herships and burning of the lands pertaining to the Lairds of Glenurquhy, and Luss, and Coline Campbell of Abirrurquhill, that they should wear no armour, but a pointless knife to cut their meat be renewed with this addition, That the said act be extended against the whole name.

This Article
agreed unto. "That some of the principal Landlords and cautioners such as the Earls of Perth, and Tullibardine, the Laird of Glenurquhie, Lawers and Weyme be charged at several dyets to enter their men for a proof of their obedience. And when they are come in, that they be demitted without trouble, their cautioners in the meantime standing obliged for them. This will be a motive to cause the rest come in, when they see that no evil is intended against them, and will cause the young ones who are not under caution give their obedience. That an act be passed finding and declaring that all the landlords who suffer any of the Clangregour to dwell upon their land and take maill and duty, plaint and court of them shall be answerable for them, and their doings, seeing sundry landlords set their land to the Clangregour for a greater rent, than poor men are able to pay which is easy for them seeing that they take from all men. That missives be directed to the Earls of Monteith, Perth and Tullibardine, to the Lord of Scone, the Laird of Glenurquhy and other barons thereabout to set out watches for keeping of the country with power to these watches to apprehend, and put to justice such masterless, broke and suspected men as they can find, with a dispensation anent whatsomever slaughter, mutilation, or other inconvenient that shall fall out in the taking of them.

This Article agreed unto.

The Act of Parliament aganis Landislordis in the Highlandis and Borderis is sufficient for this Article.

This Article agreed unto without the dispensation.

"And whereas Robert Abroche is the principal man with the sons of Patrik Aldoche that are become loose, that their cautioners be charged to enter them, and that proclamations be set out against them, discharging the resett, supply, and intercommuning with, And that a price be set upon their head to be given to any persons that will take them or slay them or present their heads

" Whereas the yearly compeirance of the Isle'smen has been a great occasion of reducing of them to obedience, that the like order be taken with the Clangregour.

" Forasmuch as the King's Majesty having taken great pains and travel and bestowed great charges and expenses for suppressing of the insolencies of the lawless lymmers of the Clan, which formerly was called Clangregour, and for reducing of them to obedience, And his Majesty in his just wrath and indignation against that whole race, having abolished the name thereof, as most infamous and not worthy to be heard of in a country, subject to a Prince who is armed with Majesty, power, and force to execute vengeance, upon such wretched and miserable caitives as dare presume, to lift their heads, and to offend against his Majesty, and his laws, whereof a great number of the principal ringleaders of that Clan have found the proof, by condign punishment, which has been executed upon them, according to their demerits In the execution whereof although his Majesty has had very good reason to have gone forward, till the whole persons of that Clan had been totally extirpated and rooted out, yet his Majesty out of his accustomed natural disposition, and inclination to clemency and mercy was graciously pleased to receive a number of them to mercy, after that they had renounced their names, and found caution for their future obedience, so that for some years thereafter they were quiet, and little or no din was heard of them, who had tasted of his Majesty's clemency, and mercy, as namely Robert Abroche, Duncane, Allaster, Patrik, Donald and Johnne McGregouris sons to umqle Patrik Aldoche McGregour, being most unworthy of the favour, and mercy shown unto them, and being wearied of the present estate, and quietness, which his Majesty by the power, and strength of his royal authority, has established throughout all the corners of this kingdom, preferring the beastly trade of blood, theft, reif, and oppression wherein unhappily they were brought up, to law and justice   They have broken loose, and have associated unto them a number of the young brood of that Clan who are now risen up, And with them thay go in troops and companies athort the country, armed with bows, darlochis, hacquebutis, pistollettis, and other armour committing a number of insolencies upon his Majesty's good subjects in all parts where they may be masters.   And they do what in them lies to stir up the whole Clan to a new rebellion highly to his Majesty's offence and contempt, and hurt of his good subjects, And whereas the liberty which these unworthy limmers have taken, to wear armour, And the reset, supply and comfort, which they find, in some parts of the country has encouraged them to break out in their disorders Therefore his Majesty with advice of the Lords of his Secret Council has statuted, and ordained, that no person or persons whatsomever who are called McGregouris, and who keep that name, and profess and avow themselves, to be of that name, shall at no time hereafter, bear nor wear any armour, but a pointless knife, to cut their meat under the pain of death which pain, shall be executed upon them who shall happen to contravene, without favour or mercy And whereas the said Robert Abroche, and the said Duncane, Allaster, Patrik, Donald, and John, sons to Patrik Aldoche, are the chief and principal ringleaders in these new disorders, and draw after them numbers of simple ignorant people, who are rather induced by their cruelty, than moved by any inclination, or disposition of their own, to assist and take part with them, so that they have forfeited, the favour that was shewn unto them, and have involved themselves in new mischief, and trouble, worthy of most exemplary and severe punishment. Therefore His Majesty with advice foresaid, promises, and declares by these presents that whatsomever person, or persons, will take, apprehend, and present, to the said Lords, any of the persons particularly above named, and failing of them their heads, that every such person, or persons, takers, apprehenders, and presenters of the limmers foresaid or any of them, shall have the whole goods and gear, with the escheat of the persons so taken, apprehended, and presented unto them, to be used by them, as their own proper goods in time coming. And ordain letters to be directed to make proclamation &a. . . . . and to inhibit reset &a. 'nor to furnish the parties above named' their followers, assisters and part takers nor furnish them meat, drink, house harbourie, nor to sell them powder, bullet, victual, armour nor any other thing comfortable unto them, nor to have intelligence with them, by word, write, nor message. But that they shoot them, and raise the fray, wherever they see them, hunt, follow, and pursue them as thieves, and traitors to God, their Prince and country, certifying them that shall do the contrary, that they shall be pursued, and punished in their persons, and fined in their goods, with all rigour at the arbitriment of his Majesty's council and such like to command, and charge all Sherriffs, Stewards, and Magistrates to burgh and land, and all justices of peace to take and apprehend all such persons, who profess and avow themselves to be McGregours, and keep that name, as they shall find them to carry, bear and wear any kind of armour, but a pointless knife to cut their meat And to present them to justice to the effect the said pain may be inflicted upon them as they will answer &a.

"1621. Sep. 24.

"'JAMES R.

"'Right Trusty &a we greite you well Wee have seen a note of your proceedings this last counsell day, and are well pleased that the proclamation which you have caused to be framed against the Makgregors be published but much is to be done in that businesse before ainie good effects, can follow according as we intende at some fitte occasioun more at length to aduertise you heirafter farewell. Given at our mannor of Hampton the 24 of Sep. 1621.'

Sep. Item to a messenger passing from Edinburgh with letters to be published at the market crosses of Crieff and Dunkeld and ther inhibit all and sundry his Highness lieges that none of them take in hand to receive, supply, or intercomoun with Robert Abroch McGregour nor with the bairns of umqle Patrik Abroch McGregour with certification to them who do the contrary, that they shall be pursued punished, and fined to the rigour, at the arbitriment of the Council. And likewise passing with letters to charge the Earl of Perth as cautioner and surety for the number of 20 McGregours who have taken upon them name of Drummond, to bring, present, and exhibit them before the Lords of Secret Council, the 19. day of Sep instant to give a prove of their obedience to his act of cautionery

"Item to messenger passing with the said proclamation to be proclaimed at Stirling, Kilmaquhug and Callender, and at Dumbarton.

"Item to messenger with letters to charge the Livingston cautioners to exhibit their charges in Oct.

"And suchlike passing with the said letters, to the market crosses of Perth, and Stirling, and Dumbartane, and there in our sovereign Lord's name and authority to charge the said McGregours, because they have no certain dwelling house, to comper personally before the council, the said day, for a proof of their obedience under the pain of rebellion.

"Item to a messenger passing from Edinburgh with letters to charge Sir Duncan Campbell cautioner for Donald Sinclair in Kintrik, and other eight of the McGregours, James Campbell of Laweris cautioner for Malcolm Robertson in Fernar (Fearnan) and other 13 McGregours, James Master of Madertie, cautioner for Gregor Ger McGregour, to comper and exhibit the same persons before the said Lords, the said day to the effect foresaid.

"Oct. 10. Charge for exhibitioun of Allaster McPatrik McGregour. forsamekle as Allaster McPatrik McGregour in Caderine, a commoun and notorious thief, sornair, and oppressour, being laitlie tane and apprehended be Alexander Campbell, prior of Ardchattane, he is now in his keeping, And the said Allaster being one of the principall lymmaris of that clan, who ar broken louse, and does quhait in him lyis, to steir up that whole clan, to new disordours and troublis necessar it is thairfoir, that he be exhibite befoir his Majesties Counsell, to the effect ordour and directioun may be gevin for his tryall, and punishement, as accords, For quhilk purpose the lordis of Secreit Counsell ordainis letters to be direct chargeing the said Alexander Campbell prior of Ardchattan, to carrye, and that said Allaster be carryet and convoyed in suretie, to Sir Dougall Campbell of Auchinbrek Kt. &a &a And to charge the said Alexander Campbell of Ardchattan, to send in to the saidis Lords suche information and dittay as he can, gif it is againis the said Allaster in write, closed and sealed.—Record of Secret Council

October 17 Precept of Remission of Sir Duncan Campbell and three sons, and natural son, for extirpation of the cursed surname, and wicked family of Makgregoris, burning of Dewletter, and the Castle of Glenstra in or about 1611.—Privy Seal

"October Item to messenger passing from Edinburgh with letters to charge

Alexander Campbell Prior of Ardchattane to carry and cause be carried Allaster McPatrik McGregour, to Sir Dougall Campbell of Auchinbrek, within three days, under the pain of rebellion, who is to transport him to Edinburgh, and likewise passing with letters to the market cross of Dumbartane to denounce three McGregours rebels and siklike passing with letters to the said Market cross to publish the price of 1000 merks to be delivered to whatsoever persons that shall present any of the three persons McGregours foresaid to the Council or bring any of their heads.

"Oct. 18.   Allaster McPatrik McGregour a notable and strong thief being laitlie tane be the Priour of Ardchattane, directioun is gevin for his exhibitioun here befoir his Maties justice to his tryall So many of the cautionaris for the Clangregour as hes bene chargeit for thair exhibitioun hes all gevin obedience, and hes enterit thair men and the lyke course is going forduart aganis the whole cautionaris whilk be appeirance will draw the whole clan to quietnes and obedience.—Denmlyne M.S. Collections of Rev. John Scot, minister of Perth, in Advocates' Library, Edinburgh.

"Nov.   Item to a messenger with letter to charge James Lord Madertie as cautioner for John Drummond of Innerzeldie, and six other McGregouris, John Master of Madertie, cautioner for John Drummond foster (forrester) of Glenthorn. and Alexander Menzies of Weyme cautioner for John Menzies sometime called John Mcillechallum glas in Stennocher and other eight McGregouris, to exhibit the persons for whom they are become cautioners before the Council on the 13. day of Nov.

"Dec. 6.   James &a.   Forsameikle as it is understand to the Lordis of secreit Counsaill that laitlie upon the 24. day of Sep. last

Callum McGregour McCoulecheir.

Duncane McGregour McCoulecheir son to the said Callum

Gillespick McCondoquhy VcAllaster

Patrik McGregour gar.

and John Dow milt McCarliche VcEwin Vcean wer ordourlie denunceit our rebellis and put to our horne, be virtue of our other letters, raisit at the instance of Kathrene Niniane VcEan the relict, John and Andrew Mcphersonis as sones with the seven dochteris, and remanent kin and friendis of umqle William Mcpherstoun in Gaspartoun.   Commission against them to the Sherrifs of Perth.

"Dec.   Item to messengers with letters making offer of 1000 merkis for the presentation of Patrik Levingstoun and Donald Balfour sons of Patrick Aldoche And Robert Abroch McGregour, or for any of their heads.

"1622. Jan. 17.   Commission against Johne Angus and others.   The persons above written have associated unto them Robert Abroche McGregour a declared rebel, traitor and lymer.

"January.   Charge against Colin Campbell of Ardbeyt to bring and present before the Council the fifth day of March next to come Ewin Mcinvallich, for whom he became cautioner so oft as he should be charged.

"Item to Andro Quhyt keeper of the Tolbooth of Edinburgh towards the defraying of the expenses of Alester McGregour alias McCartnay the time of his being in ward from the 13 day of Nov. 1621 to the last of Feb 1622.

"1622 March 5   At Edinburgh   Act in favour of Johnne Campbell.

"Forsamekle as Allaster McPatrik V^cGregour and Johnne McDonald Glas tua of the most notorious and strong lymmeris of the Clangregour haveing in the moneth of . . . . . last repairit to the boundis of . . . and according to their unhappie and theevishe trade of lyffe haueing entrit, to sorn, and oppress, and vex his Maiesties good subjecties, within the saidis boundis, and quhilk is more detestable to, force and defloir women, Johnne Campbell son to the Prior of Ardchattane, and six other persons of his servants &a, persaving thair detestable and insolent doingis, and being moved with a sense, and feilling of the distress, and greevis of the cuntrie people, They not onlie opposed thameselffis againis the insolencies of thir lymmaris bot preast to haif apprehended thame, and presented thame to justice, and the lymmaris standinge to their defens, being loathe to be tane, and feareing the event of thair triall, after a sharp conflict betuix thame, The said Allaster was apprehendit, and exhibite heir, to his Maiesties justice, in the Tolbuithe of Edinburgh, and after a condign and lawful triall by course of justice wes execute to the deade ; and the said Johnne refuseing to be tane, as said is wes killed. And quhairas the said Johnne Campbell, and the other persons that assisted him in this seruice, had no private respect of thair awin, in the execution thereof, but onlie for the weill of the countrie, Thairfoir the Lordis of Secreit Counsell findis and declares that the said Johnne Campbell, and the otheris personis, particularlie abonewritten, who assisted him in manner foresaid, in the persute of the saidis tua lymmaris, and in the takeing, apprehending, and presenting to justice of the said Allaster, and in the killing of the said umqle Johnne McDonald hes done good and acceptable service to his Maiestie, and his people, and hes fred the cuntrie of tua strong and notable lymmaris, And exoneris thame of all actioun, and cryme that may be impute to thame, thair throw, forever, Discharging heirby his Maiestie's justice, and his deputes, and all utheris officiares of his Maiesties lawes, of all calling, accuseing, or ony wayes proceding, aganis the said Johne Campbell and others persones, abone written, for the caus foirsaid and of thair offices in that pairt — Record of Secret Council.

"March 26.   The Marquis of Huntlie contra Johnne McGillechallum V^cean in Largane Allaster McRobertsoun in Aulich and others for slaughter of wild fowl

"Notwithstanding it is of truth that
    Johnne McGillechallum v^cean in Largane
    Allaster McRobertsoun in Aulich
    Alister v^cindlay v^cRobert thair
    Gregour McCondchie v^cean yair
    Archibald McCondochie V^cAllaster in Ardlariche

Johnne McGregour v^cCondochie thair
Angus McCondochie oig in Camserache beg
Auld Duncane Rioch in Phinnard
Johnne McPhatrik gar in Laren
Duncane McPhatick ger his son thair
Johnne M^{cc}anduie vig in Innerchrombie
Donald Roy McCondochie Roy in Pittigoune
Allaster Robertsoun sone to the Laird of Phascalie
Robert Fleyming appeirand of Monnes
Williame McGillechallum servitour to the Erle of Tullibardin
. . . . . M^ckane Roy vig in Camrone
Finlay Mc Wm. vic Gregour in Bonnaqr.
Allaster and Johnne his sones thair
Neill Stewart sone to Johnne Stewart appeirand of Graniche
James Stewart sone umqle Neill Stewart of Innerchumachine
Alexander Flemyng of Mones
George Malcolmetosche (M^cintosh) in Tyrmie (Tirinie)
And Angus McIntosch his brother there.—Council Fines.

"Feb. 28. Intram Allaster m^cPatrik m^cGregour in Cadderie, dilaitit and accused of the crymes following viz airt and pairt of the thiftious steilling, and away-taking of tuentie four heid of ky perteining to Mr James Grant brother to the Laird of Grant and to the Laird of Calderis tennants, and servants, committit at Mydsomer 1620 the said Robert Abroche being in cumpanie with him, at the steiling and away taking yrof. Sentenced to death.

"April 23. Another trial in the Court of Justiciary of persons out of Glen-froone, nineteen years previously Those now tried were certain of the Clan Cameron At the end of the accusations against them the following passage occurs.

"And sic like the said Duncan moir M^ceane Chamerone for being in company with Robert Abrocht [1] Johnne Dow McAllaster [2] and others thir complices eight years ago or thereby at the slaughter of umqle James Menzies brother to the Barrone of Comrie and burning of his house and so was art and part of the said slaughter and burning of the said house to the token he has confessed that he paid 3000 merks to the Barrone of Comerie and his friendis in assythement of the slaughter and burning.

"1623. January 23. Contract of Wadset betwixt Duncan Douglas formerly called McGregor and Mariot McFarlane his spouse and Malcolm Douglas their son and apparent heir on the one part and Malcolm and Walter McFarlanes elder and younger of Gartattane on the other Sum paid by McGregor 1000 merks scots, Sasine followed 10 August three years later.—Register of Sasines.

[1] Robert Abroch had received pardon in Dec. 1612 at latest.
[2] John Dow McAllaster had been killed, 1611.

"March 28. Commission to John Stewart of Ardsell against Robert Ramsay sometime called Robert Abroch McGregour, and Patrik Levinston sometime called Patrik Beg McGregour, sone to umqle Patrik Aldoch McGregour, two avowed rebels and notorious thieves, and limmers.

"July 8. Petition to the Secret Council by James Erle of Murray —— Stewart Principal of the Stewartrie of Menteith and James Stewart his depute, complainint that whereas they had received command from the Lords of Council to put Duncan moyll (bald) Campbell ane common and notorious thief, sornair, and oppressour apprehendit be the said depute within the bounds of his office in the act of theft, sorning, and oppression to the knowledge of an assise, they had tried and convicted him and pronounced upon him sentence of death to take effect on a certain day of which Robert Patrik Campbell brother to the said Duncan getting information he resolved to relieve his brother And for this effect accompanied with Dougall Gair McCondochy McGregour . . . . and a number of otheris laules lymmaris, sornaris, and outlawis come to the lands of Strongarvalt in Monteith and to the dwelling house of Patrik Stewart servitour to the said Erle and seized upon him, and carryed him, as captive, and presouner with thaim to the hillis of Glenurquhie, threatning him not onlie with deathe, bot with all kynd of most exquisite tortour yf the said Duncan his brother wer execute. Lyke as they sent word to my said depute, that yf he execute the said Duncane that he would send the said Patrick his head unto him, quhilk moved my depute to superseid the executioune of the limmer, for some certane space being loathe to expose the innocent gentleman to the merciles fury of these laules Lymmaris And my depute send to the Laird of Glenurquhie who is chief of thair limmaris they being bastard branches of his house desiring him that by his meanis the gentleman might be releeued, who returne ansuer, that he had no thing to do with these limmaris, that he had disclaimed thaim sevin yeirs since, becaus they were thievis, outlawis, and sornaris, and desire my depute to be on his advantage with thame, Quhilk seameing as it was indeid, a cauld ansuer, and my depute haueing deeplie apprehendit the dangeir of the innocent gentleman, and thairwithall resenting the indignity done to his Majestie, and to me his Maiesties officer, & he out of affection for his Majesteis service resolved to attempt the relief of the gentleman by the nearest means he could, and haueing gotten knawledge, quhair the gentleman was kept, be the lymmaris he &a accompanied with some gentlemen of the Stewartrie past to the pairt, and sent ane messenger unto thame desiring thame in his Majesties name, to restoir the gentleman prisoner. Quhilk thay not onlie proudlie refused to doe, bot out of the pryde, and malice of thair hairt, Thay entered in persute of the said depute, and the gentlemen that wer in cumpanie with him and furioushe with shoites of hagbutties pistollis and bowis invadit, and persewit thame, of thair lyvis, sua that they were constrayned to stand to thair lawful defence, In the quhilk defence it happynnit by the good providence of God that the gentleman wes relieved And the saidis Robert McPatrik —— McInteir and —— McColl wer killed and the said Dougall Gair McCondoquhy (M^cgregour) wes apprehended and deliuerit to the Viscount of Stormont.

" The Lords nominate certain Lords to be assessors to the Justice in the matter and ordains them to hear the parties and not to suffer the matter to go to an assise till they acquaint the council.

" 1624. Jan. 20.   Commission against certain McGregouris.

"Forasmuch as the King's Majesty having by the force, and strength of his Royal authority, reduced the Highlands and Isles of this kingdom to obedience, and established peace, justice, and quietness within the same, so that no part thereof, stands out in a professed and avowed rebellion ; yet, there is some few numbers of mischeant (mischievous) and lawless limmers within the said bounds, who being received to his Majesty's gracious favour wherof they were most unworthy and having given their oaths and found caution for their future good behaviour as namely,

> Robert Ramsay sometime called Robert Abroch McGregour,
> Patrik McPatrik Aldoch, and
> Callum McPatrik Aldoch his brother,

have broken loose against their faith and promised obedience, and they, with

> Callum oir McCondoquhie V^cAllaster McGregregour,
> Johnne McJames V^cEane V^cRobert alias Stewart,
> James McGeorge V^cEane V^cRobert Stewart, and
> George his brother,
> Donald Stewart, and
> Allane Dow M^ceanduy V^callaster,

all thieves and broken men and sorners, preferring their bygone wonted form of living in theft, stouth, reiff, and masterful oppression to good order and obedience They have begun to renew their former thievish doings, and go athort the country accompanied with other lawless limmers, their accomplices, and armed with un- lawful and forbidden armour, committing most heavy and violent oppressions, stouths and stouthreiffs, in all parts where they be masters, and do what in them lies, to stir up others to imitate others in their thievish doings, and so to procure new disorder, and trouble in the Highlands, highly to his Majesty's offence, and contempt, and disgrace of his government, that such an infamous byke of lawless limmers shall be suffered so long with impunity to break loose, as if they were not subject to Prince, law, nor justice, and as if his Majesty's royal arm of justice, were not able to overtake them And whereas Donald McRobert, son to Allaster McRonnald, of Gargache, to testify his willing disposition to do his Majesty some piece of service, has undertaken to hazard his own person in the prosecution of any of his Majesty's royal commandments, Therefore the Lords of Secret Council ordain a commission to be past, and expede under his Majesty's signet, giving, granting, and committing full powers, and commission express, bidding and charge to the said Donald to convocate his Majesty's lieges in arms and to pass, search, seek, hunt, follow and pursue the limmers particularly abovewritten wherever they may be apprehended And to bring, present, and exhibit them before the said Lords, to be taken order with and punished, according to their demerits, conforme to the laws of this realme   And if it shall happen to the said limmers, or any of their followers, for eschewing of apprehension, to flee to strengths and houses, with power to the said Donald to follow, and pursue them, assiege the said strengths, and houses, raise fire, and use all kind of force, and warlike engine that can be had, for winning and recovery thereof, and apprehending of the persons foresaid, being thereinto.   And if in the pursuit of the said persons they refusing to be taken, or assieging of the said strengths, and houses it shall happen them, or any, being in company with them, and assisting them, or within the said strengths, and houses to be hurt, or mutilate, or any other inconvenience, whatsoever to follow, the said Lords decern, and declare that the same shall not be imputed as crime, or offence, to the said Donald, nor persons assisting them to the execution of this commission. —Record of Secret Council.

"1624. Feb. 3 at Edinburgh   Protection to the ClanGregor.

"Forsamekle as there has been a proposition made to the Lords of Secret Council, in name of the Clangregour, proporting that they for testification of their submissive and willing disposition to become his Majesty's peaceable and willing subjects, and to live hereafter, under the obedience of his Majesty, and his laws, are not only content to redress and satisfy parties skaithed, and to find caution for their future good obedience, and for their personal compeirance before his Majesty's council upon all occasions when they shall be lawfully charged, But with that, to compeir personally before the said Lords, upon the 17 day of March now approaching, for finding of the said caution, Whereas in the meantime they be in surety to be untroubled, apprehended or warded for any cause whatsoever, And the said Lords having considered of the said proposition and finding it expedient for the good of the country, that the whole persons of the Clangregour, except Robert Abrach, who is no way comprehended in this warrant, but excepted, and reserved furth thereof, shall be secured and warranted, to come in, and to present themselves before the said Lords, to the effect abovewritten.. Therefore the said Lords upon good respect, and considerations for the peace and quiet of the country, have given, and granted, and by the tenour hereof, give, and grant, their warrant, permission, and allowance, to all and sundry persons of the ClanGregour, except Robert Abroche and his followers who are specially reserved, out of this warrant, as said is, to haunt, frequent, and repair publickly, and avowedly in all parts of the country, at their pleasure, without any search, stay, and arrestment to be made for or upon them, for whatsoever deed, cause, or occasion or by any person or persons. All which stay, and arrestment (not) to be made on any person of the Clan foresaid, except Robert Abroch and his followers, as said is, The said Lords discharge and ordain to rest until the 21. day of the said month of March next, Discharging hereby all his Majesty's lieges, and subjects of all taking, apprehending, or warding of any persons of the Clan foresaid, (except before excepted) for whatsoever deed, cause, or occasion, but to suffer them peaceably brouke the benefit of this warrant, until the day abovementioned, without anything to be done, or attempted by them to the break, or violation thereof, as they will answer upon the contrary, at their peril. Providing always that in this meantime they behave themselves as peaceable and good subjects, that they forbear theft, reiff, sorning, and oppression, and the wearing of unlawful and forbidden weapons. That they keep not companies, nor societies together, nor exceed not the number of four persons, in one company, and that they give their compeirance before his Majesty's council, upon the said 17 day of March next to come certifying them, that shall fail, in any point of the premisses that they shall be pursued, and punished as thieves, rebels, and limmers, with all rigour, and that letters of publication be directed hereupon."

The ratification of the proposed arrangement after the "armistice" does not appear to be extant.

"April 20. Precept of Sasine at Perth by Sir Duncan Campbell of Glenurquhy in favour of Gregor Murray alias M°Gregor in the 20 merkland of Glenstray, old extent.

"July 13. Sir Duncan Campbell Knight, and Colin Campbell fiar of Glenurquhy &a. Because it clearly appears, and is known to us, that the late Alexander M°Gregor of Glenstray, great grandfather of Gregor Murray, alias M°Gregour,[1] bearer of these presents, died last vested and infeoffed to the peace, and faith, of our Sovereign Lord the King in all and haill the lands underwritten viz

    In the 2 merkland of Kandroquhat
    the two merks with the $\frac{1}{2}$ merk land of Craig.
    the 1 merkland of Largachpull
    the three merkland of Adindonich with the mill of same
    the four merkland of Stroumelochan
    the 20 land of Tullich
    the 2 merkland of Castell
    the 2 merkland of Dowleatter
    the 6s and 8d land of Coronane
    the 1 merkland of Moyane
    the 6s and 8 merklands (pence) of Braeglenstray

[1] This recapitulation of the ancestor of Gregor having been infeoffed in Glenstray, proves the fact of his own legitimate descent.

extending in all to 20 merklands of old extent with all and haill the houses build-
ings gardens tofts, parts, pendicles and pertinents whatsoever lying in the Lordship
of Glenurquhy and within the Sheriffdom of Argyll, And whereas the said Gregor
Murray alias McGregor, bearer of these presents, is the lawful and nearest heir of the
said late Alexander McGregor his great Grandfather, to the foresaid lands, and that he
is of lawful age, and that the foresaid lands are held by us in capite, Therefore &a
(precept of Sasine in usual form) According to the usual form and tenour of the old
infeoftment of the said lands, with the pertinents formerly granted to the said Alexander McGregor in all points, and none other, &a, in witness whereof.—General
Register of Sasines."

From the " Black Book of Taymouth":—

" Item the said Sir Duncan Campbell sevint laird of Glenurchay in the moneth
of . . . . anno 1624 coft the tuentie merkland of Stronmelochquhan and Glenstrae
fra Gregour McEandowie V^cGregour, Patrik and Ewine McGregouris his brether,
callit all for the tyme Murrayis and gave to them for thair richtes and kindness
of the samyn landis the soume of ten thousand pundis money."

Thus the old land passed away from the Chief of the Clan representative of Joannis Gregorii de Glenwrquhay whose death is recorded in the
" Chronicle of Fortingal " as having taken place April 1391. . At that time
the Macgregours certainly did not hold their lands from the Campbells,
but in the recent transaction of "infeoftment" to Gregor MacGregor, Sir
Duncan seems to have been anxious to get the sasine properly executed
before purchasing from Glenstray the estate.

" 1624. Oct. 20. Robert Abborach ane MacGregor and great Lymmer who
had been once or twice forgiven, and remitted by his Majesty for his oppression,
upon hope of his amendment, and who yet still, continued in his courses after
there had been much searching for him in the Highlands and all his friends had
been charged to apprehend him came into Perth this day being Sunday, or preach-
ing day after sermon. He fell down upon his knees having a tow about his neck,
and offered his sword by the point to the Chancellor of Scotland. The Chancellor
refused to accept of it and commanded the Baillies to ward him, Likeas they
instantly warded him, and put both his feet in the Gadd where he remained.—
Chronicle of Perth in Scott's Collections, A.D. Lib."

1625. King James VI., the last of the Kings of Scotland exclusively,
died on the 27 March 1625, in the fifty-ninth year of his age, at Theobalds.

Of all the enemies of the ClanGregor none abused them so much, in strong words, or devised more inhuman measures of repression. He made no secret of his absolute hatred of the whole race. It should, however, be remembered that his advisers and flatterers were constantly poisoning his mind against the Clan with exaggeration and misrepresentation of facts, the Glenfroon case having been specially misjudged. Also the dauntless spirit with which fresh breaches of the peace were again and again committed particularly fretted and enraged the monarch, who had determined to quell the disorders of his kingdom, in which he certainly in great measure succeeded. In connection with his personal direction of the late affairs, the estimate of King James VI. character formed by Sir Walter Scott, as given in the " Fortunes of Nigel," may here be quoted.

"He was deeply learned without possessing useful knowledge ; sagacious in many individual cases, without having real wisdom ; fond of his power, and desirous to maintain and augment it, yet willing to resign the direction of that, and of himself to the most unworthy favourites ; a big and bold assertor of his rights in words, yet one who tamely saw them trampled on in deeds ; a lover of negotiations in which he was always outwitted ; and one who feared war where conquest might have been easy. He was fond of his dignity, while he was perpetually degrading it, by undue familiarity ; capable of much publick labour, yet often neglecting it for the meanest amusement ; a wit, though a pedant and a scholar ; fond of the conversation of the ignorant and the uneducated. Even his timidity of temper was not uniform, and there were moments of his life, and those critical, in which he showed the spirit of his ancestors. He was laborious in trifles, and a trifler where serious labour was required, devout in his sentiments, and yet too often profane in his language, just and beneficent by nature, he yet gave way to the iniquities and oppression of others. He was penurious respecting money which he had to give from his own hands, yet inconsiderately and unboundedly profuse of that which he did not see. In a word, those good qualities which displayed themselves in particular cases and occasions were not of a nature sufficiently firm and comprehensive to regulate his general conduct, &a."

Having reached the end of James VI. long reign and recorded the relinquishment of the lands of Glenstray and the final submission of Robert Abroch, it may here be well to pause, before turning to some events in the north of Scotland and following onwards the later career of the " Nameless " Clan.

Appendix

Appendix

A.—Introduction, page 2. Correspondence of Sir Robert Douglas, and John Murray, Esq, afterwards Sir John MacGregor Murray, 1st Baronet, 1769.

No. 1. Mr Murray's best compliments attend Sir Robert Douglas. He sends him inclosed three sheets of the scroll genealogical account of the family of Mac-Gregor. Gathering the materials of it has cost him no small trouble for several years past, but he has the satisfaction to think his labours have not been entirely thrown away. Dr Gregory has seen and been pleased to approve of it As this Clan is upon a different footing from all others, and have for some ages past been the football of fortune, it became absolutely necessary to enquire into and give a succinct account of the different causes of their misfortunes, in order to justify them, and render the remembrance of past actions less obnoxious than their enemies would chuse to paint them. This has been attempted as briefly as possible, and Sir Robert is left to judge how successfully. Meantime, as it is absolutely necessary to answer these purposes that the account be inserted fully with all the notes, Mr Murray begs Sir Robert may candidly say whether he will give it room as it stands, because if he does not, he insists that no part of it at all be mentioned, for to half do the affair would be in his opinion worse than silence. He knows the printing will be above the common run of the account of other families, and believes Sir Robert can have no other objection than that of the burden of these expenses Let him however understand, that if he otherways seems satisfied to give it room, these will be made easy to him. What remains of it will be sent in a day or two.—Friday, 21st September 1769.

No. 2 Sir Robert Douglas presents compliments to Mr Murray—thinks himself extremely obliged to him for the papers he has sent him, and so far as he has read of them, has not the smallest objection ; as soon as he has gone through the whole, will be glad to see Mr Murray.—Saturday, 22nd September 1769.

No. 3. Sir Robert Douglas presents compliments to Mr Murray, he has again carefully perused his account of the Clan M'Gregor, and is so well satisfied with it, that he is determined to print the whole papers, without leaving out one word of it, and intends to send it to the Press to-morrow, he'll therefore please return the remainder of it without fail.—Wednesday, October 4th, 1769.

B.—Page 254. Note in reference to the Declaration dated 1599, July 24. The document here quoted and transcribed by Mr MacGregor Stirling in the "Chartulary" about 1830 from an entry in the Register of the Privy Council, has only recently been published, 1898, in Vol. XIV. of the Privy Council Register taken from certain miscellaneous Privy Council papers; the earlier notice of it gives proof of Mr MacGregor Stirling's faithful search.—Ed.

C.—Page 279. Excerpt from "Glimpses of Church and Social Life in the Highlands in Olden Times," by Alexander Macpherson, F.S.A., Scot., the following being selected from the MSS. of the late Captain Macpherson (Old Ballid), of the 52nd Regt., who died 1858.

Battle of Glenfruin

" In an account of this battle which was fought in 1603, it is stated that early in that year Allaster MacGregor of Glenstra followed by 400 men, chiefly of his own Clan, but including also some of the Clan Cameron and Anverich? armed with halberschois, pow aixes, twahandit swordis, bowis and arrowis and with hagbutin and pistoletis advanced into the territory of Luss. Alexander Colquhoun under his royal commission granted the year before, had raised a force which some writers state to have amounted to 300 horse and 500 foot.

(Sir William Fraser's account follows.)

" Here is ' Old Ballied's ' account of the Battle, written it is believed about fifty years ago.

" It is rather singular that so little should be known of the particulars of the battle of Glenfruin, and the causes that led to it, when it is considered that it is comparatively of a late date, having been fought between the ClanGregor and the Colquhouns in the reign of James VI. No correct account has, however, been published, from which it may be inferred that the true history is lost amongst the MacGregors, for every version of the affair is more unfavourable for them than the facts would have been. One account says that it was an accidental rencontre, and another that the MacGregors were treacherously waylaid by the Colquhouns. These statements are both unfounded. The battle was deliberately resolved upon, for it was fought in the heart of the Colquhoun Country, which is of itself a proof that it was not an accidental rencontre, but what places the matter beyond a doubt is that MacGregor applied for and obtained assistance from the Clan Macpherson, with whom he had a treaty of alliance offensive and defensive, for the very purpose of invading the Colquhouns.

" There were fifty picked men sent from Badenoch to assist the ClanGregor; but the action was over a few hours before their arrival, which perhaps was rather a fortunate circumstance, for had they taken part in the battle, it is more than probable that they would also share in the proscription. Another account states that the massacre of the boys was unintentional—that a house in which they took shelter was accidentaly set on fire.

Appendix

"That the massacre of the boys was unintentional on the part of the MacGregors is very true, but still it was the deliberate act of one individual, and no doubt the ClanGregor were in a certain degree responsible for the conduct of that individual, for although he was not of their name, yet he was under their banner at the time He was a man, or rather a monster, of the name of Cameron,[1] and foster-brother of MacGregor, who was sent to take charge of the boys in order to keep them out of harm's way; and strange and unnatural as it may appear, he massacred the whole of them to the number of forty, some say sixty

"The origin of the quarrel with the Colquhouns was as follows. A party of twelve MacGregors entered the Colquhoun country in quest of stolen or strayed cattle, and in a dreadful stormy night came to a sequestered farmhouse, the landlord of which refused them admittance, although it was quite evident that they must perish in the event of attempting to reach any other inhabited place They, however, acted with extraordinary temper and forbearance, for in place of using force (which under the circumstances would be quite justifiable), they merely took possession of an out-house, where they lighted a fire, and having in vain applied for provisions, for which they offered payment, they had no alternative but to take a sheep from the churl's flock, which they killed, and handed its value in at a window Having thus provided themselves with food, they were sitting round a large fire and broiling the mutton, when the savage landlord stole quietly to the top of the house and dropped a large stone into the fire through the vent-hole, which burned several of the MacGregors severely. One of them, smarting with pain, made a spring to the door, and when the landlord was in the act of descending from the house, he shot him dead. After this accident (for it cannot be called by any other name) the MacGregors returned home, but the Colquhouns having seized several of that clan (who were on their own lawful business, and knew nothing of the other affair), they hanged them like so many dogs So gross an outrage could not be overlooked, but still the MacGregors acted with the greatest coolness, and sent a regular embassy to demand satisfaction, but every proposition was rejected by the Colquhouns, and, after much negotiation, Macgregor intimated to Colquhoun of Luss that he must hold him and his whole clan responsible for the slaughter of the MacGregors, and he accordingly prepared to put his threat in execution. The ClanGregor entered the Colquhoun country with fire and sword, and when they came to Glenfruin, and in sight of the enemy, they fell in with a number of boys who came out from Dumbarton to see the fight. They were principally schoolboys, and many of them of good families that probably had no connection whatever with either of the belligerents MacGregor, in order to keep them out of harm's way, directed that the boys should be confined in a church or meeting-house that happened to be close by, and sent his foster-brother (one of the

[1] See page 296 for Sir John MacGregor's refutation and page 295 for mention of a M'Intnach instead of Cameron

name of Cameron) to take charge of them, who, from what motive it is impossible to divine, massacred the whole of them as soon as he found the armies engaged. The battle of Glenfruin was soon over. The Colquhouns were defeated with great slaughter. Their chief was killed, and the Macgregor's scarcely lost a man. When they returned from the pursuit, Macgregor's first inquiry was for the boys, whom he intended to liberate and dismiss with kindness; but, learning the horrid fact that they were all butchered, he struck his forehead and exclaimed: 'The battle is lost after all.' The fate of the Dumbarton boys was so very revolting to the feelings of every person possessing any share of humanity, that it is no wonder that it created a deep and powerful prejudice against the ClanGregor; and yet they were, at least, morally innocent, and it must for ever be a matter of regret that such heavy calamities should be heaped upon the bravest clan in the Highlands for the act of one madman.

" The ClanGregor, however, were doomed to be unfortunate, as will appear by continuing their history a little further. Gregor Our, or Gregor the Swarthy, was the second in rank to the chief, but in deeds of arms he had no superior, nor perhaps an equal, in all the Highlands. Argyle was his maternal uncle, and his valour in defence of his clan and country, when outlawed and assailed by multitudes of foes, would appear more like romance than real facts. After various desperate actions, in which the ClanGregor displayed incredible prowess, but which considerably reduced their number, they learned with amazement that Argyle, at the head of an overwhelming force, was advancing to attack them. Upon the receipt of this intelligence, Gregor Our proposed to stop his uncle's progress, and, having communicated his plan to his chief, he set out alone in disguise. After several narrow escapes, he succeeded in making his way into Argyle's tent at midnight (by telling the sentry that he was the bearer of dispatches from the Government, the delivery of which admitted of no delay), and after upbraiding him for his cruelty and injustice, told him plainly that his life was forfeited unless he instantly agreed to relinquish the expedition. Argyle knew the determined character of his nephew, and it is also possible that he might be influenced by affection toward a relative of whom he might very justly be proud; but, be his motives what they may, he at once agreed to the proposed terms, and conducted Gregor safely out of the camp, and soon after disbanded his troops. Nor did his good offices cease there, for he became an advocate of the ClanGregor at Court, and obtained an armistice for them as well as a protection to Gregor Our, with instructions to him to appear before the Privy Council to explain every circumstance relating to the battle of Glenfruin and the massacre of the scholars. Gregor Our accordingly set out for Edinburgh with the concurrence of his chief, but he was no sooner gone than suspicions began to arise as to the purity of his intentions. Dark hints were first thrown out, and afterwards stated boldly as a fact, that Gregor, through the interest of his uncle and his own address, had obtained a royal grant of the chieftainship, as well as of the estates of MacGregor for himself. By these insinuations and reports (which no doubt had great plausibility in them), MacGregor[1] was driven to a state of absolute distraction, and, having learned that Gregor Our was on his way back from Edinburgh, he went to meet him, and, without the least inquiry or explanation, shot him through the heart with a pistol On examining his papers, it was discovered that there was not a vestige of truth in these reports. The pardon to the ClanGregor was addressed to MacGregor. His estates were restored to himself, and Gregor Our did not secure a single benefit to himself, but what he got in common with every individual of the clan. This discovery drove MacGregor to madness, and he actually became deranged. The pardon was recalled, and the proscription was enforced with greater rigour than before; nor is it at all surprising that Argyle should become their bitter (as he was their most powerful) enemy."

D.—Page 300. Dr Masson, in Vol. xiv. of the published edition of the Register of the Privy Council, edited by him, gives from certain miscellaneous papers a copy "of the original Edict for the Extermination of the ClanGregor, with offers of reward for the heads of Alexander MacGregor of Glenstrae and his principal followers," two certified copies of which he has found.

1603. Feb. 24. Letters under the Signet as follows · James be the grace of God, King of Scottis, to oure lovittis. . . Messengeris, our schireffis in that pairt, conjunctlie and severallie, speciallie constitute, gretting : Forsamekle as the wicked and unhappie race of Clangregour, quha sa lang hes continewit in bluid, thift, reiff, sorning, and oppressioun upoun the peciable and guid subjectis of the incuntrey, to the wraik, miserie, and undoing of mony honnest and substantious houshalderis, and laying waist of divers weleplenist boundis and possessiounis, they have now at last upoun the day of Februar instant, in oppin hostilitie enterit within the Lennox, quhair in maist barbarous and horrible maner, without pitie or compassion, they have murdreist and slane sevin scoir of personis, without respect to young or auld, to the offence and displeasour of God, to the grete greif and displeasour of us, and to the perpetuell reprotche and sklander of the haill natioun, gif this wyld and abhominable fact be not sua exemplarly punist as the rememberance thairof sall remane to the posteriteis · And thairfore, we, with a grete nowmer of oure Nobilitie and Counsal, haveing convenit upoun this mater, it is found that God can not be appeasit, nor the cuntrey releivit of the sklander quhilk it sustenis be that barbaritie, unless that unhappie and destable race be extirpat and ruttit out, and nevir suffereit to have rest or remaning within this cuntrey heirefter ; for quhilk purpois, ordour and discretioun is alreddy gevin how and in quhat maner they salbe prosequte, huntit, followit, and persewit with fyre and sword, ay and quhill they be exterminat

---

[1] If this relates to Glenstray, it must be absolutely untrue, and the whole of this story about Gregor Our is unknown in the clan records.

and ruttit out; and we nawayse dout bot all guid and dewitfull subjectis will hald hand to this so godlie a work, and will refuise the resset of thame and of thair guidis, and the patronizeing of thame ony way to the hinder of this oure Service: Our will is heirfore, and we chairge yow straitlie and commandis, that incontinent thir oure letters sene ye pas and in our name and auctoritie command, chairge and inhibite all and sindrie oure leigeis and subjectis quhatsumevir, be oppin proclamatioun at all mercat croceis and utheris placeis neidfull, that nane of thame presume or tak upoun hand to ressett, supplie, schaw favour or conforte to ony of the said Clangregour, thair wyffis, or bairnis, or to resett or hurde thair guidis or géir, or mak blokis or barganis with thame thairanent, undir whatsomevir cullour or pretence, nor git to entir in assuirance or freindschip with the saidis lymmairis, and gif ony assuirance or bondis of freindschip be amangis thame, that they gif up and dischairge the same, reputing and estemeing thame as traitouris and enemeis to God, thair prince, and cuntrey, undir the pane to be repute, haldin and extermit as air and pertakeris with the saidis lymmairis in all thair wickid and evill deidis, and to be persewit and punist with thame thairfore with all rigour and extremitie to the terrour of utheris, besydis the confiscatioun of all thair movable guidis to the use of the challengeair.—And to the effect the saidis thevis and lymmairis sall not eschaip thair deservit punischement, that ye command, chairge and inhibite all and sindrie ferriairis, marineris and awnairis of boitis or veschellis within our realme, that nane of thame presume or tak upoun hand to ressave ony of the said Clangregour, thair wyffis, bairnis, or servandis, within thair boitis and veschellis, nor to transport thame to or fra ferreis towardis the Illis nor to Ireland, under the pane of deid, with certificatioun to thame that sall do in the contrair heirof they salbe taikin, apprehendit, and execute to the deid without favour. And siklyke that ye command and chairge all and sindrie noblemen, baronis, and gentilmen, within quhais boundis the saidis boittis or veschellis ar that they caus diligent attendance be givin that nane of the said ClanGregour, thair wyffis, bairnis or servandis be transportit within the saidis boittis or veschellis. And, we being surlie informit that Allaster McGregour of Glenstra, cheif and chiftane of that unhappie race and clan, wes not onlie the conductair and leidair of that unhappie and mischevious cumpany, bot thairwith he with his awin handis committit the maist horrible and barbarous crueltie that fell out that day, and culd nevir be satiat in bathing of him selff, with the bluid of grit nowmeris of innocentis, thairfore we promit that quhatsumevir persone or personis will tak and apprehend the said Allaster, and bring and present him quick to us, and failyeing thairof, present his heid, that not only sall they have a frie pardoun and remissioun for all thair bygane offenssis and attemptis, albeit thay be giltie of the said barbarous and mischant crueltie committit within the Lennox, bot that thay sall have a thousand pundis money of guid and reddy payment deliverit unto thame. And siklyke quhatsumevir persoun or personis will tak, apprehend and present to us the personis undirwritten, and failyeing thairof thair heidis,—thay ar to say, Duncane McGregour V^cEwne,[1] Johnne Dow Gair Ewne,[2] and Duncan Pirdrachis,[3] Robert Abroch McGregour, Patrik Aldoch, and his twa sones, Patrik McConnoquhy in Glen,[4] Gregour McGregour, sone to Duncane Glen,[4] Charles McGregour V^cEane,[5] Callum McGregour Ruy,[6] Johnne Dow,[7] Duncan Bane McRobertis sone,[8] Allaster McGregour V^cEane Dullihaith,[9] and Allaster McRobert, his brother,—that not onlie sall the said apprehendair and presentair have a free pardoun and remissioun for all thair bygaine offensis, except for the barbarous attempt laithe committit within the Lennox, bot with that thay sall have twa hundreth merkis in present and reddy payment deliverit unto thame, as alswa quha evir will bring and present unto us ony utheris personis quhatsumevir culpable of the said barbarous crueltie committit within the Lennox, or ony utheris of the name of Clangregour quha salbe denuncet fugitives and rebellis for not compeirance, before us and oure Counsale, that the saidis apprehendairis and presentairis sall not onlie have a free pardoun and remissioun for all offences committit be thame (except and alwyse the attempt of the Lennox), bot with that thay sall have ane hundreth merkis of present and reddy payment deliverit unto thame   The quhilk to do we commit to yow conjunctlie and severallie oure full power be thir oure letteris, delivering thame be yow dewlie execute and indorsat agane to the berar.   Gevin under oure signet at Halyruidhouse the twenty foure day of Februair, and of oure regne the xxxvj yeir, 1603   (L S) Per Actum Secreti Consilij etc Ja. Prymrois "[10]

The introduction to Vol. xiv., from which the foregoing is quoted, gives the following comment ·—

"This Edict, the ruthless vengeance of the Government upon the MacGregors for their slaughter of the Colquhouns and other Lennox men in the Battle of Glenfruin, fought on the 7th of the same month, purports to have been the Act of the King with a number of his Nobility and Council 'convenit upoun this mater' It is one of the very last Acts of King James, while he was King of Scotland only , for exactly one month afterwards by the death of Queen Elizabeth at Richmond on the 24th of March 1603, he was King also of England, and the news having come to Edinburgh on the 26th March, he took farewell of Scotland on the 5th of April and

---

[1] Third son of the Tutor. [2] Second son of the Tutor, executed 1604. [3] Pudrach. [4] Both sons of Duncan na Glen [5] Not found. [6] Uncertain [7] John Dow McRob ? [8] In Craigrostane [9] Dougal Chaith.—*Ed.*

[10] The occasion of this act of extermination against the long-doomed MacGregors was their armed invasion of the Lennox, with consequent slaughter of so many of the Colquhouns, Buchanans, and others of that region in the Battle of Glenfruin, on the 7th February 1603 Within six weeks after the act, King James was on his journey southwards to take possession of the throne of England ; and it is memorable that the present tremendous decree—the first of a series of similarly ruthless edicts against the MacGregors which run through all the rest of James's reign—was among the last of his actions before leaving Scotland.—Dr Masson

began his journey to London to assume his new dignity. The dating of the Edict would on this account alone be of some consequence. Yet one looks in vain for it in its proper place, in the Official Register of the Council. Several Acts are duly recorded there as having been passed by the King and Council at Holyrood House on the 24th of February 1603; but this is not one of them. How is the absence of so important a document from its proper place in the Register to be explained? It certainly was not because the King and Council retracted it or became ashamed of it. Although there is no Record of the Edict itself on the 24th of February, there is incidental reference to it, of an almost exulting kind, in an Act of Council passed two days afterwards, *i.e.* on the 26th of February, for modifying a previous business arrangement of the King and Council. An armed muster having been ordered some time before to be in attendance on the King personally at Dundee on the 8th of March for the suppression of an intended rebellion within the bounds of Angus, this Act postpones the muster to the 1st of April, expressly on the ground that, in consequence of the late 'monstrous and cruell barbaritie' at Glenfruin, the King and Council have resolved on 'persute of that wicked and unhappie race of the ClanGregour quhill they be allutterlie extirpat and ruitit out,' and that it will be convenient at the muster on the 1st of April to conjoin this new business of the pursuit of the ClanGregor with the former business of the suppression of the rebellion in Angus. In further evidence that there was no retraction of the MacGregor Edict there are the certificates[1] on the backs of the preserved copies of it now under notice that it was duly published at the market cross of Stirling on the 5th of March, at the Kirk of Dunkeld on the 6th of March, and at the market cross of Dumbarton on the 8th of March. Clearly the Edict was then running through the country and consideration for the methods for giving effect to it, must have continued to occupy the Council till those last days of March 1603 when the news of the accession of King James to the English throne drove everything else out of their heads. That we have not more distinct proofs of this, possibly even that the great Edict itself escaped due Registration in the Council Books about the time it was issued, may be owing to that long hiatus in the extant Official Register of the Council, extending exactly from the end of February 1603 to the 7th of August 1606, which we have so many other reasons to regret. It is not from the Register, for example, but from other sources that we learn that on the 3rd of April 1603, the very Sunday on which King James took leave of his Scottish subjects in an affectionate farewell speech to such of them as were present that day in the High Church of Edinburgh, there was passed by him and his Council an Act 'whereby it was ordanit that the name of McGregoure sulde be altogedder abolisched, and that the haill personnes of thatt Clan suld renunce thair name and tak thame sum uther

---

[1] These certificates on the back have been here omitted after the Edict as less important.— *Ed.*

name, and that they nor nane of thair posteritie suld call thameselffis Gregor or MᶜGregoure thairefter under the payne of deid.' In a footnote (in a previous volume of the published Register of the Privy Council) where mention was made of this Act, it was assumed as identical with the original Edict for the Extermination of the MᶜGregors. The assumption was natural when no copy of that original Edict was accessible or known to be extant; but it must now be corrected. We can see now the real connexion between the original Edict of the 24th of February 1603, and this Act of the 3rd of the following April. The 1st of April had been appointed for the further consideration of the Macgregor business in the muster to be held at Dundee for the business of the Angus rebellion; but when the 1st of April came the King was on the wing for London, and could not think of a journey to Dundee for any purpose whatever. In order, however, not to leave the Macgregor business exactly where it was in the Edict of the 24th of February, he and his Council had been meditating a supplement to that Edict explaining that the decreed extermination of the Macgregor Clan need not be in the form of an absolute killing out of every man, woman, or child of the Clan, but might be achieved more mercifully in part by the compulsion of every man, woman, or child of the Clan that desired still to be left alive, to abjure the name of MacGregor and assume other names. By James's departure into England, the actual execution both of the original Edict and of the supplementary or interpreting Act was devolved on the Privy Council he left behind him in Scotland, and a horrible legacy it was; but both the original Edict and the supplementary Act belong really to the last weeks of King James's own residence in Scotland, and it has seemed the more worth while to explain this, because, though the original Edict of 24th February 1603 was the initiation of all the long series of subsequent Acts against the MacGregors, it has hitherto evaded search, and is now first made accessible."

E.

MACGREGOR OF RORO.

Tha mulad, tha mulad Tha mulad ga m'lionadh Tha mul-ad bochd, truadh orm, Nach dual dual domh chaoidh dhireadh. Mu Mhac-Grio-gair a Rua-ru D'am bu dual bhi'n Gleann - Liobh-unn Mu MhacGriogair na'm brat-ach, Dha'm bu-tar tar-ach piob-an.

F.—Page 413.   Quotation from Vol. xiv. of Published Edition of Privy Council Register:

" Act of Exoneration and Indemnity to the Earl of Argyle for his services against the ClanGregor."

1613 (?).   Our Soverane Lord ordanis ane letter to be maid undir the grite seale in dew forme, makand mentioun that, whereas his sacred Majestie haveing by his most prudent, wyse, and blissit government, establisheit this estate and Kingdome under a perfyte and setled obedyence, and thair being litle or no rebellioun profest and avouit in ony pairt or cornair thairof bot in the Illis, and in the personis of that infamous byke of lawles lymmaris callit the ClanGregour, who not onlie by all kynd of villannye and insolencyis opprest his Majesteis goode subjectis in all partis quhair thay might be maisteris, but gaif occasioun to utheris Yllismen and Heylandaris in imitatioun of thame to ly oute and to attend and await the event of thair rebellioun: The consideratioun quhairof as it bred in his Majesteis royall hairt a princelie disdayne that suche a handfull of miserable catives sould be sufferrit so lang in contempt and dishonnour of his Majestie to ryn louse, so his Majestie resolvit altogidder to abolische and suppres the name, and memorie of that infamous clan, and outher haillelie to extirpt and root thame oute or then to reduce thame to obedyence: And his Majestie haveing had sindrie courses and plottis anent the executioun of this his Majesties resolutioun, in end his Majestie fand that no man wes so meete to be imployit in that service as his right traist cosine and counsellour, Archibald, Erle of Ergyle, Lord Campbell, Kintyre and Lorne, not onlie in regaird of his awne pouer, freindship, and forceis to execute the said service in suche substantious forme and maner as wes most aggreable with his Majesteis honnour, bot in regaird of the bigane proofe and experience whilk his Majestie hes had of the said Erle, his fidelitie, cair and diligence in sindrie preceding imploymentis concredite unto him bothe in the Yllis and aganis thir same lymmaris of the ClanGregour, whairin fra tyme to tyme he has had a goode and happie success; lyke as the said Erll to testifie his goode affectioun and willing dispositioun to do his Majestie service, acceptit upoun him not onlie the charge and service aganis the Clangregour, bot sindrie otheris commissionis, instructionis and directionis bothe by word and wryte aganis the Yllis and Heylandis nixt adjacent, quhairin he did mony goode officeis fra tyme to tyme . . . . he and the gentilmen of his freindship who joyned with him in that service behavit thameselffis thairin with suche wisdom, courage, foirsycht and dexteritie as divers of the Yllismen and a verie grite nomber of the ClanGregour by whome the peace of the cuntrey was chieflie interruptit hes bene apprehendit, slayne and execute be justice, to his Majesteis honnour, and to the grite conforte and contentment of his Majesties goode subjectis swa that now the name of M'Gregour is in a maner abolisheit, and of that haill clan thair is not above xij personis who ar rebellis and outlawis left alive.   The Act goes on to remit all crimes, transgressions and offences which the Earl and his friends may have committed in the service assigned to them.

G.—Page 452. From Dr Masson's Introduction to Vol. xiv. of the Published Register of the Privy Council. "Account Book of Fines for Reset of the Clan-Gregor 1612-1624. Through the first seven years of King James's residence in his new Kingdom of England, the execution of his two MacGregor Edicts of February-April 1603 was part of the occupation of the Scottish Privy Council he had left behind him One of the most marked incidents in Scottish History through those years was the hanging and quartering at the Market Cross of Edinburgh on the 20th of January 1604, of Alexander Macgregor of Glenstrae, the head of the Clan, together with eleven of his principal clansmen that had been apprehended along with him; but the number of other MacGregors that were hunted to death through the seven years, or dispossessed of their native crofts and dispersed through different parts of the Highlands, to attach themselves to other clans and live on under changed names defies exact reckoning So effective had been the operation of the two Macgregor Acts of 1603 that there seems to have been a lull in the persecution of the clan from mere lack of objects to persecute But about the year 1610 the Government had to rouse itself to fresh exertions. See in the introduction to a former volume, the extraordinary series of new fulminations against the MacGregors between that year and the year 1613, and of the new Acts then passed for the future conduct of the crusade for their extermination. Our concern now is with two of those Acts in particular One is the Royal Ordinance at Greenwich, of date 29th April 1611, committing the supreme management of the crusade thenceforward to the Earl of Argyle with full powers of fire and sword, as well as of justiciary action, against all movements of the doomed clan and their abettors, and with the escheats of all their moveable goods for his reward. The other is the Act of Council at Edinburgh, of date 21st November 1611, appointing so many named landlords to act as select Commissioners in each of the districts of Scotland chiefly haunted by the fugitive MacGregors or most liable to visits from them. Each set of such district commissioners was to have the duty of co-operating with the Earl of Argyle by holding courts for the trial of all persons in the district that should be named to them by the Earl as accused of shelter or reset of any of the ClanGregor, their wives, bairns, or goods, since the 1st of August 1610, and of reporting to the Privy Council the names of those that should be found guilty, together with such an estimate of the value of the property of each guilty person as might guide the Council in fixing the fine to be imposed upon that person. The assumption in this Act is that the fines to be so inflicted upon resetters of the ClanGregor were like the escheated property of the culpable Mac-Gregors themselves, to go to the Earl of Argyle; but from a subsequent minute of Council, of date 8th July 1613, we learn that the Earl then by his own voluntary offer agreed that 22½ per cent. of all the moneys due to him or that might be due to

on the reset-account should go into his Majesty's Exchequer. His Majesty and
the Earl having thus a joint pecuniary interest in the MacGregor-reset fund arrangements were necessary for so collecting the fines and banking them, and for so keeping the accounts that the two interests should not get confused, and his Majesty's
Treasurer should be able to calculate exactly the worth of this item of his Majesty's
revenue. These arrangements were made on the 22nd of July 1613 when by an
Act of Council, Archibald Primrose, writer, and Archibald Campbell of Glencharra-
dale were, with consent of the Earl of Argyle, appointed agents for uplifting the
fines and for keeping just reckoning of his Majesty's interest in them on the one
hand and the Earl's on the other."

" One might have expected, . . . , that in the course of the year 1614 it would
have been possible to wind up the whole business of the fines for MacGregor-reset
by settling accounts between his Majesty for his 22½ per cent. of the proceeds and
the Earl of Argyle for his remaining 77½ per cent. But though there is evidence that
by this time a good deal of money from the Macgregor Reset Fund had gone into
the Earl of Argyle's pocket, and some of it into his Majesty's Scottish Treasury,
there was no hurry in closing the accounts, and no possibility of hurry. For one
thing, if it is easier even nowadays to impose a fine than to exact payment of it, one
can see what hard work it must have been for Archibald Primrose and Archibald
Campbell to ' uplift ' the fines which the Council had imposed on so many Highland Lairds, Highland farmers, and Highland cottars, and at what expense of hornings, poindings, arrests, &c., &c., they must have succeeded in ' uplifting ' even so
much as they did. In the second place the crime of Macgregor reset had by no
means been stamped out in 1614. Even as late as 1617, the year of King James's
one and only visit to Scotland after his accession to the English throne, did not his
Majesty signalise his continued detestation of the Macgregors by causing to be
passed in the Scottish Parliament held on that occasion in his own presence an Act
renewing and confirming all the preceding Acts of Parliament or of Council directed
against the ClanGregor? Why close the accounts of the Macgregor Reset Fund
in 1614, or in any subsequent year near that date when there was still a chance of
an indefinite increase of the fund by further fines to be exacted either from former
offenders for relapses into their old crime or from newly discovered offenders ?
But in the third place, the circumstances of the Earl of Argyle from 1614 onwards
were such as to postpone, so far as he was concerned, the necessity for winding up
the accounts between him and the King in the matter of the Macgregor Reset
Moneys. In 1615 the Earl was fully occupied with the business of his Lieutenancy
for the suppression of the Macdonald Rebellion in the West; from that year to
1617 his thoughts ran mainly on the acquisition of the Lordship of Kintyre as the
natural reward for that service and early in 1618 he had left Scotland and Britain
altogether, to be the amazement soon both of Scotland and of England by his apostacy

in Flanders from the Protestant religion and to be pursued by his Majesty on that account as a recreant and traitor."

Dr Masson proceeds to show that in July 1623 an Act was passed for the appointment of a Committee consisting of seven of the Councillors "for the audit of the accounts of the MacGregor Reset Fund as they should be tendered by Messrs Archibald Primrose and Archibald Campbell." The result was a Report and Audit, of date 31st March 1624, a copy of which is printed in Vol. xiv. of the published Register of the Privy Council with full lists of the persons fined. Dr Masson condenses the amounts levied in the following table (here slightly abridged).

I.	Finings in the Inverness District, concluded 30th July 1613	. . .	£36,010 0 0
II.	Do. in the Elgin and Forres District, concluded 1st Sept. 1613	.	35,736 13 4
III.	Do. in the Perth District, sundry times, concluded 31st March 1618	.	28,620 0 0
IV.	Do. in Strathearn, 27th March 1614	.	5,016 13 4
V.	Do. in Menteith, concluded 14th July 1613	. . .	5,310 0 0
VI.	Do in Dumbartonshire, concluded 17th March 1614	. . .	4,374 13 4
			£115,068 0 0

But although this was the total amount of the imposed fines, Dr Masson goes on to explain that the amount actually collected fell far short of it, an authorised abatement reduced it to £77,271, 4s., a residue of £32,606, 1s. 10d. remained due at the date of making up the account, and the whole available assets appear to have been £44,665, 2s. 2d. The proportion due to the King is set down at £10,050.

Reading over the long list of "Resetters," copied from the said "ClanGregor Fines Book," given by Dr Masson in Vol. xiv., one cannot but admire the number of disinterested friends who had thus afforded "Comfort" to the ClanGregor, at their own serious peril.

In the following Index an attempt has been made to group the names of individual MacGregors into families, extended memoirs of which may hereafter be given. To save space, reference to names of other persons or places is brief.

Index

MacGregor

3 O

[1] The above 11 traditional chiefs are all prior to the entries in the " Chronicle of Fortingal," which begin at 1390

PRINTED BY
TURNBULL AND SPEARS,
EDINBURGH